Best wishes,
Good reading.

Laurie Moran

i

THE HISTORY
of
BRANDON COLLIERY
1856 to 1960

THE HISTORY
of
BRANDON COLLIERY
1856 to 1960

by
LAURIE MORAN

Published by
LAURIE MORAN

Cover:
Two fifteen year old pony drivers (1919).
(Arthur Lonsdale and Jimmy Atess).

©1988 LAURIE MORAN

ISBN 0 9517288 1 4

First Published June 1988
Reprinted November 1988
Reprinted November 1989
Reprinted April 1991
Reprinted May 1997
Reprinted December 1999

Printed by
The Gilpin Press
Houghton-le-Spring
Tyne & Wear DH4 4BA

ACKNOWLEDGEMENTS

Supported by Durham City Arts.

Grateful thanks to Catherine Cookson who also sponsored this publication.

Extracts from Catherine Cookson's letter to the author: —

'I am astounded by your research and the compilation of it, resulting in the wonderful history of Brandon Colliery.

What is more, the book looks well. I don't know what you have done about it so far, but I feel it should be in all libraries, including those in Universities.

Thank you so much Mr. Moran, for sending me this enlightening book on conditions that should not be allowed to be forgotten.

My warmest regards and wishes for its success and yours'.

Letter from University of Newcastle upon Tyne Library: —

'Thank you for your letter and the enclosed volume on "The History of Brandon Colliery". It is a magnificent production and I am lost in admiration at the fascinating detail which you have managed to include in such an interesting way. I am not surprised that Catherine Cookson found it of great interest and I am looking forward to digging deeper into the riches it clearly contains. You must feel very proud on having completed so much first-rate research and recorded it in such an attractive book'.

B. J. Enright, Librarian.

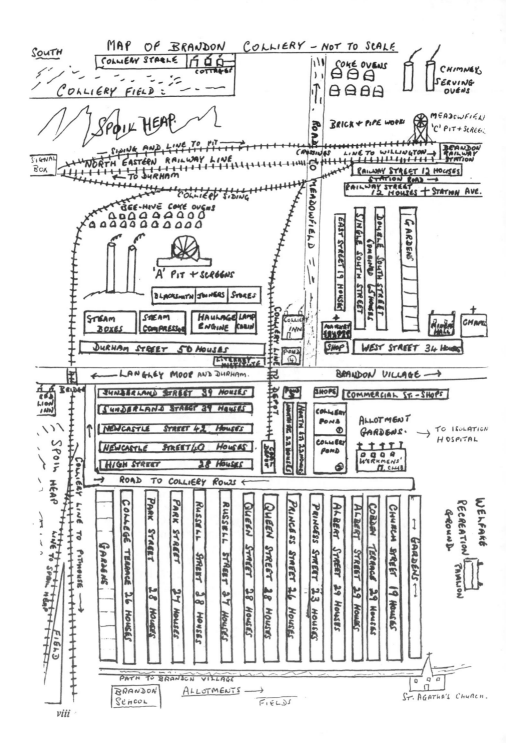

MAP OF BRANDON COLLIERY – NOT TO SCALE

PORTRAIT OF A COLLIERY AND ITS PEOPLE

1856

Viscount Boyne the Sixth, of Brancepeth Castle, died last year. He left his estate to his son who became the seventh Viscount Boyne.

Brancepeth Estate covers a vast area; for those of statistic mind this tract of land embraces the Parish of Brancepeth, Helmington Row, Stockley, Tudhoe and Willington.

Viscount Boyne is reputed the third largest landowner in the North; his farms and farmland cover some fifteen thousand three hundred and ten acres; these yield an estimated yearly rental of seventy four thousand pounds. This wealth is boosted by royalties accrued from mining operations in the area. Messrs. Straker and Love have leased over a third of the domain to work it for coal. Mr. Straker hails from Tynemouth; Mr. Love resides at nearby Willington. They share colliery interest.

Recent borings show that the new colliery to be sunk at Brandon has no Magnesium Limestone strata; a fairly easy downward passage is envisaged. Coal seams proved are:—

The Low Main with coal 1ft. 8ins. thick lies 57ft. from the surface.

Hutton Seam with coal 2ft. 8 ins. thick lies 157ft. from the surface.

Harvey Seam with coal 2ft thick lies 312ft. from the surface.

Busty Seam with coal 4ft. thick lies 418ft. from the surface.

Brockwell Seam with coal 2ft. 10ins. thick lies 522 ft. from the surface.

A layer of Seggar lies just below the Brockwell Seam; this will be used for the manufacture of fire bricks and pipes.

The shaft will be sunk to a depth of 542ft. 4½ins. to allow for the installation of pumps and to provide a sump in which to collect pit water prior to its pumping to the surface.

Brandon is situated in the Parish of Brancepeth, between the city of Durham and the Auckland coal district.

The village of Brandon, the birthplace of Tredgold, lies some three miles south-west of Durham. Thomas Tredgold, author of the 'Steam Engine' published in 1827 and other works, died in 1834.

There are several name places entitled Brandon; there is South Brandon, nearby West Brandon and East Brandon, the village on the hill. It is primarily an agricultural area; East Brandon, the largest of the three, is a self supporting community living in twenty five houses.

Brandon Colliery as this new place is named, lies one mile away on lower ground and will thus form a separate community.

Sinkers are in demand as new pits are planned in various parts of the county. The sinkers' gear is set. They begin their downward drive; boring for coal, their goal, the first seam of workable coal, the Hutton Seam which has coal 2ft 8ins. thick waiting to be worked..

1

Joe Stanger, a master sinker imported from Northumberland, is in charge of twelve men, most of whom had learned the art of sinking from their fathers. They work in three shifts which ensures continuous sinking. Joe wears a commodious leather hat with a long peak at the rear, a large waterproof smocklike coat is strapped across his chest; these afford protection from the wet sides of the shaft as he descends. He wears light, hard wearing clogs.

Shaft sinking is one of the most hazardous of jobs as the sinkers line the shaft with steel sheets. Until recently timber was used to shore the sides of the shaft. The lining or tubbing for the shaft is calculated to cost between £60 and £70 for each fathom sunk. The sinkers take pride in their highly skilled work which earns Joe Stanger's men seven shillings per fathom for the first five fathoms sunk; fourteen shillings for the second five fathoms; twenty one shillings for the third five fathoms; and so on, seven shillings extra being paid for each successive five fathoms.

1857

Sinkers, as anxious as their masters, bore steadily downward. Buildings mushroom nearby; blacksmiths, masons, joiners, are all busy. Cartmen lead stone and timber to the new site.

Houses are built; the first row has one room down, one room up. These buildings are said to have cost the colliery owners around fifty pounds each to build. The sinkers and their families are housed first.

Builders are not obliged to provide drains and sanitation but they are erecting netties across the street away from the houses. These netties are huddled in clusters of four, one netty for each household. These are brick built with a tin roof sloping to the rear; each has a sliding cast-iron plate set in front, which when lifted facilitates emptying.

Richard Hissop, a fifty nine year old cartman, born at nearby Sunderland Bridge, with other cartmen leads stone quarried at the top of the hill just approaching East Brandon, the heavy carthorses holding back swaying loads as they travel the incline down to the new colliery.

The thick walls of the first houses to be built encase a floor made up of square quarls. Until quite recently colliery houses had floors made from a mixture of lime, small coal and gravel. The fire range is large, there is an iron boiler àt one side of the fireplace, a round oven is set at the other side. The boiler is filled with water collected from a spring in the farmer's field. Hinged wooden shutters are fitted over the downstairs windows, these being fastened back to the outside wall during the day, at night they are closed and secured from the inside.

Among the first settlers are George Madgin and his wife Mary; George is a joiner. They took their new son to be christened George in the parish church of St. Brandon in the picturesque village of Brancepeth. The Rev. A. Duncombe Shafto also baptised Jane Ann Snaith. The village has a new National School, which at two miles distance is the nearest school for the colliers' children.

The new railway line running from Durham to Bishop Auckland, after four years of labour and tragedy, was opened on April 1st.

Colliery workers, together with their wives and children, gathered on this important day, alongside the new railway track at Brandon. A train carrying officials of the North Eastern Railway Company is due to leave Durham at 2 p.m. It will travel through Relly, Langley, Brandon, Brancepeth, Willington and on to Bishop Auckland.

Forgotten for the moment were the eight men and boys killed, and the numerous injured during the laying of the two and a half mile stretch of line from Durham to Brandon Colliery. Women nervously clutch their shawls, men puff on Meeshaum pipes, snuff boxes click; children, without success, try to control excited dogs.

April 1st. — April Fools' Day; a day to be remembered as the opening day of the Bishop Auckland Branch Railway. For most onlookers this was their first view of a moving train.

'Here it comes!' Margaret Hall, nine years of age; Will Leighton Jnr., seven; Isabella Parkinson, eleven; John Bell and John Coxon both ten, and Mary Garbutt, six, with her four year old sister Margaret, shout in chorus as the labouring train crosses the small bridge spanning the road to Durham.

Faces turn towards Langley. On time, ten minutes past two, the train noisily approaches Brandon Colliery. Livestock in nearby fields scatter in terror as the engineer, wind blown, operates the engine whistle. Smiling, top hatted men wave from carriage windows, the greetings are returned by the excited group lining the track. On its immediate return from Bishop Auckland, a public luncheon to celebrate the event is to be held in the New Town Hall, Durham; tickets are ten shillings and sixpence each.

Huge baulks have been erected near the shaft, these will support the heapstead. The new engine house contains machinery for winding the cage in the shaft; modern pits use a steel rope to draw the cage. Last year one hundred and thirty-six pitmen were killed in pit accidents in the Northern District, a number of them due to pit shaft mishaps.

Greater safety measures are being sought. Coal owners and others, perturbed over loss of life in pit shaft accidents, welcomed experiments which took place in December 1848 when parachutes were attached to a pit cage which stopped the descent of the cage if the shaft rope broke. Again in 1850 when Fourdrinier's patent safety apparatus was given a trial. The idea being that if the cage rope snapped in the shaft two arms would be released which would automatically bite into the sides of the shaft. Wooden tubs, a recent innovation, each built to hold eight and a half hundredweight of coal are arranged in convenient heaps for dispatch below as required. each four wheeled tub is strongly built, having two iron bands bolted round its body for added strength. A most important feature is the boiler house which produces steam to operate the winding gear.

The railway station, the title is a misnomer, as it is only a small building, is in use; it has been open for two weeks. The Parliamentary rate for train fares being one penny per mile, the colliery folk will no doubt use this swift and exciting mode of travel. Thomas Carter arranged to have his infant son christened George on the Saturday as the trains do not stop at Brandon Colliery during the week. The baby is carried the quarter of a mile from Brancepeth station to St. Brandon's.

Farmland contracts as more houses are built to provide shelter for the expected surge of pitmen. More land is buried under spoil brought out of the shaft. Richard Hissop lives at No. 8 East Street; besides leading stone from the quarry he performs other tasks: he cleans refuse from the netties which he dumps in a field lying north of the colliery.

There being as yet no shops at Brandon Colliery, people travel to the market at Durham every Saturday. Potatoes currently cost one shilling a peck; eggs are twelve a shilling; beef sevenpence halfpenny a pound; veal is eightpence a pound; chickens cost one shilling and fourpence each; coffee at one shilling and twopence a pound, is more popular than tea which is selling at three to four shillings a pound. Candles for use in the home, and in the pit, cost elevenpence halfpenny a pound. Whiskey is two shillings and sixpence a bottle; Guinness Dublin Stout is a good buy at six shillings for a dozen quart bottles.

During August a new winning was started at Brandon Colliery from the surface down to the Hutton Seam. A boring was also continued below to the Brancepeth or Brockwell Seam by Mr. Forster. The owners with great foresight have elected to operate two shafts, one on each side of the railway track and some hundreds of yards apart. In due course, when a link is forged underground, ventilation, transport and safety will be greatly enhanced.

Will Dickinson, an able twenty six year old pitman, surveyed newly built Durham Street, the first long colliery row. Will was born in Jarrow and currently works at Brancepeth Colliery about two and a half miles up the line, another colliery owned by Messrs. Straker and Love. He had left his twenty five year old wife Elizabeth, and his daughters Mary Ann and Margaret, four years and one year, at Brancepeth Colliery. Mr. Forster had engaged him to work as a sinker with him at Brandon Colliery.

Will met William Garbutt twenty eight years of age, set on as a joiner's labourer at seventeen shillings a week, he came from Yorkshire. His twenty four year old wife Sarah, their two young daughters Mary and Margaret and three year old John Henry all occupy No. 14 Durham Street.

Families are migrating from outside the North-East into the colliery areas. There is a drift from the land, argicultural wages are poor, ranging from nine shillings to twelve shillings a week. Men from Cornwall, Lancashire,

Yorkshire, Staffordshire and Derbyshire are moving into the new collieries. Scots and Irish are among the migrants.

One historian suggests that Brandon derives its name from the Scottish and Irish abbot and confessor St. Brandon; he was abbot of Clonfert in Ireland, legend says that he flew through the air in his chariot. Another interpretation is that Brandon is from the Anglo-Saxon Brun, that is brown, and dun meaning a hill. A third definition is Braun's den from which a fierce beast is said to have roamed, causing great havoc and consternation among the inhabitants. Braun's Path—now Brancepeth—is where the beast trod.

The Viscount and Lady Boyne returned to their castle at Brancepeth. They with the Hon. G. F. Hamilton Russell had spent the summer at their family residence at Stackallen in Ireland. A large, horse drawn carriage conveyed them the four hundred yards or so to the castle. The railway company built a small station at Brancepeth, here the trains stop daily.

The day following the return of Viscount Boyne saw a gig leave Brandon Colliery on its sorrowful journey to Brancepeth, it carried the remains of baby Samuel Routledge, the four month old son of Robert Routledge of No. 15 South Street.

During the year, the Rev. Shafto baptised three babies born at Brandon Colliery.

1858

A New Year turkey costs seven shillings at the market in Durham. As the pitman's wage does not run to luxuries, a joint of beef at half of that price will suffice. There is paraffin to buy at twopence halfpenny a gill; candles for use in the home and in the pit are elevenpence a pound; coffee at the same price finds favour; tea at two shillings and fourpence to four shillings a pound is beyond his pocket.

Coal is now being produced more and more abundantly at Brandon Colliery. More hewing places are prepared in the Hutton Seam; more hewers and putters are being set on. The main Winning advances, determined to leave behind the shaft precincts. Hewing places which fork to the left and right as the Winning moves forward are manned. Coal is constantly being hewed and moved in tubs by putters for transport to the shaft.

Pillars of coal measuring eighteen yards by eleven yards are left standing in the shaft area, these take roof pressure likely to be centred on the shaft and ground designated for stables.

Of the 6,000 or so acres leased to the colliery owners:—
One fifth of the coal will be left in as pillars, barriers etc.—1200 acres.
One tenth of the coal will be left in for falls, casualties—600 acres.
Estimated total to be left in—1800 acres.

This leaves some 4,200 acres of workable coal. Brandon Colliery it seems, is assured work for a number of years.

Tommy Jones, a fourteen year old putter and new arrival at the colliery, manoeuvred the empty tub into the small siding near Jack Scott's hewing place. Tommy's short coarse flannel vest, sweat soaked, clung to his frail body as he approached the hewing place. He expertly settled down on his hunkers, he avoided the water which had collected on the floor of the seam.

Tommy, all of five stones in weight, manfully appraised his biceps as they pressed against his knees. 'Have you a chow mister?' Jack Scott deftly twisted a finger length from his supply of twist tobacco; after handing it to Tommy he returned the tobacco to his stocking, there it would be safe and moist.

The single candle spluttered. Tommy squirted a stream of baccy juice against the side of the tub, he was pleased with the chow and the unexpected rest. Jack Scott busied himself spreading the coal in his nearly full tub. Tommy watched the tobacco juice run haphazardly down the side of the tub and expend itself on the floor of the seam. Jack Scott stretched across the tub which was barely clear of the roof, he could, with some difficulty, reach to the back of the tub.

'What are you doing mister?' asked Tommy.

'I'm spreading to get more coal in', came the reply. 'Up to now, the standard weight of coal has been eight and a half hundredweight', Jack Scott continued. 'A quarter of a hundredweight has been added to the standard weight making it eight and three quarter hundredweight. We are being paid sixpence extra for every score of tubs hewed'.

Jack Scott, having added more coal, finished spreading. As Tommy prepared to take away the full tub, Jack said, 'If the tub is less than eight and three quarter hundredweight Mr. Love can have it confiscated, no money beng paid for the contents'.

During May Mr. Love directed that another half hundredweight be added to the tub of coal hewed. He has set the new weight at nine and a quarter hundredweight. This entails more frequent spreading of the tub to acquire the desired weight. Jack Scott and the other hewers are playing hell and working under protest as no extra pay is offered.

While George Mann, George Coulson, Archibald Anderson, William Summers and other coal hewers were seething over the added weight, Mr. Love, an ardent Methodist, presented one thousand pounds to the Chapel fund and the Methodists' New Connexion. Mr. Love, a regular preacher, is well known in Methodist circles.

A harrassed husband, clad in vest and trousers with dangling braces, dashed urgently from the dimly lit colliery house. Down Durham Street's dark, rock-strewn waste he stumbled. He banged loudly on the rough scantily painted door. Mrs. Wilson, the buxom, unqualified but highly efficient midwife, answered his call. Some time later an infant's cries heralded a new arrival into the street. A daughter for William and Sarah Garbutt.

William had a huge fire going in the kitchen grate, two scuttles of small coal nestled on the broad fire-back for instant replenishment. William, twenty nine years of age, was born in Yorkshire, so too was his wife Sarah who is twenty five. Mary, seven years of age, Margaret five and John Henry nearly four, slept in their home, 14 Durham Street, blissfully unaware of the family drama just enacted.

William, employed as a joiner's labourer, earns seventeen shillings a week. He pays no rent for the colliery house whose owner grants him an allowance of small coal.

The baby, tightly wrapped in a woollen shawl, was carried to Brancepeth where the Rev. John Duncombe Shafto, the rector, baptised her Hannah. William and Sarah silently pray that their young family is granted immunity from the epidemics of scarlet fever and diphtheria frequently haunting the district.

William Wilkins, fed and bathed after his nine hour shift at coal hewing, settled down in his one down and one up house in Railway Street. His wife Mary Ann had climbed the steep ladder to tidy the upstairs room. William, a tolerable reader, liked reading the Durham Advertiser, a popular weekly paper just reduced from twopence halfpenny to one penny for four large sheets of news. He and other pitmen reckon they have had a champion in the paper during its forty four years of publication.

No time to relax! 'Will—we need some water'.

The rain barrel stood empty after providing his bath. Fresh water was required for household use. He laced up his boots, donned coat and cap, slung his scarf around his neck, grabbed a pail, and set off for Farmer Hepworth's field.

Shawled women, cloth capped and mufflered men, and boys sporting knicker bocker breeches awaited their turn to collect water at the spring. Men curse guardedly at the unhurried trickle; bored youngsters, forgetting their errand, leave miscellaneous receptacles to lark about. Mothers wait patiently in the colliery owned houses.

Tom Stout and Jim Sedgwick had been sent to collect water after returning from school. They and fifty eight other pupils attend the newly built school at East Brandon set just around the corner from Mr. Thornton's Bay Horse Inn. Mr. Hall is the new school's head master, he is also a collector of taxes.

Mary Garbutt and her sister Margaret, along with other colliery schoolchildren, are pleased. Hitherto they had walked to the Brancepeth Church of England school two miles away which shares the Anne Dobbinson endowment with East Brandon school.

Homeward bound, after his long wait for water, William passed Mrs. Westgarth's Durham Street home. Mrs. Westgarth admired her new cottage mangle. Its large wooden rollers turned by a heavy wheel set in an ample iron frame guaranteed halving washday drudgery. With seven in family to wash for, she considered the princely sum of thirty shillings well spent. Mrs. Walker and Mrs. Wood, her close neighbours, share her delight. Being too bulky for indoor storage, its wood and iron body, supported on four small metal wheels, stands in the corner of the yard, a large sheet protects it from inclement weather.

During September there was talk of strikes by pitmen from five counties for more pay. Although Brandon Colliery is remote, its workers, out of loyalty, could become involved. It is said that at some collieries men are working for one pound ten shillings a fortnight, this is subject to off-takes of six shillings and eightpence, leaving scarcely more than eleven shillings a week for the support of a whole family. Hewers are fined half a crown for short tubs, further depleting their meagre wages. Prospects are poor for the coal trade. Soup kitchens have opened at Durham to help the poor of the district. Fifty tickets cost four shillings and twopence—each buys one pint of soup. Will the immigrants from the rural areas find their Utopia in the coal mines?

The services of Arthur A. Phillpotts, curate at Brancepeth, are in constant demand. Diphtheria and scarlet fever stalk side by side claiming more victims, mainly the very young. Mr. John Straker, co-owner of Brandon Colliery, suffered the loss of his infant son Arthur. During November diphtheria claimed four more young souls from the colliery rows; Elizabeth Broadbent four years of age, Sarah Routledge three years of age, John Coulson two years, and William Thew also two, were victims. Joseph Love, like his co-partner, suffered a family loss, his infant daughter Susan, died at Willington House, a large mansion some three miles from Brandon Colliery.

On a happier note, five babies made the journey to Brancepeth during the year to receive baptism. They were Hannah, daughter of William and Sarah Garbutt; William, son of Thomas and Margaret Wilson—Thomas is a shoemaker; Thomas Jackson, son of Thomas and Elizabeth Dodds, the father is a blacksmith at the colliery; Jane Anne, daughter of George and Jane Coulson; John, son of Archibald and Margaret Anderson. George Coulson and Archibald Anderson are coal hewers. One feels sure that with whiskey at half a crown a bottle and sherry at one shilling and eightpence a bottle, samples would be in evidence after the ceremonies.

Sufficient coal is now being mined at the colliery to warrant frequent shipments to the London Coal Exchange. Twice during November, coal was dispatched to London fetching eighteen shillings and sixpence a ton.

1859

Thomas Rumley, aged twenty five, dropped the latch on the back door of No. 31 South Street. He instinctively trod the dark street. A nine hour shift as a coal hewer awaited him at the nearby pit whose heapstead pulsated. Tom's wife, Anne aged twenty three, like Tom, was born at South Hetton; they moved to Brandon Colliery from Nettlesworth near Durham, where their daughter Margaret, now three years of age, was born. Tom's thoughts centred on his wife and daughter, as with cloth cap perched on his head he mechanically crossed the long cloth scarf hanging round his neck, the ends of which he tucked under his trouser braces. His thick calico shirt, waistcoat and old jacket effectively cheating the January frost; his trousers, well patched, are drawn at the knees by lengths of string, strong hob-nailed boots cover thick woollen pit stockings. His bait of jam and bread, packed the previous night, nestles in the tin box carried under his arm. Precious cold water fills the tin bottle squeezed into his jacket pocket.

Tom met William Haye, another coal hewer, strong but less experienced at nineteen years of age. Will was born in Yorkshire, as was his wife, also named Anne. They have a baby; Hannah was born at Oakenshaw, another Straker and Love colliery, from which place they moved to Brandon Colliery, where they occupy No. 6 Railway Street.

Both Tom and Will on signing an agreement binding them to the colliery for twelve months, were allocated a colliery house.

Coke ovens, like so many giant bee-hives, have established themselves near the pit shaft. Gantries carry the coal to be tipped near their hungry mouths. Hewers like Tom and Will, with sweating, knot hard muscles, send up the best coking coal; sturdy Irishmen shovel the coal into the glowing ovens.

Streets have now acquired an identity; there are two short Railway Streets, two South Streets and Durham Street. About one hundred and fifty houses have been built and occupied.

James Anderson left the village school on Friday afternoon; at 5 a.m. on the Monday he went to work underground in the 'B' Pit. He had reached the manly age of eleven and started work as a trapper lad at tenpence a shift. Jim worked a twelve hour shift at his lonely job of tending a door. He opened the large wooden door through which putters brought their tubs. Wooden doors are installed to regulate the flow of air into the workings. Jim's work isn't hard. He descends first with the other lads, they are the last to ascend. His father, Archibald Anderson, a coal hewer, works a nine hour shift, some three hours less than his son.

On March 13th proud parents William and Ann Summers of South Street, had their twin baby daughters christened Georgina and Margaret in the village church at Brancepeth. William, a coal hewer in the 'B' Pit and a man of musical leanings will celebrate the event. At the same time he and his wife will take every precaution to safeguard the new arrivals against the twin scourge of scarlet fever and diphtheria still taking heavy toll in the county.

The pitmen of Brandon Colliery, eager for reform, signed a petition, they with other pitmen of Great Britain and Ireland, want an eight hour day. They would like to see that children under the age of fourteen work only half time. They say that coal owners should be obliged to use the patent safety cage; that a fund be provided by law to support disabled miners and the widows and orphans of those who have lost their lives in the mines;

and that the machinery used in raising coals should only be allowed to work nine hours a day.

The train is an established and convenient form of travel; it stops at Brandon Colliery siding on Saturdays and Sundays, passengers embark en route to Durham or Bishop Auckland.

Families are catered for at the Provision Market in Durham; potatoes are currently selling at sevenpence a peck, beef and pork sixpence a pound, mutton is dearer at eightpence a pound, a duck costs one shilling and ninepence, eggs are eighteen a shilling.

Dick Heslop helps with the weekend shopping, he finds it exciting taking the train ride to Durham on his fortnightly Saturday off, it is the highlight of his young life. Dick is fourteen years of age, he works a twelve hour shift as a putter in the same district as his mate, thirteen year old Jim Anderson who is now a pony driver. They descend and ascend in the cage together. During the winter months they see daylight only at weekends, their shift being from 5 a.m. to 5 p.m.

On most evenings around 6 p.m. refreshed after a bath and a hearty meal, Dick seeks the company of his friends. They gather at the gable end of No. 24 Railway Street whose five raised stone steps provide welcome seats. Here they gather, they come from the nearby South Streets. Any sign of frost in the air a warm spot is eagerly sought, the kitchen fire of the end house exudes warmth through the stone wall.

Dick was talking to Mary Clark. Mary is fourteen, she helps at home but hopes to start work in Mr. Smith's Paper Mill at Langley Grove about a mile away.

'What was your first cage ride like?' quizzed Mary.

'There was sickness in my belly—a bursting sensation in my ears, and worst of all, my heart almost jumped out of my mouth', answered Dick.

'What's it like down the pit?' pursued Mary.

'It's so black when my light goes out it is really frighteniing'. Mary learned that there were neither windows nor netties down the pit. Dick warmed to Mary.

Late nights become a regular summer feature. Indoor heat becomes oppressive. Catching tunes emanating from Will Summer's concertina capture the listeners as they gather at the end of Railway Street; men with their wives leave doors unlatched in the nearby streets to participate in the merriment.

The continuing hot summer favoured outdoor activities. Sunderland played at cricket, a team chosen from Brandon and Brancepeth. George Mann, a coal hewer and thirty seven years of age, plays for Brandon, his bandy legs a symbol of his trade. George is deft with pick and cricket bat. His prowess with the latter helped his side beat Sunderland.

Owing to the very hot weather and the seasonal decline in coal consumption, some pits are only working a four day week. Brandon Colliery pitmen are fortunate, the ever hungry coke oven keeps the pulleys revolving. Coal mined at the colliery is excellent for coke and coke gas.

Despite their full employment, Jack Scott, Isaac Parish, and the other coal hewers are 'acting the game'. Mr. Love has added half a hundredweight to the weight of a tub of coal. The weight he expects from the men is now nine and three quarter hundredweight. There is no mention of extra pay. Hewers grumble as they sit over their pint in the Colliery Inn; they resent having to hew the extra coal. The men expect pay for the increase in weight, especially as coal from the colliery is currently fetching eighteen shillings a ton on the London Coal Market.

During the year the Rev. A. Duncombe Shafto, aided by his curate, blessed fifteen marriages in the tiny village church. Only one couple came from Brandon Colliery.

Six babies born in the colliery rows were carried the two miles to Brancepeth for baptism. They were Georgina Summers; Margaret Wilkinson; George Crozier; John Henry Garbutt; Sarah Parish and John Caile.

Death struck ten homes during the year, six infants under the age of one being among the victims.

1860

New Year's Day. With a sigh the Rector of Brancepeth turned from his sitting room window; the castle stood majestic, a stone's throw away, a thick carpet of snow covered the approaches.

He threaded his way through the castle grounds to the small church of St. Brandon in whose grounds a small grave awaited the remains of Dorothy Robson born in Brandon Colliery only three weeks before. Her father, twenty seven year old Matt Robson is a coal hewer at the colliery.

On the afternoon the Rector's spirit lifted when he officiated at three baptisms, all the children were born at Brandon Colliery where their fathers are employed. They were George, son of Squire and Margaret Brook; Elizabeth, daughter of Christopher and Louise Richardson and Jane, daughter of Roger and Emma Hardman.

Men are realising the strength of Unions. Successful Unions are being formed in Durham and Northumberland. They are still relatively weak until they join the Miners' Federation of Great Britain. Brandon Colliery has at the moment, only a small union, not yet linked with the Federation. As more men and boys are employed the Union should develop.

On June 8th Mr. Roberts the Pitmen's Attorney General, proposed a Coal Mines Inspection Bill. Men like Thomas Bell with a thirteen year old pit lad son; Isaac Parish whose thirteen year old son Thomas is a putter; Mike Williamson whose eleven year old son works underground, and Robert Inness who has twelve year old William working in the pit, applaud the new proposals. Mr. Roberts seeks a working day of eight hours for boys between eight and fourteen years of age. He said that prior to the 1831 lockout the shift for lads in the pits had been fourteen hours a day and nine hours a day for men. The dispute went on for two months till the men had gained a twelve hour shift for the lads and various other concessions.

On the 22nd June Mr. Roberts added to his proposed Bill of June 8th 'That boys above the age of ten and under the age of sixteen be limited to ten hours a day'. As the lads work a twelve hour shift at Brandon Colliery, Thomas Bell and the other fathers anxiously await the acceptance of the Bill.

The Act of 1860 was passed. Pitmen had demanded a check-weighman of their own. This request was acceded to, unfortunately most coal owners are slow to implement it. At Brandon Colliery the banksman employed by Mr. Love checks the tubs of coal as they are brought to the surface. He is empowered to set aside any slack tubs.

Coal is coming to the surface, sufficient to warrant more frequent shipments to the London Market. Two shipments brought 18s.6d. and 19s. a ton respectively. Coal hewers say that coals sold on the Market are not subject to Set-out and Laid-out; why should theirs?

Robert Tindale; John Hindmarsh; Stephen Crozier; Jacob Brown; Thomas Suggett; Will Blades; Will Hartley; Martin Levine and their pit lad sons, putters and drivers, help make landowner and Railway Company more affluent. Since Messrs. Straker and Love leased the huge tract of land the royalties of Brancepeth Estate have leapt astronomically. The colliery owners pay to the Estate a fixed sum of money for every ton of coal mined. By agreement this coal passes over a portion of the Bishop Auckland line of railway. Taking the carriage of coke and coal of one penny per ton per mile over an average distance of eight miles the Railway Company must derive an annual revenue from this source alone of upwards of seventeen thousand pounds. As the demand for coal from this district continues to increase this annual revenue will be exceeded. It is estimated, that since the Hon. G. F. Hamilton Russell succeeded to this lucrative Estate he has added upwards of twelve thousand pounds a year to his rent-roll.

Agricultural workers continue to desert the land where wages are very poor. There are a number of jobs at the colliery offering bigger wages, most jobs qualify the worker for a house.

The following are a few examples of wages paid at the colliery—
Overman underground earns from 25s. to 33s. a week.
Overman's assistant earns from 22s; to 26s. a week.
Deputy, the next grade earns from 3s. 4d. to 3s. 9d. a day.
Ordinary wasteman earns from 16s. to 19s. a week.
Principal wastemen earns from £1 to £1. 10s a week.
Shifters and Rolleyway men earn from 2s 6d to 3s. 4d. a day.
Hewers average 3s. 9d. a day.
Putters earn 2. 2d. to 2s. 6d. a day.

Drivers earn 1s. 6d. a day.
Trappers are paid 10d. a day.
Horsekeepers underground earn 14s. a week.
Furnacemen earn 14s. to 16s. a week.
Banksmen are paid 4s. a day.
Blacksmiths and masons earn 17s. to 21s. a week.
Waggonway men on the surface earn 2s. 6d. to 3s. a day.

Joseph Addison, forty three years of age, hails from Dumbarton in far off Scotland. He has two jobs, during the day he works as a labourer, at night he and his wife, forty year old Hannah, run the New Colliery Inn. They are kept busy catering for the needs of the ever expanding work force.

Will Dickinson and some twenty men celebrated the inauguration of the Foresters' Court Pride of Brandon, No. 3333. The Foresters was founded to help the poor. Their aim is to help them financially and save them from the Poor Law. Will, being a public spirited man, had contacted Joseph Addison who joined the Court; he provided a room in which to launch Brandon Colliery's first active Society.

A gig carried twins Elizabeth and Thomas Mann,, children of George and Mary Mann, to their christening at Brancepeth. George is a coal hewer in the 'B' Pit. Jubilation was tragically terminated when the twins died two days later. No doubt George will long reflect on the cruel twist of fate as he sits on his cracket hewing coal.

John Caile, John Minto, William Bowman and William Wilson, all lads from Brandon Colliery, landed themselves into trouble by playing football in the lane running to East Brandon. They appeared at Durham County Police Court. The case was dismissed, the Bench having no desire to interfere with their amusements; but desired them, while at play, not to interfere with or annoy people. At the same time, at the Durham County Court, a labourer employed by Messrs. Straker and Love, claimed more pay. He is in charge of a colliery owned horse and cart and he empties the 'middens' and ashpits. He receives three shillings a day for three days in the week; and in order to make up his wages to such a sum as would support him, he had the privilege of screening ashes, which when screened, he disposes of to the neighbouring farmers at so much per load.

Thomas Rumley, Will Hartley, Matthew Innes and John Wilkinson, all coal hewers, were among the pitmen who renewed their twelve month bond at the beginning of December. All are married men with young families, some of whom are pony drivers, others are helpers and putters. Most men are loath to leave their job and the security of a colliery house and coals. Some of the single men, more adventurous, elect to sign on elsewhere.

'Good morning, ladies!'

'Good morning, Mr. Dunn!' replied his neighbours in East Street. Thomas Dunn, replete in blue serge pit clothes, jacket, waistcoat, half trousers fastened just below his knees by tapes, navy blue pit stockings and polished pit boots, strode towards the pit. His leather skull cap, polished black, with peak turned to the rear, shone in the wintry sunlight. His tapered yardstick swung with each measured stride as he swiftly covered the short distance to the pit.

Thomas Dunn, a widower of some years, at fifty your years of age is the colliery's first viewer; he moved from Shincliffe, near Durham. He lodges with William Dove and his family at No. 19 East Street, the end house of a short row. William at forty-one is a joiner at the colliery and came from Whickham near Blaydon. Mr. Dunn is a respected gaffer. He descends the pit every day; the men know that he must implement the owners' wishes in everything related to the pit.

Mr. Love the colliery owner moved from Willington into a huge house just up the road from Durham Railway Station and Wharton Park, he named it Mount Beaulah. His new residence is within easy reach of his colliery interests.

Intense cold weather over Christmas froze the River Wear at Durham. Robert Towers, James and Thomas Conley, Jonathan Blackett, and James Pickles, all young lads from Brandon Colliery, thought the three mile walk little price to pay for the exciting time spent on the lantern illuminated ice. Householders with gas and water taps found them frozen.

On Christmas Day, John Green only three weeks old, was carried the two miles to Brancepeth for burial at St. Brandon's. He made a sad total of twenty-four Brandon Colliery souls buried in the village churchyard during the year, of that number, sixteen were infants.

Fourteen babies were baptised during the year. Seven couples from Brandon Colliery celebrated their marriage over that period, all seven 'grooms being pitmen at the colliery.

1861

Early January brought heavy snowfalls. William Anderson, William Blades. John Garbutt, his sisters Mary and Margaret, Edward Parkinson, Mary Ann Dickinson, and Mary Raine, all pupils at East Brandon's National School, were jubilant. Snow had blocked the two lanes converging on the village, sixty pupils revelled in the enforced holiday.

Cold weather brought extra bonus. Some children were allowed the use of the chiffonier bed. The low bedrooms are reached by ladder. Cold penetrates the loose fitting windows, at such times a bed set before the kitchen fire is alluring.

Most families possess a chiffonier, this is a folding bedstead resembling an ordinary chest of drawers or cupboard, with two doors at the front. During the day it stands tall against the kitchen wall, at night the doors are opened and the bed is lowered. Most children prefer the chiffonier to a bed upstairs.

Will Dickinson, a tall thirty year old muscular pitman, finished trimming his beard; Mary Ann and Margaret, his two daughters born at Brancepeth Colliery some two miles away, long housebound by snowstorms, hungered for a walk. Eager to go, they showed impatience. The trio left their Durham Street home.

Will thought that the lane leading to Langley Moor Inn was about the dirtiest in the north country; for some two hundred yards the three travellers struggled to free their boots from the glutinous mud. He made a mental note of the inhospitable scene. On reaching Langley Paper Mill Cottages—six one-roomed cottages occupied by Paper Mill workers, and sited midway between Brandon Colliery and Durham, he found the highway flooded knee deep. The River Browney had overflowed its banks. As Will carried four year old Margaret shoulder high, he reflected on the possibility of a fatal accident as there was no fence of any kind to prevent anyone falling into the river. He made further mental notes. To avoid the two hundred years stetch of mud, they would, on their return, have to travel to Meadow Field and go a mile about by the turnpike road. Being a public spirited man, Will intended, at an early date, drawing the surveyor's attention to the filthy and deplorable state of the road. On the credit side Will noted that the owners of Brandon Colliery had made a good road from the low end of the colliery up to Brandon-on-the-hill.

Blood, sweat and tears are synonymous with colliery life. A fatal accident, the first during the five years' life of the colliery, occurred on Wednesday April 3rd. Charles Bainbridge lived two miles away at Neville's Cross, near Durham, and was employed as a screen hand at the colliery. He was riding on the waggons on the railway near the colliery, when they gave a jerk and he was pitched onto the line. On seeing a train of waggons coming in the opposite direction, he made effort to get clear of the line, but tripping on the rail, the waggons came up and nearly severed his leg from his body close to the trunk. He was taken to Durham County Hospital, where amputation was performed, but he gradually sank and died the same night. The unfortunate young man, who had served some time with Mr. Arden, chemist in Silver Street, Durham, was only twenty years of age, he leaves a wife and child to lament his early death.

During April a National Census was taken. Brandon Colliery, in five years, has a population of six hundred and seventy one in its one hundred and thirty three occupied houses. Ten years ago when the last census was taken, Brandon Colliery was unconceived. At that time the population of Brandon and Byshottles was five hundred and twenty five. Now it is fourteen hundred and eighty six; the increase being due to collieries like Brandon's with rows of new houses and large families.

The Viscount and Viscountess Boyne returned home to Brancepeth Castle after their winter sojourn in Burwarton Hall, their seat in Shropshire.

As their train puffed its way through Brandon, a lean, pale faced putter of fifteen puffed his way behind an empty tub some twenty five fathoms below ground. The place in which George Blackett hewed was stowed off. As Will Dunn ran the empty tub into the hewing place George shouted 'Get strite back, ah'll fill this one strite up'.

Will Dunn knew that the other three hewers detailed to him would also be stowed off. He had had one of those off days 'when nowt gans reet'. He hurried, bent double, his sweat grimed boyish face stinging from the heat of the candle secured to the tub, smoke seared his eyes. His heavy boots slid on the wet floor of the seam; icy water splashed his belly showing between vest and hoggers. A sudden jerk! The tub flies off the way, all four wheels; a solid immovable wall confronted him, of all the rotten luck, it had to happen where the roadway was at its narrowest, little more than the width of the tub.

Will stuck his candle holder into a nearby prop; swearing, he turned his back on the tub and tried to arse it onto the way. His struggles only succeeded in moving it an inch, the roof preventing further progress. Only one thing to do! Get to the front of the tub and try to lift that end. Pieces of stone pack were urgently removed and bundled behind him; he crawled on his side past the tub. 'Oh, God!' he hissed through clenched teeth as a jagged piece of stone grazed his back, knocking off a scab healing from the previous week. 'Fill the bloody pit in and give the farmer his bloody field back!' he screamed in agony as his rough vest touched the raw flesh. He suddenly felt all alone and forgotten. Having eased up the fore end of the tub he had to pack small stones under the wheels while keeping the tub lifted. Stomach and leg muscles knotted agonisingly, water squelched from his boots. He worked in near darkness. On feeling his sore lumbar region he swore profusely. He crawled painfully and gingerly back and treated the other end in similar manner. He had leverage now and managed to lift the tub onto a loose four foot rail, the tub being pulled back a few yards onto secure way he fixed the loose rails. As he knotted the two ends of a broken boot lace together, a candle approached. George Blackett dressed like Will in rough vest and hoggers, shouted, 'What's the matter? Do yer want a hand?' 'Yer too bloody late mister', came the reply as Will, with lungs nearly bursting, trundled his way to the flat.

Workers and their families are streaming into Brandon Colliery. On signing the yearly bond, family men are given a colliery house.

John Carroll is twenty nine years of age; he signed to hew coal at the colliery. He and his wife Margaret aged twenty four, were born in Ireland, they went to Seaton Colliery where Mary, their two year old daughter, was born. They now occupy No. 19 South Street; it is a three roomed house with a small kitchen and a low attic which is reached by a ladder. Attached to the house is a small quarl-paved yard.

John Jefferson is another immigrant, he is twenty five and was set on as a deputy overman. He moved to Brandon Colliery from North Shields with his wife twenty-one year old Jane, and their daughter Hannah who is two. No. 25 South Street is their new home.

John Watson, another official just set on, is fifty years of age, he moved from Chester-le-Street some nine miles away. He and John Jefferson will take charge of coal hewers George Maddison, William Leighton and John Wilkinson, who have just moved to South Street. George Williamson also lives in the long street. George is eleven years of age and earns tenpence a day working as a trapper lad underground.

Thomas Stout and his family also settled in South Street. There are five pitmen in the family, four children attend the village school. Mrs. Stout also has a lodger, a single young man of twenty three. She is kept busy looking after her large family.

Hugh McDermott, a thirty year old coke drawer born in Ireland, helped Alexander McDonald the twenty year old colliery cartman, load the colliery cart. The family and furniture had just arrived at Brandon Railway Siding from Bishop Auckland some eight miles away.

One chiffonier, a table, one form, a large rocking chair, a cradle and other goods of miscellaneous nature were piled onto the large flat cart. Pride of place went to the sparkling new brass and iron bedstead Hugh had just purchased for twelve shillings and sixpence. Jane McDermott, also Irish born and thirty three years of age, carrying Mary Elizabeth their new baby, had moved ahead to open up their new home, No. 16 Railway Street. Alice aged seven, born at Brancepeth, and Edward her two year old brother born at Hunwick, perched themselves high on the cart, eager to explore their new home. Railway Street, only a few hundred yards from the siding, was soon reached, the hard dirt packed road presenting the powerful Clydesdale horse no problems.

Alice and Edward were soon exploring their new home. Their mother quickly had a healthy fire going in the spacious grate; the previous tenant had left the quarled kitchen floor scrubbed clean. Hugh McDermott and the cartman swiftly transferred the furniture. Alice and her brother claimed the settle, there they would be warm and out of the way, Mary Elizabeth slept cosily in her cradle. Ann Haye, a Yorkshire woman and wife of a coal hewer, lived next door at No. 15; she welcomed her new neighbours with pots of hot coffee.

Thomas Gibbons, another newcomer, hails from West Rainton. He and his family moved to 21 South Street; Thomas was welcomed by the viewer at the colliery, six pitmen in one family guaranteed a colliery house. Dorothy Gibbons has a son aged twelve who attends the National School at East Brandon.

In just under five years of growth the colliery now boasts two Railway Streets, two South Streets, East Street, Durham Street and the Colliery Inn, shops and more houses are under construction.

More streets mean increased sale for the paraffin man whose small pony hauls the sturdy cart on which is perched the square paraffin tank. Oil for work costs one penny a day. Paraffin lamps for the home can be bought for one shilling and ninepence.

Pitmen nationwide have long agitated against child labour and their conditions of work. On July 1st a new Mines Act came into force, which amongst other important provisions stated that no boy should go down the mine under the age of twelve unless he could produce a certificate proving that he could read and write; that boys under the age of twelve should go to school five hours per day. It also stated that coal should be weighed, and that workmen should be at liberty to appoint a check weighman. Pitmen at Brandon Colliery look forward to the day when the Mines Act becomes fully operative.

On Saturday August 27th, forty members of the Court Pride of Brandon No. 3333 of the Order of Foresters, presided over by a very proud Brother Dickinson, sat down to an excellent dinner supplied by Brother Joseph Addison. The Colliery Inn, aptly named as the pit shaft lies only a short distance from the parlour, was crowded on this, the first anniversary of Brandon Colliery Lodge. Mrs. Addison and her daughters Mary aged twelve and June, ten helped serve the ample meal provided.

The businessman from the south of England arrived in Brandon Colliery. He booked a room in the Colliery Inn for the night before continuing to Carlisle. From an upstairs room emanated noise from the gathering of Foresters. The stranger sat in the smoke-filled bar, drank the strong beer, and chatted with the pitmen customers; he struggled to follow the pitmatic dialogue. Oil lamps smoked fitfully as they swung from the ceiling, spittoons, sawdust filled, liberally dotted the floor, their fresh blacklead coating conspicuous against the scrubbed floor. Through the smoky haze he selected a free clay pipe from a box on the end of the bar. He saw men ascend from the pit a few yards away, probably horse keepers homeward bound after bedding down the ponies.

As he paid his bill on the following morning he confided in his host, the belief that before his arrival, he erroneously thought that pitmen lived, like the ponies, down the pit near their work. He moved on, an enlightened man, he has supped with the men, conversed with them, and had seen them come out of the pit.

Men have moved to Brandon Colliery. Men with business acumen who know that an expanding community needs goods of every description. Richard Preston at thirty five is a coke manufactor from Lancester, his wife hails from Middlesex. They with their three young children have just moved from Brancepeth Colliery into No. 1 High Street, their new shop and home. James Jackson Ferens, forty five years old, runs a grocer shop next door at No. 2 High Street. He arrived from Northumberland with his forty seven year old wife Martha; their two sons, John sixteen and Robert fourteen, help in the shop. A servant girl, hired at Durham, is nineteen year old Jane Bowes.

The repercussions of war! During October the price of tobacco leapt from three pence an ounce to three pence halfpenny an ounce. Many pitmen, both men and lads, chew tobacco as well as smoke it. Old women bring out clay pipes, they gather round the kitchen fire and bemoan the increase in price said to be the result of the Civil War.

A. F. Forster giving evidence to the Educational Commissioners concerning all classes of Durham and Northumberland wrote 'The colliers of Northumberland and Durham are the lowest in the social scale, a heterogeneous rapidly increasing population, earning 3s. to 5s. a day (of eight hours), with a dwelling and coal free, living for the most part in the grossest sensuality, aggravated by the 'truck' or 'tommy shop' system. They dwell in isolated villages belonging to the coal owner, of 'miserable and repulsive aspect, without pavement, drainage, or enclosure in front or rear'. Few houses have more than three rooms. The consequence is that 'adultery is a matter of jest; and incest is frightfully common, and seems to excite no disgust; language even among women, boys and girls, is profane and filthy in the extreme. Attempts at improvement of dwellings are greatly frustrated by want of appreciation and liability to turn-outs'.

The foregoing remarks brought the following reply from Archdeacon Thorp of The College, Durham, a past defender of the working classes:

'I do not hesitate to express my utter disbelief in these assertions. Long acquaintance with the pit population emboldens me to do so; and I have a confidence that the voice and verdict of the county will be with me. For myself, I must say that the pitmen are a body long known to me, whose character and conduct command my respect and affectionate regard'.

William Dickinson, a Brandon Colliery pitman, took up his pen.

To the Editor of the Durham Chronicle.

Dear Sir,

Seeing an article in last week's impression of your widely circulated newspaper, headed 'Durham Miners'. I would like to make a few remarks upon the charges A. F. Forster Esq., has laid against them in his report to the Educational Commissioners. He stated that the miners of Durham and Northumberland were a set of men who made good wages. I will take that to be correct at some places, but there are other places in this district where good and industrious men cannot get what will maintain their families with the bare necessities of life. Mr. Forster says that they make from 3s. to 5s. per day of eight hours, but it is more frequently ten or eleven hours instead of eight hours per day; a man with a family of six or seven children, with only his wage to maintain them, cannot live in such gross sensuality. There are hundreds can bear me out in this assertion; and, as for living in isolated villages of miserable and repulsive aspect, without drainage, or enclosure in front or rear, any of your readers who have visited Seaham, Seaton or Brandon collieries, and many others, will give the lie to Mr. Forster. As to adultery being a jest, I cannot find words of disaprobation for such a falsehood. I do not doubt but exceptional cases of adultery are committed both in Northumberland and Durham. But are there no other counties where adultery is more rife in them? If Mr. Forster looks to the middle and higher classes, to which I take him to belong, he will find adultery more common than among the working classes; and for incest, I would like to know if ever there was such a case brought under his notice in the counties of Northumberland and Durham. I wish that his moral, social and domestic character be as good as the generality of the Durham miners are.

Mr. Archdeacon Thorp deserves the thanks of the miners for his excellent remarks in their defence, which he has given from personal experience amongst them. Well might that gentleman say that Mr. Forster had put himself into bad company, and sought out very doubtful sources for his information. If that gentleman is ever sent upon such a commission again, as to investigate into the position of miners, I hope he will make a more true statement, and not bring us below the social position of the slaves of the disunited States of America, and the Red Indians, or the serfs of Russia. I hope these few remarks will bring some abler pen to bear on this subject. By letting this appear in your next impression, you will oblige your humble servant.

Brandon Colliery, December 1861.

On December 29th Thomas and Mary Suggett had an addition to the family baptised. Michael is their fifth child. Thomas is twenty eight years of age and is a coal hewer; the family had moved from Shildon.

Nine babies were baptised at Brancepeth during the year. The curate J. C. Bulmer buried three Brandon Colliery infants; they were Jane Anne Bowes, eighteen months, George Brooks fifteen months, and Anne Garbutt, one month.

1862

Brandon Colliery, ever expanding, both below and above ground, imported ponies from Galloway in Scotland, they were allotted new stables built near the shaft.

Tired men trudged out-bye after the shift at the coal face. The sound of pounding hooves and rattling chains broke up the orderly file; bodies clung to the side of the narrow roadway, others found refuge in small recesses. James Anderson, Will Martin and John Bell, all established pony drivers were likewise homeward bound; their mounts, anticipating a meal of choppy, were galloping without guidance away to the shaft. As they passed John Watson, the fifty year old overman, each one received a resounding whack on his rear as he lay with light extinguished, and head tucked well out of sight, prone across his gallowa.

Police Constable Coverdale at twenty seven years of age is the colliery policeman, he moved from Castle Eden to lodge with John Dunn in East Street. He caught John Hepplewhite, a seventeen year old pitman, who lives with his widowed mother in the same street, setting some trucks away at the colliery. He removed the wooden drag from a waggon which ran forty yards and bumped into two coke waggons knocking off some of the coke. The Bench, after pointing out the folly and the danger of the act, ordered him to pay sixpence damages and the costs. P.C. Graham on night patrol, found Robert Carnes, a rodney, sleeping in an empty coke oven at the colliery. Damage had been done to property by vagrants who were in the habit of taking up their nightly abode in the coke ovens. He was committed to prison for three days.

Mr. Love added half a hundredweight and four pounds to the standard weight of a tub of coals. The total weight of a tub at Brandon Colliery now stands at ten and a quarter hundredweight four pounds. As no increase in price is offered, emotion is running high among the hewers, tempers are almost at breaking point. Hewers at Mr. Love's other collieries are said to suffer the same imposition. Robert Tindale, Archibald Anderson, Squire Brooks, George Maddison, Richard Lamb, Featherstone Wallace and Thomas Lamb, all hewers, are some of the men objecting to what they call the 'big filling'; to achieve the weight demanded, the men are having to flatten down the coal in the tub when the height of the seam allows them.

Putters, helpers and drivers have adopted the mood of the hewers and are 'playing hell'. James Conley 14, his brother Thomas 12, Will Leighton 11, Edward Parkinson 10, Will Levine 12, John Gibson 14, Thomas Parrish 13, John Inness 15, Will his 13 year old brother, Matt Hirst, 16, Will Hirst 13, George Hirst 12, Robert Towers 11, George 13, George Mann 15, Robert Scott 14 and 13 year old Will Wearmouth, all realise that derailment of the tub means more weight to lift.

The men await the day when their tubs will be weighed and checked under honest supervision. Mr. Love, by this latest addition to the weight acquires eleven and a quarter hundredweight of coal without cost, out of every twenty one tubs of coal the hewer fills.

Pitmen, anxious for the wellbeing of their families, are seeking to safeguard their future. Fatal pit accidents leave widows and young dependants destitute. Pitmen in the county would like to see launched a permanent fund; a fund from which a weekly allowance would be made to any unfortunate dependants of such accidents. The need for such a scheme was forcefully brought home by the news of the fearful Hartley New Pit disaster on January 16th, when two hundred and seven men and boys lost their lives. The calamity rendered four hundred and seven dependants destitute.

Every colliery village and town throughout the land has reacted to the tragedy. Funds are being raised for the dependants; Mr. Straker, co-owner of Brandon Colliery, immediately became one of a committee of fifteen set up to solicit donations for the Hartley New Pit accident fund. Viscount Boyne of Brancepeth sent fifty pounds. Both land owner and coal owner have shown positive response.

Shortly after the Hartley catastrophe, workmen at Brandon Colliery asked Mr. Dunn the colliery viewer, to chair a meeting in the joiner's shop, which he had loaned for the purpose. The workshop was crowded with men, there to find the best means to help the destitute widows and orphans. Each man was asked to pay one shilling, every putter sixpence, and other boys threepence a week towards the fund. It was suggested that any surplus arising from the fund should go towards the permanent fund for the near relatives of pit accident victims. Tom Dunn, John Watson and Archibald Thompson, the colliery cashier and local preacher, were appointed to collect the money. Ralph Jackson, Martin Lewins and William Dickinson were elected to help collect money from the men in their working area. One week after the appeal Brandon Colliery workmen gave £11:8s:6d. to the fund. Mr. Love, the colliery co-owner, gave ten guineas.

In almost every home in the colliery the topic of conversation is either the Hartley disaster or the proposed relief fund. Men forgot their own immediate grievances as they sat over their pint in the Colliery Inn; their troubles slight compared with the Hartley Colliery folks'. The colliery headstock set only a few paces from the Inn, a grim reminder of recent tragedy.

Samuel Routledge and his wife shared great personal loss; just two months after the death of their baby son Samuel they suffered further family bereavement. Sarah, their three year old daughter, died, stricken with scarlet fever, which is still rife in the county. Their neighbours in South Street comforted them on their double loss.

Mr. John Smith a local capitalist, lives in an ample house. Langley Grove is set among stately trees a few yards from the River Browney whose errant waters teem with trout. He employs sixty girls and eleven men in his Paper Mill at Langley, some of whom live at Brandon Colliery, their wages helping to support their familes.

On Easter Sunday, whole families out to enjoy the brilliant sunshine, walked to Langley Grove where Mr. Smith had organised a steeplechase. During the afternoon amid continuous sunshine, various races were run, the highlight being the steeplechase. Contestants, undaunted, splashed across the River Browney and scrambled over hedge and ditch to the great amusement of the crowd.

Business in Brandon Colliery is thriving; Jobson Magdin, a twenty three year old butcher born in Hetton-le-Hole, requires an apprentice to the butchering trade, he prefers one who has been in the business. Mr. Magdin has a shop in High Street along with Richard Preston and James Jackson Ferens who are doing brisk business. These shops obviate the weekly journey to Durham Provision Market.

Pitmen of Durham and Northumberland are jubilant. On June 7th they celebrated the launching of a Miners' Permanent Fund; they know, that in the case of accidents at work, their financial worries in future will be considerably alleviated. Collieries are asked to send one penny per man towards the Management Expenses. Subscribers to the Fund contribute and silently pray that they never have to draw on the Fund's resources.

There's talk of winding up the Hartley Disaster Fund, by the end of June the magnificent total of £78,647:8s.:5d. had been collected for the dependants. The press loudly applauded the efforts made in reaching such a staggering sum. Workmen of Brandon Colliery have sent money on three occasions to the Fund.

The ideal summer helped along the cricket programme. Brandon Colliery in form, beat Lumley on the last day of August by four wickets. George Mann and John Briggs handled their bats excellently, Mann scored nineteen and Briggs scored sixteen, it seems they are adept with cricket bat and coal hewer's pick. George and John leave behind their grievances when they are called before the wicket. They and other men at Brandon Colliery are growing restive; every week they complain about the 'big filling', they resent having to rock every tub of coal to escape confiscation of the contents.

August, while good for summer sport, has been bad for the coal trade. Several collieries are working a three day week with no sign of immediate improvement. Brandon Colliery coke ovens, now covering a large area to the south of the pit, are keeping the men fully occupied.

The most notable Act of the year was passed in November. The new law stated that colliery owners had to see that their pits had two exits. No one wanted a recurrence of the Hartley Pit disaster, when a pumping beam crashed down the only shaft and blocked escape.

Christmas Day which fell on a Thursday, was welcomed with the news that potatoes had dropped in price to eightpence a stone; beef and mutton cost sixpence a pound. Good news too, for William Dickinson and Coxon Gelson who each had a son baptised. During the year there were seven Brandon Colliery babies baptised at Brancepeth. Out of ten colliery folk buried there, five were infants. John Dunn and Catherine Westgarth both from the colliery, celebrated Christmas by their marriage at Brancepeth.

1863

Hannah Garbutt, almost five years of age, complete with bait poke containing her sandwich dinner, grasped her eight year old brother's hand. John and Hannah waved to their mother standing in the doorway of their Durham Street home. Hannah brushed a tear from her cheek and felt for the bull's eye sweet that nestled in her coat pocket. She was making her school debut; boots sparkled, as did hands and face, she wore knee length belted coat, black wool stockings, all new, the hall-mark of a new starter.

They strode the mile up the hill to the National School at East Brandon where Mr. Hall had just retired as school master. The school requires a replacement whose yearly salary would be £60 with free house and coal allowance.

Hannah would miss her daily enraptured gaze into the low window of No. 8 East Street, the operation made possible with the help of a large stone recently carted from the quarry. Bull's eyes at one farthing each, sugared fish at two for a farthing, both her favourites, occupied a prominent place in the window. Mrs. Beal's kitchen was a veritable treasure chest; a large jar of vinegar propped open the door, a round of cheese, a bag of sugar, tea, yeast, and a large roll of tobacco, were but a few of the commodities stored into one small room.

Owing to the industrial expansion with its influx of workmen, there is talk of Brandon and Byshottles adopting the Local Government Act of 1858. In the five years since the Act was passed, the villages comprising the Byshottles are in need of responsible people to run their affairs. Three people are expected to be chosen for the task.

There is a general depression in the coal trade. Brandon Colliery, among others, is only working a three day week, pitmen and their families are hard put to manage on their earnings. Pitmen at the colliery are discontented, working a short week adds to their troubles; they are 'playing hell' about the big tub and not getting a just weight. Ugly rumours are abroad; some diehards are shouting 'enough'; there is talk of strong action being taken.

Another Langley Steeplechase day! On Saturday April 18th men forgot their grievances. Mr. Smith the Paper Mill owner again organised the event. Another beautiful day favoured the crowd drawn to witness the events, the first race was at 10 a.m. The River Browney once again proved a formidable obstacle for most of the competitors in the main event. Men from Brandon Colliery and the surrounding villages took part. The North Durham Militia Band, to the crowd's enjoyment, played lively music to help make the second Langley Steeplechase a success. Success favoured Bill Cartwright when he won the Champion Belt, he beat Jack Phillips in the foot race; he also won the £2 a side bet.

Short working weeks, discontent at the pit, and smallpox, have combined to create deep depression in Brandon Colliery. An epidemic of the dread disease is taking a heavy toll of life; twelve residents succumbed during the first five months of the year, of that number, nine were infants. On June 20th, William, the five year old son of William Snowdon, became a victim. Six days later, tragedy struck again, the disease claimed the baby of the family, seven month old John Michael. Will and Sarah Garbutt lost Anne, their three year old daughter. Affluence has no defence against the dread disease. Mr. Smith's nine month old daughter, Ann Wright Smith, rests with the other victims in the village churchyard.

Messrs. Straker and Love, due to the expanding property at their collieries, have had their houses, coke ovens and other pit property re-rated under the Parochial Assessment Act. The new rates are: Engine at each pit £50 each; miners' cottages £3:12s. each; coke ovens, where the smoke is not consumed are rated at £2 each, £1:10s. to be charged where the smoke is consumed. This latter change in the rating is to encourage the reduction of smoke.

A week of heavy thunderstorms, lightning and copious showers of rain over the district caused heavy damage to wheat and uncut grass. The weather did little to cheer men in their present mood. Pitmen met in the Colliery Inn, others at corner ends, most were unwilling to continue working under the existing conditions.

Squire Brook, George Maddison, Richard Lamb and Will Hartley, all young coal hewers with families to support, left their work in the Hutton Seam on Monday 19th October. Black, tired and hungry after their nine hour shift, they were grimly determined that the time for positive action to be taken had arrived. They had heard that the collieries at Willington, Brancepeth and Oakenshaw, all owned by Straker and Love, were on the brink of a strike for similar reasons.

On the evening of the 19th a gig travelled the four miles from Oakenshaw where a meeting of colliery workers had been held. The driver of the gig, amid much gesticulation, announced that the men at Straker and Love's collieries were withdrawing their labour from tomorrow. Brandon Colliery workmen immediately followed suit.

Next day, October 20th, knots of apprehensive women gathered, worried, but totally behind their menfolk in demanding justice.

Silence reigned at the pit-head. Coke ovens cooled off as cinder drawers left their work to make a total of 308 men and boys refusing to work at Brandon Colliery, of this number 214 were members of the Union. About 1000 men from neighbouring Willington, Brancepeth and Oakenshaw collieries came out on strike. Houghall and Shincliffe collieries, under the same ownership, being sympathetic to the cause, may follow suit.

Mr. Love retaliated by having twelve of the striking pitmen arrested. Pitmen from the collieries concerned in the dispute crowded the Police Court at Durham; to their great delight, the twelve men were discharged. Triumphantly a pigeon was immediately sent off carrying the good news. The pitmen continued their strike; heartened by their first victory, they sensed some early outside support.

The strike is over the men not being paid for alleged 'slack tubs'. The banksman is the sole decider whether the tub is passed as full or slack, he works for the owner. The men want a representative at the surface to keep check on the tubs; they do not mind being paid lower wages for slack tubs sent up.

Pitmen from the four collieries feel justified in taking strike action. They have named the stoppage 'The Rocking Strike'. The name arises from the custom which obtains of setting out tubs if they are not level full when they come to bank. In order that this might be attained, the hewer walks around the tub and strikes it with his mell; he even shakes and rocks it, so that the jolting on the road out-bye does not settle the coal lower than the rim of the tub. If it settles below the rim the entire content is liable to confiscation.

This system is enforced in a glaring manner; the master's man is paid a commission on every slack tub he finds, his judgement could be at fault. The 1861 Act requires that the men have a weigh man, this is being denied them; the demands of the men are payment by weight and an advance in wages.

Four days after the commencement of the strike, each striker received a printed notice:

To the men of Brandon and Willington Collieries:

'Take notice, that by your having absented yourself from our service, you have determined and broken your contract of hiring with us; and we hereby require you to deliver up to us the possession of the cottage house which you have occupied as our servant before the 27th day of October, 1863; and in default of you doing so, you will be turned out of possession'.

Dated the 24th day of October 1863.

'The Owners of Brandon Colliery'.

Mr. Love asserts that the true origin of the strike is an advance of from 20 to 25 per cent. He further asserts that a good workman at any of his collieries can make 5s. and upwards in eight hours and that is the standard by which he fixes the price in every colliery.

He has taken the average of 20 for the last six fortnights at Brandon Colliery and finds it upwards of £3 nett to each man. The advance asked would increase the average to nearly £4 a fortnight. He goes on to say that any advance is impracticable much less the demand of 20 to 25 per cent. Finally he states, that however long the men may be able to stand out, the masters have no alternative but to resist.

The owners offered 9¼d. per ton working. This offer the men rejected as they claimed this would be ½d. per ton less than previously.

One cause of the strike: the men demanded a change from measure of coal to weight. They wanted the appointment of two men, one of whom would be paid by the men, to see that the tubs were weighed and properly accounted for.

Newspaper reporters condemned Mr. Love's action of ejection, they said that he must have a heart of stone. War could not be a greater misfortune to these desperate women and children. Men, women and children are being put out of their homes in the cold, winter weather.

Grace Anderson, twelve years of age; Will Suggett nine; Ned Parkinson, a twelve year old striker, and Will Levine, another striker at the age of fourteen, searched the spoil heap for remnants of coal. Coal which had adhered to the layer of band sent out of the pit and had been rejected to the heap.

Trespassers Edward and Will, windblown, one eye open for P.C. Coverdale, set to with manly vigour; household coal allowance now spent, they had elected to scrat for replacement. Work palling, out of shape tin dishes, battered and ejected tin bath-tubs were commandeered to serve as sledges to skim the steep slope of the spoil heap. Amid youthful shrieks the improvised toboggans careered the slope with consequent wear on breeches and boots. Grace would have to give good account of her torn skirt.

On entering its third week, the strike was reported on by a special correspondent of the Daily Telegraph, who dispatched the following:—

'Deceived by a treacherous gleam of sunshine yesterday I took an early walk along the pleasant road from the city of Durham to Willington, a distance of some eight miles. About midway, a little past a spot called Langley Moor, I fell in with a party of the Brandon Colliery men, who are out on strike with the Brancepeth, Oakenshaw and Sunnybrow pits. Conversing with them on the subject of their difference with Messrs. Straker and Love, their employers, I found these pitmen—whose decent Sunday dress, perfect cleanliness, and general appearance of sober and careful habits belied the common notion of character in the mining districts of the country—as well informed set of workmen as any I have met in a gathering of the same number.

They fell to discussing all the circumstances of their present position, with a calmness indicating their faith in the justice of the cause to which they are pledged. They had heard no news that morning from Oakenshaw, to which colliery they looked as a special source of information, it being a kind of headquarters. (The men seemed well informed having read the Newcastle Chronicle and Durham Advertiser). On walking away they met a chap who had ridden from Oakenshaw in a gig, they broke into their own mystifying dialect'.

Two days after the reporter's encounter with the striking pitmen, Mr. Love sent a letter to the public through the Durham Advertiser. He denied that there were 1200 men on strike at the collieries of Messrs. Straker and Love. He said in the statement that the Coke Burners are **Underpaid** on these collieries is an untruth. He suggests that the real secret of the conflict is whether the regulations of the Colliery are to be carried out by the Owners or the Union Committee; the latter is impossible.

John Henry Garbutt at eight years of age, sensed the dramatic change in his home. His father, once kind and patient, was morose in his enforced idleness. His mother, showing facial lines born during the struggle to manage on a pittance, seemed divorced from the mother he knew before the strike.

John Henry, his sisters Mary, Margaret and Hannah, returning home from school in the village, carried broken branches from the near denuded trees in the lane; their coal allowance from the colliery being long exhausted. They had, with some success, gathered cinders which had escpaed complete incineration on the fiery heap which had become their daily Mecca. Spent cinders poor substitute for coal, their bath night became a lukewarm game.

John Henry lived only a few yards from the now silent pithead; he missed the incessant clang of the pit cage, he missed too the beat of the clog or pit boot work or homeward bound.

Out of work ponies, brought to bank when the strike looked set to last indefinitely, revelling in their new-found freedom, their thick coats sound protection against the winter weather, scattered, startled by excited human sounds. James Anderson, Will Leighton, Will Parkinson and Tommy Dixon, all striking pony drivers, staged an impromptu rodeo; the spoil heap being an excellent grandstand for the less adventurous. Settle, Tiger, Bonny, and the other ponies were granted a reprieve on the arrival of P.C. Coverdale.

Striking pitmen, in their determination to overcome injustice, organised a march. On Thursday November 13th between 400 and 500 of the striking pitmen of Straker and Love's collieries marched through Durham bearing banners. The men went to Shincliffe for the purpose of meeting pitmen from Houghall Colliery which had struck two days previously. Houghall and Shincliffe Collieries are owned by Mr. Love.

John Dunn from Brandon Colliery addressed the meeting. He said he was no public speaker, but their case made him more able to express himself. He said they had stopped work in order to do away with the iniquitous system, under which they had been labouring for years, and which they were determined to banish from the country. He alluded to the system of 'tub rocking'. He believed that the men were determined never to 'rock' another tub for Mr. Love.

They had been bowed down by a most unjust system, without any means of redressing their grievances—without any chance of asserting their just rights—otherwise they received 'Notice to Quit'. They were anxious to raise themselves as working men and establish their position in society. They had not been treated as men. They did not want to be termed as paupers—they wanted a better state of things than had previously existed. The cause of the Union was spreading in all directions. They had shown by their conduct that they were a peacably disposed class of men; and this, he thought, was proved by the fact that they had allowed their wives and families to be turned to the door in the most wretched and miserable weather. He was convinced that their masters would repent their conduct, and eventually grant what the men required. But he was satisfied that the men would never return to their work under the system of 'rocking tubs'. The wonder was that they had so long submitted to the system. All they desired was that they should be paid for their labour; and he contended they were fully justified in the steps they had taken to obtain their just rights. They wanted justice, and the men would never raise a pick to fill a tub under the old system, and without they received extra pay for their extra labour.

John Dunn's brave and spirited remarks drew applause from the pitmen present.

Up to the beginning of November a sad cortege had left the colliery rows almost at weekly intervals. To add to the depression, thirty souls had been buried at Brancepeth, of that number, twenty five had died in early infancy. For some the journey to Brancepeth had been their only one.

Life is becoming increasingly harder for the strikers and their families; no coal, little money with which to buy necessities. Ingenuity is born through strife. Jack Brown's goat, Edward Forster's sow, Thomas Gibbon's rabbits and Tom Gill's chickens are sacrificed. Men, without money, forsake the Colliery Inn; rabbits mysteriously adorn kitchen tables, field produce fills children's hungry bellies. Shopkeepers are good, their credit seems endless.

By Thursday November 19th, the thirtieth day of the strike, the whole of the families in Willington, Oakenshaw and Brancepeth Collieries had been turned out of their houses. The settlement of the dispute seems to be as distant as ever. Brandon Colliery pitmen are perturbed, the owners are reported to be seeking the eviction of the men on strike.

The weather during November has been mild, it is hoped that it continues so for the evicted families. The men have been peaceable and orderly; to deter any outbursts of passion, all of Messrs. Straker and Love's agents have been sworn in as special constables.

A meeting was held in Gateshead by a few of the representatives of the men on strike. Matthew Charlton; a coal hewer of Brandon Colliery, gave some account of his experience at the colliery and the hardships he had borne there. He said they intended to stand out.

Adding to their worries, Will Garbutt lost his three year old daughter Ann. Matthew Brown and William Snowdon, both striking coal hewers, each had a bereavement in the family. Matthew lost his two and a half year old son, William. The Snowdons lost their three and a half year old daughter, Jane. The bereaved family lost three children in the space of five months, all were buried at Brancepeth.

Meetings are being held at regular intervals. Delegates travelled to Newcastle on December 11th. They said that the plight of the striking pitmen was serious; the men had been out seven and a half weeks, one week they got 3s. 1d. another 3. 10d. and another 4s. 5d. and last week 5s. 4d. One speaker believed it was Mr. Love's intention to starve the miners out.

It was decided to impose a levy of 1s. 6d. per fortnight on working miners as long as the strike lasts. The application of the levy would be a welcome addition to the pittance striking members of the Union are drawing.

Mr. Love sent the following letter from his home, Mount Beaulah in Durham.

Notice to Miners

Messrs Straker and Love, owners of Brancepeth, Oakenshaw, Willington and Brandon Collieries in the County of Durham, have resolved not to employ men connected with the Miners' Union.

They offer work and good wages to pitmen who are at liberty to give their labour unrestricted. Upon the above named Collieries the wages generally vary from 4s. to 7s. per day. but there are good workmen making from 8s. to 9s. per day at the present time.

House, Coals and Garden for 6d. per fortnight. Families will be removed free of cost. Brancepeth, Oakenshaw, Willington 'A' Pit and Brandon Collieries are all at work, and Willington 'B' Pit, it is hoped, soon commences work.

Application to be made to the Overman at the respective Collieries.
December 5th, 1863.

Mr. Love, in his letter, said that Brandon Colliery was at work. His information was proved to be inaccurate. As the letter was being delivered, a large meeting of pitmen was held at Brandon Colliery. Mr. Leighton again took the chair; he stated that on the morning a delegation had proceeded to Mr. Love's residence in Durham and made known their visit. They waited in the yard a short time, when a servant came to them and said that Mr. Love would not receive any more deputations from his men, and that he could not be seen.

On the motion of Mr. Dickinson, seconded by Mr. Lamb, a vote of thanks was passed, amid cheers, to the Editors of the Durham Chronicle and Durham Advertiser for the calm, clean, and temperate manner they had covered the strrike.

Another big meeting was held on Saturday, December 12th. A reporter from the Newcastle Daily Chronicle noted complaints from men whose collieries were involved in the dispute.

At Oakenshaw, forty families had been ejected from their homes. It was stated that a woman named Bird, while in a state of pregnancy, had been put out of her house, and had died in childbirth a few days later.

Jack Scott, Brandon Colliery, stated that when their pit first started, about six years ago, their standard weight was 8½ cwts. per tub for the first three months, then ¼ cwt. was added, for which 6d. per score of twenty one tubs, was paid. This continued for four months, when another ½ cwt. was added. After eighteen months ½ cwt. more. Two years elapsed, when ½ cwt. 4 lbs. extra was put, making a total of 10¼ cwts. 4lbs. no higher price being paid for any of the extra filling after the 6d. for the first additional ¼ cwt. The same dissatisfaction existed amongst them as at Brancepeth; they often remonstrated against the 'big filling' and confiscation, but it was of no use. Mr. Love told them he did not want more than one, at another time, two tubs per day per man confiscated.

For the same reasons as the Brancepeth men they joined the Union, and the same system of sacrifice was resorted to against them. Jack Scott went on to say that the cinder drawers had suffered reductions of about 4s. 6d. a week.

Young John Henry Garbutt, not yet eight, did not understand why families were being put out of their homes onto the street; even at such a tender age he realised that something was amiss.

Mr. Love had obtained a number of ejectment summonses at Durham County Police Court on Monday December 14th. Two days later the evictions began and were continued on the Thursday. John Henry would never forget the women's tears and the men's curses as their furniture was heaped in the street. Prospects looked bleak indeed for Christmas.

After weeks of struggle on their meagre strike pay from the Union, men drifted back to work. Weeks of threats, cajolery, then final eviction, had sent the last dissident pitman, cap in hand, to seek to renew his bond. All the stikers were back at work on December 28th.

Cupid was at work during the strike. John Dunn, a twenty year old pitman, married Catherine Westgarth. Another pitman, Tom Gill, married eighteen year old Mary Burrell.

1864

Jane McDermott swept away what remained of a thick carpet of snow which had drifted into her back yard in Railway Street; her kitchen mat would be preserved from her children's snow covered feet. She drew her shawl across her shoulders and leaned against the wooden partition, only a skeleton of its former self, joining the two yards, and chatted with her neighbour, Ann Haye.

They agreed that last year had been the grimmest of their lives. Smallpox had stricken the district. Their families had suffered; some more than others; the Snowdon family had lost three youngsters in the space of five months, John Michael seven months, William five years old and Jane three years and a half.

Whilst the strike had snapped the bond tying man to master, it had strengthened neighbourly ties. Edward Forster who breeds pigs in his garden across the road from his house in South Street, killed one of his stock. John Madgin, butcher of High Street, procured the cheapest cuts of beef. Many kind friends had contributed to the support of the stricken families. For the first three weeks of the strike men and their families had 8s. 3d — 7s. 5d. and 7s. 10d. to live on. Their weekly allocation reduced as the strike continued. Fortunately potatoes at the Durham Market were down to fivepence a stone.

Jane and Ann returned to their family duties, each with a sincere hope that the year ahead would blot out the unhappy memories of 1863.

Now that work has fully resumed at the colliery, pitmen with their families have moved into houses vacated during the strike. William Dixon moved to Brandon Colliery; he is a thirty four year old coal hewer born in Cumberland, his wife Maria, thirty years of age, was born at Sunderland

Bridge only about two miles away. Their home, 26 South Street, also houses two boarders, James Clark and James Kelly are coal hewers, they hail from Ireland.

Easter Saturday; whole families walked the mile to Langley Grove where Mr. Smith held the third annual sports day. Glorious spring sunshine accompanied the main event—the one mile race for the Champion Belt. As on previous occasions, the crowd enjoyed the day, pitmen from the surrounding area being grateful for a day of festivity, applaud Mr. Smith for organising the event.

Next day, whole families attended the first Easter Service to be held in the New Connexion, a Chapel built a few yards from the Colliery Inn. Mr. Love had provided the chapel cum school to obviate the walk to East Brandon school. Brandon Colliery now has a chapel, pit and inn almost within touching distance of each other.

With braces dangling from drab trousers, the vested figure shuffled across the wide street; his stocking less feet chilled inside unlaced boots. Numerous stones helped him across the wheel rutted waste. Thomas Turner, coal hewer aged thirty nine, had just recently moved to Brandon Colliery from Jarrow with his wife and family of four daughters and a son. Thomas liked a quiet read, his rowdy brood denied him the pleasure. From the second netty down, pipe smoke sneaked between gaps in the door, paper rustled, the weekly Durham Advertiser was being read in comparative peace. An old edition of the paper, cut into ample squares, is pinned to the door.

Every week the dustman calls. Richard Hissop is sixty six; he was born at Sunderland Bridge, his wife Maria, fifty two years of age, was born at Westwick. Their grandchildren, Ann and John Holliday, born in Hunwick, live with them.

Richard's shaggy coated horse patiently accepts the shower of spent ashes, refuse and excrement his master shovels from the netty into the cart. A plot of land, once farmland, lying slightly to the north of the colliery, is now in use as an ash tip. Small fires liberally dot the tip's crown. Square pieces of old newspaper await their turn for incineration, other pieces, windblown, festoon the farmer's hedge.

John Dixon, coal hewing at the age of fifty two, was tired. After a long life of labour in the pit—he started working underground at the age of ten—he desired something easier than hewing coal in a wall. His shift was half spent, yet the tub was only half full. Working in a wall is lonely work; his putter, knowing conditions in a wall would not call, would assume the tub would last out John's shift. The deputy had paid his routine visit.

John sat on his cracket and resumed hewing. Particles of coal stung his face and arms as his pick dislodged an unsatisfactory amount of coal from the solid, spiteful coal face. His supply of sharp picks was almost exhausted. His hands, sore with gripping the wooden pick shaft, were beginning to fester. John dreaded the thought of losing work through bad hands, he urinated on them, feeling some measure of relief, he once more wielded his pick.

Until the wall had been cut through the pillar of coal, John knew that his wage depended on the deputy's generosity. John's pay note, previous to working in the wall, read:—

John Dixon

Tubs hewed:

1st Week—5 shifts	97	
2nd Week—6 shifts	107	
Total for 11 shifts	204	
Hewing price	£2.6s.8½d.	
Narrow work and price		
4 yds. @ 6d.	£ 2s.0d.	
8 yds. @ 5d.	£ 3s.4d.	
Consideration	£ 0s.6d.	
Amount of earnings	£2.12s.6½d.	
Average over 11 shifts	£ 4s.9d. per shift	

Hannah and John Henry Garbutt, each cosily swathed in calico night clothes, waited expectantly on the brown painted settle built by the side of the fireplace in their Durham Street home. The long hollow brass rod supported from the mantel shelf reflected a glow from the built up fire; rain water collected from the barrel in the yard effervescent in the fireplace boiler. Their father, the story teller, lowered the oil lamp's flame and sat back erect against the warm black-leaded oven. Friday night was special for the older children, their bedtime was delayed. John Henry remembered the Christmas of last year, when a combination of spent cinders and sparse wood—a result of the strike—was inadequate to warm the kitchen. He remembered too, the song the pit lads had learned from their elders. A short defiant lyric which they called the 'Rocking Song'.

'The rocking so shocking long, long we have bore,
Farewell to the rocking, we will rock them no more'.

The Rev. E. L. Butcher, the third of a trio of curates sent to help the vicar during the year, performed his first marriage ceremony when twenty four year old pitman James Smith married Mary Roberts. Mary is twenty one years of age. Both live in the long Durham Street.

The curate's predecessors had buried twenty eight colliery inhabitants, of these half were infants, victims of the epidemic still raging in Brandon Colliery. One survivor being William, son of William and Sarah Garbutt, born at No. 14 Durham Street.

1865

Edward Forster, a sturdy fifty seven year old pit inspector, trudged through the snow, piled high across the street. It was the third day of the New Year and bitterly cold; he carried a pail, full of steaming pig swill. Edward swung open the door of the pig sty. With grunts of pleasurable anticipation, the hungry sow, of gargantuan proportions, followed the tantalising pail across the street. The expert hands of Robert Forster, a twenty eight year old colliery blacksmith, and Will his twenty six year old banksman brother, waiting in the yard of their South Street home, secured the pig.

A truly aimed downward blow sent the forty one stone sow rolling onto its side; deft hands collected the gush of blood emanating from the sow's gashed throat, into a spacious dish. Other willing hands set to and scraped the quivering flesh free of hair and dirt. Mrs. Forster kept the kitchen boiler bubbling.

Fresh pork, sausages, black pudding, brawn and pig's trotters would all be relished by the family of five strapping sons and three daughters, all of whom were born at Thornley, near Durham. The families Wood; Lidster; Green; Jackson; Ford and Dunn, neighbours who had, during the long period of feeding the monster, helped with potato peelings and vegetable waste, would not be forgotten.

More families are moving into the colliery rows. Workings stretch tentacle like underground, requiring coal hewers, putters, stonemen and lads to man them. Joiners' and blacksmiths' shops are expanding. Builders have erected almost two hundred houses, these are occupied on completion. Sunderland Street, the latest to be built, is a long row of single houses stretching almost in a continuous line from High Street. It is built across the road from Durham Street, here the workers with small families predominate.

John Brady, a coal hewer, had just finished his 'first shift', it being Monday. A twenty seven year old Irishman, he had lived in Brandon Colliery only three weeks; he had come to marry a local girl. On reaching the shaft bottom he walked into the 'cage hole', the cage descended on him crushing him so severely that he died two hours later.

On the day of the pit accident, the first fatal one underground, Mary Ellen Park, daughter of Sidney Park, died at the youthful age of four years and a half. Tragedy dogged the Park family, just three weeks after the death of little Mary Ellen, her seven month old brother John Thomas, was buried alongside her in St. Brandon's churchyard. Sisters Elizabeth and Hannah Battensby, five years and four years, were also victims of the fever.

Heavy boots flattened coarse grass, and disturbed heather, as the thin line of men, with staffs swinging, advanced. Screams rent the morning air; bodies lay inert, torn flesh and broken bones evidence of the unequal struggle.

Pitman Joe Milburn's Brandon Lad vied with George Thornton's best dog. Viscount Boyne's greyhounds took part. Beaters, spectators, greyhounds and owners, left the field of conflict on which eighteen hares had met an untimely and vicious end.

Isabella Parkinson on seeing a recipe in the Durham Advertiser, decided with the help of her sister Martha, sixteen years of age, to give the family a treat. Isabella aged nineteen decided to make 'apple pancakes' for her eight brothers and sisters, all were born in Monkwearmouth from which place their father, Will, a fifty year old coal hewer, came to Brandon Colliery.

Shrove Tuesday was a good day for pancakes.

Apple Pancakes
½ teaspoon Borwicks baking powder
A little salt
2 tablespoons of flour
Add 2 eggs well beaten
Add enough milk to make a smooth and rather thin batter
A little powered cinnamon
Grated lemon peel
2ozs. currants
6 apples peeled and chopped
Mix well together
Melt some butter in a frying pan, do not put the mixture in till quite hot.

With such a large family to feed, which includes three pitmen, the sisters knew that a busy time lay ahead watching the frying pan on the low hot fire.

On Easter Saturday the annual Steeplechase organised by Mr. J. Smith of Langley Grove took place. Contestants and spectators came from Brandon Colliery and the surrounding area. The event is much looked forward to, especially when Mr. Smith arranges the day to coincide with Baff Week when the pitmen are free on the Saturday. A noisy crowd cheered on the twenty seven valiant men who took part in the Steeplechase which was the main event of the day. As on previous occasions, the River Browney proved a formidable obstacle. Bookies were out in force for this annual gathering.

Hugh McDermott preferred the country to the crowd; he left his home in Railway Street, his daughter, twelve year old Alice, and six year old Edward, walked by his side. A delightful spring day invited a walk. With husband and two children from under her feet, Jane McDermott could better cope with household chores, four year old Mary Elizabeth and baby Catherine.

Alice, not having had a close up view of Brancepeth Castle, suggested a visit. The turnpike at Meadow Field was left behind, Red Barns Farm was next, then Scripton Farm. The raucous rookery on the rise into the village was left behind. Edward was intrigued by the steam driven saw in the mill set on the fringe of the village. Brancepeth's one row of stone built houses faced the line of stately chestnut trees which ended at the castle gate. The castle stood majestic in its own well-cared for grounds; deer and their fawn grazed at the foot of the battlement, peacocks strutted just within the iron gates, squirrel noisily scurried through nearby trees. Alice wanted to see a real live Lord, she hoped that a gig would drive under the arch of the court-yard. She was greatly disappointed, the Lord of the Manor was not in residence.

Hugh McDermott, a knowledgeable man, told Alice how the owner of the castle acquired part of his wealth.

In the agreement signed between Viscount Boyne and Messrs. Straker and Love, provision is made for royalties to be paid the Viscount for coal mined from under his land and properties.

He derives a rent of 18s. per Ten out of 4,500 acres mined and 20s. per Ten out of 2,000 acres mined being the acreage leased to the colliery owners.

As a Ten is slightly more that 48 tons, Alice's father reckoned the royalty claimed by the Viscount to be 4½d. per ton of coal hewn from the larger acreage and 5d. per ton from the 2,000 acres. Alice deduced that the Viscount received about half the amount the coal hewer himself earned for every Ten of coal he sent to the surface.

Alice also learned that since 1856 when Brandon Colliery was sunk, the colliery company had to supply annually 200 chaldrons of round coals and 100 chaldrons of small coals to the castle; these had to be delivered.

Father, daughter and son, having had their close-up view of the castle, turned homewards. Hugh McDermott, without rancour, swung Edward onto ample shoulders; with Alice by his side he retraced his steps. His possessions were of intrinsic value.

William Mewes; James Newton; John Jefferson and George Blackett, all pitmen, walked the three miles to Durham to hear Edward Rhymer, a pitman from Barnsley in Yorkshire, address a meeting of pitmen. He was a firm believer in a strong Miners' Association; he was an eloquent speaker.

Those present heard him say: 'With respect to the County of Durham he was sorry that they appeared as a blackspot in England regarding the Miners' Association. They numbered about a thousand, but there were only seventy four at the meeting. The hours of the men are eight hours working, the average wage being from four shillings to four shillings and sixpence. The hours of the boys upon an average were fourteen a day. The system with respect to the boys was the most wretched in the civilised world. They never saw the light of the blessed sun from Sabbath to Sabbath. He had authority to tell them that the district he represented begged of them through him to send help to save them from starvation and misery'.

Josh Stevens of South Street was grievously worried. His chest pained, he could scarcely breathe. Even short walks became a trial. His favourite pastime, that of walking up the hill to East Brandon, resting a while to relish the scenic panorama, then a leisurely saunter home, was denied him. He hawked dust-laden phlegm from his protesting lungs. He had not yet confided in his wife. He dreaded his daily struggle as a coal hewer; every breath, every swing of his pick, were becoming an agony. He more than suspected that he had Miners' Asthma, a disease brought on by coal dust congealing the lungs and seriously impeding breathing. He dreaded too, the thought of enforced idleness; he did not relish the idea of life as a pauper.

Sparkling eyes took in the changing vista. Brandon Siding and Durham Street were left behind. Hannah and John Henry Garbutt were off to Durham; their parents were fulfilling a promise of a Christmas treat for the labour expended in carrying water from the spring in the farmer's field. All four still found the train ride exhilarating. A circus was pitched in Durham Market Place, admission being sixpence extra to see the animals being fed. The children would be admitted at half price.

Robert Hughes, George Mather and Thomas Appleby, all Brandon Colliery pitmen, found their brides locally. They were married at Brancepeth by the Rev. Shafto. There were no baptisms of colliery babies during the year.

Hugh McDermott and Jane his wife, had baby Catherine baptised at St. Cuthbert's Catholic Chapel in Elvet, Durham.

Out of forty colliery residents buried at Brancepeth during the year, twenty six were infants. Smallpox, scarlet fever and diphtheria kept the vicar and the curate, the Rev. E. L. Butcher, busy performing the last rites. They buried seven victims during the month of March.

TEN YEARS OLD

From the few square inches exposed when the first sod was lifted almost ten years ago, an expanding, busy and smoky industry has developed. Scores of bee-hive coke ovens dominate the area south of the pit; streets run in straight lines to the four points of the compass. South, East, West and North Streets are occupied, Durham and Sunderland Street, the longest, hug the north-east side of the pit.

Men with their families have moved on, the disastrous 'rocking strike' caused an exodus. Men like Will Garbutt, Thomas Parrish, Thomas Rumley and Isaac Foster, elected to take root in Brandon Colliery. Their children attend Mr. Hough's school in Brandon Village, older sons of eleven or twelve years have been initiated to pit work as trappers or pony drivers. Daughters, with a bit of luck, find employment in Mr. Smith's Paper Mill.

Non-stop work every working day has advanced the Main Heading and extended the workings in every direction. Pillars of coal have been left in on either side of the Heading to lend support. Walls; Jenkins; Skirties and Winnings steadily advance while surface life sleeps. Coal hewers, homeward bound, meet incoming stone-men whose shots dislodge irregular shaped stone, which if not required for packing, is sent to the surface to enlarge the spoil heap.

During the coal hewing shift almost every cage ascent means that a cubic yard of coal has been hewn from the vast acreage. The nearest boundary, just a few hundred yards from the shaft bottom in a north-east direction has been reached, an estimated fifteen yards of solid coal being left untouched. Other capitalists have plans to sink a shaft and start a colliery to work the coal beyond the barrier.

There is one place in which men like to gather to talk over the events of the day—Joe Addison's Colliery Inn. Amid the pungent smell of pipe smoke, their pints of bitter adorn the round wrought iron tables, men with Edward Rhymer's spirit converse in the bar. Men of spirit, like the men, who after the strike a little more than two years ago, were blacked. Men forced to move on, hoping that their names and news of their Union activities had not reached the ears of the viewer at the colliery of their choice.

Coke drawers and coal hewers, are in the main, thirsty men. By virtue of their manual work they believe that a regular intake of beer helps replace their lost daily sweat. Joe Addison is certain, as he draws their beer, that the men shift more coke and coal talking in the bar, than they do at their jobs.

Caleb, Will and George, all pitmen, left the Colliery Inn; they had discussed pit events. All were loath to tell their wives of the sudden and terrifying cage drop, caused by the winder man's neglect. Loath to tell of the foul air in the hewing place, air so bad, due to faulty ventilation, that the candle almost succumbed. Loath to mention the time when their hewing place 'set on', and having to wait in the dark, cold and wet, until someone approached with a light to rekindle the candle snuffed out by the sudden gush of air, caused by the roof fall which had forced them to vacate their place. Loath to mention the anxious time spent dodging the flashing hooves and swinging limmers of the twelve year old pony driver's wayward pony. Loath to mention the chilling terror experienced when the steam failed and the ascending pit cage, in which they crouched helpless, swung alarmingly in the circular void of the shaft.

Jane McDermott, Ann Haye and two of their neighbours in Railway Street met for their daily gossip, they discussed a common topic—their families. Some had children attending the now crowded school at East Brandon, where they played their boisterous games in the small school-yard, and ran the mile from the village to their home in the colliery row. The women had young lads, who, on leaving school, would follow their fathers into the pit, to work as trapper boys—pony drivers—helpers—then putters. Sons and daughters would eventually court and marry other colliery residents and settle down in one of the colliery houses.

Prospects look brighter for the pitmen. After much agitation, they are to get a rise of threepence a day. There is much poverty in the area, poverty so acute among widows and their offspring, that Lord and Lady Boyne were stirred to help the needy of Brandon, Brancepeth and Willington. Two fat bullocks were killed and distributed, as was a quantity of warm clothing; this is an annual event usually performed during January.

Diphtheria and scarlet fever continue to haunt the streets of Brandon Colliery. John Jefferson, a deputy overman at the colliery, hurried home with foreboding; he had just come to bank after his shift in the Hutton Seam. His six weeks old daughter, Elizabeth Annie, was sick when he left home for work. Comforting neighbours in the kitchen of No. 25 South Street told the tale; Elizabeth Annie had died during his absence.

Margaret Batty ten years old; Edward Blackett six years; Anne Watson twenty three years of age; her ten month old daughter, Elizabeth Ann; Thomas Abbott nine months; Ellen Lamb two years; and George Maddison one week; all from Brandon Colliery, succumbed to make the early weeks of the year a time of mourning.

The colliery claimed its third victim when John Connor, while easing the trucks at the coke-ovens where he was employed as a cinder drawer, got jammed between the waggons. He was crushed so severely that he died from his injuries.

March saw the renewal of the yearly bonds at the colliery. Pitmen are once again playing hell against the system of being tied to one colliery for a full year. They wish to be free to leave a colliery on short notice without fear of prosecution.

For several consecutive years Mr. Smith of Langley Grove has organised the Langley Athletic Sports. On the last day of March, watched by an appreciative crowd, twenty nine competitors ran in the popular one mile race for the Champion Cup. Bookies' voices shouting the odds on the runners drowned the spectators' exhortations.

On the Saturday following, the sporting venue was changed. A Check Ball match was played on Mr. Minto's ball alley just up the road from Langley Grove. Baff Saturday! No work—a good day for sport. Rowdy followers of the game left the bar of the Inn and gathered to watch two men pit combined strength and skill against a solitary opponent. John Reavley and George Forster, both sripped to the buff, had accepted Jack Dixon's challenge.

The match was for four pounds, Dixon being allowed three chalks. Thomas Soulsby from New Brancepeth Colliery and Henry Errington from Brandon Colliery were appointed referees. Dixon took the lead of his two opponents and beat them after an exciting game by one chalk. The winner was throughout the game the favourite, betting was brisk, as much as six to four being laid on him. All three players are coal hewers in the same seam at Brandon Colliery. Check Ball is a popular sport among pitmen. The game provides players with much needed fresh air, it is suited to their physique, the coal hewing hardens the hands and strengthens shoulder muscles.

Six year old Minnie Lamb, born at Brancepeth Colliery and recently removed from that place to Brandon Colliery, played in the lane which ran from the colliery to East Brandon, it served as playground, West Street just completed, its muddy surrounds no place in which to play. Mr. Charles White was driving down the lane towards the colliery in a gig, the horse took fright and bolted, running over Minnie. The wood and canvas carriage was smashed to atoms; the driver, on being pitched onto the road, suffered a severely fractured head. The girl died shortly afterwards from her injuries. Minnie's father, Joseph Lamb, a twenty eight year old coal hewer, was born at Lumley, his wife Mary Ann came from Sherburn.

John Leonard, set on at Brandon Colliery, had just recently moved from Willington. He, with his wife and young family, occupied No. 8 Railway Street, the first row of single houses to be built at the colliery. Sidings for the colliery coal and coke waggons lay just a few paces from their back door, a dangerous area and out of bounds to children. Tragedy struck during the early afternoon. A six year old girl had given to drink Laudanum from a bottle, to her eighteen month old brother, John Leonard. The baby died at eight o'clock the same night.

Jane McDermott caressed Hugh her new baby son in the bed set up in the sitting room of No. 16 Railway Street. No. 8, the house of tragedy, is just across the road. Jane reflected on her good fortune and the Leonards' sorrow.

Between five and six hundred young people took advantage of a sunny August Bank Holiday. Monday and no work—what better way to spend it than attend a picnic and ball? The fun continued the whole of Monday night and the greater part of Tuesday. The youth of both sexes, from Brandon Colliery, Brancepeth and the surrounding neighbourhood, participated in the events. Brandon Colliery youth met at Mr. Bainbridge's Three Tuns Inn at East Brandon before proceeding to Morlee Pastures kindly lent by Viscount Boyne. Cricket, leaping, dancing and other games occupied the large crowd.

The Court Pride of Brandon Foresters celebrated in great style on their sixth anniversary, their festivities less boisterous than the youth of the colliery, sat down to a lavish dinner served in the Court Room of the Colliery Inn, the house of Brother Joseph Addison. The Court Pride has enrolled ninety members since its inauguration.

Brandon Colliery parents, ever alert in their fight against scarlet fever and diphtheria, were perturbed when news reached them of a case of Choleric Diarrhoea being proved in Durham. A man and his wife reside with their young daughter in the Fighting Cocks yard, the child is very ill. As this is a contagious disease, and the Inn is set among stops, the colliery folk are loath to visit Durham. Week-end trains are full of passengers as they leave Brandon Siding bound for the city.

Thirty members of the community—ten less than last year—were interred at Brancepeth. Their ages ranged from six weeks to seventy years, eighteen of the total were children.

On six occasions during the year couples left Brandon Colliery to be wed at Brancepeth. Jacob Johnson, a policeman from St. Mary the Less in Durham, married a Brandon Colliery girl, Susan Davison. He hopes to 'pound the beat' at Brandon.

1867

Tuesday, the first working day of the New Year. As arranged, two slight figures converged at the end of Railway Street; the long streets with their shuttered windows were swarthed in darkness. A diffused glow hovered over the coke ovens. The boys, with some apprehension, headed for the pit.

School days just left behind, their twelve hour shift in the pit faced them. With full bait poke swinging from an arm, the new starters paused, gulped, straightened wayward caps and nervously ascended the steep flight of wooden steps. On the pithead they met other pony drivers and a switch holder, all seasoned pit lads. 'Tom Welsh's lad?' 'Tom Conley's lad?' came from the banksman, as at 5 a.m. prompt, he withdrew the keps and signalled the winder man to drop the cage with its boy occupants.

James Welsh, twelve years of age, lived at 24 Railway Street; John Conley the same age, lived in nearby 7 South Street. Sons of pitmen, they had, tradition like, accepted their destiny and followed their fathers and brothers down the pit.

Thomas Towers, a veteran coal hewer at twenty four, on filling his sixth tub of coal in the 'B' Pit, laid aside the big mouthed shovel. January 2nd was his first shift of the New Year, the pit had been idle the day before, it being a public holiday. He had celebrated part of the day in the Colliery Inn, now he didn't feel up to the task of recovering the lost day's wage. It was bait time; his two slices of bread, sprinkled with sugar, were stored in a tin box to protect them from the ravages of the tiny black flies attracted by the candle flame. Thomas declares the flies abound in the vicinity of the pit ponies. Rats too, raid the pit clothes while the hewer sits on his cracket at the coal face.

Thomas pulled his coat over his head, tent like; this protected him from the icy roof water which dripped incessantly; he set his single candle between his legs for added warmth. Rats scurried and squeaked in the stone pack; here they played, fought, bred and became cannibals. They had presumably found their way into the pit via full choppy bags.

Under the influence of the candle's warmth, and the previous day's inebriation, his mind dwelt on surface scenes. He thought of Mary his wife, and their one year old daughter Margaret, they would be up and about at No. 14 South Street. He visualised the chimneys of every occupied house in the long street spiralling sulphurous smoke heavenwards. He thought of them on a night inclined to fog, sending their poisonous fumes down to the ground level, where, aided by smoke from the coke ovens, they seeped indoors and choked the lungs.

The rumble of the approaching putter's tub aroused Thomas from his lethargy. With a shrug he reluctantly discarded his coat, and once again wielded his pick, he knew that once he became stiff and cold, work would become doubly hard.

Alice McDermott, now thirteen years of age, left her home in Railway Street and walked the mile to the Langley Paper Mill. Alice worked on a machine called the 'Chopper', she was in the act of trying to stop it for the blacksmith to look at the knives when her hand slipped in amongst the cogwheels. She was immediately sent to the County Hospital suffering from fractured finger, severe lacerations to the hand, and shock. Kindly neighbours besieged the McDermott home to express their sympathy and wish Alice a speedy recovery.

Jackie Sayers, a nine year old outgrowing his clothes—ganzie sleeves creeping up his arm—tousled fair hair topping a sturdy frame—left his ten year old chum, Robert Strong. They had enjoyed the sport provided by the Cricket Club, when they, with other devotees of the summer sport, watched a match played between the 'Muffs' and 'Duffers' of the club. The 'Muffs' won the game. As Jackie turned into Durham Street, he envied Robert, who brought in five shillings for working his six shifts as a trapper boy in the pit behind Jackie's home, the pit in which the coal hewers are playing 'hell'. The colliery owners are paying the hewers at the rate of twenty one hundredweight to the ton. The men want it fixed at twenty hundredweight to the ton. The present system supplies the owners with one hundredweight per ton free of payment.

James Walsh and John Conley, now seasoned pony drivers, walked to work in the dark; it would be dark when they ascended after their twelve hour shift. Their schoolday friendship had carried on through that first frightening cage ride and the exciting times which followed. After five months they were adept at handling pit ponies; timid Bobby, fiery French, Jock the bright one, and Nelson the strongest of them all. The lads knew the ponies' tantrums, their likes and their dislikes.

Sorrow once again visited the Garbutt family when, on July 9th William, almost to the age of breeching, died in his third year. Young William was one of twenty infants born in the colliery rows and buried in the small graveyard lying almost at the foot of the stately castle in the beautiful village of Brancepeth.

George Battey ten months old; John Battensby only two hours; Isabella Crozier three years; Elizabeth Jackson ten months; William Soulsby three years; Will Robson six weeks; Hannah Thompson ten weeks; James Dixon three weeks; Will Soulsby's sister, Elizabeth Soulsby eight months; John Henry Hughes one year three months; Hannah Lidster two years three months; Mary Cummings two months; sisters Hannah Forster and Elizabeth Forster one and a quarter years and two weeks; Henry Hoggett two years; and Phyllis Lamb one year and three quarters, all joined William Garbutt.

The vicar's spirit lifted when he officiated at two Christmas weddings. He married Thomas Johnson to Jane Lamb, both from Brandon Colliery, at St. Brandon's; again on the next day when Thomas Watson from the colliery married Catherine Brown of Langley Grove.

1868

Heavy snowstorms over the New Year carpeted fields and streets. East Brandon village was isolated; Sleetburn was cut off, five feet drifts covered the road from Brandon Colliery. Mr. Hepworth's field and spring lay deep under sparkling virgin snow, no well worn path to denote the spring's whereabouts.

John Henry and Hannah Garbutt carried snow and long icicles into their home for conversion into bath and drinking water. The wide Durham Street lay deeply covered in soot specked snow, from every house a narrow, man-made path stretched across to the netties.

'Hurry up, John!' 'Come on, Hannah!' The reluctant pair followed their parents to the small school cum chapel Mr. Love had caused to be built almost in the shadow of the Colliery Inn. Men with neatly trimmed beards, wives sporting their best poke bonnet, and children, uncomfortably clean, attended for Sunday Service. The school obviated for some the walk to East Brandon National School.

Mrs. Wheatly, Mrs. Green and Mrs. Frances gazed in wonder; the object of their fascination--a new washing machine which Robert Preston demonstrated in his shop in High Street. At the same price as the more cumbersome Cottage Mangle, a Harper Twelvetrees Portable Rubber Clothes Wringer is a good buy. Its rubber rollers prevent injury to buttons, it can be fixed on any Tub or Washing Machine and can wring three blankets or sheets in a minute, so says the manufacturer.

The admiring women visualised, for thirty shillings, a much easier wash day than hitherto. Harper Twelvetrees also make the new 'Glycerine Soap Powder', one penny a packet will make a pound of Glycerine washing soap.

James Welsh, the bigger of the two mates, was set on as a helper to a putter; he felt ten feet tall, his daily wage now being twopence more than the one shilling and sixpence he had earned as a pony driver. Sent to work in another district he missed John's company, he missed too the pit ponies, some he had grown to love. His favourite, Jock, a well built creature with a definite horsey smell, was a bright one—he could count. Attach four tubs to his limmers, as he moved forward Jock's head nods knowingly with each coupling click, on hearing the clicks he keeps going. If he wanted five tubs moving, James kept the last coupling tight. Jock on counting three coupling clicks moved blissfully on.

Chimney smoke from pit and colliery houses hovers on the horizon. New collieries are producing coal at nearby Langley Moor, Sleetburn and Ushaw Moor.

Thomas Towers formerly of Brandon Colliery, now works at adjacent Langley Moor Colliery; challenged a man from Ushaw Moor Colliery to a game of Knurr and Spell. Pitmen from Brandon Colliery walked the mile to Langley Moor to watch the match played for a stake of £10 a side. The game consisted of thirty rises each; Towers vocally encouraged by supporters from his old colliery, won by twenty seven score.

No easing of Brandon Colliery residents' burden; they are hard pressed, the long summer drought is making heavy demands on the known springs and streams in the area. Water is scarce and slow running, the queues for water are lengthening.

John Henry Garbutt and his mates had a bonanza; whilst awaiting their turn at the spring, they scoured Farmer Hepworth's field, the bumper crop of early mushrooms being much appreciated. Farmers in the district are furious, there being much damage being done by the mushroom pickers.

The year's total of thirty one deaths, twenty three of whom were infants, spread sorrow throughout the colliery rows. Scarlet fever seriously depleted the ranks of the very young.

Eight Brandon Colliery grooms signed the register in St. Brandon's, all the brides came from Brandon Colliery's several streets.

1869

James Davison—a vagrant—doubtless after New Year cheer, taking advantage of the dark surround of Brandon Colliery Railway Station, decided on forced entry. He was caught red-handed and committed to prison for six weeks' hard labour as a rogue and vagabond.

The village of Brancepeth was in rejoicing mood on January 11th, it being the birthday of the son and heir to the Brancepeth Estates. Merry peals from the bells of the old church echoed throughout the day. Guns were fired at intervals until late at night. Sound from bells and guns drifting over fields, could be heard quite clearly in Brandon Colliery.

During three days of the revelry, George William Marshall five months; Robert Dixon one week; Elizabeth Lamb eleven months and James Forster eight years of age, all Brandon Colliery children, made their last journey, the two miles from their homes to Brancepeth's St. Brandon's graveyard. All four children were interred by the curate, the Rev. William Henderson Pritchard within sound of banquet and ball for over one hundred guests, and a lavish dinner and dancing for the estate workers.

February followed with three more bodies for burial in St. Brandon's graveyard. Hannah Lamb twenty six years of age and mother of baby Elizabeth Lamb, accompanied Mary Elizabeth Lawson one year old and John William Raine, nine days.

During March the sad cortege of death continued; Ellen Welsh aged sixty three; George Coverdale one month; Elizabeth Pearson Preston seven years and her four year old brother Robert, died on the same day. Margaret, daughter of Hugh McDermott, was buried in Durham, where she was baptised ten months ago.

James Needham, not long arrived from Ormskirk in Lancashire, left school one Friday. He was pleased with himself, hadn't he a certificate? He was eleven and could read and write. The piece of paper said so! This entitles him to leave school and seek employment.

James started work underground on the following Monday, his brother John, a thirteen year old putter, accompanied him to work. James, still shaking after the sudden cage descent, was sent some hundreds of yards inbye. Without initiation, he began his twelve hour shift. He operated the heavy, wooden door, installed for pit ventilation, this he opened on the putter's arrival. James' pay of five shillings for six shifts of work will help succour their large family.

John Henry Garbutt, his sister Hannah, Will Dippee, Isaac Lamb, Tom Lidster, Will and Margaret Ross, some had left school, others awaited their turn, were gathered at the end of their street. Durham Street's gable end making an ideal ball alley. Their boisterous play suddenly ceased. 'Look at the bonny sky!' The whole sky was filled with streamers of red and white light, which radiated from a fixed point in the heavens, called the Corona.

For the first time in their young lives they beheld the Aurora Borealis. The Aurora reached its greatest brilliance just as they, with some reluctance, retired to bed, the awesome spectacle leaving an indelible mark on their minds.

Mr. Maddison the master sinker, on orders from the owners of Brandon Colliery, continued sinking below ground from the Hutton Seam now being worked, whose 2ft. 8ins. layer of coal lay 157ft. from the surface. Sinkers planned to penetrate the Top Harvey Seam which has coal 1ft. 8ins. thick, then down to the Bottom Harvey Seam with its 2ft. seam, and on to the Busty Seam where the 4ft.1in. seam of coal is bound in the middle by a one inch layer of stone band. The sinkers' ultimate goal being the Brockwell Seam with rich coking coal in its 2ft.10in. seam, plus valuable Seggar lying 522ft. from the surface. When these seams are producing coal Brandon Colliery will indeed be a place of importance.

Discontent prevails among the country's coal hewers. In an attempt to quell the unrest, the coal owners introduced a new idea. The new Sliding Scale would fix the hewers' price per ton according to the price prevailing on the London Coal Exchange. As the Scale of prices fluctuates—so too does the hewing prices. An independent accountant is engaged to assess the Market prices over a three or four month period. From these prices he works out the rise or fall in the percentage due to the men. Will Hartley, Thomas Rumley, George Maddison, Owen Kelly and Francis Vasey are all coal hewers at the colliery, some are sceptical of the scheme, others think it will be to their advantage.

As the Sliding Scale was being launched, miners at the Boyne Pit just down the road from Brandon Colliery and almost within hailing distance, after a week out on srike, went back to work. They had rebelled against adverse working conditions.

Two weddings took place on the same day, both brides live at Brandon Colliery; James Blenkinsop Jr. of No. 1 Railway Street married Margaret Mills, they travelled to Durham Register Office. The other ceremony took place in St. Brandon's in the village of Brancepeth; the new curate, the Rev. John Harrison Bender, officiated when Thomas Ralph Hepple, a twenty two year old schoolmaster from Croxdale married Catherine Ann Ford, a nineteen year old schoolmistress. They moved into No. 24 North Street. They were given their new home, a colliery house with one room down and one room up, by virtue of their profession; school teachers being as vital to the community as the pit itself, they were assured work. The same curate baptised Harriet, the new baby daughter of William and Sarah Garbutt.

Ten year old John Kenny travelled to Durham with his widowed mother. This was no picnic outing! He had been charged by P.C. Graham with having committed wilful damage, to the amount of one penny, to a wheat field belonging to Mr. Hewitson, farmer, of Brandon. Kenny had been trespassing to get water. His mother told the magistrate, the Rev. A. D. Shafto, that they had no water at all; the boy was ordered to pay expenses of four shillings and sixpence.

Following the report of the Kenny case, a Durham Advertiser reporter visited Brandon Colliery. His remarks were published in his paper:

'In some of the colliery districts about Brandon there is absolutely no supply of water provided by the colliery owners for the families of the workmen they have brought upon the spot, and the poor creatures have to trespass upon the lands of the neighbouring farmers to procure by stealth even a limited supply of this essential of health and comfort. In such a case, who would be to blame if a fatal epidemic broke out in consequence of the enforced habits of uncleanliness in which the people are now living? Surely a grave responsibility rests upon the colliery owners, who, while enriching themselves by the rights of property are so singularly unmindful of the duties which property confers'.

Once again the Durham Advertiser has proved itself a champion of the underprivileged.

At last the pitmen of Durham County are realising that unity means strength. On November 20th the Durham District of the Miners' National Association was formed, the first meeting being held in George Oswald's Market Hotel, Durham. Although only four or five collieries showed interest enough to send delegates a new spirit is awakening among the pitmen. Brandon Colliery was not represented at the meeting. The idea of a strong Association should catch on. It is proposed that a contribution of threepence a week to the Association would secure labour protection only; sixpence a week would provide labour protection, death sickness and accident benefits.

Christmas Eve shoppers boarded the train at Brandon Siding to visit Durham's Provision Market where they found food prices steady. Potatoes were selling at sixpence a stone; chickens one shilling and sixpence each; beef sevenpence halfpenny a pound; pork tenpence a pound. For those who had saved hard—a turkey could be bought for five shillings.

Three weeks old Alice Dawson died on New Year's Eve to make a total of twenty nine deaths in the colliery rows during 1869.

1870

Rows of colliery owned houses, some single, some double, are being built to shelter workmen and their families; more pit ponies occupy underground stables, more coal hewers have signed the bond despite a report of slack time at some collieries in the county. Putters and drivers are engaged, the latter to transport the coal; underground workings are spreading tentacle like in several directions. On Saturday March 5th bond signing took place at all the collieries in the county. Pitmen at Brandon Colliery like their counterparts elsewhere, are showing a general repugnance to the system, they dislike being bound to serve a particular master for a twelve month.

Jack jumps into the train at Brandon Siding. He saw Tommy sitting with his ring of picks, ready sharpened for coal hewing at another colliery. He hadn't signed the bond. 'Where's tha gannen Tommy?' asked Jack.

'Aa's gannen to Northumberland', replied Tommy.

'Where's Northumberland?' asked Jack.

'About five mile yon side of Newcastle', answered Tommy.

Brandon 'A' Pit Busty Seam now working and producing coal, has had its prices fixed. Simon Tate, Walter Cowell, Frank Vasey and John Roper Scales, all coal hewers, hope to benefit. The whole price is settled at 7s.6d. per score of tubs filled. The score too, has been revised, it is now twenty tubs instead of twenty one. The men reckon that they can now earn 8s. 7½d. for every twenty tubs filled, which is one shilling and a penny a ton, or just over fivepence a tub after the addition of 15%.

Villagers and estate workers mourned the loss, at Brancepeth Castle, of Lady Boyne, wife of Viscount Boyne. After the funeral, the Viscount retired to his residence in Belgrave Square, London; landowner and residents of the colliery share grief, fifteen inhabitants of the colliery being interred at St. Brandon's during the first five months of the year, thirteen being infant victims of diphtheria and scarlet fever.

Large families occupy most of the three-roomed houses in Nos. 1 to 33 South Street. John Brady moved into No. 6, a three roomed house with a small kitchen and a low attic approached by a step ladder; it has a small quarl paved yard with an open channel passing from the top of the street which carries daily refuse. Ten people share the house. John, a coal hewer aged thirty one and his twenty seven year old wife Mary, both were born in Ireland and have five year old school girl Mary Ann. A fifteen year old servant girl Eliza McLaughlin, engaged at Durham Hirings helps look after five lodgers comprised of three coal hewers, a coke filler and a mason's labourer, all in their early twenties.

The servant girl's fourteen year old sister, also from Durham Hirings works for Thomas and Bridget Conley in 7 South Street. The Conleys have six sons, four of whom are pitmen; Thomas is a coal hewer, James is a putter, John and Charles are pony drivers in the Hutton Seam.

Jackie Sayers, now twelve and growing fast, relinquished his job as a trapper lad; he fancied the more active life of a pony driver, besides, he would earn one shilling and sixpence a day, almost double the wage of a trapper lad. Jackie's new job took him nearer the hewing places; he kept the putters supplied with empty tubs and removed their full tubs as they brought them from the hewer's place to the flat. Jackie's gallowa, a spirited four year old stallion, reminded him of the ponies he had seen in the colliery field during the strike, when as a lad of five, he had watched the impromptu rodeo from the summit of the spoil heap.

The literary needs of the pitmen are catered for; daily deliveries of the paper just introduced, the Northern Echo, suggests closer ties with other areas. Good news for readers of the Durham Advertiser, that worthy paper has been reduced in price from twopence halfpenny to twopence for eight pages of weekly news.

The fearful distress caused in the district due to the water shortage, caused more than one hundred colliery inhabitants to sign a petition calling on the local authorities to hold a public meeting to consider the best means to secure a supply of water. The need is so great that prompt measures are necessary.

While women and children queued for a supply of spring water—now reduced to a trickle, men gathered to watch the game of 'Fives', a popular game among pitmen. In the heat from an August sun, two men stripped to their buff, waited at Brandon Colliery Ball Alley. That versatile sportsman, George Mann, sized up his opponent, John Kelley. They prepared to do battle for six pounds a side; both men being noted for their superior playing, a great deal of money was bet on the event. Amid loud vocal encouragement, Kelley the favourite, went in first, he played five, Mann followed with three. After some good playing, Mann finished the game with nineteen chalks to spare, the final score being thirty three for Mann, Kelley fourteen. Mann lives at 26 Durham Street, Kelley at 27 South Street, both men are coal hewers.

The petition adopted at the public meeting held at Brandon Colliery concerning the water supply, was signed by a further hundred inhabitants including farmers of the district. The Rev. Shafto presented the petition to Lord Boyne and the Hon. Hamilton Russell, on behalf of the parishioners. Mr. Hamilton Russell promised to take measures to relieve the distress; he and Lord Boyne sent a letter to the Guardian of Brandon stating the importance of the matter, and gave their agents for the Brancepeth Estates instructions to take immediate action. The people of the district, for the second time in a few weeks, witnessed a sky bursting with colour. Fifteen year old John Henry Garbutt and his mates considered themselves privileged once again to behold the Aurora Borealis. Eyes gazed in wondrous awe at the heavenly display which was most brilliant between 9 p.m. and 10 p.m. when the shooting rays of light reached their zenith.

The middle of October was exceptionally good for blackberry picking; schoolchildren and others so inclined, cashed in on the harvest. Laden bushes supplied large quantities of fruit; pickers sold the berries for two pence a quart to strangers from Sunderland, who in turn sold them at sixpence a quart in their market. Farmers once again complained of damage done to hedgerow and field.

A field owned by Mr. Elliott of Brandon Hall was loaned for the occasion; followers of the sport of Knurr and Spell awaited the arrival of the contestants. George Mann from Brandon Colliery had selected as his opponent Thomas Towers, who had come from nearby Sleetburn Colliery. Both men, canny hands at the game, had such faith in their ability they bet ten pounds each, the betting on both men was heavy. An excellent match was watched from one o'clock. The result of their meeting was so close that each man was matched to play again in a month for twenty pounds a side, at the same place.

On Thursday November 10th the Primitive Methodist Chapel held a temperance meeting which was chaired by John Moralee. Archibald Thompson, colliery cashier and a preacher, made a speech of wit and humour which kept the meeting in roars of laughter.

A fruit banquet was also held in the Chapel to help pay for the new harmonium installed a short time ago. Baskets of fruit were presented for the occasion. John Wayne of the Boyne colliery greatly enlivened the company with some excellent temperance melodies.

A young couple who had recently got married decided that after tea one Sunday they would have a walk to see his marra, who happened to be living close to the chapel where they were married. On arrival at Geordie's, who is a bit of a naturalist, they found him sitting in the corner of the fireplace listening to the strains of about half a dozen crickets. At the same time the choir in the chapel close by were singing that well known hymn, 'Leave me not, for I am lonely'.

'Listen', said the newly married woman, 'What beautiful singing!'

'Ah', said Geordie, 'they do it by rubbing their hind legs together'.

Men forgot their beer as they sat in the Red Lion Inn. They were abruptly reminded of their hazardous occupation when a man burst into the bar and silenced all with the remark 'There's a man just fallen down the Boyne pit shaft'. The new sinking lies a short distance from the Inn. Being Sunday and a day given to shaft repair, William Russell was repairing a portion of the shaft when he fell from the cage into the sump and was killed instantly. Later, a verdict of 'accidentally drowned' was passed at the inquest held in Jonathan Hopper's Inn, Langley Moor.

Messrs. Straker and Love are opposed to the Union. Men at their collieries at Brandon and Brancepeth are being sacked for attending Union meetings; non Union men are making it difficult for men of the Union to improve their conditions of work.

Matthew Oliver, Henry Maddison and George Handley, all Union men, after a lifetime spent in the pit, foresee a brighter future. A momentous occasion! On December 3rd the first annual meeting of the Durham Miners' Association was held in George Oswald's Market Hotel, Durham. Fifteen collieries sent delegates to the meeting, a big increase on November of last year when only four or five collieries were represented. Membership of the Association is growing fast; after only one year it stands at 1899. Brandon

Colliery, though having a Union, is not yet a member of the Durham Miners' Association.

Tom Rumley a thirty year old coal hewer from South Hetton, worked double with Bob Deans, a coal hewer down from Cumberland. 'What's that noise Bob?' shouted a startled Tom. Their hewing cavil was near Jim Skilcorn's place from where came the sound very much like an explosion; they knew the deputy who fired the shots was not in the near vicinity. Urgent legs carried them to Jim's place. Acrid fumes filled the air and their nostrils. Their worst fears seemed justified; Jim's inert body lay sprawled on the floor of the seam. Jim, a coal hewer aged thirty seven, a widower of just one month, looked after his four daughters at 30 South Street, their ages ranged from five months to fourteen years. His late wife Mary Jane, was also thirty seven years of age.

He finished drilling the last hole in the obstinate coal, spat on his hands, and stood back to appraise his work. He had laboured the greater part of his shift at the irksome task of curving the jud; now he anticipated the mound of loose coal dislodged by the shots. Jim loaded a hole with three inches of gun cotton and placed a can of powder upon it; while in the act of forcing the stone pricker through the cotton, it exploded without warning. Jim's injuries were found to be severe; he is likely to suffer permanent blindness, part of one hand was blown off, the other being badly mutilated.

Jane, aged fifty seven, and the wife of John Raine, was the last of thirty eight Brandon Colliery residents to die during the year.

1871

There are now two hundred and sixty houses in Brandon Colliery occupied by colliery employees. Men and boys work the four seams; the Busty, Harvey, Ballarat and Brockwell seams are fully operational. The prices have also been fixed for the 'C' Pit Seam. They are, with the addition of 15%: Whole—

for 3ft. 0in. of coal and above 14s. 4d. per score

for 2 ft. 10in. of coal and under 3ft. 15s. 3d. per score

for 2ft. 8 in. of coal and under 2 ft. 10 in. 15s. 10d. per score

for 2ft. 6 in. of coal and under 2 ft. 8 in. 16s. 4d. per score.

Brandon Colliery has seen the first generation grow; born almost within the shadow of the pit's heapstead, weaned—breeched—a brief period of schooling—then work at an early age.

John Ayre at the age of ten, is a colliery labourer, he works on the screens. John's mate and neighbour lives at 31 South Street, Thomas Rumley is a screener at nine years and a half. George Blenkinsop the same age, is similarly employed, he lives in nearby 1 East Street.

Isabella Addison was born in the Colliery Inn only a few steps from the 'A' Pit shaft. At nine years of age she attends the National School at East Brandon with her two sisters Elizabeth and Mary Ann. As the colliery expands, their services will be required in the Colliery Inn.

The Coverdale, Walsh, Jefferson, Carroll, Gair, Gelley and Lythgoe families welcome the Mines Regulation Bill passed in March. It is a good one; will the Act be carried out to the letter? It suggests that boys less than twelve years of age be not employed underground. The pitmen envy their German counterparts whose boys are not allowed underground until they reach the age of sixteen.

John Carroll and his wife moved to Brandon Colliery from Seaton Colliery ten years ago, they have seen the colliery develop. Their home at No. 19 South Street houses three daughters and a son, three coal hewers and a colliery cartman lodge with them. John Jefferson, a deputy overman from North Shields, came to Brandon Colliery with his wife Jane and two year old Hannah. They, like the Carroll family, have seen the growth of the colliery in their eight years of residence at No. 25 South Street. Michael Garr and Peter Gelley live in the same street, Michael is twelve years of age and leads water in the pit, Peter is eleven, was born in Southwick and is a pony driver at the colliery.

The Coverdale family lives at No. 23 Railway Street; Mary Coverdale is thirteen, she helps her mother run the household consisting of four brothers and six lodgers; one lodger, Harry Lythgoe, is a coal hewer from Lancashire, the other five are quarry labourers employed at East Brandon, they came from Newcastle and far off Devon. William Coverdale the eldest son, is twelve and is a pony driver.

Catherine Walsh, an Irishwoman and widow at forty nine, looks after her family of six sons and two daughters in the end house of Railway Street, No. 24. There's Thomas at nineteen, a coal hewer and chief breadwinner, John is seventeen and is a putter, James is sixteen, he also puts, Edward the youngest worker, is fourteen and is a helper underground. Their sister Mary is twelve, like her friend next door, she helps run the house.

Richard Hissop now seventy three years of age, retired from his job as colliery cartman, he now enjoys the more mundane position of horse keeper. His grandson now thirteen, is a pony driver. Richard and his wife Maria have two boarders; eleven year old Tom Williamson is a colliery screener, he was born in Newcastle; Johnson Rickerby a twenty four year old coal hewer was born at Lumley. They all live in a two roomed house, No. 8 East Street.

All these families are apprehensive, having heard of three fatal cases of smallpox found in Durham during the first week of March. There are six inmates of the County Prison and two in the Union Workhouse suffering from the disease. As Durham is a busy shopping area, fears are entertained about containing the outbreak. Many Brandon Colliery folk travel the three miles to Durham for their weekly shopping.

Fr. Smith led his pony up the steep slope of Burnigill Bank. He had left Croxdale behind, just across the River Wear where his small church nestled among trees at the riverside. He straightened gaiters, buttoned up his long black coat and secured his black silk top hat. The reverend gentleman was bound for Brandon Colliery where the Catholic population sought his ministry. Mr. Love kindly provided a house in Durham Street, No. 62 is used as a church. Fr. Smith also teaches catechism on Sunday afternoons in private houses. Alice Dolan and Elizabeth Fagan, both teachers, run the small church cum school, it is sandwiched between No. 61, occupied by twenty eight year old Robert Inness and his family and No. 63 where John Cummings, also twenty eight, lives.

Fr. Smith had on the previous day, married in the chapel at Croxdale, Alice McNamara, an Irish girl living at No. 11 South Street, to Michael Keenan. Michael came from Washington to coal hew at the colliery; for the present he lives with his bride, they will be given the first available single colliery house. Fr. Smith is greatly perturbed, as are other local ministers, over the large number of deaths occurring in Brandon Colliery, six or seven every month, most of whom are children.

Great local interest was aroused; it being Saturday and a warm May day, a crowd of supporters had gathered to watch, cheer and bet on the main event. Thomas Foster had cracked out William White to a foot race, both men reside at Brandon Colliery, the race was for five pounds a side. Foster led from start to finish, amid cheers he won with a lead of five yards.

No sport or large gatherings of people during June. Early in the month smallpox spread to Brandon Colliery; four infants were stricken, all cases proving fatal, they were buried at St. Brandon's. Colliery people live in fear of their lives and those of their families; they realise that bad sanitary conditions and the absence of fresh tap water heralds such diseases.

The literary needs of the colliery work force are catered for with the opening of the new Reading Room and Institute; the ceremony took place on Monday July 3rd. Witnessed by a large and appreciative crowd, it is situated near the top of Durham Street and on the verge of the Langley Moor—East Brandon road. Sixty men immediately joined as members; Lord Boyne, the Rev. Shafto and Messrs. Straker and Love have announced their intention of becoming honorary members. The Institute will be the centre of colliery social activity.

Summer outings as always, are well attended. A Gala and Picnic were organised by the Forester's Court Pride of Brandon No. 3333. Members and their families noisily assembled outside Joseph Addison's Colliery Inn, the pulley wheels on the nearby pithead motionless after a week of almost continuous activity. The Brandon and Boyne Band led a cavorting parade round the colliery rows before marching past the fiery heap and on to a field in the beautiful valley of the Deerness, where the Sleetburn String Band awaited them. After a strenuous afternoon, during which a quoit match, handicap foot race, football match, ladies' and young girls' races took place, four hundred hungry revellers sat down to tea.

The Colliery Inn was again the meeting point when a quoit match was arranged to be played there. A spirited crowd composed mainly of pitmen, gathered to watch and bet on the encounter between Thomas Soulsby of Brandon Colliery, the favourite, and Ralph Johnson of Waterhouses Colliery. Both men, players of note, after a warming up session to get the feel of the quoits, began the game for five pounds a side, 33 chalks up. Soulsby soon had the measure of his opponent and won 33 chalks to 19. Undaunted the loser challenged Soulsby to a return match during August for ten pounds a side, the game to be played on a neutral ground, Kepier Gardens, Durham.

Baff Saturday! August 12th. Pit lads and mates, Jackie Sayers and James Needham, both thirteen years of age, walked to Durham to attend the Miners' Great Demonstration. They joined excited crowds heading in that direction; they walked through Langley Moor, Stone Bridge, Nevilles Cross and on to Wharton Park near Durham railway station where the mass meeting came to order at noon.

Jackie and James were among the five thousand who paid for admission. Four men occupied the platform; men renowned for their oratory, they came from Glasgow, Barnsley, North Staffordshire and Sunderland. After the heartening speeches a band concert entertained the crowd, £20 was offered in three prizes.

One Staffordshire man sang a melody:
'It is a glorious Union, deny it who can,
   That defends the rights of the working man'.

Mount Beaulah, the spacious home of Mr. Love the colliery owner, lies just up the road; no doubt he would sense the spirit of unity which drew men to Wharton Park. He would in all probability, have heard the defiant speakers.

Having listened to the orations and enjoyed the lively band music, the lads returned home inspired by the spirit of the day. The gathering of pitmen was the largest held to date. After evident success some talk of more and bigger meetings in the future.

Patrick Mahan, a sturdy twelve year old pit lad, sprawled across the quarled kitchen floor of 21 Railway Street. After working his twelve hour shift at putting tubs in the mine, he was too weary even to undress himself. Patrick was born in Durham; his brother James and his eldest brother Thomas, at sixteen and eighteen, are coal hewers in the same seam. Their father Thomas Mahan, Irish born, is forty years of age and is a colliery screener. Ann their mother, is two years his senior, she too, was born in Ireland.

Patrick's mother, raven hair tied in a bun, busied herself about the kitchen; twelve tins of rising dough are slid from before the hot fire to make room for the tin bath, a large pan of broth simmered excitingly on the fire hob.

After much cajoling and a little help, Patrick stripped to the waist and wearily washed his upper body. On drying himself on a square piece of harn he glanced manfully towards his mother; her billowing skirt effectively screening the door as with her back to Patrick, she gazed into the yard. Pit hoggers, boots and pit stockings add to the clothes already on the floor. Patrick completed his bath. As he shouted 'Ma, o'im hungry!' Mrs. Mahan furtively brushed a tear from her cheek.

There is a great demand for coal; the industrial revolution is well into its stride, men have arrived from all parts. Workers with their families have come from Ireland; the men came chiefly to work in the coke yards as coke drawers, coke burners and labourers. Some start as .coal hewers, their sons invariably follow them into the pit.

The colliery houses of the two South Streets, two Railway Streets, Durham Street, North, East and West Streets are occupied. The immigrants include John Dunn from Durham; James Harrison from Spennymoor; Will Hargreaves from Middlesex; Nicholas Lockey from Northumberland; Michael Keenan from Wolsingham; John Storey from Jarrow; Harry Lithgoe from Lancashire; William Garbutt and Will Haye from Yorkshire; Will Divine from Cumberland; others arrived from Bishop Auckland; Crook; Houghton-le-Spring; Ryhope; Devonshire; Scotland; Wales; Derby; Seaton; Westmoreland and nearby Sunderland Bridge. A family had come from the Isle of Man. Among the men are pitmen, coke yard workers, blacksmiths, an underground agent and a policeman.

Patrick pushed aside the large empty bowl. 'Where's me ganzie, Ma?' he piped. A familiar shout, 'Is Patrick ready?' announced the arrival of Patrick's mates.

Little John Fox, a screener at the colliery, picks stones from the coal sent out of the pit. John is eleven years of age and lives at No. 4 South Street. Brothers William and John Battey, thirteen and twelve years of age, are pony drivers in the 'B' Pit and live at No 10 South Street. John Conley, fourteen, and his brother Charles who is eleven, are pony drivers, they live at No. 7 South Street. All six work the same shift at the nearby pit. They had moved to Brandon Colliery from far off Broughton in Yorkshire, Northumberland, Northallerton, Durham and Spennymoor.

They sauntered towards the village on the hill; smoke belched from the tall chimneys serving coke ovens at the surrounding collieries. Ushaw College, Durham Castle and Cathedral stood majestic on the horizon, Pensher Monument, bold in outline, looked very much like a giant multi-legged table.

Tired after their long shift in the pit, the lads returned home. The flame of the oil lamp set on the kitchen table spluttered in smoky protest as Patrick Mahan opened the door of No. 21 Railway Street, the cries of his pals 'See you in the morning, Paddy!' ringing in his ears. Joseph Lamb who lives next door at No. 20 Railway Street is an old man of sixty three, he was born in Chester-le-Street and is the colliery caller and watcher. He would rouse the lads at four o'clock next morning for their next shift.

Hannah Haye is seventeen, she works with her friend Alice McDermott at Mr. Smith's Paper Mill. Alice is a womanly eighteen year old, her brother Edward, now twelve, is a pony driver.

October was a tragic month, seven deaths being recorded in the colliery rows. On the 10th Ann, the twenty year old wife of Charles Fox, died—five days later Charles died at the age of twenty five.

Tragedy stalked No. 30 North Street; Frank Telford a thirteen year old screener at the colliery was enjoying the ride in the empty tub his three workmates pushed along the wooden gangway at work. Youthful exuberance was abruptly stifled when the tub and its occupant careered over the side of the gangway, they fell twelve feet to the ground, Frank's chest being so crushed he died in great agony. He was one of six sons, he had two sisters. Frank was born in South Shields, his four younger brothers were born in Brandon Colliery. Robert Telford the bereaved father is a thirty year old coal hewer.

The Boyne and Brandon Brass Band was called on to render sacred music to the appreciative music lovers in the music room of the Boyne Hotel. A lengthy rendering of popular airs being well received, the band's popularity was reflected in the generous silver collection.

Sounds of merriment emanated from Joe Addison's Colliery Inn. The landlord's daughter, twenty year old Jane Addison, had on the morning married Robert Jameson Rowell, a Croxdale schoolmaster, in the parish church there. Jane and her younger sister are efficient and popular bar maids, the young bride will be greatly missed by the Inn's patrons when she moves to Croxdale.

The dreaded smallpox has again attacked the colliery inhabitants. Social gatherings are once again severely curtailed. Eleven souls died during November, some from the disease. Brandon Village too, is under attack from the scourge which is said to flourish where sanitary conditions are bad.

December will long be remembered with a death almost daily. On the 8th Harriet the daughter of William Garbutt died, she was two years and three months. A tragic yearly total of ninety deaths in the colliery rows was recorded, a shocking reminder that smallpox and other diseases greatly deplete a community.

1872

No Happy New Year for coal hewer Rowland Richardson. Rowland, thirty seven years of age, lives at No. 29 North Street. His wife Isabella died at the age of thirty five, leaving five sons and one daughter in his care. Michael, his eldest son at thirteen is a letter carrier, he was born at Portsmouth, the others were born in Brandon Colliery.

The pitmen of Durham County are showing strength and determination, at the same time efforts are being made to work in closer harmony with the coal owners. More collieries are joining the Union. Brandon Colliery long isolated, has joined the Durham Miners' Association.

On Saturday January 27th a council of delegates of the above Association met in the Guildhall in Durham Market Place. The Market Place took on a busier aspect as the one hundred and twenty nine delegates representing fourteen thousand workers gathered. Brandon Colliery Union sent a delegate to the meeting.

Delegates agreed 'That all organised collieries use their influence with their employers to get the 'fore shift' for the men put back till four in the morning'. Delegates reported the growing discontent concerning the pitmen's Yearly Bond, they say that meetings are being held in almost every colliery village, deploring the Bond, they seek a fortnightly agreement.

Pitmen Robert Metcalf, William Jones, Jonah Hudson, Joseph Lucas and others sense a significant change in their lives. Excitement is mounting; February 17th was an important day for them and all pitmen in the county, the first Joint Meeting between the Durham Miners' Association and the Coal Owners' Association took place. Hitherto some owners have acted as though their power was limitless, pitmen believe that the new arrangement will be to their advantage. About a score of employers' representatives and ten delegates representing twenty thousand workmen took part in the conference. The first question for discussion was brought forward—the controversial Yearly Binding. The owners were willing to abolish it and suggested a monthly or fortnightly agreement; the men's delegates accepted the latter. The pitmen's delegates also pressed for a thirty five per cent increase of wages; the owners after much discussion, granted them twenty per cent.

Men left the meeting and stepped out into the open, pleased with the outcome; they were convinced that a better era for Durham Mining was at hand. At the meeting it was arranged that in future a Joint Committee of masters and men should settle all disputes that arose.

A long row of houses and shops had been built. The new street runs parallel with West Street and is aptly named Commercial Street in place of High Street as the first few shops and houses were named.

The extensive population has increased the number of Primitive Methodists. Chapel-goers, anxious to erect a chapel to suit their requirements, have signed an agreement with Lord Boyne. A plot of ground situated at the top of West Street has been leased; this land covers 741 square yards and has been offered at a ground rent of five shillings per annum for fifty years, a condition being that a carriageway and footpath be maintained.

Six miners, George Maddison, Richard Kirsip, Ralph Marley, Roland Richardson, Daniel Evans and Frederick Leighton, were chosen as Trustees together with James Robson, shoemaker; Thomas Watson, coker burner; James Watson, grocer; John Pratt, labourer and John Fawell, mason. Eleven men well able to serve the Primitive Methodists of Brandon Colliery.

Colliery expansion and more workers attract salesmen from afar. Robert Sharp, a travelling auctioneer's clerk, appeared for the third time on a charge of stealing a sovereign, the monies of George Mann, a coal hewer of 26 Durham Street. Mann had called in at the sale room and bought a muffler for sixpence. He tendered in payment what he thought was a shilling and received fivepence halfpenny back in change. On getting home he discovered that he had given a sovereign instead. He hurried back to the sale being held in the Colliery Inn; the defendant repudiated all knowledge of the gold coin. Some witnesses present at the sale asserted it was a sovereign, or something like one, others averred it was only a shilling. After hearing the evidence on both sides, the Bench at Durham Court dismissed the defendant.

A man from the colliery had bought an eight day watch, he lost no opportunity of showing it to his mates, one of whom, after a few weeks, asked how his watch was going. 'Oh, fine, man', replied the owner of he watch. 'I used to wind it up every Saturday, but that was rather long for it, so I wind it up every Friday now'.

Scarlet fever is claiming more victims. Louise, the five month old daughter of Rowland Richardson, one of the trustees of the proposed new chapel, was buried at Brancepeth. She was born at No. 29 North Street; her death makes the fourteenth in the colliery rows in four months. The Rev. William Fawcett recalled that his first parochial duty was that of burying the infant's mother, Isabella Richardson, who died in January at the age of thirty five.

Peter Nyland of 13 Railway Street chatted with his friend and workmate James Allen who lives at No. 20 Railway Street; Peter is fourteen years of age and was born in Ormskirk in Lancashire. James, also fourteen, was born in Yorkshire, both are putters in the 'B' Pit. They discussed a new pit agreement which affected them personally, it referring to 'Lying Money'. Hand putters are to be paid fourpence and pony putters to get threepence for every hour they have to wait for tubs because of misadventure in the pit, when no work was provided for them. If they have to do other work, they will be paid sixpence and fourpence an hour respectively. They recalled the time when they lay about wet and cold for four hours when a tub fell down the shaft; they got no pay for that.

James Allen, a fourteen year old pony putter, sat on the limmers attached to the tub; his fiery pony made his work hard and dangerous, his legs dangled between the pony and tub; if he failed to lift his legs as the pony turned left or right he had them crushed. Whilst riding with his head well tucked in to avoid the low roof, Jim had to memorise all the turns traversed during his shift. This form of transport deemed easier than hand putting, James received less pay per score of tubs put.

Coal hewers William Haye, William Abbot and John McLeesh, as they walked inbye discussed the prices just fixed for them. They had to hew and fill twenty tubs of coal, each weighing 8 cwts. 2qts. to earn 8s. 3d. Men hewing in stooks could fill a score of tubs in a shift, depending on the putter's ability to keep him supplied with empty tubs. Men hewing in walls could hardly earn a quarter of that amount.

Putters like Peter Nyland and James Allen also had their prices fixed. Tubs put by hand brought them 1s. 10d. per score for the first eighty yards put, this to be increased by 1d. per score for every 20 yards above the eighty. Putters using a pony to be paid 1s. 4d. for every score of tubs put.

Thomas Evans, a thirteen year old driver in the 'B' Pit, sat on the first of the five full tubs of coal his pony hauled. They had travelled the drift a number of times, this was their last load down the incline, then stable and home for them, his oil lamp scarcely shining beyond the second tub as the tubs gathered speed. For some reason unknown Thomas' pony slipped, causing the tubs to veer; the tub on which he sat ran into the side of the drift. Thomas was so fearfully jammed about the head that he died almost instantly.

Edward McDermott, Thomas Clark and William Coverdale had four things in common. They were twelve years of age, worked as pony drivers in the same shift, lived in Railway Street, and were all eagerly looking forward to the Miners' Gala.

Saturday June 15th saw the noisy trio embark on the train at Brandon Colliery bound for Durham. Their mothers had baked for them on the Friday night, what young lads like. Each carried a bulky parcel, a day at the Gala would sharpen their appetites. A sunny day welcomed the second Miners' Gala, to be held this year on the spacious Durham Racecourse. The lads joined the excited gathering outside the County Hotel in Elvet. Alex McDonald (Glasgow), W. Brown (Staffordshire), Thomas Burt (Newcastle) and other speakers booked to address the expected crowds at the Gala, waved to the seething crowd from the Hotel's balcony.

The first banner arrived on the Raceourse at the early hour of seven thirty. From the first banner setting down on the Racecourse to the last arrival there was perfect order. Some sixty thousand people from one hundred and eighty collieries thronged the course. The membership of the Durham Miners' Association is now thirty two thousand, the Association paid the expenses of half of the forty policemen on duty. The police applauded the manner in which the pitmen conducted themselves. Prior to the Gala, townspeople of Durham were apprehensive about the conduct of such a vast expected crowd, their fears were allayed, businesses in Durham prospered on the day.

As most collieries produce an element of gamblers, it was not surprising to see a gathering of pitch and toss players alongside the River Wear. Men had saved hard for this their first massive gathering—they seemed to have money to burn.

A Sunday School teacher in the County of Durham was possessed with a praiseworthy desire to produce thrift among his class of lads. He had given Bill and John sixpence each for doing some work for him. 'I hope', he said, 'To hear when we meet again that you have used the money to the best advantage'.

Shortly after, they met. Bill proudly produced two sixpences. 'Well done, my lad!' said the teacher. 'I'm pleased to see my lesson bearing fruit. But what of your sixpence, Johnny?' he said to the little hopeful.

'Please sir', was the response, 'I lost it tossing with Bill'.

Women too, believe that unity means strength. Three Brandon Colliery women, tired of paying a high price for butcher's meat, and objecting to the rise in the price of milk, decided on positive action. The women, Mrs. Jane Jefferson, thirty one, wife of John Jefferson, Deputy Overman, Mrs. Knowles and Mrs. Makepeace, called a strike. Five hundred women of Brandon Colliery and nearby Boyne Colliery heeded their call and assembled to discuss their grievances; Mrs. Jefferson took the chair and the meeting was addressed by her two friends. It was unanimously resolved that no one had to buy any meat until it was reduced in price to sevenpence a pound, and milk to one penny a pint.

Arising from the determined efforts of the womenfolk regarding the price of meat, the butchers of Brandon Colliery met the men from the Brandon and Boyne Collieries at the Brancepeth Castle Inn, to state to them at what price they could sell their meat. John Jobson Madgin was the only butcher allowed to enter the room. He said that he was very sorry that such a dispute had taken place, but he could not help it, for the cattle had got to such an extraordinary high price from eight shillings to ten shillings and sixpence per stone. They would try to sell prime meat at eightpence per pound; sirloins and legs of mutton from eightpence halfpenny to ninepence a pound; inferior meat sixpence to sixpence halfpenny a pound; and second quality meat at sevenpence three farthings a pound. He also stated that the inhabitants should see that they were not buying old cows and bull beef.

Patrick Boland works at Brandon Colliery as a coke burner, he and his wife Bridget were born in Ireland. They moved from Durham to No. 2 Railway Street; they have a daughter Anne, and two sons John six years of age and George three, both lads were born in No. 2.

John Harrison six years of age, lives next door at No. 3 Railway Street, he attends school with neighbours John Boland and Thomas Needham. Peter Gelley at eleven years of age is a pony driver underground, he has just moved from Southwick to No. 12 South Street with his two brothers and two sisters. Peter's father, John, is a coal hewer. Patrick Needham is an underground switch holder; Patrick aged eleven was born in Lancashire and has just moved with his family to No. 7 Railway Street. Patrick's father readily acquired a colliery house, having six sons, a future asset to the colliery. Allan Parrish was born in No. 2 East Street and at nine years of age is a screener at the colliery; his father Isaac is a keeker on the screens, he was born in Wales. George Blenkinsop another screener, is ten years of age and was born in Brandon Colliery, the family settled in the colliery in 1860. John Deans an eleven year old, works with George on the screens, he was born in Wylam, Northumberland. John Bailey is another screener, he was born in nearby Sunnybrow eleven years ago.

Another Mines Act was passed which stated that:—

1. The employment of children under the age of 10 underground is prohibited.

2. Up to the age of 16 their hours of work would be restricted to twelve hours in any twenty four.

As the present shift for lads working underground at Brandon Colliery is twelve hours, the latter ruling does not alter existing practices.

The eight accused shuffled timorously into the courtroom; they faced the Rev. A. D. Shafto, magistrate and chairman of the Bench at Durham County Police Court. Police Sergeant Finlayson stood to attention; his silver buttons sparkled on his black serge tunic, baton protruded from his polished leather belt ready for instant action, his beard and tash neatly trimmed for the occasion.

One of the defendants had read in a recent issue of the Durham Advertiser, that a lad of thirteen living in Spennymoor, a place less than an hour away by gig, accused of stealing five sovereigns, had been committed to prison for two months with hard labour and given twelve strokes of the birch. What is hard labour like? What does a stroke of the birch feel like?

The officer stated that the accused had done wilful damage to a meadow field belonging to Francis Foster at Brandon Colliery, by treading down the grass. The defence stated that the defendants were getting water from a well in the field, which was open to anyone to go in, there being no fence of any sort around it.

Sighs of relief passed through eight pairs of lips as the Bench dismissed the case. Thomas Allen eight years of age, Stephen Allen six, George Coleman thirteen, Ann Kelley sixteen, Thomas Keenan thirteen, Mary Carroll seven, and Ann Welch, all from Brandon Colliery, were free to leave the courtroom.

The deficient water supply at Brandon Colliery was again introduced by the Rev. A. D. Shafto at a meeting of the Durham Board of Guardians; he said that Mr. Straker, colliery owner, saw the need for a better supply of water. Mr. Love, his co-partner, said that everybody was satisfied, and highly appreciated the water which was pumped out of the pit in great plenty. It was stated at the meeting that the inhabitants of the two colliery villages owe a debt of gratitude to Mr. Straker for the manliness and energy he has displayed for their benefit. There is no doubt that the object will soon be accomplished, and that the two collieries will soon have as plentiful a supply of good spring water as any other colliery village.

Six days following, the Guardians' meeting saw a public meeting at Brandon Colliery, held to hear the report of a deputation appointed to interview John Straker Esq., with reference to the present great scarcity of water there. One of the deputation informed the meeting that they explained to Mr. Straker the position of the village, and the scarcity of water there was every summer. Mr. Straker was surprised to hear such a state of things, as he fully expected there was an abundant supply of water, and promised to do all in his power to remedy the evil. Mr. Straker kindly gave the deputation £1 to defray their expenses to Newcastle to see the officials of the Waskerley Water Company. The deputation met the officials of the Water Company who promised to lay their pipes to Brandon Colliery as soon as possible, it would probably take four or five months to complete the work.

A Brandon Colliery reader took up his pen and sent the following letter to the Durham Advertiser:—

'If you Mr. Editor, were to take a walk as far as Brandon Colliery any afternoon, I will tell you what you would find. A water-tap in a small cistern. A small stream slowly dribbling out unfiltered muddy pitwater. Mr. Love says he has tasted it. So have I, so may you. I am confident nothing but raging thirst will compel even a beast to drink it. Take it home. The mud won't settle; in a short time the water positively stinks. I have known people wait their turn for three hours, and then when they have reached home they have been obliged to pour the water into the channel. I have seen it made into tea, and the tea so black, unfit to drink.

I understand that Mr. Love at the Board meeting last Saturday said that he could not understand how any person of common sense could believe that such water, after being kept in a house only a few hours, could become so offensive. But then Mr. Love must remember that common sense is a very rare thing, and if he cannot comprehend it, I have seen it, smelt it, and tasted it, much to my disgust. Mr. Love said he was prepared to prove that the water was good and wholesome. Why didn't he?

Let me tell Mr. Love, through you, Sir, that men and women go to Old Brandon in the evening to bring water. I have known men go down through Mr. Storey's field to bring water from the River Deerness. There is a little runner on the Durham turnpike, another near the new Primitive Methodist Chapel, a third above North Street. I have seen people sitting for hours at these places catching drops of water in a pint mug and putting it, when filled, into a large can. If Mr. Love has never seen these things, then I can only say he must have shut his eyes against them.

How different the conduct of Mr. Straker in this matter. He received the deputation courteously, and the deputation was satisfied, having full confidence in him, that what he promises he always performs'.

Believe me, Mr. Editor, yours truly, M.W.

The Ancient Order of Foresters organised a picnic which was held in Lord Boyne's Brancepeth Park. Lovely weather and magnificent scenery helped the school children and teachers from Brandon Colliery, Brancepeth and Willington enjoy the cricket, leapfrog and jumping. A splendid brass band entertained the gathering until nearly dusk.

A number of Brandon Colliery sportsmen walked the narrow, uneven road past the colony of bee-hive coke ovens, across the railway line to David Halliday's Brancepeth Castle Inn at Meadowfield. The quoit match between Nichol Lockey and Thomas Shipley attracted a large number of enthusiastic followers of the sport; men with week-end caps askew, best scarf knotted at the neck and velvet jacket topping best trousers covering polished boots. Nichol, a twenty two year old coke drawer living at No. 2 Railway Street, trounced Thomas 33 chalks to 18. His easy victory made him the richer by £5.

Patrick Keenan, another twenty two year old coke drawer, born in Ireland and currently one of Elizabeth's four lodgers at No. 18 Railway Street, found his bride just two doors away at No. 16. Two families in the short street celebrated the wedding when Patrick married Alice McDermott. Alice, now nineteen years of age and a Paper Mill labourer, married Patrick in Croxdale Catholic Chapel.

Two months after Alice's wedding there was a serious explosion at the Langley Paper Mill. There was a great destruction of property with damages estimated at several thousands of pounds. Alice, with some hundred employees, was rendered workless.

The excitement derived from gambling and defying the law landed three Brandon Colliery men in Durham Police Court. P.C. Kirkup was on duty at the colliery when he saw the defendants all pitmen, gaming at pitch and toss. He had received several complaints from parties living in the colliery rows, he had often cautioned the men about it. They were sent to gaol for two days with hard labour, and ordered to pay costs of seven shillings each, failing payment, a further seven days' imprisonment.

The vicar of Brancepeth and his curate were kept busy during December. Five couples from Brandon Colliery were married in the church there. During the same period, five children left the colliery rows for interment at Brancepeth. Again another dismal and tragic end to a year which has seen sixty members of the community vacate Brandon Colliery for burial at St. Brandon's.

1873

Brandon Colliery now has several streets, the longest being Durham Street; West Street has thirty eight houses; the two South Streets have a total of sixty four; East Street nineteen houses; two short Railway Streets combine to make twenty four; the two North Streets contain thirty nine dwellings.

Several blacksmiths live in Durham Street. John Postle's father is a blacksmith at the colliery; John is ten and is a screener at the pit, he was born in Durham City and now lives at No. 7 Durham Street.

The shops in newly named Commercial Street are occupied. Richard Preston a forty five year old grocer cum draper cum postmaster trades from No. 1. Next door is grocer Jacob Rowe; Jacob Jnr. is a screener at the pit. Edward Forster at sixty eight is a retired colliery time-keeper, he lives with his son Francis who runs the butcher's shop at No. 3. Next door No. 4 is another butcher's where George Gray, a butcher's servant and Gabella Scarby a hired maid live. James Jackson Ferens, a grocer and draper operates from No. 5 and has a staff of five to help run his growing business. No. 6, another grocer's shop completes the huddle of business premises.

A Knurr and Spell match held in a field at Brandon Colliery drew a large crowd. A match of £20 meant heavy gambling on the result; Ralph Steward of Clippers Colliery was favourite, his opponent local man Thomas Towers on being unable to acquire the Durham Racecourse for the game gave Steward £1 when he agreed to play at Brandon Colliery. Throughout the game Steward remained favourite and won the match, thus delighting his supporters from Clippers Colliery.

Following on the heels of the Steward and Towers tussle, another Knurr and Spell match was contested in the same field. This time George Mann of Brandon Colliery challenged George Edwards from Hunwick to a game for £20 a side. Betting was in favour of Edwards 30 to 20 being offered and taken on him. Edwards remained favourite until nearly half the game was played, amid much local encouragement Mann took the lead which he maintained to the end.

The following is the score without the odd yards:—
Mann—828899978898987010678937898888210.
Edwards—9892108108882531810999991099810911088.

After an exciting contest Mann won by eight score three yards.

Durham Pitmen finding the coal market firm, decided at a meeting of the Durham Miners' Association held in the Market Hotel in Durham, to ask for an advance of fifteen per cent in wages. A request they expect the coal-owners to resist.

On February 14th James Ritson, Will Fishwick, Richard Martin, Joe Coates and other coal hewers at Brandon Colliery were surprised and delighted when they heard that their request had been granted. Such a prompt reply was unexpected as it was less than a month since the meeting was convened. The increase would mean as much as five shillings a week to them.

The railway serving the community of Brandon has been in operation for seventeen years. Brandon Colliery residents, impatient at the Railway Company's progress, held a meeting in the Colliery Literary Institute to seek increased railway facilities. At the meeting a notice was drafted to be sent to the North Eastern Railway Company.

It was stated that Brandon Parish now had eight thousand population and the surrounding villages would have about the same number, and that in Brandon Colliery houses were being built, which will in the course of a year, increase the population one third. Mr. Will Dickinson complained of the shortage of trains on a Saturday to supply the inhabitants of Brandon Colliery, the Boyne and Browney Collieries. He said that there were three trains from Bishop Auckland, two in the morning and one in the afternoon, and only one from Durham in the afternoon. There is urgent need of a goods station at Brandon Colliery, all goods having to be carted from Brancepeth or Durham, two and three miles distance. The former place has no warehouse space whatever. On Saturday alone more than six hundred tickets are issued at Brandon Colliery.

Marion the infant daughter of John Kirkcup, police officer, died. Sarah, the widow of recently deceased John Coates, died. William and Mary Hinds lost their two year old daughter, Mary Jane. Daniel Evans, miner, lost William his five year old son. William Bridges, miner, lost his forty one year old wife, Elizabeth. William and Jane Chrisop lost their three year old son, William.

Primitive Methodists now well established in the colliery, have their first minister; Henry Pratt has been appointed to the new Mount Calvary Methodist Chapel. The imposing brick building can seat five hundred worshippers and is sited just off the colliery rows near the top of the long Commercial Street.

At 11.30 a.m. on Saturday June 13th, a boisterous crowd of some two hundred, including John Henry Garbutt now eighteen, with Hannah fifteen and William, nine, followed the Brandon Colliery banner onto the Racecourse at Durham. Mates Jackie Sayers and James Needham walked alongside. Meadowfield and Brancepeth miners followed, their banners being much admired.

One hundred and thirty banners were on parade for this the third Miners' Demonstration when a crowd of forty thousand is anticipated. The banners are said to be worth ten thousand pounds, all of them being composed of silk.

The Durham Advertiser described in alphabetical order the banners which graced the Racecourse. It said:—

'Brandon Colliery banner is well executed, but the meaning of the design it bears is not very obvious to the uninitiated.

On one side of the silk is represented a man exultingly waving a tiny flag, whilst half-way up the mound are three men apparently engaged in struggling up the steep acclivity, and seemingly anxious of emulating the exploits of the more elevated companion. At the bottom of the hill, in a somewhat undignified position, is the figure of a man who had evidently lost his footing and rolled to the bottom of the eminence, and who is being kindly assisted to regain his equilibrium by a friend. Below this enigmatical picture is this motto, "Nil Desperandum".

The symbol exhibited on the other side consists of three girls, the centre one being elevated above the others on a pedestal. Underneath are the words, "How pleasant it is for brethren to dwell together in unity". '

Speakers at the Demonstration came from South and West Yorkshire, Cleveland and London to occupy the three platforms provided.

Two weeks after the Miners' Demonstration a large and successful public meeting took place at Brandon Colliery. The purpose of the meeting was to welcome Edward Rymer a pitman from Barnsley in Yorkshire. The colliery brass band volunteered to escort Mr. Rymer to the place of the meeting, playing one of their best tunes. Will Bridges, Daniel Evans, Will Chrisop, George Maddison and Will Hartley marched with scores of their workmates in procession after the band. Mr. Davidson occupied the chair, and after a few remarks, introduced Mr. Rymer, who related his travels and troubles since 1860 in the cause of the Union. He addressed the audience on the social, commercial and political aspect of the country.

Brandon Colliery along with four other collieries sent money to Mr. Rymer for his services.

Jackie Sayers now a rugged fifteen year old putter, discussed the new increase with his mate James Needham, also a putter. It had been decided that three halfpence extra be paid for a score of twenty one tubs put for every twenty yards above eighty yards. This increase in the score price is to encourage the putter who has to shove his tub a long distance.

Robert Broomhead, Thomas Tiernan, Henry Crossley, Joseph Davidson and George Allen, all coal hewers, are worried. Their recent increase in wages could be in jeopardy. They are concerned over the price of cheaper coal; six months ago pit-head coal was twenty shillings and sixpence a ton, now it is fourteen shillings and sixpence a ton. With such a reduction in the price the owners are almost sure to ask the pitmen to make sacrifices.

Most pitmen welcome the Joint Committee which became fully operational during July. The Committee consists of six members of the Durham Miners' Association and an equal number representing the coal-owners. They will meet every fortnight to discuss the men's demands. Pitmen welcome this new approach to their grievances.

A livid glow filled the sky north of the colliery, bellowing smoke suggested a major fire. Crowds flocked to the colliery waste heap on which a set of wooden stables were built; they gazed, aghast and helpless, as the windswept inferno burned itself out. Six sets of horseshoes told their grim tale, six colliery horses housed in the stables were roasted to death.

A new quadrangle of brick built buildings was promptly erected near the colliery at Meadow Field near the Brick Flats. The horse keeper has a house attached to the stables and the space formed by the quadrangle is used to train horses and pit ponies.

Night shift workers find refuge in the Reading Room and Institute, they while away their time before work reading, playing dominoes and cards. The Institute is catering for an expanding colliery; readers among the men and boys have a choice in the two thousand volumes the library boasts.

In one of the Durham villages the secretary of the reading room walked in, and saw that there were some men there who were not members, so he said to them, 'There's some of ye here that isn't in, and ye that isn't in better gan oot!'

Brandon Colliery still awaits the promised water supply. During August the weather being so hot there was no water, an acute shortage means no tea with a meal, not enough for a good wash, and washing clothes or scrubbing the house floors was virtually impossible.

Pits invariably mean an accumulation of underground water. A number of engineers converged on Brandon Colliery on Friday September 5th to see a new set of pumps constructed by Mr. Coulson of the Merrington Lane Engine Works put into successful operation. These pumps are capable of removing one thousand eight hundred tons of water in twelve hours. The engineers expressed their opinion that the new feature introduced by Mr. Coulson rendered them much superior to what is known as the 'special pump'. To celebrate the occasion Mr. Coulson and his friends dined at Mr. Gowland's in New Elvet, Durham.

Opposition to the railway company has arisen. An enterprising body of men, under the name of Whitty and Company, has commenced to run three brakes between Durham and Brandon Colliery. They run every two hours, calling at the Browney and Boyne Collieries. The first brake which left Brandon Colliery Inn at 8 a.m. on Saturday 6th was crowded to excess, and kept running all day, setting down passengers at the King William IV public house in the North Road. This will be a boon to the residents of Brandon Colliery, especially during the week, when the trains do not stop there.

Two days after the inauguration of the brake service a melancholy and fatal accident took place at Brandon Colliery. The pit's seventh fatality involved twelve year old Cuthbert Coulson. Cuthbert, quiet and inoffensive, was employed as a waler which job entailed his climbing onto the full trucks of coal to remove any stone or waste which had escaped the eyes of the screeners. While four trucks linked together were being moved down the line he jumped onto one of them, his head became jammed between the truck and one of the solid uprights supporting the screens. His head was almost torn from his body, he died twelve hours later in great agony.

One doubts if Cuthbert Coulson, the unfortunate lad's father, could afford to pay death benefit from his meagre wage. The Durham District of the Miners' National Association formed in 1869, has after only four years, thirty five thousand members. A contribution of three pence a week secures labour protection; six pence a week secures labour protection, death, sick and accident benefits. The accumulated funds now stand at thirty seven thousand pounds.

Up to September thirty six colliery inhabitants died. Almost weekly there was a sad cortege to Brancepeth's cemetery. Twenty three of the dead were infants under the age of five.

Foresters travelled from Brandon Colliery to Durham when the Ancient Order of Foresters' Friendly Society held a meeting in the Rose and Crown Hotel in the Market Place. Brother William Dickinson represented the 'Court Pride of Brandon' No. 3333; he is founder member of the movement in Brandon Colliery and was rightly chosen to serve them on the District Committee for another year.

Pitmen at Brandon Colliery and other collieries in the county have applied for an increase in wages, they want twenty per cent. At a meeting in Durham's Town Hall, it was stated that the coal on the London Coal Market was bringing as much as six shillings extra per ton, the men feel that the industry can stand the suggested increase.

Two days after the Durham meeting men streamed up the long lane to East Brandon; a large field was the venue for a local Miners' Demonstration. Jackie Sayers and his mate, both keen Union men, joined the crowd which had arrived from the Browney, Boyne, Meadow Field, Page Bank, Croxdale and Sleetburn Collieries. Each colliery had its own band, men marched in orderly but noisy ranks to the meeting ground. Pensher Monument, Ushaw College, Durham Castle and Cathedral, together with lovely woodland scenery, created a splendid background for the gathering.

Speeches were made on the pitmen's claim to universal suffrage and productive co-operation. Mr. Joseph Cowan ably occupied the chair and a hearty vote of thanks was moved by Mr. Dunn. Jackie and James Needham learnt that universal suffrage had something to do with the right to have a vote in the running of the country. They heard that productive co-operation meant masters and men working together for the common good.

George Milner, a muscular twenty two year old coal hewer, eased his frame on the cracket, sweat glistened under fine coal dust; Friday—he was half way through his last shift for the week, he looked forward to tomorrow's sport, football cleared one's lungs of the week's coal dust. His putter found him slumped on the floor of the seam; a large stone had dislodged itself from the roof and fell on him. George was taken home with a suspected broken back, he died three days later. He had become very popular during the few weeks he had worked at the colliery.

Concerts being the order of the day, Brandon Colliery brass band desirous of fitting each bandsman with a regimental uniform, arranged a concert in the Literary Institute. John Jobson Magdin, local butcher and brass band devotee, occupied the chair. A good gathering was disappointed as the party engaged to entertain was very poor.

Another local concert was held. This time the Methodists of Mount Calvary Chapel held the concert and a Fruit Banquet towards liquidating the debt on the building. John Watson an able singer, occupied the chair. He opened the programme by singing 'Lo He comes in clouds descending'.

Several members rendered songs to make it one of the best concerts ever held in Brandon Colliery. Mrs. Pratt was well received when she sang 'The Last Rose of Summer'.

Miners throughout the coalfield are seeking to have their wages paid every week instead of the fortnightly pay day as at present. Some think it will be a blessing to the publican and a curse to the shopkeeper.

Following the tragic death of sixteen year old Peter Nyland knocked down by an engine at Brandon Colliery, another fatal accident has occurred. A young engine fireman, married, whose home is at South Shields, was crushed between trucks while coupling them at Brandon Siding.

A son arrived for Christmas to Isobel Leckonby wife of Thomas leckonby newsagent.

Crowds took the Saturday trains to Durham where the well stocked shops offered their Christmas bargains. Potatoes were eightpence a stone, cabbages one penny each, rabbits at one shilling each were popular among the low wage pitmen.

Two deaths during the last week of the year made a grievous total of sixty five from the colliery rows during the year.

1874

Parcels are much in evidence, containers of differing sizes and shape are left at Durham or Brancepeth, stations to the North and South of Brandon Colliery. The fast expanding colliery sorely needs a good station of its own. After much agitation by the colliery folk, negotiations between Lord Boyne, Mr. Straker and the North Eastern Railway Company are taking place to remedy the defect.

Coal hewers at the colliery cannot understand why the coal-owners and managers are seeking a ten per cent reduction in wages. Men earn little enough as Brandon Colliery is only working a four day week, other collieries are only working nine days in the fortnight. There are lines of trucks laden with coal and coke. At the moment coal is fetching twenty five shillings and sixpence a ton on London Coal Market.

Brandon Colliery workmen received notice of the owners' demands for a wage reduction. On Friday April 17th they were notified that from May 2nd a twenty per cent reduction would take place. Men are furious, meetings were hastily arranged at the collieries to discuss the matter, they say it is a county affair. The men agreed unanimously not to allow a fraction reduction, unless the question at issue is settled by arbitration.

On Friday May 8th Jackie Sayers, James Needham and coal hewers George Allen, Henry Crossley, Thomas Tierman, Robert Brromhead and Joseph Davison joined their mates at the colliery and came out on strike against the owners' demands.

Men and women prepared for a long strike. After abitration, the strike was settled on the following Friday much to the relief of the womenfolk who had been prepared to manage on very little money. The pitmen accepted a ten per cent reduction in wages and an eleven day fortnight, the owners' original demand had been a twenty per cent reduction and a twelve day fortnight. Men bitter over the reduction in wages, had to agree with the findings of the arbitration and reluctantly returned to work.

Durham lacks street lighting; streets around the city are dark and lonely. Will Hutton a Brandon Colliery pitman, was walking home from the city, he was coming up Crossgate Peth when two men attacked and robbed him, he was left unconscious. Two men from Littleburn Colliery were later apprehended and charged with highway robbery. Highway robbery again! Another Brandon Colliery man, Henry Will, while walking from Durham was attacked by three men at Langley Moor. A pair of trousers newly bought together with two shillings and fivepence were stolen. Luckily for the victim his assailants missed the five pound note he had in the corner of one of his pockets.

Mr. Henry Pratt became Mount Calvary Chapel's second minister, he succeeded Dr. John Eatson. There was a public meeting, tea and lecture by Dr. Watson. The congregation gave freely to aid the Chapel Funds.

Jackie Sayers and his mate were aroused early on Saturday August 15th. Band players and banner carriers sweated under the early sun as they played their way onto Durham Racecourse for the fourth Annual Demonstration. Jackie and James were among the merry cortege which reached Durham shortly after nine a.m. In all there were one hundred and thirty banners set around the ground; the palm was borne by the new banner belonging to Brandon Colliery Lodge, it is the work of a London artist and cost eighty pounds.

The Durham Advertiser commented on the new banner:—
'There are expensive hobbies, and this banner business seems to be one, if so large a sum as eighty pounds is to be thrown away—as it were—on what at best a bauble. We have no intention of saying one word against the little pleasures which the miners devise amongst themselves. They have the undoubted right to spend double or even treble the sum; but there are, after all, better investments for their surplus capital than painted silk.

There are one hundred and twenty three bands, both good, bad and indifferent; the big drums of the bands seemed to have the most prominent part'.

John Fisher Le Page the thirty two year old assistant surgeon to Dr. Robert Robson, occupies two colliery houses combined into one. Nos. 31 and 32 West Street at the top of the colliery row and a few yards from Mount Calvary Chapel, house his wife and two baby daughters in the house cum surgery arrangement. Mrs. Fisher Le Page was born in St. Peter's Port in Guernsey, one child was born in Wales, the other being born in London.

Dr. Le Page was soon called upon to administer to one of the pitmen under his care. Jack Beckworth a coal hewer at the colliery, sat on his cracket in his hewing place, a large stone fell and terminated his work for the shift. He was taken home on the colliery hand cart suffering from severely crushed legs. Dr. Le Page said that many days must pass before the unfortunate young man would be able to resume work.

The long hot summer caused an acute shortage of water. After one shower of rain two women from Sunderland Street came to blows over some rain-pipe water, each claiming that the pipe was erected in her yard. After being charged with unruly behaviour the Bench at Durham Police Court dismissed the case.

It is hoped that the water shortage will be resolved in a few months. After many discussions and meetings the inhabitants of Brandon Colliery, Brancepeth, Willington, the Boyne, Sunderland Bridge and Tudhoe are promised a good supply of water into their homes for twopence a week.

The Reading Institute is a popular rendezvous for colliery workers, it is used to good advantage, its two ornamental seats set against its outer wall are much appreciated on fine days. There was a concert there on Monday October 13th, singing, comedy, and Brandon Brass Band provided the entertainment, all the talent was local and was well received. Ten pounds was raised by admission, the colliery owners added six pounds, the money went towards the promotion of the library. Other gentlemen have promised to give books to the same laudable object.

William Dickinson of 58 Sunderland Street, once again sent a letter to the Durham Advertiser concerning the poor railway communication with Brandon Colliery. He said that since he first called the Railway Company's attention to the fact that trains did not stop daily at Brandon Colliery, the population of Brandon Parish had risen from three hundred to ten thousand. Trains were stopping daily at Brancepeth which has a population of less than one hundred. Brandon Colliery passengers had to walk two miles to Brancepeth Station; out of ninety passengers embarking there, eighty two of them had walked from the Brandon, Boyne and Browney Collieries.

During the year eighty one inhabitants of the colliery died, once again most were infants. This dreadful total may be eclipsed if the Typhoid Fever discovered at Sunderland Bridge only two miles away, is not speedily brought under control. The authorities are perturbed over the high mortality rate. In 1871 a total of ninety died many from infectious disease; sixty eight the following year, and sixty five last year.

Parents in Brandon Colliery believe that running water in each home would help contain disease; they want their children to reach school age to attend the new school opened just west of the colliery rows. The brick building erected by Messrs. Straker and Love can hold five hundred and ten in the mixed department and one hundred and twelve in the infants.

1875

After almost twenty years, church goers from Brandon Colliery and district can now attend a church built almost on their doorstep. The new church of St. John the Evangelist proudly occupies space kindly donated by Viscount Boyne. This stone edifice built in Gothic style is centrally built at Meadow Field. Its spacious chancel, nave, organ chamber and a spire containing one bell, are of architectural splendour, the tracery of the larger windows is very beautiful. Some four hundred worshippers can be accommodated.

The Rev. Joseph Lawson is the new church's vicar, being well known for his keen interest in local affairs was soon called upon to officiate at district functions. He became the first president of Brandon Colliery Literary Institute. He took the chair and the first Annual Meeting of the Institute. Mr. J. A. Moffatt, the secretary, stated that the Institute was in an exceedingly flourishing condition, there being an increase in membership of one hundred and thirty nine during the year and a further two hundred useful books had been purchased.

John Gilchrist, Sam Dunn, Edward Ward and James Patterson, all members of the Institute, played dominoes. They were well pleased with the new easy chairs provided for them, new tables were in evidence. Other night shift workers played bagatelle, draughts and chess on the french polished furniture; maps, magazines and newspapers, both daily and weekly, were in good supply. Membership is fast increasing, so much so that two rooms are to be added to the building.

Jackie Sayers now a soberly seventeen year old had served his stint at putting. He was pleased his turn for hewing had at last arrived. Putting was hard work and often fruitless, entailing strong muscles and a good heart to keep going. More hewers being required he was set on to work in the Busty 'A Pit', the Hat and Feather district, he found coal hewing less arduous than putting tubs.

Jackie and other pitmen at Brandon Colliery were much disturbed on hearing that Mr. Love had laid off Shincliffe Colliery which employs some six hundred men and boys, no reason being given for the dismissals. Would he treat his Brandon Colliery workmen in similar manner?

Hewing prices in Jackie's district just awarded by the Joint Committee are:—
Where the stone band in the coal is 6 inches thick . . . . 12s.6d. a score
Where the stone band in the coal is from 6 to 9 inches thick . . 13s.0d. a score
Where the stone band in the coal is from 9 to 12 inches thick . 14s.0d. a score
Where the stone band in the coal is from 12 to 15 inches thick. 15s.0d. a score
Where the band exceeds 15in. the price rises to 16s.0d. a score.
The new range of prices will earn Jackie sevenpence halfpenny per tub of coal hewed and filled.

Thomas Weeks, ex-coal hewer and family man, works on the screens; he cleans stone and band from the coal sent out of the pit. He was fortunate to find work on the screens when an undergound accident terminated his hewing career. His wage as a screener, fixed the same time as Jackie's, is three shillings and tenpence halfpenny a shift. Recently the pit has worked short time, he and his wife find that feeding their family is becoming a problem, especially as flour is one shilling and elevenpence a stone, meat tenpence a pound and potatoes dear at tenpence a stone.

Joseph Love, owner of Brandon Colliery and others, now seventy nine years of age, after an illness reported to be gastric fever, died at his home Mount Beullah in Durham. During five weeks of illness he was attended to daily by the minister of the Bethel Chapel, North Road, near his home, and Mr. R. N. Robson, colliery surgeon and his medical attendant.

The Durham Advertiser contained the following article:—

'Few names were more revered or more widely known than that of Joseph Love. His life was pre-eminently an eventful one, more especially when we remember the one great fact, that he rose from the ranks as a poor trapper boy in the coalmine to be one of the greatest coalowners in the county, and closed his life as a millionaire, and one of the most munificent benefactors to the cause of religious truth. To the outside world he was known as a great and successful coal owner, upon the history of which, should it ever be written, he has indelibly stamped his individuality.

The great trial of Mr. Love's mining career was in 1863, when the whole of their workmen engaged on the Brancepeth Collieries, to the number of twelve hundred turned out on strike, and almost wrecked the Durham Miners' Union, which at that time had first reached a certain degree of solidity, under the guidance of Mr. William Crawford, never before accomplished'.

The Advertiser continued:—

'A brief sketch of his life which we subjoin is pregnant with example, both to young and aged, to the former as an incentive to what accrues from honest and persevering endeavour, and to the latter Christian humbleness and simplicity while surrounded by opulance. In him we find an embodiment of the following verse

"Wise men conquer difficulties
By daring to conquer them;
While sloth and folly shiver and shrink
At sight of toil and danger, which they fear".

Mr Love was born in New York, a small pit village in Northumberland, in April 1796, when the revolutionary tempest was raging in France, threatening disaster to England, and shaking the whole civilised world. At the early age of eight he began his struggle for existence, in the Oxclose Pit near Chester-le-Street, where his father resided.

Twenty three carriages filled with funeral mourners walked Crossgate Peth, through Langley Moor, Meadow Field and on to Brancepeth, a distance of five miles, for burial in the village churchyard. Mr. Love's three brothers are left to run the collieries'.

Temple Coulson a young putter in the 'A' Pit, jumped at the chance to hew a tub of coal, the hewers assigned to him were cleaned up, the extra coppers earned would help out his pay. Temple hurriedly swung the borrowed pick. In his haste he was soon working before his timber; without warning, a large stone fell, completely burying the hapless putter. After his release and removal to his home, two surgeons immediately arrived to render aid. On examining him, they stated that both thighs were broken and at once applied the necessary splints and bandages. For two days Temple suffered the most excruciating pain. His father, Christopher Coulson, sent for Mr. Simpson, bone-setter, living at Littletown who, on his arrival, examined the boy and gave it as his opinion that not a bone in his body was broken. Before Mr. Simpson left the house he removed the splints and had the satisfaction of seeing Temple sitting up in bed taking his dinner. Mr. Simpson said that in all probability the lad would have laid in bed, tightly strapped up, until he died, or would have been crippled for life.

The coal hewer had left Chester Moor Colliery, not far from Chester-le-Street, to work at Brandon Colliery. He lived with his stepfather, also a pit-man, in Queen Street. While at Chester Moor he made the acquaintance of the nineteen year old daughter of an engineman there, they planned marriage.

The couple took the train to Durham. As the trains do not stop at Brandon Station on weekdays they walked the three miles to Brandon Colliery. On the afternoon, soon after their arrival, the tragedy occurred. While together in the parlour of the house in Queen Street, the young man drew a pistol and shot the unfortunate girl twice, the shots proving fatal. Scared and curious neighbours, drawn by the commotion, gathered at the yard gate. The young man disappeared to be apprehended four days later. He pleaded insanity at his trial and was sent to the asylum for the criminally insane during Her Majesty's pleasure. Soon after the tragic affair the family left Queen Street; some neighbours saw them take away their furniture, presumably to Wales.

Numerous pitmen breed pigs. There are pigsties erected in the allotment gardens at Railway Street, South Street and College Terrace. These animals are fed mainly from vegetable waste collected from neighbours. An epidemic disease broke out among the pigs; one man lost a sow and five pigs, several other men have seen two or three of their stock succumb to the disease.

A laden train left Brandon Colliery Station on its short journey to Brancepeth. The Primitive Methodists, now a strong religious body in the colliery, held their first annual gala and tea meeting on a blazing June day. Lord Boyne of Brancepeth Castle kindly let them use the Castle grounds. Noisy Sunday School scholars excitedly toured the grounds and surrounding woodland; they were enthralled by the number of deer, peacock and squirrel at home in the Castle's environs.

About ninety Foresters arranged to meet in the Castle grounds, their visit coincided with the Sunday School party. Proud in their regalia the Foresters paraded the colliery rows before their picnic. Lord Boyne and his family were not in residence, they were sojourning at Brighton.

Two days later on July 3rd, hundreds of pitmen lost a day's wage when they attended the fifth Miners' Gala. The pitmen from collieries on the Durham to Bishop Auckland route were greatly disappointed when the Railway Company announced the withdrawal of trains on the Saturday, they declared their inability to cope with the extra weekend traffic. Brandon Colliery band and banner paraded the colliery streets before going on to Durham. Brandon Colliery lodges arrived in Durham just before the Boyne, Browney and Oakenshaw lodges.

Despite the change of day, one hundred and twenty four colourful banners graced the Racecourse. The five speakers and agents on the two platforms impressed a large portion of the twenty five thousand people who attended the Gala. As on previous occasions the press and police complimented the pitmen on their splendid behaviour.

A few pitmen had spent the day in Durham. After getting tired with travelling about the city they made tracks for the North Road Station in order to catch their train. They were half an hour before train time and would have liked to go back to the Market Place, to while away a little of the time, but for the distance. They however, began chaffing a porter. 'Aa say', began one of the funny men, 'Whativer made them build a station se far away fra the Market Place, where it's busiest?' 'Aa divvent knaa', replied the porter drily, 'Unless they thowt it wor best to hev it up here agyen the railway'.

During July, Scarlet Fever claimed four infant victims. Joseph, son of William Reay a coal hewer living in Durham Street, at the age of one being the eldest. William suffered further depression when he received notice to quit his job. For some weeks the collieries in the neighbourhood have felt the effects of slack trade. Will and Sarah Garbutt had a daughter christened Sarah who survived the fever epidemic.

After twenty five years' hard work Alexander Macdonald, a pitmen's leader, induced seventy five thousand workmen and their masters to submit their differences to arbitration. As a result of this agreement Brandon Colliery hewers fared badly; a Joint Committee Award granted a reduction of five per cent on the score price in the 'C Pit' Brockwell Seam. The coal hewer now receives twelve shillings and sixpence for twenty tubs of coal filled. Shortly after the Brockwell Seam award, coal hewers in the Hat and Feather, Duncow and Straight North districts, all in the Busty Seam, suffered a similar reduction in their score price. Surface workers and cokemen had a four per cent reduction in wages.

Mr. Coulson brought under the notice of the Durham Rural Sanitary Board the fact that there was a great deal of bad meat sold to poor people at Brandon Colliery and in other parts of the district. Some of the meat vended was not fit for carrion, and it was sold at fivepence or sixpence a pound. People who eat such meat are only making sewers of their throats. It is well known that good meat was not sold wholesale in Newcastle Market under eightpence or tenpence a pound. Such practice was very unfair to the honest and fair dealing tradesmen. Mr. Coulson went on to say that he saw a piece of meat a woman had bought for fourpence a pound which was hardly fit to give to a dog.

Fr. Smith from Croxdale, nearing the end of his ministerial work in Brandon Colliery, the new school at Langley Moor having absorbed his Durham Street pupils, helped organise a soup kitchen for the many in need of help. Fr. Smith will be greatly missed by the people of the area, having travelled the road from Croxdale for a number of years.

John Allen, Thomas Dobson, John Storey, Will Reay and Tom Briggs, all pitmen, bored and sick of lazing around, left the Institute and slowly tread the lane leading to Brandon Village. Their notices had expired, penniless and out of work, they found the relentless June weather an excuse to escape fretful wives. Owing to the depression of the coal trade about Durham, Straker and Love closed down the 'A' Pit. Five hundred men and boys, including coke oven workers, had received notice to terminate their employment. About forty lucky men were set on at other collieries owned by Straker and Love, others moved to nearby Littleburn and Browney collieries.

Jackie Sayers and James Needham, also out of work, but free to enjoy their enforced idleness, walked the three miles to Durham. They passed the nearly completed Church of St. John at Meadow Field. A recent bazaar held in Lord Boyne's Brancepeth Park had realised four hundred and twenty five pounds towards the six hundred pounds needed to complete the work; Lord Boyne sent a cheque for two hundred pounds to hasten the parishioners' dream. The efforts of the church goers in the district wiped out the four thousand one hundred and seventy three pounds debt.

Jackie and James wishing to see the illuminated tower of the new Miners' Hall in Durham's North Road, waited until dusk. Crowds gathered to witness the lighting up ceremony. The majestic dome crowns a tower which has three clock faces which cost one hundred and thirty pounds; the thirty pounds per year estimated cost of illuminating the tower by gas flame will be borne by the town.

The coal trade recession continued throughout the summer. Furniture piled high on carts left the colliery rows at regular intervals followed by disillusioned pitmen and their families. Tearful women bade farewell to kindly neighbours.

Mrs. McGregor, Mrs. Edwards and Mrs. Stones, all of whom had suffered recent bereavement having lost a tiny infant, had known the charity and care of the departing families. They waved and wished them bon voyage. Two families had decided on Canada as their goal and destiny; others moved to other collieries, hopeful of better times to come. In ten days one hundred and fifty families left the district; streets and school were severely depleted of children. Smokeless chimneys and houses with boarded windows a grim reminder of economic decline.

Local farmers decided, at this inopportune time, to raise the price of milk from fourpence to fivepence a quart—in some cases to sixpence a quart. The increase being due to the incidence of Foot and Mouth disease in the area. Coal owners too, seem bent on adding to the men's troubles. Despite the short time working, the owners have decided to demand a reduction of twenty per cent on the underground earnings and twelve and a half per cent on the surface workers. These reductions to be applied at a later date.

Output at the collieries is halved. The Broompark and Boyne pits, almost within hailing distance of Brandon, are closed down.

Carefree pit ponies, withdrawn from the 'A Pit' for the duration of the seam's closure, were disturbed at their grazing. John Gilley, Richard Curry, Richard Robson and Richard Pepper staged their impromtu rodeo. Ponies, their shaggy coats flecked with sweat, were raced around the colliery field owned by Straker and Love. P.C. Edwards caught the lads; they were fined eight shillings and one penny each. The ponies are said to have cost the company fifteen pounds each.

Men feel that they are being oppressed from all sides. The threat of a wage cut, the loss mainly from Scarlet and other Fevers, of thirty nine of their colliery kinfolk, and the untouchable price of food, add to their Christmas gloom. Geese and turkeys are costing from ten shillings to seventeen shillings each, hares five shillings and sixpence each. Only the better off can afford such prices.

1876

The pit has been in intermittent operation for almost twenty years. Pitmen and their families have survived a major strike and various epidemics. Hundreds of families have arrived, stayed some time, made friends and moved on. Few of the first comers remain at the colliery; they have seen another shaft sunk and drawing coal at the South side of the 'A Pit'; this shaft being nearer Meadow Field is named the Meadow Field 'C Pit'. They have seen long rows of houses supersede farmland on the West side of the colliery; College Terrace, two Park Streets, two Russell Streets, two Queen Streets, two Albert Streets, and a Cobden Terrace, make a total of twenty six streets housing seven hundred and thirty six families.

The New Year saw more pits laid in. Parts of Brandon Colliery are mining coal only with men and lads accepting a seven per cent reduction on wages. Deputies were subjected to a six per cent reduction; they were told by the Owners to form themselves into a separate association, hitherto they had been members of the Miners' Association. The Owners stated that the deputies would not be subject to the six per cent reduction if they left the Miners' Association. Some deputies left the Union and were immediately dubbed 'Shakers' by men in the Miners' Union.

A deputy was rushing inbye at a time when he should have been on his way out. Meeting one of the hewers he said, 'Geordie has thoo seen owt of my westcoat in thy place 'cos As dinnet knaa where Aa can hev put it?' Geordie looked at him and smiled and then said, 'Why man, thoo hes it on'. The deputy looked at himself and said, 'Why laa thoo's reet; and mind it's a good job thoo's told us or else Aa wad hev gone hyem without it'.

George Mann left his Sunderland Street home and walked the few hundred yards, Durham direction, to Catherine Dunn's Red Lion Inn. He and twenty eight devotees of the brass band sat down to an excellent repast when they held their fourth annual supper. George, an able secretary to Brandon Colliery Brass Band, was presented with a Meershaum pipe for his services to the band, Mrs. Dunn received a dress ring. Cigars at twopence each and Taddy's snuff were appreciated during the entertainment provided.

On the same night forty men sat down to dinner in Brandon's other Inn, Robert Wray's Colliery Inn, the occasion being the fifth anniversary meeting of the brick and pipe makers of Straker and Love's Brandon Colliery. Mr. J. Davison created much amusement by his rendering of an original comic song entitled 'The Smoky Shaft'.

Hugh McDermott born in Railway Street eleven years ago, left school to work in the pit. Despite the colliery working a three or four day week, Hugh started work as a trapper lad underground. Railway Street is a short distance from Brandon Railway Siding where work is going ahead on the new

Railway Station. Fifty men are engaged in building and excavating; the Station Master's house is covered in, and the waiting rooms are far advanced. The Railway Company is building a large bridge to avoid the level crossing, a scene of many accidents. A large warehouse, for the reception of goods, is being built at the low end of the passenger station. The station is expected to be ready by July.

Proud delegates from various collieries attended the first meeting held on June 2nd in the new Miners' Hall; they met to consider the ten per cent reduction on the men's wages proposed by the coal owners. The pitmen feel that the owners should not have sought a reduction so soon after the last one. It was arranged to meet the coal owners to discuss the matter. The owners' demand caused meetings to be hastily convened.

On the Saturday following the delegates' meeting, a gathering of pitmen from Sleetburn, Waterhouses, Meadow Field, Broom Park, Esh Winning, Ushaw Moor and Brandon Colliery was held at Langley Moor. One speaker stated that if their organisation was destroyed they would be in a worse position then they were in 1852 and 1869, and instead of ten or fifteen per cent reduction, it would be thirty per cent.

A colliery ballot was taken on the issue of wage reduction. The majority of men want work not strikes; 20,190 voted for arbitration; 16,485 favoured striking. Majority for arbitration 3,785. The decision was well received throughout the county.

Jackie Sayers, now 18, took his girl friend to the Miners' Demonstration; Alice Brough, just a few months Jackie's Junior, had similar aspirations, she liked long walks and the Miners' Demonstration. They joined the two hundred Brandon Colliery folk who followed their banner to the Durham Racecourse. For the second successive year the event was held on a Monday, the same reason as last year prevailed, the Railway Company could not provide transport on the Saturday. A good and attentive crowd listened to spirited speeches delivered from the two platforms provided.

A correspondent to the Durham Advertiser made the following suggestions for improving the manner and morals of the pit population. He says:—

'Whilst wandering among the pit villages I have often thought that by a judicious arrangement a great improvement might be made of the habits of miners by having bathrooms or places wherein they could wash themselves and change their clothes immediately after leaving the pit. There is plenty of hot water about all the collieries running to waste, which could be used for baths or lavatories, and there need not be much misunderstanding with regard to soap and towels. Most of the pitmen's houses are small enough, and it cannot conduce to the delicacy and refinement of the young women of the families to have fathers and brothers "tubbed" every day often in the living room, with the family about'.

The recreational needs of Brandon and district were catered for when the new theatre was opened at Langley Moor. Mr. Parsons, a building contractor, had successfully applied to build and license the theatre and music hall.

Jackie Sayers called on Alice Brough, they were now established 'courters'. They walked the mile to Langley Moor to see a drama performed in the new 'Alhambra Theatre', a new exciting drama being booked for every performance. On the night of their attendance a beautiful silver plated teapot was offered as a prize to the first person who answered the following conundrum, 'Why ought the proprietor of Langley Moor Theatre to be more respected than any other in the diocese?' The judges were selected from the audience. Jackie noted with interest the first three dramas to be booked. 'Ticket of leave Man', 'The Streets of London', and 'The Green Hills of the Far West'.

The Alhambra has created much local interest; its popularity has spread to Durham, from which place two bus loads of theatre goers travel each week. The young people of the district are delighted, hitherto walking has been their chief free time occupation.

People representing all walks of life attended a meeting in the Colliery Mechanics' Institute; they feel that Brandon, now almost the size of a town, needed a controlling body to foster its interests. It was proposed that a Local Government Board for the Township of Brandon and Byshottles be formed; such a Board could hold promise of official investigation into the high death rate at Brandon Colliery. Eight members of the community died during the month of December, seven of whom were infants. The vicar of St. Brandon's and his curate buried an astronomical total of fifty one Brandon Colliery souls during the year.

1877

The New Year began on a depressing note. More and more pits are being closed owing to slack trade. Not half of the houses of Brandon Colliery are occupied, it is almost a ghost town. Pitmen thankfully make use of the Literary Institute, its five hundred volumes costing nearly sixty pounds, thirty two daily and weekly newspapers are a boon to its one hundred and eighty members during the bad January weather.

Jim Elliott and Tim Sullivan both staunch Union men, walked Sunderland Street's long length toward the Red Lion Inn nestling alone in the hollow lying some two hundred yards from the end of the street. They discussed pit affairs and the serious rise in the price of food. Potatoes, which four weeks ago were eightpence a stone, had doubled in price to one shilling and fourpence a stone. The colliery was working slack time, but Jim and his friend paid their Union fees at the Inn every two weeks, money which in all probability would shortly be needed as there is talk of a general strike in Durham county. Nearly four thousand men could be involved as the owners propose a reduction of fifteen per cent on wages and a readjustment of hours.

Pitmen at the colliery cannot understand that while coal is fetching eighteen shillings and sixpence a ton on the London Coal Exchange, the owners' persistence in their claim for a wage reduction.

The prices at Brandon Colliery 'C Pit' were reduced by six per cent.
Hand putters earning 1s.8d. a day reduced to 1s.7d.
Pony putters earning 1s.2d. a day reduced to 1s.1d.

Deputies per shift 4s.11d. a day reduced to 4s.8d.
Drivers per shift 1s.7d. a day reduced to 1s.6d.
Water leading 4s.2d. a day reduced to 3s.11d.
Water leading 4s.0d. a day reduced to 3s.9d.
Water leading 2s.4d. a day reduced to 2s.2d.
Trappers and Switch Keeping 1s.2d. reduced to 1s.1d.
Hewers for starting 2s.2d. reduced to 2s.0d.

Brandon Parish is formed from Brancepeth; the parish comprises the villages of Brandon, Brandon Colliery, Sleetburn, Browney, Langley Moor and Littleburn, these house a population of over ten thousand. Brandon Colliery now has twenty six streets. The colliery band draws its members from almost every street; they held their annual dinner in Catherine Dunn's Red Lion Inn. A large company sat down to a good spread; several pieces of music were performed by the band followed by songs, various toasts were given to conclude a most enjoyable evening.

Angry voices pervaded the air as men queued to pay their fortnightly Union contribution in the Red Lion; the reason for the angry upsurge was the Durham Coal Owners' request for an eighteen per cent reduction in the pitmen's wages. Tom Hutchinson, John Colman and Ralph Gray all family men, were filled with apprehension on hearing the news.

One hundred and ten men and boys, men like Tom Dickinson, John Blenkinsop, George Wilson, Dickie Bendilow and Joe Rogerson had more pressing problems than a threatened reduction in wages—they had received a fortnight's notice to leave their work.

Straker and Love, in consequence of the great depression in the coal trade, a situation worsened by the hot summer and the consequent reduction in coal consumption, contemplate closing the 'B Pit' altogether until trade revives. Some of the men will be absorbed into the 'C Pit' on the termination of their notices. The 'C Pit' is the only one being worked, the 'A Pit' having been laid idle two years ago.

Brandon Colliery has a deserted and forlorn appearance at present, and with the exodus of such a large population things will be much worse. Whole streets of houses are standing empty, and the general depression in trade has caused a marked change to come over a once busy centre of industry. Shops in Commercial Street, once a hive of activity and business, are devoid of custom. Drapers, butchers and general dealers, formerly trading in the street named High Street have accepted the more pretentious and apt Commercial Street. The long row of colliery houses next to the extensive Newcastle Street is named High Street.

On Monday July 16th, Jackie Sayers, now nineteen and courting seriously, took his girl to the seventh Durham Miners' Demonstration. Owing to the Railway Company's inability to provide sufficient trains on the Saturday the Demonstration was once again deferred to the Monday. A greatly reduced number, some thirty thousand, attended the annual event. Jackie heard one speaker, Mr. Richard Fynes from Blyth, say that he had been visiting the villages in Durham, and found that men were working ten or eleven days for one pound ten shillings or one pound thirteen shillings. That was not sufficient to enable men to feed themselves and families; and he hoped the next time they met each man would be receiving one pound ten shillings per week instead of that amount per fortnight.

The formation of a Brandon Local Board, having received the Royal Assent, the order will come into operation on September 29th. The election of nine members to form the new Local Board has been fixed for November 6th, the Rev. Joseph Lawson to be returning officer. The election will be conducted by ballot.

Voting took place in the Miners' Institute amid great local interest; something of great import was happening in Brandon Colliery. After the counting of the votes, which took place the next day, three candidates were chosen from the five nominated to sit on the proposed new Local Board. One of the three, John Fisher Le Page, gentleman, Meadowfield House, was elected to the Centre Ward in which Brandon Colliery will be situated. Mr. Le Page had at one time practised medicine in West Street, his surgery cum home, two houses combined, being set at the top of the street next to Mount Calvary Chapel.

The Chapel's new minister, the Rev. H. B. Kendall, consoled the stricken family when young William Robert Holton, son of William Holton a coal hewer, was killed at work, he was a colliery screener. The inquest was held in Robert Wray's Colliery Inn only a few yards from the gaunt wooden structure, the scene of the recent disaster. Neighbours in the short North Street, deeply shocked, mourned with the family.

The state of the coal trade is terrible; sixty pits in the county have closed down, pitmen generally are earning only about half the wages they had been receiving, most pits are only working a seven or eight day fortnight. Straker and Love have obtained a reduction varying from thirty to fifty per cent, in their colliery rates.

The coal hewers' wages are now determined by the nett price of coal; a sliding arrangement operates, which will be reviewed every four months. Men like Martin Dodd, John Edwards and James Kipling who have just recently suffered a reduction of seven and a half per cent in wages, are a little sceptical of the scheme. Will the reduction be restored?

Numbers of colliery folk are complaining about the Railway Company's attitude to the poor facilities offered to would be travellers. William Dickinson of Sunderland Street sent a letter to the Durham Advertiser condemning the Railway Company's behaviour to the conditions prevailing at Brandon Colliery. He reminded them that it was fifteen years since he first called their attention to the matter. A first class railway station had been built, it was finished over a year ago. He said that we now have the winter staring us in the face, with the dreaded Crossgate Peth before us, with all the danger of being knocked by highwaymen, who infest that dreary region on the dark winter nights. He called for an indignation meeting.

Bernard McGlen went to work on Friday November 23rd. It was his last shift of the week. At thirty one years of age he was at his prime as coal hewer in the 'C Pit'. Half way through the shift a large stone fell from the roof and injured the lower part of his body. He lingered fifteen days at home and died from his injuries on the eighth of December. His death was the tenth fatal accident since the pit started some twenty years ago. December was a memorable month for the Rev. Lawson and his flock; on December 12th the Court of Windsor granted to St. John the Evangelist (Meadow Field Place), a Chapelry. On December 18th the London Gazette contained the announcement that a new District Chapelry had been assigned to the church of St. John the Evangelist, Brandon, out of the Parish of Brancepeth.

Thirty nine Brandon Colliery residents died during the year, thankfully the number is a big decrease on that of last year.

1878

Hugh McDermott and his younger companion, Lawrence Cummings, trudged through deep snow. Homeward bound they were working men dedicated to a cause. They, with other Roman Catholics from Brandon Colliery and the surrounding district, had volunteered their services; a half built structure of galvanised iron, inlaid with wood, a testimony to their labours. Fr. James Hanley, the first parish priest in the area, knowing the need for a chapel and school for his flock, directed the work on the building destined to seat three hundred and fifty worshippers.

Hugh and Lawrence left the new site, highly pleased with the voluntary work already done on the exposed building. They passed St. John's church in the Ecclesiastical Parish of Brandon where their first vicar, the Reverend Joseph Lawson had recently read the thirty nine articles of the Church of England. Their walk home to Brandon Colliery now made easier with the laying of a new road from the south side of Meadow Field to Brandon Colliery railway station. A new path made from cinder oven ashes stretched from the turnpike road greatly enhanced the work.

On the night of Sunday January 20th a gale of tremendous ferocity raged over the district; woodwork on the new chapel was broken and considerable damage was done, resulting in the deferment of its opening. After overcoming the disappointment and the ravages of the gale, the builders and volunteer workmen had the immense satisfaction of seeing the chapel cum school opened on the 4th March. Children from Brandon Colliery, Browney Colliery, Littleburn Colliery, Langley Moor and Meadow Field attend the school, their fathers are donating one day's pay a fortnight to help erase the debt incurred.

Industry has attracted business and workers; churches, chapels and a railway station have been built, new roads have been laid. The owners of Brandon Colliery have lowered the level of Railway Street leading to the station, and made a good foundation of broken bricks.

When the railway station was opened, the people of Brandon Colliery were promised that it would soon be lighted with gas, but this has not yet been done, and the station and its approaches are in a state of obscurity every night and morning—the dim oil lamps at present in use being of little service at this dark period of the year.

The depression in the coal trade is still severely felt in the district, and many poor families are suffering greatly from want of the bare necessities of life. Brandon Colliery 'C Pit' has only worked about half time for the last two or three years, and pitmen and their families are feeling the pinch of poverty very keenly at the present, things are at a low ebb indeed.

Pitmen at the colliery have for some time had access to the Institute on Sunday mornings to read the newspapers and periodicals. A portion of the community shocked at the gravity of the offence, objected to the colliery owners, who sent word to Mr. J. J. Lishman the colliery manager to stop the practice.

A meeting of the members was held in the reading-room to consider the Sunday closing question; there was a large attendance of members; William Dickinson occupied the chair. Voting took place, the result being fifty three for the opening of the reading-room on Sundays and five against. A deputation was appointed to meet the coal owners and ask their permission to carry the resolution into effect.

The pitmen at the colliery had heard that the coal owners of Durham County are to request their men to agree to a resucitation of the yearly bond which was abolished about six years ago, the men could then enter into longer and greater contracts. The pitmen in general will not object, knowing that under the old bonding system they were sure of regular employment and compensation, whereas now many collieries are closing, and families are in extreme poverty.

Will Dickinson and other coal hewers at Brandon Colliery are once again concerned. On Saturday March 16th all pitmen and coke burners at nearby Browney Colliery received a fortnight's notice; it is not contemplated to lay the pit in, it is believed that the men will be invited to resume work at a reduction of wages. Browney Colliery one mile away is worked under different ownership.

As Will Dickinson had feared, the depression spread to Brandon Colliery. The colliery owners resolved to close the 'B Pit' or Hutton Seam which was only re-opened a few months ago; it being financially unsuccessful sixty two men and boys received two weeks notice. The pit will be laid in until better times. The 'A Pit' or Busty Seam has now been closed for nearly three years, there is no sign of its reopening. The 'C Pit', at which the Main Coal or Brockwell Seam is worked, will now be the only one left open, work is restricted there. Altogether the outlook for the area is a most gloomy one, much distress prevails.

The long hot summer days are bad for business, coal is in little demand. Even the man with the dancing bear on the end of a chain finds a tour of the colliery streets unproductive, hawkers and beggars too, fare badly.

Towards the latter part of June the depression in trade was very bad indeed in the Brandon district. Hundreds of pitmen are scarcely earning sufficient to maintain themselves and their families with the bare necessities of life, the pits generally working about half time. During the last few months a general exodus of miners and their families has taken place from Brandon Colliery and neighbourhood. Many who had the means have emigrated to the colonies and other foreign countries. Brandon Colliery, a once busy centre of industry, presents a marked change to what it formerly bore. The tall chimneys are now smokeless, or nearly so, while the long rows of coke ovens, the lurid glare of which might be seen for many a mile, are now falling to ruins for want of being used. Several rows of houses are closed, and the windows barred up, reminding the visitor of Goldsmith's deserted village.

The rows of houses are blocked up at either side by fencing, and the significant intimation, 'Any person found trespassing in this street will be prosecuted' is placed on a board at the end of each street. Trespassers, however, evidently do not care to wander about these forsaken houses, for the streets are covered with tall grass both back and front, and a capital harvest of hay is now ready for gathering.

Despite the depression throughout the coalfield, with no fewer than sixty collieries lying idle, about forty thousand representing two hundred collieries, turned up in hot blustery weather for the eighth Durham Miners' Gala. Brandon Colliery was indeed a ghost town; most of the remaining families, out for one day of enjoyment, made the three mile trek to Durham.

One week after the Gala, on July 12th, three hundred and twenty men and boys employed at the 'C Pit' received two weeks notice to cease work. Messrs. Straker and Love contend that the bad condition of trade is the reason for dismissing the men. Some of the pitmen had an interview with Mr. Hepple the manager, and offered to accept a small reduction, rather than lay the pit idle. Mr. Hepple informed the men that the owners had decided to cease operations, for the present at least, as the pit was not paying.

The ovens and brickworks at the colliery are all lying idle. During the prosperous years of 1873 and 1874 there were nearly one thousand men employed at Brandon Colliery and it contained a population of between three and four thousand; its twenty five streets are now almost deserted, and will become more so unless trade speedily revives.

After a month of closure the owners of Brandon Colliery consented to re-open the 'C Pit' at a general reduction of ten per cent. Work would be resumed first to non Union men only, about thirty pitmen connected with the Union have accepted the reduction rather than lay the pit in. Their acceptance disgusted the Union men. All the ponies and gear, having been removed from the pit, will have to be re-installed.

Great distress again pervades the district; collieries for some time past have only been working half time. During the closure a very large proportion of the inhabitants left Brandon Colliery; each day loads of furniture were seen on the road, men and their families seeking a more peaceful and prosperous existence, walking by their side.

Work resumed at the 'C Pit' on August 21st. The owners consented to re-open at a reduction of ten per cent all round, first to non-Union men only. Will Dickinson and other staunch Union men are furious over the decision.

George Mann, coal hewer and all round sportsman, died at his home in Durham Street, where he had lain ill during the mass lock-out; he was fifty six years of age.

During September another mass meeting was held in a field near Brandon Village. Ten lodges from surrounding collieries including Brandon Colliery met under the auspices of the Durham Miners' Association, all ten sported banners, the theme being 'Better Organisation of our Association and our Political Emancipation'. The object of the meeting was twofold;

it was to show the working classes the necessity of trade organisation for the attainment of their rights—the right to be remunerated fairly for their labour, and also to have the right to have a voice in the making of these laws in the country that they were bound to obey.

Early November saw an equally early winter in the form of a snowstorm, so bad, that communication with Sleetburn was again cut off.

Bad weather did not prevent crowds flocking into the Alhambra Theatre at Langley Moor. A concert of sacred music was given for the benefit of St. Patrick's Schools at Langley Moor. The building was crowded in every part, reminding the visitor of the prosperous times of four or five years ago, instead of the present depressed condition of the coal trade. The Rev. James Hanley, rector of the Catholic congregation of the district, presided. The road to Brandon Colliery was thronged with satisfied theatre goers who had heard a member of Durham Cathedral Choir sing several songs, and a programme consisting of a variety of comic and sentimental songs, principally Irish. The concert was a great success, and realised a handsome sum of money for the schools.

Once again Scarlet Fever ravaged the district, the death roll, especially among the very young, is high. During the epidemic in December, a soup kitchen was opened ay Humbersledge Farm in Meadow Field Place to supply the needy with soup during the inclement weather. The idea of opening the kitchen originated with Lord Boyne who subscribed fifty pounds. A committee has been formed, with the Rev. Joseph Lawson, the vicar of St. John's, at the head, and a meeting was held in the colliery office, Brandon Colliery, where the necessary arrangements were completed. The soup made at the farm is retailed at one penny per pint to adults, and a halfpenny a pint for children. The soup is to be sold on three days of the week.

There is still great distress in the district owing to the collieries working so badly, much sickness prevails, and many deaths have taken place, again the majority are young children.

Excited youngsters gathered to watch the sale of thirty horses and ponies just removed from Messrs. Straker and Love's Oakenshaw Colliery which is entirely laid in owing to the dullness of trade. The brick wall of the Colliery Farm stables accommodated the eager spectators as the fitful ponies changed hands, swapping their life under ground for the more sedate one of hauling a merchant's cart.

Jackie Sayers now twenty years of age, married a local girl Ann Brough on Boxing Day in the Methodist Chapel just up the lane from his home. They had decided, after a few deferments, to marry despite the fact that bleak prospects faced them. After the temperate celebrations Jackie moved from his home in Durham Street to a two roomed house in Sunderland Street which contained several empty houses. Frugal furniture adorned their first home, but being from colliery folk stock, their spirit would carry them through to better times.

1879

Continuous severe weather hit the poor people of Brandon; crowds gathered long before the time fixed for distribution. About eleven hundred pints of soup and one thousand small loaves of bread are required weekly at the soup kitchen. Soup kitchens are to be found in almost every village.

Mr. Thomas Bell; Mr. James Young; and Mr. James, all officials at the colliery, gave two shillings and sixpence each to the soup kitchen fund. Mr. George Potts and Mr. James Turner also officials, gave two shillings each to the fund. P.C. Jackson subscribes one shilling per month. It is hoped to keep the soup kitchen open until the end of March. Two weeks later further subscribers stepped forward; Mr. J. J. Madgin, butcher of Brandon Colliery, gave one guinea; Mr. Thomas Turner, Deputy, gave a second subscription of two shillings. H. J. Pearson Esq. of Brancepeth gave twenty five shillings and sixpence, Mr. Francis Forster ten shillings and sixpence, Mr. Nicholas Jenkins two shillings, P.C. Jackson sent a second monthly subscription of one shilling.

At the beginning of March the committee running Brandon Soup Kitchen appealed for further funds, there is much distress and they hope to continue the relief until Easter. Since its opening the kitchen has provided about twelve thousand pints of first class soup and eight thousand small loaves of bread.

After eight weeks of severe weather the River Browney at Langley Moor provided ice strong enough to encourage skating. Gentlemen and ladies rushed to put on their skates and many young people stayed on the glass-like ice until ten o'clock at night. Chinese lanterns illuminated the jolly scene.

Unrest and worry once again in the coalfield. The coal owners are now seeking a fifteen per cent reduction on underground wages and ten per cent on surface wages. The men want arbitration—this the owners refuse—the men reject their demand of fifteen per cent reduction.

Notices were issued to the underground pitmen of the county on Friday night and Saturday morning March 21st and 22nd, reading:

'I hereby give you notice to terminate your present engagement on the 5th April 1879. If you continue to be employed as a workman after that date, it will be at a reduction of 15% on present prices'.

A similar notice, with a reduction of 10%, was issued to the surface hands.

Seven pits in the county have accepted the owners' demand of 15% reduction in their wages. Others including Brandon Colliery have offered 10% and 7½% to the owners.

On April 5th Jackie Sayers, William Miller, Sam Bickley, Dan Veans, Tom Davison and Mick Maddison, all Brandon Colliery pitmen, joined the 70,000 pitmen of the county who refused to work. The General Strike had commenced!

One week later the coal owners said that the Sliding Scale would not be renewed unless the men agreed, as a preliminary, to the reduction in the rate of wages amounting to 20% on underground labour and 12½% on surface labour. Whilst the pitmen realised a reduction may be necessary, they are furious over the owners' further demands. Brandon Colliery's band and banner were paraded round the streets in defiance. Mass meetings are being held in these times of great distress and strife.

On Friday April 25th the Executive Committee of the Miners' Association, having rejected the Masters' offer, issued the following voting paper to each lodge:—

OWNERS' TERMS
Reduction of 10% from underground men, and 7½%
from the surface men, and refer the other 10% and 5%
to arbitration

STRIKE
Members must put opposite the question they intend voting for a cross
thus, X

At the close of the day the figures were:—

For the Owners' terms 224
For Strike 22633
_____
Majority for Strike. 22409
_____

The melancholy state of things now in operation throughout the county must be convincing evidence to most outsiders that an unwise step was taken by the coal-owners when they determined to abandon arbitration and the sliding scale.

Jackie Sayers, along with other striking pitmen received five shillings from the £6000 allotted from the Strike Fund.

During the third week of the strike the Durham Miners' Association took a ballot on complete strike action.

That every colliery be laid down. 224
That collieries now working to go on. 7
_____
Majority 217
_____

By a majority of thirty two votes to one, the county has voted to lay all the pits idle.

Jackie Sayers, always an active Union man, attended a mass meeting at Hamsteels. Ten collieries which included Brandon and the Boyne made up the gathering. Jackie heard Samuel Whitely of Brandon Colliery move 'That we recognise open arbitration as the most just and equitable means of settling the present dispute, and without it no arbitration'. This brought a great cheer from the men.

At the moment the North of England is passing through a time of trial, if not peril, the pitmen throughout the county of Durham are on strike and such is the unsettled state of affairs that it was found necessary to bring down to Durham City several troops of horse and foot soldiers to overawe the pitmen. For several months the old city looked like a garrison town.

Poor parents sadly watch their children go to school, clean but unavoidably shabby. They cannot afford two shillings and sixpence with which to buy little Joe a new knicker bocker suit, or one shilling and elevenpence for Mary a braided French Merino frock.

Two thousand determined men filled a field at Sleetburn, another striking colliery about one and a half miles from Brandon Colliery. William Dickinson presided, his colliery, Brandon was among the twelve collieries represented.

After lengthy talks the following resolution was moved and seconded: 'That this meeting pledges itself that when the present difficulty is settled, we do not return to work until it is ascertained that every man is to be reinstated in the position he had left in consequence of the strike'.

One speaker alleged that the employers opposed the application of the 1872 Bill concerning miners' checkweighmen. He said that one coal owner declared that if a checkweighman was placed on the pit heap of one of his collieries he would stop it altogether. The speaker said that the coal owner in question was making so much money out of cheating the men that he knew he would suffer a great falling off when he was compelled to deal with honest men. Yet this was the man who was representing, or rather misrepresenting, the pitmen of North Durham in the House of Commons. The speaker urged the men to be organised, if it were for nothing else but to stop the imposition, fraud, and confiscation that has been practised upon them and their fore-fathers who had hewed many long hours, filled many tubs, and gone down the shaft many times for which they were never paid. This drew applause. He wanted the men to be thoroughly organised like the army, the regiment divided into squadrons, the squadron into battalions, and battalions into troops.

The chairman, on winding up the meeting, urged the men to remain peaceable and support arbitration.

On May 23rd after six weeks of strike most of the collieries in the county were once more in production. Men of Brandon Colliery agreed to 7½% immediate reduction and had agreed to refer to arbitration the remainder of the coal owners' claim for a 20% reduction. Had the coalowners agreed to the pitmen's first offer there would have been no strike.

Arthur Robbins, secretary of Brandon Soup Kitchen, sent a letter to the Durham Chronicle:—

Dear Sir,

'Will you allow us a small space in your valuable paper to return our sincere thanks to Mr. J. J. Madgin, butcher, for the noble way he has come forward to the help of the people of Brandon Colliery during the strike in opening a soup kitchen twice a week at his expense, and he has also kindly promised to continue until the men at the above colliery receive a pay. By inserting the above you will greatly oblige. On behalf of the Relief Committee'.

Some twelve months ago a party of pitmen decided to leave Brandon Colliery and seek their fortunes in New Zealand. Recently their friends left behind received letters from them urging them to follow on to New Zealand, their letters were full of hope for the future. Letters came from the United

States of America full of glowing intelligence. This information caused a large number of pitmen to repair to the emigration offices. Cheap emigration from Durham—£4.15s. to £8.11s.6d. to Australia, forty days by steamship. Auctioneers were forthcoming to dispose of household goods, neighbours and newly-weds being ready to buy furniture which cannot be transported overseas.

It seems that workers for the Brandon Local Board, are like the pitmen, being restricted to meagre wages. The Board has instructed their surveyor, Mr. Spoor, not to pay the labourers he employs a higher wage than three shillings a day.

Jackie Sayers, glad to be back hewing coal, enjoyed his daily walk. Weather being kind he walked the lane to Brandon Village, on a clear day he enjoyed the panoramic view. He considered himself fortunate on two counts. An addition to their family was expected. Messrs. Straker and Love had just given sixty men notice to terminate their employment. The affected men are from another seam, the reason given being the inadequate price and demand for their coal. Jackie Sayers having had enough of strikes and closures, preferred to work and build up his home.

The sliding scale was re-introduced during October, having fallen into abeyance during the recent great strike, it had been in operation for two years. The sliding scale will remain operative for a further two years, after which, should either party wish to terminate it, six months notice must be given.

Despite the epidemic of scarlet fever pervading the district, crowds flocked to Fr. Hanley's Mission Church at Langley Moor. Men and women dressed in their Sunday best accompanied children arrayed in new dresses and smart velvet suits specially bought for the occasion. The roads leading from Browney and Littleburn Collieries to St. Patrick's were thronged with Catholics bent on welcoming their bishop. Bishop Chadwick preached and confirmed one hundred and thirty Catholics on this his first visitation.

Owing to the unabating fever epidemic and the closure of the Boyne Pit, a soup kitchen again serves the area. Soup is distributed every Tuesday, Thursday and Saturday at eleven a.m. Any working man can obtain soup at the nominal rate of one penny a pint, while the very poor, invalids, widows, orphans and those out of employment, received from the committee free tickets which entitle the holders to obtain soup in quantities according to the size of their families, together with a four ounce loaf of bread. Up to Christmas week eighteen hundred pints of excellent soup and seven hundred small loaves of bread had been distributed to the needy.

Christmas Eve saw an addition to the family in their small house in Sunderland Street; Jackie and Alice Sayers welcomed their first baby — a son.

INTO 1880

Several girls of school age jostled excitedly at the gate of Jackie Sayers' home, the small bricked yard glistened wet after its swilling for the occasion. Two women and a young man left the Sunderland Street house; one of the women cradled in her arms a small, shawl-wrapped infant. Jackie Sayers' son, making his debut, was bound for Mount Calvary Chapel, there to receive baptism. The Reverend L. Stafford their new minister awaited the arrival of the small party. According to custom a small package containing a piece of christening cake and a shining new sixpence was given to the first lucky girl to be met en route to the place of baptism. Baby Sayers was named William after his maternal grandfather.

After twenty four years of intermittent activity the coal seams of Brandon Colliery have produced a spoil heap of sizeable proportion. Over Christmas and New Year the duff-heap ignited. The coal, long buried, which adhered to the rejected stone, having ignited, scattered its obnoxious fumes over a wide area. Brandon, Langley Moor, Littleburn and Browney Collieries lay in the danger zone; complaints arrived from Brancepeth Village almost two miles away. Frost, snow and rain only served to aggravate the duff-heap fire which poisoned the air. It was reported that the fire could not be extinguished because water used for the purpose would carry the poison into the surrounding villages. Airborne sulphureous fumes infiltrated into the shaft and much to the pitmen's discomfort pervaded some of the working places.

During the strike a few pitmen were busily engaged in seeking coal at the colliery spoil heap. One of them, a chapel-goer, was getting coal where the men were forbidden to go, so one of the officials went up to him and said, 'Dissent thoo knaa thoo's dein' wrang, and that thoo's bricken the fifth commandment?' The man ceased picking the coal, looked up and remarked to the official, 'Wey hinney, Aa think thoo's wrang. Aa dinnet think As's bricken any commandmant, for Aa's only picking up the crumbs that's fallen from the rich man's table'.

Brandon Colliery 'B' and 'C Pits' were in full operation by the middle of January. Word reached far off Seaham Colliery, situated on the coast; twenty five families with theirs goods and chattels left the colliery to occupy vacant houses at Brandon Colliery. Will Davison, Daniel Evans, Sam Buckley and William Miller, all pitmen, welcomed their new workmates. Children in the party would soon settle into life in a new school. Not long after their arrival the immigrants from Seaham Colliery were shocked, as was the whole country, to hear of the dreadful explosion on September 16th at Seaham Colliery, resulting in the deaths of one hundred and seventy men and boys.

Brandon Colliery Court Pride of Foresters No. 3333 celebrated its twenty first anniversary in Robert Wray's Colliery Inn. Brandon Brass Band headed a procession which perambulated the streets of Brandon, Browney and Littleburn Collieries, Langley Moor and Meadowfield, before returning to Brandon Colliery. Foresters had gathered to celebrate their anniversary and to recognise the services of two of its members. William Dickinson P.S. and P.D.C.P. along with John Pratt P.C.R. and P.D.C.R. William Ayre presented William Dickinson with a purse of gold to buy a silver snuff box, the rest of the money to spend as he wished. John Pratt also received a purse of gold. William Dickinson in reply said he always felt a deep interest in the Court's welfare since he founded it twenty one years ago.

The Literary Institute is well supported, it now boasts a library of five hundred volumes. Besides readers it has a prosperous cricket team. Enthusiasts among the Institute members formed a cricket club in early May; Mrs. Wray, wife of the Colliery Inn's landlord encouraged them, in six weeks the cricket club's membership reached forty. Brandon Colliery Institute cricket team, now affectionately known as Mrs. Wray's Lads, won their first four games on a field loaned by Mr. Hepworth. The first eleven played the Boyne and beat them twenty five runs to seven. Mrs. Wray's Lads played twenty two novices from the Institute's club and beat them in the final game of the season fifty two runs to the novice's nine. Mrs. Wray provided a substantial supper to mark the club's early success.

Pitmen from Brandon Colliery paraded behind their brass band, the occasion being the tenth annual gala of the miners of Durham County. The men were jubilant, the future looked bright indeed. The long idle 'A Pit' had joined the other two seams at working full time. Men from the Brandon and Meadowfield pits arrived in Durham to join the thirty five thousand strong crowd at the gala. Glorious weather made it a day to be long remembered.

Industrial trouble raised its ugly head once again. For some time one of the flats at Oakenshaw Colliery has coal hewers who have been paid less than the county average. Some three months ago Mr. Will Marshall of Durham was called in as umpire during arbitration. He awarded the men 15% advance. Messrs. Straker and Love refused to pay, they offered an increase of threepence on a score of tubs filled, this the men refused. At a meeting of the Joint Committee it was decided that the men's notices be handed in. The Oakenshaw men's example being swiftly followed by the men of their sister collieries, Brancepeth, Willington and Brandon.

Despite strike talk, the Durham coal trade overall, continues to improve. The first small rise in wages due to the sliding scale was paid, a step in the right direction. Some hewers increased their wages by as much as one shilling.

Thrifty people welcome the new form of saving just introduced; post offices provide forms on which are twelve spaces to stick penny postage stamps, thus saving one shilling.

On Christmas Eve children streamed from the colliery rows to converge on the Colliery Institute, there to be entertained to a Magic Lantern show. While the children sat and marvelled at the wonder pictures, their parents did their Christmas shopping. They found prices reasonable except for turkeys which were selling at eleven shillings each. Christmas beef, mutton, veal and pork all at from eightpence to tenpence a pound, chickens two shillings and sixpence each, bacon fivepence to sixpence a pound, and potatoes at sevenpence a stone suited their purses.

1881

Despite the ten year depression the Durham coalfield has suffered since the last census, the population of the five wards comprising the Brandon Urban area is now 10,853 housed in 2,031 dwellings. Ten years ago the population of the same area was 4,293. Brandon Colliery with its many long streets is now almost the size of a town.

The second election for the Brandon Local Board took place. Despite heavy falls of snow voters turned out to re-elect Mr. J. F. Le Page, surgeon, to the East Eard. He was elected by a large majority; the result being 477 votes for Mr. Le Page and 62 for Mr. Coulson, farmer.

Mr. J. Tweddle took his place as minister of Mount Calvary Chapel on the departure of Mr. Stafford. To welcome the new minister, Mr. Thomas Forster of Sleetburn delivered an able lecture in the chapel, 'The Land of the Esquimax'. Mr. George Scott presided over the large gathering, whose collection greatly benefited the choir.

Another change in parochial leadership took place at Langley Moor where scores of Brandon Colliery miners and their families worship. Thirty year old the Rev. Richard Mathias Hannon took charge of St. Patrick's Mission.

Trouble at the colliery; workmen at the coke-yards took strike action. The manager wanted the men to draw eight sets of ovens in the long rows, the men refused, they said that seven was enough for one shift. After ten men had received notice to quit, fifty men in the two yards gave in their notices to leave. The dispute was speedily settled after a hurried meeting between the owners and the men at Newcastle.

Joseph Lamb, well known in Brandon Colliery for eighteen years, moved to Page Bank. Friends in both places were shocked to hear of his death in the pit there. The cortege followed by about four hundred mourners travelled the three miles to Brandon Village churchyard, the number increased to one thousand before the churchyard was reached.

He was a member of the Ancient Order of Foresters 'Court Pride of Brandon'. William Dickinson, now living in Princess Street, Littleburn, and members of the Court joined the procession at the Sawmill Lane end. Mr. Lamb had three children all of whom had died. One son, Thomas, was killed in the lane near Brandon Village when he fell from a tree. His little girl met her death in the same lane when she was run over by a gig belonging to Charles Felgate White, known as the 'King of the Beggars'.

Brandon Colliery Institute cricketers had won their last two games against Byers Green and Ushaw Moor respectively. They were beating Page Bank by nine runs and two wickets as a party from Brandon Colliery was having their annual trip to Roker and Seaburn. The day chosen by the Durham United District of Foresters was sunny as one of the two long trains pulled into Brandon Colliery railway station to embark members of the 'Court Pride of Brandon Foresters' and their families. They visited Roker, Hendon Docks, the Museum and other places.

Banners gaily fluttered from long poles at the Miners' Gala held on July 30th. An estimated crowd of thirty thousand thronged the Racecourse to hear speakers from the two platforms. Five speakers addressed the attentive gathering; one speaker said that the pitmen condemned the Afghan, Zulu and Transvaal wars as cruel and unjust, and showed that the money spent in killing men by war would be better spent in employing more inspectors for mines. Brandon Colliery banner was among the two hundred on parade at the eleventh gala.

Alarmed pitmen and women whose husbands and sons were at work hurriedly left their homes in nearby Durham, East and South Streets. Pounding hearts quietened, fears were allayed on hearing that the cause of their disquiet, the plummeting down the shaft of a cage containing tubs of coal. While coal was being drawn up the 'A Pit' shaft the rope attached to the socket suddenly broke. Although no person was injured, the workmen were compelled to cease work for the day, and were afterwards drawn up another shaft. On its uncontrolled descent of the shaft, the cage broke a great deal of buntin and crashed through to the sump.

Jackie Sayers, Hugh McDermott and other piece workers are concerned about a possible reduction of wages. They heard that according to the sliding rule, wages for the next four months will be 2½% below the present rate.

Jackie and Alice Sayers trudged through deep snow. Shopping bound, they had saved hard for baby William's first birthday. As Jackie's earnings have reached a low ebb a duck at two shillings, or a chicken for one shilling and sixpence would in all probability adorn their Christmas dinner table.

1882

. The Alhambra Variety Hall at Langley Moor has closed down, no reason being given for the closure. Supporters of this the only live show in the district, will miss the weekly variety performances it specialised in. Mrs. Love, widow of Joseph Love who owned Brandon Colliery, has offered to maintain the building as a chapel.

During January, horse owners were concerned about the Horse Epidemic prevalent in the district. Mr. Lamb, grocer and general dealer at Brandon Colliery, had two horses stricken by the disease. He sought succour from Mr. John Peele, veterinary surgeon who cured the animals.

The horse epidemic did not stop traders who have formed a Friday night market at Brandon Colliery, this move being made to divert some of the money normally spent at the Durham market. Stalls straddle the space between Mr. Lamb's shop and the Chapel, more stalls are erected across the road on land adjoining the Colliery Inn. Colliery folk welcome the carnival-like atmosphere of the market.

Swaying naptha flares direct their smoky glare on the stalls' contents. Sweets in great variety, shoes, clothing, hardware, food, basketware and jewellery are all on show. The quack doctor from Northumberland peddles his vividly coloured pills and potions. A black man, waving wicked looking forceps and claiming to be the North's best tooth extractor, awaits the brave.

Shrove Tuesday saw the inauguration of the new organ in St. John the Evangelist Church. The congregation was pleased and enthralled by Mr. Pilling's portrayal of sacred music on what is reckoned to be the finest organ in the district. It is erected on the north side of the church by Harrison and Harrison of Durham.

Allan Parrish walked his bride down the aisle of St. John's Church to the strain of the new organ's joyful notes. Allan, a nineteen year old blacksmith from Brandon Colliery, married another nineteen year old Meadow Field servant girl, Elizabeth Johnson.

Brandon Colliery pitmen were among the noisy crowd at the Demonstration held in a field at Ushaw Moor, they are in sympathy with the pitmen at that colliery in their strike against tyranny, and have promised financial aid. At the same time there was a ballot in the colliery lodges of the county re wages. Ballot papers were issued. Results came to hand from all lodges whether to strike or go to arbitration in favour of a 20% rise in wages. Brandon Colliery was among the majority which voted for arbitration. It seems that with able men to fight the cause, arbitration is the better course to take.

Mr. Heppell is leaving arbitration and wage fixing to his successor. For twelve years he has been head manager of Straker and Love's, Brandon, Brancepeth, Oakenshaw and Willington Collieries. His friends presented him with a purse containing forty two pounds in gold.

Edward, son of Hugh McDermott at three years of age moved to Brandon Colliery from Hunwick. He was one of the early settlers in the colliery. At twelve years of age he was driving a pony down the pit. At the time of his early death at the age of twenty three, he was a coal hewer. His younger brother Hugh, now seventeen, is also a coal hewer. Hugh was born in Railway Street.

The prevalence of scarlet fever in Brandon Colliery did not deter its inhabitants from following their banner and brass band to Durham Racecourse on the occasion of the twelfth annual Miners' Gala. Both Meadowfield and Brandon Colliery Lodges graced the Racecourse. The festival gains in popularity each year, this year a crowd of forty five thousand attended.

Brandon Colliery Wesleyan Choir intended visiting Roker and Tynemouth. As the day chosen fell on Miners' Gala day they decided on a trip to Finchale Abbey. After playing cricket in the exhausting heat, they had tea before returning home.

Passers by, on hearing the sounds of merriment, knew that some form of celebration was taking place in the upstairs room of the Red Lion Inn popularly dubbed the 'Blazer'. H. Taylor took the chair and T. Scott was vice-chairman when the deputies and waggonway men employed at Brandon Colliery, twelve in number, partook of a supper. Songs, recitations and toasts to the owner, manager and overmen at the colliery terminated a jolly evening.

The first query from Brandon Colliery to the new Joint Committee composed of six men for the owners and six men representing the workers and one chairman acceptable to both parties, concerned the colliery's cokemen. The men complained of having their wages paid on a Saturday, thus depriving them of the benefits and the advantages of the Friday market established at Brandon Colliery. They requested to be paid on Fridays, the same as pitmen and others of their own class in the county. This was not within the jurisdiction of the Joint Committee. This plea was followed by a complaint from the coal hewers of Brandon 'A Pit'. Men ask to have greater allowances (they want the weight of stone in laid-outs increased) and less fines for tubs laid-out. The Joint Committee was unsympathetic and moved the request off the table.

As Jackie Sayers lit the oil lamp set on the kitchen table of his Sunderland Street home he visualised brighter nights ahead. He had read that electricity supply in Great Britain had been given official sanction when the Electric Lighting Act was finally passed. Jackie joined other passengers on the special trip from Brandon Colliery railway station to Bishop Auckland to see streets and shops recently illuminated with this new form of lighting. He was intrigued by the cleanliness, simplicity and obvious safety of electricity.

The Independent Methodists of Brandon Colliery, smaller in numbers than the other religious bodies, built a chapel in North Street. The chapel is attached to the end house of the short street and seats one hundred worshippers, it is central for all the colliery rows.

Brandon Wesleyan Sunday School had its annual treat on August Bank Holiday Monday when tea and field sports featured at Lord Boyne's Brancepeth Park. Mr. J. H. Straker, colliery owner, allowed a waggon to convey the wildly excited infant classes to the grounds, he also donated money to the tea fund. After tea, two hundred being served, cricket and football were played until departure at seven thirty p.m.

In August hewers from Brandon and Meadowfield collieries together with men from Straker and Love's other collieries struck in sympathy with the Brancepeth Colliery hewers over the low price offered in the re-opened Jet Seam. A total of two thousand came out. Brandon Colliery Lodge nominated Mr. Prudhoe to represent the men in any forthcoming discussions. After four days of strike the men resumed work on the owners' terms until arbitration.

Arising from the strike eighty men from Brandon and Brancepeth collieries were summoned by the owners for a breach of the Employers' and Workmen's Act in leaving their employment without giving notice. None of the men attended court. The summonses were withdrawn on payment of costs which the Miners' Union paid.

Friday August 25th was a red letter day for local shoppers. Men of vision, seeing the need for a Co-operative Society in a large industrial area, after long meetings and delays, saw the birth of Brandon Co-operative Society when a vast new store was opened at Meadowfield Place. The store, in time, will cater for all the needs of its members.

On the day of the store's opening, Thomas Turner at the age of fifty nine died suddenly. He was a back overman at Brandon Colliery and an ardent and active chapel goer. Well known in the area, he will be sorely missed.

Brandon Colliery pitmen sent another donation to their counterparts at Ushaw Moor Colliery who have been out on strike forty weeks; there is a deadlock, families are in dire straits.

Better news for the working pitmen. A wage increase of 1¾% was granted under the sliding scale; this is the third sliding scale agreement to be entered into. Optimists say that the sliding scale could be the termination of all strikes.

Thirty eight year old Alfred Cheesey, a leading man among the Wesleyan body, married and a deputy overman in the 'A Pit' removed his thick fustian waistcoat, grasped the long handled jud mell and prepared to draw the jud. He was in the night shift. His two sons had finished work for the day, one worked in the 'A Pit', the younger one being a screener at the colliery. Two shifts of coal hewers had left a large area strongly timbered after the removal of the coal. Alfred knew that if the goaf timber was left standing, the strata unable to fall, would make the place difficult and possibly dangerous to work. John Welch and Robert Robson, both deputy overmen, handed the props one to the other as Alfred drew them from the jud, his longhandled mell enabling him to retrieve sound props from the void. Without warning a huge stone some nine feet long and two feet thick fell on him. It took his two shocked workmates and other three men half an hour to remove the stone from the dead body. The time was nine p.m.

Out of respect for the dead, Adam Simpson, Ralph Broadbent, John Clark and Joseph Cairns all pitmen in the 'C Pit', absented themselves from work on the next day, Friday November 1st. Messrs. Straker and Love claimed five shillings damages from them. The Miners' Union paid the costs.

Members of the recently formed Brandon Co-operative Society had some early Christmas cheer when the result of the first three months trading was announced. One hundred and fifty one members drew dividend at three shillings to the pound on eight hundred and thirty three pounds sales.

Ushaw Moor strikers, hard pressed after being out for one year, were sent another donation from Brandon Colliery pitmen who back the men's stand in their dispute with their colliery management.

Four Brandon Colliery infants died during December making a total of twenty nine babies for the year. Twenty five adults having died during the year making an impressive total of fifty four to leave the colliery rows on their last journey.

1883

James Storey 13; Humphrey Coverdale 12; William Stout 13; Owen Brady 13; Joseph Dowdle 14; William Connolly 14; George Batty 15 and Will Flowers 13, browsed with eager anticipation. Pony drivers and putters, they were bent on buying the best the stalls at Brandon Colliery open market had to offer. They had saved the customary Yule Do money their coal hewers had brought to the pit for them on the last working day before Christmas. The lads remembered John George Dickinson, another thirteen year old driver who had just died.

Joseph Green and Son cater for the needs of the colliery folk; shoes, suits, pit ware, ladies' clothes and utensils are all sold from their shop just above Sunderland Street. Owing to increased trade they sent to the Brandon Local Board, plans to enlarge their shop and house. Women shoppers complain that potatoes costing fivepence halfpenny a stone a year ago are now eightpence halfpenny a stone.

Three burly figures co-ordinating their movements advanced and captured their prey, not one escaped. Pitch and toss, forbidden by law, is indulged in and enjoyed by lawbreakers. Many pitmen, possibly because of their hum-drum and often dangerous work, turn to gambling for the excitement offered.

Sergeant Reed backed by Police Constables Edwards and Sherwood, cleverly netted sixty Sunday 'Scholars' in the Station Lane near Brandon Colliery railway station. The exceptionally large school of gamblers, from which could be heard 'Heads a sovereign' or 'Tails a sovereign', paid for their misdemeanour to the tune of a ten shilling fine and costs of one shilling each.

Catholics living in Brandon Colliery and the surrounding district, contemplating an Easter wedding, will be spared the journey to Croxdale, Willington or Durham for the service. St. Patrick's Catholic Chapel at Langley Moor has been duly certified according to law, as a place of Public Religious Worship and is registered for the Solemnization of Marriages.

Once again coal hewers were asked to sacrifice part of their pay when the owners applied for a reduction of hewing prices in Brandon Colliery 'A Pit'. Districts affected are Collets Shaw; South West Far-off; South West below Hitch; First West Dun Cow Broken; East Dun Cow and West through No. 1 Drift Flats in the Busty Seam—the request was adjourned.

Two weeks later the Committee acceded to the owners' demands and decided that in the Brandon 'A Pit' Busty Seam the following reduction be made: Below the Hitch 15%; South-west below the Hitch 15%; South-west Far-off 7½%; First West Dun Cow Broken 10%; East Dun Cow 10%; West through No. 1 Drift Flat and No. 2 Drift Flat 10%. Jackie Sayers, Robert Broadbent, John Doyle and Christ Storey, all hewers affected by the reductions are complaining that when coal is hard to hew they cannot earn money, yet as soon as the coal is more responsive and more tubs can be filled per shift, the owners promptly seek a reduction.

In June five residents of Brandon Colliery died, two from the dreaded Typhoid Fever. Cases of the disease were reported from other wards; advice and disinfectants were issued.

William C. Blackett, Minister of Health for the area, stated at a meeting of the Brandon Local Board that in consequence of Typhoid Fever and other fevers, he inspected Brandon Colliery streets with the Inspector of Nuisances, and they found them very unsatisfactory. The scavengers, who were paid by the colliery owners, were neglecting their duty, and the man who has charge of the houses seems to think he has nothing to do with either privvies or ashpits. As a result nuisances exist, which are prejudicial to health and ruinous to the owners of the buildings, which are rapidly becoming delapidated. At the same meeting, plans were passed which allowed Fr. Hannon of St. Patrick's, Langley Moor to go ahead and build a new class-room. This extra room will enlarge the present chapel cum school, and is needed to cater for the large families in the area.

Mr. Weeks, manager of Brandon Colliery, together with the Board's Surveyor inspected the streets of the colliery and found several of the privvies without doors, and many badly in need of repair. The manager gave orders for repair work to be done at once.

On Saturday August 10th glorious sunshine greeted contestants and spectators at the Athletic Sports organised by the committee of Brandon Colliery Branch of the Durham Miners' Association. Twenty one men ran in the one hundred and twenty yards Handicap Foot Race. Two local runners gained first and third places in the event; William Robson won the major prize of one pound, Thomas Thompson won five shillings. Twenty one players joined the Quoit Handicap; Joseph Pratt won the first prize of one pound, Robert Fenwick came second to win ten shillings. John Redhead of Brandon Colliery collected the first prize of ten shillings when he beat all opposition to win the under fifteen years competition Boys' Race. A great day's sport concluded with a grand ball held in the Literary Institute.

Not to be outdone, the Meadowfield Branch of the Durham Miners' Association held a concert in the Mechanics' Institute. Negro comics; the champion amateur singer of the north; champion juvenile clog dancer and an Irish comic, all entertained and delighted the crowded audience.

During September eight infants and three adults died in the colliery rows; funeral processions were in evidence almost every other day. The hospital was busy coping with extra cases of scarlet fever.

Owing to the incidence of smallpox at Tudhoe Colliery, all colliery managers are warned not to engage single men, or lodgers in particular, from infected areas.

Three deaths occurred during Christmas week, the last being two year old Hannah, daughter of pitman Will Lowe, making a disturbing total of fifty seven deaths for the year.

1884

January began with warm weather; it suited hare and hunter alike. Sergeant Thompson and his constables were on duty when the Brandon Coursing Meeting was held in a field adjacent to Brandon Colliery railway station. The large crowd saw numerous hares raised in the Brandon Tenants' Stake and again in the Brancepeth Stakes. Local boys augmented their pocket money by becoming beaters for the day, with luck, a freshly killed hare became an extra bonus.

Men at Brancepeth Colliery, their shift made longer owing to the length of time taken to ride the men to the surface after their shift, objected strongly. Some received notice, all the Brancepeth men handed in fourteen days notice. The Brandon and Oakenshaw Collieries came out in sympathy. The Joint Committee held a meeting at Durham; a truce was declared just before the termination of the notices.

The Joint Committee was in action once again when men from the

Brandon 'A' and 'C Pits' asked to be supplied with a better and larger quantity of Fire Coal. The Committee recommended that a sufficient quantity be supplied, and that the Owners should, as far as they are able, provide separate Coal-houses for the householders. The Brandon 'C Pit' men had sent in their request three months previously, nothing had been done.

More depression hit the colliery rows; smallpox broke out, disinfectants were issued to use in and around the infected houses, one of which was whitewashed. Five cases of scarlet fever housed in Brandon Hospital proved fatal.

Tragedy struck once again. John Mills, a thirty year old coal hewer in the 'C Pit' started work at four a.m. Shortly after eating his bait at eight a.m. a stone nine feet long, four feet broad and seventeen inches thick, without warning, fell on him. Matthew Garthwaite a putter, and Thomas Gilpin coal hewer, heard the crash and the cries of the stricken man. The unfortunate hewer was frightfully crushed about the bowels and back. His injuries proved so severe he died six hours later. John was much respected and after the inquest a number of pitmen preceded the cortege, bearing aloft the Lodge banner in memory of their hapless comrade.

Brandon's Blue and White cricket tram played East Rainton on the spacious colliery field which lies just east of the colliery. The visitors won handsomely scoring one hundred and thirteen runs to Brandon's twenty. Brandon made amends when they travelled to Byers Green and beat them sixty four runs to twenty eight. James Ashcroft was Brandon's most prominent player when they visited Pity Me from whom they squeezed victory by two runs after two thrilling innings. Brandon I.O.G.T. Blue and White retained their good form when Hamsteels came to Brandon with an unbeaten record; they returned the losers having scored sixteen runs against Brandon's twenty six.

Byers Green, out for revenge, sent their best eleven cricketers down to Brandon. James Ashcroft again scored well for Brandon, his twenty five runs helped his team cruise to victory with seventy runs against Byers Green's twenty eight.

While a crowd of twenty thousand gathered to watch fifty banners parade Durham's Racecourse on the fourteenth Big Meeting day on July 11th when six speakers including a woman and a rector graced the platform, Sunnybrow cricket club challeged Brandon Colliery's eleven to a game at Sunnybrow. The game was sparsely attended owing to the greater pull of the Gala no doubt. Brandon finished worthy winners seventy eight runs to forty seven. James Ashcroft shone once again, he and Benjamin Lightfoot being Brandon's principal scorers.

Joseph Broadbent the thirteen year old son of Ralph Broadbent was one of four colliery residents to die on Big Meeting day, he was the victim of the dreaded Typhoid Fever. Anxious dwellers in Durham Street's long row saw Ralph Broadbent drag the bed and bedding from No. 39 where young Joseph had lived and suffered. They saw Ralph transorm the bed and bedding on which his son had lain into a germ killing pyre. On applying to the Brandon Local Board, Ralph Broadbent who had spent every penny during his son's illness, was awarded two pounds ten shillings compensation for the loss of furniture.

The pits being idle on the second Saturday of August allowed crowds to gather in good time for the sports; Mr. Lishman the colliery viewer, kindly granted the sports committee the use of the colliery field for the annual sports day and gala.

Brandon Colliery entrants did well in all the events. Gowland Redhead beat all comers in the one hundred and twenty yards handicap foot race; Robert Pouton was first to collect the twenty five stones in the stone picking handicap race, Thomas Lawson was third out of the thirteen entries.

Eager boys gathered for the one hundred yards handicap race, all were under the age of fourteen, they came from Brandon and nearby Browney and Littleburn Collieries. Amid intense rivalry from visitors and raucous support from locals, Thomas Felton and James Redhead landed first and third prizes.

Pigeon fanciers were not forgotten at the gala. Entries for the pigeon flying handicap were liberated at Flass Inn, Ushaw Moor; Ralph Watson's Royal First creed first in Brandon Colliery, Abraham Turner's Blue Girl came in a close second, followed by Charles Holme's Oyster Lad out of thirteen entries.

A cricket match between a team of married men and one of single men ended a great day of sport. All players were from Brandon I.O.G.T. Blue and White. William Rounding's score of twenty six runs gained the single men victory.

Pitmen cyclists, Jack Dixon and Jim Wood, both from Brandon Colliery, cycled to Spennymoor where they entered the one mile amateur bicycle race at Wood Vue, after an exciting race they finished second and third.

The North of England Hand Bell Ringers with their peel of one hundred bells, entertained an appreciative audience in the Primitive Methodists' Chapel to a musical treat. The rendering of the 'Hallelujah Chorus', 'Blue Bells of Scotland', 'Bid me Discourse' and 'German Clock' made the evening a brilliant success.

At a local chapel the minister was preaching about going to Heaven, and after he had been preaching for a time, he said to the congregation, 'Those who would like to go to Heaven, please stand up'. All stood up except one man, and the preached noticing him, went up to him and said 'My dear man, wouldn't you like to go to Heaven too?' 'Yis sir', came the reply, 'Aa was like te gan te Hiven an all, but here, Aa say, Aa's not gannen wi this trip'.

During November three cases of small pox were discovered in the colliery rows, one of which proved fatal. On the twelfth day of the appearance of the disease a man died in Queen Street. In early December there were five caes of smallpox, three men and a woman suffered severely, the other victim, a young girl, had mild smallpox. The health authorities, hard pressed to accommodate the victims, requisitioned four houses in College Terrace, which after repair were fenced off and kept for cases of smallpox. Parents and their school children gave the row a wide berth.

Jackie Sayers by-passed College Terrace on his way to Brandon Colliery

Mixed School to enrol little Will Sayers. The school, owing to the large number of new entrants expected, had been enlarged. At the other end of the colliery, parents Patrick and Anne Moran had their son baptised Patrick, he was carried to Langley Moor on 27th December where the ceremony was performed in St. Patrick's Chapel. Both Jackie Sayers and Patrick Moran Snr. had cause for alarm, slack time once again at the colliery and the smallpox scourge cast a gloom over the district.

The year ended on a dismal note, the sixtieth death in the colliery precincts during the year being recorded on December 31st.

1885

The New Year was heralded with first footing when all the local collieries blew their buzzers at midnight. During the day there were chapel services and celebrations, band parades and concerts.

The sombre legacy continued from 1884; during January four infants and four adults died in Brandon Colliery. During the month sixty four houses were stoved and disinfected against smallpox.

A spontaneous feeling has arisen among the pitmen and other workmen of the district in favour of presenting the lady nurses of the hospital with a testimonial, in recognition of their valuable and disinterested labours in nursing the sick patients since the visitation of this dreadful scourge. Nothing can exceed the care and tender devotion with which these ladies are discharging their onerous duties, and there is little doubt that, but for the aid thus rendered, many of the patients who are now restored to health would have died, and the disease would have assumed much wider proportions.

Charles Holmes, a twenty year old putter, being next on turn for coal hewing, jumped at the chance of a shift at hewing, it would be good practice for the day he would become a coal hewer proper. He was sent to work double with Dick Robson a coal hewer in the Busty A Pit. They filled five tubs when the putters had to wait for empty tubs arriving from the shaft, they continued hewing. Charles nicked into the top coal which unexpectedly fell, a large piece striking his head; he was knocked unconscious from his cracket. He died four days later from his injuries.

While men hewed coal underground, others furtively picked bits of coal which had reached the spoil heap via the screens. A mason was fined five shillings and costs for taking about seven or eight stones of coal from the heap. He had just moved into a big house and had no fire. On the same day, Hugh Stones, an old blind man, was charged with stealing two hundredweight of coal, value twopence, from a heap belonging to Messrs. Straker and Love. The man was seen by a policeman helping himself with coals and putting them into a bag. It was proved that the prisoner had no authority to take the coal. Defendant pleaded guilty and said he had nothing to say. He was living on four shillings a week from the Permanent Fund, and out of that he had to pay the rent. The Chairman: 'Well you should not do this; you will have to pay a fine of two shillings and sixpence'. Defendant: 'Well, you have guessed my pocket; that is just the amount I have brought with me'.

Smallpox claimed two victims during March. Brandon Hospital took in three more cases for treatment. Forster Lamb aged seventy five years, a retired pitman and one of the first coal hewers to arrive when the colliery began, died from the disease. A mild form of measles had assumed almost epidemic proportion in the area, it is reported to come from Sunderland.

As colliery owners go, Mr. John Straker senior partner in Straker and Love's Brandon and other pits, was liked and respected at the collieries he controlled. He died at Stagshaw House, Northumberland on Saturday 4th April. His pits were laid idle for one day out of respect.

After eight months of sinking, three shifts daily, the Air Shaft at Brandon Colliery was finished. It had reached a depth of eighty seven fathoms. With four arches and four rings it is one of the best finished shafts in the county. The Hutton Seam was passed at twenty six fathoms depth; the Busty Seam at a depth of sixty nine fathoms; the Brockwell Seam being reached eighteen fathoms on. The underground workings far extended inbye, requiring a greater intake of air meant this addition to existing ventilation.

Despite the loss of thirteen members of the community during June, eleven of whom were infants, the church authorities at St. John's, Meadowfield decided on having Confirmation. One hundred and seventy people being confirmed, a good number arrived from Brandon for the ceremony at which the average age was twenty four years. The service had been postponed for three months due to the epidemic of smallpox in the area.

The inhabitants of the colliery were helped to forget the gloom fifty deaths in the first half of the year had left when a sports day was organised. A quoits handicap; kite flying for lads; sack race; three legged race; bell ringing; obstacle race and one hundred yards flat race were arranged. Cricket also featured, Brandon St. Agatha's Mission cricket club invited Croxdale Church Choir to a game. Supporters cheered on St. Agatha's who won sixteen runs to seven. Tom Clennell scored five runs for Brandon, he also bowled well, only three players scored for Croxdale.

Pigeon racing attracts many fans. Heavy betting was evident among the pigeon men when for ten pounds, a race took place from Brandon Colliery to Sunnybrow Colliery. John Charlton's Bonny Mary flew the five miles in five minutes thirty seconds. Benjamin Gordon's Black Watch landed fifteen seconds later. Joe Rawlinson was the referee and John Robertson was stakeholder.

The very physical side of the game of hand-ball attracts a good crowd when a match is arranged. Betting was heavily indulged in when two Littleburn men, favourites, challenged Peter Higgins and Thomas Elliott both from Brandon Colliery to a game at Littleburn Recreation ground. Sweat flowed freely as the four men, stripped to their waists on a hot summer day, battled for ascendancy. Stephen Pattinson and John Hall lost the twenty pound stake ball match; Higgins and Elliott played remarkably well and won the hard fought game thirty three chalks to twenty six.

Measles, scarlet fever and whooping cough continue to haunt the parents of the young in the colliery rows. Of the seventy three deaths reported up to the end of August, forty seven were infants. Two old standards died during the month; Richard Chrissop, having spent most of his eighty years in Brandon Colliery, was an ardent Methodist and a trustee of Mount Calvary Chapel, an ex-coal hewer he had witnessed the changes in Brandon Colliery since he first arrived. Thomas Wilson, another local character, never reached the age of retirement. Whilst performing his task of truck man at the colliery sidings, he was fatally crushed between coal waggons and a wall. He was sixty four years of age.

Another depression hits the coal trade. Brandon Colliery now a member of the Durham Miners' Association, feels the pinch once again, it is only working half time. The plight of some pitmen being so acute the Durham Miners' Relief Fund helped to the tune of ten shillings a fortnight. Despite near starvation no deaths were recorded in the colliery streets for two whole weeks. Was disease and tragedy on the wane? Following an influx of deaths, the year ended on a tragic note when the body of a young woman was recovered from the colliery reservoir behind single North Street. She had suffered from depression having for long attended an ailing husband. P.C. Sherwood and Henry Pinkney shared the onerous task of removing the body and carrying it to Queen Street.

One hundred and three deaths occurred in Brandon Colliery's rows during the year—a grim total—almost double that of 1884.

1886

As per custom, the buzzers of the surrounding collieries welcomed in the New Year, their strident chorus a signal to first footers waiting at doorstep and corner end.

Despite a show of festivity, the immediate future looked black for the pitmen and their families. Would trade in the coal industry pick up soon?

The New Year brought a change in the ministry of Mount Calvary Methodist Chapel. Mr. Tweddle, after five years of service to the community, left to minister elsewhere. Mr. R. Shields was welcomed as Brandon Colliery's new leader.

A change took place at Langley Moor when the parishioners of St. Patrick's, most of whom reside in Brandon Colliery, built a brick Presbytery for their priest, the Rev. Richard Hannon. The large, sturdy structure is built only a few yards from the present chapel cum school. The Brandon and Byshottles Local Board granted a certificate of occupation.

Hugh McDermott, Henry Turner and Joe Pritchard, all coal hewers in the Busty Seam's East under No. 2 Drift, were advanced five per cent on their coal hewing price. The increase is an incentive where the coal is of a hard nature and few men earn a decent wage. Men in the South-west broken district in the same seam are playing war; conditions being more favourable for hewing, they are being subjected to a reduction in wages. Joe Graham, Jim Foster, Bob Brown and Joe Bell have been earning good money, they have had their wages reduced twelve and a half per cent. Prices were also fixed for the Brandon Colliery 'C Pit' Third West-way No. 1 South broken:—
When the seam is 36 inches and above, 6s. 10d. per score;
When the seam is 34 inches and above, 7s. 6d. per score;

When the seam is 32 inches and above, 7s. 10d. per score;
When the seam is 30 inches and above, 8s. 1d. per score;
When the seam is 28 inches and above, 8s.10d. per score.

The depression continues in the coal trade. Three weeks after fifty men at nearby North Brancepeth Colliery had received notice, twenty eight hewers, four cinder drawers and one leveller at Brandon Colliery were given fourteen days notice.

Pigeon fanciers had their birds conveyed to Bearpark about two and a half miles away across the valley from Brandon Colliery. After liberation the birds were welcomed amid tremendous excitement into their home lofts. J. Cairns' Pearl Eye flew the distance in the extremely fast time of two minutes and ten seconds; second was W. Nelson's Engine in two minutes nineteen seconds; third to land was R. Marbel's bird Jonathan Hutchins to clock two minutes twenty seven seconds; two seconds later J. Goodall's Sheffielder arrived in fourth place.

Pearl Eye figured in a race with Grey Bird of Sacriston, they flew from dovecote to dovecote, a distance of five miles. The former won easily. Another shorter race took place between birds owned by T. Hartley of Brandon Colliery and J. Skillcorn of Sleetburn, again the local owner won the honours when his bird won the dovecote to dovecote race.

Early February saw renewed activity among the pigeon fanciers. A pigeon flying match between two birds belonging to J. Jackson and N. Dodds of Brandon Colliery was arranged. The race of about three miles from Durham Railway Station to Brandon Colliery, was won by Jackson's bird in five minutes five seconds, its challenger came home nine seconds later. Twelve birds competed in a sweepstake flown from Elvet Cottage ro Brandon Colliery; M. Hutchinson's Cripple flew the distance in two minutes five seconds, Atherstone's Hungry Lad was second in three minutes twenty three seconds just beating Grant's Swell by one second.

Spite matches draw big crowds. As the pigeon sweep was being decided, two men clashed in a fives match. Pat Higgins of Brandon Colliery, who had previously clashed with R. Ainslie of Langley Moor, accepted the latter's challenge to a game for five pounds, the game being thirty three chalks up. Higgins delighted his supporters by winning thirty three chalks to Ainslie's twenty two.

Higgins and his brother travelled to Langley Recreation Grounds on Easter Saturday to take part in another fives match. They challenged Robert Temperley and Will Harrison of Langley Moor to a game for ten pounds. Temperley, a sound player was handicapped, he had to use his right hand only. William Ainslie was avenged; Temperley and his partner won by eleven chalks.

Sportsmen made the most of the warm summer days. Five cricket teams operated in the colliery area; Brandon I.O.G.T. (Blue and White), Brandon Mission, Brandon Y.M.F.S., Brandon St. John's and Brandon Institute were all active. The most notable game decided was between Brandon I.O.G.T. and Kimblesworth at Brandon Colliery; the home team won one hundred and forty three runs to sixty. W. Rounding scored forty five and J. Crabtree thirty four for Brandon.

On Saturday July 10th twenty coal hewers in the A Pit and twelve in the C Pit, together with nine cinder-yard men, received notice to terminate their engagement at the end of fourteen days. A number of cinder ovens will stop production. The depression in the coal trade is the reason for this step.

Depression did not figure in Dr. Blackett's report as Minister of Health to Brandon and Byshottles Local Board. He stated that there need be no fear of cholera while the district was kept in its present thoroughly clean and sanitary condition. It only required that the Board should support its officers in their endeavours to maintain it in such condition.

Heavy, day long rain failed to dampen the spirits of men determined to separate this day from all others. On July 31st Brandon Colliery lodges joined the fifty present at the sixteenth Durham Miners' Big Meeting. Most collieries represented reported sackings and short time working.

Thirteen residents of the colliery died during July, all but three were infants. There being a great need for a mortuary to serve the needs of the district, one was erected in the Brandon Village graveyard at a cost of eighty pounds. It occupies a prominent place at the entrance.

Chapel-goers crowded into the spacious Wesleyan Chapel in the Station Road. Mr. Issott had brought his portable show to Brandon Colliery. Mr. Issott of Sheffield, delivered a lecture entitled 'Buy your own Cherries' illustrated by the new monellous pamphenhos lantern. Scripture pieces and stories were told which enthralled the gathering. 'Washing the black boy white' being well received. There were moving views and chromotrophe, which kept the crowded room spellbound.

Brandon Colliery fife and drum band, being low in funds, gave a musical concert in the Literary Institute before a good audience. Mr. Bendilow of South Street ably led the band which played a stirring overture. Mr. J. Mearman played the piano, E. Mearman and others sang. The Institute is used to good advantage, being in demand for concerts and other worthy gatherings.

During September thirteen residents of the colliery died; all but three were infants, making a grim total of fifty deaths for the nine months.

Brandon St. John's cricket club played their last game of the season on October 2nd. After the game, played in one of Mr. Hepworth's fields, they proceeded to the Bay Horse Inn in Brandon Village, where a good supper was provided by Mrs. Thornton. Prizes were given to members who had made the highest score during the season. George Jackson being head scorer, received a splendid belt, with his name inscribed on it. John Gibbons and William Thornton, the second and third highest scorers, were each provided with a very neat cap. Several songs completed a great night of entertainment. The Bay Horse, much frequented by the colliery men, lies only a few yards from the village school, which is less crowded now that Brandon Colliery School absorbs its pupils from the colliery rows, thus allowing the village schoolgoers more space for study and play.

Neighbours, ever willing to help in times of stress, consoled the parents of young John Storey, a driver in the A Pit Busty Seam, who on bringing out a set of tubs with a pony, accidentally fell between the horse and the full tubs of coal which were in motion. The first tub ran over him causing serious injuries to his head and chest.

On the same afternoon, James Sexton coal hewing in the C Pit, met with a serious accident when stone fell on him, severely bruising his back and legs. The colliery cart trundled pain racked James home over rough ground to be attended by Dr. Binnie of Meadowfield House.

John Mearman, Matt Martin, James Wilson and John Copeland, all had family bereavement in the last week of October. John Mearman lost his nineteen year old wife Elizabeth, the others lost young members of their families.

Almost at the end of the pigeon flying season a flying match took place for a stake of four pounds, between George Winter's blue bird and J. Simpson's check bird. After being conveyed in baskets the three miles to Durham's Elvet Pit, the birds were liberated to speed back to Brandon Colliery. Simpson's check bird, quicker off the mark, won by twenty five seconds.

Young lad to old gent waiting in the railway carriage: 'Where are you going mister?'

'To Hades, you young rascal', retorted the old one.

'Well take this basket and let out the pigeon when you get there', said the lad, handing him a small basket.

Crowds gathered to watch and bet on their favourites; J. Higgins and J. Harrison, both of Brandon Colliery, had challenged M. Haley and M. Maley to a game of Fives. Betting was brisk at the Brandon Ball Alley, at six to four on, the local men allowed the visitors from Sacriston ten chalks start in the game of forty one chalks up. The twenty pounds stake money was won easily by Higgins and Harrison who chalked up forty one against their opponents' twenty four.

Pitmen and cokeyard workers applauded and good news. Early in December fifty of Brandon Colliery's long idle coke ovens were restarted. It being estimated that the ovens would consume five hundred tons of coal each week, more coal hewers and coke yard men relish the idea of a healthy Christmas pay.

With more working days now the rule, women enjoyed doing their Christmas shopping. Pork at eightpence a pound, beef and mutton at sevenpence, and bacon at fivepence, ensured a festive season.

1887

First footers braved the gale which heralded the New Year. Fierce winds whipped off house tiles and dislodged long lengths of wooden guttering from their horizontal perches under the eaves of the colliery houses. Durham, Sunderland, Newcastle, East and the two South Streets suffered most damage.

On Monday January 3rd Michael Doyle, a fourteen year old pony driver in the C Pit met with a singular accident. No explosion, fall of stone or runaway tubs terminated young Michael's Life. As he passed a pony which was unattached to tubs, the animal rolled over on him. Gowan Redhead, a putter boy, witnessed the tragic incident. Michael was among the nine colliery residents who died during January, of the nine only two were infants. John James Carr, pitman, lost his three year old son Peter. Tom Sutton, another pitman, lost his infant son William Edward.

Tragedy, its appetite already whetted, struck again on February 25th. Ralph Harland, a deputy in the C Pit was killed at his work. Ralph at forty years of age was an experienced workman and adept an drawing juds in the seam. Thomas Hepple and George Miller were among the eight men it took to lift the huge slab of blue stone from Ralph Harland's lifeless body. He had been killed instantly when the massive stone fell as he drew the very first prop of the jud in Thomas Hepple's place almost at the end of Thomas' shift.

Still recoiling from the recent tragedies in their seam, George Robson, Robert Curry, George Bragon, John Moore and George Watson received a further shock. The owners sought, and were granted a reduction in the coal hewers' wages; Brandon C Pit's Second North, First West, Second West and Third West Flats suffered a four per cent cut in pay. Other coal hewers working the East Thro' No. 1 Drift suffered a reduction of twelve and a half per cent. Again men complain bitterly that once the coal becomes workable and better wages are earned, the owners step in with a massive cut in the hewing price.

Mary Cummings survived the ravages of typhoid and scarlet fever which continue to haunt the area. Baby Mary was born at 19 South Street and is the first daughter to Lawrence and Mary Jane Cummings, she received her name in St. Patrick's Chapel at Langley Moor.

At the seventeenth Miners' Gala held in Durham at which six notabilities including Alderman Fowler of Durham spoke, the new Mines Act was discussed. Brandon Colliery pitmen, like others in the country, applaud the Act which states that no boy under the age of twelve shall be employed underground.

Brandon Local Board ordered that all privvies be whitewashed with quicklime, colliery managers were asked to help.

Whole families mustered when Queen Victoria celebrated her Golden Jubilee. One thousand excited school children from all parts of the district, lessons forgotten for the day, assembled for a grand demonstration of loyalty and a tea. About five thousand joined in procession for the long walk under the blistering sun. Tired children thankfully settled down alongside the River Wear at Sunderland Bridge after their journey from Brandon Colliery through Browney Colliery down Burnigill's steep bank to the riverside. There were contingents from Brandon, Browney, Boyne and Sleetburn Collieries, each carrying a distinctive banner. After tea each scholar was given a Jubilee medal to commemorate fifty years of reign.

To culminate the rejoicings, at precisely ten p.m. an escending rocket announced the lighting of the huge bonfire; the expectant gathering on the highest local point at Brandon Village cheered as the immense pile of faggots, furze and trees illuminated the countryside.

1888

On January 6th Brandon Colliery school re-opened after being closed for seven weeks owing to fever and measles, only sixty per cent of the children turned up for lessons. Despite precautions taken by the Brandon Local Board, the diseases' incursion accounted for many victims. Coal hewer Henry Wood lost his two year old daughter, Jane, exactly one week later his three year old son Henry joined her.

Hugh McDermott, a twenty two year old coal hewer had spent his life in Brandon; he was born in Railway Street. Hugh married Catherine Donoghue, a Durham girl, in St. Godric's Chapel there. He continued his life as a coal hewer at Brandon Colliery. Hugh would, in all probability, take his bride to the Durham Miners' Gala which was celebrating its eighteenth yearly appearance. Forty thousand enthusiasts thronged the racecourse to give ear to the five speakers. Brandon Colliery's banner displayed the fluttering black ribbon drape announcing to all that life had been forfeit at the colliery; a thirty year old coal hewer and a boy of fourteen being the victims.

Shortly after the Miners Gala James Bragon, John Clark, John Allen and Will Todd, complained bitterly over the second successive reduction of one and a quarter per cent under the sliding scale agreement. Most pitmen resent the continuance of the scale and seek its termination. Tom Hartill, another complainant, suffered further loss when within one week, infectious diseases claimed his infant children Robert and Elizabeth. Disease is still resident in the colliery rows.

The train left Brandon Colliery railway station after embarking a goodly number of Fives match devotees; they went to see their champion, Peter Higgins, play Jack Clark of Page Bank, the venue being the Bee Hive Ball Alley, Willington. Odds of two to one were laid on Clark the favourite, who gave Higgins a start of five in thirty three up. Clark started badly, the vociferous spectators saw Higgins win by twelve chalks to take away the thirty pounds stake money.

At the Annual General Meeting of the Brandon and Byshottles Co-operative Society it was decided to further child education in the district. The management offered ten free scholarships to local school children whose parents were members of the Society. Children who fared well in ordinary school subjects were eligible. Each scholarship was to the value of one pound and tenable for one year.

The annual meeting of a local trade society was being held—the treasurer reading out the financial statement after detailing the various items, gave the total income and expenditure, which left, he said, a debit balance of £30. 'Hear, hear', roared one of the members.

'I see no reason to shout hear, hear', said the treasurer, 'the balance is on the wrong side of the book'.

'Ne matter!' retorted the member. 'This society has had se many difficulties that it's a wonder it hes any balance at arl'.

Brandon Warriors made the five mile journey to Esh for their match with Esh Excelsior. Warrior supporters shortened their walk by taking the fell route after passing through Brandon Village. Excelsior, playing good football, won easily by four goals to the Warriors' one.

Brandon Colliery Excelsior Cricket Club, while the football season was in progress, was preparing for its next season. They held a meeting in the Red Lion Inn, whose landlord, Matthew Bates, himself a keen sportsman, helped and encouraged others. They chose as their officers for the 1889 season the following: W. E. Forster, secretary; W. Rutherford, president; H. Martin, vice-president; W. Simpson, captain; W. Rounding, assistant secretary. All were active cricketers.

James Simpson at the age of fourteen became the eighteenth victim of fatal accidents incurred during the thirty two years life of the colliery. A screener on the belts at the C Pit, he was caught in the moving drum, he survived the accident about thirteen hours.

For the coal hewer, the year has been one of hewing price fluctuation.
The Brandon A Pit Dun Cow Way, reduced 5%;
The Brandon A Pit North Flat in Third East Way, reduced 20%;
The Brandon A Pit First South Broken in Cross-Cut Way, reduced 8%;
The Brandon A Pit Cross-Cut District-South Whole Flat, advanced 5%;
The Brandon A Pit North Headways-North Flat, advanced 10%.

The Committee decided that owing to the men's inability to earn that Brandon's A Pit hewing prices in Third East South Flat be advanced 12½%. The men complain that it is 'robbing Peter to pay Paul'.

Another year ended on a melancholy note. A total of fifty six colliery inhabitants left the streets for burial.

1889

Michael Greenie, John Battenby, Matt Robson and Mick Robson were among the law-breakers present in Durham Court. They were charged with having played at pitch and toss at Brandon Colliery; they were fined sixpence each and ordered to pay the costs.

Local man Samuel Galbraith, the colliery check-weighman, and colliery owner H. H. Cochrane of Sleetburn were nominated for a seat on Durham County Council. Thomas Lamb, grocer and draper Joseph Green proposed and seconded the local candidate. Both nominees collected a high vote; Galbraith 933, Cochrane 888. The new councillor makes up the seventy three forming the Council. One hundred and sixteen pounds seventeen shillings and sixpence was spent on running the election at Brandon Colliery.

Gloom reigns supreme; the colliery once again works slack time. Seven people died during January, only two of whom were infants. At such times people seek solace in the Chapels. Crowds turned up at the Methodist New Connexion when the much publicised Canadian Evengelists, Mr. and Mrs. Braddan and Miss Knox held daily religious services. Their eloquence made a number of converts during their week of religious revival meetings.

Pigeon racing, very popular among pitmen, exploded into activity. Men were eager to show their undoubted skill of pigeon training. Fifteen birds were entered for the sweep run by Matt Bates, mine host of the Red Lion Inn, who added ten shillings to the one pound seventeen shillings and sixpence subscribed. The race from Old Clay Lane near Lowes Barn to Brandon Colliery was won by George Lee's Cut Tail in two minutes forty seconds, followed by Tom Warriner's White Flite, George Brunskill's Slatey and Ben Marple's Old One were joint third in three minutes five seconds.

Another pigeon sweep took place, this time from Pit House Gate to Brandon Colliery, a distance of one mile and a quarter, again fifteen birds took part. Ralph Smith's Wild Duck proved superior, clocking in at one minute thirty one seconds, George Brunskill's Slatey and Tom Warriner's Red One arriving nine seconds later to share the second prize.

Pigeon flying, it seemed, was the most popular sport during the early months of the year. Men and lads trundled home made conveyances the two and a quarter miles to Sunderland Bridge, the pigeon baskets being too bulky to carry. A large entry at five shillings a bird, with the addition of Matt Bates' twenty shillings, augured well for a most exciting race. George Lee's birds, Cranky and Cut Tail, were first and third. Tom Warriner's Little Star was second.

A week later excitement ran high both at Brandon Colliery and Oakenshaw Colliery. A pigeon flying match between Archie Robson's Red Flight of Brandon Colliery and Marshall's White Flight of Oakenshaw Colliery had been arranged. The pigeons' owners laid down a stake of ten pounds, the race being from dovecote to dovecote. White Flight was given a start of one minute; with the help of a strong tail wind he won easily in four minutes fifty nine seconds. The adverse conditions affected Red Flight who took seven minutes and sixteen seconds to cover the distance.

On the same day, flying from Elvet Hill near Durham to Brandon Colliery, were twenty eight pigeons entered at five shillings each. Matt Bates added ten shillings to the pool money. Amid tremendous excitement, Bob Garbutt's Fan Blast, George Brunskill's Slatey and Jim Turner's Dicky clocked in at one minute fifty second to share the first three prizes. Bob Smith's Wild Duck was fourth.

Good Friday saw the pigeon men at their lofts. Pitmen patronised the colliery's two public houses, the Red Lion and the Colliery Inn. Others with gardens took the opportunity of a day off work to set their allotment or garden. The large number of Methodists thronged the chapels for the Easter Services and their annual tea. The Catholic fraternity attended the Good Friday afternoon service.

Hens' eggs at fourteen a shilling were in demand; dyed egg competitions were attracting big entries. Easter brought the traditional egg jarping. Local shops sold chickens for two shillings and sixpence each, ducks at two shillings each, a rabbit at one shilling and fourpence, beef at sixpence to ninepence a pound, potatoes at sevenpence a stone.

Coal hewers Archie Robson, George Brunskill, Bob Taylorson, George Brabbon, George Thompson and Bob Smith anxiously awaited news from Brancepeth Colliery, their sister colliery in the Straker group. The strike in its second week, had laid some four hundred and ten men idle, threatened to involve all six thousand employed at Straker and Love's collieries. Happily the strike was resolved at the end of two weeks, the Brancepeth Colliery hewers and putters returned to work.

Robert Pratt, a muscular putter, sweated and heaved the tub of coal forward, his helper-up Will Robson, puny by comparison, shoved alongside. The incline in the A Pit required their combined efforts. Without warning a large stone fell on them; Robert's thigh was broken, young Will suffered a badly crushed back and severe cuts to his head and shoulders. Doctors Binnie and Gosforth were in attendance on the victims' painful arrival at the surface. If a helper-up is unavailable and a coal hewer takes his place, he is paid six-pence a shift extra if the distance helped is ten or twelve plate lengths.

Thomas Swaddle, a twenty eight year old C Pit coal hewer, was hewing in double with John Gibbon in a broken jud. A large stone, without warning, fell on Thomas, crushing him. Only half an hour after reaching home, his wife and four children mourned his death, his back having been broken. Thomas' dependants will be chargeable to the Miners' Permanent Relief Fund.

Men hurriedly left their homes, others vacated the nearby Colliery Inn. The quiet of the Sunday evening was rudely shattered by the incessant blowing of the colliery buzzer. What had happened? Continuous blowing of the buzzer was reserved for serious colliery accidents. The extensive wooden gangways spanning the coke-ovens were on fire. The boiler men and fan engineman on duty spotted the flames, they notified the resident engineer, Mr. Rutherford, who took immediate charge of operations. The fire, being clear of the pithead and shaft did not affect the working of the pit.

The cricket season saw Brandon Colliery's three cricket teams in action. Brandon Red Rose played Littletown on the Colliery field. the home team batted first and only lasted fifteen minutes, devastating bowling allowing only twelve runs. Jim Evans being Brandon's highest scorer with six runs to his credit; six players scored ducks. Littletown's one hundred and eighty one runs confounded Red Rose. On the same day Brandon Y.M.F.S. beat Sunnybrow Colliery sixty eight runs to twenty five. Brandon Mission Juniors played a draw with Shadforth, scoring thirty nine runs to Shadforth's seven, eight of whose players did not bat.

George Jackson, Daniel Johnson and James Roxboro, sporting pit-men, forgot their cricket when they joined other Durham County pitmen in their demand for a twenty per cent advance in wages. They applaud the termination of the sliding scale which has been in operation for twelve years. Pitmen of the county have never been totally satisfied with the arrangement.

Officials of the Durham Miners' Association met the Durham Coal Owners to discuss the twenty per cent advance asked. After four hours deliberation the owners offered ten per cent increase. A ballot was taken, the owners offer being accepted by a majority of one. Voting was one hundred and sixty nine to one hundred and sixty eight. At the same meeting a list of twenty six requests has handed to the coal owners, the most important being:—

4. That men be paid their money at the colliery office as they leave their work.

6. That the first Monday in August in each year be observed as a general holiday.

8. That boys commencing work at 13 years of age be paid one shilling a day. That boys 14 years of age be paid one shilling and nine pence a day. That boys 16 years of age be paid two shillings and three pence a day. That three shillings a day be paid to those reaching 18. On reaching the age of 20 they be paid men's wages.

10. That men be paid a uniform rent allowance of three shillings per week.

21. That all boys under 16 years of age work no more than nine hours a day.

26. That screenmen's daily wage be not less than three shillings and six pence as a standard wage.

These requests would affect pitmen like family men William Forster, Peter Bragan, Ritson Golightly, William Dickinson, to name but a few.

No huge field with massive poles erected at each end for William Freak and William Whiteman when they met in combat. Iron hobs set eleven yards apart and four quoits met their requirements. Their presence attracted a large crowd to the new running grounds at Thomas Towers' Boyne Hotel. Both contestants being Brandon Colliery men, their supporters travelled the mile to witness and bet on the game. The quoit match was for twenty pounds, William Freak won easily, he had been made favourite at two to one to win the game.

Another publican sportsman, Matt Bates of Brandon's Red Lion Inn, celebrated when the long awaited water supply was switched on in the isolated building. The Weardale and Shildon Water Company had laid pipes from the colliery rows to his place lying in the depression north of the pit. Matt Bates was delighted—instant water at the turn of a tap. Hitherto the elements and a trek to the spring supplied his needs.

The large assembly appreciated the Penny Readings given in the Primitive Methodist schoolroom. The building situated at the top of Commercial Street reverberated with joyous sound when members of the choir under their able leader James Richardson, sang several choruses. One, 'Laugh and grow fat', had to be repeated; the audience relished the medicine. After a coffee supper, all departed, well pleased with the proceedings.

A newsman reporting that good sugar costs twopence a pound, decent sugar three halfpence a pound, flour one shilling and three halfpence a stone and good potatoes at fivepence a stone, asks, 'How far off is the millennium?' Knowledgeable men are puzzling over his remark.

During the year thirty three colliery inhabitants succumbed, mainly infant victims of measles still prevalent in the district.

1890

Pitmen on learning that the January price of coal had risen to twenty three shillings a ton in the London Coal Market, asked a fifteen per cent advance in wages, a ten hour day and ten days per fortnight. The coal owners turned down the request.

George Liddle, Thomas Riley and Alexander Seed, all pitmen at Brandon Colliery, would be among the fifty thousand men affected if the Durham miners decided on strike action, a ballot is being considered.

After much deliberation, the owners offered five per cent advance as against the fifteen per cent asked for. A ballot was found unnecessary when the miners accepted the much reduced offer.

James Rushford, fore overman in the C Pit talked to the fore shift hewers gathered at the shaft bottom prior to their long walk inbye. The overman gave them details of the new advances and reductions worked out for them.

Mick Robson who hewed in Second South Cross-Cut whole in No. 3 west, learned that he had been advanced five per cent, this was one shilling to the pound earned. He received the news without visible emotion. His hewing place being whole no pressure softened the two feet ten inches of coal, therefore defying Mick's effort, even with the advance, to earn a fair living.

Francis Brown and John Bevans had been doing decent in South-west brokens in Third West; the coal was friable owing to roof pressure, coal hewing was made much easier. They with the hewers in Second North-West were to suffer a five per cent reduction. Hewers in Fourth West district First North were told that their reduction would be eight per cent.

Joseph Johnson and Thomas Clarke, coal hewers in No. 3 West found the hewing hard, even with a fifteen per cent increase a good wage could not be earned. Robert Routledge and William Gilbert, coal hewers in Jubilee North were equally unimpressed with their five per cent advance, it was nigh impossible to earn a living wage.

The night shift workers in the C Pit were deeply concerned when John Joseph Lishman the colliery manager, notified them that their shift was to be discontinued. Work would be resumed when the owners deemed it necessary. The men contend that there is an abundance of coking coal and seggar in their seam.

William Dickinson, a resident of Brandon Colliery since the pit was sunk thirty four years ago, has long agitated for better travel facilities for Brandon Colliery inhabitants and their near neighbours. He suggests that a tram line could be laid, at little cost, the two miles from Crossgate Workhouse to Meadowfield which lies close to Brandon Colliery. He asserts that some three hundred to four hundred people have to walk to Durham on a Saturday, the existing railway station at Brandon Colliery being too remote.

Brandon Rovers exit in the second round of the Durham County Challenge Cup in their football match with Hunwick Rovers who won three goals to two, fostered revenge. Brandon Rovers supporters made their presence felt when they visited Durham to witness the much talked of clash between Durham City and their team. Durham City's players lighter than their broad shouldered, stronger pitmen opponents, contributed to a fast moving, exciting game. Cries of 'Gan on Brandon' and 'Well kicked hinny' encouraged Crooks, the best player on the field, to score the only goal of the match which Brandon won. The win whetted Brandon's supporters' appetites when they watched the Football Association match between Brandon Rovers and Sunderland Swifts. Spectators, including several vociferous women, savoured Brandon's four-one win.

Brandon Albions, Brandon Rovers and Brandon Juniors, three active association football teams, cater for the sporting fraternity. Brandon Mechanics and Brandon Mechanics second team, two rugby teams, provide sport for the elite. Durham's Henderson's Creelers, Durham St. Cuthbert's, Hamsteels and Jarrow St. Peter's were among the rugby teams to visit Brandon.

Brandon Excelsiors made an early start to their cricket season, they welcomed Lumley Thicks. The visitors had the Excelsiors all out for seventy-seven runs; W. Rounding and J. Ritchies batted well. Lumley Thicks won their first game of the season easily, they scored ninety two runs for the loss of only three wickets.

Thomas Condron, John Horsley, Tom Crossings, Bob Storey, Jim Lee, Caleb Lee, Tom Olger, Peter Bragon, George Hury and John Stanton, all miners at Brandon Colliery, were among the seventy thousand present at the twentieth Miners' Annual Gala and demonstration. Over two hundred collieries had band or banner on display at the largest Big Meeting so far. Five speakers, all Members of Parliament, occupied the two platforms erected on the racecourse running alongside the River Wear in Durham.

While Brandon Colliery's two public houses were almost deserted, Durham's one hundred and twelve public houses did brisk business on the day. Two of the public houses being exceptionally busy, one took sixty pounds while the other took fifty pounds.

With the population nearing fifteen thousand there's a growing need for a hospital in the area. Messrs. Straker and Love have for some'time allowed the Local Board to use the cottages in the short Railway Street in which to store hospital requirements. With the expanding coal trade the owners require the three houses for their workmen. They could do with fifty more dwellings.

Five plans and estimates for a new hospital were sent to the Board. One to be built of corrugated iron was selected, it was decided to erect it between Brandon Colliery and Brandon Village. The surveyor considered both the site and the plan very suitable.

The iron hospital to be built in Watergate Field below Brandon Village would be seventy five feet long and twenty feet wide with eight feet to the eaves. An acre of land was available for five pounds six shillings per annum for the new hospital estimated to cost four hundred and fifty pounds. Three wards would be built to hold ten beds each. A double iron cottage would be erected for the caretaker and nurse at a cost of two hundred and fifty pounds. As the proposed site is well away from the colliery rows and pits and set in healthy environs Brandon Colliery people applaud the choice. Judicious use of a hospital could effectively reduce the death toll in the colliery rows. Fifty-seven inhabitants died during the year, most were infants, victims of fever and attending diseases.

Brandon's large population suggests the need for a spacious new Mission Chapel. A sale of work was held in the colliery school by members of St. John's Church for that worthy cause. At the present time the colliery owners allow a house in Newcastle Street to be used as a Mission Centre. Viscount Boyne has promised land at Brandon.

1891

The New Year saw bricklayers and joiners busy enlarging Brandon Colliery school. The population increase of three thousand three hundred and ninety in the Byshottles since the last census ten years ago, necessitated more school space. The building now accommodates seven hundred and thirty five children.

Viscount Boyne granted Messrs. Straker and Love right of way to the proposed Staple to be sunk at Brandon Colliery near Cobden Terrace and on the road to Stobb House. John C. Straker; Joseph H. Straker and Joseph Horatio Love, the colliery owners signed the papers. The new drift from the surface will shorten the walk to work and eliminate the cage ride. It will allow more time to be spent at the coal-face for men and boys employed in the B Pit's Dunn Drift and the Tichbourne and East Districts.

Hugh McDermott, now twenty five years of age and a coal hewer in the C Pit's Brockwell Seam, visualised healthier pay packets. After negotiations between R. C. Weeks for the owners and William Barnes and Thomas Condron for the men, a list of awards was compiled and displayed at Union room and pit.

Brandon Colliery C Pit Brockwell Seam:
No. 1 North District, North broken—advanced 7½%.
No. 2 West District, narrow Bord whole—advanced 7½%
No. 2 North-West whole—advanced 5½%
No. 2 Jubilee Cross-cut, South whole—advanced 5½%
No. 3 West district, second South whole—advanced 5½%
No. 4 West district, second North-west whole—advanced 5½%
No. 4 Jubilee district, North-West whole—advanced 2½%

Thirteen days into the New Year. Men who had been cheered by the colliery awards, and the news that a seven hour shift from bank to bank had been granted them, sorrowed with the Carroll family. William Carroll, a twenty two year old coal hewer, had lived all his life at Brandon Colliery, having been born in No. 19 South Street. His father, John, also a coal hewer, was born in Ireland; he married Margaret there and moved to Seaton Colliery. With their daughter Mary they moved to Brandon Colliery. Three more girls were born in South Street.

William's Davey lamp only gave out enough light to amplify the darkness. He sat, erect on his low cracket, his pick acquired a rhythmic swing, coal dislodged from the coal face on the floor of the seam. The roof in his work place had been 'jowled' and deemed safe. Half way through his shift a large stone fell from the roof and terminated William's life.

The long rows of bee-hive coke ovens, some with iron doors, fascinated the five colliery row lads. All around the age of ten, they were wont to wander over colliery property. Robert Douglas, James Moran, Tom Wilkinson, James Carroll and William Rowland met after school. Boisterous youth damaged the iron oven doors; each was fined sixpence and one shilling damages at Durham Police Court.

Excited youngsters gathered as Mary McLoughlin prepared to leave her home for her marriage to Paddy Cahill in St. Patrick's Chapel. Vantage points were secured from which to swoop on the pennies and halfpennies thrown out to the expectant pack on such occasions. The couple's new home would be in South Street near the colliery where Paddy hewed coal.

During February scarlet fever once again ravaged the colliery rows. Robert Stephenson lost his two year old daughter Sarah Elizabeth and five year old Susannah Jane within twenty four hours. Similar tragedy dogged Will Raine who lost daughters Martha and Mary on one day. Parson and undertaker were active during a drab February when scarlet fever claimed eleven infants and one adult. The epidemic was especially severe at Browney Colliery about one mile from Brandon, some Brandon Colliery children attend school there and concern is felt for their health. Ash-pits were ordered to be emptied and quicklime put in to retard the disease.

The owners of Brandon Colliery issued an order forbidding their workers to keep dogs in their houses. There are some valuable racing dogs in the colliery. 'What's a pitman to do wi'oot his dog?' The order caused a great deal of dissatisfaction, some men declared that they would rather leave the colliery than part with their canine pets.

The associated coalowners have suggested a seven and a half per cent reduction in miners' wages. This is to pave the way for a general drop in the price of coal.

Pitmen at the colliery resolved to resist the owners' demands. Patrick Riley, John Brown, George Bragon, Pat Smith, John Dowdall, John Poulton, Mat Smith, Edward Welch, Pat Solan, John Pratt, Owen Moody and John Humphreys back their Lodge's resolution to the full.

Newcastle South End travelled to Brandon for their match in the Football Association Competition; there were other three entries for the competition. A blazing June day helped the shirt-sleeved spectators enjoy a one sided game in which Brandon Rovers scored five goals, the visitors failing to score. Brandon's two football teams, the Rovers and the Rovers second team, were in good form. The latter beat Hedley Hill Rovers one goal to nil; on the same day the senior team beat Benwell Hill one goal to nil. Blaydon visited Brandon to lose four goals to one, a large crowd was entertained to a sparkling display of football.

Jane Cummings, a lively four year old, played in the bedroom as her mother, Jane Cummings, cleaned the room. A bottle of pink liquid attracted little Jane, she drank part of the contents. Doctor Halliday arrived immediately, he pronounced little hope of recovery. The child's father, Lawrence Cummings, on returning from work, found his daughter in a critical state, she died twenty four hours later. The bottle of Carbolic Acid was kept under the bed for safety, it was used for disinfecting and killing vermin.

News of Will Dickinson's death shocked Brandon Colliery folk. Will, sixty seven years of age, died at Langley. He was thirty years of age when he came to Brandon Colliery in 1857 to help sink the pit shaft. He founded the Brandon Colliery branch of the Foresters, he was well known for his other public interests. Will left Brandon Colliery some years ago to live at Littleburn Colliery. He agitated right up to the time of his death, for a railway station at Langley Moor.

Another early settler in the colliery was Isaac Parrish. The same age as Will Dickinson, he hewed coal on the day before his death. His widow, one year his junior, died exactly one month later. Their son John Isaac Parrish, having courted Mary Jane Dickinson for some time, married her at Brandon Parish Church three days after John's mother's death. Both families experienced sorrow and joy in quick succession.

Brandon Colliery pitmen seeing the need for better accommodation, put forward plans for the erection of an iron building intended for use as a miners' hall and social room.

Proudly, pitmen gathered in the new hall sited at the top end of West Street. The Mayor of Durham, Councillor Matthew Fowler, a champion of the pitmen, had just performed the opening ceremony. An expanding union necessitated more spacious premises. Saturday November 7th was an important day as the members viewed the new building's interior; neatly lined with wood it possessed a raised platform in the large room which would hold three hundred people. The outer corrugated frame covered a well designed entrance porch. Pitmen's contributions had raised the three hundred pounds needed to erect the building.

Just up the road from the Union room stands Brandon Hospital, the building was recently insured against fire, the sum insured being six hundred and fifty pounds, the cost of the insurance was very small. There are three cases of scarlet fever in the hospital, all being from one house. A bad case of typhoid fever was admitted from a house in Commercial Street. The hospital awaits a steam disinfecting apparatus advertised at seventy five pounds plus ten pounds for package.

William Cummings went to work in the 'back shift'; he missed his four year old sister Jane whose life was so tragically terminated. She had almost reached school starting age. William at fifteen years of age was a putter in the C Pit. One of his hewers was twenty eight years old John Stoker. John, like William, had only just started his shift. On running the empty tub into the hewer's place William sensed tragedy, all was silent at the coal face. Horror stricken, William sought out a chap called Barnes in the next hewing place, he in turn informed the deputy. They found John Stoker lifeless under a stone measuring three yards by one yard. Alec Stoker, John's father, was immediately notified.

Coke ovens generate warmth. Recently emptied ovens retain inviting heat, this in turn attracts tramps. Police Constable McIntyre was involved in an incident which caused some stir in Brandon Colliery. He accosted a tramp loitering in the vicinity of the ovens. The tramp, also known as a 'rodney', drew a knife and threatened to stab the constable who had received several complaints concerning the defendant stopping little boys going to the pit in the early hours of the morning and taking their 'bait' from them. The tramp was sent to prison as a vagrant for one month.

Brandon C Pit men who had been granted pay increases early in the year were asked to suffer an all round reduction. Surface and underground datal hands to be affected.

Joint Committee Award: Brandon C Pit.

(a) Underground men and boys:
At or under 2 shillings reduced 1 penny per day
Above 2 shillings reduced 2 pence per day
Above 3 shillings reduced 3 pence per day
Above 4 shillings reduced 4 pence per day.

(b) Surface men and boys:
At or under two shillings eightpence reduced one penny per day
Above two shillings eightpence reduced two pence per day

The Committee further decided that:

Brandon A Pit — Reduction of stonemen's datal wages in the Busty Seam to be paid three shillings and eightpence.

Brandon B Pit — the same as above.

Brandon C Pit — as above.

Lower wages and a total of sixty three deaths in the colliery rows during 1891 left its inhabitants with little room for rejoicing.

1892

Thomas Hutchinson, Oswald Hedley, John Thompson and Joseph Ashcroft, all pitmen at Brandon Colliery, began the New Year on a cheerless note. All had suffered a wage reduction and the death of an infant.

Severe snowstorms struck the area, roads were blocked, coffins en route to the Brandon Village cemetery had to be manhandled.

During the first six weeks of the year eleven inhabitants of the colliery died. John Jobson Magdin died at the age of fifty two, he came to Brandon Colliery as a young man to occupy a shop in High Street. The premises still trade as a butcher's in the renamed Commercial Street.

Grave unrest prevailed among the county's pitmen. All pits were affected by the coalowners' decision to reduce wages by ten per cent. On Saturday February 20th Durham's pitmen refused to accept the cut. With the view of averting a strike, the owners adopted the following resolution, 'The final offer of the Owners' Association is that they will accept seven and a half per cent immediate reduction; or five per cent immediate reduction and five per cent on May 1st. In the event of neither of these proposals being accepted, the notices will be given on 27th February to terminate the present contract of hiring'.

Immediately the Durham Miners' Association issued a ballot paper containing four propositions to its members:—

(a) Immediate acceptance of seven and a half per cent reduction.

(b) Immediate acceptance of five per cent reduction and a further five per cent reduction on 1st May.

(c) Leave settlement in the hands of the Durham Miners' Federation Board.

(d) Strike.

The ballot was taken — result, an overwhelming majority in favour of a strike.

The owners' notice expired, they immediately made public a letter which said that the Durham men 'have refused all the proposals made by the employers' and therefore the employers declared a 'lock-out'. On March 12th the 'lock-out' began; tools, gear, horses and ponies were removed from the pit.

Joe Stead, Cornelius Ferguson, Will Hunter, George Neesham, Ed Walsh and other pitmen from Brandon's three seams, noted the withdrawal of the pit ponies and other activities quietly taking place. Desperate times loomed ahead.

Northumberland levied sixpence a week on its miners on behalf of the Durham men on strike. The levy allowed for six shillings a week strike money to be paid to the striking men.

Nearly three thousand met on a bit of unoccupied ground at Langley Moor. Samuel Galbraith of Brandon Colliery presided at the meeting; Samuel Whitely also from Brandon Colliery moved 'That this mass meeting representing a large proportion of the Federation Board, believes that the colliery owners' demand for a ten per cent reduction of wages is unjust and uncalled for'. Mr. James Mulhall, checkweighman of Littleburn Colliery, seconded the motion.

On Friday and Saturday evenings from March 25th and 26th there was a partial renewal of the disturbance at Brandon Colliery, strikers broke the windows and doors of the house occupied by Mr. Bainbridge, one of the officials at the colliery. Extra police were standing by at the General Post Office in Durham.

On April 25th after six weeks of 'lock-out' the pitmen were hard put; the pitmen's fund was exhausted, their meagre savings spent, their families starving on a strike pay of three shillings a week and their children going to soup kitchens. On alternate days and after school hours over one thousand children crowded Brandon Colliery school where Mr. Richardson from Durham gave every child an orange. The elderly of the colliery were provided with soup and bread on alternate days. Lord Boyne donated twenty pounds to Brandon Workmen's Relief Committee, the Rev. A. D. Shafto gave five pounds.

On May 25th the twelve weeks 'lock-out' ended. The owners wanted a thirteen and a half per cent reduction. The Bishop of Durham, himself a substantial coal-owner, acted as mediator. The owners consented to re-open the pits on a wage reduction of ten per cent. Brandon Colliery was among the majority of pits to resume work during the first half of June.

Local interest among the racing pigeon fraternity was aroused when three of the best pigeons from Brandon Colliery were released from Burnigill. The race, from Burnigill Bank to Brandon Colliery, a distance of one mile and three quarters, was won by George Galley's Little Bob in one minute fifty six seconds, Woodward's Sheffielder and Turner's Graney arrived together two seconds later.

Paddy Moran, a nine year old schoolboy, wandered the colliery with his pal George Miller of similar age. With no local football to watch, they drifted along to the allotments. Pigeon crees abound near Brandon School from which Bobby Sayers, now thirteen, had just left to follow in his father's and grandfather's footsteps, to work in the pit. He began his career in Brandon's A Pit as a pony driver. Valuable pigeons are bred in crees on the fringe of the colliery rows. Galley's Little Bob; Hewitt's Tony; Turner's pair—Jimmy and Graney; Woodward's Sheffielder, were all class birds likely to clock two miles two hundred and ten yards in two minutes fifteen seconds.

Garden produce was trampled underfoot as two sets of youthful footprints headed towards the pigeon loft. Great concern was shown, a valuable racing pigeon had been abducted from its loft. Enquiries directed the local police constable to Paddy's home in South Street, which with Single South Street, houses so many Irish coke oven workers that the area became known as 'Little Ireland'. A box containing a pigeon was found hidden under a bed, the bird was unharmed. Paddy was fined four shillings and sixpence, a whole year's pocket money.

Noisy, shirt-sleeeved pitmen, free on the sultry August Saturday afternoon, bet and speculated on the forthcoming quoit match. William Wilson of Moorsley and John Smith of Brandon Colliery each handed over to the stake holder ten pounds. Each man being noted for his skill at the game kept betting to even money. The two inch iron pins were driven into the ground ten yards apart, the four quoits each weighed four and one quarter pounds. The game was very exciting throughout. Wilson vocally encouraged by his friends from Moorsley, playing in splendid form at the finish, won by one point. Wilson forty one — Smith forty.

Hot weather helped spread disease. Nine cases of typhoid fever were admitted to Brandon's hospital, one case being from Brandon Colliery. At the same time ten cases of scarlet fever were treated at home. The houses containing the typhoid fever victims were stoved with sulphur and the ceilings were disinfected. Brandon Local Board decided to purchase a ton of carbolic dusting powder for keeping the drains clean at a cost of six shillings a hundredweight, and that the ashpit contractors be supplied with a barrel each in order that they may sprinkle some of the powder in the various ashpits after they have cleaned them out.

The hospital is still without a conveyance, it was proposed to buy a cab for £29. A very strong vehicle would be needed owing to the bad state of the road from Langley Moor to Brandon Village. The road would cost an estimated £1000 to adequately repair.

Nurses at the hospital decided to cheer up their nine patients over Christmas. A Christmas tree was bought; Watson the mineral water manufacturer, sent aerated waters; Thomas Lamb, grocer, sent grapes; Mr. Thompson a chicken; Mr. Hedley sent toys. Lord Boyne donated a tree of evergreens for decorations. Shopkeepers in the area contributed; Uncle Toby's toys were sent to the hospital to brighten the younger patients' Christmas.

Thirty seven couples danced throughout the night. Highly polished laced boots pounded the unyielding floor of the schoolroom when Brandon Colliery's Quadrille Party held its annual ball. John Mearman supplied the band consisting of piano, cornet and violin, whose lively music kept the dancers on their toes. Deep Christmas snow greeted the square dance revellers on their leaving the school at six a.m.

Christmas it seems, is a time for jollification. School-children gave dramatic renderings of 'Blundering Barney' and 'Love in a collar-box'. School-boys Ward, Shepherd, Connolly and Pinchin, together with Miss Malone, sang excellently in St. Patrick's Chapel at Langley Moor. Father Hannon an able tutor, trained the children.

John Wilson's infant daughter, Elizabeth and John Henry, son of Simon Thompson, joined the fifty four colliery row inhabitants who died during the year, a large number being victims of infectious disease.

1893

Members of the Co-operative Society had long awaited a butchering department. Mrs. Devine, Mrs. Robson, Mrs. Curry, Mrs. Hunter, Mrs. Jones and Mrs. Laverick, all Brandon Colliery women, took full advantage of the offer of first class beef or mutton at one penny per pound for one week, when the new butchering premises were opened at Meadowfield Place.

The high infant mortality rate continued throughout January. Much sorrow and distress prevailed in the colliery rows. Charles Hall, John Fox, Josh Storey, William Dixon, George Jones, Jim Smith, all pitmen, and John Storey assistant school-master, each lost an infant; William Maddison lost his wife Mary Ann. During January nine inhabitants died.

In early February another depression struck the coal trade. Brandon Colliery was put on a four day week owing to slack business. Straker and Love's nearby Willington, Sunnybrow and Brancepeth pits were put on four-teen days notice to close. To avert a closedown, the Coal Federation Board persuaded the miners to accept a five per cent reduction.

There was rejoicing in Brandon Colliery on April 20th when St. Aga-tha's Mission Church was opened.

The new church built entirely of pitch pine, seats five hundred with a total cost of £1,050 which includes furniture. The sixteenth century period building replaces a mission room which provided accommodation for only two hundred worshippers. The mission church founded in a house in New-castle Street is expected to collect the cost of the new building during the opening services. Viscount Boyne and Messrs. Straker and Love each gave one hundred pounds.

Brandon Albion Football Club held their annual supper in Bob Wray's Colliery Inn. Members of the team Bob Cairns, Bart Plant, Tom Pattinson, Morty Maddison, Tom Jones, Will Gustard and Alex Cook, entertained the thirty-two members present with lively songs and recitations. Jack Crooks on retiring from the post of treasurer to the club, was presented with a Meershaum pipe. Jim Mearman ably presided on the piano. The Albions ended their successful season with Brandon St. Agatha's as opponents in a friendly match.

Colliery lodges in the county were notified that owing to the need to collect crops, at the farmers' request, the twenty third Miners' Gala would be deferred two weeks from July 15th to July 29th.

The Durham Chronicle, just reduced from twopence to one penny for eight sheets of news, reporting on the Big Meeting, stated that Brandon Colliery lodge banner evidenced a characteristic which is particularly strong in the Durham miner, that of veneration. Upon the front of it is a capital portrayal of Alderman Fowler of Durham, whose name is revered among the miners of the county, and by his side is the well known form of Mr. Whiteley the lodge secretary. The other side of the banner illustrates the valuable truth that 'unity is strength'. Five speakers occupied the platforms at the Gala, the twenty third to be held, three of the speakers being Members of Parliament.

On the day of the Big Meeting, July 29th, members of St. Agatha's Church Choir went on an outing to the coast. Sixty choristers were conveyed to Sunderland and Roker in brakes where they thoroughly enjoyed themselves in bathing, boating and other seaside amusements.

There being thirty two deputies employed at Brandon Colliery, the Deputies' Association applied to Brandon Miners' Lodge for clearance papers for the deputies in the Durham Miners' Association.

The coal-owners seek a reduction of twenty-five per cent in miners' wages, a deadlock ensued. There is talk of a county strike; the men countered with a demand for an advance of fiteen per cent on their wages. After much haggling the men settled for a six per cent reduction.

After Daniel Doyle and George Simpson screenmen at Brandon Colliery sought a rise in wages, the Union forwarded their request to the Joint Committee who turned it down. At the same time screenmen and labourers throughout the county had their wages settled; the county average now is 2s.7½d plus 22% making 3s. 2½d. per day of ten and a half hours.

The parents of a young boy named Hedley were spared the agony of seeing the addition of his name to the list of eight deaths in Brandon Colliery during July. The eight died from natural causes. The Sunday afternoon peace was shattered when the twelve year old, the eldest of James Hedley's large family, found a box containing a few detonator caps, the type used by pitmen for detonating shots in the mine. He was playing with one of them when one exploded. His hand was severely shattered.

News that three cases of smallpox were found in Durham's lodging houses added to local gloom. Bills were posted throughout the district cautioning people against exposing themselves while suffering from any infectious disease—ashpits and privvies were disinfected with carbolic powder.

Brandon Rovers, ever desirous of helping the unfortunate, played Durham City football at Meadowfield Place. The former winning five nil at half time, the game eight nil. The proceeds from a collection and concert were given to the widow and children of Mr. Turnbull who died suddenly while attending service at the Primitive Methodist Chapel in Brandon Colliery.

A good crowd watched an exciting game between Brandon Albion and

Burnmoor Rovers. Albion won by one goal to nil. On the same day Brandon Rovers visited Hunwick to play a draw—three goals each. Brandon Rover Reserves easily beat St. Agatha's two goals to nil.

Despite the report of two cases of typhoid fever and six of scarlet fever in Brandon Colliery, the Brandon Youth Amateur Variety Company gave a concert to a large and appreciative audience. Tom Brain and Ralph Land instrumentalists; Richard Chrisop, Tyrolean yodeller; John Russell, Tyneside reciter; George Hodgson and Will Todd, duettists; Harold Nesbitt, stump speaker and nigger comedian; Henry Brain and Chris Rutherford, sentimentalists; George Hodgson, mouth harmonica, performed well, as did John William at the piano. Two sketches were also warmly appreciated.

On Christmas Eve the 'Pride of Brandon Lodge' of the Shildon and St. Andrew's Equalised District Order of St. Druids held their annual celebration on the Three Tuns, Brandon Village. Brothers Edward Mearman, Henry Thrower, Steve Jones, Steve Brown and Sara entertained the company of forty diners with a selection of songs.

Sixty eight residents of the colliery rows died during the year, fourteen more than last year.

1894

The following letter was read by the clerk at the January meeting of the Local Board:— 'The members of the Brandon Lodge (which includes the workmen of the A and B Pits) have had under consideration two or three questions, which we conceive to be of high important to the district and which we humbly ask you to lay before the members of the Board at your next meeting, and we hope that the questions will have your careful consideration.

The first question to which we wish to call your attention is the road between Brandon Village and the Boyne. The condition of this road has never been too good, we assure you that it is frequently bad. An improvement is highly desirable.

The second question is in regard to the lighting of the colliery rows and the surrounding district. This is a matter that we have had under consideration for some time, and we think that an improvement in this direction would add greatly to the comfort and convenience of the inhabitants of the district.

The third question is with respect to the making of a road through the wall at the top end of West Street. We can assure you that great inconvenience is experienced on account of the top end of this street being blocked. It would be of great advantage to the people if a way was opened at the end of this street.

We are, yours sincerely on behalf of the workmen.

L. Cummings, W. Kay, Thomas Smith, John Kendrew,
John Futers, F. Smith, S. Whitely.'

Mr. Green, a member for Brandon East Ward, said at the Council Meeting that he had no hesitation in declaring that Brandon was one of the darkest and most polluted parishes in the Durham Union. Some months ago he called the attention of the members of the Board to the condition of the reservoir. One day he, along with a member, visited the reservoir and what did they find in it? Three dead dogs! He said that if there were three or four hot days the stench from the reservoir would be sufficient to cause disease to spread into every house in Brandon Colliery.

George Elliott's meat display in his butcher's shop proved too great a temptation for two Brandon Colliery men, they broke into his shop and stole six pieces of meat. On conviction they were sent to prison for six months at the Durham Quarter Session.

A Durham pitman (a correspondent says) was asked the other day what was the meaning of a 'living wage'.

'A living wage, maun, whoy enough ter keep the dawg and mesel, forbye the wife and bairns'.

During January horses and ponies at the colliery consumed choppy to the amount of
4 tons 18 hundredweights at 7s. 6d. per hundredweight—£36.15s.
Bran 6 hundredweights at 6s. per hundredweight—£1.16s.
Old hay 18 hundredweights at 5s. per hundredweight—£4.10s.

On Sunday night February 11th a furious storm of rain and wind raged over Brandon doing considerable damage to house property and other buildings. The Miners' Hall, a comparatively new building built of corrugated iron, suffered the most, the roof of which was about stripped off and carried for a considerable distance by the wind. Several chimneys were blown down, and the roofs of many of the houses presented a very dilapidated condition the following morning. Houses in West Street and Commercial Street suffered most damage, fortunately the tenants escaped injury.

John Mills, Sheill Bell, Edward Ramsey, John Strong, Elijah Genna, George Brown, were among the many coal hewers dissatisfied with the Committee's decisions re Brandon A Pit. (1) That hewing prices be reduced 2½% in the following districts:— North West broken in Orton district; First West broken, Second West whole, and North Headways whole in Hat and Feather district; Second and Third West broken in Tichborne district; South, West and North, West North-west whole, and East Cross-cut whole in Cross-cut district; and first broken in Third East district in Busty Seam. Orton district, Narrow Bord high coal reduced 6%; Narrow bord under band whole North-west broken reduced 15%. Hat and Feather district, First West broken reduced 12½%; Second West whole reduced 17½%; North Headways whole reduced 12½%. In Cross-cut South district broken reduced 17%; West broken reduced 10%; North broken reduced 15%; North-west whole reduced 5%; East Cross-cut whole reduced 7½%. (2) Hewing prices in North Flat whole in Orton district in the Busty Seam to be advanced 7%.

Henry Clark, Tom Reed, James McKay, George Burlison and Tom Lowther, all coal hewers, some of whom hewed in the A Pit, others in the B Pit, were among the coal hewers of both pits who refused to descend the pit on Monday March 19th. They objected to go down as one of the men in the B Pit was not a member of the miners' union. Settlement was reached and both pits resumed work on the Wednesday.

In June Messrs. Straker and Love decided to sink the A Pit shaft a further fifteen fathoms so as to work the Brockwell Seam found at that depth. The sinking will in no way interfere with the normal working of the pit. All shots fired in the sinking will be detonated by electric cable, which will considerably lessen the danger to those engaged in the work.

Robert Meagher of Princess Street hewed coal in the A Pit. On Monday June 25th half way through his shift he was buried under a huge mass of stone and was killed instantly. He had played the harmonium for many years at the Primitive Methodist Chapel. He had taken part in the anniversary services the day before at which his wife and two children attended.

Danger on the surface! Brandon Fever Hospital is kept in a state of readiness owing to the outbreak of smallpox in Durham. There are five cases in Durham County Hospital. A twenty one year old pitman lodging in Brandon Colliery died from typhoid fever.

Heavy rain greeted the colliery band and banner as they set off for the 24th annual Durham Miners' Gala. Colliery folk joined the expectant 50,000 present on the racecourse. Despite the continuing rain, crowds listened to the speakers from the two platforms. Five had been booked to address the gathering, among them being two M.P.s and the Durham Miners' solicitor, Isadore Isaacs.

Packed trains ran from Durham to Brandon Colliery at regular intervals during the afternoon. Old friends took advantage of the day to visit and stayed overnight. Men who had worked at the colliery sought out ex-workmates to reminisce in the crowded Colliery Inn or Red Lion Inn.

If anyone knew the taste of ale for miles around it was Geordie; but one day while in the city he heard of another house where it was reported to be extra special ale. That very night he made a detour in order to call at this particular tavern, and being on horseback, he rattled the sign with his whipstock, which brought out the maid. 'They tell me ye have some good beer here', he said. 'Fetch me a quart, and A'll test it for mesel'.

Geordie drank it in one draught, smacked his lips like a connoisseur, and said 'Fetch me another'. The second quart went the same way. 'Wey', said Geordie, 'they said ye kept good beer here, and by God ye dee. A'll get off and hev some'.

John Roper sent birds as did the Plant and Ritchie lofts; the occasion being the pigeon race from Ventnor in the Isle of Wight to Brandon Colliery. Owing to a mistake the birds were liberated at Dover in very bad weather which caused heavy loss of life among them. John Roper's pigeons won him two silver medals and a special prize.

Two thousand five hundred people attended Brandon's first floral show and horticultural exhibition in a field adjoining the school. Flowers, fruit, rabbits, iron work, pigeons, poultry, rabbits etc. were shown. A foot-race, bowling at the wicket, kicking at goal, and a bicycle parade entertained the crowd.

It was stated at a meeting of Brandon Ratepayers that four dead dogs and one cat were found in one reservoir and four dead dogs in another.

There was grave risk of disease from the evil smell. The colliery manager sent men with a pail and tar brush to dab the fencing surrounding the ponds. At the same time there were eighteen cases of scarlet fever, four of typhoid and three of diphtheria in Brandon Hospital. Twenty three houses have recently been stoved to help combat the diseases.

The funeral cortege passed the hospital on its sorrowful journey to Brandon Village cemetery which was crowded for twenty eight year old Will Draycott's burial. The Army band from Durham played the Dead March from his South Street home to the cemetery. Will was in the 2nd Durham Artillery Volunteers and had served seven years in the army throughout the Egyptian campaign.

Brandon's football teams were active and had fared well during the season. Brandon Rovers played and beat Consett Town 4–2. High Fell Temperance beat Brandon Albion. Brandon Rovers avenged the Albions when they beat Durham City second team 5–1 at Brandon. The result of the return game was a 2–2 draw.

The Local Government Act was passed. The Act places the management of parochial affairs in the hands of the people. At the same time pitmen decided to run a candidate of their own choosing at the meeting of Brandon and Byshottles Parish Council.

1895

At the first meeting at the North Bailey in Durham of the Brandon and Byshottled Urban District Council on Monday January 11th Mr. Green said that a young woman had died from the stench emanating from the reservoir. He had received several complaints of ashpits not being cleaned out. Mr. Green, Brandon's East Ward member of the Council, declared that the scavengers were not honouring their contract. It was stated at the meeting that the cost to the Council for the removal of snow from two miles of its roads was eighteen pounds.

School attendances in the area were severely depleted owing to measles and heavy falls of snow. The weather in January was so severe as to cause crows to become cannibals.

Fourteen members of the community died during January, twelve of whom were infants, victims of measles.

Brandon Unionist Association held their Annual Ball and social gathering in the school. A good crowd defied the very bad weather to dance in the holly decorated school room. The same room was crowded on the following night when Brandon Floral Society held a Ball and social in aid of the funds.

Brandon Colliery Private Quadrille Party held their last Ball of the season. Sixty couples assembled for dancing from 9.30 p.m. to 5.30 a.m. They danced with great spirit to the music supplied by Mearman and Bell.

On May 1st pitmen throughout the county suffered a reduction of 7½% in wages. Pitmen Herbert Martin, George Willis, George Liddle, William Dodds and Harry Furnival, all employed at Brandon Colliery are playing hell! They say it is uncalled for. Men maintaining the roads are now jubilant, they have had their wages increased by two shillings a week making them twenty two shillings.

Collieries are working slack time. To add to the gloom, April claimed fifteen victims from the colliery rows, seven of whom succumbed to measles.

The ratepayers held a meeting in Brandon's Miners' Hall. It was stated that the road between Brandon Village and Langley Moor was in a deplorable state. Lord Boyne had promised £200, Straker and Love the same amount. Many farmers and tradesmen, who use the roads, have promised to lend their horses and carts to lead the stone from the quarry at Brandon Village.

The committee of Brandon Colliery Literary Institute opened their new billiard room with a handicap for the first and second teams. A crowded room watched the battle for prizes. First prize for each team, an electro-plated teapot; second a silver albert; third a silver mounted pipe; fourth a silver medal. Hedley Emmerson and Tommy Taylor were appointed markers for the occasion.

Disease is still prevalent in the area. In the first six months of the year sixty four victims were claimed.

Bobby Sawyers now fifteen years of age, after a spell of helping-up, got his turn at putting. He and his mates travelled to Durham for the 25th Durham Miners' Gala at which five men spoke, all of whom were Members of Parliament who had come from all parts of the country.

Doctors Stewart and Denholm, colliery doctors, were appointed joint medical officers to Brandon Colliery Hospital at a salary of £10 each per annum.

There being no street lights in Brandon Colliery, residents are tripping over deep ruts. A walk at night is a positive hazard.

At a special meeting of the Urban Council the surveyor Mr. R. Gardner presented a scheme and estimate cost of lighting the district with oil and gas lamps. The estimated cost of laying down sixty oil lamps was £165, and maintenance would be about £100 a year. Fifty gas lamps would cost £150, and their maintenance would amount to between £120 and £130 a year.

Dark nights meant more indoor entertainment. St. Patrick's gave their annual concert in the schoolroom. The first item was an overture by members of St. John's String Band, 'The Caliph of Baghdad'. Sentimental and comic songs passed away a most pleasant evening. Mr. Tom Connelly's comic song 'The brick came down' received a well deserved encore.

Footballers were busy at the end of the year. Leadgate Exiles beat Brandon Rovers 2−1. Boyne Stars were playing a 2−2 game with Brandon Swifts when a third goal was claimed by the former, the referee disallowed it. Stars being dissatisfied with the referee's decision, the players left the field.

Brandon Rovers beat Oakenshaw Heroes 7 goals to 1 an Brandon. Brandon Rovers were again the victors when they beat Cockfield 2−1. Brandon St. Agatha's were also in good form around Christmas.

A billiard handicap held over Christmas holidays in the Literary Institute drew thirty-eight competitors who were divided into two divisions. The prizes in each section being 1st−Turkey; 2nd−Goose; 3rd−Hare; 4th− a couple of rabbits. Eighty-five competed in the domino handicap which offered the same prizes as the billard handicap.

Ninety-seven colliery folk died during the year, thirty-three more than in 1894. The measles epidemic, so active during the year, boosted the total.

1896

Brandon Social Quadrille Party let in the New Year with its annual dance which was held in the schoolroom. Miss Caislaw and Miss Gibbons were M.C.s when fifty lively couples danced to the music supplied by John Bell. Mr. Connolly and Mr. Mearman entertained with songs. The Quadrille Party sent two guineas to Brandon Fever Hospital towards buying toys for the children.

Durham pitmen showed their disapproval of the Conciliation Board which has been in operation for one year. During January a ballot was taken; 30,000 voted against retaining the Conciliation Board, 14,894 voted for the maintenance of the Board.

The Joint Committee awarded thirteen young helper-ups an advance of one penny per day. They were F. Graney, S. Cutler, R. Gibbs, J. Harker, W. Howden, G. Gill, R. Rumley, W. Richardson, J. Liddle, M. Murphy, C. Bullows, W. Jones and J. Woodward. John Gilbert an engine plane man was awarded fourpence a day. They were among the 1150 men and boys who draw coal from Brandon Colliery's three seams the Hutton, Busty and the Brockwell. Three shafts are in use. The former seam produces gas from its coal while the deeper seams produce coal to make the best quality coke. A forty five feet Waddle fan ventilates the Brockwell and the thirty five feet Gurbal fan serves the Hutton and Busty seams.

Bob Sayers followed his grandfather and father into the pit. At the age of fifteen, after awaiting his turn, started putting in the Busty seam. As Bob began his pit career, so to speak, Hugh McDermott ended his. Hugh died at the age of sixty-three after having spent the greater part of his life in Railway Street. Hugh's son another Hugh, at thirty-three is a coal hewer.

The Sayers family attend Mount Calvary Methodist Chapel where Mr. J. Williams ministered since 1889. He left the area and Mr. J. G. Bowran took over his duties. The new minister arrived as the measles epidemic reached its peak. Measles had claimed four infants during the month of January; fourteen infants and two lads of school age fell to the disease during February. The outbreak of measles combined with whooping cough accounted for the low percentage of attendance at Brandon Colliery and Langley Moor St. Patrick's schools. The majority of the latter's scholars reside in Brandon Colliery.

The field adjoining the school provides for Brandon Colliery's two football teams; Brandon Rovers and Brandon Swifts entertain a good crowd of pitmen supporters, they fell to Coundon Exiles and the Boyne Stars. Brandon Swifts beat the Dunelmians 3—1 and played a draw with Newbottle Villa.

On Monday April 13th devastating news engulfed the colliery rows. News of a terrible explosion having occurred at Brancepeth Colliery lying just over two miles up the road, reached Brandon Colliery. Both pits are in the Straker and Love group of collieries. Many workmen, at present at Brandon Colliery, had worked at the ill-fated pit, they were acquainted with some of the identified victims. The disaster claimed the lives of twenty men and boys. A deputy overman was sent from Brandon Colliery to render aid underground.

A week following the Brancepeth disaster tragedy struck Brandon Colliery. Fifty-five year old Matthew Peel hewed coal in the C Pit; on Tuesday April 21st he was buried beneath a large heap of stone. William Bailes—deputy overman—heard the stone fall, he and hewer Tom Lee rushed to the scene. It took a team of workers twenty minutes to recover Matt Peel's extinct body.

More gloomy news! On Friday July 17th, the day before the twenty-sixth Durham Miners' Gala, between fifty and sixty Brandon Colliery workmen received notice to terminate their engagement at the colliery. The owners are desirous of restricting output, and will therefore close a working district in the colliery until such time as an improvement in the coal trade justifies them in re-opening it.

Brandon Colliery Horticultural Society held its third annual show. The North Eastern Railway Company ran a cheap excursion from Newcastle to Brandon Colliery. Despite showery weather five thousand enthusiasts visited the show in which fifteen hundred exhibitors from all parts of the the North of England participated. A Bishop Auckland solicitor said that the exhibits proved that there was a love of gardening in the place, and a vast amount of skill and industry.

Visitors to Brandon Colliery usually get lost in the dark labyrinth of long streets, coke-ovens, railway lines and coal waggons. Strangers and residents alike rejoiced, when on November 5th one hundred gas lamps illuminated the East and Centre Wards of Brandon and Byshottles for the first time. Hundreds of Brandon Colliery folk, being in the bigger Centre Ward, turned out into the main thoroughfare to witness the lighting of the streets. Guy Fawkes' day was celebrated with a profuse display of fireworks. The night being dark, the lamps were seen to their best advantage.

Brandon Rovers met Sunderland Nomads in the third round of the English Amateur Cup; good football had forced a draw on two occasions. At the third meeting of the teams a jubilant crowd saw the Rovers win 4—2 when the game finished in semi-darkness.

Brandon Colliery Literary Institute provided more sedate Christmas cheer when it held its annual billiards, dominoes and draughts handicaps. The results being, first team billiards: G. Christie, goose; second: Robert Cairns, stone of beef; third: J. McDonald, leg of mutton. Second team billiards: first Matt Hayes, goose; second: Arch Robson, stone of beef; third: Hedley Emmerson, leg of mutton. Winners on the domino handicap were first: Chris Hedley, goose; second: W. Cook, stone of beef; third: Tom Batey, leg of mutton; fourth: H. Selway, leg of pork; fifth: J. Felton, a duck; sixth: Peter Campbell, a pair of rabbits. The winners in the draughts games being Jos. Pybus, leg of mutton; T. Graham, duck; W. Hutchinson, couple of rabbits.

Fifty-nine Brandon Colliery residents died during the year, the majority being infants, victims of measles and whooping cough.

1896—UNDERGROUND LAYOUT OF BRANDON COLLIERY 'A' PIT —BUSTY SEAM. *(Not to Scale).*

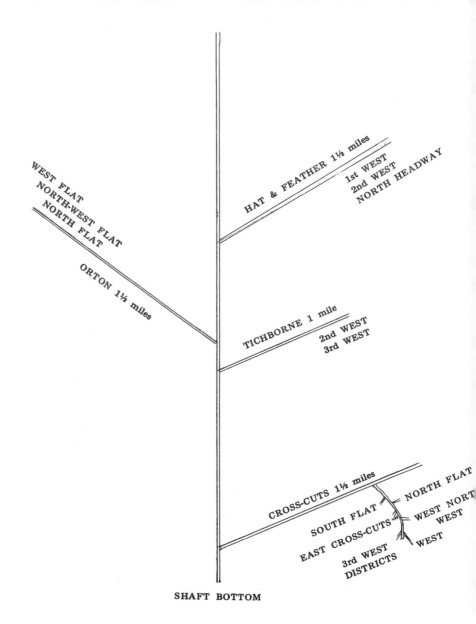

SHAFT BOTTOM

1896–UNDERGROUND LAYOUT OF BRANDON COLLIERY 'B' PIT —HUTTON SEAM. *(Not to Scale).*

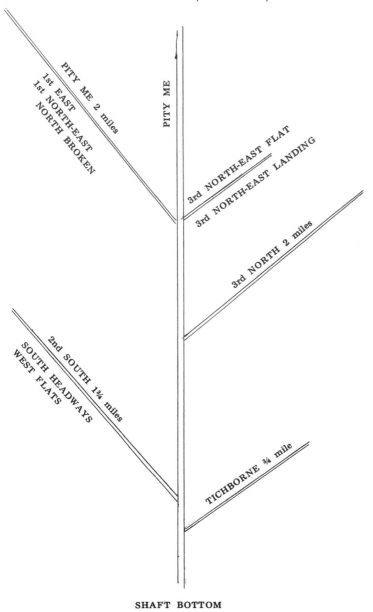

SHAFT BOTTOM

1897

The golden orb shed its brilliance on the scene below. Brandon Colliery's streets, hitherto in half shadow despite the recent installation of lamps, stood out in shining relief. The 'man in the moon' seemed to smile as he watched the antics of the colliery folk.

Figures, all male, tall and short, stood at every street end and numerous yard gates. Driver lads, helper-ups, putters, surface workers and even older coal hewers were in evidence. Midnight approached; restive 'first footers' awaited the signal. Prompt twelve o'clock, buzzers from the surrounding collieries joined Brandon Colliery buzzer to welcome in the New Year. Before the buzzers ended their raucous symphony, 'first footers' were banging on doors shouting, 'Happy New Year missus!' On the kitchen table, awaiting the first man or boy to cross the doorstep in the New Year, stood the usual piece of spice cake, drink and money. Strong drink was strictly reserved for the older 'first foot'.

Jack had asked his marra to be his 'first foot'. Geordie duly turned up on the stroke of midnight. After sampling the proffered whiskey, Geordie said to Jack's wife, 'Why Meg, there was nivver owt like this when Aa was a lad'.

'What, nee whiskey?' said Meg.

'Nay, plenty of whiskey', said Geordie, 'but nivver such a small glass!'

Two football games delighted crowds on New Year's Day. Brandon Rovers played Cockfield, both teams are in the Wear Valley League; Brandon Swifts versus Meadowfield United both in the Mid Durham League made up the other game, this local derby game aroused great interest. Brandon Swifts had vanquished only two days before, a much fancied Langley Park United, another member of the Mid Durham League.

William Lee, general dealer; John Woodward, Bob Johnson and John Grieveson, all miners, lost a son in the space of a few days. An epidemic of measles took eleven infants in one week. In an effort to control the epidemic, Brandon School was closed from April 17th until May 17th.

Bob Sayers, now a robust seventeen year old, after a spell of putting in the A Pit, joined three more putters and started coal hewing. As per custom their places were taken by four helpers-up, in their turn drivers took over from the helpers.

Paddy Moran, born and bred in double South Street, left St. Patrick's School at the age of thirteen. Tall and wiry, he started on the following Monday as a helper up, he was spared the apprenticeship of driving. Paddy's sister Mary, had just married John Ryan in St. Patrick's Chapel the couple moved straight into a house in single South Street.

Ten colliery men landed themselves into Durham Police Court; nine were fined sixpence each and costs for playing pitch and toss, the other defendant was fined five shillings for drunkenness.

Great excitement prevailed on the occasion of Queen Victoria's Diamond Jubilee. The District Council decided to give each child in Brandon and Byshottles district a steel enamelled mug as a memento to commemorate the sixtieth anniversary of the Queen's accession to the throne. Seventy pounds was the sum of money seconded to pay for the mugs. Four thousand one hundred and seventy mugs at a cost of fourpence each were distributed. Thirteen hundred children from Brandon Colliery and Brandon Village each received a mug.

On Diamond Jubilee day, June 22nd the owners gave twenty guineas towards providing a tea for the colliery children. Brandon Miners' Lodge (A and B pits) celebrated the Jubilee by giving a substantial dinner and tea to the permanently disabled pitmen, superannuated members and widows. The dinner consisted of mutton, pork, lamb and veal pie; plum pudding followed as sweet. After tea field sports were run for the old men and women, foot and other races were organised. The old men were given three shillings each. The day's highly successful celebrations ended with the lighting of a massive bonfire on a vantage point on Pit House Fell.

On the third Saturday of July Durham miners held their 26th Annual Gala. Six speakers graced the two platforms, four of whom were Members of Parliament. Mr. Jim Robson of Brandon Lodge seconded a resolution from No. 2 platform. During the afternoon, under a merciless sun, crowds flocked from the racecourse to Durham's cathedral for the first ever Miners' Day service; the cathedral was packed to the doors on this especial occasion.

Brandon's representative on the .Brandon Urban District Council referred to the dire need for better lighting at Brandon Colliery railway station. The gas lamps promised twelve months ago have not yet been erected.

There were over one thousand entries in the livestock section, eight hundred in the floral department, and four hundred in the industrial section when Brandon Colliery Flower Show held its annual event in the field adjoining the school. Three large tents were erected to hold the exhibits. There were one hundred and fifty three entries for the foot handicap in which fifteen pounds were given in prizes. Bookmakers attended in force to cater for the betting fraternity. The judge for the racing had to be escorted from the grounds by several policemen, his verdicts not being popular. Trains ran from York — Sunderland — Newcastle — Middlesbrough and Hartlepool for the occasion. Two weeks after the foot handicap at the flower show, the judge's ruling was objected to and the race was re-run at the same venue. Thanks to the efforts of the Committee of Management: H. Goundry, H. Martin, W. Rounding, R. Robson, W. Brumley, E. Rowland, F. Lightfoot, and J. Ramsey, the event was a resounding success.

By the end of August forty-four residents of the colliery had died, once again the victims were mainly infants, a high percentage for eight months. Despite the high death rate there was an absence of infectious disease. Four children died from diarrhoea during that period.

At the meeting of the Brandon District Council it was stated that the open channels in single South Street and low Princess Street were very much in need of repair. The owners were served with notices to put in proper drains with traps.

During August Brandon Colliery's Busty Seam's agreement was confirmed;

Hat and Feather Fouth West advanced 12½%.

North Flat advanced 12½%.

Second West reduced 12½%.

Tichbourne's Cross-cut Second West reduced 5%.

Tichbourne's North Flat reduced 2½%.

The men in the B Pit Hutton seam asked for an advance on hewing prices in South Headways Landing East; Southways Landing South; Pity Me Narrow Bord whole; Pity Me 2nd North broken; Pity Me 1st North-east; 3rd North broken and 3rd North-east whole. Their request was not entertained, as the hewers concerned are not carrying out the decisions of January 8th 1894.

Putters in Brandon A Pit after a dispute with the overman, left work, the walk-out affects a number of coal hewers who are laid off work pending a settlement. Some of the hewers and putters affected help to make up Brandon's football teams. Five teams operate in the colliery area: Brandon Black Watch; Brandon United; Brandon Albion; Brandon Celtic and Meadowfield Rovers entertain lovers of the sport. Their games with Waldridge Fell, Gilesgate Moor Albions, Sleetburn Rising Stars, Sunnybrow Olympic and the Boyne Rising Star, produced a superabundance of goals. Consistent scorers for the local teams were Pat McVay, Edward Cummings, Tom Cahill, James Moran, Joe Smith and Jack Healey.

The Christmas season began with a heavy snowfall through which troops of carol singers plodded on their tour of the streets. Special services and entertainments were held in the various chapels.

1898

As usual the colliery buzzers welcomed in the New Year. First Footers were once again out in force, chanting hopefully, the rhyme,

'Happy New Year t'ye
God send ye plenty!
Where ye have one pound note,
I wish ye may have twenty'.

During the morning Brandon Celtic played Quebec St. Michael's in an Association Football game which Celtic won 6–4. Edward Cummings, Jack Healy, Joe Smith, Danny Doyle and Edward McVay entertained the fair crowd with skilful football. Brandon won 6–0 in the return visit in which Jack Healy, James Moran and Joe Smith shone. Yet another team has sprung up in Brandon; Brandon Villa versus Sherburn Hill Rovers produced good football which enabled the former team to win 2–1. Jack Clennell and George Robson scored for the Villa.

The sound of the New Year buzzers had barely faded when the hewers and putters of nine districts in the C Pit Brockwell Seam were asked to accept lower wages. The reductions varied from five per cent to seventeen per cent. One district was advanced eight per cent.

Open channels run alongside all colliery houses. One sink is provided for about twenty houses; as the channels are a serious threat to health, Brandon District Council asked the owners Messrs. Straker and Love, to put a sink in every two houses.

During March one case of typhoid fever and one of erysipelas were reported; these cases were treated at home as the hospital was kept in readiness for any case of smallpox that might occur in the district.

The surveyor reported that the scavenging contractor had not been doing his work. He had written to him four times, and had given him notice to clean out forty ashpits and privies which he had neglected.

A charity concert originally planned for the Miners' Hall had to be held in the much larger Brandon School. Seven hundred tickets were sold for the show, the proceeds went to nineteen year old John Graney who suffered an accident six months previously. He is now totally blind. All the artistes gave their services freely; Peter Keenan sang 'Milly Clare', Widow of Wicklow', and 'Death of Nelson'. Tom Connolly and Jim Mearman gave several pieces. These two young men are great favourites and their 'comicalities' proved most amusing.

On Tuesday night May 26th Mrs. Cahill waited anxiously in her South Street home. Her husband Paddy, a coal hewer in the C Pit, was long overdue from work. Paddy's deputy in the back-shift lived next door, he had returned from work, bathed and was dressed, ready for his night out. As he closed his door behind him, Mrs. Cahill shouted across the intervening yard wall, 'Paddy hasn't got home yet, have you seen him?' Fearing the worst, the deputy rushed to the pit. Paddy was found in his work place, he had been trapped, suffering a broken back, for two hours under a large stone. Paddy was taken home on a stretcher in the colliery ambulance.

Brandon Colliery Home Society's members organised the first old bird race of the season. Nine members sent ninety birds to Normanton for liberation. Great local interest was shown in the new Barker timing machine. Mr. Tom Bartle manipulated the instrument. Bart Plant's birds won first, second and third places with 794, 784 and 774. J. Richie and J. Johnson gaining third and fifth places for their lofts.

Another fatal accident in the B Pit. Adam Todd, driver lad son of William Todd a colliery brakesman, was killed in a most unfortunate accident. As Adam was driving a load of tubs, firing shots in the distance dislodged a stone, which falling on him, terminated his life. Young Adam Todd was buried in the graveyard at Brandon Village at the same time as John Henry Wharton, a twenty-three year old Sleetburn pitman who had been killed by a fall of stone in the Old Pit there. Over one thousand sympathisers from the two collieries crowded into the churchyard.

Excellent work by the committee guaranteed success for Brandon's fifth Flower, Livestock and Industrial Show. Mr. Bowes an able bandsman, conducted Brandon Brass Band which played throughout the day. One hundred and eighty doughty runners fancied their chance in the one hundred and twenty yards foot handicap race for prizes worth sixteen pounds ten shillings.

Tom Clennell of Brandon Colliery took a day off scoring for his local team when he married Jane Stronach of Ryhope at Durham Register Office. The couple moved into a colliery house provided by the owner.

In a colliery district the school Inspector was questioning the children as to their knowledge of the Bible. 'Why did Noah build the Ark?' asked the Inspector. The class was silent, then suddenly a bright-faced boy put up his hand.
'Well, Tommy?' said the Inspector.
'Please sir, it was 'cos 'is feyther cuddent get a colliery 'ouse', was the bright boy's reply.

The ever popular quoits attracted a large gathering of spectators when William Freak of Brandon Colliery challenged George Hunter of Sleetburn to a game for twenty five pounds a side. The conditions were ten yards on the sward. After a good game Freak emerged the winner by nine; the final score being Freak 41, Hunter 32.
A game of 'fives', another popular sport, took place on the alley adjoining Robert Richardson's hostelry at Broompark over the valley from Brandon Colliery. Gamblers and non-gambling spectators left the colliery environs to witness the battle. They took the narrow road skirting the fiery heaps, crossed the Sleetburn road and the River Deerness and up the incline to Broompark. The contestants with leather gloves on work hardened hands came over from the colliery. J. Liddle took on two men; J. Duffy elected to partner Peter Carey in a game of thirty-three chalks up for ten pounds a side. Bob Montgomery also from Brandon Colliery, was stake holder and referee for the game which Liddle who was five to four on favourite, won 33 chalks to 17.
On Christmas Eve Brandon United played a draw with East Howle 1—1 in an exciting football match watched by pitmen enjoying a long weekend rest. As Christmas Day fell on a Sunday they will take the Monday off. The day after New Year's Day will also be a holiday. To save friction the lodges were asked to send delegates to the colliery manager notifying him of their intention. It had been agreed in July 1881 that Christmas and New Years' Days should enforth by kept as holidays.

1899

The first pit casualty of the year occurred on January 11th. James Kidman, a twenty two year old putter, left his home 64 Sunderland Street just before six a.m. His journey to the A Pit was a short one. His shift was due to finish at four p.m. At three fifteen p.m. all tubs having been filled and put to the landing, James was standing alongside the full set which was ready and awaiting the arrival of the empty set. The oncoming run of tubs became derailed and knocked down several props and displaced two long baulks. A fall of roof engulfed James, he sustained severe injuries to his head and abdomen, and died the same night.

Ralph Cairns, a Brandon Colliery pitman and a regular player for the Institute team, was in good form. A billiards handicap was staged in Langley Moor's Grand Hotel; fourteen players participated in the two hundred up contest. Ralph notched second place, he had forty five start. His prize was a billiard cue in a case.

Ralph scored 127 for his team Brandon Colliery Institute when they travelled to Newton Cap near Bishop Auckland to play them in the Durham Miners' Billiards League in which all collieries in the county were eligible to play. Brandon's team scored 531; R. Cairns 127, T. Pattinson 150, J. McDonald 150, B. Walker 114, J. Doran 104. Newton Cap's team replied with 520.

In the same league run by Burroughs and Watts Ltd., Brandon beat Sunniside 521 to 501 who hope to reverse the decision when they come to Brandon for the return match.

The four year old daughter of Tom Turner, a colliery waggonway man, died in the Brandon Infectious Diseases Hospital. Four cases of scarlet fever and four cases of typhoid fever, three of whom came from one house, were reported. Sulphur candles and steam were recommended for stoving out the infected houses.

Sorrow too, for Robert Wray the popular landlord of the Colliery Inn, when he lost his fifty-four year old wife Mary. Mrs. Wray helped run the cricket team she had founded, she helped on of the Brandon Colliery football teams. Colliery sporting fans flocked to Brandon Village for her burial. Their twenty year old son Tom William died two years ago.

The twenty three stone Father Richard Mathias Hannon was a familiar figure in Brandon's streets. For the last nineteen years he has been in charge of St. Patrick's Mission at Langley Moor. He died in Durham County Hospital at the age of forty-nine. His successor, the Reverend Father Thorman from St. Mary's Cathedral in Newcastle, took over the Mission. A few days after his arrival he performed his first marriage ceremony when he married a Brandon Colliery couple, Edward Jones and Winifred Carrol. On Easter Sunday Peter Keenan married Mary Ann Doran from Crook.

The Reverend J. Lawson married ten couples in the space of two weeks in St. John's Church, all from Brandon Colliery. W. Humphries married Miss Jane Aberdeen at Durham Registry Office.

Geordie got married to a widow, and one morning as he was sitting at the Kist his marra, named Jim, said to him, 'Thoo's fond of a treat Geordie, getting married te the widow'.

'Nowt of the sort', replied Geordie, 'Aa think hev gettin' a bargain'.

'Hoo's that?' queried Jim.

'Wey', said Geordie, 'thoo sees she hes five lads workin' an' two big wenches, an' a fat bacon pig in the sty, an' thoo sees Jim, it only cost me a seven an' a tanner licence'.

Friday July 21st was no ordinary Friday, it was the day before the twenty-ninth Durham Miners' Gala. Paddy Moran, now fifteen and a putter in the A Pit, was finished for the week. He knelt over the tin bath set in the middle of the kitchen. His sister Mary washed his back, she was after a few pennies to spend at Brandon's Friday market. Paddy and his mates would not patronise the market on the eve of the Gala, they wanted their money for the 'big day'. Mary, proceeding with the back cleaning, inadvertently erased the button on Paddy's back exposing the raw flesh. 'Ouch!' howled Paddy. Later he smiled to himself. He almost shouted 'Close the bloody pit in and give the farmer his bloody field back!', an epithet often passing the lips of harrassed putters and helpers-up.

Brandon Lodge sent a request to the Joint Committee that three unmarried coal hewers working at the colliery who keep their parents and are heads of families, be allowed colliery houses free of rent. The three C Pit hewers are granted free colliery houses by the Arbitrator, Thomas Lambert Esq. Other collieries in the county seeing this as a test case, applaud the award.

Men and boys preparing themselves for work, women making school-children's breakfast, were aghast at the terrible news. Accounts were rife concerning the explosion which had occurred at 8 a.m. in the East Flat 'Jubilee' district at Brandon Colliery C Pit.

The seam employs 200 men, 70 of whom were at work at the time. The explosion was confined to a small area of the mine where shot firing operations were in progress one and three quarters of a mile from the shaft.

Francis Murphy a twenty year old putter and son of John Murphy, a retired pitman of Brandon Colliery and Enoch Griffiths, coal hewer, thirty years of age with a wife and two young children at 28 Park Street, were instant victims of the explosion.

Four other pitmen, William Carr, deputy; Frank Robson, putter; Ralph Broadbent, hewer and George Robson, putter were so severely injured that they died later at their homes. A total of six lives lost in this the second disaster in two years, twenty having died at Willington in a sister pit, another of the Straker and Love group of collieries.

James Liddle, deputy, although injured in the blast, together with another deputy Ralph Rumley, had to encounter foul air for a considerable distance in order to recover William Carr, whom they dragged out in an unconscious condition. Among the rescuers was Mr. Dakers, the overman who was overcome by stythe and had to be removed to the surface where Doctors Denholm and Green rendered medical aid.

Hundreds of people journeyed to Brandon Colliery both by road and rail causing obstruction near the pithead, seeking more news of the worst pit accident of the year in Durham county.

On Saturday August 19th the bodies of Ralph Broadbent, William Carr and George Robson were carried to their last resting place. Two other victims had already been interred. Brandon Colliery Band playing the 'Dead March' headed the procession of about one thousand sorrowing people.

It was the saddest sight Brandon Colliery's inhabitants have had to endure when the three victims were carried to their allotted places in Brandon Cemetery.

A survivor gave testimony of the brave and unselfish action of William Carr. As a deputy, charged with the safety of other men, and even though most seriously burnt, he deliberately put on one side the invitation to escape and went back. We are not rich enough in human life to pay a price as we paid in the explosion.

'Deeds have been done in the darkness of the mine, and amidst the most appalling dangers, which enoble our nature, and which if done in the light of day and before the world, would have covered those humble miners with glory'.

Two weeks after the disaster the sixth annual exhibition of the Brandon Society drew a record crowd. Visitors discussed the tragedy with survivors and rescuers as they moved round the three large marquees in a field near the pit. The number of livestock—poultry—pigeons—rabbits was also a record, being one short of a thousand. Many of the exhibitors were well known fanciers from distant parts of the country. There were one hundred and seventy four entries for the Handicap Foot Race, the handicapper was Matthew Bates, landlord of the Red Lion Inn.

Forty-seven cases of typhoid fever were reported at Bishop Auckland. As trains take shoppers to the stricken area every Saturday, there are fears of the disease spreading. Seven cases of typhoid fever at Brandon Colliery were admitted to the hospital. Disinfectant was distributed and infected clothing ordered to be destroyed. Thomas Burt, a twenty-five year old pitman, died from typhoid fever.

Owing to an epidemic of measles at the same time, both Brandon Colliery and St. Patrick's schools had a low percentage of attendance.

Supporters of quoit player William Freak of Brandon Colliery walked the mile to Langley Moor to bet and cheer him on in his game against J. Vickers of Toft Hill for £50. Despite the crowd's vociferous encouragement Freak trailed behind Vickers who won 41 chalks to 23.

At Christmas the Durham Provision Market had on offer beef from 6d. a pound, pork 6d. a pound, mutton 6d. a pound, veal 8d. a pound, bacon 4d. to 6d. a pound, hams 5d. to 6½d. a pound, potatoes 7d. a stone, tea at 1s. and 1s. 4d. a pound. Trains picking up at Brandon Colliery were full of eager shoppers and children keen to shop gaze.

1900

Brandon Colliery station employees gathered in Matt Wray's Colliery Inn. They began the New Year by celebrating with a dinner held annually. Their station master, Mr. Fothergill, tok the chair. After toasts to the 'Queen and Royal Family', 'Subscribers', 'Host and Hostess', Messrs. Nesbit, Rutherford, Brice and Roper entertained the company with harmony.

Paddy Moran, now sixteen, finished putting to start coal hewing as the Durham miners' wages were advanced five per cent. The increase to remain until the August meeting of the Board of Conciliation and not to be touched under any circumstances. The miners welcome the thought of a stabilised wage for six months.

Five years ago Mr. Green, draper, of Brandon Colliery and member of the Brandon Urban Council, stated that Brandon was one of the dirtiest and darkest places in the county. Once again he brought the matter up at the

Council meeting; he said that sanitary improvements are required in Brandon Colliery streets. In most cases there was only one sink for a whole street of houses, and during wet weather they overflowed onto the streets, several of which are in a bad state of repair. Another member of the Council said it was an abominable state of affairs, and a disgrace to a firm like Messrs. Straker and Love. Scavengers are not doing their job—they never saw the bottom of the netty.

Schools had a low percentage of attendance owing to the epidemics of influenza, whooping cough, measles and eczema. Jane and Matthew Wood lost their fifteen year old daughter, a victim of typhoid fever. One case of erysipelas and one of scarlet fever were reported.

The first quarterly meeting of the newly formed Brandon and District Anti-vaccination League, which, according to the promoters, has been formed for 'purposes of aggression and mutial defence' was held on Saturday, March 31st. Numerous people had been summoned for not having their children vaccinated against infectious diseases. It was stated that in Brandon alone something like ninety per cent were against vaccination.

A thirteen year old Brandon Colliery boy was summoned for a breach of the Mines Regulations Act. He unlocked his lamp while down the pit. He had used a nail to dismantle it, took out the gauze to get more light, then fitted the lamp together again. The court decided not to convict but ordered him to pay the court expenses. His father had given him a good thrashing. The court thought it the best deterrent.

On May 17th the Boers raised the siege of Mafeking. The next day it was declared official. The news called for celebration. The streets of Langley Moor presented a very gay appearance. An evening procession was formed consisting of representatives of mounted infantry, Boers and leading spirits of the war, and various other personages arrayed in grotesque outfits, the rear being brought up by an effigy of Kruger. Headed by the Browney Brass Band, the procession proceeded by way of Meadowfield to Brandon Colliery, the way being lighted by blazing torches which the processionists carried. The streets were thronged by eager sightseers, who gave hearty cheers for the hero of the hour, Lord Roberts, and the officers commanding the relief party. Burlesque bands, composed of 'Tom and Jerries', bugles, tin whistles and jews harps, caused much merriment, and there was a splendid display of fireworks. Collections were taken in aid of the Reservists' Fund.

Brandon cokemen collected £1.0s.3d. for the Durham Soldiers' and Sailors' Fund, Brandon A and B Pits donated £8.19s. while the Mechanics' and Enginemen sent their sixth instalment to the Fund, £1.11s.2d.

Corporal Shell of the 82nd Battery Royal Field Artillery now serving with the 6th Battery Western Division Durham Light Infantry in South Africa, wrote to his brother residing in Brandon Colliery. He sent a lengthy and interesting letter in which he said he had just finished six rough months fighting but had escaped injury. He thought the war would last another twelve months unless the British Government try some sterner methods— such as hanging or shooting all rebels, train wreckers, abusers of the white flag, and those who take no notice of the rules and usages of civilised warfare.

Let the Boers who are still in the field see that we are determined to put an end to their guerilla tactics etc. It is not the fighting but the marching which knocks the hearts out of the troops.

The football season got into swing with Brandon Rangers playing in the Durham and District League when they beat Dene Burn six goals to one; they beat Browney Rangers by the same margin. Stanley Moor were Rangers' next victims when they came to Brandon, they lost three goals to one.

The Good Templars gave a lantern entertainment in their Hall. A good audience appreciated the pictures thrown upon the screen which illustrated 'A tour round the world in 100 minutes'.

Mr. J. Jenkins, the new minister to Mount Calvary Methodist Chapel in Commercial Street, arrived in time to officiate at the Christmas services. He followed Mr. J. G. Bowran and he is the Chapel's ninth minister since it was opened some twenty-seven years ago.

Shops stocked up for Christmas with hams from sixpence halfpenny a pound and tea from one shilling and twopence to one shilling and ninepence a pound.

For the adventurous! A Guinea Hamper produced:—
One bottle of fine Scotch Whisky
One bottle of fine Irish Whisky
One bottle of fine Old Cognac Brandy
One bottle of fine London Gin
One bottle of fine Old Port
One bottle of Dinner Sherry
One bottle of fine Jamaica Rum
One bottle of fine British Wine.

A NEW CENTURY

The colliery buzzers and hordes of first footers seemed extra exuberant in their welcome to a New Year and the start of a New Century.

Ramsay Guthrie writes at length about the custom of first footing and yule-do's in his new book, 'Kitty Fagan'. The scene is laid in Brandon.

Brandon Miners' Lodge provided a dinner in the Miners' Hall for the old people of the colliery. Tables laden with beef, pork, mutton, turkeys and puddings greeted the guests. Tea was laid on in the afternoon. Afterwards the men received tobacco and pipes, the women each got a half-pound of tea. The old folk were further entertained in Brandon Colliery by the Jackson Minstrel Troupe. Songs and choruses were well rendered, and a burlesque sketch 'The Demon Phonograph' which closed the concert, was very amusing.

The nation mourned the loss of Queen Victoria who died at Osborne at half past six on Tuesday evening January 22nd after a reign of nearly sixty-two years and a half. Queen Victoria was crowned on June 28th, 1838.

The Brandon and Boyne Brass Bands led the procession from Langley Moor to St. John's Church, Meadowfield where the Rev. Joseph Lawson conducted a memorial service. The bands played the 'Dead March' from 'Saul'. Tradesmen in Brandon and the Boyne kept their shops closed all day on Saturday, February 2nd, the day of the funeral.

The coal depression continues—one pit in the county has given eight hundred men notice to quit work, another colliery has handed out two hundred notices. Miners at Brandon Colliery are apprehensive for the future.

Brandon Colliery deputies, despite the dim outlook in the coal trade, held their first social, it was a huge success. Mr. Thomas Parrish in the name of the deputies, asked Mr. T. L. Elwin the colliery manager to take the chair.

There were sixty applicants for the posts of Surveyor, salary £120 per annum and Inspector or Nuisances, salary £100 per annum. Surveyor Mr. R. Gardiner had hitherto done both jobs for Brandon and Byshottles Urban District Council.

By the end of March eighteen Brandon Colliery residents had been buried. During the month the measles epidemic spread to Brandon Colliery and caused five deaths. Browney British, St. Patrick's and Brandon Colliery schools had a low percentage owing to the eipidemic.

Brandon Institute played the final game of the season when they played Ryhope Miners' Hall before a large crowd at Brandon. Both billiards teams were in good form and spectators enjoyed one of the best games to be played in Brandon Institute. Ralph Cairns and Bob Cairns each scored 150; J. McDonald 141; J. Pratt 109 to narrowly win by twenty points.

Brandon finished in the middle of the Houghton and District Billiard League consisting of seven colliery villages. They climbed to second position in the Burroughs and Watts Miners' League.

Friendly Societies held a Church Parade. The procession was headed by the Brandon section of the 2nd Durham Volunteer Artillery, and the Sleetburn section paraded with Brandon, Meadowfield and Langley Moor to the Brandon St. Agatha's Mission Church. The following societies were also represented: Druids, Free Gardeners, Rational Association Oddfellows, Sons of Temperance, Rechabites, Brandon and Langley Moor I.O.G.T. members. Eight pounds ten shillings was collected en route.

John Allsop, Bob Thompson, Thomas Kane, James Gillings and George Bainbridge, all miners, lost an infant during August. Scarlet fever and measles claimed most of the fifty-three victims who succumbed during the first eight months of the year.

There were seventeen cases of mild typhoid fever. The large and insanitary privy-ashpits were an important factor in the spread of disease. Ten patients occupy Brandon Hospital, six scarlet fever and four typhoid fever.

Despite epidemics of typhoid fever, scarlet fever and measles, newcomers came to sample what the colliery had to offer. Owen Woods decided to leave his homeland. The potato crop had failed; times were hard. Owen, the eldest son of a family living in Dundalk, Ireland, managed the family farm. He left the farm to his youngest brother and set sail to England and Brandon Colliery. Owen married Jane Keenan, they bought a house in newly-built Station Avenue built by a New Brancepeth building contractor also named Woods.

Brandon's population is now 15,573, an increase of 1,333 since the 1891 census was taken.

Coal owners and pitmen were united on one issue. The government put a Coal Tax on export duty of one shilling per ton to help fight the Boer War. Durham's miners bitterly opposed it, as did the owners. The latter consented to closing the pits for two days to allow pitmen to hold mass meetings in protest.

Fifty-eight year old Alex Welch spent his shift shunting trucks back and forth at the A Pit. He ran his loco into the engine shed. He collapsed in his cabin and died before medical assistance could be procured. Brandon Variety Social Party held a dance for his widow. Seventy couples attended, the proceeds amounted to £2. 3s. 6d.

The truce between master and man was short lived. The owners, despite the favourable state of the coal trade during the last three months sought a reduction of 6¼%. The men's representatives eventually secured the reduction of 5%.

Another year ended on a dismal note, seventy colliery folk having died, the last one on New Year's Eve.

1902

Two hundred and forty four coke ovens each with a ten feet diameter and two hundred and sixty four with a ten and a half feet diameter lie sprawled on the south side of the colliery. When in use their dull red glow hovers over the colliery rows and can be seen from miles away. Straker and Love appealed to the Assessment Committee respecting deductions when the August rate for the coke ovens is assessed.

The conversation turned upon the earth revolving, when an old man said, 'A'll nivvor believe the world gans roond, Aa've heard it monny a time, but nebody will persuade me that'. One of the company drew an imitation of the globe and was proceeding to explain when he was stopped by the old man. 'It's nee use', he said, 'It's nee use trying ter push that doon me throat. Aa've had far arder men than you at me, and it's arl nee use'.

'Well, but listen', the other replied.

'No, no', continued our old friend. 'Aa can prove Aa'm reet. Aa've worked in the pit since Aa was nine years old, Aa've gone in both first and back shift, and Aa've gone hyem at all times of the neet; and the coke ovens were always opposite our back door'.

The walls of the Red Lion Inn failed to veil the sound of men's angry voices. Some dispute concerning the racing of pigeons would have ended in blows but for the intervention of the landlord.

Next day, January 4th saw trains converge on Durham. A crowded train carried excited passengers en route for the city, a distance of two and a half miles from Brandon Colliery's railway station. Without ceremony the shops in the old city were illuminated by electricity. Shoppers were delighted; the new form of lighting greatly enhanced the window display.

The recent death of William McKay left a sad gap in the ranks of the local colliery Union Lodge. He had been a member of the Durham Miners' Association from its commencement. Many parts of the county had seen William work actively in the cause of the Union in its earliest days. Brandon Miners' Lodge sent a letter of sympathy to his widow.

Thomas Wright finished his coal hewing shift at twenty minutes past four on pay Friday afternoon. Thomas headed homewards; his sister Catharine would have a meal ready for him in their colliery house in Sunderland Street. A long night lay ahead. Thomas liked a drink of beer, he would turn out around eight o'clock; his favourite pub, Matt Bates' Red Lion Inn, lay snug in the hollow at the foot of the colliery ballast heaps whose summits lay quite near his home.

Thomas, a quiet lad, had moved with his family into the colliery rows eight months previously, he was little known in the colliery of twenty-six streets and several hundred houses.

Just after eight p.m. Thomas crossed the ballast heap on which James Auton of 56 Park Street and a miner at the colliery, had erected a potato chip van. A cold January night with a thin covering of snow. Jim looked forward to good trade; besides the regular pedestrian traffic between Brandon Colliery and the Boyne people came from the rows for delicious fried chips. Customers called on the way home after Red Lion Inn closing time. Friday night being pay night was his best night.

At half past ten Thomas Smith, a putter living at 18 South Street, and his mate Andrew McGregor also a putter, from Durham Street, called into the pub having spent the earlier part of the night at the Boyne. They saw James Lynch from Sunderland Street, a coal hewer, seated in the taproom in heated conversation with a swarthy twenty eight year old Brandon Colliery coal hewer. Their talk, a continuation from two weeks previously, concerned the flying of racing pigeons. Robert Wilson, Joseph Pouton and Caleb Lee, all miners, were present in the taproom.

At closing time Thomas Wright climbed the heap's acclivity on which the chip potato van and several pigeon crees were perched. He ordered his usual three-penny worth, a drink of beer had put an edge on his appetite.

An argument and scuffle took place just at the fringe of light thrown by the chip van's single oil lamp. Blows were exchanged. The noise of the battle attracted some thirty people from nearby colliery houses. People returning from the Boyne joined the inquisitive crowd. James Pouton and the swarthy miner had words, more blows were struck. Thomas Wright pulled Pouton away from the conflict. Thomas fell; a fierce pain gripped him, he felt his body, low down; blood saturated his fingers.

Catharine Wright, attracted by the commotion, left the house at eleven thirty, her brother had not arrived home. She joined the milling crowd. Thomas Wright was carried home in a state of shock; he was placed on the kitchen mat. On examination he was found to have stab wounds in the bowels, part of which were protruding.

Police Constable Forrest was called. Dr. McIntyre was sent for to attend Joseph Pouton in his home 16 Durham Street, he had a cut in his right thigh, a suspected knife wound. The doctor was requested to call on James Lynch who suffered from a cut on the left thigh, also thought to be knife inflicted. Whilst attending to James he was asked to call on the Wright's home. Dr. McIntyre on examining Thomas Wright, diagnosed stab wounds and ordered an ambulance for his prompt removal to Durham Hospital. The swarthy miner was immediately put under arrest.

There were four applicants for the post of Surveyor for the Brandon and Byshottles Urban District Council. Mr. J. McKenzie of Leighton Buzzard was chosen. A salary of £140 a year—payable quarterly—goes with the job.

A successful cafe chantant was held in the colliery school by members of the Wesleyan Society. Two of the most interesting items of the three day entertainment were a nigger sketch, 'The Darktown Parish Council', and the highly acclaimed 'Melodious Aldiborontophoscophonium Band'. The latter is to give a performance in the Durham Town Hall. Photos and curios from South Africa were viewed with much interest.

The recent stabbing affair took precedence in colliery gossip. Eight days after the incident, tragic news was discussed. Thomas Wright had died in hospital from peritonitis. The man in custody was given a further remand; the case was now one of murder.

People left Brandon Colliery in the early hours to hear the case at the Assize Court in Durham. One man walked six miles from Chester-le-Street and appeared at the door of the courthouse at seven a.m. Most of the seats in the court were taken by women.

After five hours' deliberation the court was cleared. Women and girls grumbled—they would miss the verdict. A chastened and repentant prisoner received his sentence. On a recommendation to mercy the prisoner was sentenced to twelve years penal servitude.

The death rate in the colliery rows was very heavy in April; a month during which twelve cases of scarlet fever and one of typhoid fever were detected, it was twice that of a normal month. Five patients were removed to the Isolation Hospital. Thirty houses were stoved to prevent the spread of the disease.

It was proposed to built a caretaker's cottage near the hospital. The caretaker at present lives in a house some distance away in the colliery rows. Lord Boyne has agreed to lease the site of the Fever Hospital and additional ground for the building of a caretaker's lodge for fifty years at the yearly rent of £7. 10s. These generous terms were made mainly on account of the building being a public hospital. At a meeting of the Brandon Urban District Council it was decided to carry on with the work.

James Liddle at forty-two was a popular and efficient deputy overman. He was president of the local Deputies' Association and a member of Meadowfield Store committee. James was injured in the C Pit explosion in 1899, despite his injuries he assisted in the rescue operations afterwards. He was drawing timber in the same seam when a fall of stone killed him instantly. Andrew Houghton and Martin Tunney, hurrying to the spot, removed the stone.

Hugh McDermott also involved in the 1899 explosion rescue, a miner keen to learn, was elected secretary of Brandon Technical Education Committee for twelve months. He replaces John Gillis who has left the district.

As 50,000 attended the 31st Miners' Big Meeting in Durham, Edward Hoare mourned the loss of Winifred his infant daughter. Edward Hewitson and J. T. Gates both miners, each lost an infant son.

After long delays due to the Prince's illness, August 9th saw the coronation of sixty-one year old Edward and Princess Alexandria.

The coronation festivities coincided with the declaration of peace. The Boer War was finished after 20,000 lives had been forfeit. Trooper Huntley, Corporal Shell and Private Storey, all Brandon men, have served in South Africa. The latter was seriously ill with fever while serving abroad.

To help make the celebrations a success Brandon Literary Institute gave £25; Straker and Love £25; Brandon and Byshottles Co-op Society gave £15. The Committee has £108 in hand. The Committees of the A, B and C Pits together with the Literary Institute provided a further £20, which when shared out amounted to seven shillings to each old person living in the colliery.

The Brandon District Council procured 3,572 coronation mugs at four shillings per dozen. Each child received a mug, while children between the ages of three and sixteen, together with the aged, infirm, poor and widows, were provided with a substantial tea.

Local volunteers and members of Brandon Band arranged sports in the colliery field—the torchlight procession, display of fireworks and the bonfire on the hill drew ecstatic crowds.

Another great Peace Parade in which prizes were given for the best comic horseman, best comic cyclist toured the area. Fancy dress was the order of the day; revellers on horse and on foot vied with one another for prizes. The parade meandered through Langley Moor up Brandon's long Sunderland Street, round Meadowfield and on to Littleburn. Streets en route were decorated with banners and an assortment of streamers.

Brandon Colliery provided a field on which an old men's race took place. There was a putters' contest; rails being laid on which young putters displayed their prowess at the job. Rockets were fired, a balloon was released. At ten p.m. a huge crowd cheered as the colliery manager, Mr. E. L. Elwin, lit a massive bonfire.

Residents of the area are glad that some progress is being made with the scheme for the construction of an electric railway between Durham and Brandon. Plans are out for the sheds to be built at Brandon.

A provisional committee has been working hard in Brandon with a view of establishing a Workmen's Club. There is only one public house, a tied one, which is considered inadequate for a village of some five thousand inhabitants. At a large meeting presided over by James Turner, the following resolutions were unanimously agreed to:—

1)   'That in the opinion of this meeting the proposal to establish a workmen's club in Brandon deserves the hearty support of all classes'.

2)   'That those present at the meeting pledge themselves to use their best exertions to make the undertaking as successful as possible'.

James Turner was elected President, George Winter Secretary, James Wilkinson Treasurer, and a committee of ten members.

Mr. Turner spoke of the needs in the district of a club of an educational character. He urged all present to make the club worthy of its name, and not a drinking club as it had been so-called by some people who did not know the intentions of the Provisional Committee.

The publication of the foregoing brought a swift response. At a public meeting of the various religious and temperance societies presided over by the Rev. Mr. Day, it was unanimously resolved that each society petition the promoters of the proposed workmen's club with a view of showing the evil results which the meeting·believed would necessarily follow from the increased facilities for drinking such a club would provide. It was also decided to hold an open-air meeting on the subject at an early date.

The Durham Light Railway was the dream child of William Dickinson, an active worker in local affairs, who died in 1896. He spent most of his working life at Brandon Colliery, he founded the Brandon Colliery Order of Foresters. A commencement will be shortly made with the construction of the tramway from Durham to Brandon. Garden holders at Meadowfield have received intimation that all garden produce must be cleared up by September, as the land is required for the construction of sheds for the tramcars.

When the Brandon line is completed there is to be a terminus near the Saint Margaret's Cemetery, Durham. A flippant citizen remarked that there will then be a new version of Gray, something after the style—

'The path of the tramcar
Leads but to the grave'.

After six months of work the new club inaugurated by the Brandon Centre Ward and Meadowfield Social Club and Institute Limited, was formally opened by Mr. Thomas Carr in the absence of the treasurer, Mr. Turner. The premises occupied by Mr. Robert Hedley and owned by Mr. Frank Foster were bought at a cost of £500. Membership is confined exclusively to workmen residing or working within the limits of Brandon Centre Ward and Meadowfield, up to the present time over 200 workmen have signed their willingness to become members. The shares are of the value of £3, which can be paid by instalments, the lowest instalment being 2s. 6d.

During December eighty-four children were absent from Brandon Infant School, victims of measles and scarlet fever. Miss Kirkup is their mistress, Thomas Ralph Hepple is headmaster.

Brandon, last season's champions of the Houghton Billiard League, met the sunners-up, Silksworth Miners' Hall in Brandon Literary Institute. A large crowd gathered to watch the play-off of a League fixture. Great excitement prevailed. A brilliant game was played, the best ever witnessed in the Institute. For Brandon John Pratt compiled breaks of 51, 27 and 17 (unfinished). Brandon players Robert Cairns 139, Ralph Cairns 85, John Pratt 150, Archie Robson 150. Total scores Brandon 524: Silksworth Miners' Hall 521. Brandon won by three points.

1902 saw the birth of the Brandon and Byshottle Co-operative Store at nearby Meadowfield. The building has a frontage of 152 feet. A butchering department has an area of 264 feet done out in glazed bricks. Upstairs is a large Central Hall big enough to accommodate about six hundred people. The building cost about £14,000 and is lit throughout by electricity.

Bannerettes and streamers stretched across the street at Meadowfield presented quite a festive appearance. At 1.45 p.m. a procession headed by the Brandon and Browney Bands traversed the principal streets. Motor cars driving wagons laden with products of the Wholesale Society were a feature of the proceedings. Of the 2,420 electors in the Brandon area, 1,094 were full members of the Store on its opening day.

1903

Peter Keenan, a labourer at Brandon Colliery, died on New Year's Day at the age of fifty-two.

Brandon Colliery school is poorly attended due to the prevalence of measles and scarlet fever. William Simpson, a labourer, lost two infant sons; Thomas Jones and James White, both pitmen, each lost a son, all were victims of scarlet fever. Seven cases of smallpox were reported in Durham City. Colliery folk are fearful of the dread disease spreading.

While the new schools for the children of St. Patrick's, Langley Moor, was nearing completion, a serious fire occurred at Brandon. The wooden stable housing three horses and a large quantity of harness belonging to the Barnes brothers was left a total wreck. Crowds, drawn by the huge blaze, were helpless. The three animals suffocated from heat and smoke. The brothers suffered a great loss as the stable and contents were not insured. Great public sympathy went out to the brothers in their misfortune.

Tired dancers emerged from Brandon School at four a.m. at the end of the first March dance. The spiteful wind struck steamed up bodies; couples were whisked home by the March gale which whipped along at ninety miles an hour. Many scared inhabitants, awakened by the unearthly howling, dared not retire for further rest. Broken roof slates crashed to the ground, chimney pots, bricks, ridging and spouting were dislodged. Glass in several of the street lamps was blown out and broken by the force of the gale.

Thankfully the gale favoured the new St. Patrick's School at Langley Moor which was opened to take up to three hundred pupils. Straker and Love, Brandon Colliery owners, made a donation of fifty pounds towards the cost of the building.

Hugh McDermott, the able secretary of Brandon Science and Art Classes, desirous of helping the funds for technical evening classes, organised a lengthy concert. Artistes from Newcastle, Durham and Darlington entertained a crowded Central Hall in the new Meadowfield Co-operative Society building.

Stables to house one hundred pit ponies nestled near the Busty Seam A Pit shaft. Nearby a drift was begun down to the Brockwell Seam. George Miller, an eighteen year old sinker together with the two Bragon brothers, was assigned the task of firing and removing the debris. On completion of the arduous task the management had about five score of Busty coal tubs lowered down daily. These inferior coals were mixed with the Brockwell Seam's best coking coal and sent to the surface to feed the coke ovens. Farmer, the big horse, manoeuvred the tubs when they reached the Brockwell level.

Hugh McDermott, Mark Bell, John Felton, William Rutter, William Attess, John Pinkney, Michael Murphy, all miners, were vociferous in their protest to the removal of the one and a quarter per cent increase in wages the Durham miners were granted just four months before. It was a Red Letter Day for pony putters when their wages were advanced threepence a day.

The first August Bank Holiday granted to miners, albeit without pay, was duly celebrated by the Brandonians. To commemorate the occasion a walking competition and sealed handicap were arranged. Ex-Superintendent Burrell of the Colliery Inn gave money prizes; a local business man Mr. Dodgson, gave a suit of clothes and one guinea.

Sixteen stockily built pitmen of varying ages, whose pale skin denoted their occupation, gathered in the precincts of the A Pit. Cage pulley wheels were conspicuously silent. The route took in the Station Road — Browney Colliery — Burnigill Bank — Sunderland Bridge — alongside the River Wear to the Dairy Lane — on to Brancepeth Road to terminate at the starting point, a circular race of six miles. A. Tullock was first, Masher Kennedy came in second. The winners of the sealed handicap were Masher Kennedy first, Bob Freeman second, and A. Tullock third.

Some miners, especially the younger ones, talk of emigrating to British Columbia where they are promised plenty of work; with wages from nineteen shillings to twenty-eight shillings a day a move could be lucrative. Mr. John Wilson, M.P. had a letter from the President of the United Mineworkers of America discouraging men going to the Fernie District of British Columbia where wages are not high as promised and conditions of labour are not favourable.

Work is assured; George Emmerson, son of George Emmerson a Brandon Colliery miner, has been awarded a first class certificate of competency, thus qualifying him as a mine manager. He has passed examinations each year since 1897.

Tragedy dogged the Crozier family. Thomas Crozier, married and living at No. 6 Single Sinderland Street, at the age of twenty-seven was a coal hewer in Brandon Colliery Hutton Seam. Whilst outbye bound at his shift's end he detected the approach of the fast moving set of empty tubs running inbye. Whilst showing concern for the safety of a lad following behind, Thomas was struck by the set. A very large crowd attended the popular young man's funeral. The Crozier family has been connected with the colliery since coal was first found in 1856. Thomas' father was killed whilst at work at nearby Browney Colliery; two of his wife's brothers also met with a similar fate at the same colliery.

Talk of the Crozier accident had barely subsided when news of thirteen year old Albert Peel's fatal accident was reported. He was an underground pony driver.

As the Christmas festive season approached Edward Rumley, a twenty-nine year old coal hewer was buried under a fall of stone. He death completed a trio of fatal accidents at Brandon Colliery during the year.

On Christmas Eve a conversazione was started in the Colliery School in connection with the Mount Beaulah Lodge of the I.O.G.T. A good crowd enjoyed a programme of songs and other items which were rendered in first class style. Two capital sketches, entitled 'Wanted a lecturer' and 'Saved from crime' were given by the Grand Templar Sketch Party composed of Brothers J. Young, Tom Clark, M. Porter, Robert Forster, J. Young and Misses Naisbitt, F. Skelton, A. Tynen and M. Naisbitt.

Mr. J. Roxby newly arrived in Brandon Colliery as Minister to Mount Calvary Methodist Chapel on the departure of Mr. Jenkins, was busy up to the year's end performing burial rites. He interred Thomas the infant son of Steve Stringer, miner. The child was the forty-fourth colliery resident to die during the year. the majority of whom were infants.

1904

Out of forty-two applicants for the post of surveyor to the Brandon Urban Council just vacated by Mr. J. McKenzie, Mr. George Donkin was chosen to fill the position. The appointment is worth £140 a year. He is well known in the area having served in the City Surveyor's office.

Three cases of scarlet fever and one of smallpox were admitted to Brandon's hospital in the first week of the New Year. There were also two cases of diphtheria from one family. Four deaths occurred with startling suddenness: R. Ewens, Tom and Edward Pattinson, all miners, each lost an infant. Twenty year old Catherine Kennick joined the children.

After a long lay off the pits were re-opened. Jubilation was short-lived; owing to trade depression the pits fell to working slack time. Matt Pigford, Alf Laws, Nichol Adamson, Robert Howe, John Thornton, Edward Hoare and Paddy Moran were among the four hundred men who were put onto the relief fund.

George Emmerson junior had not long to wait for a post of importance. His workmates at Brandon Colliery presented him with a handsome rolled top secretaire on his leaving to take up the more lucrative position of Under-manager at nearby Oakenshaw Colliery under the same firm, Straker and Love. Mr. Elwin, manager of Brandon Colliery, made the presentation in Brandon School. A pleasant evening was spent and concluded with the National Anthem.

Sixteen students won a total of nineteen certificates at the Brandon Technical Instruction Classes. A free concert was arranged by Hugh Mc-Dermott and held in the Co-operative Hall. Mr. William Whiteley of Durham successfully coached the various classes for the examination. Society of Arts — Arithmetic — shorthand and book-keeping being taught.

The junior examination for shorthand was held in the Brandon Miners' Hall where eight students, George Dowson, W. Wylde, George Curl, F. Adamson, Thomas Green, Thomas Reed, Harold James and George Bainbridge gained a Pitman's Elementary Certificate. They received their awards in a crowded Brandon School along with ambulance students, billiard players, medal winners of the Houghton-le-Spring Billiards League and members of the Brandon and District Carbine Club Morris Tube Competition. Fr. Thorman of St. Patrick's, Brandon's vicar and curate, doctors and local officers graced the proceedings.

Doctors McIntyre and Denholm attended William Barnes, a thirty-seven year old coal hewer. William, whilst at work hewing a jud in the 'A' Pit was buried under a fall of stone which severely crushed and broke both legs. He died at his home 3 Russell Street at eight o'clock the same night. His widow and five children mourn his loss. The children are pupils of nearby Brandon School which is closed owing to an epidemic of measles in the colliery.

Only a month after Will Barnes' accident another fatal incident oc-curred in the same seam when twenty three year old Thomas Coleman was trapped under a fall of stone. William McCabe, a putter to Coleman, notified James Wilkinson, deputy overman who found Coleman under a four feet square stone. He had died instantly with a broken neck and back.

At the Brandon Urban Council meeting reference was made to the proposed Durham to Brandon tramway. The chairman said the scheme had been dropped, presumably through lack of money. It was suggested that buses run between Brandon and Durham would do a 'roaring trade' especially at the pay weekends. Durham City shopkeepers regret the collapse of the Brandon tramway scheme, they believed it would bring them increased custom.

News of the Council's intention of lighting the district by means of electricity helped offset local disappointment regarding the tramway pro-ject. The estimated cost of the work is £1893 to replace the few gas and oil lamps in the area.

Joseph McDonald, James Connolly, Bob Grimes, Tom Goundry, Tom Cameron, William Cummings and Thomas Smith, coal hewers and family men, after suffering a five per cent reduction in wages, had little money to celebrate the thirty-third Miners' Gala at which bands and banners moved in continuous procession from eight a.m. to noon. Brandon Colliery banner, preceded by a concourse of colliery supporters and cavorting youths, was played in by a proud prize silver band. The band only two days before had travelled to Marske where their Horticultural Show held a band contest. Brandon Colliery played the test pieces 'Songs of Schubert' and 'La Favorita' superbly to beat all opposition. They had also been successful at Witton Park, having won the first prize of £8 in the band contest there. They also came a close second to win 10s. in the March contest; the band's solo cornettist W. Gordon won the cornet medal.

Brandon Colliery once again harbours infectious disease. Enteric fever struck West Street. On inspection only one of the houses was found defective, having a damp pantry. One of the enteric cases occurred in the house which had a cesspool under the pantry window. Ten houses were stoved out and thirty-five articles disinfected by steam. Disinfectants were supplied for use in the infected houses.

A typhoid fever victim was removed from 18 East Street to Brandon's Isolation Hospital. The two roomed house with eight occupants, six of whom sleep in one bedroom which averages seven feet in height from floor to ceiling, is one in a row of nineteen sprawling a few yards from the 'A' Pit where a number of miners have just received notice to cease work.

The slackness of the coal trade has seriously affected the coke works. It has meant the closure of a large number of nearby coke ovens. 'Little Ireland' comprising South, East and Railway Streets houses sturdy Irishmen who operate the coke ovens who are worried for their large families.

A further outbreak of enteric fever necessitated the removal to hospital of twelve of the eighteen cases found in the colliery rows, one of whom died there. Dr. Smith reported that he could not find the cause of the enteric fever, but was of the opinion that the disease has been spread by means of the open channels which exist all over Brandon Colliery. The hospital is full and the services of another nurse are being sought. West, Newcastle, Durham, North and East Streets supplied most victims. Eleven of the colliery's twenty-six streets contributed to the total.

A Littleburn fruiterer drove his cart the one mile to Brandon Colliery. The collecting box nestling among the cart's contents proved tempting to the twelve year old boy, he stole the book worth one shilling and sixpence. He was fined ten shillings and ordered to have six strokes of the birch rod.

Geordie was in possession of an old, feeble, half-blind horse, and a few of his friends are always poking fun about it. Meeting Bill recently, the latter asked sarcastically, 'Wey Geordie, hoo much can thee galloway draa?'

'Bi gox', sharply retorted Geordie, 'he seems te be yable ta draa thor attintion of aa'll thor fyeuls in the plyece!'

The third fatal accident of the year occurred when William Crozier, a twenty seven year old coal hewer in the 'B' Pit was buried under a fall of stone.

Two years ago the premises in Commercial Street were taken over as a Workmen's Club for the Centre Ward of the district and Meadowfield, for the initial outlay of £500. Increased accommodation was needed for the four hundred members. The major portion of the work in alterations has been helped out by members, owing to the tenders for the job being too high. Some £1,615 has been spent on the Club.

The day's programme included a tea in the Miners' Hall where six hundred guests were catered for. Following the meal a concert was held in the club's new billiard room at which a gold key was presented to James Turner, the club's first president. Silver mounted umbrellas were presented to the secretary James Wilkinson and the treasurer George Winter.

The fever epidemic, having raged for weeks in the colliery rows, shows no sign of abating; two more deaths occurred, just as the old October fatal case is that of Mr. Thompson of Sunderland Street, who had just completed arrangements to emigrate to Canada, but now leaves a widow to mourn his sad loss. Brandon Hospital now houses twenty seven enteric fever cases. Three of scarlet fever, together with three cases of diphtheria. Two nurses have been engaged to nurse the victims. Seventeen houses were fumigated and sixty two articles disinfected by steam. There was a low percentage of scholars attending Brandon Colliery school owing to the prevalence of whooping cough, typhoid and scarlet fever.

The drains in West and Durham Streets are in a very bad state. There's need for sanitary reform in Brandon Colliery. It is known that there are people living on the top of drains, which, in the event of heavy rains, burst through the ground floor, compelling the residents to take flight to the upper rooms. Householders aver that such conditions foster diseases of every nature.

One of the finest treats ever was given in Brandon School over Christmas, when the Mount Beulah Lodge I.O.G.T. gave its fifth annual conversazione. The programme consisted of songs, humorous recitals, duets, dances and sketches. Seventy four of Brandon Colliery's old people were admitted free to the front seats. The four day event was concluded with a substantial tea for the old folk.

On New Year's Eve the colliery school was once again the time of activity when five hundred sat down to good things provided by the lady members of St. Agatha's Mission. Games and dancing were indulged in afterwards to make their annual social a success.

1905

In a New Year game Brandon Institute played Langley Moor in the Houghton League Billiards series. J. Pratt, W. Cairns, J. McDonald and A. Robson each scored 150 to beat the visitors 600 to 401.

St. John's Church draws a good number of worshippers from Brandon Colliery; to satisfy the needs of a growing congregation the church was thoroughly renovated and enlarged, a north aisle being added at a cost of £4,000. The church now seats four hundred and fifty.

Mary Jane Hunter bid her husband Thomas good morning. Thomas, a forty-six year old deputy, left his home in Queen Street for another shift in Brandon Colliery's 'C' Pit. He was drawing a jud at 10.30 a.m. some two hours after leaving home, when a fall of stone engulfed him. Ralph Rumley and Thomas Robson, both coal hewers in the First West District of the West Flat recovered the body in half an hour. A large concourse of mourners attended his funeral in Brandon Village graveyard.

Tragedy followed tragedy. Seventeen year old Phillip McKenna, a strong seventeen year old pit lad, was assistant onsetter in the 'B' Pit. His job was to help unload the empty tubs from the cage and replace them with full tubs of coal for removal to the surface. He lived in 2 South Street and was a member of the Catholic Drum and Fife Band. His father, Phillip McKenna, is chairman of the United Irish League. Young Phillip whilst at work was fatally crushed between the cage and the shaft buntin.

On March 8th followers of John Wesley, who since 1872 assembled every Sunday in one of Brandon Colliery's two roomed cottages, celebrated the laying of the foundation stone for a new church in the Station Road. Three months later on June 12th the New Wesleyan Church was opened. The building cost £1,500 and holds about two hundred people.

Builders were again busy when the library of the Colliery Institute was enlarged. The Institute, a much used building, caters for the literary needs of the five hundred and eighty two who work the colliery's A. B and C Pits.

Three M.P.s attended the thirty-fifth annual Miners' Gala, one of whom was Kier Hardie, a great fighter for miners' rights. Brandon Colliery banner was among the eighty-nine banners which could be seen at one time from Durham's Saddler Street.

Meadowfield Co-operative Society opened a Kinema showing films and variety shows. Patrons from Brandon Colliery and district are now spared the journey to Durham hitherto involved when such entertainment was sought.

William Underwood at twenty-eight years of age had worked underground since the age of twelve when he left Brandon Colliery school. He lived in the long High Street and hewed coal in the 'A' Pit. Thomas Hewitt a putter, ran William's empty tub into the hewing place. Thomas had gone some thirteen yards with a full tub of coal when he heard William Underwood shout. On returning to the place Thomas found him dead, he had been almost buried under a fall of stone. William was the forty-seventh fatal accident victim of the colliery's forty-nine years of existence.

FIFTY YEARS OF AGE

Colliery buzzers, as usual, announced the entry of the New Year, a year during which the colliery celebrates its fiftieth year of existence. Three seams employing nearly six hundred men, twenty-six streets with their hundreds of houses, innumerable coke ovens, four chapels, a school, two inns, a workmen's club, literary institute, a street of shops, a weekly market and gigantic colliery spoil heaps have emerged since the first sod was lifted almost half a century ago.

Hundreds of families have drifted into the colliery, some stayed on. The majority, nomad like, ventured further afield, some of whom even elected to seek work abroad. A railway was nearing construction as the first immigrants arrived. Those who chose to settle, to work and watch the colliery grow, experienced a major colliery strike and soup kitchens, distress and sorrow in the wake of numerous epidemics, shock and overwhelming sympathy at the time of the 'C' Pit explosion when six lives were lost. They expressed horror when crimes of passion claimed the lives of two victims, pride on the safe return of volunteer soldiers from the African Boer War.

Business men Robert Wray and Matt Bates, both publicans; John Hedley and John Longstaff, grocers; Andrew Glass and Thomas Long also grocers; Green and Willis, drapers; Barbara Madgin, butcher; and the Workmen's Club all look to the day when the Orton, Cross-cuts and South-East Districts, naming but a few of the many scattered seams at the colliery work full time. Success in their business is centred on a thriving colliery. The Literary Institute is a haven for out of work miners where draughts, billiards, dominoes and library book reading are indulged in.

There was great excitement when the intrepid Colonel Cody manoeuvred his flying machine over Brandon Colliery. The aeroplane was seen to descend in the vicinity of Pit House. Twenty-one year old Paddy Moran, Billy Miller and a number of temporary unemployed miners, excitedly ran the one and a half miles to give Colonel Cody a towing start. Amid cheers and much hand waving the machine passed over Ushaw College and eventually arrived at Newcastle Town Moor.

An expectant crowd gathered in the colliery field to greet the arrival of the diminutive pit pony on whose flat cart perched a huge ball. Ample ropes held the sphere, its bulk overflowing the sides of the carriage. Brandon United football team had challeged Crook United to a game of push ball. Cheered on by their many supporters, both teams finished the game in a state of physical exhaustion. A drawn game was deemed a fair result.

John Lee and Thomas Graham descended to the Hutton Seam at four p.m. At six p.m. the two men, both stonemen, were taking down stone to make height for the following shift. The premature fall of strata covered both men, John Lee being killed outright and his workmate seriously injured. Nicholas Westgarth, another stoneman of 3 Albert Street, on returning with a hand saw he had borrowed, found the hapless men. John Lee the twenty-seven year old miner, left a widow and a baby in their Newcastle Street home. Hundreds of mourners walked in procession the three miles to Red Hills cemetery in Durham for interment.

The pit claimed yet another victom when Isaac Robertshaw, a twenty-three year old coal hewer on the 'C' Pit was buried under a fall of stone. The accident occurred at five a.m., despite all-out rescue work, his body was not recovered until eight a.m.

When Brandon Colliery banner with black drape fluttering in memory of the recent fatalities, was carried aloft at the thirty-sixth annual Miners' Gala which drew a record crowd of ninety thousand, it joined the banners from one hundred and ninety Lodges to grace Durham's racecourse.

Accidents occur despite the fact that some seams are closed and others are on short time. On August 30th the colliery claimed its fiftieth victim in fifty years of working when at ten minutes to three, twenty-five year old Joseph Hoyle was killed. He rode in the empty set with eight other men from the shaft to the Ballarat Seam in the 'C' Pit; at the Third West off-takes he jumped from the moving set to be hit by the rear tubs.

Local churchgoers lost the services of two popular clergymen when the Vicar of Brandon, the Rev. W. Ransome left for missionary work in Zanzibar, Africa, and when the Rev. Joseph Thorman left St. Patrick's, Langley Moor to take up duties at St. Andrew's in Newcastle. Fr. Thorman had in his last week at Langley Moor seen a beautiful new altar fitted in the church. During his eight years at Langley Moor he had seen new schools built and a big organ installed in the church.

The Rev. Harry Hayward, B.A., of the Royal University of Ireland, was inducted as Brandon's new vicar in time to perform the Christmas services. Brandon folk welcomed Fr. John Parker when he came to St. Patrick's Langley Moor on December 29th.

1907

John George Fenwick, petticoat swirling around his short legs, ran from No. 33 Sunderland Street, he unerringly crossed the road and the wide rock-strewn street to Durham Street's No. 46 where Hannah Rutter lived; he sought his usual treat. John George's father, Will Fenwick, had retired to bed after his early shift at the pit. The child's mother worked in her kitchen, blissfully unaware of John George's intentions. Hannah's brother Thomas, a coal hewer, after his bath in a tin set before the bright red fire in the big grate, had ascended the stairs to bed, the time was one thirty in the afternoon, he had worked the fore-shift. It was wash day. Hannah, with the week's wash ready on the table, lifted the large pan of boiling water from the fire and put it on the kitchen's mat covered floor. Like a magnet, the glowing fire drew John George, his small hands extended for warmth. He stepped back and fell into the boiling water. Thomas Rutter, on hearing the splash and screams, rushed downstairs. He applied olive oil, sweet oil, lime water and whiting to the child's injuries. Mr. McIntyre found the child so terribly scalded he ordered his immediate removal to hospital. The flat cart, horse-drawn, left deep ruts in the January snow as it began the three mile journey to Durham. On the cart lay the badly blistered body of John George Fenwick born just two years and three months before.

St. Patrick's Church, Langley Moor

**Right Rev.
Joseph Thorman**
*Bishop of Hexham
and Newcastle*

*Rector of
St. Patrick's,
Langley Moor, from
April, 1899 to
Dec., 1906*

Fr. Hanley

Fr. Hannon

**Rev.
John Parker, P.P.**

*Parish Priest of
St. Patrick's,
Langley, from
Dec., 29th, 1906*

Brandon Colliery Miners' Union Hall, 1891

St. Patrick's New School, 1902

Six hundred men and boys employed at Brandon's A and B pits handed in their notices. There had been hell on in the Union Hall, after bitter argument the drastic strike action had been decided on. The dispute was not over wages, the miners had just been awarded a wage increase of three and three-quarters per cent. There was friction over the employment of miners who are non-unionists. Three men had refused to join the Union, twenty-eight men had let their Union fees lapse; the rule allowed no more than three missed fortnightly payments.

After a ballot the majority favoured striking. Tom Carr, head of Brandon Miners' Union said it was not a question between master and men, but one solely confined to the miners. Two weeks later, just as the notices had expired, the strike was settled, all but one of the twenty-eight men had paid up their dues to the Union.

A new cemetery to serve Brandon and Byshottles area was acquired at Meadowfield. At a total cost of £2,700 it is large enough for five thousand single graves. It is expected to last about thirty years at the present rate of burial. The Council bought five and a half acres of land from Lord Boyne at a cost of £150 an acre.

Site of Burial Ground, 1904

Tom Gibson and his wife were the oldest standards of Brandon Colliery; their connection with the Primitive Methodist movement reached back some fifty nine years. After a burial service by the Rev. Joseph Roxby, Mrs. Gibson was interred in the new cemetery at Meadowfield, she was the first Brandon Colliery resident to repose there.

For ten years Brandon's gas has been fed from Durham. A new form of street lighting emerged when Straker and Love erected a power station at the colliery from which electricity was generated to all streets, back and front, in Brandon Colliery, Brandon Village, Browney and Meadowfield. Dismal bye-roads and back streets were lit up. Dark corners of East and West Streets, the Market Place and corner ends were illuminated and made safer for the pedestrian.

Miss Ramsey, daughter of a pitman lived in the colliery rows, she had attended Brandon School before training to teach. She was appointed Superintendent in the Mixed Department in the school just a short walk away. At the same time Miss Florence Hannah Thew was promoted to Head Mistress of the Infants' School at a salary of £100 per annum. Mrs. Hayward, wife of Vicar Hayward, distributed prizes for good attendance at the school, fifty-six children received books.

William Green, draper, stood again for the Centre Ward of the Brandon and Byshottles Urban District. He has been a member of the Council since 1894 during which time his motto has been 'The greatest good for the greatest number'. He avers that during the last three years over £8000 was spent in new sewage works, bridges, electric lighting, a new cemetery and other projects.

Some months after the departure of the Rev. Joseph Thorman from St. Patrick's, Langley Moor, Catholics and non-Catholics subscribed to a testimonial fund. During his parochial leadership he made many friends in Brandon Colliery who gave generously. His gifts took the form of an oak file pedestal and a purse of gold from the parishioners, and a polished oak spirit and smoking cabinet from the teachers and scholars of the school.

James Murphy, Norris Woodward, Philip Lynch jnr., Thomas Williams, John Tunney, Frank Tunney and James Duffy, all pitmen living at Brandon Colliery, were married during the year. Patrick Moran now twenty-two and a coal hewer, lived at 20 Railway Street; he married twenty-one year old Mary Cummings from nearby 19 South Street. They had attended the same school at Langley Moor.

1908

On January 6th crowds gathered in the hitherto quiet village of Brancepeth; seventy-seven year old Gustavus Russell, the eighth Viscount Boyne, who died on December 30th was buried in the family vault in a corner of the little churchyard. His home Brancepeth Castle, towered over his resting place. Viscount Boyne owned a vast tract of land which included Brandon Colliery from which he drew royalties from coal mined there. He left more than £600,000.

Matt Bates had been landlord of the Red Lion Inn, affectionately known as the 'Blazer' for twenty-five years. A great sportsman, he was very popular in the area. On his retirement from public life a concert was held in his public house. Hugh McDermott, Brandon's Union Lodge chairman for the past twenty years, presided at the gathering. A gold mounted walking stick, silver snuff box, and a mounted guinea were presented to Matt Bates. His daughter, a teacher at Brandon School was handed a beautiful gold brooch. John Mearman played the piano, Hugh McDermott sang, as did other six artistes to make the night a memorable one.

The colliery's miners look to a brighter future. A new Act of Parliament has just been passed which states that no man is to work more than eight hours out of twenty-four; it is called the Eight Hour Act. Good news, too, when Durham Miners' Association joined the Miners' Federation of Great Britain.

Twenty year old Miss Florence Pilling was engaged to teach at Brandon School where Miss Bates teaches twelve year old Billy Miller.

A daughter was born to coal hewer Patrick Moran and his wife Mary; Norah their first child arrived in their new home in single Sunderland Street.

John Boyle of Sunderland Street; Michael Tunney, Newcastle Street; and William Graney, also from Newcastle Street, all young miners just recently married, are bitter over the coal owners' decision to reduce their wages 3¾%. Some nine months ago, the county's miners had, after long negotiation, been granted an increase of 7¼%.

Careful household budgeting enabled music lovers to acquire the popular machine, the phonograph, much used at wedding receptions, for two pounds ten shillings. Sound is recorded on wax cylinders and is played by winding up a clockwork motor.

George Burton, forty-seven year old husband of Anne Burton, left his West Street home after breakfast, to join Joseph Bell, another coal hewer, to work double in the 'A' Pit. During the shift a large stone fell on them as they worked side by side. Joseph Bell luckily escaped with a scraped back and bruised arms. The falling stone on striking George's back and neck killed him instantly.

1909

Good news for the elderly. They no longer dread outliving their savings. From January 1st an old age pension was given to all over seventy years of age with an income of less than ten shillings a week. A couple will receive seven shillings and sixpence and a single person five shillings a week.

Heavy January snowfalls cost Brandon Urban Council £18:3s:4d. This was the sum expended in clearing the roads, the snowplough being out, certain blocked parts, too deep for the plough, had to be dealt with by hand. The Council needing an ambulance, accepted tenders for a vehicle. T. Farr's tender from Bishop Auckland for £55 was chosen. The tender was the lowest of twenty-two sent in from various parts of the county.

Three Brandon Colliery pitmen left Durham Police Court after being fined for fighting and disturbing the Christmas peace. One was heard to say, 'I haven't a meg'. Another remarked, 'We cannot change our shirts'.

The magistrate frowned severely from the Bench upon the prisoner in the dock. It was the fifth time the same lad had been before him for poaching. 'Do you realise', said his worship, turning to the boy's father, 'that this boy of yours has been before me too many times? In fact, I am thoroughly tired of seeing him here'.

'Not half so tired as me', said the father.

'They why don't you take him in hand and teach him the right way?'

'Aa've shown 'im the reet way', said the disgusted parent, 'but the young fella alwis gans and gets catched'.

Almost every week sees trains pass through Brandon Colliery railway station carrying miners and their families en route to Australia. Miniature flags are waved from carriage windows; men and women search for the acquaintance likely to wave to the emigrants. Men tired of the conditions prevailing in the coal trade, after saving from their meagre wage and selling off furniture, have managed to raise the £17 required as fare for the six weeks sea voyage.

Devastating news reached the colliery on February 16th. West Stanley Colliery, one of Durham's pits suffered a terrible explosion in which one hundred and sixty eight lives were lost. A number of Brandon Colliery pitmen recall the anguish of the much smaller disaster which struck underground at their colliery some nine years ago.

On the day of the West Stanley disaster thirteen year old Billy Miller descended the pit for his first shift; he had left school where Miss Bates had taught him, he was immediately set on at the colliery. The wooden cage swaying alarmingly in the 'D' shaft as Billy descended. He started as a flatter and spent ten hours collecting tubs together in the flat as putters brought them from the coal-face. Pony drivers took the full tubs out to the main landing prior to removal by the outbye hauler to the shaft bottom.

Brandon Colliery Silver Prize Band gave a sacred concert to help alleviate the distress left in the wake of the West Stanley pit disaster. The band marched through Brandon Colliery and on to the Central Hall, Meadowfield, which was kindly granted free of charge for the occasion. The musical treat was poorly patronised as only £2:1s. was collected.

Easter Saturday! Norman Smith aged eleven, and eight year old John Tullock left behind the colliery rows and wandered through the maze of coke ovens to the disused quarry where deep murky water had drained after heavy rainfall. The younger lad on reaching for birds' eggs on the quarry side, overbalanced and fell into the water. Norman jumped in to the rescue; the coke ovens surrounding the lonely quarry effectively cut out the lads' tragic cries for help.

Pitmen Gavin Parkin, John Walton, Jonathon and Tom Stevens were relieved when Lord Collins, sitting as umpire to deal with a dispute which had arisen between Durham's coalowners and miners of the county with reference to wages, gave his verdict. The coalowners contended that circumstances justified a reduction of 7½% in the men's wages, while the men's representatives offered to accept a reduction of 5%.

Lord Collins' award is in the following terms: 'I award and determine that the Durham Coalowners' Association are not entitled to claim any deduction from the said current rates in wages'.

After a long agitation by the Council's representative for the Centre Ward, Mr. Green, Messrs. Straker and Love wrote to the Council stating that they had built four hundred and one new ash-closets at Brandon Colliery out of a total of six hundred and eighty-five, and would continue to build the others at their earliest convenience.

Best suits and bonnets were charmingly displayed as their owners thronged the road from Brandon Colliery to Meadowfield, where the vicar of Brandon had one hundred and five candidates ready for Confirmation in St. John's Parish Church. A proud Rev. Hayward greeted the Bishop of Jarrow in his Whit Sunday visitation. Choirs from St. John's, St. Agatha's and St. Catherine's stirred the packed church was they entered singing 'Onward, Christian Soldiers'.

On the same afternoon Brandon's Silver Band headed the Sunday School Union parade, and accompanied the hymns at the service held in Wharton Park. The band gave a concert on Durham's racecourse bandstand in the evening; a fine programme of music was rendered.

Hewers, offhand men, stonemen, deputies and banksmen of Brandon Colliery donated £36:2s.6d. which the Brandon Union Lodge sent to the Stanley Pit disaster fund.

On Monday June 21st, two putters hewed in the Brockwell 'C' pit. Eighteen year old John O'Neill and William Prudhoe of Sunderland Street after their shift at putting, decided to earn extra pay. It was midnight when they began hewing in a spare place in 3rd West District. A 'roll' in the roof loosened and fell on John O'Neill's legs; he died at six a.m. in Durham Hospital.

Two days later James Oban, a thirty-six year old married man of 3 North Street was busy packing stone in his work place, he had half an hour of his shift to work. A stone four foot long, two feet broad and fourteen inches thick fell on him. The pit was again laid idle according to custom pertaining to fatal accidents.

Brandon and Meadowfield Social Club held its second annual sports. School-children residing around Brandon and district met in Commercial Street where the club is situated. They formed into ranks and marched to the field one thousand two hundred strong. On entering the grounds each child was presented with a bag of sweets, and a penny to treat themselves to any of the amusements there. Sunnybrow beat Brandon Stars in a competition for a set of medals presented by the club, the football was watched by an enthusiastic crowd.

On Big Meeting day Thomas Atkinson of Brandon Colliery took his turn with the pony and trap in the hackney carriage rank at Langley Moor; business was always good on the day when all traffic seemed Durham bound. He was fined two shillings and sixpence for not having a licensed number on his trap. Robert Jackson was fined one pound and costs for a like offence.

Brandon Colliery Prize Silver Band in cracking form visited Newburn on Tyne to enter the band contest promoted by the Spencer Steel Works. The band won two first prizes and a total of eight pounds in cash. They also took the Newburn Challenge Cup valued at thirty guineas and medals for soprano, trombone and euphonium. Six first prizes and one third had been won in the space of five weeks. Colliery folk turned out to cheer when the band paraded the streets before holding a 'smoker' in Beattie Burrell's Colliery Inn where an excellent supper was served.

Thomas Condron, George Lee, Hugh McDermott, John Clennell, George Winter and Thomas Lee were coffin bearers at the funeral of fifty-five year old William Hardwood, checkweighman at Brandon 'C' Pit who died suddenly. He was held in high esteem by management and men alike. Workmen bore aloft the black draped banner usually reserved for fatal accidents at the colliery.

George Emmerson at sixty-seven had worked fifty-three years for Straker and Love. Born in 1842, he began his pit career at the age of fourteen on the opening of Brandon Colliery. He worked twenty-eight years as heap keeper for the 'A' and 'B' Pits up to his recent death.

October saw a typhoid fever epidemic in Brandon Colliery. Thirty cases of the disease being reported; the Isolation Hospital is full. John Elliott a twenty-five year old Sunderland Street man, died from the fever. The day following his burial, his mother Mrs. Elliott succumbed. Another son, Simon, aged nineteen died shortly after. Another son, Charles, is prostrated at the hospital. The bereaved husband lost his wife and two sons within a week.

One hundred and twenty old folk celebrated Christmas in style. Workmen of the 'A', 'B' and 'C' pits gave them their annual tea where each couple received fifteen shillings and each single person was handed five shillings. Carol singers were busy touring the streets on Christmas morning until mid-day.

1910

Workmen at the 'A' and 'B' Pits resumed work on January 24th. They had been on strike since January 1st; the dispute, a county one, was named the eight-hour strike. Brandon Workmen's Social Club financially aided the needy cases arising from the dispute. Members of the club received one shilling for each child and the same for their wives. Tickets varying from two shillings to ten shillings were given out to them. The Co-operative Society had a busy time next day, when about three hundred tickets were handed in for supplies of groceries and meat, the total amounting to about £60. On the next day club officials were again busy when tickets were given to anyone off work, whether members of the club or not, who were affected by the dispute. A sum of about £120 being disbursed, which alleviated many sad cases of distress.

The coalowners' again sought a reduction of the miners' wages. The latter agreed to arbitration; Lord Macdonnell's award was that the reduction be 6¼%. This award leaves wages 33¾% above the basis of 1879.

Due to slackness in the coal trade, four of Straker's six pits are idle, only Brandon's two pits are at work albeit only three or four shifts a week.

Viscount Boyne made a gift of 1,500 square yards of ground close to St. John's Church for the purpose of building a parochial hall. The vicar, Rev. H. Hayward, said it wasn't exactly a gift; they had to pay the sum of five shillings per year for ninety-nine years. He introduced a Freewill Offering Scheme. Around the same time a plan for a new Catholic church at Langley Moor, to accommodate the large number of catholics in the Brandon area, was passed by the Urban Council.

When King Edward VII died, Friday May 20th, the day of his funeral, was observed as a day of mourning. Brandon Colliery was idle for the day; men at the collieries could ill afford the loss of wages as slack time was once again the rule. Services were held in St. John's, St. Agatha's and St. Patrick's; H. Hayward, J. H. Ellis and J. Parker are the respective ministers.

The colliery caller toured the colliery streets ringing his handbell, and declaring to all that 'the pits are idle the morn'; Brandon's pits were not working on the Saturday owing to slack trade. The loss of a day's wage did not prevent the happy exodus from Brandon Colliery railway station, the occasion being the annual excursion promoted by Brandon Social Club. Club officials had been busy on the Friday night handing out tickets, which if bought at the railway station would have cost the recipients two shillings each. Between three thousand and four thousand departed from the station in four packed trains which visited Tynemouth and Whitley Bay. Never has such a crowd left the colliery in one day.

It was Miners' Gala Day, and Jack, having taken too much 'bad beer' was lying drunk, when a policeman approached and said 'Come on, lad, get a move on!'

'Dis thoo knaa we Aa is lad?' asked Jack.

'No, who are you?'

'Aa's Jack Smith cc'.

'What! Are you a county councillor?'

'Wey, not a county councillor; Aa's a colliery caaler'.

Owing to the strike of North Eastern Railway workers, business in the Brandon district was greatly inconvenienced. The cattle purchased by butchers at the market had to be driven the sixteen miles from Newcastle. Local butchers collected their beasts at midnight.

Robert Felton and Thomas Lawson left Brandon Colliery; their vociferous companions acclaiming the coming contest. On their way to do battle they passed the Red Lion Inn where Matt Bates had reigned as mine host for some twenty-seven years. His lamented death leaves a vacancy on the Durham Board of Guardians.

A game of 'fives' had been arranged between the two colliery men and two Langley Moor men, Pat Mulhall and Frank Burns. Spectators paid £13.13s. gate money to watch, bet and cheer on the four contestants. The game, 33 up was played for a stake of £15 a side. Brandon men cheered as Felton and Lawson went eight chalks up to their opponents' two. Joy was short lived; the Langley Moor players won by twenty chalks, they had been warm favourites to win.

Two pitmen, William Allen, deputy overman of Cobden Terrace, and George Winter, miner of Sunderland Street, elected to stand as Brandon Centre Ward's representative on the Durham Board of Guardians. Out of eight hundred and eighty three electors only two hundred and eighty four residents decided to exercise their franchise. The result after the voting in Brandon Colliery School was George Winter one hundred and fifty-two; William Allan one hundred and twenty-nine. There were three spoiled papers.

Parishioners of St. Patrick's Langley Moor, long in need of a bigger church, most of whom come from Brandon's twenty-six rows, were jubilant on hearing of the proposed new church. The edifice will be faced with stone, will consist of nave and aisles, sanctuary and apsidal end, and side chapels. There will be two sacristies attached to the church. The interior will show an arcade of five arches to each side of the nave, resting on octagonal columns with foliated capitals. The roof will be an open one of hammer beam construction. Electric lights will be installed.

In the last game of the cricket season Brandon travelled to Durham City. The City declared with a score of one hundred and thirteen for eight wickets, then skittled Brandon for fifty-five runs.

On October 1st crowds converged on Langley Moor; the sixpence admission charge meant a good view at the laying of the foundation stone. Thirty-two years have passed since the corrugated iron building, to serve as chapel and school was built. Bishop Collins laid the foundation stone of the church which will cost £3000 and seat four hundred and fifty. It was a Red Letter Day for the Catholic community of which Fr. Parker is leader. He has £1200 in hand; £170 was raised during the day. Pitmen who are parishioners continue to contribute a 'day's wage' every fortnight to help pay off the debt incurred.

Edmondsley Heroes were drawn against Brandon United in the Brandon Nursing Cup. A poor crowd saw Dave Oakley and Will Ramsey score two each for Brandon United whose better football produced a 6—2 result. The United are also in the Durham Central League lying second behind Durham Rovers.

In the first round of the Deerness and District Aged Miners' Cup, Langley Moor Temperance played Brandon United to a 2—2 draw. Goodall, Pennington and Bowes played well for United in a hard game. Brandon still in form, neat New Brancepeth Villa 2—1 in the Brandon Nursing Cup Competition.

In the Durham Hospital Cup Langley Moor St. Patrick's versus Brandon United attracted a good gate. It being too dark for extra time to be played, the game finished a goalless draw. Dave Oakley was prominent for the United; Selway in goal for St. Patrick's saved two penalties in a hard fought game.

George was supporting the home football team. During the match he was shouting to the referee to watch the game, get his eyes chalked, etc. At half time the referee went over to him and said, 'Look here, my man, who's refereeing this match, you or me?'

Geordie looked him up and down, then he replied, 'Neether of us'.

Christmas entertainment was assured when the Boyne Electric Theatre was opened. The new Royal Hippodrome, built of wood and covered with corrugated iron, holds 800 persons, it cost £1000 and is fitted throughout with electric radiators. A splendid orchestra, all local talent, is engaged. W. Jackson (bass), T. Chadwick (cornet), T. Green (flute), E. Mearman (drum), Miss Hartnell (pianist). Excellent pictures were shown and variety performers also contributed to the entertainment.

Prizes of Christmas fare awaited the winner of the annual billiards, domino and card handicaps promoted by the committee of Brandon Colliery Literary Institute. The games were as usual well attended.

One hundred and twenty old people received their annual Christmas cheer when Brandon Lodge distributed £74. Each couple was given 15s. and a single person 10s.

Carter Watson, James Welsh and Joseph Reynolds, all Brandon Colliery pitmen, had cause for double celebration; their marriage dates coincided with news of a wage incease of 2½%.

During the year Patrick and Mary Moran's second child was born, a brother for two year old Norah. The baby was carried the one mile from Sunderland Street to St. Patrick's chapel-cum-school, where he was baptised and given the name James.

Dry fine weather favoured carol singers and the local band when they patrolled the district. All places of religious worship were well attended.

1911

Clusters of men and boys waited patiently. A heavy fall of snow enhanced lounging figures ready to spring into instant action. Mufflered males swarmed the twenty-five streets the colliery boasted. In scores of the seven hundred and four houses in Brandon Colliery built and owned by Messrs. Straker and Love, sat man or woman, or both, ready to respond on hearing the knock on their door.

Buzzers at Brandon, nearby Littleburn and Browney collieries, as per custom, heralded the New Year; their raucous, albeit joyful sound set off the midnight scramble. Ere the cacophany had ceased, first footers had entered their chosen house, others taking 'pot luck' ran from door to door, hopefully shouting 'Happy New Year, missus!'

It was New Year's Eve, and the colliery buzzers had ceased. Geordie sat by the fireside holding his ferocious dog by the collar, waiting patiently for his chosen first foot. Suddenly a low timid voice shouted through the key-hole,

'A Happy New Yore, m-mister'.

'Is that thoo, Bill?' inquired Geordie.

'Yes, lad; hes the got the d-dog t-tied up?' asked Bill.

'Wey aye, ho'way in, dinnet be freetened', replied Geordie, 'Aa jus gave 'im a good feed afore the buzzer blew'.

Brandon Centre Ward has a population of 4,732 consisting mainly of colliery workers and their families. The Durham County Council published its report on the Sanitary Circumstances and administration of the Brandon and Byshottles Urban District. The Assistant Medical Officer reports:—

Brandon Colliery

Nos. 1—12 Railway Street:—

Defective floors and roofs, causing dampness. Low attics poorly lighted and ventilated. No stair-head lights. Pantries improperly ceiled. Small yards defectively paved. Insanitary open channels.

Nos. 1—33 South Street:—

Three-roomed houses. Small kitchen and low attic, badly lighted and ventilated. Yards small and defectively paved. Insanitary open channels.

*Nos. 34—64 South Street:—

Two-roomed houses. Low attic bed-rooms approached by step-ladders and defectively lighted and ventilated. Poor pantries and defectively paved kitchen floors. Small yards defectively paved. Insanitary open channels.

*Nos. 1—20 East Street:—

Similar to preceding.

*Nos. 1—40 Sunderland Street:—

Similar to preceding.

Nos. 1—38 West Street:—

Two-roomed flats with defective floors. Defective paved yards. Insanitary open channels.

Nos. 43—82 Newcastle Street:—

Two-roomed houses. No stairhead lights. Small yards defectively paved. Insanitary open channels.

Nos. 1—14 High Street; Nos. 1—60 Park Street; Nos. 27—52 Princess Street; Nos. 1—52 Albert Street:—

Similar to preceding; also insanitary open ash-pit privies in Park Street and Albert Street.

*Nos. 1—23 North Street

Two-roomed houses. Step-ladders to attics which are badly lighted and ventilated. No fireplaces. No stair-head lights. Poor pantry accommodation. Defectively paved ground floors. Small yards defectively paved. Insanitary conveniences and open channels.

Nos. 26—42 North Street:—

Three-roomed houses with defectively paved ground floors. Low attic bedrooms defectively lighted and ventilated. No stair-head lights. No fireplaces. Small yards defectively paved. Insanitary conveniences and open channels.

*These houses are not reasonably fit for habitation

Slaughter houses:—

Premises were for the most part attached to butchers' shops and generally were located much too close to dwelling-houses. For instance, I was surprised to find that slaughtering is permitted on the premises of a house in Station Avenue, a new row of small self-contained houses at Brandon Colliery. Most of those that were inspected were clean, but some premises in Commercial Street, Brandon Colliery, were in very bad order.

Isolation Hospital:—

This is a temporary structure of poor design situated close to Brandon Village. The two wards, the kitchen, and the accommodation for the staff are under the one roof. Each ward is stated to have a capacity of 4,000 cubic feet and is, therefore, suitable to hold two beds (adopting the usual standard of 2,000 cubic feet per bed). This accommodation is inadequate and it is also unsuitable for the treatment of two or more infectious diseases concurrently.

Disinfection:—

In cases of infectious diseases liquid disinfectants are supplied by the District Council, and the occupiers of the houses concerned are instructed to disinfect all washable articles with the same. The houses are also fumigated, under the supervision of the Sanitary Inspector, with sulphur. At the Isolation Hospital there is a small single-ended steam steriliser (on wheels). I understand that it has not been in use for some months. It should be repaired, or preferably a larger disinfector, which could be used for articles such as bedding etc., should be obtained.

The Rev. James Courtney Bevin, L.Th. of Durham University moved to his new post in Brandon Colliery. He is curate in charge of St. Agatha's Mission Church. The church adjoins a plot of land designated for another row of houses next to Cobden Terrace.

With engine wheels barely visible behind escaping stem, the lengthy stopping train to King's Cross halted at Durham's railway station. A pale faced young man, tall and smartly dressed, entered the compartment occupied by three men, all mature in years.

The train eased away from Durham. Its wheels soon acquired a regular rhythm. 'Are you going far, sonny?' enquired one of the trio. The young man fidgetted and put a hand into his jacket pocket; reassured, he replied, 'I'm going to the plate ends—the end of the line'. Meaning King's Cross. One of the friendly passengers suggested a game of cards to while away the time on their long journey. Some miles on, the young man eyed his winnings approvingly. There was talk of playing for higher stakes — much higher; the three older men seemed keen.

A perceptible slowing of the train announced its approach to a scheduled stop — York. As the train braked to a halt, the young miner pocketted his winnings and said, 'Gentlemen, this is where I get off!' As he sought anonymity in the departing crowd, he withdrew from his pocket the Third Class return rail ticket to York.

Paddy Moran, a twenty-six year old coal hewer in Brandon Colliery's 'A' Pit, four years married, had left his wife Mary, three year old Norah and baby James one year old, at home while he did the York Races. His recent windfall enhanced the day's sport.

George Cooke, the deputy in charge of the 'C' Pit's 2nd West District, showed signs of impatience and swore as he left his kist and headed for coal hewer Ellis Reed's place. Thomas Bullows, a putter, was filling a tub in Ellis's cavil. It was the end of the shift; other coal hewers were homeward bound.

'Come on Ellis! And you Tommy!' remonstrated the deputy, 'We are late!'

The three men began their walk to the shaft bottom, they travelled in single file. Strong wind fanned into the district struck their faces. A sudden reducing of the air velocity warned them of something amiss. George Cooke was worried; normally the wind blew with force only about a mile from the shaft. A solid wall of immovable stone barred their path; the only way to the shaft was effectively blocked. All three men, shocked but in no immediate physical danger, pondered their predicament. How long was the fall? How long before their absence would be discovered? A horrific thought shared by the trio—did the men who left earlier escape the fall of stone?

Ellis Reed carried a blunt pick, the pick sharpener on the surface would have it ready for Ellis's next coal hewing shift. He energetically rapped on the metal way; a primitive S.O.S. which, if the would-be rescuer puts an ear to the rail, can hear the entombed's plea for help. No early reply was expected as their absence would have as yet gone undetected.

Three oil lamps missing from the day's issued warned the lamp cabin attendant of possible mishap—a search party descended the mine. Meanwhile George Cooke kept Ellis and Thomas busy renewing timber in the area of the fall—more to occupy their minds.

On reaching the fall, one of the rescuers jowled the metal way, the call was immediately answered from beyond the barrier. Were all three men safe? Volunteer coal hewers descended. It was agreed to skirt alongside the fall of obstinate rock. Eager men, scantily clothed in vest and shorts, with expertise hewed and timbered in relays.

After six long, agonising hours and the removal of twelve tubs of coal from the narrow confines of the 2ft. 10in. seam of coal the twelve yard long fall of stone was bypassed. Immediately the joyous news was conveyed to the surface where the worried kin of the rescued men waited. Hot coffee was sent down to cold and hungry men.

Two hundred and ten pounds was raised from the penny rate. On June 22nd George the Fifth was crowned King of England and the Commonwealth. The children of Brandon Colliery aged from three to fourteen years were each presented with a Coronation mug and provided with a tea to mark the occasion.

The long hot summer attracted swimmers; the colliery ponds were a handy distance from the colliery rows. Thirty-three year old Bob Gillis, a miner and a strong swimmer, was found drowned in one of the reservoirs. At nine p.m. crowds saw his lifeless body drawn from the water and carried to nearby 7 Single Sunderland Street.

On Sunday October 8th a new Catholic Church was opened at Langley Moor, the foundation stone of which had been laid on October 1st last year. Solemn High Mass was celebrated, Brandon Colliery's Catholics forming a large part of the packed congregation. The Mission was founded thirty-five years ago.

John David Higgins of Queen Street married Catherine Jennings of Railway Street. Maurice McAloon of Sunderland Street married Sarah Ann Brown from the next street, Durham Street.

A double wedding took place when two sisters, Catherine and Jane Condron of Queen Street were wed to James McIntyre and Peter Harrison Sewell respectively. Theirs were the first nuptials performed in the new church by Fr. John Parker, a very happy minister.

The local football team, Brandon United, smarting from last year's defeat at the hands, or feet, of Langley Moor Temperance were avenged when they beat them before a large crowd of home supporters on Christmas Day.

Christmas was a happy time for one hundred and ninety eight old people, an increase of seventy-six upon last year, when each couple received eleven shillings and seven shillings was given to each single person.

A manager of a small colliery gave an invitation to all his workmen to attend a Christmas dinner. One of the guests—a young coal hewer—seated himself at the end of the table. Presently a large dish consisting of a couple of hot geese was brought in and place in front of Geordie, ready for carving. 'Why by gox', said Geordie to the waiter, 'She's rather a biggish plateful, but ye beggor Aa'll try me best te doon her'.

1912

Jos Pybus, Bob Stirling, Will Carr and Archie Robson, Brandon Colliery's Best billiards players had a game on with Langley Grove Club. The Brandon team had good support when they travelled to the Grove Club set in picturesque scenery alongside the River Browney at Langley Moor. All four Brandon men scored 150 each to finish worthy winners 462—600 chalks.

Brandon Workmen's Club has sufficient members with skill to form a billiards team, one which will keep the Institute side on its mettle.

Thomas Solan lived in No. 3 Church Street the newly-built street in Brandon Colliery. Had the street been built last year the intention was to name it Coronation Street; Church Street is apt as St. Agatha's Mission Church is set near the end house of the street. Thomas married Jane Anne Dodds from Framwellgate in Durham. James Cummings, 55 Sunderland Street, another Brandon Colliery miner also wed a Framwellgate girl, Amy Chicken.

Baby Mary Moran, born 10th February is the third child of Patrick and Mary Moran. The family increase necessitated a house move from single Sunderland Street to Durham Street just across the road; four year old Norah and two year old James now have four rooms in which to roam.

Unrest over men's wages reached boiling point—the country's miners struck on March 1st—they wanted a Minimum Wage. On that day anxious men and boys saw seventy-three ponies drawn from the 'A' Pit and thirty-nine from the 'C' Pit. The onlookers wondered how long the ponies would roam the Colliery Field. Ponies' drivers knew that their charges would be quite a handful when they returned underground after a lay-off. The men's last working pay was drawn on March 8th.

Private purchases of coal just before the pits stopped had to pay a hundred per cent upon the ordinary price of coal. At Brandon Colliery the price advanced from 12s.6d. to 25s. per ton. Miners carried what was left of their coal allowance into their houses, as coal houses had already been cleared of their contents by pillagers.

Women, worried for their families, and fearing a long strike have laid up provisions for a few weeks. Some miners have stored two sacks of flour—most have stored one and a half sacks.

Time seemed to press very monotonously for many of the miners, some of them standing in groups at the corner ends, while others stroll around the countryside. Those who make a hobby of gardening are taking full advantage of the enforced holiday to put their plots in trim.

Brandon Colliery was one of the 200 Lodges comprising the Durham Miners' Association to share in the pay-out of the first fortnight's strike pay. The total disbursed was £114,000.

After three weeks of lethargy the miners of Brandon and district amused themselves in earnest. A singing contest was held in the Miners' Institute; Brandon Councillor Tom Carr presided over a large attendance, about five hundred spent a thoroughly enjoyable time. George Taylor and Jim Millward were judges. Jim Welsh won the first prize of five shillings' worth of groceries; tenor Joe Lidster came second to win a 3s.6d. watch; third prize, three shillings' worth of groceries, went to J. W. Brown; fourth prize, a shirt valued at 3s.6d. was won by E. Goodall; Anty Cairns came fifth, his prize being three shillings' worth of mutton; sixth prize, three stones of potatoes and half a pound of tea was won by Ralph Rumley; seventh Tom Connelly the Brandon comedian won 2s.6d. worth of goods; J. Blenkinsop won the final prize of two shillings' worth of goods.

Next day a 'go as you please' race was promoted, the route round the colliery streets lined by cheering colliery folk who encouraged the contestants taking part. Thomas Lee, William Ayre, Charles Powton, William Rowe, J. Straughan, John McCall, Henry Blenkinsop, John Carr, Frank Lynch, Edward Moses Chance and Thomas Smith, all Brandon Colliery men, did not figure among the winners; Mr. Carney came in an easy first.

On the following day sports were promoted by the ambulance men of the colliery; a football match was held, racing and skipping were freely indulged in, again good crowds followed the events.

Coals are becoming scarce, every day hundreds are seen at the tips seeking the precious mineral. All sorts of vehicles are used to convey the spoils, flat carts without horses, barrows with wobbly wheels, and old perambulators are put to unaccustomed use.

The Central Hall, Meadowfield Picture Company have reduced their prices to half, and hams are given away to those who give the nearest number of persons in the Hall on certain nights. These prizes are most welcome to many at present in the district.

The final result of the Durham Miners' ballot on the question of resuming work was available on Wednesday April 3rd. The wording of the ballot being as follows:—

'Are you in favour of resuming work pending a settlement of the minimum rates of wages in the various grades by the district boards to be appointed under the Mines (Minimum Wage) Act?'

The result of the ballot was:—

Against resuming work	48,828
For resuming work	24,511
	————
Majority against	24,317
	————

As the majority fell short of the two thirds of the vote which is required by the rule, the men accept that it is a return to work.

Brandon Colliery 'A' and 'B' Pits voted 264 against resuming work with 179 for. Meadowfield 'C' Pit, her sister pit voted 83 against resuming work and 75 for.

At Brandon Colliery the news of the settlement of the strike on Saturday April 6th was received with a certain amount of indifference, though many expressed satisfaction at the Executive's ballot. Brandon miners will resume work as soon as the management are ready.

On the day before the announcement of the strike's termination, Good Friday, four hundred children started to arrive at noon for a four p.m. tea. The Station Road Wesleyan Church Sunday School superintendents, teachers and their friends helped to feed the hungry gathering. Each child received an orange on leaving the church.

Soup kitchens were active during the strike. Brandon and Meadowfield children being fed in the former's Miners' Hall. It cost an average of twopence per child for each breakfast consisting of tea, currant bun, with unlimited bread and butter.

After thirty-seven days of strike all pits were at work once again. The new Act became operational. Coal hewers minimum wages is fixed at five shillings and six pence per day. Under 16 years of age, two shillings per day and from 16 years to 18 years, two shillings and ninepence per day. The stoppage had flung one million men out of work, the largest so far in any dispute.

News of an advance of 3¾% in wages—the last one being nine months ago—came as the men settled down to work. The current increase is to last three months. With time on their hands and with little money in their pockets, striking pitmen gathered in the field adjoining the 'Blazer' pub. The summit of the colliery spoil heap, lacking a 'watcher out', became a vantage point for P.C. Ward. Eighteen Brandon Colliery men were two shillings and sixpence poorer when they were fined for playing pitch and toss.

William Rutter, Nicholas Adamson, Thomas Hewitson, Robert Gill, James Robson, all miners, and other workers at the colliery took part in the ballot. No friction with management or owner this time. They sought a weekly pay-out of wages instead of the present fortnightly pay. Their efforts bore fruit, a majority voted for the weekly pay. On August 24th Messrs. Straker and Love conceded their request. Men and their womenfolk welcome the weekly Saturday pay.

Patrons of the Colliery Inn, whilst seated in the bar viewed the building activity nearby. The colliery owners decided to greatly enlarge the premises near the 'A' Pit shaft. A high structure destined for use as a storehouse and weigh cabin was in course of erection near the colliery Ambulance Room.

Temperance Legislation: At the weekly meeting of the Mount Beaulah Lodge Brandon Colliery the following resolution was sumbitted by Bro. J. E. Chance the electoral superintendent:– 'That this meeting relying on the promise of the Prime Minister to introduce a Bill on the lines of the 1908 Licensing Bill in the lifetime of the present Parliament, respectfully and earnestly urges the Government to bring in the promised temperance measure as the first Bill of the session of 1913, and to secure its enactment'. The resolution was accepted and recorded.

Geordie had been imbibing, and on his way home had accidentally dropped into a temperance meeting, where the lecturer had a very red nose. Of course the highly coloured condition of his nasal organ was brought about by indigestion etc., but Geordie was disinclined to believe that, and passed many rude remarks about it. At last the watery one was fed up, and shouted wildly in the direction of Geordie, 'That man will make me angry in a minute, I'm not often put out but when I am put out you may be sure–'
'That it's closing time!' yelled Geordie triumphantly.

Scarlet fever and other diseases once more haunt the colliery rows, six cases of scarlet fever from three homes being treated. Four cases of the fever and one of enteric fever were removed to Brandon Hospital. One case of erysipelas received home treatment.
The new Parish Hall adjoining St. John's Church reverberated when the first parish social gathering took place. The Rev. H. Hayward and Mrs. Hayward led sixty couples in the first dance; twenty-four items kept the perspiring dancers engaged until two a.m. Earlier, a hat trimming competition for men, a nail driving event for the ladies, a darning contest for the men, and a baked cake competition helped make a most enjoyable day.
There were seventy-nine applicants for the post of steward and stewardess for Brandon Colliery Social Club at a salary of five pounds five shillings a week. Mr. and Mrs. Bell of Gateshead were selected, William Isles of Brandon Colliery being second choice if needed.

In a club not far from Durham a party of workmen were discussing their late steward, who had been dismissed, when a traveller for a well-known brewery entered and began making enquiries about the change of stewards. Turning to one of the men he remarked, 'I believe there have been some serious discrepancies in your late steward's account. Is that a fact?'
'No hinney', replied the man, 'thor's nowt been the matter that way; nivvor had a rang word wi' neebody, but', (leaning forward in a confidential manner and whispering) 'but thoo knaas he was about thirteen pund short'.

For the year ending December 31st, 1911–
Average tons of coal drawn from Brandon Colliery's seams per day:--

'A' Pit Busty	713
'B' Pit Busty	609
'C' Pit Busty	367
Total	1689

One hundred and thirty nine coal hewers employed in the 'B' Pit hewed 3.68 tons of coal per man shift. Naked lights were in use in the 'B' Pit, Colza oil being used.

Of 590 lamps in use in the 'A' and 'C' pits, 320 were secured by lead rivets and 270 by screws.

Coals drawn for the same period:—

'A' Pit Busty	209,449
Ballarat	459
'B' Pit Hutton	177,422
'C' Pit Brockwell	88,650
Ballarat	20,036
	—————
Total coals	496,017
Fireclay (Seggar)	8,934
	—————
Total	504,951
	—————

Total number of coal drawing days:—

'A' Pit	294½
'B' Pit	291½
'C' Pit	296
	————
Total	881½ days
	————

Number of horses and ponies in:—

'A' Pit	73
'C' Pit	39

1913

New Year sorrow gripped the Graham's home. Joseph Graham, a truck lowerer at the colliery, was fatally injured when he was crushed between trucks.

Intense cold and slack work at the pit greeted the colliery inhabitants on the dawn of a New Year. The Co-operative Society and local tradesmen are complaining of sluggish business, they are hoping for an improvement in the coal trade.

Thirteen hundred underground and four hundred and seventeen surface workers man the three pits comprising the colliery. Mr. T. L. Elwen is the colliery manager; John Gilchrist second class ticket, George Moore second class, and John Dakers also second class, are respective under-managers of the 'A', 'B' and 'C' Pits. Mr. R. L. Weeks has, for a number of years, been Straker and Love's agent for their group of collieries.

The 'A' Pit sends up coal for commercial and manufacturing use from its Busty, Ballarat and Three Quarter Seams. The 'B' Pit yields similar coal from its only seam, the Hutton, while the 'C' Pit provides commercial and manufacturing coal plus fireclay for the making of bricks from its Harvey and Brockwell Seams.

Anxious men, a good number of whom had just returned from the pit and had sacrificed much needed rest, filled the Miners' Hall to overflowing. Councillor Carr chaired the important meeting. Only a limited number of coal hewers and putters were needed to supply the demand for coal, hence the convening of the assembly.

Worried and tired faces creased with smiles as names were drawn from the cap. Management and men agreed that in fairness all hewers' and putters' names be placed in a cap and drawn at the most convenient time. Lucky men hastened home to put an end to the family anxiety—they had gained a reprieve! 'Gentlemen this is the last place to be drawn for'. Only one more fortunate and delighted workman; the rest being left in the cap. All the unlucky miner could say to his dependants was, 'Ah was left in the cap'.

After years at Brandon Colliery several coal hewers and their families left after the men had been 'set on' at one of the newer coastal collieries. Most emigrant pitmen dislike lifting their roots; their wives have to make new acquaintances, their children have to settle in new schools, and they themselves have to adapt to new working conditions and workmates.

Two miners having got work hewing at a colliery started on the Monday. They happened to be working near each other. On the same morning the overman went into the first man. 'Wee's here?' he asked.

'A stranger', said Geordie.

'The overman said, 'Hoo many hes thoo filled?'

Geordie replied, 'This is ma forst 'un half full'.

'Wee's this chap hewing in thy side here?'

Geordie replied, 'That's another stranger'.

'How monny hes he filled?'

'Nay. he'll hev filled nyen yit; he's just been alang te me seekin' a bit coal for the heartburn!'

Glorious May sunshine greeted the troop of colliery folk as they left their homes. The throng consisted mainly of miners and their wives; the younger generation had gone diverse ways. Brandon Colliery workmen, like their counterparts across the county, had elected to ease the lot of their retired miners. They followed the Brandon Colliery Silver Band and the unfurled Lodge Banner to the assembly point midway between the colliery and Brandon Village. Lord Boyne provided the site, at a nominal rent, on which to build twelve homes for aged miners and their wives. The foundation stone for the row of one storey dwellings was laid; over £500 had been subscribed towards the estimated cost of £15,000. Three days after the ceremony many of the miners, observers at the function, had to be hastily withdrawn, by another route, from the 'A' Pit. An electric wire fused in the shaft and set fire to buntin. Burning timber caused dense smoke; Mr. Elwen the colliery manager, was promptly on the scene, his timely action prevented what could have been a disastrous accident.

Hawkers are regular visitors to the colliery rows. Graney, the paraffin man; has his regular customers among the 'B' Pit miners, his oil is favoured for their lamps. Blocks of salt for sale, are carried from house to house.

Mussels sold by the pint, are sold in similar fashion. Billy Thompson sells yeast by the twopenneth from the large square basket carried on his good arm; Billy, a Brandon Colliery lad, has a paralysed arm which prevents more strenuous work. Tommy Harker, another industrious local man, shovels in the miners' coal allowance at twopence a load.

The band and banner toured the streets for the second time this year on the day of the Durham Miners' Gala; crowds left with the banner en route for Durham's forty-third gala. Good weather welcomed a record attendance; all two hundred banners connected with the Durham Miners' Association.

Shortly after the 'Big Meeting' miners of the county were awarded an advance of three and three quarters per cent on their wages. Ninepence in the pound increase on wages can mean as much as one shilling and sixpence extra to take home.

Pigtailed Norah Moran, sporting new laced boots and clothes newly acquired fron nearby Green and Willis the drapers, now five years of age, started school at St. Patrick's R.C. school one mile away at Langley Moor.

Norah had matured in 48 Durham Street; her mother appreciated her help about the house, Mary at one year old was exploring the oil-cloth covered kitchen and the sitting room overshadowed by the nearby pit's pulsating dynamo, compressor and massive steam boilers. When the door of the cupboard under the stairs housing the colliery coal allowance being inadvertently left open, Norah's vigilance prevented Mary and three year old Jimmy from scattering coal and dust in gay abandon.

Norah chaperoned Jimmy on his visit to the nettie across the street; she was on hand in case of mishap, there being three stone steps to ascend before perching him on the wooden throne covering the ash-pit. Norah and her friends, sisters Kitty and Maggie Bone together with Mary Dowdle, played at the top of the street which always seemed to have men coming and going from the lamp cabin almost part of Durham Street. They never ventured down the awe-inspiring rear of the street which housed the colliery cooling box where scalding water cascaded incessantly into effervescent water in the huge sunken tank surrounded by close fitting rails. Women ingeniously slung a pail with rope attachment into the steaming depths and retrieved clean hot water which considerably eased washday drudgery.

Joiners and masons were busy in North and West Streets where all staircases were completed; stairs replaced the steep ladders which had been in use about fifty years since the rows were built. Sunderland and East Streets are shortly to follow suit.

The services of the colliery band and banner were once again called upon when only four months from the laying of the foundation stone, the Aged Miners' Homes were ceremoniously opened. Poor weather greeted the day. Councillor Carr introduced the colliery agent Mr. R. L. Weeks, who handed over the keys to the new homes which face south and are delightfully situated adjoining the road leading to Brandon Village. Twelve grateful and happy couples look forward to settling in their new residences which have a porch overlooking a garden and a cluster of fields.

People thronged the road outside Holly Garth the residence of the manager Mr. T. T. Elwen; the large house lies just above the new Aged Miners' Homes. The colliery band with drum draped in black turned out; the band played the 'Dead March' while the cortege escorted the popular manager's body to nearby Brandon Village for burial. Fifty-three year old Mr. Elwen had, up to a few hours before his death, attended to his managerial duties at Brandon Colliery.

John William Dixon; John Willy Richardson; James Burns and Joseph Condron were among the Brandon Colliery pitmen to marry during the year. Mary Anne Condron, Joseph Condon's sister, married William Mulhall from Langley Moor.

Brandon Colliery men attending their meeting in the Miners' Hall heard of the fine edifice to be built. The Durham Miners' New Hall is estimated to cost £21,357 and will occupy a site not far removed from the present Hall in Durham's North Road.

Well stocked shops drew seasonal shoppers despite the stormy Christmas weather. Beef in abundance at 6d. to 9d. a pound, mutton 6d. to 10d. a pound, potatoes 8d. a stone, rabbits at 1s. 3d. each and apples from 2d. to 4d. a pound graced the shops.

1914

Littleburn and Brandon colliery buzzers commenced to blow in the New Year a few minutes to twelve o'clock and continued until midnight.

The Workmen's Institute, in need ot a full-time caretaker, prompted a mini election. Five candidates, J. Richardson, H. Armstrong, J. Martin, J. Carmedy, and G. Witson submitted their names to the Institute for consideration. Five hundred and thirty two cast votes in favour of Joe Richardson whose total votes swamped the other four candidates who polled eighteen, fifteen, seven and seven respectively.

Kathleen the fourth child of Patrick and Mary Moran was born on February the fifth. Baby wear and clothes for the young family were bought at Green and Willis, Brandon Colliery's largest drapers who allowed credit to the colliery folk.

The Centre Ward of Brandon Urban District Council has a population of 4732 houses mainly in Brandon Colliery's twenty seven rows. Councillors for the Ward are Thomas Carr, and William Green.

A greater demand for coal meant money to be spent at Jane Dodd's shop; George Lamb's grocer cum butcher shop; George Pratt's general dealers; Mrs. Ethel Kelly's milliner shop; Frederick William Render's drapery and Jacob Rowe and his brother Joseph who each have a butcher's shop. Beattie Burrell, Brandon's Colliery Inn and William Harle, Red Lion cater for the drinkers.

There being no place of entertainment in the colliery, its folk frequent the Royal Hippodrome in Langley Moor, where large audiences applauded the cast in the fine acting of 'The Bonny Pit Lad'. The players were requested by the appreciative patrons to stay for a further week to perform the play 'Her One False Step'.

St. Patrick's Chapel cum School, 1878.

*St. John's Church,
1875.*

Mount Calvary Methodist Chapel, 1873.

Brandon Rovers and Brandon United give the sporting fraternity their own special entertainment—football. They are in the Durham Central League. The Rovers visited Langley Moor where the latter team won 3—0 in a League game.

Brandon's indefatigable Councillor, William Green, said regarding Brandon Colliery houses, that there was no better housing accommodation at Brandon Colliery now than there was five years ago, and no signs of getting any either. Nineteen houses had been built, but not a single one altered in accordance to promise given. In some houses the ceiling came down to a low window, and such places should be condemned as unfit for human beings to live in. It had been allowed to go on despite the renewed promise of the Colliery Company that the work would be done as quickly as possible. He thought the time had arrived when the Council should take some definite steps to enforce better housing at Brandon.

Messrs. Straker and Love wrote to the Council regarding overcrowding and unsatisfactory lighting at Brandon Colliery. Mr. Weeks the colliery agent would have the Council's letter before him, on his return.

On Tuesday June 23rd fore shift men at Brandon Colliery 'A' Pit met with an accident that might have been attended by serious results. The set containing about eighty men, was going inbye, about forty got off at their places, the others resuming their journey. After the set had been started and had proceeded only thirty or forty yards it came in contact with an obstruction, which in examination was found to be an iron pipe, the tubs only clearing this by about an inch, the men, being inside the tubs, their heads protruded above the bar, with the result that each man received a blow, from the neck upwards, some of them receiving severe injuries, having teeth knocked out and faces cut. The worst injuries were sustained by William Bainbridge, Robert Kennedy and Thomas Hughes; other twenty-six received slight injuries. The set was at once pulled up, it was clear that if it had been running at its usual speed the consequences would have been very serious. The men were attended at their home by Drs. James and George Denholm.

Mr. R. Walton left Brandon Colliery after serving six years as Minister to the Mount Calvary Methodist Church. His successor, Mr. G. B. Richardson, arrived to take over the pastoral duties, he is their eleventh cleric to fill the post.

Glorious weather helped make the forty-fourth Durham Miners' Gala, held on 25th July a numerical success, most of the county's two hundred and seventy-nine pits being represented on Durham's racecourse.

Brandon Silver Prize Band paraded, with the Lodge Banner, through the colliery strets before embarking to Durham. Trains and horse traps were kept busy during the day when most of Brandon Colliery's work force of thirteen hundred and eighty-one were off work. The traps travelling by way of Langley Moor—Stonebridge—Neville's Cross and on to Durham, had the busiest day of the year doing the three-penny journey.

A very stout old lady was seen alighting from a trap plying to Durham and upon reaching the ground stiffly turned and said to the driver, 'Now mi canny man, how much is Aa in thee debt?' and the driver said, 'Thippence, missus'. The old lady paid her fare and was about to pass the horse's head to get on the pavement when the driver shouted, 'Hi missus, dinna gan roond that way for goodness sake'.

'What for?' inquired the old lady.

'Why', replied the driver, 'if my aad hoss sees what's he's pulled for thrippence he'll drop doon dead!'

The Big Meeting carnival spirit was dampened somewhat by trouble on the continent which had brewed up when on Sunday 28th June the Archduke Francis Ferdinand, heir to the Austrian throne, and his wife were assassinated in Sarajevo, the capital of Bosnia, to which they were paying a State Visit. War clouds were gathering over Europe. The three M.P.s among the five speakers at the Gala spoke at some length on the subject.

George Gray, Newcastle Street and Martin Cairns, Colliery Stables, Meadowfield, married young women from Langley Moor in early summer.

On 28th July Austria declared war on Serbia. This first step was followed by the mobilisation, in rapid succession, of the armies of Europe. On 31st July, Sir Edward Grey, the British Foreign Minister, asked both France and Germany for an assurance that Belgian neutrality, guaranteed in 1831, would be respected. France immediately gave a definite promise, but Germany quibbled.

On 4th August Sir Edward Grey demanded from Germany an explicit pledge on the subject, but by two o'clock in the afternoon news reached him that the Germans were already in Belgium. At midnight Britain declared war on Germany.

Wives and mothers were worried. The other war, fought in far off South Africa, seemed so remote and only a handful of Brandon Colliery men volunteered to fight. This conflict had brought the fighting much nearer home.

Men on the Reserve List were immediately called up. Private Michael Tunney, a miner at Brandon Colliery, a reservist, having served in India, was among the first men to leave Brandon Colliery to do battle with the Germans.

Just four days after the declaration of war, Edward McDermott, Queen Street and Thomas Carey, Railway Street, sought their brides in Langley Moor and Brandon. They were married in St. Patrick's, Langley Moor.

John Pennington of High Street, Brandon Colliery, enlisted in September. He had served two years in the Boer War. Tom Ramsey from the same street, joined up at the same time. Brandon Colliery's seams, The Hutton, Busty, Brockwell, Main Coal, Low Main, Harvey, Three-Quarter and Ballarat had been worked in the area of Brandon Village. Pitfalls occurred when coal had been removed from seams nearest the surface, in consequence, damage was done to Village houses. An agreement between Viscount Boyne and Messrs. Straker and Love, resulted in the latter awarding £4000 in compensation to the property owners. The award was made one week before Christmas.

Christmas festivities were restrained; men had left home to train as soldiers. Services were held in all churches and chapels in the district where prayers were offered for a speedy end to the conflict.

1915

Colliery buzzers, as per custom, let in the New Year. Unlike former years, celebrations were muted.

January saw the departure of more men and youths to join the colours. Straker and Love reverted to the two shift system owing to the scarcity of hands.

Corporal Christon of the Colliery Inn, one of Brandon Colliery's first volunteers, arrived home on ten days leave from the front. Corporal Christon is a despatch rider; he carried a German helmet when he arrived by train in Durham. Local interest was aroused when the helmet was on show in the bar of the Colliery Inn.

Private Michael Tunney was welcomed home, he hobbled about with the aid of a stick. He thought he would never see Brandon Colliery again. There are five members of his family in the army, but Michael is the only one to have served at the front. Though his nerves are shaken, he would like to be with his regiment when they march back in triumph at the conclusion of the war.

It was decided to hold the Annual Brandon and District Cage Bird Show. Three hundred and fifty entries were on show in the Miners' Hall, an increase of forty upon last year's exhibits. Forty classes were on view, including canaries, British and foreign hybrid birds.

Ninety-one Brandon School pupils were stricken with measles, all streets in the colliery being affected. The school was closed as was Browney School and St. Patrick's R.C. Infants. When the schools re-opened, parents sent notes to say that some of their children were still suffering from measles and whooping cough. Measles, followed by pneumonia, caused fifty-one deaths in the district during the month of March.

The spacious Castle situated in the quiet village of Brancepeth was converted into a hospital for wounded soldiers. Mrs. Burrell, President of Brandon Working Party, allows the use of a room in the Colliery Inn where members are kept busy providing comforts for them and their fellows at war. Five hundred and twenty one garments have been sent to the front made up into parcels by the ladies of the working party and their honorary secretary, Mrs. Emmerson.

It was a sobering thought; war's casualties being nursed just two miles away. The battlefront seemed only a gunshot away.

A batch of wounded Tommies, amongst whom was a miner had just arrived, and fresh clothes were being served to them in the hospital. Suddenly, after a long and rueful contemplation of his new garment, the miner called out, 'Aa say, norse, whaat de ye caal them cats what hes nee tails?'

'Manx cats, silly', replied the busy nurse.

'Wey, by gum, this must be a Manx shirt thoo's given me', replied Geordie.

Work at the colliery continued despite the large number of men leaving for the front. Thirteen year.old Bob Garbutt left school and started work in the 'A' Pit. He collected his first pony as a driver lad at 2nd North stables whose eight stalls housed ponies Banker, Larry, Patch and others. The animals' needs were cared for by three keepers under the watchful eye of head horse keeper Bill Bromley. Ralph Holmes, not long started as a driver, earned seventeen shillings and eightpence for six shifts worked.

Paddy Moran, now thirty-one and father of four children, three girls and a boy, went away to war with his mate George Thompson Naisbitt; they left the humdrum world of coal hewing at Brandon Colliery.

There being no Miners' Gala owing to the war with Germany, week-end relaxers visited the recently re-opened Empire Theatre at Langley Moor. The Paramount News, a two part comic and variety turns were featured for the admission of sixpence and ninepence downstairs. Courting couples paid their shilling for an upstairs seat.

Destructive ants are once again active in the long Newcastle Street. The Council recommended that the colliery owners attend to the nuisance; they suggest that the old woodwork of the ground floors be removed, the inside walls stripped, concrete floors be put down, and the concrete continued some distance up the walls. After the floors and old materials had been removed, copious sprayings with some powerful disinfectant, or strong solution of chlorine and lime should be carried out. Joints of mutton had to be destroyed after infestation by the pests.

Names of war casualties from amongst Brandon's soldiers serving overseas, reach the colliery with alarming regularity. Lance Corporal T. R. Turner, son of Brandon Co-operative Society's secretary James Turner, whilst serving with the 2nd East Yorks, after one month at the front, received shrapnel wounds in the right fore-arm. Private T. W. Hewitt of the 8th Durham Light Infantry lies wounded in a Prisoner of War camp in Germany. There was great joy and relief at 28 Park Street as Private Hewitt had been reported missing. Private Frank Tunney is reported missing; he too is in the 8th Durhams as the regiment is affectionately named, it is composed mainly of miners.

Twenty year old John Smith, after joining the 8th Durhams last November, completed his army training. After a short leave he left his College Terrace home on April 19th bound for the front; five weeks later he was wounded near Boulogne, he was transferred to a British hospital where he died. Private Smith's funeral was one of the largest in the district, the streets were lined with people as the sad procession wended its way to St. Patrick's Church in Langley Moor where Fr. John Parker officiated at the burial.

James Lidster, Jack Worrall, Jim Ellwood, Ralph Appleby, R. Thompson and Thomas Hughes, all miners at Brandon Colliery, gathered outside the Colliery Institute. After sad farewells the men, accompanied by Mr. Nelson the colliery manager, left for Durham; they had volunteered for the Army to dig mines and trenches.

Between eight hundred and nine hundred officials and workmen employed at Willington, Brancepeth, Oakenshaw and Brandon Collieries are now serving in the Army and Navy—a splendid record. More recruits are expected from these areas. The 8th Durham Light Infantry Pipers' Band accompanied the speakers when they arrived in Brandon Colliery on a recruiting campaign. After stirring speeches and martial music and the names of twenty volunteers secured, the campaigners moved to Meadowfield and Browney to boost their total.

Bob Roxborough, Patrick Brennan and James Dunnegan were among the Brandon pitmen who received their annual money from the checkweigh fund, thet were each handed six shillings. The money is usually paid on the eve of the 'Big Meeting'. This year owing to the large number of miners serving the colours, the event has been abandoned. The Gala has for forty-four years taken place annually until this year.

Despite a year of war food seems plentiful and reasonably priced, with beef and mutton from 10d. a pound, cheese 10d. a pound, eggs eight for 1s., butter 1s. 5d. a pound, turkey and duck eggs at six for 1s., potatoes 1s. a stone.

The dreaded war telegram stated that Pte. Francis Tunney, 8th D.L.I. previously reported missing, was killed in action four months ago on April 26th. He is Brandon's first reported fatal war casualty. Pte. William Mills of 12 East Street also in the 8th D.L.I. is also reported missing. Pte. William Rowan, killed in action adds to the growing list of casualties.

On the home front neighbours comforted the mother of five year old James Moran. His father was away fighting the Germans. On returning home from school a little boy was knocked down and killed by a train on Brandon railway crossing. Great sorrow for Thomas Doran and his family in

Cobden Terrace when the victim of the accident was identified as five year old James Doran. Indescribable relief filled the Moran home.

The New Empire at Langley Moor was officially opened by the Vicar of Brandon, the Rev. Harry Hayward; it had cost £3000 to renovate the building. Great interest was shown in the new front scenery which depicted a group of wounded soldiers recuperating. They were gathered in the grounds of Brancepeth Castle with the ancestral home of Lord Boyne majestic in the background.

The four stone statues, each an effigy of a well-known Union man, after being wrapped in sacks and secured by ropes, were transferred from Durham's North Road to their permanent location in the grounds of the new headquarters of the Durham Miners' Association in Redhills.

At a local colliery the master shifter was having a row with two of his men, whom he could not persuade to do the work properly. At last he exclaimed in exasperation, 'Aa wish Aa cud faal in wi' fower gud sound upreet and honest styenmen!'

'Wey', said one of them drily, 'Aa think Aa knaa the only pleyce ye can git them. Trey them fower that stands on the front of the Miners' Haal at Durham!'

The postman's call invariably brings ill news; shaking hands open the buff coloured envelope bearing the official stamp. T. Turnbull, John Hamilton, James McVean, Edward McVay, Thomas Watson, J. Gill, A. Smith, Alfred Gill, R. Gill and Hugh McDermott, all Privates in the Army are reported wounded. They serve in the 14th and 15th Durham Light Infantry. Private McDermott crawled one mile to a First Aid Post after being shot in the knee.

Tragedy on the home front! It was five thirty a.m. and the end of the shift for sixty-three year old shifter William Hamilton. He was riding outbye in the set, as the tubs reached the curve he was fatally injured.

Exactly one week later, another fatality occurred when sixteen year old Thomas, eldest son of George Ainsley Parrish, was struck by a derailed set of tubs. Workers at the colliery observed the age old custom of taking the day off work on both occasions.

The King and Lord Derby made special appeals for more recruits for the forces. Robert Carr of 29 Albert Street was one of fifty from the colliery to volunteer, he joined the Royal Artillery. Mr. and Mrs. Tunney have six sons and eleven nephews serving in the Army.

Notices were posted at the pithead which stated that men working underground who are willing to fight for their country will be given an armband to say so. They must return to their work of producing coal until the authorities send for them. The armband is made from khaki cloth on which is imprinted a red crown.

Sapper William Gerrard of the Royal Engineers Tunnelling Company, after serving six months at the front without suffering a scratch, received a warm welcome on his arrival home on leave. He said that the Germans had used liquid fire against them. He had met another Brandon Colliery man at the front. He and Ike Herrington had received gifts when Brandon 'Women's' Working Party sent sixty woollen shirts and sixty pairs of first class socks to Brandon Colliery lads serving in the Forces.

A football match was played at Brandon between Spennymoor United and Brandon Institute; an exciting game produced a draw. At night a smoker was held in the Institute, the whole of the proceeds were handed to a grateful Ladies' Committee.

Pte. Henry Clark, a twenty-six year old Brandon Colliery miner, left his home on September 13th. Two months later he was killed in the Dardenelles. Nineteen year old Pte. Richard Burlison was killed in action on the same day; George and Maggie Burlison his parents, mourn his loss.

MINUTE

PASSED AT A MEETING OF

THE ARBITRATION COMMITTEE

OF THE

DURHAM COLLIERY OWNERS' MUTUAL PROTECTION ASSOCIATION

AND THE

DURHAM MINERS' ASSOCIATION

HELD AT

THE COAL TRADE OFFICES, NEWCASTLE-ON-TYNE, ON

Monday Dec 6 1915

No. 2841.—Brandon "A." William Hamilton, 63, shifter.— Killed on October 15th, 1915, through being crushed between a tub and the side.

Full liability admitted, £247 16s. 0d.

Dependants :—

Mary Ellen Hamilton, 54, widow.
Annie Hamilton, 24, daughter.

Awarded £247 16s. 0d. : the same to be invested in the Newcastle Savings Bank for the benefit of the several dependants, the shares of the several dependants, and the payments out of each share to be as follows :—

Mary Ellen Hamilton, £237 16s. 0d. (25s. per fortnight).
Annie Hamilton, £10 (forthwith).

REGINALD GUTHRIE } Secretaries.
WILLIAM HOUSE }

186

MINUTE

PASSED AT A MEETING OF

THE ARBITRATION COMMITTEE

OF THE

DURHAM COLLIERY OWNERS' MUTUAL PROTECTION ASSOCIATION

AND THE

DURHAM MINERS' ASSOCIATION

HELD AT

THE COAL TRADE OFFICES, NEWCASTLE-ON-TYNE, ON

Monday January 10th 1916

No. 8023.—Brandon "A." James Bell, 30, shifter.—Claiming in respect of injuries to his face received on February 4th, 1910, by a blow from a winch handle. The colliery doctor reported on November 23rd, 1915, that Bell is apparently recovered from his accident and is fit for his ordinary work.

Awarded compensation at the full rate of 15s. 8d. per week from October 18th, 1915, to November 22nd, 1915, and after this latter date at the rate of 8d. per week.

REGINALD GUTHRIE ⎞ Secretaries.
WILLIAM HOUSE ⎠

Pte. Fred Bailes of the 15th D.L.I. was among the December casualties from Brandon Colliery, he was reported missing on September 25th. Pte. Fred Storey who emigrated from Brandon to Canada two years ago is expected to receive a posthumous award—the Victoria Cross. After losing an eye and being gassed, he returned to the trenches and died at his machine gun.

Christmastide in Brandon Colliery was very quietly spent. The young folk especially the lads, patronised the Central Palace at Meadowfield where a serial of twenty-two hair raising episodes starring Eddie Polo in 'The Broken Coin' was booked. For the more mature, Langley Moor's Empire presented a play 'Pitman's Daughter'. Owing to the persistent rainfall, the streets were in a very unpleasant condition, but a few carol singers ventured out in the inclement weather. Many homes are in mourning at present through the war, many sons and husbands have been wounded since last Christmas. Very few soldiers arrived home on leave from the front on Christmas Eve and Christmas Day.

1916

After one year and five months of war the casualties from the district total sixty-six, twenty-five of whom have been killed or are missing. Despite the growing number of war casualties, recruits for the forces are still forthcoming from among the young miners.

'Halloa, Geordie', said Bill the other morning, 'Aa see the Government wants some mair money ta help carry on the war'.
'Aye', said Bill, 'An' weel they might'.
'Hoo's that?' asked Geordie.
'Wey, leuk what a happetite wor Tom hes', said Bill. 'Aa tell'd wor Meg it wad myek a bonny difference when he 'listed'.

Not a Happy New Year for Matthew Waddle and his family in 37 Durham Street when they received official word that their youngest son, twenty-two year old Pte. A. Waddle, had been killed whilst serving with the 15th D.L.I. He had been in the trenches for three months and was looking forward to a few days leave. He will be missed by the players of Brandon Albion A.F.C. of which he was a member; he was also a noted local billiard player.

The Government passed a 'No Treating Order' to help the nation conserve vital foodstuffs. Viscount Boyne had an audit day every month in Beattie Burrell's Colliery Inn; it had been customary for each of his estate lease-holders on paying their rent to receive a sixpenny ticket for refreshment—or cigarettes. There was general disappointment when the practice was discontinued.

Various schemes were conceived to brighten the lot of the man on active service. 'The Trench Tobacconist' promised to send seventy Woodbine cigarettes or four ounces of 'Arf a Mo' tobacco to any of your beloved fighting abroad, at a cost of one shilling which included postage.

Over four hundred and fifty parcels, each one containing one pair of good socks, two ounces ot twist tobacco, eight packets of cigarettes, one slab of chocolate and sixpence towards paying the postage were made up by Langley Moor and District Tradesmen's Associaton. Many grateful thanks go out to the secretary, Brandon shopkeeper Joseph Close, and to all the tradesmen involved in the scheme.

Children attending Brandon School on January 12th were subject to Arctic conditions; the heating apparatus, being defective was not in use. The temperature in Room 1 was 46 degrees, in Room 2 46 degrees, the temperature in Room 3 was 45 degrees. On 13th and 14th the rooms were even colder.

War is taking a steady toll of Brandon Colliery's young fighting men, three of whom were mourned in quick succession. Pte. George Thompson Naisbitt leaves a widow and four children. Another Brandon Colliery war widow and four children mourn Pte. J. E. Welsh killed on the same day. Both men served in the 15th D.L.I. Pte. Joseph Tunney of the 26th Northumberland Fusiliers was killed in action. Twenty-one year old Pte. William Lee died from wounds sustained in a bayonet charge. His father S. Lee and family live in Durham Street.

The Curfew Bell at Durham Cathedral, often heard from Brandon Colliery, was stopped from ringing when the city had its first Zeppelin scare.

The other day Jack was noticed wandering about the streets anxiously gazing into the sky; Bill, who had seen Jack in this manner, asked him what he was looking for. 'Wey, A'm lookin' for Zeppelins', said Jack.

'But thoo dissent want Zeppelins ter come ower here, dis tha?' replied Bill.

'Wey, aye', replied Jack. 'A've insured mesel for a hundred pund against loss of life be aircraft, an' tha knaas A'as arfully short of money'.

Crowds of curious sightseers gathered on Brandon Hill; men, women and boys had come from the colliery rows. The object of interest, a military aeroplane, had landed only a short distance from the spot where Col. Cody had landed a few years ago. Many visited the scene during the three days the plane was grounded.

A war bonus of two shillings a week was granted to workers on the home front. Miners received an increase of 3¾%; this brings their wage 88¾% above the 1879 basis, it is the highest ever recorded. Deputies working at the coalface now earn 8s. 10d. — 46d. a shift; deputies working backbye are paid 7s. 10d. — 84d. a shift.

Arthur Slater a whistler of renown, and 'His Master's Voice' gramophone have nightly delighted audiences at Langley Moor Theatre. Many Brandon Colliery patrons enjoyed his performance with the picture portion 'The Prisoner of Zenda'.

A War Tax is imposed on seats in the Empire Theatre.

1d. Tax is payable on the 3d.—4d. and 6d. seats;

2d. Tax is payable on the 6d.—9d. and 1s. seats.

There is no War Tax on tickets at the children's matinee.

Pte. Thomas Fox 8th D.L.I. who was gassed on the battlefield a year ago, after many weeks on the sick list, returned to duty. His wife on West Street has been notified that Thomas has had his left arm amputated.

Pte. John Emmerson of the same unit has been wounded a second time.

Sergeant Thomas Tyson, Army Service Corps and Corporal J. Roxborough left their jobs in the pit to enlist and are now serving in France where they have met other warriors from Brandon Colliery.

Sergeant J. Metcalfe and Pte. W. Darling joined the list of Brandon's wounded heroes. P. McDonough left South Street in October 1914; the twenty-two year old Private is in hospital after being wounded in the arm.

A crowded congregation, listened with pride tinged with sorrow, when the Rev. Harry Hayward, St. John's Parish, Brandon, preached his farewell sermon prior to his taking up duties as Army Chaplain. He has been in the parish for ten years, and he hoped he would be remembered as he served Holy Communion to the troops at the front.

The khaki clad figure of the private in the 8th Durham Light Infantry crouched in the wet, vermin infested trench, his thoughts were miles away in Blighty. Norah his eight year old daughter, James a six year old, Mary four, Kathleen two years of age, and his wife Mary expecting their fifth child—'What would it . . . .' The insidious creeping barrage of Jerry shells directed towards his trench abruptly ended Paddy's dream of home.

During May Laurie joined his brother and three sisters in their colliery house. His father Patrick Moran 8th D.L.I. was serving at the front when his fifth child was born.

News arrives almost daily of loved ones being wounded in action. Three families in High Street pray for their wounded lying somewhere in France. Lieutenant John Pennington, D.L.I. has been wounded in the left leg, he joined up almost two years ago.

A near neighbour, Pte. Tom Ramsey, enlisted at the same time, suffers shrapnel wounds from the eye to the neck.

After six months in France Pte. Robert Felton, Tyneside Irish, has sustained a bullet wound in the left shoulder. He was near neighbour to the two previous casualties. Lance Corporal John Gill, D.L.I. has been wounded for the second time; he is now in hospital suffering from wounds in the lower part of the body. Pte. William Fenwick, Royal Iniskilling Fusiliers, is reported wounded.

Pte. George Fairless of North Street lies seriously wounded in hospital; a compound fracture of his right arm necessitated amputation of the limb.

Lance Corporal John D. Higgins, Northumberland Fusiliers, has an injury to his right leg.

Pte. William Cummings of Sunderland Street, also a Fusilier, is wounded in the right arm. He is the son of Lawrence Cummings.

Pte. John McDermott D.L.I., son of Hugh McDermott of Queen Street has been wounded for the second time.

Privates John Ainsley and John Robson, neighbours in Newcastle Street received wounds in battle as did Pte. Thomas Robson, Yorks Regiment.

Brandon, Browney, Langley Moor and Meadowfield Workmen's Clubs pooled resources and held a sports day on behalf of the wounded soldiers recuperating at Brancepeth Castle. £17.19s.4d. was collected from the crowd gathered in Brandon Colliery field. A crutch race, three legged race, sack race, egg and spoon race, fifty yard sprint, stone picking, quoits and a singing contest entertained the spectators.

A couple of wounded Tommies were lying in a local hospital, one having lost a leg, and the other all the fingers of one hand.

'What are ye gannen te de when yer get fit?' enquired the latter one day of his mate.

'Oh, A'am thinkin' of gannen doon ter Kent te de a bit hoppin', was the reply. 'And what are ye gannen te de?'

'Why', answer the other, 'Ar wis thinkin' ev luckin' oot for a job as a shorthand writer'.

News of another Brandon fatal war casualty; Sergeant Joseph Tumulty, Northumberland Fusiliers, who served in the Boer War and has two medals with bars.

The list of wounded casualties lengthens:—

Pte. J. A. Brannen, Yorks Regiment is wounded for the second time.

Pte. W. Dowdle, D.L.I., has shrapnel in the knee. He lies in a Scottish hospital.

Pte. James Tunney, Northumberland Fusiliers, suffered from shell shock and back injuries.

He wrote to a friend:— 'I will tell you a bit about the big battle now. It was on the first day of July, on Saturday morning, at 7.30 a.m., that we got orders to go over the top. It was a grand sight to see every man Jack marching over to no man's land. We soon reached the Germans' trenches and when we got about 30 yards from them we made a rush with fixed bayonets and rifle fire. They asked us to spare them, but we let them see how we could use cold steel. They put up their hands and said 'Mercy, Kamrade; me got wife and five children'. It was man to man, death or glory to us. As time went on, under heavy shell fire and machine gun fire, we got to the second line of German trenches. They came to meet us to fight for their trench back which we took from them. Our line began to get weak from the loss of men who had fallen down the field, but nevertheless we marched on in spite of gunfire and shells bursting here and there. It was 10 a.m. I was blown up in the air by a shell which killed some of our men and wounded a lot. I was knocked sick, and was lying in no man's land for two hours before I knew where I was. Then, hearing the rattle of rifle fire I crept into a big shell hole, and lay there for about two hours. It took a bonny long time to creep 400 yards back into our trenches again. I was lost a bit in no man's land. I pulled myself together a bit by drinking my water which I had on me, then found my way out of the trenches on to the road, where the Red Cross vans were taking badly wounded men back to safety. I was put in a Red Cross van and taken away down the country'.

Pte. J. Bond joined the Northumberland Fusiliers eighteen months ago. Thirty-nine year old Jonathan went through several engagements including Ypres and Looes without a scratch, has been reported killed at the front.

Pte. Welsh is suffering from head wounds.

Pte. William A. Parrish, Tyneside Scottish is another Brandon Colliery war fatality.

Pte. J. Travers of Sunderland Street and Pte. J. Mills, both of the D.L.I. have been killed in action.

Brandon Tribunal re exemption from call up. Straker and Love asked for the continued exemption of a cashier and sixteen other workers mostly at Brandon Colliery cokeyard. It was stated that over two hundred tons of coke were lying on the benches, and they could not get it lifted. The coke-men would be required so long as the war lasts. Further exemption of four months was granted.

Pte. A. Dumbleton of the East Yorks has been wounded for the second time.

Corporal James Chance, Northumberland Fusiliers, has been missing over a month.

Pte. J. Watt, D.L.I., is wounded.

Pte. John Staff, Northumberland Fusiliers, of Albert Street, died from wounds. Pte. Staff, married, leaves a child whom he has never seen.

Twenty-eight year old gunner in the Royal Artillery, Pte. Robert Dixon, went to France three months ago. News reached Brandon Colliery of his death when shrapnel pierced his heart.

Pte Edward Ryan, Northumberland Fusiliers, was wounded in the chest and left leg, and lay in a shell hole for two days before he could crawl back to the trenches.

The Daylight Saving Act has been voted a great success. Clocks were pushed forward one hour on May 22nd. It was feared that the decreased consumption of gas would lead to an increase in price of the illuminant.

Brandon suffered heavily during the first month of the great offensive on the Somme; twelve local men having laid down their lives, two are missing (believed dead) and forty one have been wounded.

Casualties continue to mount. Sorrow and grief re-haunting some homes.

Pte. James Mills, D.L.I., killed by a shell. He lost his only brother last year.

Pte. George Johnson of East Street, has been wounded.

Pte. Michael Bailes, Northumberland Fusiliers, wounded in the forearm by an explosive bullet.

Sergeant Robert Foster, D.L.I., wounded in the thigh.

Pte. John Carr, D.L.I., wounded in the left arm.

Ptes. R. Kennedy, T. Harbottle and J. Carr, all Yorks Regiment, are wounded.

Ptes. Alf Gill, J. Humphries and James Turner, all Durham Light Infantry, are wounded.

War crossed the Channel when Zeppelin raids were made on the North East Coast, only about twenty miles from Brandon Colliery.

While a party of miners was discussing the damage done by the recent bombardment of Hartlepool a poor woman who had been gathering sea-coal on the beach passed at the time. 'Hey, missus', asked one of the group, 'Hey ye ony bits of shell doon heor what the Jarmens fired?'

'No canny man', answered the woman.

'D'ye knaa where we can get any, we'll buy it, ye knaa?' said the collier.

'Aa doot ye're ower late, but if ye'd comed doon that day ye'd hev seen plenty, for the Germans were throwing 'em at ye for nowt'.

Pte. Michael Lynch, a twenty-two year old soldier in the Northumberland Fusiliers, has been reported missing, no word being received of his whereabouts. He has four brothers in the army.

Pte. J. McCall lies in hospital--wounded.

Lance-Corporal Ralph Bee, Yorks Regiment, is suffering from shell-shock and wounds.

Six dreaded War Office telegrams sent to Brandon Colliery families announced that Corporal George Johnson, R.G.A., Pte. John Cornish; Pte. Titus Hutchinson, R.A.M.C., Pte. Fred Bailes, D.L.I., Corporal R. Trow, East Yorks and Pte. J. Bond, Northumberland Fusiliers, had been killed in action.

More Brandon men are reported wounded:—

Pte. Robert Ritson, D.L.I., seriously wounded in leg and back.

Pte. Thomas Blenkinsop and James Gardner, another Private in the Royal Medical Corps, have been gassed.

Lance Sergeant Kenneth McVean, D.L.I., lies in a Dublin hospital with shrapnel wounds in his right leg.

Ptes. Frank Kennick, Northumberland Fusiliers and J. T. Corms are in hospital.

Pte. James Robinson, West Yorks, bullet wound in left hip.

Corporal Ernest Wetherall, Machine Gun Corps, shell wound in thigh.

Pte. Philip Rome, D.L.I., wounded in left arm and side.

Pte. George Clarke, wounded in the legs.

Pte. F. Alderson, D.L.I., serving with the King's Own Light Infantry, wounded in the right arm.

Pte. William Welsh, wounded in the left arm.

Brandon Colliery's latest war fatality is Pte. J. W. Wilson, who leaves a wife and three children.

Two Brandon soldiers on leave and a civilian were fined £1 each for playing banker at Brandon Sports; they denied the charge and said they were playing nap, they had paid to go in to have a bet. At the same court a Brandon woman was sent to prison for one month for drunkenness.

The Chairman: 'What is your husband?'

Defendant: 'A shifter'.

The Chairman: 'He shifts the coal and you shift the beer'.

Two Brandon Colliery soldiers have been mentioned for bravery in the field, Pioneer David Anderson, D.L.I. was found worthy of a Certificate of Merit for great bravery and hard work under enemy fire. On being promoted to Sergeant he was awarded the Military Medal. Corporal William Gerrard, Yorkshire Green Howards, became the third Brandon Colliery soldier to win the Military Medal.

Men and women filled the local halls nightly. The Central Palace, Meadowfield, showed the film epic 'The Battle of the Somme'. This remarkable true record shows the horror and futility of war and depicts the struggle on the slopes of Picardy. School-children were admitted to matinees on two days at 4.30 p.m.

Councillor Carr stated at the Council Meeting that nine houses in Brandon's Double Newcastle Street Nos. 3 to 11 were closed owing to an infestation of ants. Although the houses were closed other people were living under the same verminous conditions. It is no fault of the people, who are very clean in all their habits, and as clean as in any other part of the Colliery or any other colliery in the county. They could not get rid of the ants, and the people were living under conditions which no member of the Council would live in. Instead of being better the houses were practically worse. Some houses had been closed, but the ants were increasing in others.

Memorial services for local soldiers who had left their work, signed up and received the 'King's Shilling' then fell on the battlefield, were held in all the Churches and Chapels in the district. Well attended ceremonies brought great comfort to families in their bereavement.

At the Brandon District War Tribunal the thirty-nine year old steward of Brandon Club with five children, and guardian of another family of six children, had their appeal against Military Service refused. A Brandon Colliery farmer, aged thirty-six, with a farm at Shincliffe was granted conditional exemption. The Chairman of the Tribunal said that a million trained men are wanted for military service.

Three more families mourn their dead:—

Pte. E. T. Coulson, D.L.I., has been killed in action.

Lance-Sergeant B. Carr, Yorks. Regiment, killed.

Pte. Robert Defty Freeman, Gloucester Regiment, has been killed by a sniper. He leaves a widow and nine children.

Lance-Corporal L. Wandless lies severely wounded in hospital, he lost his right eye and has thigh wounds.

Pte. M. Bousfield, D.L.I., Pte. J. Liptrot and Corporal W. Jones joined the list of wounded.

Brandon Colliery 'B' and 'C' Pits were idle one day. Both 'A' and 'B' pits idle the next day due to the shortage of trucks which had been diverted for war purposes.

Corporal Richard Trow, formerly reported wounded, died from wounds.

Pte. James Craggs, D.L.I., killed in action.

Mrs. J. Liptrot of High Street, Brandon Colliery had word that her husband Pte. J. Liptrot, formerly reported as being wounded, was killed in action.

Pte. C. Jackson, D.L.I., is also among the dead.

Pte. Ben Carr, D.L.I., twenty-six years of age, lodged with Mr. P. Lynch of Brandon Colliery up to the outbreak of war, has been killed.

War has hit the Ryan family of South Street. Pte. Thomas Ryan and his brother James having been killed at the front, another brother is reported missing, and Edward was badly wounded.

Wounded: Sergeant T. Lightfoot, Royal Field Artillery and Pte. J. O'Connor, D.L.I.

Brandon, Meadowfield and Browney Amalgamated Clubs once again visited the sick and wounded soldiers at Brancepeth Casthe, they provided a concert, tea and cigarettes.

The vicar of a certain country parish decided to make a collection of eggs for wounded soldiers and sailors. After going round for one month collecting these eggs, he grew rather tired, and on the following Sunday after making all the announcements, he said, 'My dear sisters, you would greatly assist this collection if each of you, when coming into church, would kindly lay an egg in the font'.

Brandon Colliery workmen gave the aged people their annual Christmas treat. The old folk were once again guests when Brandon Social Club handed out two stone of flour and two loaves of bread to each couple. Each member received ten shillings.

Christmas-tide was spent very quietly no doubt in deference to war victims. There is hardly a family among the people one knows that isn't more or less in deep mourning. The telegram was the terror by day. Mothers go pale and fight for control at the sight of a telegraph boy coming to the door. They opened the yellow envelope with trembling fingers. During the big battles the sight of a Post Office boy in the street caused agonies of apprehension; a sharp knock on the door was the signal for panic.

1917

New Year's Day, for the first time within recollection, was ushered in without the sound of pit buzzers.

Thirty-one year old Pte. Edward Cummings of the East Yorks was killed at the front just after his return from Christmas leave. One of three brothers serving in the army, Edward, a football enthusiast, played for Brandon Athletic Football Club. One of his brothers, William, has been wounded. Also wounded, Sergent Ralph Rumley, Northumberland Fusiliers, and Corporal R. Kennedy of the York and Lancaster Regiment.

At a crowded concert held in Brandon Social Club, Corporal Bill Gerrard, on leave from the Army, was presented with a gold albert and seal, in recognition of conspicuous gallantry on the Western Front, for which he was awarded the Military Medal. Another Brandon Colliery man, Able Seaman Thomas Tierney has been honoured. He won the Meritorious Service Cross.

At the Brandon Urban Tribunal Messrs. Straker and Love applied for exemption on behalf of a number of pipe workers and others at the coke-yards. They had had seven substitutes, all of whom had gone back, being unfit for work. One was a billiards marker, and he did not know how to fill coke. One started to fill a truck at eight o'clock and had not finished it at the end of the day, and he never started the next day. Another went to the works, but could not wheel a barrow. Another man had tried to throw up into a truck a gripe full of coke and it struck against the side of the truck, and coming down the man ran away. Six coke drawers were granted conditional exemption from war service. Local coke yard workers complain about these 'soft fingered' workmen who are sent as replacements.

Number 18 of the long Single Sunderland Street houses eleven persons in its kitchen and one upstairs bedroom.

One hundred wounded soldiers accompanied by their nurses left behind Brancepeth Castle to be entertained by the members of the Primitive Methodist Church to an excellent tea. A concert presided over by the Rev. G. B. Richardson was greatly appreciated, as were Orchestras from the Central Palace and the Empire Palace.

Pte. John Gibbons, Yorks Regiment has been killed. He joined up in 1914.

Corporal J. W. Bird, King's Own Light Infantry; Pte. A. McAllister, D.L.I. have been wounded. Pte. Robert Gibbons, Northumberland Fusiliers, wounded for the second time.

Due to the continuance of the war, food is becoming harder to get, there is talk of rationing. An order came to 'Plough up Britain'. Three hundred allotments have been provided in the district. There is a demand for more.

Smith was struggling laboriously up the stairs at his club, holding his hand to his back in a typical 'Every picture tells a story' manner, when he met Brown.

'Hello, old chap. I didn't know you suffered from rheumatism. I'm sorry to see you so bad'.

'Rheumatism be hanged', replied Smith. 'It's not rheumatism, it's allotmentitus'.

Mr. Deighton's Red Lion Inn, the Colliery Inn and Brandon Working-men's Club, survive despite 2d. increase on a pint of beer—now 6d. a pint; whisky up 2d. to 8d. a glass; Guinness Stout and Bass are up 1d. to 5d. for a half pint.

Pte. Paddy Moran, 8th D.L.I. arrived home on leave. The joyous reunion with his wife and young family which included Lawrence, the latest arrival whom he had not seen, compensated for the several months he had spent in the hell-hole of the trenches. Paddy, with knowledge learned from the previous leaves, was soon soaking in the large wooden poss tub his wife Mary had filled with hot water. Soapy water splashed around the small colliery house yard as he scrubbed his lice infested body. His army uniform, gingerly handled, was subjected to hot water and steam to rid the seams of lice. Paddy would miss the friendship of Pte. George Thompson Naisbitt and the riotous times spent together. Alas his chum was one of the many to fall in battle.

The Rev. H. Hayward, M.A., long settled in France, sent a letter to his parishioners in St. John's Church. His Pierrot Troop the 'Somme Black Cats' has performed with great success before thousands of 'Tommies' behind the firing line.

Brandon Volunteers tired of travelling the long walk to and from Durham to do their training, are talking of forming a Platoon of Volunteers in the Brandon district. Mr. Weeks, agent for Messrs. Straker and Love, has promised to provide a shed for drill purposes.

Pat had not been long in the Army when he was ordered with his Company to go on a fifteen mile route march. Pat, who had always been a poor walker, had fallen out of the ranks for the fifth time during the march, when the officer came up to him and said, 'Pat, I think you have made a mistake and joined the wrong corps'.

'Shure, and how's that, sor?' asked Pat.

'Well', the officer replied, 'you should have joined the Flying Corps, they only drop out once there'.

Local cinemas, keen for trade, advertised the special film in glowing terms. 'Come and see the tanks advance at the Front'. It was the Battle of the Ancre. 'Take the wife and children'. 'Nothing faked'. 'Among the sights to see, the sea of mud which covers everything and in which even the horses sink knee-deep'.

Geordie's son had been at the front, and a week of two ago he came home on leave. Geordie, anxious to get some news from the son, began asking him questions. 'Why Jack, hinney', he said, 'What's these tanks folk tark se much aboot?'

'Why, feyther, they're just wobbling thing-a-ma-bobs full of what-you-may-callems, and they blaze away like billyo', replied Jack.

'Aye', said Geordie, 'Aa heard they were wonderful things, but As could nivver get any details afore'.

Empire Day inspired the schoolchildren to bring flags to decorate the school. The children saluted the school flag. and during the afternoon they paraded the streets and sang patriotic songs. A collection of money was made and the 'Over Seas Club' received £2:2s:9d.

Durham Street once again felt war's impact when Privates R. McGregor and H. Maddison died from wounds.

Pte. H. Davison, killed in action.

Wounded: Privates J. Tunney; H. Colwell; R. Hewitt; J. Kennedy; M. Waddle; A. Woloughan. Wounded for the second time, Corporal Thomas Robson, Yorks Regiment.

Owing to vastly reduced attendances a ballot of Brandon & Byshottles Co-op Society among its members on the question as to whether the Society should carry on the Central Hall as at present. Voting showed For 281; Against 953.

After three years of war the list of killed and wounded goes remorselessly on. Killed: Pte. Will Freeman, Machine Gun Corps. His father was killed in December 1916.

Wounded: Sgt. J. Lynch; Pte. J. Sherrington, Joseph Ball, J. Woodward, M. Franklin, Driver C. S. Tibbett, Sgt. Joseph William White, Yorks Regiment; Gunner C. Donovan, Gunner J. Barkas, another Military Medallist.

Sorrow, detached from war, struck the Blythe home in Durham Street. After one week of intensive searching five year old Thomas Blythe's body was found in the colliery pond near Lamb's general dealer's shop. A Brandon youth saw what looked like a bundle of sacking lying in the corner.

Sgt. Flem Farrish, Royal Engineers Heavy Branch Machine Gun Corps faced the noisy crowd of men in the concert room of the Brandon Social Club. Their subscriptions bought the gold albert, silver cigarette case and match-box about to be presented to him. The chairman of the Club, Mr. Hugh McDermott, on handing over the gifts, referred to the Card of Honour and the Military Medal awarded to Sgt. Farrish and said that he was the third member of the Brandon Social Club to gain distinction in the war.

Sgt. Farrish recalled that he enlisted in the Tyneside Irish and was discharged. When the call came over two years ago for skilled miners he rejoined with several other Brandon men and proceeded at once to France.

He was twice under fire at the Messines Battle. Mr. Mearman's party provided the night's entertainment.

More Brandon casualties, Wounded: Sapper James Lidster; Sgt. W. Dixon; Ptes. R. Spirit, R. Ritson, Ike Hewitt.

The families of Bombardiers Sam Cully, M.M. and Stout were notified of their deaths in action.

Christmas was a time of gloom, albeit tinged with pride when Sgt. J. White, Yorks Regiment, was awarded the Military Medal. Again when Sgt. Major George Bird received the Distinguished Conduct Medal.

Pte. George Bowman, wounded.

Signaller James O'Hara, wounded.

Lance-Corporal John Humphries, killed.

Pte. William Jarvis, killed.

Pte. Thomas Hutchinson, wounded.

The list of casualties for the year ended with the news that Pte. Johnson was reported as missing.

1918

Food is becoming increasingly scarce. After three and a half years of war beef queues and margarine queues made their first appearance. Housewives clamoured in the streets for margarine.

A miner arriving home from work was making preparation to wash himself and change his clothes, when his wife stopped him and asked him to go and try to get a pound of margarine. 'Wait till Aa hev weshed an' changed, can tha?' asked the miner.

'Noa', she answered, 'Gan as thoo is; then cum hyem, wash an' change thesel', an' gan for another pund. They winnet knaa thoo is the syem chap'.

Early in the year saw the arrival of food rationing. Meat the first commodity to be rationed, could only be obtained on production of an official meat card.

A Brandon man has been elected public auditor for the Durham County branch of the Workingmen's Club and Institute Limited. James Turner shares this important post with another man. Mr. Turner's son, Pte. James Turner has been wounded for a third time.

Brandon Council School was crowded for the whist drive and dance held in aid of Lady Anne Lambton's Fund for Soldiers and Sailors. £32:13s. was sent for a worthy cause.

Men are still joining the Colours. After a brief spell of training they are despatched overseas.

At a certain camp in Durham County the orderly officer was on his usual round.

'Any complaints?' he asked.

'Wey, aye, sor', replied Geordie, 'this 'ere bally meat's raw'.

'Look here', said the Officer, 'Do you know that Captain Webb trained on raw beef in order to swim the Channel?'

'Aye', replied Geordie, 'bi gox, Aa thought as hoo we wor gannen across in boats'.

Three times the family of Pte. J. A. Brannen received word that their Yorks Regiment soldier had been wounded, each time he returned to the front. Word has reached them of his death in action.

Brothers Pte. James Tunney, Northumberland Fusiliers and Pte. John Tunney, both stretcher bearers in France, have each been wounded a second time. They are the sons of Martin Tunney, Brandon Colliery.

Wounded, another stretcher bearer, Pte. Robert Gage, D.L.I.

Wounded, Pte. John Bailey, North Staffordshire Regiment.

Mary Moran and her five children in Brandon Colliery's Durham Street were notified that Pte. Paddy Moran, D.L.I., is in hospital, serously wounded with shrapnel wounds in the back.

Wounded, Ptes. W. T. Eastham and George Bell, Northumberland Fusiliers.

Killed, Lance-Corporal Thomas Liddle, King's Own Scottish Borderers.

Killed, Lance-Corporal James Brown.

Edward Mearman of 17 Newcastle Street married Mary Ann Middleton of Trimdon.

At a full meeting of Brandon 'A' and 'B' Pit Lodge of the Durham Miners' Association it was agreed to nominate Councillor Carr for the Miners' Executive Committee for the No. 2 Ward. Tom Carr has been four years an active member of the Urban District Council; he is chairman of the Aged Miners' Homes Committee of the colliery lodge.

Total exemption from war service is rarely awarded; a Brandon Colliery coal hewer was granted exemption from the Army by the Brandon Tribunal, having three married brothers in the Army, and another ready to go, and himself the support of a widowed mother.

The Four Horsemen of the Apocalypse were War, Strife, Pestilence and Famine. The first two have been rampant for almost four years; Pestilence the third horseman arrived. Throughout the world the epidemic of Spanish influenza wiped out more than had fallen on all the battlefields. Civilians were dying like flies. Most expired in their beds, suffocating slowly, some dropped in the streets and fields.

All schools in the Brandon district, Brandon, the Boyne, Browney and St. Patrick's R.C. were closed for a week, prior to the summer break. The output at the pits suffered owing to the large numbers of men and boys on the sick list. Cinemas were closed; even public houses lacked customers for their watered beer.

The fourth horseman, Famine, sheered away after giving the nation a bad fright. In the summer ration books were issued for meat, bacon, sugar and fats.

The good weather meant a good supply of milk. The Advisory Committee for the Brandon and Byshottles let the good news be known that milk whch had sold for sevenpence a quart during April, May and June would sell at a maximum of sixpence a quart during July, August and September.

More reported killed, missing or wounded.

Killed, Pte. James McArdle, D.L.I., twenty-two years of age.

Killed, Pte. John Hamilton, D.L.I., twenty-four years of age, after two years and nine months in the Army.

Two Privates, William Winter, three years a soldier, and A. Kirtly are reported missing.

Good news for the Hutchinson family. After anxious weeks hungry for news of Pte. A. Hutchinson, it was announced that he was a prisoner of war.

Wounded, Bombardier M. Hodgson, Royal Field Artillery.

Wounded, Privates Richard and Ralph Harland, brothers.

Men on leave from the war were besieged for news of serving acquaintances. Reluctance to return to the horrors of trench warfare is nearly always evident. A few precious days at home slip remorselessly away.

O'Flaherty is the proud father of five stalwart sons, and prouder still that four of them are in the army and one in the navy. They all managed to be home a few weeks ago, and O'Flaherty displayed them to the admiring villagers.

'Sure, an' it's a foine fam'ly ye hev, Mike', said a friend.

'They are that same', replied the father.

'An' did ye hev much trouble with them—in the rearing I mane?'

'Trouble is it', scoffed O'Flaherty. 'Trouble, say ye, why be dad I've nivver had to lift a hand to wan o' thim, save in self-defence'.

Bill, invalided home from the war, was asked by one of his relatives what struck him most about the battles he took part in.

'What struck us most?' said Bill, 'wey, the greet number o'bullets fleein' around es that didn't hit es'.

Mr. H. McDermott of Queen Street has received a copy of the Army Orders by General Sir H. S. Rawlinson, Bart., commanding the Fourth Army and also a certificate awarded to Pte. H. McDermott, Sherwood Foresters, for gallantry and devotion in action on the field, for which he gained the Military Medal. Since being awarded the above Pte. McDermott has been made a prisoner of war in Germany. There is also another son, Pte. Edward McDermott, who was reported missing three months ago.

Among the wounded is Second Lieutenant W. H. Denholm, D.L.I. who has been admitted to hospital in Rouen seriously ill and suffering from gunshot wounds in his right shoulder. He is the second son of Dr. Denholm of Brandon, he was educated at Durham School, and afterwards became a medical student at Durham University. His brother, Dr. George Denholm has been appointed on the staff of a general hospital in France.

There was a capital attendance at the annual sports day promoted by the Brandon Institute Football Club. The principal attraction was the choral contest in which six choirs took part, the local Browney Choral Society was placed fourth. There was also a good entry for the hundred yard foot handicap for £25. Refreshments were again served from public subscriptions, £25 being collected. Twenty-one war widows of Brandon Colliery helped with the tea. The day ended with a successful dance held in the schoolroom. The day's proceeds were shared among the war widows. M.C.s for the dance were R. Barker, Tom Dickinson, Tom Lawson and Mark Pratt; the music was rendered by the Institute Band.

The football club has a good following—men keen to get away from the stringency of war, travelled to Quebec about five miles away to see their team lose by one goal in the Durham Central League game. Langley Moor were beaten by a similar margin when they played Brandon Institute in the Durham Hospital Cup competition.

More war casualties:— Pte. James Lee died from pneumonia following war wounds. Wounded, Pte, Alf Brown, Northumberland Fusiliers.

Further tightening of belts on the Home Front; the butter-margarine ration reduced to five ounces on October 20th, making it one ounce of butter and four ounces of margarine. During the month a curfew was imposed. Every night blinds must be drawn at 6 p.m. and during November lights are to be blacked out at 5 p.m.

Wounded, for the second time, Pte. John Bailey.

Wounded, Sgt. George Bird, D.C.M.

Wounded, Pte. John Higgins for the third time.

Wounded, Privates John Gill and Robert Davison.

Killed, Pte. John Kennedy, Northumberland Fusiliers.

During October the German Imperial Chancellor, Prince Max of Baden, asked for an armistice.

After fifty months of war, hostilities ceased; peace was declared on 11th November. Crowds flocked to services of Remembrance and Thanksgiving.

Mercifully the spate of messages carrying news of wounded kin had reduced to a trickle. The whereabouts of men listed as missing was anxiously awaited.

With the black cloud of the most terrible war in history rolled away and the sun of peace shining once more brightly in the sky, we can welcome home our soldiers and settle down to a peaceful future.

Tragic news reached three Brandon Colliery families. Only a month before the Armistice, Pte. Philip Rome died from pneumonia. Privates Thomas Smith and John Hopkins were reported killed. Pte. Hopkins was stationed in Italy; a keen musician and sportsman, he was a member of Brandon Colliery Prize Silver Band and played as half-back for Brandon United Football Club.

Another Brandon Colliery man, Sgt. Alex Simpson of the Royal Garrison Artillery has been awarded the Distinguished Conduct Medal. He has been twice wounded and slightly gassed.

On one occasion, although wounded, he kept his gun in action, and fired continuously for many hours until exhausted from loss of blood, and with only one gunner left. Another time he organised rescue parties and extracted a number of men who had been buried under tons of debris caused by emeny shell fire. He remained quite cool although the enemy continued shelling very heavily. Sgt. Simpson is regarded as one of the coolest N.C.O.s in the battery, and one of the bravest, and is a real credit to the district to which he belongs.

Welcome Home flags festooned part of Brandon Colliery on December 1st when Pte. J. S. Richardson returned home after two years in captivity. He is the first prisoner of war to arrive back into Brandon Colliery. He went to France in April 1915, was wounded in June 1915, and again in October and was taken prisoner in December 1916. He received neither letters nor parcels until the following August. The generosity of Belgian civilians in an internment camp kept him alive.

Nineteen year old Pte. Robert William Liddell had only been in France six days when he was made a prisoner of the Germans. His parents have been notified that he had been killed by a bomb dropped by an Allied aeroplane on June 1st, 1918.

Heartbreaking news reached the Bailey family. Pte. John Bailey died from wounds on Armistice Day, November 11th, 1918.

Deeds of valour are still reported:

Corporal James McVean, D.L.I., of Brandon Colliery has been awarded the Military Medal for devotion to duty in Italy. Corporal McVean was wounded in the knee when crossing the River Piave with his Lewis gun, and, although wounded, he stuck to his gun throughout the day and kept back the enemy. He has been wounded three times.

Curfews lifted—the lights shone again. Familes settled down to the first peaceful Christmas and New Year for four years.

ROLL OF HONOUR
BRANDON SERVICEMEN – GREAT WAR 1914–1918

1915

Pte. Frank Tunney
Pte. John Smith
Pte. William Mills, D.L.I.
Pte. Fred Bailes, 15th D.L.I.
Pte. Willian Rowan
Pte. Harry Clark (26)
Pte. Richard Burlison (19)
Pte. Fred Storey

1916

Pte. A. Waddle (22)
Pte. George Thompson Naisbitt, 15th D.L.I.
Pte. J. E. Welsh, 15th D.L.I
Pte. Joseph Tunney, 26th Northumberland Fusiliers
Pte. William Lee
Sgt. Joseph Tumulty, Northumberland Fusiliers
Pte. J. Bond, Northumberland Fusiliers

Pte. William A. Parrish, Tyneside Scottish
Pte. J. Travers, D.L.I.
Pte. J. Mills, D.L.I
Pte. John Staff, Northumberland Fusiliers
Pte. Robert Dixon (28), Royal Artillery
Cpl. George Johnson, Royal Artillery
Pte. John Cornish
Pte. Titus Hutchinson, Royal Army Medical Corps
Cpl. Richard Trow, East York Regiment
Pte. J. W. Wilson
Pte. E. T. Coulson, D.L.I.
Lance-Sgt. B. Carr, Gloucester Regiment
Pte. James Craggs, D.L.I.
Pte. J. Liptrott, D.L.I.
Pte. C. Jackson, D.L.I.
Pte. Ben Carr, D.L.I.
Pte. Thomas Ryan
Pte. James Ryan

1917

Pte. Edward Cummings
Pte. John Gibbons, Yorks Regiment
Pte. R. McGregor
Pte. H. Maddison
Pte. H. Davison
Pte. Will Freeman, Machine Gun Corps
Bombardier Sam Cully, M.M.
Bombardier Stout
Lance-Cpl. John Humphries

1918

Pte. J. A. Brannen
Lance-Cpl. Thomas Liddle, King's Own Scottish Borderers
Lance-Cpl. James Brown
Pte. James McArdle, D.L.I.
Pte. John Hamilton, D.L.I.
Pte. James Lee
Pte. John Kennedy, Northumberland Fusiliers
Pte. Philip Rome
Pte. Thomas Smith
Pte. John Hopkins
Pte. Robert William Liddell
Pte. John Bailey
Pte. William H. Allchurch, Northumberland Fusiliers

Let their names never be forgotten.
For the blood of heroes is the seal of freedom.

R.I.P.

1919

The old folk of Brandon Colliery were awarded their annual treat in the New Year when nine shillings were given to each single person and fourteen shillings to each couple. About eighty pounds were distributed amongst the one hundred and eighty old people.

News that Pte. William H. Allchurch, twenty-one year old Northumberland Fusilier, had been killed on October 27th last, has reached Brandon Colliery.

Another Colliery man, soldier prisoner of war Pte. J. T. Cooper, has arrived home. News of his impending arrival meant the sudden appearance of welcoming flags and excited friends; all returning soldiers were treated as individual conquerors and given a hero's reception.

Mr. I. Graham succeeded Mr. Richardson who left Brandon Colliery after serving four years from 1914 as minister to the Methodists of the Mount Calvary Chapel. Mr. Graham is the Chapel's thirteenth minister since the building was erected in 1873.

The new minister was soon called upon to officiate at the funeral of Thomas Rumley, a well-known eighty-six year old Brandonian. Thomas had lived in Brandon Colliery for fifty years having arrived in 1870 at the age of thirty-six. A large cortege visited Brandon Village cemetery for the burial.

A crowded St. Agatha's Mission Room witnessed a presentation made to Lance Corporal Jim McVean D.L.I. in honour of his award of the Military Medal. Lance Corporal McVean, a member of the Brandon Institute A.F.C., was saluted by his fellow members. He was presented with a gold keyless watch. The watch was inscribed, 'Presented to Lance Corpl. J. McVean, M.M. 12th D.L.I. by members of the Brandon Institute A.F.C. February 22nd, 1919'.

Mr. Ward the Nuisance Inspector for the Brandon Urban Council reported that during the month of March he had inspected houses in Newcastle Street. He said that while the tenants of Nos. 1—42 come and go, the ants still remain. One resident said that she had lived in the same house for thirty years; the ants were tenants when she came, though she thinks they have reduced in size during the thirty years she has been acquainted with them.

A good number of Brandon Colliery's Catholics were present in the crowded hall at St. Patrick's Langley Moor when a presentation was made to the Rev. John Parker. He was the recipient of a handsome illuminated address and two hundred war savings from the members of the congregation on his semi-jubilee as a Catholic priest, he having been ordained on April 29th, 1894. The Rev. gentleman succeeded Rev. Father Thorman, at Langley Moor some twelve years ago, and has rendered devoted service to the church during his stay in the district. The illuminated address was in the following terms:—

'We, the members of St. Patrick's R.C. Church, Langley Moor, desire you to accept this gift, together with two hundred war savings certificates of the value of £155 to mark the occasion of your twenty-fifth year as a priest, and as an attempt to show our warm regard for you and the high esteem we have for the great services you have rendered the parish during your twelve years as our pastor. To your untiring energy we owe the building of the new church and the establishment of the men's club, both of which are testimony to our zealous interest in the welfare of the parish. We hope that you may have long life and good health to continue your good work amongst us'.

A special meeting was held at Brandon on May 15th for the purpose of making arrangements for the forthcoming Peace celebrations in the Brandon Central Ward.

Chairman, Mr. Thomas Carr; Vice-Chairman, Mr. George Nelson, colliery manager. A secretary, assistant secretary and a treasurer were elected, as was a Procession Committee of eleven plus the school staff. Thirty were elected on the Tea and Refreshment Committee; twenty-four were chosen for the Sports Committee. An open air Divine Service will be held in the morning at 10.30, weather permitting.

At the recent election for councillors to the Centre Ward, J. W. Bird, W. Green and Joseph Robson were successful candidates.

Brandon Institute won no trophies at football but they shared honours with Quebec when they shared the highest points in the Durham Central League.

St. Agatha's Mission Room was once again crowded when the Brandon Institute Juniors, after having had a good season, held a Social. During the interval, the four leading scorers were awarded suitable prizes. 1st Prize, Tom Staley—a sold gold medal suitable for inscription. 2nd Prize, Norman Cook—sterling silver medal with gold centre. 3rd Prize, James Abson—electroplated case filled with cigarettes and a cigarette holder. 4th Prize, J. Humphrey—a Russian leather wallet.

Brandon Institute A.F.C. held their two day annual sports in the Institute field. Tom Staley and James Abson again figured among the prize winners; Tom came in second in the hundred yard foot handicap to win two pounds, James collected the third prize of twelve shillings and sixpence, W. Bartram came in fourth to win five shillings. P. Campbell won the go-as-you-please sealed handicap over two miles, his prize was two pounds.

Forty-three year old Christopher Simpson of Sunderland Street had worked in the district since leaving school at the age of thirteen. Chris, a coal hewer, was knocked down by a tub and his head was so severely crushed he died before reaching home, where his wife Isabella awaited him. It was the end of his shift.

Some seven months after the signing of the Armistice a Peace Treaty was signed at 3.55 p.m. on Saturday June 28th. The news spread with great rapidity; flags and bunting were soon displayed. At night there were scenes of great animation, fireworks being set off until the early hours of the morning. The news was put on the screen at the picture houses, audiences responded with loud and prolonged cheers.

Brandon Colliery folk entered whole-heartedly into the Peace celebrations. For a few months the colliery workmen had contributed by levy to make the day a huge success, so that there was no lack of funds.

The proceedings started about noon with judging etc. A procession started from the schools headed by the Colliery banner and the Brandon Colliery Silver Band, there followed decorated vehicles, comic cyclists, children in fancy and comic costumes, and the schoolchildren with flags, forming a most attractive spectacle. Sports followed in the nearby colliery field, and tea was provided in the school, each child receiving a Peace mug.

The soldiers had special events, including squad drill, bowling at the wicket, and egg and spoon race. The sum of ten pounds was divided, ten shillings each for the best decorated houses, some of which were tastefully adorned with fancy lamps, flags and evergreen.

To end a memorable day a Victory Ball was held in the school, when fancy dress was worn.

Twenty-one runners of the newly formed Harriers Club sent two packs to run the six mile course. The fast pack caught the slows about one and a half miles from home. Great local interest is shown when the Harriers turn out; pitman David Hopkins is the Club's most effective runner, he and another pitman, J. Cairns were among the one hundred and twenty-four runners in the paperchase of six miles organised by Saltwell Harriers. David finished in twelfth place, his club mate being close behind to finish fourteenth. Brandon Harriers sent seventeen runners to Saltwell.

Brandon councillors let off a good deal of 'steam' at their Council Meeting. They reported bad cases of over-crowding; at 62 Durham Street five persons slept in one room, one of whom suffers from consumption. Ten persons, eight children with their father and mother, occupy three rooms at 43 Durham Street; in 30 Durham Street three rooms house eleven persons—four married couples and three children, no houses being available. The medical officer recommended the Council approach the Colliery Company with a view to getting a larger house for the family in 43 Durham Street.

The surveyor submitted plans for Brandon Colliery houses which needed house-yards. The need for some of the houses needing their roofs raised was discussed. The inspector and surveyor were instructed to see when the building of house-yards would commence in Park Street and College Terrace. Mr. T. Dickinson on behalf of the Brandon Labour Party suggested at the council meeting that the Council take over the scavenging of Brandon. The present state of affairs was a menace to public health.

St. Agatha's Allotment Association not to be outdone by the splendour of the Workmen's Club annual shows, held their annual exhibition in the Brandon Social Club. Jim Grieveson won seven placings while Bob Fairless secured six for parsnips, turnips, potatoes, celery, cabbage and bouquets.

Another Brandon Colliery man gained further honour; Driver H. Eley, 128/129th Brigade has been awarded a Bar to his Military Medal.

The district is settling down to peace-time activities. Several Brandon men returned from war showing wounds of varying intensity. One is sharply reminded of war's savagery in the greatest conflict in history.

Thomas Fox and George Fairless each lost an arm, others lost a leg, Eddie Ryan is condemned to hobble around supporting a useless leg by the aid of a crutch. Patrick Moran carried eight pieces of shrapnel in his back which cannot safely be removed by surgery. Pity goes out to the young man who shuffled forward on toes, fighting to retain his balance, saliva continually dripping uncontrolled from trembling lips. His silver ex-serviceman's badge confirming that he suffers from severe shell-shock acquired during active war service. Jack Worrall and others find it increasingly hard to follow their employment owing to the effort to breathe through the inhaling of poison gas on the battlefield.

On the day Brandon Colliery together with the local pits was idle owing to the railway strike, the Brandon Labour Party held an open air meeting at the 'Pond Corner'. The corner, really a spot where out of work meet to chat, is overshadowed by one of the colliery's four ponds. A big Labour campaign is planned in favour of the nationalisation of the coal mines. Since such aspirations directly affect every miner at Brandon Colliery the meeting was very well attended.

It is stated that in the days when the landscape of Durham County was not hidden by clouds of colliery smoke, a remarkably wide area of country was to be seen from the summit of Brandon Hill on a clear day. The view extended to the north as far as the Cheviot Hills and Scotland, to the south was far as the Cleveland and Hamilton Hills in Yorkshire, conspicuous among them the 'Roseberry Topping', to the east as far as the sea, and to the west as far as the mountains of Cumberland and Westmorland. No fewer than sixteen castles could be seen at one time.

Pigeon flying, restricted during the war, is once again active. Birds are often conveyed to Brandon Hill for liberation to Brandon Colliery only a short burst of speed away.

Pigeon flying from time immemorial has been a ruling passion in the North Country—strong even in death. Legend relates that a young curate administering the Last Sacrament to a Durham collier was suddenly asked whether they would wear wings in heaven, and incautiously replied in the affirmative. 'Then', said the dying man, 'I'll flee thee for a sovereign!' And he died with the jest on his lips.

Norah Moran with Jimmy, Mary, Kathleen and Laurie, together with their parents, lament the loss of baby Anne, the sixth child of the family.

BRANDON MEN WHO SURVIVED THE WAR
AND RETURNED HOME

1914

Lieutenant John Pennington, D.L.I., enlisted September
Pte. Tom Ramsey, D.L.I., enlisted September

1915

Pte. Ralph Appleby, enlisted—volunteered to dig mines and trenches
Cpl. Christon of Brandon Colliery Inn, enlisted
Pte. Jim Ellwood, enlisted—volunteered to dig mines and trenches
Pte. Alf Gill, wounded

Pte. J. Gill, wounded
Pte. R. Gill, wounded
Sapper William Gerrard, home on leave
Pte. John Hamiltoñ, wounded
Pte. T. W. Hewitt, wounded—taken prisoner of war
Pte. Ike Herrington, home on leave
Pte. Thomas Hughes, enlisted—volunteered to dig mines and trenches
Pte. James Lister, enlisted—volunteered to dig mines and trenches
Pte. Paddy Moran, enlisted
Pte. A. Smith, wounded
Pte. J. Thompson, enlisted—volunteered to dig mines and trenches
Pte. T. Thompson, enlisted—volunteered to dig mines and trenches
Pte. Michael Tunney, wounded
Pte. T. Turnbull, wounded
Cpl. T. R. Turner, wounded
Pte. Hugh McDermott, wounded
Pte. Edward McVay, wounded
Pte. James McVean, wounded
Pte. Jack Worrall, enlisted to dig mines and trenches

1916
Pte. John Ainsley, D.L.I., wounded in right arm
Pte. F. Alderson, D.L.I., wounded
Pioneer David Anderson, D.L.I., Certificate of Merit—awarded Military Medal
Pte. Michael Biles, N.F. wounded in forearm
Lance-Cpl. Ralph Bee, N.F., shell shock and wounds
Pts. Thomas Blenkinsop, Royal Army Medical Corps—gassed
Pte. M. Bousfield, D.L.I., wounded
Pte. J. A. Brannan, Y.R., wounded a second time
Pte. John Carr, D.L.I., wounded in the arm
Pte. J. Carr, Y.R., wounded
Cpl. James Chance, N.F., reported missing
Pte. George Clarke, wounded in the legs
Pte. J. T. Corms, wounded
Pte. William Cummings, N.F., wounded in right arm
Pte. W. Darling, wounded
Pte. W. Dowdle, D.L.I., in Scottish hospital with shrapnel wounds in knee
Pte. A. Dumbleton, E.Y., wounded for second time
Pte. John Emmerson, 8th D.L.I., wounded a second time
Pte. George Fairless, wounded—right arm amputated
Pte. Robert Felton, Tyneside Irish, wounded—bullet in left shoulder
Pte. William Fenwick, R.I.F., wounded
Sgt. Robert Foster, D.L.I., wounded in thigh
Pte. Thomas Fox, 8th D.L.I., wounded—left arm amputated
Pte. James Gardner, Royal Army Medical Corps, gassed
Cpl. William Gerrard, Yorkshire Green Howards, won Military Medal

Pte. Alf Gill, wounded
Pte. T. Harbottle, Y.R., wounded
Rev. Harry Hayward, M.A., took up duties as an Army Chaplain
Lance-Cpl. John D. Higgins, N.F., injured right leg
Pte. J. Humphries, D.L.I., wounded
Pte. George Johnson, wounded
Cpl. W. Jones, wounded
Pte. R. Kennedy, Y.R., wounded
Pte. Frank Kennick, N.F., wounded—in hospital
Sgt. T. Lightfoot, R.F.A., wounded
Sgt. J. Metcalfe, wounded
Pte. J. McCall, wounded
Pte. John McDermott, D.L.I., wounded for second time
Pte. P. McDonough (22), wounded
Lance Sgt. Ken McVean, D.L.I., im Dublin hospital with shrapnel
wounded in right leg
Pte. J. O'Connor, D.L.I., wounded
Pte. T. Ramsey, wounded by shrapnel
Pte. R. Ritson, D.L.I., seriously wounded leg and back
Pte. James Robinson, W.Y., wounded—bullet in left hip
Pte. Thomas Robinson, Y.R., wounded
Pte. John Robson, wounded
Pte. Phillip Rome, D.L.I., wounded in left arm and side
Cpl. J. Roxborough, enlisted
Pte. Edward Ryan, N.F., wounded
Pte. James Tunney, N.F., wounded—shell shock and back injuries
Pte. James Turner, D.L.I., wounded
Sgt. Thomas Tyson, Army Service Corps—enlisted
Lance-Cpl. L. Wandless, wounded—lost his right eye and has thigh
wounds
Pte. J. Watt, D.L.I., wounded
Pte. William Welsh, wounded in right arm
Cpl. Ernest Wetherall, Machine Gun Corps, shell wound in thigh

1917

Pte. A. McAllister, D.L.I., wounded
Cpl. J. W. Bird, K.O.L.I., wounded
Sgt-Major George Bird—awarded the Distinguished Conduct Medal
Pte. Joseph Bell—wounded
Gunner J. Barkas—Military Medal, wounded
Pte. George Bowman, wounded
Pte. H. Colwell, wounded
Sgt. W. Dixon, wounded
Gunner C. Donovan, wounded
Pte. M. Franklin, wounded
Sgt. Flem Farrish, Military Medal, Royal Engineers Heavy Branch
Machine Gun Corps
Pte. Robert Gibbons, N.F., wounded a second time

Pte. Ike Hewitt, wounded
Pte. R. Hewitt, wounded
Pte. Thomas Hutchinson, wounded
Pte. Johnson, reported missing
Pte. J. Kennedy, wounded
Cpl. R. Kennedy, Y. and L.R., wounded
Sapper J. Lidster, wounded
Sgt. J. Lynch, wounded
Signaller James O'Hara, wounded
Pte. R. Ritson, wounded
Cpl. Thomas Robson, Y.R., wounded a second time
Sgt. Ralph Rumley, N.F., wounded
Pte. J. Sherrington, wounded
Pte. Bob Spirit, wounded
Able Seaman Thomas Tierney, honoured, won the Meritorious Service Cross
Driver C. S. Tibbet, wounded
Pte. J. Tunney, wounded
Pte. M. Waddle, wounded
Sgt. J. White, Y.R., wounded—awarded the Military Medal
Pte. A. Woloughan, wounded
Pte. J. Woodward, wounded

1918

Pte. George Bell, N.F., wounded
Pte. Alf Brown, N.F., wounded
Sgt. George Bird, D.C.M., wounded
Pte. Robert Davison, wounded
Dr. George Denholm, appointed to a general hospital in France
Second Lieutenant W. H. Denholm, D.L.I., gunshot wounded in shoulder
Pte. W. T. Eastham, N.F., wounded
Pte. Robert Gage, D.L.I., stretcher bearer, wounded
Pte. John Gill, wounded
Pte. Ralph Harland, wounded
Pte. Richard Harland, wounded
Pte. John Higgins, wounded for the third time
Bombardier M. Hodgson, R.F.A., wounded
Pte. A. Hutchinson, prisoner of war
Pte. Hugh McDermott, S.F., won Military Medal—made prisoner of war
Pte. Paddy Moran, 8th D.L.I., seriously wounded—shrapnel in back
Cpl. James McVean, D.L.I., awarded Military Medal in Italy
Pte. J. S. Richardson, home after two years in captivity
Sgt. Alex Simpson, R.G.A., awarded the D.C.M.—twice wounded and slightly gassed
Pte. James Tunney, N.F., stretcher bearer—wounded a second time
Pte. John Tunney, N.F., stretcher bearer—wounded a second time
Pte. James Turner, wounded a third time

1919
  Pte. J. T. Cooper, arrived home from prisoner of war camp

List of abbreviations:—
  D.L.I.—Durham Light Infantry. E.Y.—East Yorks. K.O.L.I.—King's
  Own Light Infantry. N.F.—Northumberland Fusiliers. R.A.M.C.—Royal
  Army Medical Corps. R.E.—Royal Engineers. R.F.A.—Royal Field
  Artillery. R.G.A.—Royal Garrison Artillery. R.I.F.—Royal Inniskilling
  Fusiliers. S.F.—Sherwood Forsters. T.I.—Tyneside Irish. W.Y.—West
  Yorks. Y.G.R.—Yorkshire Green Howards. Y. & L.R.—York and
  Lancaster Regiment. Y.R.—York Regiment.
  M.M.—Military Medal. D.C.M.—Distinguished Conduct Medal.

1920

Snowstorms raged over the New Year. Snowdrifts of eight to ten feet
being prevalent in the district. The Co-op grocery and butcher carts could
only operate from street ends; sledges came in handy to deliver goods to
houses in the colliery rows.

Snowbound streets and the shortage of scavengers prompted the
Council to seek the services of Tommy Harker of Commercial Street; he was
paid the sum of one pound a day as fee for cleaning out the 'netties', he
had to find his own horse and cart.

The New Year was only ten days old when forty-six year old John
Boyle, a well-known and likeable man, met his fate. John, a coal hewer,
was killed by a fall of stone in the 'A' Pit. On Sunday January 13th a very
large crowd attended his funeral. The Brandon Colliery Prize Band preceded
the cortege with muffled drums, playing the Dead March from 'Saul'.

An accident reminiscent of war: fourteen year old William Burlison
and his mate played in the long colliery row. Two copper pencil-shaped
objects were picked up from the street now cleared of snow. After pocketing
one of them, William put a match to the other, which exploded in his left
hand blowing nearly all his hand away, while his chest and chin were severely
burnt, and his face marked. The object in his pocket exploded, blowing his
waistcoat to ribbons, while his jacket was torn and burnt. He was removed
to hospital in a critical condition. They had been unfortunate to find two
detonators, the type used in the pit to blast coal or stone.

Archie Robson, caretaker of the Brandon Literary Institute, a place
much frequented by the miners of the colliery, after securing windows and
locked inner doors, left for home and supper, the time being 9.20 p.m. He
lived in Durham Street only a few yards away, his house lay near the colliery
yard and one of the colliery's ponds. Four hours later Archie was aroused.
The Institute, buit in 1872 was severely damaged by fire to the extent of
£2000. Three billiard tables were destroyed.

Woodbines, by far the most popular cigarette among miners, hitherto
costing 3½d. for two packets of five, now cost 2d. for one packet of five.

Other dearer brands, formerly costing 5½d. for ten have been increased to 6d. at the same time whiskey was increased in price to 12.6d. a bottle of which the Government takes 9s.4½d. back in tax.

Brandon Harriers and friends filled the large room in the Red Lion Inn when presentations were made to the successful competitors in the Good Friday Handicap. David Hopkins was presented with a cup and gold medal, he was the club's most consistent winner. Thomas Dickinson who presided, said that Brandon Rovers Football Club which was founded thirty years ago, held their meetings in the same room.

War dead were not forgotten; in the presence of a large congregation a war memorial and roll of honour were unveiled and dedicated in St. John's Church; the memorial consists of a dwarf chancel screen wrought iron placed on a stone base, with chancel gates four feet wide. The names of 123 men from Brandon, Langley Moor, Boyne, Littleburn and Browney are inscribed on six brass oak foundations. An east window and roll of honour bearing over six hundred names, is the tribute of thanksgiving for the men who returned safely. 'Let their names never be forgotten. For the blood of heroes is the seal of freedom'.

Forty houses in Newcastle Street, being defective and infested with ants, are to be reconstructed by the owners Straker and Love. There has been much bantering over the years concerning the same property and the unwanted tenants.

Thomas Carr who has long campaigned against Brandon Colliery's poor housing, received 249 votes against Wilson Allen's 143 to become checkweighman at the colliery, Sam Whiteley Sen. having resigned after holding the post for thirty-five years.

The 'A' Pit's second fatality of the year occurred when Sidney Lee, seventeen and a half years of age and a pony driver of two and a half years experience, was killed by a fall of stone in the landing. Another boy named Cairns, had a narrow escape when he and Sidney brought their pony set into the landing for transference to the shaft. A prop supporting one end of a long girder stretched across the landing being dislodged, a fall of stone resulted in the death of Sidney and the removal to hospital of his mate in a precarious condition.

A tragic affair occurred in Albert Street when a sixty-two year old woman who had suffered rheumatic neuritis for four months, ended her life. She was found at 1.45 a.m. kneeling on the bedroom floor endeavouring to vomit. She was quite conscious, and said 'That man under the bed said I had to take the stuff out of the bottle'. She had taken thymol cresol which had been kept in a bottle to be used for sanitary purposes.

A case of enteric fever at Brandon Colliery was reported by the Medical Officer. No definite source of infecion could be established. The street in which the case occurred was drained by an open channel which was not a satisfactory system, especially in hot weather. There was a certain amount of over-crowding in the house. One man complained that he could spend all his spare time chasing beetles out of his house.

Miners at Brandon Colliery and their wives are apprehensive, there is talk of possible strike involving coalfields throughout Britain.

At a delegates' conference of the Miners' Federation one hundred and sixty-eight voted for a strike ballot, only three voted against. In view of the Government's refusal to concede Federation's request for a reduction in the price of domestic coal by fourteen shillings and twopence a ton, and an advance of wages of two shillings a shift for members of eighteen years and upwards, one shilling per shift from sixteen to eighteen years old, and ninepence a shift below sixteen years. Are you in favour of strike action to secure these claims?

At the shadow of the crisis drew nearer excitement rose in the colliery. The voting strength of the County is 127,000. On 30th August the strike ballot for the County was declared; for strike action 76,869; against strike action 32,783. The majority showed an excess of 3768 over the two thirds necessary to carry out their wish.

As the ballot favoured a strike, notices were handed in on September 3rd. The strike notices expired on 18th and the strike began on September 20th.

More tragedy! During the strike more time was spent swimming in the River Wear at Croxdale. Fifteen year old Jacob Rowe of Commercial Street, a token boy on the pit head at Brandon Colliery, walked alone the three miles to bathe in the river at a place much frequented during the summer months. Unfortunately no-one witnessed his plight; he was missing for two days, volunteers from the colliery searched assiduously since Jacob failed to return home. Amid scenes of intense grief his body was found, in his father's presence, in twenty feet of water, presumably having been caught in willows.

The strike did not prevent cricket enthusiasts from enjoying their sport. Brandon visited Esh Winning to play a Wear Valley League game. Esh declared; eight wickets for forty-five runs. Brandon were all bowled out for forty runs. When Brandon played Stanley the final score being eight-nine--ninety-two in Brandon's favour.

Churches, chapels and business establishments are erecting Rolls of Honour in memory of fallen members.

Roll of Honour and brass shield were unfurled at a commemorative service held in the Commercial Street place of worship. The inscription read, 'Primitive Methodist Church, Brandon Colliery. To the glory of God and in loving memory of the members of our church who fell in the Great European War 1914 to 1919. Adam Beadle, G. W. Gibson, Isaac Jackson, James Teggart, who made the supreme sacrifice'. The Roll of Honour also contained the names of twenty-seven members who had served with the forces.

The following words were illuminated, 'Primitive Metodist Church, Brandon Colliery. The following served their King and country in the cause of right and liberty in the Great War. "The blood of heroes is the shield of freedom".'

During October the striking miners received one pound strike pay. Coal is very scarce at Brandon Colliery. Since the strike started men and boys have been going to the colliery heaps getting what scraps of coal they could to keep the home fires burning.

Ponies withdrawn from the pit grazed happily in the colliery field. Some pit ponies were taken to Durham and ridden round the town to the great interest of citizens.

Another ballot was taken, 'Whether or not in favour of continuing the strike'. Brandon Colliery showed a majority of seventy-six against restarting. As the majority was not two thirds of the vote the Miners' Executive declared the strike off and advised men to resume work.

Pit ponies, barely identifiable by name under their thick coats acquired during their six weeks romp on the surface, were rounded up for dispersal underground. Youngsters perched on the spoil heap, watched in safety as the skittish animals headed for the pithead.

After the strike a group of miners were standing near the pit shaft watching the officials put the ponies down the pit prior to the final settlement. The first few ponies walked straight into the cage as though they were glad of the ride down the shaft. Then the fifth one resented all endearing terms to enter the cage, and even objected after a little force had been applied. At last it slipped down and the men dragged it into the cage. One of the miners was heard to remark, 'Aa doot that yen hesn't accepted the terms', which made even the officials laugh.

Eight year old little Michael Solan left Brandon Colliery. His father, Thomas, had been 'left in the cap' at the colliery. After obtaining work at Easington Colliery, some twenty miles away on the coast, Thomas moved there with his family.

Michael is back among his former mates. His father dying at Easington Colliery, the family had to give up their colliery owned house and move. Michael now a robust seventeen year old, started work in the 'B' Pit where deputies Jack Lightfoot and Tommy Strong are in charge. Michael descends by the Staple to the 'B' Pit where Ralph Holmes, another putter, works.

St. Agatha's Mission also paid tribute to the fallen of the Great War. An illuminated Roll of Honour bearing the names of eighty men who had made the supreme sacrifice was installed. Also inscribed were the names of over four hundred local men who had served in the War.

1921

None of the local buzzers ushered in the New Year which fell on a Saturday, no reason being given for the omission.

Residents in the colliery rows are pleased with the new lighting installed. The streets look less drab now that electric lighting has been introduced; gas having hitherto been used for lighting purposes. Better illumination enhances the filthy state of the streets. One man wrote, 'Oh, thou bottomless abyss. I am almost swallowed up in this'.

On New Year's day Brandon A.F.C. visited nearby Browney, a noisy crowd in festive mood saw the Athletic return home winners by two goals to one. Brandon Institute Reserves beat Freehold Albion 4—1 in a Durham Central Leagie game.

Brandon A.F.C. held their first Ball in the New Parochial Hall. Supporters from Brandon Colliery travelled the short distance to Meadowfield to help make the club's first social function a success.

Three hundred club members all ex-Servicemen, marched with military gusto, through cheering crowds lining Brandon Colliery's streets. A substantial meal awaited them in the Miners' Hall. Hugh McDermott the Workmen's Club president handed each man an inscribed War Medal with the compliments of the club. The widows and parents of the twenty-three fallen members received medals on their behalf.

The Miners' Hall was once again crowded when Mr, Whiteley retired after a long and active working life. Mr. Tom Carr on presenting a gold watch and albert, also a wallet containing fifty-four pounds and ten shillings, said that Mr. Whiteley had been Lodge Secretary and colliery check-weighman for thirty-five years. The recipient in reply said that he commenced work at Oakenshaw Colliery in 1856 at the early age of seven years. Two years later he came to Brandon Colliery to work as a helper-up. He was pleased to see, that at the moment all the seams with the exception of the Busty were working a two shift system.

In March the miners were once again worried for the future. The conference between representatives of the Mining Association and the Miners' Federation revealed almost insuperable differences—there was a deadlock.

One coal owner declared that a reduction in the wages of all workers was essential for the recovery of the trade. If the miners resisted this process, he said, it was inevitable that collieries would be closed down on such a scale that the whole of the country would be brought to a standstill.

James Lidster a miner at Brandon Colliery, claimed £32.6.6d., the balance due to him of the allowance paid by Messrs. Straker and Love, owners of Brandon Colliery, during his military service. It will be recalled that James, along with six more Brandon miners, after volunteering, was bid bon voyage by Mr. Nelson the colliery manager. In June 1915 the company posted up notices inviting employees to join the Army. The manager, Mr. Nelson, promised the plaintiff and other workmen that they would be allowed two shillings and sixpence for the support of their wives and one shilling for each child per week. James claimed the money due to him from January 1917 to December 1918. Judgement was given in favour of the defendants, the colliery company.

Brandon schoolboys are having a successful football season; in the semi-final of the Chester-le-Street District Cup they inflicted a four-nil defeat on Grange Villa. Their opponents in the final will be either Chester-le-Street Victoria or Framwellgate Moor. Brandon are not going to be content with only one cup this season.

Black Friday! On Friday April 15th after the failure of talks with the coal-owners it was announced that all workers are to be withdrawn from the pits. Safety men included. The miners, railwaymen and transport workers, forming the Triple Alliance, definitely announced a strike from 10 p.m. In reality it was a lock-out as the owners had forced the issue.

Mr. Joseph Batey, one of the Durham Miners' agents, addressed a crowded meeting under the auspices of the Labour Party at Brandon. He called upon miners to stand shoulder to shoulder in the present difficulties. He said that the Durham coal-owners' offer is equal to a reduction of five shillings a week.

Brandon Harriers set off on their championship run and sealed handicap on Good Friday morning. The six mile course ran from Brandon Post Office–Brandon Station–Browney–Sunderland Bridge–Dairy Lane–Brancepeth Road to finish at Brandon Post Office. David Hopkins, winner of this year's North East Counties Cross Country Championship, won the race.

Many homes are fireless. Although the lock-out has only been in operation three weeks, there is a great scarcity of coal, and many miners are industriously employed,securing what they can from colliery heaps. An old man named Stout while gathering coal was badly gassed by carbon dioxide fumes arising from the fiery portion of the heap. Despite the dangers of scrambling over fiery heaps, a few miners have hired ponies and flat carts, and are becoming coal dealers on a small scale.

The absence of strike or lock-out money for the Durham miners is a serious matter and is causing a great deal of anxiety. Distress in Brandon has not yet become acute, though there are many applicants for the relief given by the schools. The tradesmen of Langley Moor have offered to give credit to any members of the local miners' unions subject to the union standing bond for repayment within thirteen weeks after commencement of work. So far the offer has not been received favourably by the miners.

Meanwhile the miners have adopted a very determined attitude. They are occupying their time in the gardens and with impromptu sports, and the local 'fiery heaps' have their daily contingent of coal seekers.

At a colliery, idle owing to trade depression, a group of miners was standing at a corner end engaged in conversation. One of them was lucky enough to have a fat pig in his cree, and an envious neighbour said to him,

'Thoo'll not be lang in killin' the pig noo, Billy?'

'Aa'll not that's a certainty', replied Billy.

'And Aa warn't thoo'll waste nowt', said the other.

'Aa'll not waste a thing, not even the squealin' when the butcher fetches it out of the cree', added Billy.

'What will thoo mak of that?' said the other.

'A new record for wor Jack's gramophone', was the answer.

There was great excitement in Brandon, not in anticipation of hearing that work at the collieries would be resumed at an early date, but eagerly awaiting the news of the schoolboys, who were appearing in a final football tie at Chester-le-Street. A pigeon brought the intelligence that Brandon stood a great chance of winning, and everybody was elated. Later, came the result, and there was great disappointment when it was known that the Chester-le-Street team had vanquished the Brandon schoolboys.

Nothing daunted, forty men and women supporters of Brandon Schoolboys gathered in the Red Lion, commonly called the 'Blazer'. A jazz band was born. The musicians paraded the streets of Brandon in fancy costume and collected four pounds three shillings and sixpence en route to Durham. A football crowd of five thousand on Kepier ground to watch Brandon do battle with Framwellgate Moor schoolboys in the final of the Durham County Schools' Cup invited a collection. Brandon Schools' soup kitchen fund was richer by eight pounds and sixpence halfpenny collected at the 'Schools' Derby'.

Jim Teggart and his wife have supervised, over the last seven weeks, the feeding of six hundred necessitous children every day. Members of the volunteer staff include Jim Ellwood, Thomas Lawson, Tommy Dickinson, Jack Jones and Joseph Bell.

The local relief committee organised a fancy dress parade. Brandon Colliery Silver Band followed by the Red Lion Jazz Band, headed a decorated lorry conveying the triumphant Brandon Colliery School football team with their trophies and medals. Brandon Miners' Lodge with their banner joined the procession on its way round Brandon, Meadowfield and Langley Moor. A matinee concert was held in the Empire Theatre. The generosity of the owners, Messrs. Wood and Briggs is a household word in the district.

What was scheduled to be the forty-seventh Miners' Gala was cancelled owing to the national lock-out. Brandon Colliery banner, like others in the country, was furled and put away until the advent of better times.

Laurie Moran, having reached the exploratory age of five, started school. His daily walk, the one mile or so to Langley Moor, filled him with wonder; hitherto the world beyond the 'netties' set across the wide wheel-rutted street was out of bounds. He passed the coke ovens whose fiery glow, before the lock-out, had filtered rose tinted into his bedroom the window of which permanently rattled as if in tune with the colliery compressors incessant beat. Laurie marvelled at the sprawling, decrepit sixty year old Meadowfield 'C' pit down which his father hewed. He saw the extensive brick and pipe works managed by Thomas Green, also the two majestic chimneys overlooking everything. He crossed the N.E.R. line, a place where more than one unfortunate had tangled with a moving train. He saw the grotesque spoil heap which relentlessly encroached the field in which the locked-out pit ponies ran free and frisky. A last look back as he relinquished his sister's hand, the daunting length of the man-made mountain leaving an indelible memory.

On June 17th a ballot was taken—for or against the new offer by the coal-owners. Voting at Brandon Colliery showed, by a substantial majority, acceptance of the offer. Meanwhile the Brandon Miners' Lodge paid out ten shillings to each full member and five shillings to each half member, the result of a grant from the local Aged Miners' Fund. The men greatly appreciate the gesture in a time of stress, the money will be repaid when full working is resumed.

On July 1st the Miners' leaders accepted the Premier's terms. Peace in the coalfields is assured until the end of 1922. The temporary period is to last three months in which reductions in wages are to be two shillings a shift during July, two shillings and sixpence during August rising to three shillings a shift during September. The men are not very happy over the outcome of the lock-out.

There is much concern over the re-opening of the seams at the colliery. Seams will not be ready for weeks owing to defective ventilation and other causes. The seams near the shaft; the Harvey, Low Main and Three Quarter will be re-opened immediately.

R. Foster, J. Plant and T. Dowdle, all ex-servivemen who served in the Durhams, and Cameron Highlanders, looking for a rosier future, applied under the Overseas Settlement Scheme, their goal being Australia.

Mr. and Mrs. R. Foster and family together with the Plant family, sailed for Australia in early September. Streets were crowded as neighbours and friends bid them good-bye; they were bound for Aberdare in New South Wales, there they will join Mr. and Mrs. R. Rumley who left Brandon Colliery at the beginning of the year. Quite a little colony of Brandonites has been formed 'down under' this year; amongst them being Mrs. J. Parkinson, Mrs. W. Foster, Mr. and Mrs. T. Foster, Mr. and Mrs. R. Hunter, Mr. Clem Parkinson, Mr. and Mrs. R. Curnow, Mr. and Mrs. J. Brown and Mr. and Mrs. R. Rumley, all of whom left behind the dim prospects the colliery offered, and undertook the six weeks voyage into the unknown but hopefully better future for their families.

Brandon Harriers turned out three packs for their weekly run, twenty runners in all. The slow pack paced by J. Richardson and whipped by W. Wilson, was given three minutes start by the medium pack, which in turn was allowed four minutes start by the fast pack paced by David Hopkins and whipped by Ralph Brown. The fast pack took the lead near home at the end of the six mile run.

The club took part in the Paperchase League run at Sunderland. Eighty-four runners turned up in bad weather to run the five miles across country. Of the first twenty home David Hopkins was second, other Brandon Colliery runners were Percy Hall, A. Rainbow and William Harrison who took fifth, twelfth and nineteenth places respectively.

It was a third class railway carriage, and a young fellow had talked so long and loudly about his running powers that an old miner in the corner thought he would take the young braggart down a peg or two. Leaning over, he tapped him on the knee and asked,

'So thou can run a bit can tha?'

'Aa can that!' came the ready reply.

'Aa'll race tha if thoo'll give me a yard start', said the old miner.

The young man laughed sarcastically, 'Aa'll tak tha', he said. 'That's easy money for me. Where will tha run?'

'Up a ladder', came the answer amid laughter from the other occupants of the carriage.

John, the seventh child to Patrick and Mary Moran, was born on Armistice Day, November 11th. Patrick, now affected by seam closures, has to bring up his family of six on reduced wages, cuts enforced by the nation's coalowners.

The lead up to Christmas is bleak; the men have received a fortnight's notice to cease work, over one hundred men are affected. Miners' wages were reduced in December; before the stoppage the coal hewers rate was 16s. 6d. a shift, for December the rate will be 8s. 4½d., a decrease of practically fifty per cent. Labourers' meagre earnings will be reduced 9d. to 3s. 3d. a shift.

Wesleyan Chapel, 1905.

St. John's Parish Hall, 1910.

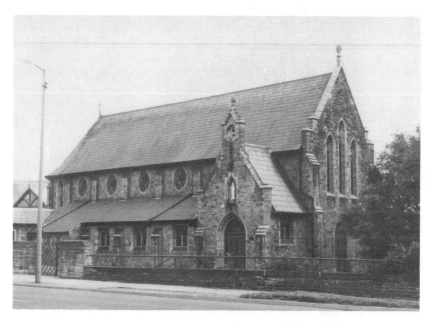

St. Patrick's R.C. Church, 1911.

Christmas festivities did not affect the prowess of four Brandon Colliery runners who finished among the first twenty when the Gateshead Congregational Harriers held their open race on Boxing Day. They were W. Harrison, 4th; David Hopkins, 5th; Percy Hall, 14th and George Harrison, 20th.

1922

The spectral symphony of strident buzzer, raucous greetings and diligent door knocking, woke five year old Laurie Moran. His mother waited downstairs in their Durham Street home; it was midnight—New Year's Eve—first footing was taking place. The usual gifts of drink, cake and money lay on the oil-clothed kitchen table awaiting the first foot.

At a colliery not far from Brandon, Meg had given Geordie a glass of whisky, and after Geordie had finished his drink he exclaimed,
'Wey, Meg, there was nivvor such a thing in my young days'.
'What!' exclaimed Meg, 'Nee whisky?'
'Plenty whisky, Meg, but nivvor such a small glass', replied Geordie.

On New Year's Day Brandon Silver Band paraded the streets playing carols and short 'toe tapping' dance pieces. Nearly all of the bandsmen are miners; despite the threat of impending wage reduction, their hearty rendering of topical music thrilled the colliery folk.

Durham miners and their leaders were bitter, when in early January they were called upon to suffer a further reduction in wages.

A worrying time, too, for four families, whose menfolk were not colliery employees. They are tenants of houses in North, South, West and Park Streets. Application was made by P.C. Patterson for the possession of four houses. He is empowered by Straker and Love to house colliery workers and evict when necessary.

David Hopkins was Brandon Harriers' only entry to travel to North Shields to run for the Clive Cookson Cup. Out of ninety-nine runners he returned second, beaten by one second in the five and three quarter miles race.

Several members of Brandon Harriers ran at Blaydon, the event being the Northumberland and Durham Paperchase League in which one hundred and eighty runners competed. In the team placings the Harriers took twelfth place. David Hopkins came in seventh.

January brought a serious epidemic of 'flu; there were many deaths in Brandon Colliery, even hard frost and snow, generally an ally, failed to prevent the 'flu's rampage. James Ellwood and his wife suffered severely; they lost their eleven year old daughter to be followed in two weeks by James, their seven year old son. An eighteen year old daughter, another 'flu victim, was taken seriously ill.

Sorrow gripped Number 8 Albert·Street when six months old Herbert Rodgers Russell died from burns to the lower part of the body when a detonator exploded in the kitchen fire grate.

The screams of the sixteen-month old child of Joseph Kennedy at 37 Queen Street brooked investigation. A hot cinder having fallen from the fire onto the hearth rug, had adhered to the child's lower body causing severe burns which proved fatal.

The whole of the coal hewers of the Busty and Ballarat Seams signed on at the colliery office. After a stoppage of nearly twelve months the seams are to re-open. The men's jubilation turned to anger when the manager proposed to work a third shift with men of his own choosing. After fierce objection, the matter was settled when the coal hewers' names went into a ballot.

News reached Brandon concerning the recent emigrants from the colliery to Australia. Luke Elmore and Robert Foster are working in the Victoria coalfield in New South Wales. Their colliery, the Sibria Colliery, is neighbour to the Abermain Colliery down which Robert Hunter, Ralph Rumley and Tot Foster, also Brandonians, work.

John Payne Cairns was nineteen years of age when he suffered a fractured spine in the accident in which seventeen year old Sydney Lee lost his life. John lay at 16 Princess Street for two years until his recent death. He was employed as a rolley-wayman at the time of the tragedy.

After a severe public outcry it was suggested that the colliery company abolish the open channels which run alongside the houses and are directly below most pantries, and provide sewers, and that such facilities be immediately introduced in East, West, South and High Streets at Brandon Colliery.

The existing depression in the coal trade is keenly felt at Brandon Colliery. For some time four days a week being the maximum time worked. The colliery sidings are congested with unsold trucks of coal and coke; there is no immediate sign of improvement. Brandon only worked one day in the first week of June. Durham miners' wages, unfortunately again show signs of decline, but, as the Irish hangman said to his victim, 'It will only be a tiny drop, so cheer up and look pleasant'.

Forty-three year old Charles Bell of 54 Newcastle Street served four years in the Army during the War; he returned home unscathed. His job was packing stone in Brandon's Ballarat Seam. As a packer he had to dispose of stone which had been broken by blasting. A large stone fell on him, causing instant death. The pit was laid idle for the day. The future of the colliery is dependent on the export trade—work at the coke-ovens is temporarily suspended. Prospects are grim in Durham County. The Miners' Gala was not held for the second year running due to the depression after the lock-out—too many pits idle being the reason.

Some miners train whippets; both man and dog enjoy the bonus of more fresh air and exercise short time working brings. Thomas Rodgers and Will Pouton promoted a whippet handicap which took place in Jack Barnes' field adjoining the Red Lion Inn. Thirty dogs ran in ten heats. Walter Hardy's Union Jack won, his Laughing Jack was second and Billy's Little Ivy came in third.

November saw the twenty-fifth anniversary of the lighting up of the streets of Brandon. In 1897 residents in the district assisted members of the Urban Council in the lighting of the oil lamps.

As Thomas Carr was made secretary of Brandon Colliery Miners' Lodge the Rev. J. Dyson took over as minister to Mount Calvary Methodist Church which stands alongside the Miners' Hall. He succeeds the Rev. I. Graham who has served the Methodists of the colliery for four years.

Laurie, at the age of six and a half, wondered why men and women unashamedly wiped moist eyes. The colliery band led the sad cortege to the cemetery; a deep gloom descended on the colliery rows; the pit had claimed another victim.

Some thirty men and boys huddled in the set of tubs hurrying them from the shaft bottom in the 'B' Pit to their district inbye. Young Thomas Clennell sat in the last occupied tub with John William Lightfoot, both were fifteen years of age and fellow pony drivers. Thomas, better known as 'Little Pompey' was a footballer of local renown, he had won seven medals whilst playing for Brandon School team. His ambition was to play for a First Division football team. His father was a coal hewer in the same pit. 'Little Pompey' started work down the pit on leaving school at the age of fourteen; there were six younger brothers to help feed and clothe.

Warning shouts were muffled by the rattle of the wooden tubs as they swung round the curve; a loose iron band, swinging on the curve, had grazed some twenty six fellow travellers causing shock and minor injuries. 'Little Pompey', struck on the head, slumped against John William, death was instantaneous.

Miners appreciate music; Gramophone contests were popular; one was run in the Red Lion Inn where forty-eight entrants played miscellaneous records over two week-ends. Joseph Harland, an old member of Brandon Band, acting as judge, gave his decision as follows; first George Reed; second Frank Lynch; third Robert Brown; fourth John Gates.

A gramophone contest was also promoted by the Brandon Social Club Committee. Tom Connelly judged thirty-five entrants in a humourous selection, results were, first Joseph Fenwick; second, George Reed, third James Lynch; fourth Pat Moran, fifth Robert Brown, sixth Norman Isles.

A miner bought a fiddle and started to play upon it. His wife, hearing the unusual sounds, went to the bottom of the stairs and shouted,

'Geordie, whaat's that aaful noise thoo's makin' up there?'

'Aa's only tryin' mi new fiddle', replied Geordie.

'Great goodness', said his wife, 'Aa thowt thoo was shiftin' the bed'.

Two special events were promoted by the Brandon Institute A.F.C. during Christmas week. A balloon carnival on the first occasion and a fancy dress carnival, very well attended, on the second. On Christmas Eve another gramophone contest which attracted twenty-two entries, took place in the Red Lion Inn where Jim O'Hara chaired a lively farewell smoker and presentation ceremony. A crowded concert room evidence of William Morris and his wife's popularity. Their friends had gathered to wish them 'bon voyage' they were bound for Australia where a number of their one-time neighbours had settled.

Norah Moran, now fourteen and left school, is most useful about the house; besides seeing to the wants of her younger brothers and sisters, she earns a weekly two shillings cleaning old Mrs. Doyle's home in the long High Street, money much appreciated by her mother and skilfully spent to help feed the growing family.

The Harvey and Three Quarter Seams have been closed for months owing to the poor demand for coal. The families of the hundred men affected are in dire straits.

Paddy Moran is experiencing great difficulty earning sufficient to feed and clothe his family, there being Norah, Jimmy twelve, Mary ten, Kathleen eight, Laurie six and baby John, one year old. Prior to December last, Paddy's wage as a coal hewer was rated at 16s. 6d. a shift, now it is 8s. 4½d. a shift. A savage clash in wages which has made him and other Durham pitmen very bitter indeed.

Since the arrival of John into the family their mother has been awaiting a bigger house as an extra room is most desirable. Sunderland Street two rows away has a small extra room—an attic with a rectangular hinged window set into the sloping roof facing the back street. P.C. Patterson the colliery policeman hands out keys to new tenants as colliery houses are vacated.

Thomas Rodgers took over the tenancy of the Red Lion Inn; with pitmen's wages at a low ebb he looks set for a lean time. Jane Beresford, tobacconist; William Green, draper; George Lamb, grocer; Jane Routledge, Mary Scott and John McAllister Wood, shopkeepers, long for colliery prosperity.

As Thomas Carr was made new secretary of Brandon Colliery 'Miners' Lodge the Reverend J. Dyson succeeded the Rev. I. Graham as minister to the Mount Calvary Methodist Church, Mr. Graham having served four years as Brandon Colliery. The Miners' Hall with its exterior built with zinc sheets lies only a few yards from the more pretentious Methodist Church built some fifty years ago.

During November William Whiteley, formerly a local miner, and Joseph Batey were elected Labour Members of Parliament for the first time. They ceased to be Agents to Durham Miners, posts they had held for several years.

1923

Geordie invited his friend Bill to his home on New Year's Day, and after a few preliminaries brought out the bottle.

'Noo, Bill, hinney, say when', Geordie remarked as he slowly poured. Time passed, and as Bill remained tongue-tied, Geordie stopped and stared.

'Gan on, say when. Can't thoo see Aa's still pouring?' remarked Geordie, letting a few more drops fall.

'Wh-wh-wh-wh-when', exclaimed Bill at last.

'Aa diddent knaa thooo stammered', said Geordie, attending to his own glass.

'Aa divvent as a rule', replied Bill, smiling. 'But Aa cannot help it on speshul occasions'.

Both Brandon United and Brandon Institute were busy in their respective Divisions. The Institute are fifth in Division One of the Durham Central League; Brandon United who are lying second in Division Two, beat Sunnybrow five goals to one in the Durham Amateur Cup.

A heavy course of nine miles which included a quarter of a mile of ploughed field, faced Brandon Harriers' David Hopkins and Percy Hall when they took part in the Senior Championship of the North Eastern Cross Country Race held at Houghton. Percy, last year's Junior Championship winner, finished fourteenth.

On the winding up of the Brandon Harriers Club some of the members joined Sunderland Harriers. David Hopkins soon made his mark. Out of one hundred and forty-nine runners the Brandon man finished second, being beaten for the winning position by only three seconds, the occasion being the race from Monkseaton to Heaton for the Longfield and Watson Memorial Cup.

Some families in the colliery augment their income by stocking a few household commodities and selling them to their neighbours. Local tradesmen are up in arms over shops of which there are over seventy in the twenty-nine streets in Brandon Colliery. They pay neither rates nor taxes.

Measles is once again rampant in the colliery rows. Three miners, Thomas Lawson, Matt Pickford and Tom Strong, each lost an infant to the disease.

Measles did not prevent twenty pupils of Brandon School from sharing in the Dobbinson Charity prizes for school attendance. The prizes were distributed by Vicar Hayward who is chairman of the school governors. The pupils had made the full total of four hundred and five attendances. Miss Dinah E. Muckle was engaged as temporary teacher at the school, her salary being twenty-eight shillings and sixpence a week.

The Joint Committee which had been in existence for fifty-one years was disbanded. The Committee's decisions had not always been to the men's satisfaction, most men feel that the Committee had served its purpose.

Excitedly, seven year old Laurie Moran helped pull the heavily laden colliery hand-cart. P.C. Patterson, in charge of the colliery house keys, had sanctioned the removal from Durham Street to Sunderland Street, two streets away. Furniture swayed alarmingly as the long handled bogey trundled over the rough ground. Laurie and his brother has decimated the swarm of gigantic black beetles as they scuttled across the kitchen floor. The move into a bigger house was made necessary on the arrival of baby Edward into the Moran family which already houses three girls and three boys.

There was jubilation in Brandon Colliery when the Ambulance Team won the Donald Bain Shield, fifteen years having elapsed since the trophy was last in Brandon. The team consisting of George Lee (captain), G. W. Hoggarth, R. H. Farrell, Ken McVean and W. Abson, scored thirty-eight points more than their nearest rival, Wheatley Hill.

On the following Sunday the colliery streets were lined with well-wishers when the victorious team paraded, showing their trophies, the Donald Bain Sheild, the Durham County Club Union Challenge Shield and medals. The men were exceedingly smart in their well cared for uniforms and military marching.

A group of pitmen were being examined by a doctor in ambulance work. 'Supposing', said the Doctor to one of them, 'a man was blown up by gunpowder, what would yo do?'

'Aa wad wait till he came doon', replied Geordie.

Another much larger parade took place on May Day when the workers of the district celebrated in style. Three miners' lodges, Brandon, Browney and Littleburn Collieries, with their officials and banners, paraded the principal streets headed by the Brandon Colliery Silver Prize Band. The lively throng headed for Langley Moor's Empire Theatre where Joe Batey, Labour M.P. for the area, addressed a large crowd.

Brandon Miners' Hall was packed when the result of the election of officers of the Brandon Miners' Lodge—Durham Miners' Association was made known. Great interest is taken in the yearly event. Thomas Dickinson was elected president; secretary, Thomas Carr; treasurer, Norman Richardson; assistant weighman, John Clennel; delegate, William Robertshaw; representatives on Minimum Wage Board, T. Carr and T. Dickinson; hewers' average-takers, J. Harland and Tom Connelly; stonemen's representative J. Jones; auditors Tom Tyson and Charles Grice; crakeman, W. Robson; local pit inspectors, T. Tyson, Abel Hopkins, Jack Higgins, T. Davis, Tot Underwood and J. Goodall; the committee of eight being William Thompson, Flem Farrish, Jackson Hewitson, William Dowdle, J. Cairns, T. Davis, J. Walker and T. Taylor.

An estimated crowd of 200,000 attended the 47th Durham Miners' Gala. Brandon Lodge was among the 190 Lodges present and its banner shared the racecourse with 113 colourful silken banners. Greater interest in the Gala being shown this year as it was abandoned in 1921 and 1922. Despite the twelve hour opening of Durham's public houses only one man was charged with disorderly conduct.

At the Miners' Gala the people were all eagerly watching the different bands and banners marching onto the field. By the side of a pitman stood a Scotsman, and when a banner appeared, played in by a band of Scottish pipers in kilts, Jock was all smiles and cheers. 'That's all right', he said. Next came a local colliery band, and the weather being rather hot, the drummer had taken off his coat and was banging the drum with both drumsticks flying round.

'Why, he's daft', said the Scotsman.

'No', replied the miner, 'he's aal reet; he didn't hev te tak his troosers off te blaw the bagpipes'.

On the Monday following the Big Meeting the miners had a day's holiday, it being August Bank Holiday Monday. Brandon sweltered in the summer heat; crowds left behind the colliery rows and walked to Morley Wood and Pit House Fell where the cool breezes were appreciated—picnics being the order of the day.

Robert Cairns was born eighty years ago, he lives with his seventy-nine year old wife in Brandon Aged Miners' Homes. Robert commenced work at Sherburn Hill Colliery at the tender age of eight, being frequently carried to and from the pit by his father. He retired at the age of seventy after forty-two years as a deputy overman. They celebrated their Golden Wedding in great style, a supper and dance being held in the Brandon Institute in their honour. They have seven sons and four daughters, twenty-six grandchildren and twenty-three great-grandchildren, most of whom made it a noisy, albeit joyful occasion.

Brandon Homing Society sent twenty-seven birds to Hastings. Bad weather delayed liberation; it took seven and a half hours for the winner to finish in a storm. First, T. Collins 1106; second, J. Lee; third Adam Bailes and fourth Jack Walton.

A week later a similar race was flown, this time with nineteen birds. Jack Walton won the silver cup given by Charles Christon of the Colliery Inn, the secretary of the club. The birds were timed in with a new clock costing £8.

In another pigeon race, James Lee's bird, the only one to time in owing to the pigeons being liberated late, won for its owner a pair of racing pigeons donated by Mr. Potts, and a gold medal valued at four guineas by Mrs. Beattie Burrell, Colliery Inn.

Brandon's cricketers enjoying a successful season and a good crowd of supporters, played Sacriston in a Deerness League game. Brandon, having won thirteen of their fifteen games, were fancied to win. An exciting game ended in a draw, each team recording 83 runs. N. Huntley took seven wickets for Brandon at a small cost.

Despite the persistent coal trade depression the Indian summer attracted crowds to the coast. The fine little resort of Blackhall was invaded by visitors from Brandon and Langley Moor when hundreds travelled by char-a-banc and bus. After a long hot day all returned home without mishap.

Sunderland Stadium rang with cheers from hundreds of Brandon supporters when their promising young boxer, Steve Ryan stepped into the ring. Jack Rose from nearby Broompark had elected to fight Steve for £25 a side. The match was a keen one and productive of much clever ringcraft, but in the tenth round Ryan floored his opponent, the latter being counted out. The result was a popular one and the winner had a great ovation.

Mrs. Burrell gave a Bowl for which footballing schools in Brandon and Byshottles would compete; the Burrell Charity Bowl Competition looked like a very popular innovation. Owing to dissatisfaction existing among the controllers of school football with respect to the rules governing the competition, Mrs. Burrell withdrew the trophy from the football competition and transferred it to the local Homing Societies for long distance flight contests.

A race was flown from Hastings; a gold medal valued at £2. 10s. was given with the Bowl. Brandon Homing Society concluded an interesting season by taking part in a race from Luton.

Brandon's Catholics trudged through thick snow to attend the customary Midnight Mass at St. Patrick's Langley Moor on Christmas Eve. Extra seating had to be provided to cater for the occasion. The Rev. John Parker celebrated High Mass at which the choir sang admirably under the direction of Mr. John McGough, organist and choir-master.

1924

The dissonant midnight intrusion of the colliery buzzers stirred would-be harbingers of good fortune into frenzied activity; the bitter cold and the prospects of a warming glass of spirit set first footers' legs pounding the streets.

Geordie was visiting his friend, and it being Christmas time he was offered refreshment. 'Noo, Geordie', said his host, 'will tha hev a glass of rum or whisky?'

'Aye, Aa divvent mind Bill, lad', was the reply. Bill filled the whisky, and handing it to Geordie, said,

'Here's another nail i' thee coffin'.

'Howay', said Geordie, 'Aa's not nervous, so when thoo hes the hammer i' thee hand thoo can knock anuther one in'.

Full members of Brandon and Byshottles Co-operative Society received an early New Year's bonus. Sales for the quarter had reached £53,938 of which £7,331 was handed out to them at a dividend of 3s. 2d. in the pound.

The chairman of the Society, Mr. Wilson Allan, made the proud boast that the Society's balance sheet was one of the finest in the County of Durham. The committee decided to provide a silver cup for competition amongest the four schools' football teams in the district, Brandon Council, Browney Council, North Brancepeth (Boyne) Council and St. Patrick's R.C. Proceeds of all the matches to be devoted to the Durham County Hospital. This will supersede the Burrell Bowl Competition which is in future to be contested between Homing Societies instead of football teams.

The district is once more well supplied with football teams. A discerning crowd saw Tot Bartram score two fine goals for First Division Brandon Institute against their Second Division neighbours and rival Brandon United in the second round of the Brandon Aged Miners' Cup. United defeated Durham Shire Hall two goals to one to head the Durham Central League Division Two.

Pit lad David Hopkins forced the pace in the gruelling five and a half miles road race to South Shields. He finished fourth out of a total of ninety-six runners. He was awarded a prize for being among the first six home; his time of twenty-eight minutes eleven seconds was only forty-four seconds behind the winner. David, a member of Sunderland Harriers Club, entered the six and a half miles race at Heaton, he came in second out of one hundred and twenty-nine runners.

On the first Monday of April at 2.45 a.m., school leavers fourteen year old Jimmy Moran and his mate of similar age, having been set on as pony drivers, walked silently in the dark to the 'A' Pit pit-head. What would this new life hold for Jimmy and Tommy Parks? Jimmy was shown how to gear up his fractious young gallowa and detailed to drive him from the top of First Incline in the Ballarat Seam to the bottom of the Second Incline also called the Cross-Cut. Jimmy became accustomed to the strong horsey smell as he rode on the first of the four tubs the pony hauled. Jimmy and Tommy Parks drew eighteen shillings for their six day week.

Two horse-keepers tended the large number of ponies operating in the Busty and Hutton Seams. A Brandon Colliery man, Thomas Ridley, cared for the ponies stabled in the Busty while farmer Milner's son from Primrose Farm near New Brancepeth, daily descended the nine spiralled steps of the Staple to the Hutton Seam where his animals were stabled. Some twenty stalls comprised the Hutton Seam's stables set about one and a half miles from the shaft. Professor; Stick; John; Donald; York; Duncan and Bullet were some of the pony occupants. Bullet, deemed dangerous, was muzzled and gagged.

More football! Brandon Institute's large following accompanied their team to Durham's Holiday Park to see them take on Ushaw Moor in the final of the Brandon Aged Miner's Cup. Ushaw Moor returned victors having won three goals to two.

It was proposed to amalgamate Brandon Institute with Brandon United, both teams having accomplished good work during the season. At a final meeting held in the Institute A.F.C. Hall it was decided to run teams in the Durham Central League (first and second divisions) and to enter for the following cups: Durham and Deerness Aged Miners', Durham Hospital, Sherburn Convalescent Homes' and Brandon Aged Miners'. The new team is to be called Brandon Colliery A.F.C.

Schoolboy George Tones, seeking newts to take to school, knelt at the edge of the colliery pond, he was the only human inside the boundary fence. John Thomas Mortimer, better known as Jack, a Brandon Colliery miner, retrieved George's lifeless body. The pond had claimed another victim. Sorrowing neighbours gathered on the hot summer day to witness the brave miner carry the fourteen year old boy's dripping body the full length of Newcastle Street to the Tones' home.

Newcastle Street figured in the discussion at the Brandon Urban Council meeting. Members highly praised Straker and Love for the work done in that street. Brandon Councillor Tom Carr declared that the work had been done at the expense of other improvements at Brandon Colliery. In College Terrace the tenants were without coal-houses and were compelled to keep coals under the stairs. Some of the people were living under wretched conditions. It was his opinion that the reconstructed houses in Newcastle Street were for people who were to be brought into the place in connection with the development of the colliery.

September was a month of calamity. All house repair and rebuilding ceased. On Saturday August 30th Jimmy Moran and Tommy Parks, after five months of work, joined the 1300 workmen and officials of Brandon Colliery who received fourteen days' notice to terminate their employment. Puzzled and dejected men brought their gear out of the pit; all ponies and tubs were drawn from the mine to the surface. All unusual activity pointed to a lengthy spell of idleness. The coal industry was in a worse position today than at any time since 1878. Recently the coal hewers had suffered a loss of threepence three farthings a shift with other classes of labour in proportion.

Harry Young, a deputy and a victim of the lock-out, forlornly viewed his two roomed Railway Street home just gutted by fire. Colliery engineer John Brown had organised firefighters who prevented damage to adjoining houses.

John Studholme, known locally as 'Little Johnnie' was a simple minded man who loved children and dumb animals, he attended all local funerals, weddings and receptions. People lined the streets when forty-two year old 'Little Johnnie' was buried; his end was sudden and unexpected.

Brandon's reshuffled football teams fared poorly; nearly half-way through the season saw Brandon Colliery lying third off bottom in the Durham Central League. Coxhoe United beat them five goals to one in the League Cup Competition. The United Methodists beat Brandon Juniors.

After almost four months without work the colliery inhabitants faced a bleak Christmas. Pit ponies revelled in the smoke-free atmosphere as they grazed and grew long cold excluding coats.

PONY POEM

We hear praise for the flowers,
The sun, and the stars that shine,
But a praising word is seldom heard
For the ponies down the mine.
Year in, year out these ponies toil,

Never seeing the light of day,
Oft covered with sweat, they pull a set
Of tubs along the way,
And often when they have to stop,
Beat by too big a set,
A whip or stick, aye, oft a kick,
Is the only help they get.
The inventors have done wondrous things,
And it's hoped they may
Invent something which at last will bring
These ponies to the light of day.

1925

Long-suffering miners' wives queued for their quarterly 'divi' payout. Despite the fact that Brandon Colliery has been closed down since last September, the sales of the Brandon and Byshottles Co-operative Society haven't been greatly affected. Paddy Moran's wife, expecting an addition to the seven in family already in Sunderland Street, along with fellow members of the Society, was delighted to draw dividend of 3s. 2d. in the pound. Norah, her eldest daughter, now worked as a maid in Yorkshire, she earned seven shillings and sixpence a week of which she sent five shillings home to help relieve the financial distress.

Hugh McDermott of Railway Street, miner, was elected to represent Brandon on the Store Committee when he polled 506 votes.

Out of work pigeon fanciers spent more time tending their birds in Brandon Colliery's conglomeration of pigeon crees. James Campbell and partners sent birds to Northallerton for the race back to the colliery, one of which won first prize of a young pig kindly donated by Mrs. Burrell of the Colliery Inn.

Geordie and Bill were homing pigeon fanciers, and they sent some of their birds to a race, but, unfortunately, Bill's birds failed to return. Annoyed at this, he went to Geordie and asked whether his pigeons had arrived or not.

'Aye, Bill', said Geordie. 'Aa'll mine's in the cree'.

'That's queer', replied Bill, 'Nyen o' mine hes come back hyem'.

'Wey, dis thoo knaa what thoo should dee, Bill?' said Geordie.

'What hinney?'

'Bi, gox, thoo should cross 'em wi' a parrot', was the answer, 'an' then they cud ask their way hyem'.

During recent months several families have left Brandon Colliery bound for distant shores. Pit lad Charles Jones, a Brandon Colliery bandsman from boyhood, left the colliery for Australia with his mother and three sisters to join his father, Robert Jones, already there. Many tears were shed on their departure to a new life; friends were left behind—friends they would never see again.

Young men, out of work, passed away the time in diverse ways. Some acquired proficiency on the green cloth of the Colliery Institute's billiard tables, others endeavoured to breed the fastest racing pigeon in Brandon Homing Society, others opted for more energetic sport. Out of work David Hopkins ran for his club the Sunderland Harriers in the fifth of a series of paperchases organised by Durham and Northumberland Harrier Clubs, he came in fourth.

Seventeen year old Norah Moran walked with her cousin Mary Cummungs and Mary Ellen Lynch of similar age the torturous route to Ushaw College, a four mile walk over the Deerness Valley where they were employed as maids. Their wage was 7s. 6d. a week plus board. Most of Norah's money went towards the upkeep of the family which now numbers nine with the arrival of baby Teresa.

Brandon Colliery is one of the seventy-five pits closed in the County during the last twelve months. Owing to the heavy pressure on the funds of the Durham Miners' Association the unemployment allowance at Brandon Colliery suffered a further substantial reduction, the second since last September, and the local sick relief fund was discontinued. Although to all outward appearances the people are maintaining a cheerful disposition after nine months' enforced idleness, yet the distress is widespread and acute, and the children in particular are 'feeling the pinch'.

Despite the crisis in the coal trade people forgot their worries on Whitsuntide Monday. Whole families trekked to Morley Wood, a picturesque spot between Brandon Village and Brancepeth; it was an annual event generally favoured with hot sunny weather. Scores of makeshift tents dotted the ample space alongside Morley Wood. Raucous gramophone music encouraged dancing; Morley Farm sold out of one penny a pint milk.

Forty local men will be employed for four months making the proposed new road from Brandon Colliery Railway Station to the top of the long Commercial Street. The project will cost £3,800.

Councillor Tom Carr has fought hard to bring sorely needed employment to the area; forty fortunate men will shortly work on the scheme he fostered. As the newly elected chairman of Brandon Urban Council he took the oath and qualified as County Magistrate during his period of office. He was first elected on the Brandon Urban Council in 1910 and retained his seat until 1919. He sought election in 1922 and was successful.

The surrounding colliery spoil heaps made ideal grandstands for non-paying spectators, mostly out of work miners, when Brandon Juniors were 4–2 victors of Eldon Juniors playing in the Auckland Junior League. The field adjoins the Red Lion Inn where Brandon Juniors hosted Willington Juniors in a 2–2 drawn game.

As Brandon Colliery entered its second year of idleness the plight of its workless miners is acute. Home coals are scarce. Two Brandon women were fined for raiding the coal trucks stored in the colliery sidings which had been filled at Pit House Colliery.

Owing to the industrial depression prevailing in the area, the Co-operative Society reduced its dividend to members from 3s. 2d. to 2s; 6d. in the pound and are to close their departments at Meadowfield all day on

Wednesdays and at twelve noon on Saturdays.

Local police helped distress caused by the prolonged pit closure; they held a whist drive and dance to raise money for the Police Boot Fund. In six months one hundred and forty pairs of boots costing around seventy pounds, have been handed to necessitous cases in the district.

Hundreds of tobogganers converged on the steep hill running from Brandon Village to the Red Lion Inn below Brandon's long Sunderland Street; the slippery surface of ice and snow afforded endless delight to adults and juveniles alike. Laurie Moran, now nine years of age, used the boots donated by the police to good effect on the glass-like pavement of Sunderland Street.

There being no sign of work resuming at the colliery, the workless and their families suffered their second bleak Christmas of unemployment. Keeping a house fire going was only made possible by assiduous visits to the colliery spoil heaps.

A miner took his wife to the pictures one night, but remembered that he had forgotten to lock his coal-house door so he turned back and locked it. Three hours later he was met at his yard gate by another man who asked in indignant tones, 'What hev ye deun wi' my missus?'

'Aa hevn't seen yor missus', replied the other.

'Hesn't tha?' exclaimed the indignant one. 'What's she deein' locked up in your coal-house then?'

1926

Colliery church and chapel goers attended the Christmastide services. There was financial distress wherever one turned. Despondent pitmen passed the time wandering the roads; others still scratted for precious coal fragments and spent cinders on the unyielding fiery heaps; others frequented the Colliery Institute from breakfast to supper; Jimmy Moran at fifteen years of age became a proficient billiards player.

Great news! A limited number of coal hewers, putters and pony drivers were set on; 'A' Pit Ballarat Seam, about one mile from the shaft, had reopened. Pony drivers Jimmy Moran and Thomas Parks, after their long lay-off, were recalled. Jimmy was disgusted when the colliery company, to save a few pence weekly, set the youngest drivers on. Brothers Pat and Jim Robinson and George Jackson had been pony drivers prior to the lock-out; they live in Church Street, their fathers Mr. Jim Robinson, overman and Mr. Tommy Jackson, deputy are in charge of the Ballarat Seam.

Jimmy and Tommy, both diminutive, were given the daunting task of handling skittish pit ponies which had been running free for some months. Jimmy did not know his pony's name as its coat had grown; after four days they clipped the animal's hair, which was a brownish colour and its hide was roan coloured. It was Clam! Jimmy was scared because Clam had the reputation of being the worst pony to handle in the 'A' Pit before the stoppage. Jimmy avoided Clam's flying hooves except on one occasion when they shattered his knuckles, resulting in a further two weeks off work for Jimmy.

Not long ago, at a certain colliery, a little driver lad not more that four feet in hieght was struggling with a pony. He tried several times to get the pony to move, but it would not budge, and the perspiration came pouring from his brow. The manager came up to him and said, 'Halloa, sonny, I see you are sweating like a horse'.

'Aye sor', answered the lad, looking into the manager's face, 'Aa is reet enough, but Aa only get a cuddy's wages'.

During Jimmy's enforced inactivity the family moved from Sunderland Street to Newcastle Street not many paces away, the colliery barrow was once again put to good use. Number 14 was a vast improvement, recent innovations included a new attached brick built wash-house and an outside flush lavatory, the latter much more desirable that the netty in Sunderland Street.

The colliery, as just arousing from its torpor, absorbed a few more men, coal hewers and others. Despite the slight show of prosperity miners of Brandon Colliery and elsewhere in the country were perturbed. A depression was spreading all over the industrial world; wages were reduced— the miners were hardest hit. The Trades Union Congress supported the miners in their fight and called a General Strike from May 2nd. Men and ponies were once more out of work.

Jimmy, his return to work short-lived, vowed he would never go down the pit again; he had the satisfaction of seeing Clam returned once more to the field alongside the pit.

Strike support for Britain's miners soon evaporated. Other striking workers returned to work on May 12th. The miners decided to carry on with the struggle.

Out of work miners, James Hamilton of Queen Steet and Thomas Byrne of Albert Street, decided to wed their sweethearts. James married a Sleetburn girl while Thomas' bride came from Esh Winning. Thomas' sister, Rose, married Roderick Jennings, another striking miner from Bearpark. All three pitmen fervently hoped that the strike would be of short duration.

Miners, their household coal allowance spent, had to search nearby woods for branches from trees, they collected cinders from the ash heap, a mound made bigger with the addition of the weekly netty emptying, and scoured the colliery spoil heap for discarded long-buried morsels of coal. Shallow veins of coal, found near the silent 'C' Pit shaft, were claimed by some miners who left a son to guard the excavation while the digger was absent leading coal home.

As the strike proceeded, poverty reared its ugly head. Children went to school, their shoes in a pitiable state of repair. Police officers toured the classrooms inspecting children's footwear. Those children whose fathers had ingeniously mended boots and shoes with strips cut from motor tyres and their inner tubes, were deemed suitably shod and did not qualify for new footwear. Some people sold the new boots—this caused the authorities to mark boots supplied to the school children.

Soup kitchens were set up at Mount Calvary Chapel in Commercial Street and St. Patrick's Club-room at Langley Moor. Gallant miners and their wives saw that the children attending the soup kitchens were provided with hot meals, their time and energy were given without stint. Some Brandon Colliery men, taking on a new role, borrowed a van and begged for bread and other foodstuffs at coastal towns some fifteen miles away. They kept the boilers of the soup kitchens going.

Paddy Moran, his slim figure bent almost double, dragged his heavy burden along the deep, rutted path; Croxdale Colliery some two and a half miles from his home is left behind; miners on strike, seeking warmth for their families, have come from afar to riddle the heap for coal.

Perspiring freely, Paddy gratefully lowered the long handles of his barrow, Croxdale Bridge being his first stop. With cap askew and shirt sleeves rolled to elbows, he thankfully rested awhile; he perched on his coat and scarf laid on the barrow. After a few minutes his patched up boots pointed to Brandon Colliery. For the next three hundred yards the going is flat, the wheels of the barrow, ex cottage mangle handles, wobble alarmingly as he advanced. The foor of Burnigill Bank is reached, its sharp slope daunting. A veritable Calvary! Heaving, straining, puffing his laborious zig-zag way up the hill, Paddy, between the shafts, muttered 'Bloody pit gallowas running about free'. After much perspiring the top is reached; Paddy looked back wistfully to where Laurie his ten year old school truant son, ant like on the distant heap, awaited his return.

The terrified hare, probably disturbed from its lair on the heap, long legs stretched, ears laid back, fled up Sunderland Street. Bored out of work miners, stood at the rusting railway crossing at the top of the street. Some ten strikers kicked their heels idly. On seeing the human barrier, the hare shot off to the right. Knowingly, one of the group, tall and lithe, took up the chase. 'There's Paddy fancies his chance with the hare'. Other scathing remarks were tendered as Paddy planned his campaign. Sunderland Street is swiftly left behind, so is Newcastle Street. Three coal bunkers towered at the end of North Street; long since emptied, they are normally used to store workmen's coal.

The pursued hare raced up the railway incline to the depot. No escape! The animal flung itself into the first empty bunker, its pursuer followed suit. A hole in the dividing wall of the bunker attracts the hare; Paddy, undaunted, climbs out to peer into the second cavernous bunker. The hunted creature crouched, momentarily safe; a short length of steel rail crashed unerringly downwards.

Just as the coal seeker, refreshed, was picking up the barrow handles, a small pale green van of five horse power chugged its way up Burnigill Bank and stopped, boiling after its steep climb.

'Buy your coals, mister?' shouted the driver.

Paddy, gazing down the steep slope, surveyed the distant spoil heap with its ant-like coal pickers, retorted, 'Yes, at the price of your baccy', pointing at the van on which was painted in gold letters the words, 'Sinclair's Thin Brown Twist Tobacco, 9d. an ounce'. With a grunt he set off on the two mile journey home.

Laurie, ten years old, returned from school. 'What's for tea, ma?'

'Look behind the pantry door, son', answered his mother. Laurie gazed in awe at the still warm body stretched from a nail; he touched the blood-soaked head.

'Who caught it ma?' he asked.

'Your da', came her reply.

'Get away, he couldn't run fast enough'.

Forty-two year old Patrick Moran, Dickie Mearman, Pat Cassidy, Mick McDonough and Jack Wilson, along with thousands more out of work miners, were denied the pleasure of attending the Miners' Gala generally held in July. This year the Gala had been abandoned owing to the national lock-out.

During July the Seven Hours Act of 1919 was amended to give eight hours per day for all classes or pitmen with the exception of deputies and hewers who were to be increased to seven and a half hours a shift. There was general dissatisfaction among the country's miners. The men remained out of work.

The Jones and Barr families, having friends in far off Australia, friends who had left Brandon during an earlier strike, seeing nothing but gloom in the foreseeable future, decided to emigrate. Neighbours waved them good-bye as they left Brandon Colliery Railway Station en route overseas. One family chose Canada in which to start a new life.

The son of an old miner was to go to Canada to seek fame and fortune on the prairie. When the time for his going drew near, the old man put on his best coat and hat and went to the neighbouring town where the booking office was situated. He took the ticket but as he was about to leave the place he saw in a glass case a stuffed animal with horns on its head.

'What's that animal?' asked the old miner of the clerk.

'Oh', was the answer, 'that's a Canadian moose'.

'Oh', said the old miner decisively, 'then Aa'll hev me money back. Aa'll nivvor let any son o' mine gan ter such a place. If that's a mouse, what will their bloomin' rats be like?'

The emigrants were still afloat when the dreaded smallpox struck Brandon Colliery and the surrounding area. Apprehensive men, women and children, lined the Colliery Ambulance Room. Ten year old Laurie Moran timorously rolled up his ganzie sleeve to receive the injection against small-pox. Thousands were innoculated. For many hundreds it was long before the sickening effects of innoculation wore off. Scores were left with prominent scars in the region of the biceps. Deaths from the contagious disease became commonplace.

Paddy Moran with five pitmen acquaintances, bored with standing idly around, sauntered through the fields beyond Brandon Village. After long months of inactivity their spirits were low—no money—just a pittance from the Public Assistance Committee (known as Packy), an indeterminate amount repayable on the recipient starting work. They recognised the mounted gent confronting them as the local farmer. He accused the men of stealing from his fields and threatened dire penalties. The incensed innocent sextet had the satisfaction of seeing a very scared farmer retreat, no doubt pleased to escape unscathed.

After seven months of struggle the miners decided to accept the owners' terms and return to work. Their martyrdom to no avail; the miners' lot was to be worse than pre-lockout. On November 30th the terms of settlement imposed on the miners were:—

1.   A reduction in the percentage addition to basic wages cut from 110% to 89%.
2.   A reduction in subsistence wage from 7s. 6½d. to 6s. 8½d. per shift.
3.   An increase in hours from 7 to 8 per day for all classes with the exception of deputies and hewers, who were to be increased to 7½ hours.

The disastrous National Stoppage, the worst in history, meant the loss of 27,814 days work in the pits. Over 26½ million days' work were lost during the stoppage.

During November smallpox raged in Brandon and Byshottles, three hundred died from the disease. A Brandon Colliery baby of seventeen days succumbed.

A clamorous crowd cheered on the two contestants in the Colliery Institute Christmas Billiards Final. Jimmy Moran, not yet seventeen, faced the formidable Billy Craddock. The latter, more experienced, won the day. Jimmy as runner-up landed a grocery voucher valued at a princely £1. 10s. The resultant pile of goods on the kitchen table evidence of Jimmy's prowess with a billiard cue.

December heralded the decline of deaths from smallpox; one hundred and seventy five fatal cases being reported in the Brandon and Byshottles area.

The year saw three changes at Brandon Colliery. Mr. Nelson the colliery manager died at his home Hollygarth, he was its first tenant. Mr. Walter Armstrong took over as Brandon Colliery's new manager.

Jack Higgins at forty years of age, became Brandon Social Club's new secretary. After a term of Government Training, seventeen year old Jimmy Moran kept his promise, he left home to work in the south of England.

1927

The new colliery manager toured the 'A', 'B' and 'C' Pits with George Moore, the under-manager. Fifteen years ago Brandon Colliery's three seams, the Busty, Three Quarter and Harvey Seams, employed 1717 men and boys. Besides a manager, three under-managers, John Gilchrist, J. Dakers and George Moore, were employed. Today the total work force is 158 men and boys with George Moore, holder of a second class certificate, the only under-manager.

After the 1921 struggle Paddy Moran earned 20s. 0½d. a day coal hewing; now after the lockout of 1926 his wage has plummeted to 8s. 10½d. a shift. He and other coal hewers in the Durham coalfield are hard put to maintain a family.

Smallpox continues to rage in Brandon Colliery; of the 170 fresh cases in Brandon and Byshottles area notified during December, 71 were found in the colliery rows. Councillor Dickinson emphasised the importance of people refraining from collecting together and from visiting patients stricken with the disease. Councillor Tom Carr remarked that the Council appeared powerless. The matter had been discussed at the Miners' Lodge meetings. He said that despite the epidemic only a few hundred have been vaccinated. Many object on conscientious grounds and others because they do not regard the disease as serious. Some even look upon the disease as a chance for a rest and holiday.

Brandon Colliery after working regularly since the lockout was idle on the first Saturday of February and on the following Monday and Tuesday owing to slackness of trade. Despite short-time working the colliery is setting on more men. Mechanics employed at the colliery formed a Union branch for themselves on non-political lines.

David Hopkins the Brandon 'pit lad' won the championship of his club the Sunderland Harriers for the fourth successive year. He did the five and a half miles run in just over twenty-seven minutes. David is also a prominent member of Brandon Colliery Band. He was an easy winner at the North-Eastern Counties' Cross Country Championships run on Stockton Racecourse. There was a field of two hundred runners over a course of nine miles which David ran in fifty minutes thirty-two seconds. He was fourth in the event last year and has been champion of his club for the past three years.

The corrugated framework of the Miners' Hall reverberated when the young men of Brandon United Methodist Church gave their nigger minstrel concert. A good audience enjoyed the programme which comprised vocal items, solo and choir, coon melodies, monologues and cross-talk. A screaming farce entitled 'A Black Breach of Promise Case' set the audience away smiling.

The Evergreens' Concert Party are always sure of a good welcome wherever they appear. Jim McKenna, tenor; Bob E. Connolly, humourist; and versatile John McGough, tenor vocalist and piano accompanist, comprise the party.

Geordie and Bill went to a local concert recently, where one of the artistes was singing that old song, 'I'll hang my harp on a willow tree'. Unfortunately she broke down twice, trying to reach the high note.

Geordie said to Bill, 'Bi gox, that's aawful, Bill hinney'.

'Aye', replied Bill.

As the artiste failed on a third attempt, Geordie shouted out, 'Aa say, hinney, thoo might try a lower branch'.

During February there were thirty-three cases of smallpox in Brandon Colliery of which only one proved fatal. The Moran family was spared the disease, an addition to the family of eight was expected.

One hundred and seventy men employed in the Harvey and Busty seams received a fortnight's notice to terminate their employment. The present pit heap is somewhat antiquated, and a scheme is being drawn up necessitating the dismantling of the existing surface plant and provision for drawing coals up one shaft instead of at the 'A', 'B' and 'C' pits as previously. It is also intended to electrify the pit so as to save coal consumption. When the work is completed in about a year, work should be found for about 700 men.

Paddy Moran and the other hewers in the Busty Seam brought their gear to bank. Dismantling was begun at the 'A' and 'B' Pits in preparation for new structural alterations.

Owing to the long drawn out spell of unemployment at Brandon Colliery, it was decided at a meeting of the Lodge that Brandon Colliery lodge would not be officially represented at the fiftieth Durham Miners' Gala. Brandon Colliery Band will accompany the Littleburn Miners' Lodge to the Gala.

The Reverend G. Davies took over as new minister to the Mount Calvary Chapel at Brandon Colliery; Mr. Dyson left for service in Thornley. Mr. Davies arrived at a time when about eight hundred men and lads at Brandon had not worked for three years. A proposed new sewer at nearby Browney and the building of a new road at Brandon could help them.

Volunteer work helped to add a new cricket pitch and a tennis court to the Brandon Colliery Recreation Ground. Brandon had challenged Browney Colliery to a game of cricket on the new pitch. Incessant drizzle foiled good cricket. Brandon scored 97 runs to Browney's 35. For the first time tea was served in the new pavilion.

The colliery cricket team won their third successive match when they played Coxhoe under the Coxhoe and District League auspices by 116 runs to 60. Joe Mawson the Brandon footballer currently playing for Bishop Auckland scored 26 runs and took four wickets for nine runs in his game for Brandon. Arthur Stott took three of Coxhoe's wickets for nine runs.

When Kelloe cricket team visited Brandon they scored 77 runs all out after the latter had declared at 181 runs for nine wickets.

Geordie was an ardent supporter of the local cricket club, and at the end of a recent game in which his team had lost he was not quite satisfied with the umpire's decisions. He went up to him and said,

'Hey lad, wheor's thi dog?'

'I haven't one', said the umpire. 'What do you mean?'

'Wey', replied Geordie, 'thoo's the forst blind chep Aa've knaan whe didn't keep a dog'.

Brandon Colliery was declared free from smallpox after two cases had been removed to Shincliffe Hospital. During March twenty-six cases had been reported in the colliery rows.

The four local school football teams ended a good season of sport. Crowds had enjoyed a season of youthful rivalry when Brandon Council, Browney Council, North Brancepeth (Langley Moor) Council and St. Patrick's R.C. schoolboys participated in the struggle for the cup presented by the Brandon and Byshottles Co-operative Society. Football fever gripped the area when the teams were locked in conflict. The four teams were treated to a free film show at the Co-operative Kinema; each player received a suitable present from the committee.

Twenty-five years ago, in June 1902, two Brandon publicans were refused an extension of time limit on Coronation Day. They were asked the reason for application. 'There's to be a bonfire on the hill', was the reply.

'Bonfires don't want drink', commended Canon Greenwell of Durham, in refusing the application.

Two women and a man were fined at Durham Police Court for pulling down railings surrounding one of the colliery ponds at Brandon Colliery— they had no coals. Three colliery lads were caught red-handed stealing coal to the value of one shilling and sixpence. These acts are brought about by the severe depression still prevailing in the coal trade.

Laurie Moran aged eleven, lost in the expectant crowd lining Station Road, awaited the destruction of a long familiar landmark. Adults and school lads watched the preparations for felling the square brick chimney towering one hundred and seventy feet above the pit and surrounding colliery sidings. Awed cheers arose as the monster toppled, its half million bricks spreading dust over the area it had dominated for thirty years.

Laurie's brother Jim, now seventeen, moved from Watford to work in Samuel Clough's woollen mill in Steeton, Yorkshire where he earned 24s. 6d. per week as a 'Spinner'. Their new brother christened Francis, the Morans' tenth child, was born on September 11th. The family now comprises five sons and four daughters.

Workers in the Durham coalfield were threatened with further reductions in wages; there is an immediate and acute crisis.

Miners at the colliery, some working, others not so lucky, had spent their spare time to good advantage. Brandon Colliery Allotment Holders and Protection Society held their first annual vegetable and flower show in Brandon Social Club. Local man and keen gardener, Bob Fairless, was judge. George Abson, Harry Lamb and Nichol Huntley were helped by committee men Harry Nichol, Harry Ball, John Coulthard, Isaac Pybus, Harry Gerrard, Herbert Winter, Frank Turner, Jim McCormack and Bob Grieveson to make it the best show ever held in the district.

William Ward of Brandon Colliery in a newspaper article recalled that the first patient admitted to Brandon Hospital on its opening on 8th September 1892 was an enteric fever victim. Dr. Binnie the medical officer sent sixteen year old Thomas Ashcroft of 46 Queen Street for treatment. In thirty-five years 2108 patients have been dealt with, including scarlet fever, enteric fever, diphtheria and smallpox.

At Durham County Hospital William Oakes, a well-known Brandon Colliery figure, reputed to have circus connections. The old comedian, better known as 'Billy Mackney', fell out of a bus and sustained severe injuries to his knees, he was detained.

Brandon's hills and streets were crowded with happy youngsters; the early winter snow and ice brought out the sledges. The retinue of tobogganists careered the slope from Brandon Village. Good sledges ran from the village, past the Fever Hospital, the colliery manager's spacious house, the Aged Miners' Homes, down Commercial Street and Sunderland Street, then on to the Red Lion Inn nestling down in the hollow at the foot of Brandon Colliery, without stop.

The new Sanitary Inspector for the Brandon Urban Council took up his new duties; he moved into the house adjoining the hospital. Mr. Wilkinson reported two cases of overcrowding at Brandon Colliery. In a two roomed house in Sunderland Street he stated that there resided father, mother and six children, whose ages ranged from three weeks to twenty one years. In a similar dwelling in Park Street there were father, mother and seven children.

During the month 55 stones 8 pounds of meat had been condemned as diseased and unfit for human consumption. The Inspector was congratulated for the manner in which he was discharging his duties.

Christmas was one of a succession of lean Christmases. There's unemployment and short time at the colliery. An investigator reports, 'It is reckoned that one out of every four miners in the Durham coalfield is out of work, and many men have not worked a day since the slump burst on the district in 1925. There are boys of sixteen who have never had a job since they left school at fourteen, and many have worked only a few months in the two years. There are hundreds of elderly men who will never be taken on again.

The rough, hearty, often careless living of the miner, his magnificent independence have given way to a struggle to snap up what the community can give him. That compliance with the rules of relief should become the main preoccupation of one of the most self reliant of the British working class is a saddening social change'.

1928

Heavy falls of snow and severe wintry conditions greeted the New Year. Celebrations were somewhat muted probably owing to the year beginning on the Sabbath. Bell and buzzers sent forth their customary greeting.

Durham County Hospital benefited when £5.11s. was collected in the colliery rows. Choir leader J. H. Myers and the Brandon Male Voice Choir singing carols of which the colliery folk approved.

Business men out to capture what little money there is to spare, arrive in Brandon Colliery. The multitudinous flare-lit stalls hug the walls of the little Market Chapel, encroach the space outside Lamb's store and overflow across the road to almost surround the Colliery Inn. Friday night is market night, the carnival atmosphere of better times sadly missing. Pennies for pocket money change hands; one penny procures eight boiled sweets, each fish-shaped and multi-coloured. Mr. Turnbull the owner of the four wooden swings promises a long ride for one penny. If hunger assails one penny buys either a penny dip or duck at nearby Tommy Holmes' butcher shop. The former is a bun sandwich containing pork cracknel and onions, while the latter is a concoction known only to the butcher, which when prepared is cube shaped and has a hint of a fatty veil. The travelling coloured dentist is in evidence—he offered free extractions.

The Vicar of Brandon, the Rev. Harry Hayward, congratulated his opponent Wilson Allan who had just been re-elected President of the Brandon and Byshottles Co-operative Society. Wilson Allan procured 578 votes to the Vicar's 469.

Brandon St. Agatha's accomplished Concert Party performed Sullivan's short comic opera 'Trial by Jury'. Pleasing musical effects and dramatic skill delighted a crowded audience. Miss Edith Grayson proved a convincing actress and vocalist; Mr. Tom Gill's sweet tenor voice being a great asset.

Brandon Colliery Silver Prize Band visited Brandon Social Club and gave a concert, consisting of selections and solos. Messrs. David and Wilf Hopkins, William and A. Tyrie, Masters Bullows and Robson were the chief contributors to the programme on the cornet, trombone, euphonium, bass, horn and cornet respectively.

There was a good attendance at the Irish concert held in St. Patrick's Club Hall, all the performers being local. Miss Johnson, soprano; Peter Lockeron, tenor; Miss N. Morgan, ballet dancer; and Tom Connolly, the quaint patter comedian of Brandon, made the night a success.

More musical talent has been unearthed at Brandon. The Operatic Society of Brandon Primitive Methodist Church gave a performance of 'Aladdin and Out'. Their efforts realised £12.15s.9d. which was handed over to the Durham County Hospital.

Sixty teachers applied for the post of Headmaster of Brandon School. Long-serving headmaster Mr. W. Ashcroft is retiring after twenty-one years service. The successful applicant being Mr. Arnold Ross whose yearly salary will be £418.

As the old school has been condemned by the Board of Education a site at the western end of Station Avenue, near the footpath between Brandon Railway Station and the Saw Mills has been chosen. The school will contain three departments for 228 infants, 336 juniors and 440 seniors, a total of 1064 children. The expenditure authorised for the building scheme is £22,499. Some local labour will be used thereby alleviating distress still prevalent locally.

The Brandon Council School football team has had a most generous supporter in Mr. Joseph Close during their strenuous hunt after cups and medals. Mr. Close is a well-known Brandon tradesman, and in addition to giving the boys' competitions the utmost publicity by window-dressing advertisements, composing sonnets on their successes, and patronising their games, he awarded cash prizes to all the members of the team upon bringing home the Brandon Co-operative Society and the Ushaw Moor Miners' Cups.

Mr. Charles Robinson, manager of the Meadowfield Kinema, gave free seats to a show which all the players of the four local schools enjoyed. All of the teams had played on 'Barney's Field' alongside the Red Lion Inn on the Langley Moor road. Jack Barnes of Brandon had leased the field of three acres—for the purposes of providing recreational facilities for the North Brancepeth School, Langley Moor.

There's distress in the coalfield. The umpire, Sir William Plender, to the miners' great chagrin, awarded in Durham the reduction in the subsistence, or minimum wage, of twopence a shift from 6s.8½d. to 6.6½d. Some colliery workers are in dire poverty and in many instances were having their wages subsidised by the Guardians. Within seven years the wages of the Durham miners, which includes Paddy Moran and his fellow coal hewers, have been reduced by more than half, while output and working hours have increased. In spite of the foregoing, the mineworkers of the county had to submit to a twenty-four per cent reduction which reduced them to a standard of life that is a disgrace to any civilised community. Yet the owners sought a reduction of percentage that would not only arrest their losses but would give them a profit of tenpence halfpenny per ton—this when the miners are living in poverty.

So many people have heard repeatedly the story of the miners suffering that it is now being looked upon as a natural sequence and taken no notice of.

Despite rumours of it not being held this year, the Miners' Gala will take place on July 28th. Three M.P.s and Emmanuel Shinwell have been chosen to speak at the fifty-first Gala.

Brandon Colliery is still closed down, its men and boys, like nearby Browney Colliery's 567 men and boys, foresee a bleak future; the latter pit is not paying its way. It is not to be abandoned however, it is hoped to resume work in about two months on a day to day basis.

It is exactly fifty years ago, in 1878, that the whole of the men and boys of the 'C' Pit Brandon Colliery, received fourteen days' notice to quit their homes as their services would not be required at the colliery.

Geordie, being out of work, took a stroll to a neighbouring colliery, where the work was good but difficult to obtain. Whilst passing the colliery pond he heard cries for help, and looking round saw a man struggling for his life.

'Where does tha work?' cried Geordie.

'Wey Aa work at yonder colliery', gasped the drowning man.

'An' what's thy name?' asked Geordie.

'Bill Dixon', was the reply, 'and get me out of this'.

'When Aa cum back', said Geordie, and he went to the manager's office and told him about Bill Dixon's plight.

'Oh', said the manager, 'and what do you want?'

Geordie said, 'Aa want his work'.

'Oh, said the manager, 'you're too late. The man that shoved him in got his job'.

Parents, determined to see that their children had at least one day by the sea, organised events to raise money. Chapels and churches responded in various ways. From monies raised by jumble sales, dances and whist drives, seven hundred adults and juveniles journeyed by rail from Brandon Colliery London-North Eastern Railway Station to South Shields. Twelve year old Laurie Moran collected his free rail ticket on the eve of the trip after waiting his turn in St. Patrick's Club-room. Another good day followed when buses ran from the Club-room to Sunderland and Sea Lane.

The local chapels had combined to form an excursion that took all and sundry from the colliery village down to the seaside town for a day's outing. In the early afternoon one of the ministers, making his way down to the beach, met a group leaving the vicinity of the pier.

'Now then, my friends', he greeted them. 'I suppose you'll have been drinking in the ozone?'

'Wey, now', said Geordie, the spokesman, 'Aa canna tell ye whaat they caal the pub, but it's tha' one strite opposite the pier end!'

Some men put their leisure time to good effect. Out of one hundred and six candidates in the Durham Union of Working Men's Clubs who applied for admittance to the Ruskin College Summer School, J. Tyson, W. McKay, S. Richardson and J. Hutchinson, all members of Brandon Social Club, were successful students.

Faced with the necessity of changing their vocation because of the long-continued trade depression, many Durham miners have set their wits to work and have secured an entry into other callings. Among them Eunoch Edwin Howden, eldest son of Mr. and Mrs. Teddie Howden of Park Street, Brandon, who is an example of what grit and determination may accomplish in the face of adverse circumstances.

As a Brandon 'pit laddie' he served his 'apprenticeship' at the 'A' Pit and was always recognised as a good workman, but was thrown out of employment by the industrial slump.

Launching out on his own account as a cinema pianist and studying harmony and instrumentation in his spare time, he became musical director to a popular touring revue and variety syndicate.

He has appeared at the principal threatre in Newcastle as well as most of the important centres throughout the United Kingdom.

After four years' unemployment and its attendant hardships, prospects are brighter at Brandon Colliery. A meeting of miners was held in the Miners' Hall to discuss cavils, seam transfers, and the arrangements of the manager Mr. Walter Armstrong.

Preparations are being made for the re-starting of the Busty Seam with seventy coal hewers in addition to stonemen, and more will be absorbed as time progresses. The re-starting of the Harvey Seam at full working capacity is also under consideration. The general outlook of Brandon's pits is much brighter, and a more optimistic feeling is prevalent amongst all classes of the community than has been the case for the past four years.

One of the twelve successful candidates from the Durham Johnston School in the Cambridge Higher School Certificate Examination, taken by scholars in all parts of the country, Master Fred Grice of Brandon, son of Mr. and Mrs. Charles Grice, gained distinctions in French and English. He has been awarded one of the State Scholarships set apart for proficiency in these subjects. Three more Brandon Colliery young people gained distinctions. Master G. N. Westgarth, French and English; Master A. Hutchinson, Physics and Chemistry. Miss T. C. Caislaw was one of the successful candidates in French and English subjects from the Durham Girls' County School.

Great credit must go to the late headmaster of Brandon School. For a considerable time the school has been playing a part almost equal to that of the average secondary school and, under Mr. Ashcroft's direction, there had not been a single failure in either the senior or junior Cambridge examinations.

Laurie witnessed the felling of another pit chimney. Durham Street, lying almost at the foot of the lofty, square, one hundered and ninety-nine feet tall landmark built fifty years ago, was strangely quiet. Its occupants watched the busy preparations for the chimney's destruction. Carefully placed blasting powder, on detonation, razed the monster. On falling neatly into the Durham Street bee-hive ovens' gullet, the street, nearby 'A' and 'B' Pits, the general workshops, and the offices of the colliery escaped mishap.

Sammy Crooks, the marvellous young Derby County outside right footballer, who graduated from Brandon Juniors to more important clubs, got his first chance of qualifying for an International cap. He has been selected by the Football Association Selection Committee for the outside right position in the team to represent them against the Lancashire Football Association XI.

Kathleen Moran, with brothers Laurie, John and Eddie, had friends and playmates among the families in Newcastle and Sunderland Streets; streets divided by a wide, cart wheel rutted back road with the string of netties set in groups of four along the entire length. The two long rows housed the Sykes, Mortimer, Welsh, Walton, Reynolds, Clough, Tones, Bussey, Douglas, Egglestone, Clennel, Harker, Pye, Duffy, Kennedy, Dowdle, Richardson, Attess, Pybus, Worral, Brown, Clough, Mearman, McCormack, Bullows, Spirit, Beer, Stock and Welsh families. All householders were employed at the colliery.

The three Moran lads soon acquired skill at guiding their tin toboggan, unusually the flattened side of a discarded bath tin; Brandon Colliery had a number of spoil heaps which provided hair-raising sleigh runs. Bowler and hoop, colliery made, can be seen propped against the wall of almost each house which harbours a young male; a journey to either Langley Moor a mile away, or to Meadowfield the same distance, is run non-stop at speed without fatigue if the hoop is kept moving by the operator.

The girls' pastimes are playing with skipping ropes and flicking buttons into a bay chalked on the pavement. They are called upon to help with the housework and look after the younger members of the family, they shop and some love to have a go at cooking.

David Hopkins, the Brandon Colliery runner, took part in the North East Counties Cross Country Association Championship meeting at Gosforth Park. Dave was sixth man home, only two minutes behind the leaders. A worthy performance by the miner who enjoys the challenge of a hard race even after a week of underground work.

Mr. Ashcroft, the able headmaster of Brandon School, retired from his post. A testimonial fund has been inaugurated of which James Turner the able secretary of the Co-operative Society and Robert Wood, undertaker, both of Station Avenue, will operate as secretary and treasurer respectively. Mr. Ashcroft had been headmaster at Brandon for twenty-one years having taken over from Mr. Heppell in 1907.

A big crowd watched the cricket match between Brandon Colliery and Brandon Village under the auspices of the Deerness Valley League on the Colliery Recreation ground—a local Derby eagerly anticipated. Expectations of a keen struggle were not realised; the Colliery team gaining a hollow victory, 103 runs to 29.

Considerable activity was witnessed at Brandon Colliery in connection with the re-starting of the Busty Seam with a complement of 120 men and boys as a beginning, an exceedingly welcome 'turn of the tide' for many anxious wives and mothers. More workers are expected to be absorbed week by week. The first batch descended and ascended at the Meadowfield (C Pit) New Side.

Forty-four year old Paddy Moran descended with the first batch of men; he was thankful to don pit clothes after a long period of Public Assistance. His wife, forty-two year old Mary, is delighted at the prospect of having a tangible wage to work the family budget. Norah, now twenty, faithfully posts off a postal order every week from Keighley in Yorkshire where she is a domestic servant. Jim's meagre earnings at eighteen in the mill are just sufficient to pay his board.

Despite the depression prevailing in the coal industry, there being forty collieries in the Durham Coalfield idle, by the exercise of strict economy and excellent management the Brandon and Byshottled Co-operative Society is paying the same dividend as last quarter, namely, 2s.3d. in the £. Mary Moran used her divi to good effect when she bought boys' wool jerseys 2s.11d., gent's socks at 1s.4½d. a pair at·their sale.

Efforts have been made to bring life to a sorely depressed area. Herron's Empire Band of Brandon commenced a series of weekly dances in the Central Institute Hall. Forty members of Brandon Harmonic Male Voice Choir entertained at various functions. Brandon Social Club held a singing contest which Jacob Lawson judged; from thirteen entries Robert Fraser was elected winner, John Ayre second, Adam Bailes third, and Anty Cairns fourth. The pianist was William Rounding.

The officials of Brandon Social Club arranged a change of entertainment when twenty-five competitors entered their favourite gamophone record. Only half the entries could be played on the night, the rest being booked to play on a later date.

Colliery folk took advantage of the glorious weather August Bank Holiday offered. The Moran family joined the exodus from the colliery rows to Brandon Fells adjoining Morley Wood set just beyond Brandon Village.

Tents mushroomed on the day; raucous gramophones played Woolworth's sixpenny records, seven year old John with schoolmates Joe Lynch and Charlie Fenwick roamed the Fell. Games were played until dusk forced an evacuation of the pasture.

For years local trade has been slack. John Higgins, secretary of two years' standing, stated that owing to the depression, Brandon Workingmen's Club's takings had been as low as £40 a week—hardly enough for overhead charges.

Brandon area suffered a great loss on the death of the Rev. Harry Hayward. He survived his wife by six months. For twenty-two years he served the community; a diligent pastor and effective preacher, he found time apart from his spiritual duties to assist in the public and social work of the district. For many years he was an ardent supporter of the Co-operative movement, and his interest in the affairs of the local society brought him into office as its president.

The local collieries are working well and an increasing number of men have been engaged at the new pit ('C' Pit), but unfortunately the wages they are able to earn are exceedingly low, and often do not exceed the amount of the 'dole'.

Twelve year old Laurie's whistle died on his lips. On entering the darkening kitchen he saw his mother, her slim shoulders heaved with every sob, her white hair limp on the tear-soaked oil-cloth covered table.

'What's the matter, Ma?' anxiously enquired Laurie.

'There's nothing for Christmas, son', — Laurie thought of his three younger brothers and a sister.

Disconsolate he wandered into the little used sitting room, also swathed in gloom. He stumbled over an object lying near the front door. Laurie carried the heavy straw bag into the kitchen. Timid hands undid the parcel. A large plucked turkey lay exposed to view. No sender's name, no accompanying note. 'The postman made a mistake. This isn't ours!' Laurie's mother whispered. Laurie's father exchanged the bird for a more practicable leg of pork—he got a Christmas drink into the bargain.

Norah in domestic service in Yorkshire had, without preamble, taken on the role of Santa Claus.

1929

Unemployment and a job scarcity greeted the New Year. Some families are living, or existing, on as low as three shillings and fourpence halfpenny per head per week.

The old year departed amid bleak, bitterly cold weather. The old custom of 'first footing' was maintained, and all the churches well filled for the usual watch-night services.

Peals from church bells and the blowing of colliery buzzers ushered in the New Year. First footers were out in force.

On New Year's Night crowds of Brandon's Methodists converged on their Chapel in Commercial Street, a social night had been arranged for them. Simultaneously the United Methodists of Brandon Colliery held a pie supper and social in the adjoining Miners' Hall. Both functions were well patronised.

Ushaw Moor sent a team to play Brandon Colliery at billiards. There are seven teams in the Deerness and District League, Brandon is currently lying fifth. Skilful play from both teams enthralled members of the Brandon Institute who witnessed a nail-biting contest. Brandon scraped home, winning by three points—529 to 526. J. Lumley 115; J. Pinkney 114; J. McKay 150; J. G. Tolley 150 comprised the home team.

In the Club Union Tournament Games held in the Workingmen's Club, Brandon came first in whist, fourth at dominoes and second in billiards.

Two young unemployed miners, who spent nearly all their time watching the billiards players in the Welfare Hall, went to see Willie Smith and Joe David play. After watching Joe Davis silently pile up a huge break one said to the other, 'Whaat's the caal this gam', Billy?'

'Wey, billiards, ye fyeul', said Billy.

The other was silent for a few minutes then turning to Billy again he said, 'Wey, whaat's the nyeum o' thaat gam' wor mates play in the Welfare Harl?'

Brandon Colliery is catered for in the world of football. The United Methodists have a successful team playing in the Deerness and District League, the team is dubbed the U.M.'s.

Joe Mawson, son of Mr. and Mrs. Mawson of Brandon, is a popular footballer and useful cricketer. He has been playing football for the Washington N.E.L. Club after playing for Brandon, Bishop Auckland, Crook, Durham City and Langley Park. After signing for Stoke he left his native Brandon to display his undoubted skills to a wider audience. Joe, a good all-round cricketer, was a useful member of Brandon Colliery Cricket Club during the last two seasons, during which they won the Coxhoe and District League Championship and the Deerness Valley League 'Knock-out Cup'.

Increasing activity is the keynote of operations at Brandon Colliery. More men are being absorbed week by week. Paddy Moran joined the batch of hewers and putters who started work in the Busty 2nd North District. Prospects are definitely brighter.

At three thirty in the afternoon, Laurie aged thirteen and two of his classmates left their classroom, the last school bell of the week having been sounded. They rubbed shoulders as they ran home to Brandon Colliery. Across the colliery field they trespassed, skirted the forbidding spoil heap, the heap on which Mr. Caislaw a colliery official had caught Laurie perched on the new steam operated crane, and had administered a painful reminder of their encounter, up the railway embankment and slunk across the Bishop Auckland to Durham London North Eastern Railway line. Laurie and his mates knew that both Mr. Caislaw and P.C. Brown, the colliery police force, would be on duty elsewhere.

They ran along the railway track leading from the colliery to Pit House colliery. A short distance beyond Brandon's Council School their journey ended.

Prior to leaving the classroom Laurie's teacher, Mr. Tonge the headmaster, had assembled the school and offered prayers for the victims of a terrible accident at the very spot at which they stood. Laurie looked up the single railway running in a continuous rise to Pit House colliery.

Laurie gazed at the awesome spectacle. The rotund six wheeled colliery engine lay on its side in the field, steam still hissed from its exposed belly.

The locomotive was being tested at Pit House colliery. To it was attached an empty wagon and six twenty tonners and a twelve tonner laden with coal. Whilst Bob Halkier the foreman fitter was off the engine attending to the brakes, the engine moved forward on the slippery line and quickly gaining speed, went rapidly down a steep gradient. The hook by which the wagons were attached to the engine snapped and the trucks left the metals and fell into a heap. Four hundred yards further on the engine left the rails and turned a couple of somersaults into a field.

The steam safey valve was broken and the following occupants in the cabin died almost instantly from scalds—

T. W. Taylor, aged 58, Master's Weighman, 44 Princess Street.

Norman Brown, aged 29, Fitter, 46 Princess Street.

Fred Watson, aged 32, Winding Engineman, 7 Princess Street.

Ralph Johnson, aged 44, Fireman, of Meadowfield.

By this disaster the metals over a considerable distance were torn up, electric cable poles were mown down like matchwood and cables were smashed. The result was that the electric current was cut off at all the collieries. The news of the catastrophe quickly spread. Heart-rending scenes were witnessed as neighbours rushed to succour the bereaved.

The Rev. G. Davies spoke at the funeral of two of the victims.

'For quite a long time the district of Brandon has been passing through a period of exceptional industrial depression. There has been a great deal to make the hearts of the people of this neighbourhood exceedingly sad, but not for many years has there been such an occasion for sadness as that which brings us together. The whole community has been plunged into grief, and that grief is bewildering and blinding in its suddenness. To have left home strong and well, and happy, and to be brought home mangled, brought home with the spirit gone, is a tragedy that makes us almost speechless. There are many in this congregation, there are many men and women outside this church, who feel "it might have been my husband; it might have been my father; it might have been my brother". Only as we take the tragedy to ourselves does something of the overwhelming sorrow of the widows and fatherless come home to us'. Friday the first day of March—a black day in the annals of the colliery.

Two hundred applicants in the Brandon and Byshottles area sought assistance from the Lord Mayor's Relief Fund. The needs of Brandon are at present being ascertained. No assistance can be given to households whose average income exceeds seven shillings and sixpence a head.

As the minimum wage is not paid until the men have worked a month, wages are pitifully small. Men with badly bruised hands, caused through long unemployment, make little impression on some of the hard coal seams in the colliery. One man drew eleven shillings and fourpence for four days' coal hewing.

Bill and Geodie were waiting at the pay office for their turn when, suddenly, Bill said, 'Hes tha ivver wondered what tha'd dee if that had the boss's income?'

Geordie, 'No, but Aa've often wondered what he'd dee if he had mine'.

Nearly all the workmen have been absorbed at the colliery. The feeding of school children is carried on periodically from the Cookery Centre at Brandon. Mary Moran whose husband Paddy enjoys the fashionable low pay packet, with her large family to cater for, seeks the best out of the current food prices. She found butter at 1s.4d. a pound, hens' eggs 1s.8d. a dozen, duck eggs the same, pork 1s.3d. a pound, beef 9d. a pound, mutton 10d. a pound, lamb 1s.7d. a pound, rabbits 1s. to 1s.6d. each, potatoes 6d. a stone, new potatoes 1½d. a pound.

During May Brandon Colliery senior cricket team made their debut in the North-East Durham League when they played the Hazard Colliery team. Despite Brandon's Thornton, Abson and Stott who bowled splendidly in the cold and cheerless conditions, they were beaten by two runs 46 to 44.

A tremendous success attended the introduction of the 'talkies' to the Langley Moor Empire Theatre. Crowds from the Brandon area helped fill the Empire to capacity. Last year's Armistice Ceremony at the London Cenotaph was shown. The audience thrilled on the performance of the bands and the shouted military orders.

Billy Buxton left Brandon School, a short distance away from his home in Albert Street, last Christmas at the age of fourteen. His headmaster Mr. Ashcroft on his recent retirement had been lauded for the school's successful handling of pupils for higher education.

Billy's brother Tom, a past pupil of Brandon Village Church of England School is currently attending Durham Johnston School. Their father, miner Ernie Buxton who works at Brandon 'C' Pit, arranged an underground visit for his two sons; seeing is believing—both elected to seek other careers.

Brandon and Byshottles Co-operative Society required a youth for its butchering department. Billy approaching fourteen years and a half, with Bobby Gibbon, John Bainbridge and Edwin Robson, all Billy's ex-school mates, sat an entrance examination—an apprenticeship in the department. Billy landed the job which paid nine shillings and sixpence per week. Dapper James Turner who lives in Brandon's Station Avenue is the Society's active secretary.

Once again the colliery people flocked to Brandon Fells, an annual Mecca; August Bank Holiday Monday, next to Durham Miners' Gala, is the colliery's favourite holiday, albeit an unpaid one. Other places visited on the day include Holliday Park, Relly Woods, Brandon Recreation Ground and the Stepping Stones over the River Browney; while for the young and energetic a day spent by the River Wear at Croxdale where swimming is a favourite activity, is a must.

A miner, his wife and family went to Sunderland last Bank Holiday, taking with them a well filled luncheon basket. The crowd in the streets was very dense, and Geordie said,
'Let's have the basket Nan, an Aa'll carry it'.
'Aa'll carry it a bit langer, Geordie, Aa's not tired yit', she replied.
'It's not that', said Geordie, 'Aa might loss tha in this crowd!'

Tom Buxton did well at school; he left Durham's Johnston School to study at Bede College in Durham City. Patricia Anderson, daughter of David and Mrs. Anderson of Brandon, a member of the teaching staff at Blackhill School, has won one of the twenty-two Board of Education scholarships for the short course in music at Oxford University.

Brandon Village as it was in 1911.

Brandon Vicarage built 1911, Residence of the Vicar of Brandon.

Brandon Aged Miners' Homes built 1913.

There was a queue at the local picture palace, and a cheeky little chap about twelve came pushing into the queue.

'Hi', said a man, 'Where's tha tryin' te get te? Hadaway back an' tak' thee turn'.

'Wey, Aa was here afore man', said the lad. 'Aa only went te buy some bullets'.

'Wey, but hoo dis tha knaa thoo's in the reet place?'

'Cos As put a cross on thee back wi' chalk'.

The Medical Officer recommended the Council to consider the following needs: the closing of the houses in Durham Street, one of the first to be built at the colliery, and the enforcement of the demolition of the property and clearance of the site; the completion by the owners of twenty-six empty houses in Brandon's Newcastle Street.

Brothers Doctors George and William Denholm entered the underground workings in a vain attempt to render aid. On Wednesday, June 5th Deputy George Abson, a married man from Albert Street, was fatally injured by a fall of stone. The colliery was laid idle for the day.

Brandon's streets presented a lively appearance when Brandon Silver Band, conducted by Fred Bowes paraded—and followed by joyous youth who danced under the banner with its splendid colours blowing in the breeze. All were en route to the pitmen's Mecca. Paddy Moran took his young family to the fifty-second Annual Gala to enjoy a fine day with the 120,000 revellers.

In May Sam Whiteley aged 56, of Russell Street, suffered injuries to the back caused by his having been crushed between a tub and the roof in the Hutton Seam. Samuel, for twenty-two years an overman at Brandon Colliery Hutton Seam, died in August from the delayed accident injury to his spine. He was a patient in Newcastle Royal Infirmary at the time of his death.

Three former pupils of Brandon Council School, Masters W. N. Hall, H. A. Harker and Proud, are the sons of three very proud miners working at Brandon. They attend the Durham Johnston Secondary School in Durham and took part in the recent Oxford and Cambridge Universities Local Examinations. Master Hall gained honours, the other two obtained passes.

Dutch rabbit specialist Herbert Winter was again successful with his rabbit at the Tursdale Fur Society's Show. He secured the first prize and a special prize for the best rabbit on show. He won prizes at Edinburgh, Grimsby and Tursdale in three weeks. He has had successes at Sunderland and Durham against some of the foremost fanciers in England. His Dutch rabbit was fifth in the Leicester National Show.

Man travels far to indulge in his hobby. Another Brandon Colliery miner who is also interested in the breeding of rabbits and cavies for exhibition is also having a successful season; George Aither, the secretary of the Brandon Fur and Feather Society, having won numerous prizes with his rabbits.

Residents of Commercial Street savoured the singing of the 'Old Hundredth' by the choir at the entrance of the church. Members of the Mount Calvary Primitive Methodist Church gathered for the re-opening of the church after being closed for the purposes of renovation and to allow for the installation of a new organ. Erected behind the pulpit, the organ is a two manual instrument with pedals enclosed in an oak case. The front pipes are silver with gold moulds and there is pneumatic action to keys and pedals and octave couplers.

Club members like musical harmony. Tommy Lawson introduced the concert party composed of local artistes. A large gathering applauded the first of the autumn and winter concerts. A. Cairns, Jake Lawson, S. Coulson, Kit Harrison and Jack Ruddick set the ball rolling in merry fashion. Jack acted as solo pianist and accompanist.

Geordie bought a piano on the instalment system. He invited his neighbour in to see it, who remarked 'Aa'll tell tha what Geordie, before tha's able ter play a tyune on't Aa bet tha sends it back in disgust'.

Three weeks later Geordie was struggling with the piano trying to put it on to a cart.

'What did Aa tell tha?' shouted Geordie's neighbour, his face beaming with apparent satisfaction.

'Dinnit thoo gan an' kid thisel up like that, lad', retorted Geordie, 'Aa'm just gannen for me forst lesson'.

Amongst the many 'pit laddies' who have shaken off the pit dust and joined the ever increasing ranks of professional footballers may be mentioned Geordie Bartram, who has rendered fine service to Rochdale for a long time; Joe Mawson, a recognised member of the Stoke City first team and a consistent scorer; Sammy Crooks, one of the 'stars' of Derby County and formerly a Brandon Junior, and Tom (Duck) Freeman, at one time the idol of the Brandon public when attached to the Brandon Council School team, who has signed forms to play professional football for Middlesbrough. All the players are shaping well and are comfortable in their new homes—the reward of steadiness and reliability.

Nineteen year old Alfred Stanley Thompson, son of Mr. and Mrs. Charles Arthur Thompson, has been transferred to Brighton and Hove Albion from Durham City A.F.C. 'Stan' is also a keen cricketer, and showed promising form while playing for Brandon Colliery Cricket Club.

It is proposed to place in the Parish Church, Brandon, a brass tablet in memory of the late Vicar, the Rev. H. Hayward, testifying to the parishioners' appreciation of his twenty-two years' service as Vicar and his widespread activities in other directions. Framed photographs are also to be placed in the Sacristy and Parish Hall, which he was instrumental in building.

Christmas-time brought sorrow to the Flather family with the death of the father, Fred Flather. Fred was badly wounded during the war; he leaves a widow and family of three to mourn his loss.

1930

Without regret the disastrous year of 1929 was allowed to depart and the New Year was entered into with a spirit of hopefulness. Men are facing the New Year optimistically; it is reported that the colliery still has a working life of fifty years.

Brandon Colliery was hard hit during the prolonged depression in the mining industry, and nowhere has the turn of the economic tide been more thankfully welcomed than in this populous area. Extra hands are being employed at the colliery. Preparations are being made for the introduction of electric coal-cutting machines into more seams.

Joseph, the Moran's eleventh child, arrived on April 1st, making six sons and four daughters surviving. Eight are at home. Paddy Moran and his coal hewing counterparts are grateful that the colliery has reserves of coal to last their lifetime.

More work for Tommy Harker and Sons. They have secured Brandon Council's scavenging contract—District No. 11 with a tender for £148.

Brandon School football team, its players now established scholars in the new school which holds 1200 pupils, began the New Year with a busy programme. They play East Hedley Hope in the Ushaw Moor Aged Miner's Cup; Hamsteels in the Ushaw Moor Nursing Cup and Langley Park in the League Medal Competition. They have a vociferous crowd of Brandon men and women who egg them on.

Bill and Geordie, members of the colliery football team, which had just won the local cup, were returning from a luncheon given by the colliery manager in honour of the occasion.

'Well, Bill, what did you think of it?' asked Geordie.

'Te tell ye the truth, Geordie, Aa think it wud hev been forst class but for one thing—them buns was far ower hard'.

'Begox, Bill! That's just what Aa thowt. Now Aa knaa what the maid meant when she said, 'Take your pick!'

Brandon Social Club met Langley Moor Social Club to play off their billiards, double whist and domino games, the games were in connection with the Durham City and District Inter-club Tournament. Brandon won at billiards and whist but lost at dominoes. Percy Shell 150; Ernie Buckley 140; Robert Kennedy 150 and J. McKay 77. Their points at billiards gave Brandon a winning total of 517 points.

Doctor George Denholm of Hillside, Brandon Colliery had lived in the Brandon district since the age of ten. His early death at the age of forty-six came as a shock to his many friends in Brandon. Following an impressive service in St. Agatha's Mission Church he was buried in Brandon Village Cemetery. The bi-annual concert promoted by the members of the Brandon Harmonic Male Voice Choir was postponed for two weeks—Dr. Denholm was its president.

Three worried lads watched the ten ton truck career down the slope from the colliery depot, knock down the colliery yard gates, and run out of sight. It travelled a further quarter mile after passing over two crossings, before coming to a standstill near the engine house. The guilty trio were summoned for committing wilful damage by removing the iron sprag from a wheel of the truck.

The day's business began as usual in the old inadequate Brandon Colliery officer formerly two small cottage houses joined together. So speedy was the transfer that work for the day was concluded in the Higher Tops School adjoining the Old Colliery School, but separate and distinct from the latter. The clerical department, near the 'A' Pit had closed down, the furniture and documents having been moved to the more suitable and commodious building in a few hours.

Young and old were buried on the same day. After a brief illness eight year old George James, son of Mrs. Ralph Galley, died. His funeral coincided with Lawrence Cummings', an old retired miner; his grandson Laurie Moran, fourteen years of age and just left school, was one of a large gathering of mourners, friends and old comrades to pay their last tributes.

Laurie and his friend Steve, both left school, with no immediate prospects of securing work, resorted to other means of earning coppers. Laurie picked cinders from the spacious 'fiery heap' which he sold to old Mrs. Hoare who lived in No. 5 High Street. Old 'Crocker' Bailey lived in No. 1 while Granny Doyle and David Anderson occupied houses in the middle and the top of the street. The twopence Laurie received for his labours on the 'fiery heap' ensured two tickets to the afternoon matinee or one to an evening programme. Laurie loved the likeable old couple. Mrs. Hoare's husband, white haired Teddy had served a prison sentence in Durham Goal with his father, they had been victimised for trying to establish a Union among their fellow pitmen.

All of Brandon's pits were idle for one week prior to the fifty-third Miners' Gala due to take place on July 26th. The men were instructed to draw their unemployment cards from the colliery office with a view to signing on at Durham Labour Exchange. Office staff, well settled in their new place, the Higher Tops' buildings, were kept busy handing out the cards on July 19th.

Laurie, oblivious of his parents' pending financial worries, enjoyed his day at Whitley Bay, a seaside trip organised by Church volunteers. He joined the scores of Brandon youths parading with the colliery band and banner to add to the one hundred and ninety-eight banners on parade at the 'Pitmen's Carnival' on 26th July.

Geordie was decidedly tipsy, and when he arrived home late from the 'Big Meeting', his wife had gone to bed. He saw a basin on the table, and eagerly devoured the contents and retired to rest also.

'Did thoo find thi supper aalreet, Geordie?' she said sleepily.

'Aye, hinney, Aa liked the gravy varry weel, but ye begger, Aa had a bonny job wi' the tripe. Aa think thoo hadn't stewed hor plenty!'

'Tripe!' cried his wife, 'Tripe!'

'Aye, tripe, in the basin on the Tyble!'

'Wey, by gum, if thoo's ate whaat was in the basin thoo'll hev te buy thesel some mare collars, 'cos thoo's eaten collars an' starch. Thi supper was on a plate i' the yuven'.

Tramps and beggars frequented the colliery rows. One well known character, Manny Pecker of no fixed abode, was a weekly visitor, as was the Durham-based professional beggar who called on the Moran household every Sunday morning. Laurie's mother always contrived to hand the clean, affable old gent a sixpenny piece. Laurie's father called him the 'weekly insurance man'.

Carts and vans hawked their goods in the colliery streets. One enterprising baker from Ushaw Moor, another colliery place which could be seen in the distance across the Deerness Valley, did good business every week. His familiar cry 'Three pies—three teacakes and a brown loaf for a shilling' or 'Cakes sixpence a dozen' was eagerly awaited.

Laurie's father arrived home from his shift in the pit. On entering the house his wife Mary said, 'I took fourpence out of your waistcoat pocket to buy a dozen callow herring'. The multi-pocketed garment was strewn over a chair in the sitting room with coat and cap, awaiting its owner's return from work. 'What did the man say when you handed him the money?' inquired Paddy. 'Oh! He just turned them over before putting them into his pocket'. 'You have just lost me a fortune', said the unhappy Paddy. He had carried in his waistcoat pocket four pennies, two of which were double headed, the other two being double tailed coins. Paddy sometimes indulged in the illicit game of 'pitch and toss' and had gone to great trouble and considerable expense to acquire his double-sided coins.

Laurie, now eager to earn money which his mother so desperately needed to help out his father's meagre pay and help bring up the young family, sought temporary jobs. Joseph, the latest arrival, had joined his three brothers and a sister all under the age of ten. Laurie with his mate Steve were grateful to earn two or three shillings caddying at Brancepeth golf links. The look of relief on his mother's face when handed the small amount was ample reward for labour exerted carrying the heavy bag of golf clubs.

Laurie and Steve eyed the potato field. The decided that potato picking would provide a substantial sum to help out the family resources. Monday eight a.m. to noon; Tuesday eight a.m. to noon; Wednesday eight a.m. to noon. Twelve hours of back breaking labour. The farmer having no change requested the mates to call back on the Thursday for their three shillings each pay, the rate being two shillings per day of eight hours. Much to the lads' chagrin he asked them to return the next day for their money.

The death of one of Brandon's oldest residents in the person of Mrs. Philip Lynch senior, occurred at her home in Commercial Street. Mrs. Lynch, 76 years of age, was a woman of strong character and possessed of a loveable temperament, in addition to a rich Irish wit which is handed down to members of her family.

Another Brandon stalwart, George Bainbridge aged 84, foreman mason for many years at the colliery, died. He was a brilliant conversationalist, and could relate many remarkable incidents in connection with his occupation. His house was stoned and besieged during the pitmen's strike of 1863.

Mrs. Enoch Griffiths made up the trio of old standards to pass away within a few days. Aged 85, she died in Brandon Aged Miner's Homes. Her thirty-year old son Enoch, was killed in the 'C' Pit explosion of 1899 when six pitmen lost their lives.

After seeking numerous jobs without avail, Laurie secured work on the screens at Browney Colliery, a mile from his home in Brandon Colliery, he was fourteen and a half. His first pay, two weeks after starting work, was seven shillings and eleven pence out of which his mother bought him a pair of pit boots for five shillings.

Some three months after commencing work on the screens, work which entailed picking stone from the coal sent to the surface, and the use of a shovel, Laurie sustained a 'beat hand', a much dreaded condition amongst miners. The hand swells and fills with pus; the painful condition relieved only by application of the surgeon's scalpel. Laurie created medical history—he was the youngest victim to have sustained 'beat hand', a condition reserved for the more mature coal hewer. He was awarded compensation of three shillings and seven pence which he drew for six weeks.

Three thousand race goers paid for admission the modest sum of one penny, when Brandon Carnival closed with a bumper race meeting at Langley Moor. Forty-three horses entered the various handicaps which included pony races, steeplechases, leaping and musical chairs. Billy Mac, Banana, Fire Coal, Brown Bread, Ice Cream, Some Pep, Show Boat, Corn Thresher, Dark Fire, Done In, Farmer Giles, Mick and Good Faith were some of the mounts of various types which entertained the crowd. Not all finished the course; some flatly refused after one circuit and decided on a sit down strike. Out of £11.6s.6d. gate money, £9.11s.6d. was sent to Durham County Hospital.

At five a.m. on November 21st, two coal hewers, John Rutter and Jack Carter, were working at the coal face of a heading in Brandon Colliery's Harvey Seam, when an explosion of firedamp took place. Thirty-six year old John Rutter was hewing at the face by the light of an acetylene lamp, thirty-two year old Jack worked with a candle. Suddenly there was a report and a flash of flame which extinguished the naked lights and seriously burned both men. Rutter subsequently died from his injuries. One of the most impressive funerals ever seen in Brandon took place on Sunday November 30th when John Rutter was buried.

Thomas Davison, a single man of Newcastle Street, was killed by a fall of stone in the pit while hewing coal.

Two of Brandon's miners spent Christmas in Durham County Hospital. David White, a married man of Park Street, was filling coal in the new South East Cross-cut of the 3rd South District. He sustained serious injuries to his back. William Foster of Russell Street was badly injured in the Hutton Seam whilst coal hewing. A fall of stone caused severe cuts to his head, face and legs.

A new road was opened by Councillor Carr. The road is 553 yards long and cost £5,139 and was aptly named Carr's Avenue after Councillor Carr. Tom Carr had brought much needed work to the area at a time when unemployment was high and prospects low.

On New Year's Eve an old gentleman overtook a poor woman pushing a pram up a steep bank. He asked if he might help her and she accepted his offer, thanking him.

By the time he got to the top of the bank he was nearly exhausted. He said to the woman, 'What a fine, heavy baby this is, missus'.

'Oh, hinney, it's not a baby. It's two dozen bottles of stout for wor Geordie', replied the woman.

1931

Hundreds of people were perambulating the streets in the clear frosty air, when the colliery buzzers heralded the New Year. The orderly crowd quickly dispersed to follow their custom of calling upon householders for admittance.

Singers out on New Year's morning entertained with their:—

'Ring out the old, ring in the new,
Ring happy bells, across the snow,
The year is going, let him go;
Ring out the false, ring in the true'.

Men are facing the New Year optimistically despite the dark cloud of industrial depression. Churches, chapels, schools and social clubs all helped to spread cheer. Brandon Intermediate Primary School and St. Patrick's R.C. day school pupils were treated to refreshments, sweets, fruit and toys. Brandon Social Club provided its members with free drink and sandwiches.

The young people of Brandon's United Methodist Chapel held a very successful social on two occasions when the Rev. Stephen Park of Taunton,

Somersetshire preached. Stephen is a native of Brandon, was at one time a colliery workman.

After being open on Sunday evenings for many years, the three local cinemas have been closed down with the result that the streets are crowded with young people wandering aimlessly about. Joseph Close, draper and general dealer of Brandon Colliery, wrote to the Durham Advertiser condemning the closure of Sunday cinemas.

Residents of the colliery are delighted with the latest hygienic move. One of the most unsightly landmarks has been removed. The evil smelling pond at the foot of West and Commercial Streets having been drained and filled after being for years a depository for dead animals and every kind of filth. It is proposed to use the site in future as an omnibus station.

Brandon's doctors were kept busy. 'Flu raging in the district meant almost house-to-house visitation, the disease being of the most virulent type. Deaths have taken place; both schools and business establishments are being heavily affected.

Brandon Colliery, with the exception of the Hutton Seam is working full time, coal cutters are being introduced into the Ballarat and Busty Seams. News is eagerly awaited of the success or failure of the venture. The seams were idle on the first Friday of March owing to a shortage of trucks. On the afternoon the caller came round the streets making good use of his 'crake'; he announced to all that, 'The pits are working the morn'.

Laurie Moran left his home in Newcastle Street; the quiet of the pitch black morning did nothing to lessen his trepidation. Not yet fifteen, he had worked on the screens some six months. He was given an ultimatum—either go down the pit or take his notice; he accepted the former. With mixed feelings he entered the pit cage for the first time and was introduced to pony driving. He had never handled a pony.

Laurie joined the queue in the Club yard. Carling Sunday night, and as per custom the Committee of Brandon Social Club dished out boiled Carlings to members and their families. A concert, free beer and sandwiches were provided for the adults.

May brought slack time once again to the pits. On one of the three days worked in one week John Thomas Liddle, a filler in the 'C' Pit Busty Seam, was severely injured about the legs and ribs. Albert Rodgers, a South Street man, sustained serious injuries to his back; he was a stoneman in the 'C' Pit Ballarat Seam.

Members of the Brandon Colliery Prize Band formed their own Silvertones Dance Band; they played to May Day Carnival dancers in the Parochial Hall. Next Day, May Day, the band followed by miners and banners, paraded the colliery streets as a prelude to the mass meeting held in the Empire Theatre, Langley Moor. Councillor Tom Carr presided. Mr. Peter Lee, secretary of the Durham Miners' Association, said,

'We do not want strife in the coal trade. I am the last person to advocate a stoppage if it can be avoided on honourable terms, but the policy of cutting down selling prices and then turning to the miners for a reduction in wages in order to made the concern profitable must cease'. This drew applause from the large audience.

One lad who did not follow his father into the pit; Master H. A. Harker, son of Mr. and Mrs. Harry Harker of Newcastle Street, has been successful in gaining an entrance scholarship to York College tenable for one year.

It was revealed at the monthly meeting of thr Brandon Urban District Council that tenants of council houses who were on the dole were in many cases in a financially better position than those who were working. The chairman, Councillor Dickinson, said he could not accept the fact that a man was unemployed as an excuse for not paying rent, especially when he was in receipt of 38s. per week unemployment benefit. This figure, which represented the income for husband, wife and six children, was higher than the minimum wage earned at the colliery. Yet many tenants who were in work on this basis had continued to pay their rent without falling into arrears.

In July preparations were made to participate in the fifty-fourth Annual Miners' Gala. Although Littleburn Colliery has been closed the Miners' Lodge is still functioning and it was decided that they attend the Gala accompanied by the Brandon Prize Band in conjunction with the Brandon Miners' Lodge.

The band displayed their new musical instruments. £2,000 had been borrowed from Brandon Social Club for their purchase. Brandon Miners' Lodge agreed to repay the loan through quarterly instalments. A workmen's levy of twopence a week helps finance the band.

On the eve of the Gala men streamed into the Miners' Hall at the top of Commercial Street. No speaker graced the platform; it was pay-out night for contributors to the Weigh Fund. Piece workers who had paid into the Fund throughout the year each drew twelve shillings. A handsome sum to take to the Gala.

Sam Bussey, Bill Burnet, Tom Blenkinsop, Fred Johnson, Billy Bainbridge, Tommy Lockey, Dave Pinkney and Isaac Kendall having been selected out of a cap holding three hundred names each received £1 granted to banner carriers at the Gala.

It was Big Meeting and Geordie was wending his way through the crowd when he noticed a bit of commotion. Seizing his opportunity, he dashed into a house nearby.

'Have yet got any whiskey?' he asked the householder. 'A woman hes fainted i' the crowd'. A bottle was produced and handed to him, whereupon he drew the cork, took a good long drink from the bottle, handed it back and calmly said, 'Thanks, hinney, thoo knaas it always upsets us te see a woman faint'. Then he went on his way.

Joe Mawson, the Brandon Colliery cricketer and Stoke City footballer, a product of the Brandon football 'nursery', was drafted into the Stoke senior team against Manchester United. He scored two fine goals for his side with some splendid headwork and enabled Stoke to win by three clear goals. The Saturday night Chronicle and Pink are eagerly scanned for news of former Brandon footballers' exploits on the field.

Concern was once again felt in Brandon Colliery when 250 men at Straker and Love's Brancepeth Colliery received fourteen days notice to terminate work. Two hundred men were given notice at Oakenshaw Colliery, another one of the Straker group of collieries. Brandon's 'C' and 'B' Pits continue to work slack time—the future is uncertain.

The result of a final ballot for an additional check weighman at the colliery between Councillor Tom Dickinson and Councillor J. Clennell was announced, the former being elected with a majority of 97 votes. According to lodge rule two ballots had been taken. Dickinson 256; Clennell 159.

Mr. Dickinson has worked at the coal face since the age of fourteen and was coal hewing before he was seventeen. A few weeks ago while following his occupation he suffered severe injuries as the result of a fall of stone. Appointed chairman of the Brandon Miners' Lodge over eleven years ago, he interested himself in public affairs, and in 1924 was elected as one of the representatives on the local Urban Council, of which body he has been chairman since April 1930.

'It is an ill wind!' The inhabitants of Brandon Colliery were treated to a most unusual spectacle; a coal heap between seventy and eighty feet in height, caught fire at the base. A disastrous fire near the 'C' Pit was imminent. Miners were called out during the night to fill the coal into trucks which were led to the depot for miners' coals—miners received overdue household coals.

Brandon produced a winning boxer when Jack Benyon beat Young Jacks of Coxhoe. A colliery contingent visited Durham New Markets to see their man in form, the referee stopping the fight in the fourth round.

After working irregularly for the past six weeks during which time the Durham Miners' Association paid out relief allowances in cash, all the pits and drifts at Brandon Colliery worked a full week—which made for a 'Merrier Christmas' than hitherto expected.

Geordie who had been off work for a considerable time, had just started work again. Upon arriving home from his first shift he was surprised to find a travelling photographer waiting for him.

'Now', said the man, after Geordie's wife had put his dinner out, 'how about taking your photograph to be enlarged?'

'Photograph!' exclaimed Geordie, 'Aa'll tell thoo what te de, lad, thoo sees that pudden on the table? Take a photo of that and enlarge it; it's the first Aa've seen for sixteen month'.

1932

Mild weather greeted the time honoured custom of 'first footing'. Colliery buzzers set the scores of 'first footers' on their quest; slack time of late no doubt reflecting on their 'takings'.

Father John Parker, now twenty-five years a priest, was honoured by his parishioners, most of whom hail from Brandon Colliery. At a tea and social Fr. Parker was presented with an easy chair, a set of brevaries and an umbrella on behalf of the different sections of the church. Fr. Parker judged a fancy dress parade, and a fine entertainment was given by St. Patrick's Pierrot Troupe.

The Vicar was walking down the village street the other day. He was met by one of his parishioners, Geordie, who told him he had had a dream.
'What were you dreaming about?'
'Wey, Aa dreamt Aa was in Hivin'.
'And did you have a good time?' asked the Vicar.
'Aye', he replied, 'As met an aad sweetheart of mine and we travelled about for three weeks'.
'And did you not think of getting married?' asked the Vicar.
'Aye, but there was nee parsons there', replied Geordie.

Mr. N. Brough took over as Minister to Mount Calvary Methodist Church on the departure of the Rev. G. Davies who had served Brandon Methodists for five years.

One of Fr. Parker's parishioners, John Duffy, a fifty-five year old coal hewer, worked in 'double' with coal hewer Dickie Danby in the 'C' Pit's Busty Seam. John was casting coals out to Dickie in the wide hewing place, when he shouted, 'Oh, Dick!' The shout of alarm preceded his death caused by a fall of stone. John's family at 21 Newcastle Street mourn his loss.

Consternation spread when a rare case of spotted fever was discovered in Brandon Colliery. The victim was removed to Sherburn Hospital in a serious condition. Visitors were barred from the hospital for two weeks.

The yearly club ballot was held at Brandon Club. Members returned Councillor Jack Clennell as President; Rop Miller, Treasurer; and five men to the Committee, Steve Dennis, Harry Blenkinsop, Paddy Moran, Tommy Lawson and William Ramsey Sen.

Two hundred and eighty-one underground miners and one hundred and twenty-eight surface workers began the New Year by working full time. They work the coal from the Three Quarter Busty, Harvey and Ballarat Seams of which W. H. Armstrong is manager; second class ticket holder H. Marley is under-manager.

Slack time soon returned. The 'C' Pit worked only one shift in one week whilst the 'B' Pit was idle throughout. Shortage of trucks being the cause of the pits' irregular working.

Owing to slack time, shops reduced food prices. Mary Moran shopped at Meadowfield Co-op where sliced bacon was reduced to fourpence halfpenny a pound, Danish butter to tenpence halfpenny a pound, lard fourpence halfpenny a pound, sugar twopence and cooking margarine fourpence halfpenny a pound. Fifty years ago Meadowfield Co-operative Society was born in a small rented shop in Meadowfield. The Society has grown and during its trading life sales have reached £5,100,000 and the net surplus allocated to members as dividends amounted to £866,000.

Ralph Smith Sen. was for many years a colliery caller at Brandon Colliery. Seventy-three year old Ralph died at the Sawmills Cottages, Brandon. His son Ralph is secretary-manager of Durham City Association Football Club. Brandon has a new football club it is named Brandon Argyle F.C. and will compete in the Durham Central League and various cup contests. The secretary is George Hewitt of Newcastle Street.

Brandon Argyle F.C. members of the Durham Central League had a promising beginning to their football season. Mr. Mark Bell, manager of the boot and shoe department of Meadowfield Co-op Society presented the club with a new football and ten pairs of football boots. Mr. Walter Armstrong the colliery manager is helping the club in many ways.

Over one thousand spectators flocked into the Red Lion Inn field, others watched from the summits of the surrounding spoil heaps, to see North Brancepeth Boys and Brandon Boys draw again in the replayed final of the Deerness Valley Schools' Medal Competition. Ross gave Brandon the lead, Drennan scored to level the score and Peart put North Brancepeth ahead. James put Brandon level just on time. It was decided to give medals to both teams as the finalists in the competition.

Robert Cheesey owned a house and shop in Commerical Street. He had worked as a stoneman for many years under Messrs. Straker and Love at their Brandon 'A' Pit, he left the pit after acquiring an interest in an omnibus firm (the United Bus Service). His initiative was short lived, he died at the age of sixty-five.

The depression in trade still exists at Brandon Colliery pits, the 'C' Pit, Meadowfield being idle for two weeks and the 'B' Pit the same.

The result of the slump showed at the fifty-fifth Big Meeting, there being little money to spend on this much looked to occasion. Brandon Colliery banner took its place with other eighty-nine silken drapes bordering the racecourse. The portrait of Ramsey McDonald has been erased from Brandon Colliery banner. Herbert Seed, a Brandon miner did a fine artistic job when he replaced the portrait with a view of the west side of Durham Cathedral.

Bill (on the racecourse on Gala Day), 'Did thoo hear that chap what's just been speaking'?'

Geordie, 'Ae, Aa did noo'.

Bill, 'And wat sort o' crack had he?'

Geordie, 'He dealt wi' the coal problem and said we'll aalwes stick i' the mud until aal the pits is marmaladed tegither'.

Brandon Colliery saw the largest funeral for several years when Hugh McDermott Jun., the third son of Mr. and Mrs. Hugh McDermott of Railway Street, was buried. Hugh McDermott Sen. was at one time president of old 'C' Pit Miners' Lodge, and also of the Brandon Social Club.

Another well known Brandon Colliery figure—old Enoch Griffiths, died at the age of eighty-seven. He worked for many years as coal hewer and wasteman. He lost his son Enoch in the 'C' Pit explosion thirty-three years ago when Hugh McDermott Sen. was a noted rescuer.

Seventy-eight year old Ralph Kell died at Brandon Colliery where he was an underground official for many years at the 'C' Pit. The family lost two promising sons a few months ago.

Twenty year old Fred Humphries left Brandon Colliery two years ago to work in Cortonwood Colliery in Yorkshire. He was one of the unfortunate seven victims of the recent explosion at that colliery. He had lived at his sister's home in Wombwell.

After a month's spell of enforced idelness in the 'C' Pit Busty, Ballarat and Harvey Seams started work on the Tuesday following August Bank Holiday Monday. The quarterly cavils had just been drawn at the weekend. Fillers are paid ninepence a ton for filling coals, if the coal seam is under eighteen inches high tenpence a ton is paid.

Billy was unlucky every time the cavils went in, he always got the minimum. His mate said to him, 'Wey thoo wants te get married tiv that lass thoo's gannen with. Thee luck might change for the better'.

Billy took his advice and he and the lass were in a taxi on the way to the Registrat's Office. As they sped on, Bessie began to cry.

'What's that cryin' for, lass?' asked Billy.

'Aa hev a secret to tell that', said Bessie.

'Aye, what is it?'

'Aa canna bake', she replied.

'Oh, haad thi gob, lass', exclaimed Billy. 'If Aa gets as much money after Aa's married as what Aa's gettin' noo, thou'll hev nowt to bake wi'.'

Brandon Argyle, now established as a fighting team, took on Durham Reserves in the Brandon Aged Miners' Cup; they beat Birtley in the sixth round of the Durham County Challenge Cup; Crook Nomads fell victims in the second round of the Durham Amateur Cup.

Brandon Colliery miner Ernie Buxton and his wife are proud people; Tom their eldest son, after three years of study at Bede College, took up teaching at Brandon School. William their seventeen year old son, is a Co-op Store butcher.

Prospects for Christmas look bright—market stalls prosper when full time is worked at the colliery.

There was revelry after the Boxing Day wedding of the Moran's neighbour in Newcastle Street. Miss Mary Ellen Lynch married William Smith of Horden Colliery. William was a miner at Littleburn Colliery before moving to Horden Colliery.

1933

The coal trade showed an improvement in the New Year. Sixty men were set on when at the Meadowfield 'C' Pit the Busty and Ballarat Seams started to produce coal.

While some colliery folk enjoy the popular weekend concerts provided by 'Connolly's Entertainers' of Brandon, others are supporting the new Brandon British Legion Boxing Club where Tom Bohill and Tom Farrage train aspiring boxers. Boxers Hill, Smith, Tweddle, Parnaby, Gibson and Brown were the contestants when they met Hetton. The Legion Club won five of the eight fights before a large crowd.

After fixing up fights with Chester-le-Street, Fence Houses, Hetton-le-Hole and Sunderland clubs, the local club did battle with Newcastle Amateur Boxing Club. Height and reach enabled the Newcastle team to win all seven of the three round contests. Robert Stoker, Pat Hutchinson, Miles Walker, Bill Smith, Robert Hill, Ralph Tweddle and Pat McAloon hope to do better in the return contests.

Joe Bell and Teddy Reynolds of Brandon were two of the five judges chosen for the Boxing Tournament arranged by the Brandon British Legion. Two well known boxers, Jack Casey of Sunderland and Mickey McGuire of Newcastle, pledged their support and promised a visit to the Club at an early date.

To be numbered among the last eight in the Durham County Challenge Cup Competition with the prospect of reaching the final is the proud position of Brandon Argyle, a club in its first season of football and is a member of the Durham League. Its secretary George Hewitt, after guiding his team to the third round proper of the Durham County Challenge Cup, appeared before the Council of the Durham Football Association. The Commission of the Association reported that he had attempted to mislead them when they went to inspect the ground of the Brandon Club.

The case arose out of a protest by Annfield Plain with whom the Argyle were drawn to play in the Challenge Cup, that the ground was unsuitable for the tie. It was alleged that the club secretary took them to the ground of Brandon Juniors. Supposing Annfield Plain had not protested about the ground, the secretary was asked where the game would have been played.

'We would have taken them to the graveyard'. (Laughter)

Colonel Dowling, 'Which ground is that?'

'Where we have beaten all the "big pots".' (Renewed laughter)

It being his first season as secretary George Hewitt was dismissed with a caution.

After a long spell of continuous working the 'C' Pit Busty, Ballarat and Harvey Seams are once again on slack time. In one week in March the 'C' Pit Seams worked only one day owing to the colliery sidings being snowed up. At the same time the locomotive and carriages carrying workmen to Pit House Colliery on the fells—had to be dug out of the snow.

April saw the Diamond Jubilee of Mount Calvary Church. The Brandon Women's Guild Gypsy Choir held a special effort in the school in connection with the event.

Paddy Moran with other hewers of the colliery and the county are disgruntled. Their coal hewing output has risen by more than half a hundredweight a shift yet the average in wages has fallen to the extent of 1s.4½d. a day. Fully one third of the miners employed are drawing the subsistence wage of 6s.6½d. a shift.

Geordie was on the 'Minnie' and he had the job of splitting the pay for the four marras for the past two or three weeks. The job had been difficult without the aid of a ready reckoner.

Being in the 'toon' at the weekend he asked for one at the bookstall.

'Sixpence', said the bookseller.

'Hoo far dis this yen reckon te?' asked Geordie.

'Thouands of pounds', was the reply.

'Hev ye not something smaaler and a bit cheaper?' asked Geordie, 'One that staps calkilatin' roond about six and sixpence ha'penny'.

Kathleen, the Moran's third daughter, now nineteen is a mother's help in Keighley, Yorkshire. Eddie their fourth son, is ten; his friends at school and in Sunderland Street being George Whitfield, Dennis O'Hara, Reg Sykes, Jackie Mortimer, Jimmy Lynch, Jim Mulhall, Tommy Sewell and Fred Maguire.

Laurie Moran aged seventeen, was pleased with himself as he followed Brandon Colliery banner and band; he had just been awarded his First Aid Certificate. All roads led to Langley Moor's Empire Theatre on the occasion of the annual May Day parade and mass meeting. Laurie was early astir to join the band and banner on the parade round the colliery streets before being joined by the Browney and New Brancepeth Colliery Bands before proceeding to the Theatre where a large crowd assembled.

After the meeting the theatre was prepared for the evening performance of Little Mary Hagan. Despite slack time working colliery folk flocked to hear the sweet notes of the Tyneside 'Wonder Girl Singer'.

There are four generations in the family of Terence Kennedy and his wife of Newcastle Street, Brandon Colliery. They were married in Durham on July 27th, 1887 and have had three sons, six daughters, forty-six grandchildren and one great-grandchild. Several members are ex-soldiers and were badly wounded in France.

Brandon Schoolboys brought honour to the colliery when they beat Ushaw Moor Schoolboys in the final of the Ushaw Moor Aged Miners' Cup. Brandon team comprised Swainston, Collins, Bon Richardson, Bellis, George Keys, Potts, Guy, Kay, Bobby Ross and Lister. Guy, Thompson, Ross each scored, followed by a fourth scored by a penalty taken by Richardson. Five minutes from the end Ross scored his second goal to make a convincing win five goals to nil.

There has not been much 'close season' for the officials and members of the Brandon Argyle's A.F.C.—they have been busily engaged putting the ground in order, and as a result of their labours visiting teams will now have no cause for complaint. The club secretary George Hewitt, is determined to place upon the field a team worthy of support.

Artificial flowers on graves and the erection of memorials in the form of a heart and tree trunk were deprecated by the Vicar of Brandon the Rev. E. F. Tallents in the course of an address to a large crowd when he conducted a service of dedication of a new oak gate at the entrance to the cemetery at Brandon Village.

August saw a return to prosperity at Brandon Colliery. One hundred and seventy men and boys who have been idle for six weeks due to coal trade depression re-started work.

In a certain local village one of the 'dole' officials happened to make an unexpected call upon one of his 'clients', and unfortunately found him sitting on the doorstep reading the morning paper.

'Are you aware that you should be looking for work at this time of the morning?' asked the official.

'Wey, man, that's exactly what Aa'm deeing', answered the victim. 'But you don't mean to tell me that you are looking for work when you just happen to be reading the paper?'

'Sartinly, man, can thoo not see Aa'm looking doon the "Situations Vacant"?'

Five hundred spectators crowded into the newly reconstructed football ground. Brandon Argyle won their first game of the season on Deepdale Ground beating Durham City Reserves 3–1. In the draw for the first round of the Brandon Aged Miners' Cup the Argyles played Sherburn Hill while Brandon Y.M. (Young Methodists) took on Spennymoor Amateurs.

T. Collinson conducted the Brandon Silver Prize Band when they played at Egglestone in the dales. They took first prize in the selection 'Rossini' and first in the March 'Victor's Return' at the Agricultural Show.

A house-to-house collection was taken when the Band played selections in the streets of the colliery when James Tyson lost all the household furniture in his South Street home in which the family escaped injury.

All schools in the district hold evening classes; interest in adult education is greatly on the increase. Economics is the subject at Brandon new School.

Brandon Argyle—managed by George Hewitt—heads the thirteen teams comprising the Durham Central League. Five hundred Brandon and Sherburn spectators visited Deepdale to see the exciting battle; Carter scored the only goal ten minutes before time when Brandon Argyle entertained Sherburn Hill. Deepdale ground resounded when eight hundred fans saw the Argyles beat Wooley Colliery in the Durham Hospital Cup. Disorderly scenes were witnessed at the close of the game; on time spectators rushed onto the field and free fights were indulged in. The game was the most thrilling seen for some time; the goal scorer Edmund Carter, at nineteen years of age, stands at five feet eight inches, is Brandon Argyle's inside left with a promising future and is to have a trial with Hartlepool United.

Christmas spirit was absent when more than a thousand spectators visited Browney Colliery to witness the Browney Social Club and Brandon Argyle clash, the latter team won 2–1 in the third round of the Durham Amateur Cup. Having won the twelve previous games Browney were confident of including Brandon among their victims. At the end of the game the referee left the field under police escort to the accompaniment of jeering from the hostile crowd.

Laurie Moran was among the eighty members and friends at the Christmas dinner organised by the Brandon Colliery Division of the St. John Ambulance Association where he was presented with his First Aid Certificate. At the age of seventeen and an underground worker, Laurie reckoned that a knowledge of first aid would, one day, stand him in good stead.

Geordie was visiting his friend, and it being Christmas time he was offered refreshment. 'Noo, Geordie', said his host, 'Will tha hev a glass o' rum or whiskey?'

'Aye, Aa dinna mind, Bill, lad', was the reply.

Bill filled the whiskey, and handing it to Geordie, said, 'Here's anuther nail i' thee coffin'.

'Howay', said Geordie, 'Aa's not nervous, so when thoo hes the hammer i' thee hand thoo can knock another one in'.

1934

A large number of first-footers began their many house calls as the colliery buzzers ushered in the New Year.

Ninety men and boys started at Brandon's 'C' Pit. With improved trade the 327 underground and 116 surface workers employed at the colliery can look to a better future. Twenty-one men and boys from Oakenshaw Colliery, one of the Straker and Love group, were set on at the 'C' Pit. It will mean a three mile each way journey for them.

Fr. John Parker welcomed eighty old people to a New Year tea and concert in St. Patrick's Hall, also forty children from St. Mary's Orphanage, Tudhoe.

Brandon Colliery's two ambulance teams 'A' and 'B' travelled to Willington to compete in the Straker Trophy for First Aid. The former team's 224 points and the latter's 243 points won the Silver Cup with replicas and silver means with gold centres. Eighteen year old Laurie Moran had just won his medallion in the First Aid examination held in Brandon Ambulance Hall.

Nineteen Brandon boys successfully passed the Safety in Mines Examination. They were: George Brown, Alex Bullows, George Charlton, John W. Coulthard, Cecil Cumisky, George Felton, James R. Fox, Sidney Kay, Aaron Kay, Harry Lee, Joseph McCall, Alfred Myers, Leslie Peacock, Irving Pigg, William Reed, Ralph Rutherford, Roderick Strong, John J. Wilkinson and Ralph Wilson.

Albert Johnson presided at a meeting of the Brandon & Byshottles Milk Retailers' Association where it was decided that the price of milk during the summer months would be fixed at sixpence per quart. Farmer Albert bemoaned the recent loss of a five ton haystack in a fire at his Staple Farm, the fire brigade could not save the stack in the farm buildings overlooking Deepdale football ground.

Brandon business man John George Rowe died in Station Avenue. Sixty-seven year old John George was born in Brandon and was a butcher for fifty years. He was a keen sportsman and took an interest in greyhoud coursing.

What is believed to be a record in the county is claimed for two Brandon Colliery brothers. Stan and Ron Simpson of 28 Russell Street have a combined eighteen years' of unbroken attendance at school. The eldest, Stan, now fifteen, had completed ten years and two months without being late or absent. Ron at thirteen has not been absent or late for eight years.

Another Brandon Colliery born man claims a record. Aged seventy-nine, James Welsh began work at the colliery at the age of ten. After fourteen years he left with a desire to sample work at other collieries. Roving about, he worked at twenty-two pits in Durham, two in Northumberland and, emigrating to America, he worked in six there, a total of thirty. He retired at Easington Colliery on his seventieth birthday after spending sixty years in the mines.

Tom Carr the checkweighman and Union leader, lived in a small house in the colliery's Albert Street. The miners of Brandon's two pits, Pit House and the 'C' Pit, had decided at a Lodge meeting to impose a levy of one shilling and sixpence drawn from their pay every week. A new house built on the slope next to the Aged Miners' Homes was the result of their sacrifice. Tom Carr and his wife occupied the pretentious dwelling. Some pitmen objected, they could hardly afford the weekly one shilling and sixpence.

Coal hewers' and putters' minimum wages had just been fixed:—
Coal hewers' minimum wage 7s. 1d. per shift.
Putters' minimum wage 6s. 7d. per shift if over 21.
Putter's minimum wage 6s. 2d. per shift if under 21.

Most of the seven hundred spectators left Deepdale football ground bemoaning the fact that Brandon Argyle had lost their replayed seventh round cup game with Tyzacks. Brandon had been firm favourites to win the Durham Amateur Cup Competition game but lost 4—2. The Argyle avenged their defeat when they played Browney Social Club a second time in the semi-final of the Sacriston Aged Miners' Cup Competition. A month ago the teams took part in a 5—5 draw. Browney players were not allowed to score—Brandon winning by six goals to nil. Staley scored three, Lowes, Pinkney and Fineran a goal each for Brandon.

On Easter Saturday a jubilant holiday crowd saw Brandon Argyle trounce Cornsay Welfare 10—0. Tom Staley (Pompey) Brandon's prolific goal scorer took no part in the game. As the teams met, Tom was married to Miss Florrie Mason of Esh Winning.

Parishioners from Brandon Colliery attended the crowded funeral service of sixty-five year old Father John Parker. When he came to Langley Moor St. Patrick's twenty-seven years ago the services were held in what is now the Church Institute, and the present beautiful stone church will remain as a monument to his memory. He was greatly loved and held in very high esteem by his parishioners and his death will be a great loss to the church. It took twenty-two years to pay off the debt on St. Patrick's Church and it was known to be one of Father Parker's ambitions to live to see it cleared of debt and to see its consecration. This was done in October of last year.

Another Brandon resident died at the age of eighty-three. Mrs. Hannah Gray lived with her son John Felton, at 17 College Terrace. Mrs. Gray came to Brandon Colliery fifty years ago and leaves five sons who are all well known in the district.

Seventy-two year old Ellis Jones, also lived in College Terrace; he moved to Brandon Colliery forty years ago and was one of the rescue party at the 'C' Pit explosion on August 15th, 1899. His funeral attracted a large number of friends.

Brandon banner and band attended the 57th Miners' Gala. Families from the colliery joined the 200,000, the largest crowd to date to invade Durham City. Some chapels elected to visit the seaside on that day. Brandon's club and two public houses were well patronised on the night.

Geordie had gone in to the Big Meeting but on the way home had the misfortune to meet with an accident so he was rushed to the hospital. As soon as Meg heard the news she dashed up to the hospital, straight to her hubby's bedside where she met the nurse just leaving Geordie. 'Oh, nurse', she exclaimed, 'Hoo is he noo?'

With a smile the nurse answered, 'Oh, he's coming round now; he's just been trying to bloth the froth off a drink I was giving him'.

Brandon Colliery Silver Prize Band competed at the Crystal Palace Tournament; colliery folk deem it an honour to have their bandsmen travel to London for the event. The band holds the following record for 1933: Winners of the Murton Aged Miners' Cup, the Boosey Shield and fifty guineas, the Ecclestone Challenge Cup, Newsome Cup, six firsts, four seconds and three third prizes.

Brandon Social Football Club continued their successful season; they head the Durham Central League having won all nine games played, with eighteen points they are five points in front of Langley Park. Ushaw Moor team returned home, another Social Club victim being defeated nine goals to nil.

During December the 'Mount Calvary' Methodist Sunday School presented the Eastern Opera 'The Rajah of Rajahpore', which drew applause from large audiences.

Miners at the colliery had a brighter Christmas than normally, the pits having worked full time for some weeks.

1935

Tuesday, New Year's Day, saw a wedding at Mount Calvary Methodist Chapel when William McKeen travelled from Wingate to marry Catherine Howden, the daughter of Mr. and Mrs. Edwin Howden of 7 Park Street. On the same day Eileen Paulin, only daughter of Charles Paulin, married William Bartlett of nearby Langley Moor. Eileen's mother died a few months ago.

Laurie Moran, almost nineteen, and Steve his mate, took advantage of the excursion trip from Brandon Colliery railway station to Newcastle. After paying their shilling fare they enjoyed the sixteen mile train ride. Sixpence procured a meal of pie, peas and potato in the market there. A good day was made complete when for ninepence they enjoyed a variety show in Newcastle Empire.

Brandon Club's football team beat Page Bank Rovers 4–0 in the sixteen team strong Durham Central League taking them top of the league with twenty-nine points. The club was leading 4–2 in the Brandon Nursing Cup-tie in their game at Brandon against Langley Park when the weather, in the form of a heavy snowfall occurred, causing the abandonment of the game.

Football fever has gripped the colliery sportsmen and women. One thousand supporters saw their team fall 4–1 to Wingate in the seventh round of the Durham Amateur Cup. Brandon recovered in later games, George

Hewitt's team won the Brandon Nursing Cup by beating Oakenshaw Colliery 3–0. Their captain Arthur Stock received the cup which they will hold for twelve months.

Brandon Social Club were committed to play six league games in one week, five of which were played away from home, eleven points were required to win the league. Brandon won all six games to take twelve points. They concluded a successful season by winning the Durham Central League, the Brandon Nursing Cup and the Deerness Aged Miners' Cup. A good deal of the club's success is due to their popular centre half and captain, Arthur Stock. Brandon received medals to the value of twelve pounds.

Over the weeks there had been feverish activity at Brandon Colliery. Eager to outdo rivals, a monster bonfire had been erected; Straker and Love supplied barrels of tar and railway sleepers, more combustible material had been collected. Lighting up time was scheduled for ten p.m. Jubilee night; it was to be Brandon's event of the year, children's bedtime had been pit back on the night. Bonfires had been erected on vantage points throughout the British Isles to commemorate the Silver Jubilee of George V's and Queen Mary's coronation. About midnight prior to the official day of celebration, flames were seen to erupt from the bonfire site, it had been mysteriously and wantonly set on fire. Later a Brandon youth received a month's imprisonment for his misdemeanour.

Brandon band and banner joined others at the May Day demonstration of the Spennymoor Labour Division. Langley Moor's Empire Theatre was crowded to hear Will Lawther speak. Union officials, banner carriers and miners posed for a group picture outside of the Empire.

The election meeting was in full swing when Geordie who was the worse for drink, stopped to listen. Each time the speaker finished his sentence Geordie insisted on calling out, 'Yer a silly ass'.

He was ignored until the member could stand it no longer and turning to Geordie, said, 'Look here, sir, I may or may not be what you say I am, but you are beastly drunk'.

'Yesh, it's true', replied Geordie, 'I'm beashly drunk, but in the mornin' Aa'll be sober, but you (hic) you'll still be a silly ass'.

Brandon's band and banner were honoured when they were chosen to attend the impressive Miners' Service in Durham's cathedral on the day of the fifty-eighth Miners' Gala. Bands from Brancepeth Colliery and Burnhope Colliery accompanied Brandon to the service. Laurie Moran and his mate left the 200,000 strong Gala crowd to follow their band and banner into the House of God.

A rise in wages and shorter working hours were the concern of one speaker at the Gala. He referred to the recent pit shaft mishap, when at one colliery the cage fell thirty feet with twenty miners in. Fortunately no serious injury was incurred. The speaker stated that the incident was generally accepted by the men as one of the risks to which a miner's calling is susceptible. People who are not as close to pit life may not feel inclined to accept that stoic view of a colliery mishap. Possibly they visualise the danger more clearly. If so they will get nearer to an understanding of the miners' claim for a wage commensurate with the work he does and the risk he runs in the quest for coal.

Thomas Crich survived wounds inflicted on three occasions whilst serving in the Great War before being discharged from the army. A miner shifter of 68 Newcastle Street, he died from an abcess on the left lung believed to have been caused more than twenty years ago when he was gassed in the campaign.

During November a National Miners' Ballot took place. Miners demand a flat rate increase of two shillings per day. An overwhelming vote—in excess of the requisite two thirds majority—was forthcoming:—

For a strike 409351
Against a strike 29215
                                                                    _____

Majority for a strike   380136
                                                                    _____

Ninety-three per cent of the workforce voted, the largest proportion of any ballot in the history of the Miners' Federation.

Brandon Colliery's corrugated Miners' Hall buzzed once more on the occasion of the drawing of the cavils. Lady Luck plays her part on the day. Some miners turn the fireside fender upside down for good luck in the draw, others put the cat in the oven (cold of course), while others place chairs on the bed upside down.

Every day the deputy puts cavils in for putters to go their different ways. He usually chalks them on his saw. One morning, expecting to have fun with them, he said, 'Rub away, lads, Aa've got the cavils in my head'.

'Gie me the one next to the watter', came the quick response from one of the lads.

John Moran, just left school, started as a van boy at Nevilles Cross Co-operative Laundry, his wage at fourteen is twelve shillings a week less twopence Insurance and twopence National Health stamp.

Joseph, the baby of the family, now five, attends Langley Moor St. Patrick's R.C. school. Teresa, ten and Frank, eight attend the same school. Connie Bird, Jenny Clennell, Jenny Watson and Alice McGough are Teresa's friends.

Over Christmas Brandon Social Club football supporters were cheered when their team beat Edmondsley Temperance in the Brandon Aged Miners' Cup, and again when Bowburn Welfare returned home defeated in the Durham Hospital Cup.

1936

Football enthusiasts boarded the excursion trains at Brandon Colliery railway station on New Year's Day when the London North Eastern Railway Company organised the trips especially for them. Newcastle and Sunderland, both first division sides, attracted crowds for their home games. Fares to both towns were one shilling and sixpence return from Brandon Colliery.

Whilst the trains were puffing their way to the games the Rev. Steve Parks, son of a Brandon Colliery miner, and himself a former colliery worker preached in the Market Square Methodist Chapel. Steve's father, like all of the country's miners, had anxiously awaited the outcome of the strike threat.

The threat of strike was removed. Miners were advised to accept the owners' offer:—

To datal workers (over 18) 6d. per shift.

To datal workers (under 18) 3d. per shift.

Piece workers' rise according to scale.

Mrs. Elisabeth Lamb had lived in Brandon Colliery for over thirty years. She died at her home in the Market Place where she had helped her husband George run their grocery shop.

Ex Brighton and Hove and Brandon player Stan Thompson, at present playing for Hartlepool, was married at Durham Registry Office. Winifred Steele travelled the long journey from Brighton to marry Stan. Members of the Hartlepool club attended the wedding and then the reception at the Langley Grand Hotel in Langley Moor, the home of Mr. John Saville, the best man.

Twenty year old Edmund Carter the popular Brandon Social Club inside right whose club currently heads the Durham Central League, went on a month's trial with Bradford City. Edmund played for Brandon Juniors then Willington in the Northern League before being spotted whilst playing for Brandon Social Club whose secretary George Hewitt, recently passed his referees' oral examination.

Brandon Social Club's players had the measure of Kimblesworth. They were leading 2—0 when play became very rough. One of the Kimblesworth players was cautioned and later sent off, but refused to leave the field. The referee brought the game to a swift close amid thunderous catcalls.

From an entry of over two hundred clubs, Brandon Social Club emerged the winners of the Durham Amateur Cup. Some seven thousand spectators savoured the game with ninety minutes of thrills between Brandon and Mackay's Social on Easter Monday at Durham's Holiday Park. A ding-dong battle ended with Brandon the victors with a 3—2 win. The victorious Braddon supporters expressed their sorrow for Arthur Stock the popular Brandon Colliery lad who at one time played for Brandon, but being a Mackay's employee he had elected to wear their colours. After the game he congratulated Brandon Social Club on being winners of such a spirited game.

Brandon Social Club retained possession of the Brandon Nursing Cup when they beat Framwellgate Moor 3—2 before a large crowd.

As usual pace eggs were in abundant evidence over the Easter, dyed egg competitions being held in various establishments. The Working Men's Clubs provided their colourful displays as did the members of the chapels in Brandon. Patients of Brandon and Durham Hospitals polished off the entrants of the pace egg competitions.

Tragedy struck the Paulin home — 2 Cobden Terrace. The news stunned the colliery folk. Eighteen year old John Charles Herbert Paulin's decapitated body was found on the railway line near Brandon Colliery. He was a brilliant young scholar for whom Brandon residents mourned.

Thomas Carr the newly elected chairman of the Brandon Urban District Council, presided at the May Day meeting held in the Empire Theatre. Brandon Colliery band and banner joined their counterparts from the three local collieries.

At the 1936 Meadowfield Carnival three of the six entrants for the Beauty Queen Contest, Misses Mary Ord, Mary Anderson and Lavinia Liddle, were from Brandon Colliery; the latter contestant emerged the winner. In conjunction with the carnival a football match was arranged between Langley Moor Social Club Veterans and Brandon Social Club Veterans for the Allison Challenge Cup.

Brandon Colliery Prize Silver Band won the Newsome Challenge Cup in the band contest at Middleton-in-Teesdale Carnival. Brandon band were winners of the trophy last year. The two Ord brothers won medals for the best cornet solo and the best soprano.

The leader of a local band which had earned for itself, not without reason, the unenviable title of 'the .waarst in the fower counties', was approached recently by a man with the request that the band should play at his brother's funeral.

'Is it a military funeral?' asked the leader.

'Wey no, man, not at aal', was the reply, 'but it was me bruthor's express wish that yor band should play at his funeral'.

Very surprised and flattered, the leader said, 'Is that so?'

'Yis', answered the other, 'he said he wanted ivvory body i' the place to be sorry he'd deed!'

Laurie Moran, now twenty years of age, severed connection with Browney Colliery. He started work at Brandon 'C' Pit—he was now a true 'Brandonian'!

R. D. Glass, holder of a First Class Certificate, took over as under-manager of the 'C' Pit under Walter H. Armstrong, the colliery manager.

There had been some disagreement in a local mine recently, and as a sequel Geordie and Jack were ordered to the colliery office for fighting underground. In his defence, Jack declared that there would have been no blows struck had it not been for the terrible language used by his opponent.

Asked by the manager to repeat it, Jack declined on account of its terrible nature.

'Come, come', said the manager, 'there is no need to be squeamish here, you know'.

'No, really, Aa cuddent, sor', Jack remonstrated. 'De ye knaa, it simply wassent fit for one respectable man to hear'.

'Is that so?' meditated the manager. 'Well, I'll tell you what to do. Just step over into that corner and whisper it to the under-manager'.

The colliery's five seams, the Hutton, Busty, Brockwell, Three Quarter and Ballarat employ 447 men and boys, 78 more than a year ago. The surface complement is 131, some six less than 1935.

Durham's miners have for some time agitated for a rise in wages, their average wage being £2.0s.9d. a week.

Laurie followed his colliery band and banner as they marched onto the racecourse in Durham. Brandon Colliery was well represented at the 59th Big Meeting at which three M.P.s and other two notabilities spoke. Arthur Greenwood, Major C. R. Attlee and Emmanuel Shinwell, all beloved by the miners, graced the platform. Mr. Samuel Watson, affectionately known as Sam, was present as the newly-elected agent to the Durham Miners' Association.

Laurie started work after six weeks' enforced idleness; he had drawn compensation of 19s.3½d. a week. He shuddered as he recollected standing in the Cross-cuts landing of the Busty beside the six full tubs of coal brought from the hewing places by putters and hearing the sound of approaching havoc. Sixty empty coal tubs running at speed had jumped the way on entering the landing; coals showered the immediate area, dust from coal and floor hovered. The derailed set came to a thunderous halt at its regular mark. Laurie shakily surveyed the dislodged length of steel waggon-way protruding from the bowel of an empty tub just a few feet from his incumbent body.

A resolution was passed at a Lodge meeting that full members pay one shilling each and half members sixpence each from one week's wage to the widows of workmen killed at the colliery. One widow whose husband, a Lodge member, received maximum compensation of £600 on his death by pit accident. At the same meeting it was decided that full members have sixpence and half members three pence deducted from one week's pay for the Sunderland Eye Infirmary. This to be a yearly contribution.

Brandon Social Club won their first game of the season when they travelled to Waldridge Welfare whom they beat 3–0 in a Durham and District League game. Brandon met Pittington in a first round tie of the Durham Hospital Cup Competition in which thirty-two teams are taking part.

A thousand spectators thronged Deepdale football ground to see Brandon Social Club beat Leasingthorne Village 4–1; two days later Brandon gained a victory over Willington in the first round of the Crook Nursing Cup. Bullyment, Brandon's centre forward and captain, scored a 'hat trick'. Brandon entertained Middlestone Moor in the first round of the Durham Aged Miners' Cup. Fifteen teams are competing.

In a Christmas game Pittington Sports Club sprang a surprise when they dismissed Brandon Social Club in the second round game for the Durham Hospital Cup. A lone goal decided the issue.

On Christmas Night an 'At Home' and Silver Tree were held in Commercial Street's Mount Calvary Methodist Chapel. A musical evening concluded with the stripping of the silver tree which realised £5. Robert Cairns, a society steward, was chairman and M.C. On the same evening two hundred and fifty parishioners and friends held their annual reunion and concert, whist drive, supper and dance in St. Patrick's Club Hall. John Higgins of Brandon Colliery was steward for the whist.

1937

Seasonal weather greeted in form Brandon Social Club football team. They began the New Year well when they entertained Pittington in the second round of the Brandon Nursing Cup and won by three goals to one. Members of the Durham and District League, they are having a successful season and have made application to join the Wearside League next season. They have already qualified for the semi-finals of six competitions.

Brandon avenged their Christmas Day defeat against Mackay's Social Club when they beat the Durham side 2–0 in the return Durham and District League encounter at Brandon.

George Lamb aged 64, died at his home, Market Place, Brandon Colliery. He was born at Brandon Colliery and was the son of the late Thomas Lamb, grocer. George succeeded his father in the grocery business, his wife Elizabeth died a year ago. His son Fred takes over the shop situated in the Market Place.

Brandon's business people include Miss Sarah Cheesey, shopkeeper; William Freek, hairdresser; Harry Pinkney, hairdresser; Thomas Gill, newsagent; Mrs. Lily Waddle, shopkeeper; William Woodard, shopkeeper; Walter Robinson, Colliery Inn; Thomas Nutter, Red Lion Inn.

A miner the worse for drink came out of a pub the other day, and on seeing his mate this question was put to him,

'Is there a free hoose up there, Jack?'

'Yes', said Jack, 'But there is only one fault, the landlord's got the heartburn'.

'Why', said his mate. 'Thoo should ha' telt him that chalk was good for it'.

'Aye', said Jack knowingly, but that's what giv him it'.

February was half yearly election time for club members to elect club officers of their choice. Councillor John Clennell (re-elected president, unopposed); secretary John Higgins (re-elected unopposed); treasurer Rop Miller; committee, Tommy Lawson, Jim Bartle, Jack Heron junior, Paddy Moran, Harry Pybus, Joe Freeman (reserve), were Brandon Social Club members' option.

Laurie Moran, now classed as an adult worker, shared in the best wage settlement ever negotiated by the Durham Miners' Association. His daily wage is now 4s.6d. plus 70% – making 7s.8d.

Laurie crouched over the small electrically driven hauler–commonly called a 'tugger'. The protesting one drum machine hauled six full coal tubs up the incline from the Red Lion district, so called because the coal hewing places were being worked immediately under the Red Lion Inn. Laurie had just attached the six tubs to the others waiting in the landing prior to removal to the nearby shaft.

Unable to contact by phone, a shaft worker had hurried the short distance to convey the tragic news. Laurie, together with the Red Lion coal hewers and their putter, immediately downed tools and returned to the surface.

Nineteen year old Ernie Staley had met his death under tragic circumstances while working as a shaft lad at the 'C' Pit Busty. The cage had moved as he tried to enter, he fell down the shaft to his immediate end.

Laurie shuddered when he recalled the time he sat 'hunker like' beside the glowing embers cleaned from under the fish shop pans. His companions, twelve year old Ernie Staley and his elder brother Jeff, discussed the future. Sturdily built, the younger brother fancied playing for Sunderland or some other big team.

Ernie of 1 College Terrace never attained his boyhood ambition of playing football for a First Division club.

Around the time of the accident steps leading from the surface were officially opened. Five hundred and thirty seven concrete steps had been built during the descent of four seams—the Low Main, Harvey, Hutton and Busty levels. What normally took one minute to descend by cage was achieved in ten minutes laborious descent by the steps. It took some time for the workmen to acclimatise their shaking legs to the change over. Coal hewers sweated profusely while carrying an eight pound electric lamp, tokens, shot powder, sharp picks and an occasional new shovel or other impedimenta.

Norah and Kathleen Moran are in domestic service in Keighley, Yorkshire, where Jimmy aged twenty-seven married Winnie Johnston in St. Anne's R.C. Church. Twenty-one year old Laurie was his brother's best man. Jimmy and Winnie live in nearby Steeton where they are mill workers.

John Moran, having worked one year as a van boy, worked a similar term for Billy Freek, a go-ahead Commercial Street hairdresser. Billy started an electric washer business at the rear of his shop and required a lad to deliver finished washing to his growing number of clients. On reaching the age of sixteen, John seeking a permanent job with more pay, started work underground at Brandon Colliery 'C' Pit.

Eddie Moran, two years John's junior, delivered newspapers for Tommy Gill, another Commercial Street businessman before finding employment with Sacriston Motor Company.

Ten year old Matthew Eales left Washington Colliery with his parents to live in Brandon Colliery. Sixty years after his arrival he died at his home, 17 Albert Street. Seventy year old Matt was well known in football circles, having begun his career as a player with the former Brandon Rovers. He later became a referee in Northern League football.

Three of Brandon Colliery's old standards died in quick succession. John Dacres succumbed to a long illness at his home, 13 Station Avenue, at the age of seventy-eight. He came to the colliery over forty years ago, and for several years was under-manager of the 'C' Pit where he also worked as a fore-overman and back-overman until his retirement at the age of sixty-nine. Well known horsekeeper Thomas Cairns worked until he reached seventy-one years of age. He worked at the colliery for fifty-five years until his retirement. For thirty-eight years he was head horsekeeper. His smart figure, dressed in neat tweeds and highly polished leggings, was well known throughout the county and he acted as judge as many of the principal horse shows. He enjoyed a retirement of two years before his death at the age of seventy-three. The Aged Miners' Homes lost one of its oldest tenants on the death of seventy-nine year old John Maddison. He had lived in Brandon Colliery more than seventy years and was a miner for sixty years and during that time was an ardent worker for Brandon Mount Calvary Methodists.

Fifteen year old Reuben Ditchburn of 25 Newcastle Street received injuries to his right leg when caught by tubs in the 'C' Pit. He was treated at Durham County Hospital. Reuben's mother Mrs. Kate Ditchburn, born in Cumberland but had lived nearly all her life in Brandon Colliery, died just three months ago at the early age of fifty-one.

Two Coronation Year weddings took place. All four participants were from Brandon Colliery. George Gill married Margaret Ross in St. John's Church, Meadowfield. Ralph Teasdale married Miss S. Jones at the Bethel Church, Durham. George lives in Commercial Street and is the son of Brandon Colliery's newsagent. Ralph is a deputy in the 'C' Pit's Whin Ballarat, a seam of high class coal and four low working faces. A seam which has had a coal face as low as twelve inches — so low that a wooden frame, termed 'the wooden cutter', was attached to the front of the twelve inch high coal cutter of some five tons in weight. Where the wooden contraption travelled the coal cutter would follow.

Teams of fillers among whom were Pud Liddle, George Liddle, Teddy Bailes and Joe Bell, cleared the coal from each face which averaged one hundred yards in length. They are paid eightpence per ton for their labour.

Austin Keenan, Tommy Pickard and Jimmy Gray, marras who worked the three shifts as deputies on one face. The latter deputy had resumed work after a lay-off of some weeks; whilst firing a shot he was severely injured in the face, he was removed to the surface with a coat covering his head and shoulders. After a spell in Durham County Hospital he was discharged; a coal embedded, heavily scarred face, a testimony of his lucky escape from death.

They were telling 'tall' stories about tall seams, and Geordie thought he had reached the high coal mark when he described a nine foot seam he had worked on in Yorkshire. But one never knows.

'Wy, that's nowt', said Bill. 'Aa worked in a seam in Staffordshire where you had to 'jowl' the top with a catapult'.

On the closure and sealing up of the Red Lion district, Laurie Moran was transferred to the Whin Ballarat. He joined Wilf Sherrington, Michael Solan, Billy Cairns, Teddy Mearman junior and other datal hands working in the Whin. This district had no regular time of starting; men and boys were called to work as their face became ready for production. In the regular event of mishap during the course of operations the caller shouted 'Lie back till seven'. This system caused great inconvenience to the family concerned.

Brandon's new Workingmen's Club has taken shape since the first sward was cut in May. The bulk of the cost is expected to be borne by members' shares. The present club situated in Commercial Street, is deemed inadequate for the growing membership.

Club members, mainly miners, joined the crowd estimated at a quarter million on the occasion of the 60th annual Gala. Drenching downpours failed to dampen their spirits and those of the representatives from the county's 253 pits.

The Gala scenes were still a vivid memory when William Tyrie a twenty-four year old pitman, met his death. The peaceful cycling jaunt, a regular weekend pastime, was suddenly and tragically terminated as Willy rode just ahead of his twenty-one year old sweetheart. He was knocked off his bike by an overtaking car to die almost instantly from head injuries. Sunderland Street mourned his death. Willy, a popular neighbour, was a good cornet player, he played in Brandon Prize Silver Band and was a member of the local Salvation Army Band.

Brandon Social Football Club, newly elected members of the Wearside League, have signed four professionals and three prominent amateurs for the forthcoming season. The club made a highly encouraging debut in the Wearside League when Seaham Colliery Welfare fell victims eight goals to two. Four days later, before a crowd of over one thousand, Brandon beat travellers West Auckland in a most thrilling encounter when they finished winners by two goals to one. Another nail-biting contest took place when Bearpark lost to Brandon 2−1 on the first qualifying round of the Durham County Challenge Cup.

The local club is going great guns in the Wearside League. At home to Dawdon Recreation, they prevailed by three goals to one, thereby winning their fourth successive league fixture. Football enthusiasm is at a high pitch in the Brandon area. The reason is obvious. Since the local club applied for and secured admission to the Wearside League there has been an almost continuous run of success, for which George Hewitt, the secretary, can take considerable credit. An astute judge of a player, he set himself out in the close season to get together an experienced side and the value of his knowledge is to be seen in the results so far recorded. Brandon's successful team is Hedley, Hall, Matthews, Blades, Bragan, Ferguson, Hobson, Halliday, Hole, Carter, Fannen. Edmund Carter, Brandon born, is the idol of the crowd. A clever purveyor, he is regarded as a player with a great future.

During November, Robert Ferguson centre half and captain of Brandon Social Club team, suffered a compound fracture of the ankle while at work at Pit House Colliery. A falling girder terminated his football for some time.

Youngsters have caught 'football fever'. First Eleven cigarettes, a new brand selling at ten for 4d. contains a cigarette card depicting a football 'star'. There is keen competition and much swapping of cards among colliery youths.

St. Patrick's Amateur Dramatic Society has a number of Brandon Colliery miners among its stars and cast. Laurie Moran was a member of the 'chorus of citizens' when the musical play in two acts 'A Slave in Araby' was performed. The proceeds were in aid of the proposed new school to be erected at Broompark.

On Christmas Day representatives from Barnsley, Bradford, Wolverhampton and Stockport Football Clubs watched Brandon Social Club's outside right Tom Drennan. He had another fine game and the four scouts offered him trials with their clubs.

Geordie is a hard-hearted individual. The spirit of Christmas never troubles him. He better half, however, is different. She entered the kitchen with a troubled look on Christmas Eve. 'Oh, Geordie', she said, 'Wor Mary swalleyed a tanner, whaat hev we ter dee?'

'Dee?' repeated Geordie, 'Wey, hinney, Aa suppose we'll hev ter let hor keep't. Onyhow, she'd hev expected a Christmas box'.

1938

On New Year's Day, Geordie fell in with his old pal, Bill. Geordie, who happened to have a bottle of whisky in his pocket, asked Bill if he wad have a drink.

'Wey, Geordie, Aa'll hev a toothful', replied Bill, and he put the whisky to his mouth and drained it. Geordie looked at him, then looked at the bottle and replied,

'Bill, if ivvor thou gets that tooth drawn Aa'll buy it off tha'.

Thomas Edwin Genner died at the age of sixty-four. He had lived in Brandon for over forty years, twenty of which he was a local reporter for the Durham County Advertiser and Chronicle. At one time he played in Brandon Colliery Silver Band and for a number of years he was the band's secretary.

Brandon Social Club, the only unbeaten team in the Wearside League were fortunate to retain their record when they travelled to Ouston and returned with one point. Sadly Brandon's run of success ended when Lumley Sixth Pit Welfare returned home the victors by four goals to nil.

Brandon Social Club supporters, still smarting over the dismal performance of their club, joined the crowd of nearly five thousand who paid a total of £113 gate money, to witness the demise of Bishop Auckland from the Challenge Cup Competition. Brandon's supremacy was never in doubt, they played typical cup-tie football to beat them by two well-taken goals.

A former Brandon Argyle Football Club player, Joseph Pybus, son of Isaac Pybus of Princess Street, took a day off work; he is a putter in Brandon's 'C' Pit Busty, to marry Lillian Sargent of Langley Moor. Joe's brother George is an ex-Chelsea and Bradford footballer.

For thirty-six years the Workingmen's Club in Commercial Street had served the needs of its members. Men with vision, seeing the need for more commodious premises, had launched the project of their dreams. James Wilkinson, John Clennell, James Turner, Jack Higgins and committee men, eyed with approval the new club built a short distance from their first venture into the land of club life. The club's president, John Clennell, opened the £6000 venture which contains a large bar, billiard room, reading room, board room, three sitting rooms, a secretary's room and a spacious entertainment hall with accommodation for two hundred people.

On the opening of the club, the residue of the old club's beer stocks was served out free to members in the new club's bar. A festive crowd enjoyed the spree. 'Can I have my share in Woodbine cigarettes?' came from a slight figure at the bar.

James Wilkinson did not long enjoy the social life of the new club he had helped evolve, a club in which he had served as first secretary, and at one time as chairman. Jim Wilkie as he was affectionately known, died at the age of seventy-two. He came to Brandon Colliery as a baby; at the age of twelve he started work at the colliery. For fourteen years prior to retirement he was a well respected deputy overman who knew his job.

A keen horticulturist, he was widely known throughout the county and helped judge many flower shows. For several years he was secretary of the Brandon Colliery Flower Show, which was at one time one of the best in the county.

Miners nationwide are jubilant. The holidays with pay agreement—this year to be three days—the first in the history of the coal mines, was signed to take effect in August. An historic occasion! The principal agreement which is to continue for five years provides that as from next year all workmen in the industry shall have seven consecutive days' holiday annually in addition to the eight existing recognised public holidays.

The rate of pay offered for the annual holiday is:—
married men, widower having families living with them, and employees in receipt of rent or coal allowances—£2.12.
Single men of 18 or over—£1.10s.4d.
Boys under 18—£1.1s.8d.

The three days granted for 1938 will be paid at half the rates provided in the principal agreement.

The coal industry was taken over by the State. Miners in Great Britain looked forward to a more stable future.

The colliery caller knocked up Tommy Warriner, Billy Stewart, John Worral and Laurie Moran. They with fillers working one of the Whin Ballarat faces had been called to start work at three a.m. Due to mechanical breakdown the coal on the low face had not been filled away, the fillers lay awaiting resumption of work.

The quartet of shover-ups removed the full tubs from the loader set up on the main heading and shoved them up the landing to await removal to the shaft. The end of a normal working shift had long passed. There being no sign of a renewal of work, the four cold, hungry and tired workers decided to leave, come what may. On their journey outbye to the shaft they met the colliery manager and under-manager hurrying in to the scene of the breakdown. 'Where are you buggers going?' screamed the manager.

'Home', came a chorus from the four delinquents.

'If you don't come back you'll get this bloody stick over your rumps'.

As the defiant four turned homewards, the manager, waving his stick, almost choked. 'I'll see that you will all get other jobs tomorrow'.

True to his word, the four offenders were drafted to other parts of the mine.

Laurie started work next day—with a difference—he knew that at his shift end he would go home, whereas the length of shift in the Whin Ballarat depended on what time it took the fillers to clear all the coal from the face. Some weeks saw the caller knocking up the men at four or five different times, depending on the completion of operations. The men's wives and mothers never knew the time of their arrival home from work. Laurie and his mother were delighted to be rid of an invidious system.

Geordie had gone to the river for an afternoon's fishing, when the colliery manager, who by the way, was very unpopular with his men, came along and entered into conversation with him. Presently the official left and Geordie resumed fishing, only to be startled a few moments later by a loud splash and a cry for help. Realising that the manager had fallen in, he rushed to the spot whence came the noise and sprang in to the rescue. After some difficulty he brought the manager to the bank, and the latter, gasping his thanks, exclaimed, 'What can I do for you? Is there anyhting I can do for you?'

'Well, sorr', replied Geordie after a moment's hesitation. 'There's only one favour Aa hev ter ask'.

'What is it?' asked the manager.

'Well,' said Geordie, with a twinkle in his eye, 'Divvent tell me mates Aa saved your life, or they'll chuck me doon the shaft!'

Brandon Social Club's supporters were disappointed when they visited Gateshead to watch their team play South Shields in the replayed final of the Durham County Challenge Cup. Shields won on their merits by four goals to one. The final was not productive of good football, Brandon's attack being very weak. Brandon Social Club started the season with a debit balance of ten pounds and finished with a credit balance of forty pounds.

George Hewitt, the club's secretary was informed at a meeting of the Wearside League of complaints that Brandon had no stripping room. If adequate accommodation is not forthcoming for next season the club might be asked to tender its resignation from the league, of which at the moment they are only probationary members.

The hot summer brought out cricket enthusiasts when Brandon Colliery one of the ten teams forming Division II in the North-East Durham League, handsomely beat Hazard Colliery. Only two of Belmont's batsmen reached double figure in their league game with Brandon and their innings closed for fifty-six runs. James Abson played a great part for Brandon, taking eight wickets for twenty-two runs. Brandon knocked off the runs with five wickets to spare. Brandon's team: Joe Swinburn, Robert Charlton, Alex Lidster, Fred Brown, James Abson, Tucker Thornton and Alf Brown.

Six familes were rendered homeless and two families had miraculous escapes from death when a disastrous fire broke out in the long colliery row. Numbers 21 and 22 High Street occupied by Mr. and Mrs. T. Mawson and Mrs. and Mrs. J. Gray were completely gutted.

Numbers 23 and 24, the homes of Mr. and Mrs. R. Robson and Mr. and Mrs. Leslie Blenkinsop, were badly damaged, while numbers 19 and 20 housing Mr. and Mrs. Walter Harker and Mr. and Mrs. Jim Beer were only partly affected. Forty-nine year old Mr. Gray jumped for his life as the stairs and bedroom floors of number 22 were ablaze and almost ready to collapse.

Mr. Gray, a miner, in whose home the fire originated, owes his life to a passing busker playing the bagpipes, who raised the alarm. Mr. Gray said, 'We lost everything, including a new suite of furniture and a new wireless. We had booked rooms at Redcar for a week's holiday in August, but all our holiday money which was in the house, has gone'.

Brandon girl Miss Winifred Welsh of 9 Newcastle Street married Norman Henry of Front Street, Browney Colliery. Their July wedding took place in St. John's Church.

Brandon Colliery band and banner, like those from neighbouring collieries, paraded the main thoroughfare before proceeding to Durham for the sixty-first Durham Miners' Gala. The band with Brancepeth and Burnhope bands joined in the playing of voluntaries in Durham Cathedral.

Brandon's banner depicted Thomas Carr on one side and a picture of the cathedral on the other. Earlier photographs reveal that the same banner once bore two portraits, Thomas Carr and Ramsey McDonald. Many miners called Ramsey McDonald a traitor, hence his removal from the banner.

One of Brandon's oldest inhabitants died in South Street. Anthony McDonough was born in Ireland's County Mayo and came to England at the age of nine. At thirteen he worked as a blacksmith's labourer. He worked for five years in the mines in America before returning to Brandon Colliery where he resumed his employment in the coke-yard.

Brandon Social Club football team began the season in sparkling style when they beat Crook 5–1 on their own ground. The occasion was a Ferryhill Nursing Cup game. Brandon beat Tow Law in the preliminary round of the F.A. Cup.

Brandon's new signing, Reggie Brown, the old Murton centre half and captain, failed to stop Langley Park Villa in their runaway victory in the first qualifiying round of the F.A. Cup when the Villa won 5–0. Reggie will be challenging Bob Ferguson for his position in the team. Bob is currently recovering from a broken ankle.

A Brandon miner who was entombed in the pit for sixteen hours before being rescued, told a story of grim humour. Through hours that seemed an eternity the imprisoned man was considerably heartened by a bluebottle that kept buzzing round him in the dark. He was thirty-four year old John Edward Lumley. Johnnie, a coal hewer of 53 Single Sunderland Street, was trapped in a space about four feet square and four feet high when a large fall of rubble, clay and small stones occurred.

'I seemed to be living through eternity', Johnnie said afterwards. 'But I was thankful for one thing—a large bluebottle was imprisoned with me. It was a great comfort to me as it buzzed around in the dark, and seemed quite friendly. When my lamp was shining it nearly put out the flame while it was buzzing around. How grateful I was later, in the darkness, that I had resisted the temptation to kill it'.

William Bailes, a hearty eighty-six year old, on receiving his Diploma for being a member of the Durham Miners' Association for fifty years, recalled many miraculous and exciting incidents during his life. He began work underground as a trapper boy at the age of nine. At the age of fourteen while working underground as a pony driver, the steam boiler at the surface burst and blew away the winding-engine house which operated the cage to and from the mine. He, along with other lads, had to be raised out of the pit by means of a crib. He also relates his experience during a sixteen weeks' strike at Sunnybrow Colliery; how he and his parents and other mining families were victimised and evicted from their homes, and spent a Christmas in the dyke back.

He was one of the survivors of the 'C' Pit explosion at Messrs. Straker and Love's Brandon Colliery, which occurred in 1899, while he was following his employment as a deputy-overman.

William was among sixty members of Brandon Colliery Lodge and eighteen members of Littleburn Colliery Miners' Lodge at the presentation.

Fred Bowes finished his coal hewing shift in Brandon's 'C' Pit Brockwell seam. The seam is reached after a long walk from the shaft which terminated in the region of Brancepeth Castle. A steeper than usual incline runs down from the Busty level; six tubs of coal being deemed enough for a safe hauling. A set of full tubs moved from the bottom of the incline. Fred succumbed to the temptation of an easy ascent, he lay prone on a tub. Failing to jump clear before reaching low ground at the top of the incline, he was crushed between tub and roof. He survived a fractured spine for two months.

Fred was forty-nine and lived at 46 Queen Street. His wife Ethel died in June at the early age of forty-four.

Brandon and Byshottles heeding the threat of war and desirous of taking air raid precautions, appointed the Rev. G. H. Greenfield, Vicar of Brandon as chief warden. J. P. Addison the Council's surveyor, said that volunteers were coming in gradually and that 200 out of a total requirement of 450 had come forward.

William Garbutt of 7 Sunderland Street, a putter at Brandon 'C' Pit, married Lena Evans of Station Avenue. Billy is well known in the district as being a capable dancer who would in all probability sample the delight of dancing on the new maple wood dance floor. The floor, certainly the best for miles around, was a big attraction when a newly built building replaced the old zinc structure of St. Patrick's Catholic Men's Club. A dance was held to commemorate the event.

A discerning group of miners attended the annual meeting for the election of Miners' Lodge officers held in the Miners' Hall. The voting by show of hands produced the following result: Chairman, Councillor Thomas Dickinson (re-elected); secretary and compensation secretary, Councillor Thomas Carr (re-elected); auditor, Tot Underwood; pit inspectors, David Hopkins, Edward Duffy, Will Robson, George Taylor, Matt Robinson. Committee, 'C' Pit, George Hewitt, Isaac Pybus and Dave White.

Supporters of Brandon Social Club football team were elated around Christmas. Their team, Batey, Bowden, Matthews, Blades, Brown, Spencer, Thomas, Rochester, Williams, Holliday and Evans had qualified for the semi-finals of three cup competitions—the Sunderland Shipowners' Monkwearmouth Charity and Ferryhill Nursing Cup—and they are still interested in the County Challenge Competition.

1939

The New Year was ushered in by the usual custom of 'first footing'. Members of various churches in the district as well as the Salvation Army braved squalls and storms to entertain with carol singing.

Brandon Social Club's first game of the year was at home against Washington Chemical Works. A good crowd braving atrocious weather was rewarded with a glut of goals—four being scored in each half, all by Brandon players. Four came from Williams, while Carter, Matthews, Brown and Holliday netted one each. Brandon now lie second in the Wearside League.

Playing on the same day under similar weather conditions, Blackhall Colliery Welfare and Shotton Colliery Welfare collected gate money of seven shillings and sixpence.

Brandon Social Club beat West Stanley 6–1 in the second round game for the Durham County Challenge Cup. Brandon followed up their magnificent County Cup performances by trouncing Hetton United 6–0 at Brandon. Their 12–1 win over Houghton Colliery Welfare puts Brandon at the top of the Wearside League.

Brandon Urban District Council at their monthly meeting decided to build shelters to provide temporary cover and safety in the event of air raids. The trenches will be constructed on suitable sites to accommodate a tenth of the population. Brandon was one of nine proposed sites; the allotment site behind Commercial Street could hold a shelter for four hundred people.

Councillor Tom Dickinson observed that at Brandon Colliery there were probably the finest places for air raid shelter in this county or any other. 'There are cement steps into the pit and all is ready made', he said. 'It will house not only the population of Brandon, but that of the whole area'. He stated that the idea had been mentioned before, but he thought the Council should get on with it. The pit was in the centre of the village and could be utilised with greater benefit than any trench or covered shelter.

Preparations are being made to change over the electric current from direct current to alternating current. Hitherto Messrs. Straker and Love have supplied the needs of the colliery houses and streets; it is feared that the change over will affect some old wireless sets.

Despite its lack of publicity, Brandon 'A' team heads the table in the Durham and District Table Tennis League, having won all 15 games played. William Allchurch is a constant winner for the 'A' team. Brandon 'B' team have played 17 games, three of which they won.

Finalists last season, Brandon Social Club reached the semi-final of the Durham County Challenge Cup competition when they beat Reyrolles the leaders of the Tyneside League 5–1.

A strong wind proved a severe handicap at Brandon, where Seaham Colliery gained a 2–1 victory and thus put a sprag in the Social Club's championship aspirations.

Laurie Moran and Billy Taylor applied through Brandon Colliery Miners' Lodge to savour two weeks' convalescence in the Durham Miners' Convalescent Home at Ulverston in Lancashire, which was acquired in August 1930.

Laurie was recuperating after the removal of a torn cartilege in the leg sustained while at work in Brandon's 'C' Pit. He was paid compensation for ten weeks at the rate of twenty-three shillings and ninepence per week.

The authorities at Ulverston deemed it wise to prepare for possible war casualties; they has stored two hundred hospital type beds in the spacious Priory.

Some 310,000 conscripts—all men between 20 and 21 will receive six months training in warfare under the Government's Conscription Bill. Brandon Urban Council members were unanimous in their decision to protest strongly against the introduction of conscription in peace time. At the same meeting it was proposed and passed that new Council offices be built at a cost of £17,000.

One of the founders of the Indpendent Methodist Church at Brandon Colliery, Mrs. Prudence Pritchard, had lived in Brandon for sixty years. She died at No. 12 Aged Miners' Homes. Aged eighty-four, she is survived by her husband Joseph Pritchard, three daughters and two sons. Another founder member, Mrs. Mary Robson, died at the age of eighty-three at 11 Russell Street; she too had lived in Brandon for sixty years.

Nine clergymen, one doctor and a layman played a team of police in a charity football match on Brandon's ground. The Rev. E. E. Eddon, Brandon's vicar, lined up with the clergymen. The 1939 Cup Final referees Mr. H. Nattrass and Mr. A. Joseph, were linesmen. The police won the game by the only goal scored, during which thirty pounds was collected for charity.

Joseph Pritchard survived his eighty-four year old wife Prudence by less than one month; he died at No. 12 Aged Miners' Homes. Joseph started work in the mine as a boy of eight. He was a miner for sixty years and retired twenty-four years ago.

Laurie had saved for his first official week's holiday from work. Britain's miners had been granted their first full week off work — with pay! A new suit costing forty-five shillings at Burtons the Tailors, saw him smartly dressed as he left for a break in Yorkshire.

The sixty-second Miners' Gala was held in July. Laurie Moran and Steve joined the 200,000 strong crowd to hear the three Members of Parliament address the gathering of miners; their theme — trouble on the Continent; there was murmur of war.

Undeterred by talk of international crisis, Laurie and Steve followed Brandon banner into Durham's majestic cathedral for the annual Miners' Day Service at which Brandon Colliery, Blackhall and Craghead contingents accompanied the singing.

A portrait of Durham Cathedral graced one side of Brandon's silken banner. Thomas Carr, the Miners' Lodge secretary, procalimed to all his popularity with his men by having his likeness impressed on the reverse side. At one time Ramsey McDonald shared the honours with Thomas Carr. Many miners called the former a traitor, hence his removal from the banner. A colliery worker was commissioned to erase Ramsey McDonald's likeness.

Tommy Simpson (Bomber), a putter in Brandon's 'C' Pit, married Miss Chittock in St. John's Church. Their reception took place in the nearby Ex-Servicemen's Hall. Another wedding was solemnised in St. John's Church when Joseph Bell, a filler in Brandon's 'C' Pit Whin Ballarat, married Elizabeth Richardson who hails from Meadowfield.

A Brandon Colliery couple, James Bartle and Sarah Martin, were married. Jim is a colliery engine driver and he had as his best man his engine driver's mate, Frank Robson.

Good cricket weather did not enhance Brandon Cricket Club's fortunes, they lie sixth in the Deerness League comprising eight teams, having played four games—won one and lost three. They are at the bottom of the eleven team Mid-Durham League, having played eight games and lost all of them.

End of August — the gravity of the existing situation in Europe, with a devastating world war looming, was the uppermost topic in home, mine, office, shop, factory and street. Prayers were said in churches and chapels for peace.

On September 1st the tanks of Nazi Germany rolled into Poland, and Europe was plunged into war.

On September 3rd while Laurie was waiting to see his colliery undermanager about starting to put in the 'C' Pit, the air raid warning sounded. Britain had declared war on Germany. The early sounding of the sirens caused a hasty cessation of business. Laurie had to wait until the next gathering of officials in the office before he could leave his datal job and take up putting.

Gas masks were in attendance. An official order stated that all must carry a gas mask even if you wish to attend a performance at any cinematograph hall. Without the gas mask admisson will be denied.

George Renwick the colliery caller groped his way through the darkened streets; despite the complete wartime blackout he trod the rows almost by instinct. George felt the loosening of his shoe and bent to fasten the offending shoe lace. Thump! A heavy object struck him from behind. Turning to meet his blackout assailant he retrieved his gas mask which had been suspended by string from his shoulder before colliding with his skull's base.

Early war jitters were displayed when loud booming sounds were heard. Great relief was displayed when it was learned that blasting operations had taken place in the vicinity of Littleburn Colliery about one mile away.

Brandon Urban Council, at its monthly meeting, decided to pay seventy-five per cent of the differences between service pay and salaries in respect of employees serving in His Majesty's Forces, subject to the combined income not exceeding £225 a year.

Ten houses were built and occupied — the first of thirty-eight to be built at Brandon Colliery to re-house tenants of the demolished colliery rows. Coun. Carr named the site Grey Ridge Estate. Coun. Dickinson and Coun. Clennell were present to formally open blocks of houses.

Laurie now inured to the rigour of putting, had descended to the 'C' Pit Busty level at three a.m. one week after the declaration of war. He carried his bunch of numbered tokens, one of which he attached to every tub he put into the hewer's place, this being for verification purposes. As he walked inbye with other established putters he had been apprehensive of the future; now he was on 'piece work'—no results, no pay! Gone was his fixed datal wage.

During November miners were granted their first National War Wage advance, eightpence for adults and fourpence for the under eighteens. Accumulated awards up to two shillings and eightpence for adults per shift to be spread over to 1st July, 1941.

Colliery folk spent the blacked out Christmas quietly in deference to their loved ones fighting on foreign soil. Churches and chapels were well attended. May peace be with us in 1940.

1940

No raucous colliery buzzer to greet the New Year and the trickle of blackout defying first footers. On the home front blackout accidents were mounting.

By a majority of more than seven to one the miners' lodges in the Durham coalfield voted in favour of the resolution passed by the Mineworkers' Federation Conference rejecting as inadequate the coalowners' wage offer of fourpence a shift increase to men and twopence for boys.

The owners countered with an immediate offer of fivepence per shift, which the miners accepted. Fivepence and twopence-halfpenny is retrospective and will operate from January 1st.

'Gee! Just missed that pole!' chuckled Steve. Wham! Steve collided with the solid street lamp stanchion set only a stride away from his imaginary one. Laurie and Steve groped their blacked-out way; Saturday night—what mysteries had the fish shop to offer? Dimmed fish shop illumination revealed an angry looking bump—hen's egg size—on unfortunate Steve's head.

The annual meeting and election of officers and committee of Brandon Colliery Workmen's Social Club took place. As usual great interest was taken in the ballot; results, President, Councillor Jack Clennell; Secretary, Jack Higgins; Treasurer, Rop Miller; Committee, Jim Bartle, Bill Ramsey, Bill Powton, Tommy Lawson and Paddy Moran.

During March the need for conserving food stocks resulted in the ration of meat to one shilling and tenpence her pead per week.

Men from the Brandon area fighting in His Majesty's Forces were remembered by the British Legion.

Pte. William Welsh
Sgt. Henry Stoker
Pte. R. Jackson
Pte. Joe Duffy
Lance Corporal Ralph Smith
Pte. W. H. Jones
George Grainger, R.A.F.
T. Wood, British Expeditionary Force
Sgt. J. Reavley
A. C. Ogilvy, R.A.F.
Pte. Jim Richardson
Pte. Robert Adair
Pte. Edward Duffy

All wrote in glowing terms their thanks for comforts sent.

Well known Great War veteran Harry Draycott, 72, died at 1 East Street. He had lived in Brandon for about sixty years. He served in the Boer War and four and a half years during the Great War with the Durham Light Infantry in France.

Fifty-six year old William Thompson died at 3 Princess Street after spending the whole of his life in Brandon Colliery. He was formerly treasurer of Brandon Colliery Miners' Lodge. For years he was a familiar figure seen collecting the miners' union fees in the Miners' Hall.

Recommendations to improve coal production, minimise absenteeism, the absorption of unemployed miners, and inviting the men to forego their annual holiday but not the holiday pay, were approved at a Council meeting of the Durham Miners' Association. The scheme was outlined by Samuel Watson on behalf of the Executive Committee and was the subject of a lodge vote. Laurie and Steve with other miners gave up their holiday. Being miners they were exempt from war service; they joined the Home Guard for the duration of the war.

Brandon Cycling Club, formed just before the start of the war and all but faded into obscurity, has experienced a promising revival. Under the guidance of Jack Hutchinson and secretary Wince Cole, cyclists in the Brandon area will be catered for during the war with a programme of social and sporting events. The first run is to Alston and will start from Brandon Co-op Store corner.

There was consternation in Brandon, and elsewhere, when the sirens wailed, shattering the Sunday afternoon quiet; the aircraft approaching warning had not been heard for some time. Some said that it was a test, others averred it was for real. It was announced later than a monthly test would be carried out at two p.m. on a Sunday.

Soldiers who survived the horrors of Dunkirk are in temporary billets around the area, schools and halls being comandeered; they are being lauded for their courage and tenacity during recent months.

On the resignation of Neville Chamberlain, Winston Churchill became Prime Minister. He invited members of the Labour Party under Clem Attlee to join the administration. The Labour Party decided that they should take their share of responsibility as full partners in the running of the war.

The capitulation of France resulted in loss of coal exports and dislocation of the coal industry in Durham; pits are laid idle or working short time. It is expected that by the end of the year there will be a loss of man power exceeding 23,000 in Durham coal industry with men transferred either to other coalfields or other work of national importance.

Brandon Colliery continued to work full time. Laurie Moran, now twenty-four, has been hand putting since the beginning of the war. When opportunity arises he visits recently opened British Restaurant built behind Durham's Silver Street which seems to cater for all and sundry. With eight to feed of whom four are miners, Laurie's mother, a hard-working wife and mother at fifty-four, appreciates any outside assistance which helps stretch the wartime rations.

Laurie took his turn in the queue for Earl's pies; the ever lengthening line savouring the aroma wafting from the shop in Durham's Saddler Street. After a considerable wait Laurie hopefully whispered, 'There are eight of us'. Sadly the ration was two pies, sadly undersized, per customer. On leaving the shop Laurie reasoned that two into eight was not much; a nearby public house had just received its long-awaited ration of watered down beer; Laurie had two pies and two halves of ale for lunch. His mother forgave him his over indulgence.

Eddie, now seventeen, had started work at Brandon's Pit House Colliery working on the screens. He had been employed by Sacriston Motor Company for three years helping demolish hundreds of abandoned coke ovens, relics of the colliery's heyday, scattered around the 'A' and 'C' Pits' heapsteads. The crushed brick had been used in the construction of Browney sewer system and for road repair work.

Councillor Clennell at the monthly meeting of Brandon Urban District Council, stated that the back of Russell Street, Brandon Colliery was in a deplorable condition. Councillor Clennell who lives in Russell Street said that one portion of the street was eighteen inches lower than the rest, and only part of the roadway was finished properly. It was difficult for pedestrians to walk along the street even in daylight, and the blackout made it even more difficult. You can neither walk on the footpath nor walk on the road. Councillor Clennell remarked, 'I have been insulted by my neighbours. When I leave my house I have to step down eighteen inches off the footpath into a quagmire'.

A number of organisations are helping to provide comforts for local men serving in the Forces. Brandon School Infants under Miss Stodhart the headmistress, are doing a great work, they have sent a large parcel of comforts to the Mayoress' Fund for the Fighting Forces. The boys of the school have taken one penny each week to the school and have disposed of small articles in the locality by which they have raised money for the purchase of wool for the school.

Brandon Miners' Lodge paid out ten shillings to each member away on active service. At the same meeting which approved the resolution it was also resolved to send a letter of complaint to the management of the colliery regarding the inferior quality of miners' household coal allowance.

While on his way to work Jim happened to meet the coal leader, to whom he said, 'By lad, that was a champion load of coal thoo fetched this mornin'!'

'Oh', replied the cartman, 'Aa's pleased to heor it'.

'Aye', continued Jim, 'Just efter thoo had tipped them at the door wor hoose tyuk fire, and dis thaa knaa, Aa wasn't a couple of jiffs in puttin' the fire oot wi' them!'

Kathleen Moran the third daughter of Patrick and Mary Moran of 14 Newcastle Street, married Joseph Walsh from Wakefield in Yorkshire. Laurie, Kathleen's younger brother, was best man.

Laurie was stirred when Durham Miners' Executive passed a resolution recording their unspeakable horror of the manner in which the peoples of the Belgian and Dutch coalfields have been hunted and butchered by savage murderers. The resolution proceeded, 'We have made an unflinching resolve that these crimes shall be avenged, and that those who have made these brutal assaults on the lives and liberty of peace loving peoples shall be utterly destroyed.

In the full knowledge that in the dark days ahead we will pay an incalcuable price in blood and sacrifice, we pledge ourselves that in invincible combination with the peoples dedicated to the cause of freedom we will fight until the days of bondage are ended and peace and liberty restored.

In this conflict there will be no neutrals. All must play their part, be it large or small, and we appreciate the desire of the Labour movement to play its part in this struggle'.

Mr. Will Lawther, president of the Mineworkers' Federation, said in an interview, 'Whatever may be the opinion of any individual in the Durham coalfield, be he a Member of Parliament or otherwise, there can be no mistake in the attitude of the Durham miners and their enthusiasm to do their bit'.

Two Brandon Colliery families received sad news of the deaths of a son on active service. Mr. James Monley of 56 Sunderland Street has been informed that his son Gunner John Monley (30) has been killed in action during the retreat to Dunkirk.

In next door Newcastle Street Mr. and Mrs. Joseph Reynolds were notified of the death of their son Gunner Frank Reynolds (28), killed in action in France. Both men were Reservists and were among the first to go to war.

Mr. and Mrs. Park Pratt, 12 Greyridge Estate, have been informed that their only son Pte. William Pratt (20), is missing.

Pte. Wilf Cummings from the same estate is a prisoner of war. He joined the Royal Scots three years ago and served one year in Palestine.

Pte. Irving Pigg reported missing three months ago, much to his parents' relief and joy, is listed as a prisoner of war.

Another prisoner of war, Pte. Jack Hunter of Newcastle Street, served in India for five years and was a Reservist for two years before being called up for action in France. All the above servicemen had worked at Brandon Colliery.

As the coal faces in Brandon 'C' Pit Whin Ballarat were worked out fillers and stonemen were transferred to Straker and Love's other nearby colliery, Pit House. Whin Ballarat coat was at one time twelve inches high. A wooden contraption nicknamed the 'Wooden Cutter' was placed in front of the coal cutter as it cut the face; if the 'Wooden Cutter' travelled in the low seam so would the five ton cutter. When the wooden article got wedged between the roof and the floor of the seam it was much easier to extricate than its iron counterpart.

Four faces were in operation in the Whin Ballarat, all were low. Fillers and lads had no fixed time to start their shift; they were called on as the cycle of work was completed. Stonemen, cutters and face advance men, were under the same handicap.

The Rev. Albert Wilson became the eighteenth minister to the Mount Calvary Methodist Church, he replaced the Rev. W. Harrison who had served for four years.

On December 31st firewatching became compulsory. Straker and Love employed Mr. Lynch (Paddy) to douse the glowing spoil heap situated near the Red Lion Inn (Blazer). The heap frequently burst into flames which were discernible from a distance. Paddy was one of the six men employed in three shifts of two to give a twenty-four hour surveillance of the heap. Firewatchers were also employed to guard colliery property; it was feared incendiary bombs would be dropped on the colliery during an air raid.

1941

What would 1941 bring? The second blacked out wartime Christmas and New Year passed quietly at home; a few hardy first footers braved the somewhat eerie streets, silent pit buzzers once raucously announced the New Year; places of worship were once again well attended.

'Safety in Mines' Laurie was busy at his work putting in the 'C' Pit Busty Seam when the newly appointed local pit inspectors visited his district.

A National Agreement between the Mining Association and the Miners' Federation of Great Britain resulted in the compulsory partial pit inspection. The cost of the scheme is shared equally between coal owners' and workmen. The pit inspectors in the 'C' Pit had been nominated from the Miners' Lodge. The men reported their findings to the management and Union. It is thought that much good will accrue from regular safety visitation.

Ninety-two year old Dr. James Denholm died. He was for many years Medical Officer for Browney and Brandon Collieries. His two sons, Doctors George and Will Denholm have served the needs of the Brandon area from the surgery at Hillside, Brandon Colliery.

The state of the burning pit heap at Brandon Colliery was discussed at the Urban District Council meeting. It was stated that the heap would take three months to extinguish; the first consideration was to stop the glow and eliminate the stench emanating from the fire and pervading the area.

Another well-known Brandonian died. Robert Cairns (Bob) was seventy four. Back shift overman for many years in the 'C' Pit, he started work underground at the age of twelve at Brandon Colliery where he worked for sixty years, retiring two years ago. Bob was formerly an active player of the Brandon Rovers' Football Club and an enthusiastic billiards player.

Brandon born William Hopkins had been a chorister of St. Agatha's Mission Church choir. After a prolonged illness, William died in Sherburn Hospital at the early age of forty-two.

Miners of Great Britain were asked to forego the Easter break. Brandon Colliery worked on Good Friday in compliance with the request. Gardeners were asked to plant and sow every available inch of garden. Food is being conserved; cheese being rationed to one ounce per person per week. A special ration of eight ounces is allocated to underground miners and agricultural workers.

News from the battlefield reached Brandon Colliery. Three more Brandon men are listed as prisoners of war in Germany; Rifleman Arthur Wilson, Pte. Harry Huntley, Royal Army Service Corps and Pte. George Felton. The latter, serving in the Middle East, was taken prisoner at a dressing camp in Crete. He was an enthusiastic first-aider and served with the Royal Army Medical Corps.

Cavilling time once again. Laurie worked six shifts every week and considered himself fortunate indeed in being spared the dangers and rigours of active service. Laurie was sure to land a dry working cavil because his seam was dry whereas most places in the Hutton Seam were wet.

Sammy had been cavilled to a wet flat, and at supper complained to the wife about pains. When the rude awakening of the alarm came next morning he said to his wife, 'Aa'll not bother ter gan this morning, lass'.

'Ay, man', said the wife, 'thoo'll be aal reet if tha had a good sweat'.

'Arl reet', said Sammy, 'shove another blanket on'.

There was a grand all talkie Cinema Show in Mount Calvary schoolroom. An interesting programme of sound film presented by the Ministry of Information was shown to a large audience. A collection was taken for comforts for the Sunday School young men who are serving with His Majesty's Forces.

Every week Mr. J. Green, manager of the colliery pipe works, presides at the meeting of the Men's Fireside Fellowship in St. Agatha's Mission Hall. Mr. Charles Paulin gave an instructive talk on 'Coal'. Piano accordian and mandolin music entertained. £9.3s.2d. was raised in aid of the Centralised Soldiers' Comforts Fund.

November saw the potato picking retarded owing to a shortage of labour. Children of twelve and over were excused school when elementary schools were closed to them for one week to enable them to assist in harvesting the crop.

A nineteen year old Brandon Colliery lad was fined ten shillings for not screening his hand torch while out in the black-out. He was among seven people fined for the same offence.

Pit activity on the surface. After hauling sets of tubs from all parts of the Busty Seam, the powerful machine based on the surface was dismantled. Hitherto ropes ingeniously run down the 'A' Pit shaft had done prodigious work for a number of decades. A new electric hauler was installed at the Busty shaft which required less steel haulage rope to operate.

At the same time a bore-hole was made from Weatherhill Farm at Littlewhite near Brancepeth down to the Busty Seam to accept an armoured electric cable which obviated the use of some two miles of similar cable stretched underground. Demand for electricity to serve coal-cutters and other machinery in the Whin and South Districts necessitated the change.

Miners waiting to descend the steps into the pit for the three a.m. shift gazed anxiously skywards; the air raid siren had sounded about an hour ago. They would be safe from enemy air attack once they were underground; what of their families at home? The raid was confined to a town on the coast. Cheers rang out when an aeroplane, caught in the defence's searchlights was seen to plummet earthwards, its flaming crucifix-shape visible to excited miners some fifteen miles away. Time to descend. As he walked inbye Laurie shuddered at the thought of the burning holocaust, a visible reminder of the horror of war.

A year filled with almost continuous gloomy war news had run its course. The New Year held hopeful prospects now that Russia and America have joined Great Britain in her struggle against Germany.

During the year, Laurie as a miner, had been granted War Additions to his wage. On January 1st a War Addition of sixpence a shift was announced, followed in July with one of fourpence a shift. In July an attendance bonus of one shilling a shift was paid on condition that all six shifts per week were worked. In September the attendance bonus conditions were dispensed with. On December 1st there was an increase of sixpence a shift for boys working underground—plus percentage.

At the same time 'points' rationing began in Britain. Certain types of tinned and dried foods went 'on points'. Each person received up to twenty points a month.

1942

Fifty-five year old Ralph Wilson survived only one day of the New Year. He died at his home, 28 Sunderland Street where he had lain since July after a fall of stone in the pit crippled both legs.

Brandon and area joined with Durham when a 'Warship Week' was promoted. The former's contribution apart from savings included two football matches on the Welfare Ground organised by Brandon Home Guard, also whist drives and dances. The target of £210,000 sufficient to pay for the hull of a destroyer, was passed with £12,000 in excess. £167,000 had been raised in four days.

Brandon Home Guard football team was kept busy. It was drawn against Ferryhill Home Guard in the first round of the Brandon Aged Miners' Cup.

Complaints from occupants of several houses in the colliery's West Street regarding the uninhabitable state of their houses was discussed at the Brandon Urban District Council meeting. Householders complained that water was dripping through the bedroom ceilings. The trouble was due to fine snow having drifted through the slates and settled in the ceilings. When the thaw came the water found its way through the ceilings of the eighty year old houses.

Sad war news for two Brandon Colliery families. Sgt. Pilot John Porter (22) son of Mr. and Mrs. John Porter of 47 Albert Street died in a plane crash in England. In his schooldays he was a keen player of the Brandon Council School rugby team.

Private John Pratt (19), missing since May 1940 is now presumed killed.

Three of the older generation passed away. Mr. Green died at the age of eighty-three, he was well known in Brandon and district. An outspoken councillor of many years standing, he also owned a drapery business in Brandon Colliery.

George Tones had lived seventy of his eighty years in Brandon Colliery. He died in College Terrace and was buried in St. Agatha's Mission Church.

Caleb Lee seventy-three years of age died at 21 Commercial Street.
The long-awaited Easter break brought an appeal from the Government to stay at home—that no roads or railways be used for pleasure. Walking, cycling, better still — dig for victory, was advocated.

There being no annual holiday, Laurie as a single adult person drew £1.10s. holiday pay. Married men and youths drew £2.12s. and £1.1s.8d. respectively.

Savings groups were active—streets vied with one another:—

Grey Ridge Estate's target, £50 for a Bren gun.

North Street's target, £50 for a Bren gun.

Sunderland Street's target, £140 for a Bren gun and a machine gun.

Princess Street's target, £90 for a machine gun.

Russell Street's target, £90 for a machine gun.

Brandon Council School, £750 for a twelve pound gun and three machine guns.

Three more Brandon men, Pte. Frank Laurence Shevels, D.L.I. of 6 College Terrace; Gunner Samuel George Lockey of Railway Street and twenty year old Sapper Ralph Guyll, Royal Engineers, are missing, presumed killed, the latter being lost at sea.

Corporal Albert Duffy, Royal Artillery and Pte. Alfred Myers are reported missing somewhere in the Middle East. Also missing is twenty-seven year old Pte. James Durkin, D.L.I.; his home is in North Street. Word reached 17 Newcastle Street that Jack Hunter is a prisoner of war in Germany.

Glorious weather favoured the 'Stay at Home' holiday field day. A fancy dress parade and abundant sports in the Welfare Ground made it a memorable occasion.

The seventy year old wife of Coun. Tom Carr died at their home Hillcrest View, she had lived in Brandon for forty-six years. Representatives from Brandon Miners' Lodge of which Coun. Carr is secretary were Coun. Tom Dickinson, David Hopkins, Jack Peart, Tot Underwood, Tommy Lawson, Harry Blenkinsop, Eddie Duffy, William Dowdle, Michael Parkin, Sam Bussey and Jack Stronach.

Brandon Home Guard played Bearpark Home Guard at football. Brandon are lying eighth in the ten team league, Bearpark hold the sixth position. Stanley United trounced Brandon Home Guard six goals to one; Brandon suffered another defeat at the hands of Langley Moor Athletic when Langley's two goal win knocked them out of the Durham Hospital Cup competition. The Welfare Ground was the popular venue on each occasion.

Four months of anxious waiting ended when the parents of Pte. Alfred Myers received notification that Alfred is a prisoner of war in Italy.

Thankfully owing to miners being exempt from war service, reports of war fatalities are less frequent than during the last war when scores of Brandon Colliery men joined the Colours.

After the recent Allied victories in Africa, and the fear of an invasion of Britain had passed, Winston Churchill announced that church bells could be rung. The glorious sound of Durham Cathedral and Brancepeth Church bells could be heard pealing forth the glad tidings.

Another Brandon man joined the band of war heroes. Twenty-two year old Captain Greenfield, Royal Field Artillery, has been awarded the Military Cross. His proud parents are the Rev. George and Mrs. Greenfield of the Vicarage, Sawmills Lane.

Mr. J. D. Murray the new Labour M.P. for Spennymoor and a resident of nearby Meadowfield, asked two questions of the Minister of Transport, one of which is, 'Whether on the London North Eastern Railway (Bishop Auckland Branch Line) arrangements can be made, in view of the recent curtailments in the omnibus services, whereby the 11.17 p.m. Durham to Bishop Auckland train could stop at Brandon Colliery station en route, every night, in addition to Saturdays as at present.' People in the Brandon area are greatly inconvenienced having to walk some three miles if the earlier finishing buses are missed.

Prisoners of war were not forgotten when a successful concert organised by the Brandon Colliery Division of the St. John Ambulance and Nursing Association was held in St. Patrick's Hall, Langley Moor. A miscellaneous programme of singing, dancing, conjuring, ventriloquial entertainment and piano accordian items pleased the large audience. The proceeds were in aid of the St. John and Red Cross Prisoners of War Fund.

Collectors were busy during the year when £117.12s.5½d. was collected for the Brandon and District Centralised Comforts Fund. Many letters expressing deep gratitude have been received by the committee.

During the year a National Minimum wage was granted to miners; all underground workers' minimum wages being set at £4.3s. and surface workers £3.18s. a week. The Greene Award meant an increase of 2s.6d. per shift to all persons over 21, also an addition to wages of all underground workers between the ages of 18 and 21. A graduated addition to wages to under 18s underground and to surface workers.

'Wet work' 6d. per shift extra was granted to persons over 18 years of age and 3d. to persons under 18 years. Wet workers were allowed priority over other workers ascending in the cage at the shift's end. When piece workers stayed overtime to complete the cycle of work on the face they were paid 10d. per hour basic rate.

Agreement as a condition of employment—all manual workers should be members of their appropriate union.

There was a change in colliery managership. On Mr. Walter Armstrong leaving Brandon Colliery after sixteen years in residence his place was taken by Mr. Peter Welsh from Monkwearmouth Colliery.

Mr. F. Humble settled in as new minister to Mount Calvary Church.

Brandon's Workmen's Club built just five years ago, was paid off. Its capable secretary signed a cheque to clear the Bank.

1943

Good New Year news for local late travellers; Mr. Murray, Labour M.P. has been granted the two concessions he asked for in the House of Commons. Late trains from Durham now stop at Brandon Colliery Station en route to Bishop Auckland.

Laurie now into his fourth year at hand putting, worked six shifts every week. He had just been cavilled to the midnight shift. Every day was a challenge to his slight frame; Laurie avowed sheer spirit saw him through.

The weary putter was finding the going rough. Every obstacle assumed gargantuan proportion. Laurie knew that the four coal hewers whom he had to supply with tubs would be stowed off; every minute he spent resetting plates and lifting on the way the numerous derailed tubs, meant more coal hewed and waiting to be put. Laurie hurried along, his sweat-soaked back and the tub top barely missing the low roof; his cap lamp's glare rebounding from the floor of the seam. Would he ever clear the men's places of coal? Their livelihood depended on him.

A sickening thud! The tub of coal was off the way 'all four wheels'; all progress being effectively halted, the tub appeared an impassable barrier. Laurie sized up the situation; no help was forthcoming, first he must get to the other side of the stranded tub. He divested himself of hat, lamp and belt holding his battery, and proceeded to remove the obstructing stone pack, an arduously slow job. He squeezed his perspiring body past the tub, his horizontal frame flinching as the stone's coldness. 'Oh God!' he hissed through clenched teeth as a jagged piece of stone clawed his back, knocking off a scab just on the mend from a previous encounter with the roof. Pain and frustration forced a 'Fill the bloody pit in and give the farmer his bloody field back!' through parched lips. He managed to ease the heavy tub a few inches, meanwhile kicking small stones under the wheels to retain the height thus gained. Laurie crawled gingerly back to the other end of the tub to treat it in similar manner. Loose plates being laid under the tub wheels the tub was pulled onto secure way. He swore profusely on rubbing his sore lumbar region.

As he fastened the two ends of a broken bootlace together, a voice shouted 'What's the matter—do you want a hand?' the coal hewer continued. 'Yer too bloody late mister!' shouted Laurie as he trundled his painful way to the flat.

There was a large audience for the presentation in Brandon Workmen's Club to Mr. Walter Armstrong on his leaving Brandon Colliery to take up a more important post under the same firm at Willington.

Coun. Tom Carr said that when Mr. Armstrong first came to Brandon Colliery the state of the colliery was desolate, having been closed down from 1924 to 1928. He gradually got a few men to work and in a short time the colliery was very active, and at the present time is one of the most prosperous collieries in the county.

A crowded room in the Social Club appreciated a film 'Modern Life of the Russian Peasant' depicting the production and distribution of coal for essential war purposes. Mr. R. Atkinson, a representative of the Ministry of Information, showed the film.

Mr. Atkinson advocated a two shift working Saturday to help step up production. Mr. Welsh the newly installed colliery manager spoke. Mr. T. Robertshaw, Langley Park, addressed the gathering; he deputised for Mr. William Lawther. At the close a vote of thanks was moved by Mr. Charles Paulin, supported by Mr. Alf Firth.

On Brandon joining the 'Scrap Week' Drive a local man commented, 'Take down all the useless light poles and accidents will be averted in the black-out. Work will be provided when they will need replacing after the war'.

Sgt. Pilot George Firth, eldest son of Mr. and Mrs. Alf Firth of High Street, Brandon Colliery, serving with the R.A.F. in Africa, obtained his 'wings' as he celebrated his twenty-first birthday.

Another Brandon youth, Keith Gould, serving as a Second Lieutenant in the Royal Indian Army Service Corps, has qualfied at the Officers' Training School at Baradore, India. Mr. W. A. Gould of Church Street was notified of his twenty year old son's success.

Airman Frederic Grice, only son of Mr. and Mrs. Charles Grice, 10 Princess Street, has gained his commission in East Africa. Brandon man Guardsman Joseph Ord serving with the Grenadier Guards in the Middle East, has been wounded and is in hospital. He joined the army three years ago and has been in Africa for five months. Joe is an enthusiastic student of pen etching and painting.

Pit deputies, shot-firers and chargemen's basic wages were increased from 5s.9d. per shift to 6s.9d. per shift.

Miners Geordie and Bill were at Newcastle and happened to meet two of the opposite sex. After a jolly afternoon the ladies expressed their desire for a little refreshment, so they all went into the nearest cafe.

Geordie handed one of the girls the menu, asking what they would like. After scanning it for a few minutes, she replied, 'Well, what about some chicken, jellies and a bottle of champagne?'

Bill looked at Geordie and remarked, 'Howay, Geordie, let's gan. They think we are deputies'.

Due to the war the Durham Miners' Gala was cancelled for the fourth year running. The miners' holidays coincided with the date usually reserved for the Gala. Laurie with single miners received £1.16s.5d. holday pay while married men drew £3.2s.5d.

Laurie appreciated the colliery canteen's facilities. Ever hungry, his arduous underground work called for constant interior replenishment. The canteen and British Restaurant helped eke out the official food ration due to each person in the household.

Coun. Carr opened a British Restaurant in Commercial Street. The project started by the Urban District Council was constructed in three months at a cost of £600; £755 was the original figure quoted to convert the old club building into a restaurant. Brandon folk were delighted.

The sight of foreign fruit is a rarity. Attracted by the window gazing crowd, Laurie craned his neck for a better view. A banana reposed in glorious isolation in the centre of the window space. It was not for sale; the precious fruit was earmarked for a sick child.

A Brandon mother was sent some bananas by her Royal Air Force son; they raised £5 when raffled for the Red Cross War Fund.

Sgt. Raymond Wilkinson, Royal Army Medical Corps, son of Brandon's Health Inspector, brought back some Algiers fruit comprising one lemon, two bananas, one orange and a grapefruit, which on being raffled raised £4 for the Red Cross.

A Brandon Colliery man, Able Seaman Patrick McAloon, wrote home to 19 Railway Street to say that he met Mr. J. D. Murray the local M.P. Mr. Murray wished Pat the best of luck and good hunting when he visited the British destroyer in which he served.

A 'Back to Brandon Night' was organised at Aberdare, New South Wales, Australia. A meeting of exiled Brandon Colliery folk took place at Weston, on the Maitland Coalfields.

Mr. R. Foster, Greta Street, Aberdare, N.S.W., Australia, reported that, 'A very pleasant evening was spent by people formerly of Brandon Colliery. There were about sixty people present. The gathering included Mrs. Parkinson, Mr. and Mrs. R. Curnow, Mr. and Mrs. Brown, Mr. and Mrs. W. Douglas, Mr. and Mrs. Wilf Brown, Mr. and Mrs. Elam Parkinson, Mr. Andrew Swan, Mr. and Mrs. Tot Foster, Mr. and Mrs. E. Rumley, Mr. and Mrs. Bob Foster, Mr. and Mrs. T. Brunskill, Mr. I. Hadfield, Mr. and Mrs. B. Clogg, Mr. Hadfield, Mr. W. Greig, Mr. Robinson, Mr. and Mrs. T. Robinson, Mr. and Mrs. Wilson, Mr. Jack Plant, Mr. and Mrs. Bob Jones, Mr. Charlie Jones, Mr. and Mrs. McFall, Mr. and Mrs. Green, Mrs. Barrass, Mr. and Mrs. Ike Hewitt, Mrs. Elmore, Mr. and Mrs. J. Elmore, Mr. and Mrs. Ellis Reed, Mr. and Mrs. Butler and Mr. Joe Stimson.

Mr. Ike Hewitt was chairman and gave a welcome to all. They drank the toast "Brandon". The evening was opened by the grand march led off by the two eldest present from Brandon, Mrs. Parkinson (87 years) and Mr. Andrew Swan (76 years).

Everyone voted it the best evening ever, and it was decided to hold "Back to Brandon" on the last Saturday in July of future years as that is always the date of the Durham Miners' big meeting on the Racecourse, Durham City'.

A number of Brandon men have been reported held in a Prisoner of War Camp. Held in Italy, Pte. Richard Connelly, Royal Signal Corps in Africa. He is the son of Mr. and Mrs. Tom Connolly, 31 Greyridge Estate.

Mr. and Mrs. William Bennetts, 14 Railway Street, have been informed that their eldest son James Robinson Bennetts (32) is a P.O.W. in Japanese hands.

Two Brandon men, previously unacquainted, met in Stalag IIID Camp in Germany. Pte. Harry Huntley, Royal Army Service Corps and Pte. George Felton, Royal Army Medical Corps. Both were captured at the fall of Crete in June 1941.

Posted missing since November 1942, Pte. Andrew McKay, Leicester Regiment, to his parents' joy, is reported now P.O.W. in Japanese hands.

Sgt. Pilot Henry (Harry) Halkier, son of Mr. and Mrs. Robert Halkier, 4 Church Street is reported missing in action.

Another prisoner of the Japanese is Pte. Thomas L. Rounding (25), Northumberland Fusiliers. He is the son of Mr. and Mrs. William Rounding of 27 Princess Street.

Colliery folk were saddened when the news of the death of Pte. Ernest Gibbs was released. Ernie served in the Pioneer Corps which he joined at the outbreak of war and went through the evacuation of Dunkirk. His parents Mr. and Mrs. Samuel Gibbs, 33 Queen Street, mourn Ernie who died serving the First Army in North Africa.

Missing some two months, Pte. James Durkin is now presumed killed in action.

Captain Peter Greenfield mentioned in despatches for the second time, is the son of the Rev. G. H. and Mrs. Greenfield, Brandon Vicarage. In the last phase of the Battle of Tunisia Peter was responsible for getting ammunition to his battery under heavy enemy fire, and thus enabled the fire of his guns to be maintained on enemy positions.

Apart from the British Army's success on the African Front, good news comes from Sicily where British forces advance. Heartening news from the Russian Front and Allied victories in South-West Pacific combined with the R.A.F.'s ability to bomb at will the heart of Germany, prompted Winston Churchill's speech. The Prime Minister said, 'Now those who sowed the wind are reaping the whirlwind. There is no halting place at this point. We have now reached a point in the journey where there can be no pause. We must go on!'

Mining, being of major importance to the war effort, was added to the list of priority industries in preference to military service. Ernest Bevin introduced Bevin Boys into the pits; young men were encouraged to work in them. Some lads settled into the new life, others rebelled. Laurie heard of a Bevan Boy who on being drafted into the mine, wrote to his father, a Vicar, and declared that 'the best pit is a pulpit'.

Manager of the Colliery Inn, Brandon Colliery for thirty years, Mrs. Beatrice Burrell (79) died at the home of her son-in-law and daughter Mr. and Mrs. John S. Blackett. Mrs. Burrell popularly known as Beattie, was a well known local woman. Her public house was almost taken over as headquarters for the committee running the Comforts Fund for Brandon men serving in the Great War.

1944

Brandon Colliery folk settled down into their fifth year of war. News from the war front is encouraging; the Allies are victorious in many areas across the world.

Miners were granted a Porter Award in January. The National Union of Mineworkers' Minimum Wage increase of 17s. for underground workers and 12s. for surface men, making the new Minimum Wage per week of £5 and £4.10s. respectively.

At home, teachers and scholars attending the Market Square Methodist Sunday School held a New Year Party in St. Agatha's Mission Hall. More than fifty were entertained to tea and games. Each child was presented with a sixpence.

Councillor Carr died at the age of seventy at his home Hillcrest View, Brandon Colliery. He had been in the Brandon district for forty-seven years. He began a public career as delegate of Brandon Miners' Lodge and held the chairmanship for twenty years, afterwards succeeding the late Samuel White-ley as secretary and checkweighman twenty-five years ago. He was a former chairman of Brandon Workmen's Social Club, and performed the opening ceremony of the first club in Brandon.

In his younger days Mr. Carr, better known as Tom Carr, was a keen fives player, and took an interest in sword dancing, of which he was an instructor.

In 1930 he opened the new road for which he had fought for eighteen years. He was revered in Brandon and the road bears his name, Carr Avenue.

Crowds attended the funeral service. Members of the Miners' Lodge were preceded by the banner and the colliery band under the conductorship of Mr. James Oliver, Lowes Barn. Laurie Moran as a member of the Lodge committee .was privileged, along with other Lodge officials, to represent the workmen.

News was received in Brandon of the death of the Rev. F. E. Tallents who served Brandon so well from 1929 to 1934.

Good news and bad. Brandon Welcome Home Committee made presentations to Misses May Davis, L. Futers, V. Ward and Ethel Bowes, members of the Women's Auxiliary Corps.

Twenty-four year old Private Alfred Myers has been transferred to Germany as a P.O.W. He was posted as missing from 27th June 1942 while serving with the Middle East Forces, and eight weeks later his parents were informed that he was a prisoner of war in Italy. Since his arrival in Germany, Alfred broadcast a Christmas greeting to his mother and father at Brandon Colliery.

Thirty-seven year old Norman Tunney, Royal Navy, was lost at sea in the service of his country.

David Hopkins of Russell Street, Brandon Colliery, was unanimously elected a member of the Brandon Urban Council to represent the Centre Ward in succession to the late Thomas Carr.

Holidays with pay—all restrictions were lifted. If a man was on the Colliery books on the pay day preceding the holiday he would receive the agreed payment of £5.5s. for adult workers, £4.4s. for those between 18 and 21 and workers under 18 to get £3.3s. for the week's holiday.

After a series of heavy blows to the enemy, the nation was cheered on hearing the Prime Minister's speech,

'Britain . . . has never flinched or failed. And when the signal is given, the whole circle of avenging nations will hurl themselves upon the foe and batter out the life of the cruellest tyranny which has ever sought to bar the progress of mankind'.

The Rev. Stephen Franklin Park left his ministry in London on a poignant visit to the North. Stephen, a one-time Brandon Colliery worker, returned to his birthplace to officiate at the funeral of his sixty-seven year old mother Mrs. Mary Park who had spent the greater part of her life in Brandon. Her husband is coal hewer Bob Park.

Another resident of Newcastle Street was added to the list of pit fatalities when William Bromley, a fifty-nine year old underground mason, suffered spinal injuries whilst at work in Brandon's 'C' Pit.

More war grief! The Air Ministry notified Mr. and Mrs. Tom Ridley that their youngest son Sergeant George Ridley (Smiler) air gunner and wireless operator, posted missing three months ago has been killed. The Lancaster bomber was flying over Berlin when it was brought down. 'Smiler' was among those lost; he had accomplished twenty-four operations over enemy territory, nine of them with the Pathfinders.

The target of £250,000 fixed for the 'Salute the Soldier' week in Durham District was easily surpassed. Brandon, Langley Moor and Meadowfield savings groups beat their £21,000 share of the target comfortably to buy seven armoured cars.

Mr. Edward Welsh (84) had lived in Brandon for more than sixty-five years, he was for many years an underground official at Messrs. Straker and Love, Brandon Colliery. He died at the residence of his son-in-law and daughter, Mr. and Mrs. Norman Suddes.

John Thomas Thompson had lived his sixty-five years in Brandon Colliery. He died at his home in North Street after a prolonged illness. Formerly employed as a miner, he was for a considerable number of years a mines inspector. In his younger days he was a well-known local footballer. He was a member of Brandon Colliery Literary Institute Committee.

Tuesday 6th June, 1944! Topic at home, mine and factory. 'The invasion is on'. Wireless sets are eagerly tuned in for up to date news. Prayers for an Allied victory said at hastily arranged services. The pits worked as usual. All day the talk concerned the invasion of Europe.

One of Brandon Colliery's first reported invasion war casualties was Sgt. Alfred Ditchburn, D.L.I., wounded while with the North-West European Forces in Normandy. He joined the army at the outbreak of war. His brother, Sgt. Major Robert Ditchburn, D.L.I., was killed at the evacuation of Dunkirk.

Sergeant Walter Duffy, 32 Newcastle Street, who is in the Maritime Royal Artillery, the branch of the army which mans the A.A. guns of merchant ships, has sailed the seven seas with our convoys, but it was his first ocean voyage that proved his undoing. On the return crossing from Canada his convoy was picked up by a pack of submarines, and the days and nights were filled with alarms.

Sgt. Duffy's ship was torpedoed within sight of the coast of Greenland, and they could see the U-boat in the moonlight only four hundred yards away. The ship went down in seven minutes, and Sgt. Duffy was in the icy cold water for two hours before being picked up by a Norwegian timber boat. He is the son of Mr. and Mrs. Edward Duffy. Mr. Duffy is a coal hewer at the colliery.

After more that four years of hand putting, Laurie Moran took his turn at coal hewing. It is generally accepted that putting is the hardest job in the mine, and Laurie, pleased with the change, teamed up with coal hewing brothers Jackie and Freddie Miller; they worked the fore shift, back shift and night shift in the 'C' Pit's Busty Seam.

Laurie hewed away at the sold wall of glistening coal; he had acquired a rhythm to his swinging of the pick, it made for easier hewing, his body now comfortable after having his first good sweat. Dislodged coal fell onto the floor of the seam, the mound slowly rising. Laurie removed a token from his bunch; the numbered metal disc being fastened inside the tub, which he began filling, using a large round mouthed shovel.

Tommy, the young putter, came into Laurie's hewing place to exchange the full tub of coal for an empty one.

'How's things, Laurie?' he asked.

'Very fair, Tommy', replied Laurie.

After filling his fourth tub of coal Laurie reckoned it to be about bait time. On seeing that his place was safely timbered, Laurie squatted near his folded clothes and enjoyed his two slices of bread and jam; he took a liberal drink of water and returned to hewing. He did not want to cool off by sitting around.

When Tommy put the eighth tub into the hewing place Laurie said, 'That's my last one, Tommy'.

On his way out to the shaft at his shift's end Laurie met Billy his back shift marra and said, 'I've filled eight, Billy'. Freddie the night shift marra would follow Billy on.

Eight tired men crouched in the ascending cage. They had walked down the five hundred and thirty seven steps from the surface to the Busty Seam; they were allowed the use of the cage at the end of the shift.

A hot meal awaited Laurie — potatoes, dumplings and what goes to revitalise a tired body. Laurie soon stripped to the waist, knelt over the oval tin bath set before the kitchen fire. After washing his upper body, still in his short hoggers, he washed his legs and thighs.

Laurie retired to the welcome bed he had left some eleven hours before; four or five hours sleep would make a new man of him.

Laurie reckoned that he had earned twenty-four shillings for the three and a half tons of coal hewed and sent to the surface — just a few shillings more that the minimum wage.

Four more wartime weddings. Thomas Clough married Doreen Pattinson fron Broompark; Miss D. Jones, Brandon, wed Sgt. J. T. Powell, Leicester; Robert Richardson married Miss D. Rothwell from Ushaw Moor and Richard Pearson married Miss Audrey Hanson, Bearpark.

Mrs. J. Oliver, landlady of the Red Lion Inn, Brandon, received tragic news from the Admiralty stating that her eldest son, Stoker Robert Nutter Oliver, Royal Navy (20) has been killed by enemy action at sea. He enlisted with the Royal Navy in June 1943.

Mrs. Eliza Davis (39) of 18 Railway Street, Brandon Colliery, a warworker machinist, has been presented with a brochure for front line duty, and in recognition of her valuable services by the works superintendent with her photograph inserted showing her at work, with the following inscription, 'Mrs. Davis is a fine example of a woman who is putting up a splendid fight against great odds.

Eight years ago her husband was injured in a pit accident. Overnight, the bread winner became a dependant invalid, and Mrs. Davis was left with a burden which would daunt the stoutest heart.

There are eight children—the eldest a girl of 19, and the youngest a boy of seven, five are still at school and utterly dependant on their mother for all needs of childhood. In December, 1941, Mrs. Davis started work at the factory, and the job of filling shells was quietly added to her other jobs. Nothing is used by Mrs. Davis as an excuse for absence from duty. On one occasion she was sent home suffering from shock after a "blow". The very next day she was back at her machine as if nothing had happened.

If this operative is worried and anxious about her husband and children—as she must often be—she does not show it. Her work here is done conscientiously and efficiently, and it is to her great credit that, in almost two years, she has missed only two shifts'.

Football returned to Brandon when Brandon Welfare played Waterhouses Home Guard in their first game of football in the Durham and District League. Fifteen teams make up the league.

Good news for two Brandon families. Laurie Moran lived at 14 Newcastle Street. His near neighbour Billy Allchurch left 16 Newcastle Street in November 1939, he joined the Royal Army Medical Corps as a Private. Pte. Allchurch was reported missing at Arnhem. Word reached his mother that he is now a prisoner of war.

Another Arnhem hero, Paratrooper Jack Etherington, Station Avenue, son of Mr. and Mrs. George Etherington, is a captive in a German internment camp. Jack was a member of the heroic Airborne Division who put up such a daring resistance at Arnhem.

Sadly James Carter died at the age of 46. James had been an invalid at 40 Princess Street since he sustained a fractured spine in the pit explosion in which his workmate John Rutter was killed in 1930. James was sometimes seen in the street being pushed along in a low basket affair; he was condemned to lie in a prone position due to his injuries. He joins the long list of pitmen killed or who died from injuries incurred during the working of Brandon's A, B and C Pits.

There now being no fear of invasion of Britain by German Forces—the Home Guard was 'stood down'. Laurie and Steve of the 25th Platoon 'F' Company of the 11th Battalion Durham Home Guard, mercifully never having been tested, handed in their equipment.

Brandon Miners' Lodge paid ten shillings to each member serving with the Forces. At the same time the annual election of officers took place. Laurie Moran, Joe Pybus and Jim Byrne were elected to serve the 'C' Pit as committee men.

The year ended with good war news. The Allies recaptured several towns which fell during the major counter-offensive on the Ardennes.

1945

The Allied armies are victorious on all Fronts. The home Front is working and praying for an early end to a lengthy and calamitous war.

Three Brandon stalwarts figure in the New Year deaths list: Jonathan Simpson died at the age of 82; born in 1863 he had lived in Brandon for over seventy years. He was employed as a miner at Brandon Colliery, formerly a keen quiots player he was also librarian for Meadowfield Social Club for twenty years.

John Brown celebrated his 90th birthday on Christmas Day. He retired from colliery work as a joiner and shaftman twenty-seven years ago. He died at 38 Russell Street. In his youth he was a keen pole jumper, footballer and cricketer.

Mr. Tom Brain is the third veteran to die in the first week of the New Year. At the age of 82 he had seen a full life; a pioneer of the Independent Methodists in Brandon Colliery, he was the last of the seven who founded the I.M. Church forty years ago. He was injured in the pit accident in 1922 in which young Pompey Clennell was killed.

The second week of January brought sorrow to two more Brandon Colliery families. George Tunney died suddenly at the age of 53. He left school at thirteen to work at the colliery where he toiled for forty years. Official word was received from the War Office that Charles Thomas had been killed in action in Italy. Before joining the army as a private he was a miner at the colliery.

Flight Sergeant George Gill, R.A.F. Wireless Ooperator Air-gunner joined Brandon's Roll of Honour; he is presumed lost 16th/17th April, 1943.

Four of the six sons of Mr. and Mrs. Joe Winter of.61 Sunderland Street are in the forces. Joseph the eldest is in the Army, George is in the R.E.M.E., William is a Signalman and Charles is a Royal Navy Wireless Operator.

Brandon Social Club organised a whist drive in aid of Brandon Colliery Welcome Home Fund. The club secretary John Higgins and Mrs. Lidster arranged the highly successful event. Supplies of drink in the club are still severely restricted; Johnny Walker whiskey at twenty-five shillings a bottle is scarce. A singing contest under the direction of the secretary took place in Brandon Social Club. Mr. T. Nixon of South Moor won the first heat being the best of six contestants.

Laurie Moran spent a long, cold day on Pit House Colliery heapstead. He had been elected with others, at the Miners' Lodge meeting, to assist in the taking of a ballot for the first National Union of Mineworkers' President. Laurie handed each workman a ballot paper before he descended for his shift. The result of the ballot declared Mr. Will Lawther president.

The Premier Mr. Winston Churchill broadcast an announcement at 3 p.m. on Tuesday, May 8th. Almost every radio set in the land was switched on; streets denuded of people evidence of the importance of the occasion. Eager listeners heard him say that at 2.41 a.m. the Germans had signed an Act of Unconditional Surrender of all their forces in Europe to the Allied Expeditionary Forces.

On the same day His Majesty the King broadcast to a rejoicing nation, 'We kept faith with ourselves and with one another; we kept faith and unity with our great Allies. That faith, that unity, have carried us to victory through dangers which at times seemed overwhelming'.

Rejoicing, too, for the families of Brandon Colliery men Private Jack Hunter, D.L.I. and Private Irvine Pigg, D.L.I., who have returned after five years of captivity in Germany. Private Alfred Myers, D.L.I., returned home to 19.Cobden Terrace after three years in a P.O.W. camp.

News reached his parents of the death in action of Nicholas Tweddle with the North West Forces on 8th July, 1944.

Thomas Rounding, Brandon Colliery, died in Japanese hands on 26th July, 1943.

Private James Little (23) Royal Scots Regiment, died of wounds in S.B. Emergency Hospital on 13th September, 1944. He was given a military funeral.

Private William Ramsey left his home, 4 College Terrace at the beginning of the war. He was killed in action on June 17th, 1940. His family mourn the anniversary of his death. William Ramsey Sr. was among the first of Brandon Colliery's miners to join up as a Private in the 1914-18 war; he survived four years of trench warfare;

World peace was announced on Tuesday midnight, August 14th on the occasion of the Japanese surrender to the Allied Forces. Nine days later it was Victory Day in Brandon area — all available halls were filled with old folk and school children invited to celebrate with tea and sports.

Private J. W. Coulthard, D.L.I. settled down to twenty-eight days well earned home leave. He had returned to Brandon Colliery after an absence of five years. He came through the trauma of Dunkirk. In 1940 he was sent to the Middle East where he served until his return to England. He was a miner at Brandon Colliery before he enlisted.

There being insufficient time to revive the Durham Miners' Gala, none was held for the sixth consecutive year.

Disappointment at not having their treasured 'Big Meeting' was soothed for Durham's miners when the Labour Party was triumphant in all sixteen Divisions in the county. A Labour government was elected with a clear majority over all other parties.

In the early days of the century the newly-formed Labour Party sent its first members from Durham to Parliament.

J. D. Murray who serves Brandon Colliery in his Spennymoor Division came out of his first election with flying colours. In his election campaign in the area he expressed his opinion that mines should be under state control. Laurie's near neighbour took over as M.P. from Mr. Joseph Batey on his resignation in July 1942.

In September Brandon Parish Church youth held their excursion, formerly an annual one, for the first time since the war started. Some two hundred expectant parents, teachers and scholars went by coach to Seaburn.

Two Brandon Colliery men are now safe having been held captives of the Japanese. Pte. Cecil Cumusky of Princess Street has served overseas for eight and a half years having joined the army at the age of eighteen. He was taken prisoner on the fall of Hong Kong. Cecil, an ex-miner arrived safely in Australia from a P.O.W. camp.

Mr. and Mrs. William Bennetts of 14 Railway Street received the glad news of their son's release from the Japanese. ACI James R. Bennetts has been in a P.O.W. camp for three and a half years.

After three years of active service Corporal James Chance returned to his home in Brandon Colliery. An ardent worker and member of the Independent Methodist Church, his colleagues organised a pie and peas supper held in St. Agatha's Hall in his honour.

ROLL OF HONOUR
IN MEMORY OF
THE MEMBERS OF THIS CLUB
WHO GAVE THEIR LIVES
IN THE WORLD WAR
1939 — 1945

Pilot Officer Walter Tonge
P. Sergeant Major Robert W. Ditchburn
Flight Sergeant George Gill
Aircraftsman Charles McGarry
Able Seaman Norman Tunney
Guardsman Albert Stokoe
Private Ernest Gibbs
Private James Little
Private Samuel Lockey
Private Edward Stewart
Private Nicholas Tweddle

"WE SHALL REMEMBER THEM"

From the plaque in Brandon Social Club

ROLL OF HONOUR
BRANDON SERVICEMEN
SECOND WORLD WAR, 1939 — 1945

1940
Gunner Frank Reynolds (28)
Gunner James Monley (30)
Private William Ramsey
Private William John Pratt (19), D.L.I.
Sergeant-Major Robert Ditchburn, D.L.I.

1942
Sergeant-Pilot John Porter (22), Royal Air Force
Private Laurence Shevels, D.L.I.
Gunner Samuel George Lockey
Sapper Ralph Guyll (20), Royal Engineers
Private James Durkin (27), D.L.I.

1943
Sergeant-Pilot Henry (Harry) Halkier, Royal Air Force
Private Ernest Gibbs, Pioneer Corps
Private Thomas Rounding
Aircraftsman Charles McGarry

1944
Norman Tunney (37), Royal Navy
Stoker Robert Nutter Oliver (20), Royal Navy
Private James Little (23), Royal Scots Regiment
Private Nicholas Tweddle

1945
Private Charles Thomas
Flight-Sergeant George Gill, Royal Air Force

REST IN PEACE

All the males in the Moran family, six in number, being employed, Mary Moran now fifty-nine arouses her family at different times during the working week; the only daughter at home also works.

Frank Moran is now eighteen, after working one year at Nevilles Cross Co-operative Laundry where he began work at the age of fourteen years and a half as a van boy with a wage of 17s.10d. for a forty-four hour week, joined the London North Eastern Railway Company as a number taker of mineral freight traffic operating in the Brandon area.

At sixteen Frank's wage as a number taker at Brandon was £1.5d. per week of forty-four hours; his work centred round Brandon Colliery and Station where Ivy Kelly, Eileen Wilby and Marion Round were clerks and George Curry and George Fawcett the porters.

On reaching the age of seventeen and a half, Frank joined the Loco-motive Department as a cleaner in the loco sheds at Durham; he was allotted another task, that of knocking up train crews around Durham City for early morning turns of duty.

After six months, at the age of eighteen, Frank was promoted to fire-man on local passenger trains. He was thrilled to raise steam on such notable engines as the 'Flying Scotsman' and 'The Streak' of the world famous Mallard class − no mean feat in the blackout imposed by the war.

Eddie Moran now twenty-two, after working three years on the pithead screens, keen to earn a bigger wage, elected to team up with the coal-cutters in Meadowfield 'C' Pit; a hazardous and unhealthy job for which he was paid the new minimum underground wage of £4.3s. per week.

Teresa their sister now twenty, had been directed to Ammunitions at the age of seventeen and a half.

John Moran worked in the 'C' Pit Busty as did Laurie another brother, who after four years of gruelling wartime putting, took up coal hewing.

All the men folk of the family are clients of Harry Pinkney nicknamed 'Slasher'−a facetious title for the Commercial Street based hairdresser. Jackson Hurst a Brandon youth was lather boy in the shop next door to the one-time Brandon Social Club premises. Harry, a well-known local character, was noted for his swift removal of head growth for twopence; Jackson often took charge as his employer visited the new club where his young clients' fathers paid for the haircut.

Mr. Thomas Lawson presided at the annual meeting of the Brandon Miners' Lodge. A final 'welcome' presentation was made when upwards of fifty members returned from the forces, each received a voucher valued at twenty-five shillings.

Miners were granted an extra day's holiday, the agreed holidays for Christmas 1945 being Christmas Day, Boxing Day and New Year's Day.

1946

The year 1946 was welcomed by the colliery buzzers and the customary 'first footing'. The colliery comprises the Ballarat, Busty, Hutton and the Brockwell Seams employing a workforce of 394 underground and 79 surface.

A large crowd thrilled at the New Year's Day match between Brandon and Ferryhill Athletic. Despite the home crowd's vociferous backing, Brandon could only take a point from the Northern League game. Brandon rallied and Pinkney quickly equalised after Ferryhill took the lead after seven minutes play. In another Northern League game Shildon scored a 5—3 victory, beating Brandon on their ground. Brandon took a thrashing of 4—0 from Shildon on their previous encounter.

Brandon Welfare Reserves lost heavily to Waterhouses Social Club in a Durham Central League game, score 6—2.

Seventy-seven years old Oliver Johnson died at 54 Park Street. He came to Brandon Colliery more than fifty years ago; he was associated with the former New Connexion Church (Market Square), and later with the Mount Calvary Methodist Church of which he was a trustee for fifty years.

Councillor George Jackson, Chairman of Brandon Urban Council in his message says, 'I believe that the year 1946 will see the accomplishment of many of the Council's desires in relation to planning, housing, industry and employment in the area. The full housing programme provides for: Centre, South and West Wards 2000 houses and 2,500 houses for the other four Wards'.

One new post-war building was ceremoniously opened. The spacious pit canteen was erected almost on the steps of the lamp cabin serving Brandon Colliery's 'C' Pit workers. The canteen will also cater for the needs of the 'C' Pit's sister colliery Pit House. Hitherto business had been conducted from the nearby Colliery Ambulance Room which had no facilities for cooking hot meals for workmen.

Mr. and Mrs. Dave White of 25 Princess Street, received word from the War Department that their son Laurie has been wounded and is detained in hospital at Singapore. Laurie enlisted with the Durham Light Infantry in 1944 and went to Burma in 1945.

Brandon Officials' Association arranged a social to welcome home four of its members from the Forces. Mr. J. P. Welsh, colliery manager, made the presentations of a wallet of Treasury notes to Robert Gibbon, weigh office clerk, who joined the Royal Navy as a signalman and served five years, mainly on North Atlantic convoys and was stationed in Iceland; Ralph Rutherford, masters' weighman, recently demobilised as corporal with the Royal Air Force, enlisted in August 1940, served thirteen months in Palestine and twelve months in Iraq; Lance Corporal John Felton, R.E.M.E.; Lance Corporal Harry Huntley, R.A.S.C., formerly colliery clerk, enlisted in March 1940, went to France, came through Dunkirk, went to the Middle East and was taken prisoner at Crete, and transferred to Germany for five years.

Well known in Brandon Colliery, sixty-eight years old Mrs. Eleanor Strong died at her home 3 Cobden Terrace, after a brief illness. Her husband Thomas Strong, three sons and a daughter, mourn her passing.

Mrs. Mary Moore, 83, died suddenly at 18 Queen Street. Born at Tow Law she came to Brandon Colliery from Sunnybrow at the age of seventeen. She was the widow of the late George Moore, who for a number of years was under-manager of Brandon A, B and C Pits. After the interment an auctioneer did brisk business disposing of No. 18's valuable household contents.

Three young Brandon Colliery men sought their brides from out of the area. John Farrell wed Miss Ellen Cole, Durham; John Joseph Worrall married Florence May Waltham of Sherburn; Wilfred Cummings, returned prisoner of war, Greyridge Estate, married Margaret Dickson.

A derailed mineral train attracted the curious. Six wagons ran off the line near Brandon Railway Station. Special buses were run between Durham and Bishop Auckland to carry would-be rail travellers. Crowds watched as heavy lifting gear was used to re-rail the wagons.

Anthony Howden, born in Brandon Colliery, left school at the age of twelve to start work at the colliery. Now at the age of seventy-three he has completed sixty-one years of work for Straker and Love where he is employed every day. He and his sixty-nine year old wife Ada have just celebrated their golden wedding.

More post-war weddings: Miss M. Grice of Princess Street married Mr. E. Connor of Gilesgate. Margaret is the third daughter of Mr. and Mrs. Charles Grice. Miss Mary Walton, 29 Newcastle Street married Reginald Reed of 43 Albert Street; Reg is in the Royal Navy. Ex-prisoner of war Alfred Myers married Miss O. Minns at St. Edmund's Church, Bearpark.

Good football returned to Brandon Welfare ground when Brandon Colliery Welfare entertained Bishop Auckland on Easter Monday. A large and enthusiastic crowd enjoyed the Northern League game from which Brandon emerged the winners four goals to one.

For many years a Brandon Colliery butcher, seventy-four year old Joseph Rowe died at 6 Commercial Street. He was the son of the late Mr. and Mrs. Jacob Rowe. During the 1939—45 conflict Mr. Rowe was employed as a butcher by Mr. Tommy Holmes of Brandon Colliery.

William Bowman of Willington married Brandon Colliery girl Jenny Garbutt at Brandon Parish Church. Henry James, Broompark, wed Miss Ruby Grayson of 19 Church Street, Brandon Colliery and John George Clarke, Brandon Colliery married Durham girl Miss E. Brennan.

The Mayor and Mayoress of Durham visited Brandon Colliery on the occasion of a garden party being held in Dr. Denholm's 'Hillside House'. The event was in connection with the restoration of bombed Methodist

Churches. The Mayor (Councillor J. L. Robson's) late mother was a former organist at the Market Square Church in Brandon Colliery. The successful fete raised £43.7s.8d. for the Bombed Methodist Churches Fund.

A well-known Brandon Colliery man, Tom Blenkinsop, had been awarded a medal for thirty years' unbroken service with the St. John Ambulance Association. Tom, born in Brandon Colliery, was one of the founders of the St. John Ambulance Brigade in the area. He possesses a long service medal for fifteen years' service, bar for twenty years, bar for twenty-five years, and a bar for thirty years.

Laurie Moran and Steve Murther joined the estimated crowd of 250,000 at the first post-war Durham Miners' Gala, the sixty-third, held on July 20th. Victory atmosphere prevailed. After an absence of six years bands, banners and followers invaded Durham to hear and cheer their Labour Leader, Prime Minister the Rt. Hon. Clem Attlee, M.P., Aneurin Bevan, Minister of Health, Hugh Dalton, Chancellor of the Exchequer, Ebby Edwards, Secretary of the National Union of Mineworkers. Despite the shortage of food, beer, cigarettes and tobacco on the day, representatives from Durham's two hundred and eighteen pits thronged the Racecourse.

A miner entered a public house in a village near the city carrying a brown paper bag. He called for a drink. His want was supplied. A second was handed to him. The customer left the bar after a few minutes.

Shortly afterwards men began to arrive, and soon the bar was crowded. The inn-keeper was kept busy pulling the pints until his supplies were exhausted. How did it happen?

The first customer had a carrier pigeon in the brown paper bag, and when he found apparently an abundant supply of drink he released the bird, with a note attached to its legs. The news was out!

Councillor Mrs. Sanford, a member of Camberwell Borough Council, speaking at a meeting of Brandon Co-operative Society Women's Guild, told of a visit to a six-roomed house in Double Newcastle Street, Brandon Colliery. 'To my horror', she said, 'I found that not one room had a ceiling'. She urged miners' wives to go forward for election on local councils to get rid of the 'appalling sanitary conditions' in which the mining community lived and worked.

Seaside resorts boomed—it was the first year of peace; day trips to the coast were organised. The start of the summer outing season saw six coaches leave Mount Calvary Methodist Church; two hundred scholars, parents and Sunday School teachers were en route to Redcar.

More than ninety members and friends of the Brandon Debating Society had their first annual outing to Whitby and Scarborough. They had lunch at Simpson's Cafe, Whitby and high tea at the Grand Annexe, Scarborough. The Society is most active with a membership of one hundred and eighty-eight with colliery manager J. P. Welsh as its first President.

Houses which had survived ninety years as homes for Straker and Love's colliery workmen were deemed unsatisfactory for human habitation. Two Railway Streets, two South Streets and East Street had been replaced by the Greyridge Estate. Tenants of West Street, the last remaining row on colliery's south side, were being re-housed.

Members of Brandon Urban Council, bricklayers and other workmen, and colliery folk, witnessed the 11 a.m. official opening of the first eight modern council houses forming the Carr Avenue Housing Estate.

The workmen, engaged in the initial stages of Brandon Urban Council's re-development plan, had downed tools at the invitation of the architect, Mr. Fred Hedley, to enable them to take part in the ceremony.

Council officials afterwards had lunch followed by a housing discussion in the Cock of the North Hotel.

'From cottage to palace' might well describe the experience of eight families at their good fortune and fulfilment of dreams which seemed to be totally out of their reach.

The last to leave West Street—and heartily glad to see the back of it—were Mr. and Mrs. Jim Bartle and their three small sons. Ever since their marriage seven years ago they have lived in two rooms which were inconvenient for a growing family. Mrs. Bartle described how her kiddies had had to play in the muddy lane to the ruination of their clothes and her carpets. She has had to replace the linos on many occasions.

The most acute overcrowding was experienced by Mr. and Mrs. William Ullathorne, now of 16 Victoria Avenue, For twenty-seven years they lived in West Street and reared a family of three sons and a daughter. Mrs. J. McCall, a widow with three grown up daughters, is now established in 29 Grey Ridge after sixteen years in West Street. Mr. and Mrs. Davison, parents of two girls and a boy, Mrs. M. J. Hutton and Mr. W. Thompson are living at 30 and 31 Greyridge and 14 Victoria Avenue respectively. Everyone is completely satisfied.

A Langley Moor reader of the Durham Advertiser sent in the following letter:—

'Sir—Brandon Urban Council opened eight new houses on Saturday September 14th. Afterwards the councillor and a few friends went to an hotel out of the district for lunch. It would have been better if this money had been spent at some hotel in the Brandon district.

No Beer'.

Geordie and Meg were going for a walk taking with them their three weeks old baby, when they met Sam, one of Geordie's pals.

'Is thoo taking him to be christened?' queried Sam.

'Wey, no', was the reply, 'Aa'm gannen ter get his name doon for a council hoose'.

Brandon Welfare played Wearmouth Colliery Welfare in the first qualifying round of the English F.A. Amateur Cup. Eight hundred spectators saw Brandon win 3—1. Brandon's side being Johnson, Ross, Sharp, Gregory, Davis, Drew, Croudace, Quigley, Graham, McKibben and Hope. To qualify for their encounter with Wearmouth Colliery, Brandon had beaten Stanley United 3—1 after a replay. A game witnessed by nine hundred wildly excited spectators.

Brandon Welfare have signed centre forward Jimmy Halliday, who is connected with West Auckland and Ferryhill in Northern League circles. Jimmy is a playing member of Durham City cricket eleven.

In a mid-season game Brandon Colliery Welfare suffered their biggest defeat ever when South Bank beat them 12–0 before a small attendance.

Mrs. Hannah Bailes died suddenly at the age of 60 at her home, 34 Russell Street. A cheerful person, Hannah had spent nearly all her life in Brandon Colliery and was the wife of Adam Bailes. The wartime comforts fund greatly benefitted from her prowess as a knitter.

After a long illness Dickie Brown died. Thirty-nine years of age, he was a miner and a member of Brandon Colliery Welfare Football Club whose players and their opponents for the day stood in silent remembrance when his death was announced.

Mr. R. Foster, Aberdare, New South Wales, Australia, wrote to the Durham Advertiser of activities of the 'Brandonians' in his town. The 'Back to Brandon' night was held last month at Weston, and people from Cesswock and Aberdare bussed to the event.

Mr. F. Hewitt opened proceedings and all stood for two minutes in memory of Bob Lumsdale and Bill Barnes, who died since the previous meeting.

The 'Grand old lady', Mrs. Parkinson, aged 92, who lived in High Street, Brandon, and Mr. Andrew Swan, now over 80, were guests of honour. Mrs. Parkinson received a pair of slippers and Mr. Swan was presented with a pipe. There were eighty people present – all natives of Brandon.

Joseph Lynch of Sunderland Street married his Christmas bride, Phoebe Mollen of Durham, in St. Patrick's, Church, Langley Moor.

Mates Laurie Moran and Steve were pleased with the decision of the Government and the Coal Board to concede a five day week to miners from May of next year. They look forward to more leisurely weekends.

1947

Colliery buzzers once again welcomed in the New Year. During the morning services were held in the chapels and churches, street carol singing took place.

The main event of the day was much talked about. New Year's Day was Vesting Day in connection with the coal mining industry, the day on which all the mines in the country were formally transferred from private to public owndership under the terms of the Mines Nationalisation Act.

Representatives of all sections of mineworkers paraded the streets behind the lodge banner and colliery band before proceeding to Brandon 'C' pit-head. There, in the presence of a large gathering, the National Coal Board's flag in blue with the initials of the Board in white in the centre, was hoisted to the top of the flagstaff and a board fixed to the winding engine house proclaiming that as from that day

'This colliery is now managed by the National Coal Board on behalf of the people'.

Unfurling of the flag was performed by a recently retired mineworker and the youngest entrant into the mine. The former was Mr. Edward Jameson, Station Road, who spent 62 of his 75 years in the pit at Brandon, 40 of them in charge of the engine plane. The boy was James Johnson, who recently removed with his parents to a new council house in Victoria Avenue.

Having hoisted the flag to the mast, Mr. Jameson said, 'I hope that the young fellows who follow on will put their backs into it. The opportunity is there for them now'. Jimmy Johnson said 'I am going to do my best under the new system. I hope everybody will do the same'.

After the pit-head ceremony an adjournment was made to the Kinema, Meadowfield, where speech-making was resumed under the chairmanship of Councillor Dickinson. Councillor Carr giving the new undertaking his blessing, said,

'The public expects you to make a success of it. It is an act of humanity and as such it cannot fail. In return the Council would provide better housing conditions, and every effort would be made to give the children better education and improve their health'.

Mr. J. D. Murray, M.P. and Mr. Welsh the colliery manager, addressed the crowd.

A Durham miner is quoted as saying, 'The pits belong ter us noo; whaat aboot sellin' them an' makin' a profit?'

The colliery has now worked intermittently for ninety years. Each generation of workmen probably had produced 'crack' men in almost every grade of work.

The dictionary definition of crack is: special, smart, of great reputation for skill or fashion.

Even before the lifting to the surface of the first nut of coal hewed from the first workable seam there would be men qualified to be hailed as 'crack'.

Skilled cartmen were employed to lead stone from the quarry at East Brandon, the village set on the hill about one mile from the colliery site. Men on deserting the land for better wages, offered their services to supply house builders and their labourers the material for the job. Men who deftly controlled their powerful Clydesdale horse on the steep run down from the quarry, and supplied the goods despite the weather, would be regarded as special.

The first stone built houses flanking the colliery were occupied by the foregoing men; houses too, were built for the all important master sinker and his gang of sinkers; men whose prowess at sinking the circular chasm to its required depth acquired a reputation for skill and were in great demand throughout the county. Expert sinkers would enable the colliery owner to dispatch coal to the market town in record time.

On the shaft reaching down to the first seam, the Hutton Seam, the production of coal began. A banksman, surrounded by the gangling pit heapstead, and stationed by the gaping mouth of the shaft, was employed to extract the full tubs of coal sent up by the onsetter. Empty tubs took their place and the banksman signalled the cage's descent to the shaft bottom.

When a banksman developed speed at loading and signalling the cage's descent almost without stop, he was looked upon as a 'crack' workman, much prized by the colliery owner.

Coal hewers installed in places near the shaft were easily supplied with empties and made rapid advance. Men had come from all parts on hearing of the need for coal getters at the new colliery; some of whom soon acquired the title of 'crack' by virtue of their ability to hew and fill tubs of coal.

Working at the shaft bottom is the onsetter who operates the underground shaft traffic. He replaces the empty tubs sent down by the banksman with full ones. Like the banksman, a good onsetter is most dextrous in keeping the pit cage moving; such a man is sought after by owners when production begins.

As the workings of the seam advanced, more hewers were set on; hewers need someone to exchange their full tubs of coal — a putter is employed to perform the task.

Ninety years ago the putter worked ten hours a shift, his hours having just been reduced from twelve hours. At the age of fourteen or fifteen years and most certainly, at that age, be of slight build, he would have to supply three or four hewers with empty tubs. He had to conserve his strength by memorising every twist and turn leading to the men's hewing places; he knew that derailed tubs resulted in loss of energy, time and money for himself and his team of hewers. He learned to be good at his task.

Pony driving called for courage and skill. The good driver on being 'broken in' to underground work on leaving school at the age of eleven or twelve got to know his pony. His control of the often fractious animal enabled him to keep the putter well supplied with empty tubs, resulting in greater output and a bigger wage packet for the putter and coal hewer. He too, was in demand.

The helper-up, the next grade up from driving—when good was an asset to the putter who required the helper's service when two were needed to push the laden coal tub up an incline. The helper was capable of putting tubs himself thus allowing the putter to earn extra by hewing a tub of coal; yes! A skilful helper could certainly enhance the putter's wage.

Some ninety years ago there would most likely be a screener whose nimble fingers earned him a reputation on the pithead screen. The diminutive lad would deftly remove spoil from the coal sent out of the pit; he would remove more than his elders, thus ensuring clean coal for trucking. Even at the youthful age of ten a 'crack' screener would emerge.

On the introduction of coke producing, scores of bee-hive ovens sprang up near the pithead; coke drawers were required to operate the ovens which when filled with coal were fired and sealed off. First grade coke was the result of the firing process.

Sturdy men, usually Irishmen having left an impoverished country, sought work at the colliery; these men were housed in nearby Railway and South Streets, soon to be known as 'Little Ireland'.

Seemingly with tireless effort, a skilled operator could empty seven cooled off ovens in a shift; sustained no doubt by more than one two quart can of ale conveyed from Joseph Addison's nearby Colliery Inn by a mercenary colliery lad. At tenpence an oven the coker drawer — more likely with a sizeable young family to support — had to be 'crack' at coke drawing.

Stoneman, mature pitmen who prefer the high workings of the main heading, generally men who have progressed through the other grades, come next; they drill holes into the solid stone, after firing the charges of powder they can remove the resulting mound of stone.

There is always one stoneman who gains a reputation for skill in knowing the length of shot-hole required and how much explosive to insert. He knows how to split large stones with mell and wedge with the minimum of effort; how much stone needs removing to enable a girder or baulk to be erected across the wide headway. He is a champion packer of stone into the void left on the removal of the face coal.

Since the introduction of electrically driven coal-cutters into the low seams, cutter men have been adept at handling their machines. The 'crack' cutter man precedes the five ton monster as it noisily cuts its way along the low coal face; he expertly guides and controls it, thus ensuring a maximum undercut and high output of coal.

There is the face driller who travels the long length of coal face, pulling his heavy drilling machine and attached cable drilling shotholes four feet apart. Sometimes a lithe man, below average weight, drills the face in the shortest time — he is a champion.

A team of coal fillers crawls onto the face after the driller's shotholes have been stemmed and fired. The filler in the low seam of eighteen or twenty inches high who consistently fills off his stint first is a 'crack' filler; he is sometimes of such girth and size one wonders how he manages to manoeuvre in the low seam to scoop coal into the path of a 'scraper' which carries it from the face to the waiting tub.

Before full mechanisation of the mines, the pony came into its own; a pony's physical condition reflected the ability of its keeper. A good horse keeper with a string of sturdy ponies to tend, acquired a love and affection for his charges stabled in the white-washed underground gallery. On occasion a pit pony was brought to the surface; its sleek appearance and sprightly bearing a great credit to its keeper, whose ambition rose to securing top honours for his entrant in the 'Best Pit Pony' section of the show. He was without doubt special to his ponies.

Reckoned to be a key man in the mine, the deputy is the most versatile workman of all. A semi-official in charge of men and lads in a district, he caters for the needs of his men; he supplies hewers with timber and four foot plates to advance his place; fires shots as required and is on call for any emergency. He is adept at handling men and master in a job which takes knowledge and skill to perform. When a person comes across such a deputy he has indeed met a man with great reputation for skill.

When a pitman began his coal hewing career astride his small wooden cracket, he generally expected to hew coal for the rest of his working days. Sadly a pitman's career is fraught with daily danger and liable to early termination due to Miners' Asthma, Nystagmus or falls of stone. The former disease which in latter years has been diagnosed as Pneumoconiosis, caused by dust inhalation destroying the victim's lungs, being the most common. Nystagmus, an eye disease, consisting of involuntary and spasmodic movement of the eyeballs and sometimes resulting in permanent blindness, is a malady brought on by poor light at the coalface and the coal's fluorescence.

Needless to say that the hewer's daily concern was the fickle strata, part of which, without prior warning, could displode itself to terminate life or disable limbs. A dismal amount of compensation being meted out to all such unfortunate victims.

Of all the champions in all the grades, the coal hewer must hold pride of place; he is the most talked of pitman when men gather to discuss their workaday affairs, be it at workmen's club, public house or corner end, one is almost sure to hear, at some time, the exploits of the 'crack' hewer. With coal hewers numbering around three quarters of the underground workforce there is more likelihood of hearing the word 'crack' than among other grades.

When Laurie Moran started work down Brandon Colliery's 'C' Pit some eleven years ago there were two hewers who symbolised the term 'crack', one in each seam; inoffensive and of ordinary physique they would be the last on earth to think of themselves as 'crack'. They were Jimmy Twist, a coal hewer in the 'C' Pit's deepest seam the Brockwell, and Joe Bell, a hewer in the Busty Seam. Both seams had coal of similar height; the former being noted for its quality coking coal and seggar which when brought to the surface made excellent bricks, while the Busty produced top grade household coal. The word seggar needs explaining: it is the thin layer of stone in the Brockwell Seam containing suitable ingredients for the brickworks. The crust of stone has to be removed to make height for the tub to travel.

Jimmy, only about five feet seven inches in height, looked the essence of fitness and ruggedness – a natural pitman – if one was to be found. He lived for his family, work and pigeon breeding; he also liked a spot of gardening, the tidy fresh rose in his button-hole evidence of his skill. Jimmy also liked a couple of pints in Brandon Workmen's Club.

At work in the yard seam of coal, he was lethal; Jimmy was credited with hewing coal where other men baulked.

Hewers unfortunate enough to be cavilled to a 'wall' were excused and paid the minimum wage without query; if only one tub of coal per shift was hewed from their narrow width of rock-hard virgin coal they did not lose face with their workmates. When Jimmy found himself in a 'wall' his sole ambition was to split the pillar of coal to loosen it thus enabling him and his marras to earn money. Jimmy always contrived to hew three tubs of coal from the 'wall'.

Jimmy Twist had a number of children of school age; he had to be 'crack'. Jimmy could manoeuvre in the lowest of places; his large mouthed coal shovel scooping coal tubwards from every conceivable direction. Other men seeking to emulate him would likely develop a hernia. It must have been daunting being his marra to keep pace with him while working together in the double cavil.

Joe Bell, slightly taller despite one bent leg, probably a legacy of a fall of stone, was a man of simple tastes. A keen gardener and teetotaller,

Joe could be seen most nights doing the rounds of the picture halls — first the Kinema and then the Empire for a change of programme; Joe's wife trailed some yards behind her spouse as they plodded their way either to Meadowfield or Langley Moor.

Joe was a wizard at getting coals; like Jimmy Twist he seemed able to hew coal in places where others baulked. With a young family to feed he too had to be good.

Laurie Moran put during four long war years. During that time he saw little of Jimmy Twist as Jimmy was a Brockwell Seam hewer. It was when the Brockwell seam was worked out and Jimmy and the other hewers were transferred to the Busty Seam on the next level above that Laurie had occasion to see Jimmy in action. Joe Bell being a Busty man sometimes hewed in Laurie's district, or conversely Laurie was cavilled to put in Joe's district.

Laurie marvelled! The empty iron bound tub settled over the plate ends in Joe's hewing place; with not a piece of loose coal in sight Laurie breathed a sigh of relief, he could relax a little.

'Come straight back', piped Joe from behind a steamy curtain of sweat. Laurie returned in a short while; besides the full tub of coals, more were strewn on the floor waiting to be tubbed.

On one occasion Laurie was supplied with a helper-up; Joe's place was on the dip' as were the places of two other hewers, when Laurie changed their tubs it took the combined shoving power of Laurie and his helper to clear the place. Putters descended three quarters of an hour after the hewers, thus enabling the latter to hew coals ready for the putter's arrival. At the shift's end putters took the opportunity to hew coal for themselves when the hewers left their places.

It was time to get Joe Bell's last full tub from his place; as Laurie and his helper set off, they were dumbfounded on meeting Joe who had shoved the tub up the long incline from his place, his bare head pressing against the tub.

Will the 'crack' worker emerge under nationalisation?

Champions on the surface must not be forgotten.

Masters of the art of billiards playing are legendary; Archie Robson, Bob Stirling, Joe Pybus, Will Carr, George Craddock, Jimmy Moran, Percy Shell, numerous members of Club and Institute were capable of entertaining a crowd. Dominoes produced Joe Ayre, Joe Kitching and others who excelled in inter-club games.

The sport of running produced Harriers David Hopkins, Percy Hall, A. Rainbow and Will Harrison.

Pigeon racing's clientele boasted Tommy Collins, Jim Lee, Adam Bailes, Jack Walton and James Campbell.

Boxing, Steve Ryan and up and coming young Dave Ogilvy.

Football had stars in Tom Freeman, Edmund Carter, Bobby Lowes, William Ashurst, Brandon Juniors' Sammy Crooks and schoolboy Pompey Clennell.

A renowned musician, Eunoch Edwin Howden, rose from pit lad to musical director.

Good gardeners were profuse, allotments being worked on three sides of the colliery rows. Men with green fingers, R. Grieveson, R. Fairless and H. Winter, contributed to the success of the local flower and vegetable shows.

The supreme title of special, smart and skilful, must go to well known Brandon character Tommy Harker. Tommy never descended the mine to hew coal. He excelled in the art of putting miners' household coal allowances through the small square hole of the coalhouse.

Tommy, an ardent Salvationist and expert drummer, could be seen every weekday at his onerous task. The twelve or fifteen hundredweight of mostly inferior coal tipped in the street gutter was speedily scooped into the eighteen inch square hole set some six feet above floor level; like Jimmy Twist, he could shovel coal from all angles. At twopence a load, he had to dispose of one hundred and twenty loads to earn £1.

Tommy saved and acquired a horse and cart. Refuse had to be cleared from the street netties and tipped on the ever expanding ash heap set away from the colliery rows. Tommy submitted a tender and Brandon Urban Council accepted it. Tommy Harker became the official scavenger; he with horse and cart was paid £1 per day by contract. Business required more mobility; a small lorry, driven by a son was seen touring the colliery rows delivering miners' coals.

Tommy's days of retirement were spent as passenger in one of his fleet of four lorries occupied in their multifarious tasks.

Fred Hedley, architect to Brandon Urban Council, had a proud moment at a luncheon in the Three Tuns Hotel when he was described by a local M.P. as one of the finest architects in the country. The first four new council built houses on the Red Courts estate were occupied.

At the annual meeting of Brandon Colliery branch of the Durham County Deputies' Association, Laurie Moran now a shot-firer of a few months standing, together with Anthony Howden, was elected pit inspector ('C' Pit). Both members were also elected onto a committee of six.

A colliery strike occurred recently near Durham. During a meeting of the Miners' Lodge held to consider the dispute a miner made this remark, 'Look here men: we buried the hatchet on New Year's Day, but some fella's howked it out agyen and hit us on the back o' the heed wint'.

Coal hewing marra with his brother James and Paddy Moran for a number of years in Brandon Colliery's 'C' Pit Brockwell Seam, Richard Morrissey died at the age of 68. A native of Kilkenny, Ireland, he came to Manchester, stayed a while and moved to Brandon Colliery forty-one years ago. He retired from mining in 1942.

Joseph Reynolds and Michael Robert Parkin, both Brandon Colliery men, were among the several Easter 'grooms. Joseph married Miss Mary Hartley of Durham, while Michael wed Teresa McCall of Greyridge Estate, Brandon Colliery.

Brandon Colliery Welfare Football Club, wooden spoonist of the Northern League with eighteen points from eighteen games played, suffered heavy defeats against Bishop Auckland in Eastertide matches. At home on

Good Friday they lost 7—0 and at Auckland on Easter Monday the margin was a 7—1 defeat. Sandwiched between these reverses was a 4—0 beating at Evenwood. Brandon had conceded eighteen goals and registered one.

Hubert McDermott (82) formerly of 35 Greyridge Estate, died in the Royal Infirmary, Sunderland, following an accident. Born at Brandon Colliery, his parents were among the first emigrants to occupy houses in Railway Street, he began work when a boy of eleven in the mine at Brandon Colliery as a trapper lad, and worked at the same pit up to his seventy-fourth year. He was in the 'C' Pit at the time of the explosion forty-eight years ago, and was the first man in and brought the first dead man out. Hugh was for twenty years chairman of Brandon Colliery Miners' Lodge, and had his photograph on the Lodge banner.

Mrs. Priscilla Tones (77), died at her home, 9 College Terrace. A native of Norfolk, she had spent nearly all of her life at Brandon Colliery, and was the widow of George Tones, who predeceased her five years ago.

A crippled woman from Brandon Colliery, who has walked with crutches for thirty-four years, was Mr. Edwards' first patient. He knelt before her on the platform and applied treatment to her legs. 'I am trying', he said, 'to break up a condition which has become set over a period of thirty-four years'. He helped her to stand and walk across the platform.

With 2,500 people looking on, men, women and children, some limping, some aided by crutches, some carried in arms, others bent low with pain, and some blind and deaf, appeared on the spacious platform at the City Hall, Newcastle where Mr. Harry Edwards, London, gave a healing demonstration under the auspices of the Spiritual Evidence Society. In the audience were people from all parts of the Durham coalfield.

Mr. W. A. Helm was installed as the twentieth minister to Mount Calvary Methodist Church; he arrived in time to welcome home the members of the chapel from the Forces.

May saw the start of the five day working week for Britain's miners, one of the early fruits of nationalisation of the mines. Wages were the same as at January 1944, negotiations are in hand regarding a wage increase.

No Gala attendance for Laurie Moran's mate Steve. He married Ann Cleary of Langley Moor at St. Patrick's Church. He elected to honeymoon away from the record crowd attending the 64th Durham Miners' Gala.

Laurie now a shot-firer did not qualify for the sixteen shillings Brandon Miners' Lodge paid out to each member of the checkweigh fund at the start of Brandon Colliery miners' holidays during which many motor tours have been arranged.

Prices have spiralled since the end of the war. Beer then tenpence a pint is now one shilling. The Durham Advertiser had been increased in price, from twopence; it is now threepence a copy owing to dearer newsprint.

Mary Martin of Park Street married Frederick C. Bragazie, Derby, at St. John's Church, Meadowfield.

Another soldier, P.O.W. Irving Pigg, youngest son of Charles Pigg, Cobden Terrace, married Margaret Balmer from nearby Dorlonco Villas, Meadowfield. They too, were married in St. John's.

Doreen Ruddick of Brandon travelled the short journey from Church Street to Commercial Street to be married to R. C. Lamb of Bearpark, in Mount Calvary Methodist Church.

A fancy dress parade led by the beauty queen (Miss Doreen Spirit) and accompanied by Brandon Colliery Silver Prize Band preceded the opening of the first annual field day of the Flower Show and Sports organised by Brandon Colliery Welfare Committee when 6,510 paid admission fees to the sports ground.

The event was an all-out effort to revive the show for which Brandon was noted about thirty-six years ago.

Eddie Moran after three years of coal-cutting desired a change as it was an onerous occupation with no regular shift, he was called on for work at any hour depending on the cycle of face work preparations. He left home and joined the peacetime Royal Navy in which he served before meeting and marrying Yorkshire girl Mary O'Hara at St. Joseph's Church, Keighley on September 3rd.

Earlier in the year Teresa Moran married Ronald Bailey from Langley Park; the reception was held in the bride's home, 5 Newcastle Street, in Brandon.

The fifth re-union of Brandonians in Australia has been held and Mr. R. Foster, Greta Street Ext., Aberdare, N.S.W., reported that a great crowd of Brandon people, their married sons and daughters and grandchildren gathered in the Aberdare Hall, aboue ninety adults were present.

A birthday cake inscribed with icing 'Brandon's Fifth Re-union' welcomed Mrs. Parkinson, Mr. and Mrs. Cairns, Jack Brown, Wilf and Mrs. Brown and family, Mr. and Mrs. E. Rumley and family, Mr. and Mrs. Bob Rumley and family, Mr. and Mrs. Tot Foster and daughter and son-in-law from Shell Harbour, Mr. and Mrs. Wardle and son and daughter-in-law from Corrinal, Mr. and Mrs. Bob Foster and sons Bob, Bill and Terry, Mr. and Mrs. Morris and family, Mr. Clem Parkinson and wife, Mr. and Mrs. Bill Brunskill and family, Mr. and Mrs. Tot Robinson and family, Mr. and Mrs. J. Robinson and family, Mr. and Mrs. W. Robinson and family (in fact all the Robinsons and Brunskills), Mr. and Mrs. Bob Jones and all their married daughters and families, Mr. Charles Jones, Mr. and Mrs. Ike Hewitt, Mrs. P. Elmore, Mr. J. Elmore from Sydney, Mr. Parks, Mr. and Mrs. Barrass, Mr. and Mrs. Mick McFall, Mr. and Mrs. Green, Jim and Mrs. Snell, Matt and Mrs. Armstrong, Joe Simpson, Jim O'Hara, Mr. and Mrs. Browell, Mr. Bill Douglas from Musselbrook.

At midnight there was the singing of the 'Maori Farewell' and 'Auld Lang Syne'.

For the fourth week in succession the target has been broken. Brandon 'C' Pit and Pit House collieries produced 9,127 tons, 477 tons above the combined target of 8,650 tons.

A national wage increase for miners was granted in time to help Christmas shoppers when the minimum underground wage was increased by fifteen shillings per week, and surface workers by ten shillings per week, making the new minimum underground weekly wage £5.15s. and the surface minimum £5.

Hospitals and Institutions were not forgotten at Christmas. Santa Claus (one of the staff) distributed presents on Christmas morning and dinner was a sumptuous feast of turkey. plum pudding and mince pies when a party was arranged for the children in Brandon Isolation Hospital.

One time next door neighbour to the Moran family, Mrs. Margaret Bussey (60), died at her home, 15 Newcastle Street. Born at Chester Moor she had lived in Brandon for thirty-two years. Her husband Joseph, five sons and three daughters mourn her death.

1948

On January 3rd, Laurie Moran married Theresa Minns of Browney in St. Patrick's Church, Langley Moor.

The week preceding the New Year saw Brandon's two pits exceed their target of 8,650 tons by 363 tons.

A large crowd gathered on Brandon Colliery Walfare ground witnessed the demise of Brandon in the semi-final of the Brandon Aged Miners' Cup. Ushaw Moor, their visiting opponents, won easily 6—2. Gage scored for Brandon by heading in Nyland's centre; Graham scored their second goal.

The team played one of its best games of the season when visitors New Brancepeth United were beaten by two clear goals. New Brancepeth's league championship aspirations were put in jeopardy.

Pat Robinson presided over Brandon Colliery Welfare A.F.C. meeting in the Miners' Hall when George Hewitt (secretary) reported a successful season. The club had reached four semi-finals and had been finalist in the Durham County Hospital Cup competition. Election of officers: President Abel Hopkins; secretary George Hewitt; treasurer Jack Robson.

William Teggart (58), 20 Russell Street, whilst filling at Pit House was killed by a fall of stone at the end of March. He leaves a wife, son and daughter.

Councillor David Hopkins was elected Chairman of Brandon Urban District Council in succession to Councillor J. Meldrum. David is secretary of Brandon Miners' Lodge and has served on the Council for five years, having succeeded the late County Councillor Thomas Carr.

Ruby Futers, daughter of Mr. and Mrs. Jim Futers, Queen Street, a former pupil at Brandon School, met her husband during the war. Ruby, now Mrs. Colescott, of Sunbury, Pennsylvania in the U.S.A., addressed several gatherings there on 'Conditions prevailing in England'. Unknown to Mrs. Colescott, the Rev. W. Hunt took a collection at one of the meetings. The money raised procured over two hundred and fifty bars of milk chocolate which were distributed to Junior and Infant scholars at Brandon Council School.

A life-long resident of Brandon, Thomas Davison with his wife, celebrated their golden wedding at 48 Sunderland Street. Tom, who is 73, began work in the mine as a boy of eleven and worked three days at the pit and three days at school. He completed 55 years in the mine at Brancepeth and Brandon Collieries.

Sir Hartley Shawcross, K.C., M.P., Sir Stafford Cripps, M.P., A. Bevan, M.P., and A. L. Horner, General Secretary National Union of Mineworkers, helped attract the crowds to Durham's greatest gala in 75 years. The occasion was the 65th Big Meeting.

Brandon Colliery Silver Prize Band visited Durham City again on the Saturday following the Gala when they led a parade of over 300 ambulance men, nurses and cadets through Durham from the County Hospital to participate in a service held in Durham Cathedral.

During the holiday week at Brandon Colliery, a record was set up at the local railway station when the largest and most efficiently organised excursion, comprising 1809 members and wives and children of members of Brandon Social Club, left for Scarborough. Three trains were used and there was hardly a hitch. Newly elected committee members Bill Poutin, Chris Hedley, Charles Winter, Joe Freeman and Aaron Robinson, helped marshal the crowd.

Walter Mercer, Langley Moor, an invalid for sixteen years, had to travel in his invalid chair. It was decided that he should travel by the second train and when they arrived his wife and friends entered a compartment on the understanding that Walter was to be put into the luggage van, but owing to the exceptional length of the train this could not be done and he was left behind.

The train was well on its journey before Mrs. Mercer found that her husband was not on the train. Walter and his friends, however, travelled on the third train and arrived ten minutes later at Scarborough. He commented, 'I was all right. My wife had the pies, but I had the purse'.

More than 350 old folk, widows and friends were taken for an outing to South Shields as guests of the officials and committee of Brandon Colliery Literary Institute. Members and wives over 65 years of age and widows of past members aged over 50 were given a free ticket, lunch and tea. Each person also received a gift of five shillings. The oldest man on the excursion was George Miller (84), of Greyridge Estate and the eldest woman, Mrs. Maddison also 84, of the Aged Miners' Homes.

Brandon Colliery Band, under Joseph Mains, finished second in both events at the Murton Flower Show Band contest. They were twelve points behind the winners of the selection event and only two behind the match event winner. Brandon, however, won the event for C section bands.

Charles Collins, 41 North Street, married Councillor Thomas Dickinson's daughter, Mary who lives at Hill Crest View, Brandon. They were wed in St. John's Church, Meadowfield.

More than 7,000 attended the record annual flower show and sports at Brandon. A fancy dress parade was led by beauty queen Doris Ryan. Eighteen years old Doris was winner of a baby show at the first Meadowfield and District Charity Carnival seventeen years ago, among sixty-two entrants.

A brass band contest attracted ten bands. A baby show, Punch and Judy show, fancy dress parade, rabbit section, industrial section, sports events and a boxing contest combined to make a memorable day.

A Boxing Tournament was given by National Coal Board finalists under the direction of J. P. Welsh (Brandon Colliery). Featherweight Ray Herron (Brandon) beat Ray Blewitt (Darlington). J. Gilroy (New Brancepeth) beat Ron Ogilvie (Brandon). R. Blenkinsop (Brandon) beat M. Lawson (New Brancepeth).

Three years after the end of hostilities; the sweet ration is to be increased by four ounces during the next rationing period. When will rationing end?

John Simpson came to Brandon forty-five years ago at the age of eighteen. Well known as a cyclist, cavie rabbit breeder and keen gardener, John of 28 Russell Street, was fatally injured while following his employment at the shaft bottom of Pit House Colliery. He was a familiar figure astride his cycle which could be seen almost every day on Brandon's streets.

David Anderson lived in nearby High Street; he died after a short illness. Born in Brandon Colliery, he began work in the mine at the age of thirteen and rose to be a deputy overman and retired three years ago at the age of sixty-seven.

On Durham Miners' Gala Day, John, the third son of Patrick and Mary Moran, 5 Newcastle Street, married Margaret Lockey of Commercial Square, Brandon. Margaret and John are lifelong Brandonians. John was the fourth member of the Moran family to wed in the space of fourteen months.

One of two clubs before the Durham Football Association, Brandon Welfare Football Club was fined £1 and issued a warning about the future conduct of spectators. The club was also ordered to pay one shilling expenses to the referee, who had undertaken to officiate at the game owing to the non-appearance of the appointed official.

Another Brandon stalwart, James Thorpe Bell (72), 3 Commercial Street, died in hospital at Durham. He came to Brandon at the age of two, began work in the mine at the age of twelve and worked at Brandon and Brancepeth Collieries for fifty-nine years, retiring two years ago.

After nearly fifteen years of service to Brandon community, the Rev. George H. Greenfield is leaving to serve Herriard with Lasham in the Diocese of Winchester.

When he arrived early in 1934 the Bishop of Durham (Dr. Hensley Harrison) said to him, 'Brandon Parish is one of the most difficult parishes in my Diocese; if you serve there for five years and make good, you will deserve preferment'.

Miner's wife Mrs. T. Crick, 12 Victoria Avenue, has received a birthday parcel from Princess Elizabeth, having given birth to a male child on November 14th (the birthday of Prince Charles).

Steve Goodall, Brandon Colliery, was bridegroom at Bethel Church in Durham on Christmas Day. The bride was Jean Stobbs of Durham.

1949

Brandon's football ground was crowded with football enthusiasts on New Year's Day when the Welfare team, Potts, Williams, Hutton, Cooper, Egglestone, Gibbs, Gage, H. Grayson, Charlton, A. Grayson and Foster played

Cornsay in the second round of the Brandon Aged Miners' Cup. Both teams provided entertaining football.

The fresh and more contented outlook adopted by the miners of the Durham coalfield since the nationalisation of the industry, is reflected in the present day designs of lodge banners. Gone are the days of the sentimental pictures depicting the sufferings of the miner and his family. One of the banners which will bear the 'new look' at the next gala will be that of Brandon Colliery Lodge.

According to Sam Watson, general secreary of the Durham Area, National Union of Mineworkers, it is the finest flag ever to be commissioned by a miners' lodge, because it depicts 'the greatest assembly in the world'— the miners' gala on Durham Racecourse. The River Wear occupied the foreground in the picture, and thousands gather round the two platforms, with the Cathedral and Castle in the distance.

The combined collieries of Brandon beat their weekly target of 9,200 tons by four tons. The 'C' Pit's target is 2,225 tons, produced mainly from the Ballarat Seam which has four long wall faces where the height of the coal varies from sixteen to twenty inches, three of which are over one hundred yards in length while the other is sixty yards long. These faces are about one mile from the shaft. These working places are cut by electrically driven machines, after being drilled, are fired by shot-firers. Laurie Moran is a shot-firer on one of the longer faces.

Coal is also drawn from the waggon-way pillars of the Busty Seam. These pillars of coal were left in for security as the workings advanced some ninety years ago. Coal is drawn too, from the Hutton and Brockwell Seams where coal hewing predominates. All three seams send coal up the one shaft; seggar for use at the brickworks, is sent up from the Brockwell Seam. It is said that there is twenty or thirty years work in the Ballarat Seam.

A champion coal hewer could never find a 'marra' up to his standard. One day he met a tall negro stoker in a pub and asked him to forsake the sea and start work in the mine. Meeting him one day coming out of the flat, Geordie asked how he had got on. 'Aa filled ten of dem l'il boxes', he said. The champion went in, and by exerting himself managed to fill ten tubs of coal.

Next day the negro said he has filled thirteen. 'But', he added, 'that is an unlucky number so ah filled another'. Geordie threw down his pick in disgust and swore he was finished with coal hewing. The negro looked at the pick and asked, 'What's that?'

'Why that's a pick to cut the coal'.

'Oh', said the negro, 'Aa'll have to get some of dem. My finger nails are getting a bit sore'.

Harry Gerrard left his native Lancashire at the age of eighteeen, he had worked in the mines there from the age of twelve. He continued his pit career at Brandon Colliery where he worked until his retirement two years ago. He died at the age of sixty-three at his home 21 Russell Street.

Near neighbour Elizabeth Jane Russell, sixty-seven, died in Park Street; she too had lived in Brandon for more than forty years.

"Village Simpleton," Billy Davis, on parade before Brandon Colliery folk at the Brandon Flower Show, 1947.

*Mary Moran,
aged sixty one,
mother of ten.
1947.*

Laurie at Conishead Convalescent Home, 1939.

Laurie Moran after a hard shift, 1936.

Laurie and mate Steve Murther, 1940.

Theresa and Laurie with baby Anne outside of a one-roomed cottage at Stonebridge, 1949.

Mark Franklin, 78, died at his home, 7 Aged Miners' Homes. He had resided in Brandon for more than half a century. He began as a trapper led at the age of twelve and rose to be deputy-overman. He retired thirteen years ago after working for fifty-three years in the mine.

Forty-two year old colliery locomotive driver James William Bartle died suddenly at his home, 15 Victoria Avenue. James was treasurer of the Brandon Social Club, a member of Brandon Flower Show Committee, and a member of Brandon Welfare and Pit Canteen Committees.

Large crowds went to Brandon Welfare Ground on Easter Monday to see the final of the Brandon Aged Miners' Cup, when Brandon accounted for Durham St. Giles, winning by four clear goals. Amid tumultuous cheers H. Grayson scored two while A. Grayson and Harding added one each.

Brandon's new banner was much admired when 250,000 people and 120 colliery banners graced the Big Meeting on Durham's Racecourse for the sixty-sixth Durham Miners' Gala.

Brandon's claim to be the first miners' lodge to put a picture of Durham 'Big Meeting' on their lodge banner is challenged. Councillor Sam Usher, the genial veteran of Pelton Fell Miners' Lodge, says he can remember that one of his lodge's old banners bore such a scene.

Three hundred parishioners and friends welcomed the new Vicar of Brandon, the Rev. John Newman Ellwood, M.A., they had assembled in the Parochial Hall for a social function.

Over seven thousand people attended Brandon's third Flower Show and Sport Day. The fancy dress parade and the 'Beauty Queen' Miss Barbara Wood with her escorts presented a colourful spectacle. The Dagenham Girl Pipers and Brandon Colliery Prize Silver Band provided enjoyable music much appreciated by the sun-soaked folk lining the route. Bandsmen proudly displayed new uniforms and shining newly acquired instruments, the latter having been provided by Brandon Miners' Lodge.

The colliery lodge agreed that the men should work one Saturday a month. They produced 991 tons of coal on the first Saturday worked. Total output from the two collieries being 10,450 tons, thus exceeding the target by 1,250 tons. A laudable effort! Collieries throughout the county have responded to the appeal for more coal.

Sunderland and Newcastle Streets with their squatly built houses, and the uneven grass-grown streets, are soon to disappear. Occupants of the four streets will take over houses being built on the new Sawmills Estate, others are envisaged. Some £500,000 has been spent on the Council's ambitious building scheme to date.

Miss Mary E. Johnson died suddenly in hospital while on holiday. Thirty-eight years of age, she was the eldest daughter of Albert Johnson, farmer, of 1 Commercial Street. She was employed as a bacteriologist at the Milk Marketing Board factory at Langley Moor.

Alice Ann Reynolds and Thomas Willian Warriner did not survive to experience life in a new home on the Sawmills Estate.

Alice, a neighbour of the Moran family for some years, had lived in Brandon all her life; she died at the age of sixty after a brief illness, at her home at 49 Newcastle Street. She was the widow of the late Joseph Reynolds who pre-deceased her by two years.

Thomas, a coal hewer, died at the age of fifty-seven at his home, 22 Newcastle Street. A teetotaller and non-smoker, he had spent the greater part of his life in Brandon. He leaves a widow and family of six sons and two daughters.

Brandon has produced some quality players in its football history; it has had five teams with different names. They were Brandon United in 1908 when they won the County Challenge Cup, Brandon Albion, Brandon Argyle, Brandon Social Club and now Brandon Colliery Welfare. Throughout its history Brandon has had several football teams bearing the name of a local chapel.

Private Tom Darbyshire (22) has a future in football. Goalkeeper Tom, son of Mr. and Mrs. Tom Darbyshire of College Terrace, at present serving with the East Yorkshire Regiment Police in Austria, has been invited to play a trial for Sunderland A.F.C. when he comes home on leave. He has also been offered the same by Ipswich Town Football Club. He kept goal for Brandon Colliery Welfare. He has won a silver cup for jumping, two medals for tug-of-war and two medals for football.

Mrs. Lucy Teggert, 29 Commercial Street, celebrated her ninetieth birthday. Born at Willington in 1859, she came to Brandon fifty-six years ago. With her husband Jim, she supervised for seven weeks the daily feeding of six hundred hungry children during the 1921 miners' stoppage.

1950

The New Year was welcomed throughout Brandon district by the customary 'first footing' with shouts of 'Happy New Year, missus'.

Councillor Clennell and Mrs. Clennell, 52 Russell Street celebrated their golden wedding. Mr. Clennell (Jack) who is 73, was born at Downs Lane, Hetton, and came to Brandon Colliery in 1880 at the age of three years. For five years he was a surface worker and retired three years ago.

Frank Lightfoot came to Brandon Colliery from Silksworth at the age of thirteen where he started work in the mine. He was a keen harrier and a member of Brandon Harrier Club. A devoted Methodist and a member of the Male Voice Choir, he died at the age of sixty-three at his home, 21 Princess Street.

Three Brandon Colliery officials have retired; they are George Dobson, George Lee and Charles W. Pye, they share one hundred and fifty years' work in the mine.

A husband and six sons survive Emma Winter (58) of 61 Sunderland Street, who died in Dryburn Hospital. Born at Willington, she had lived in Brandon for more than half a century.

John Clennell's and Lucy Teggart's celebrations were short lived. The former died at the age of seventy-four. He was a member of Brandon Urban Council for twenty-five years. Mrs. Teggart died at her home in her ninety-first year.

Brandon is a member of six Welfare Leagues in the National Coal Board's No. 5 Area. They are senior billiards, junior billiards, snooker, darts and table tennis. Healthy positions are maintained in each league.

Brandon Colliery Railway Station was swelling at the seams on a fine July Tuesday when 1,851 members and wives and friends assembled for the outing to South Shields organised by Brandon Workmen's Club.

Four days later buses carried one hundred and eighty adults to Tynemouth where fine weather prevailed throughout the day.

In his early days Tom Connelly was a popular comedian and entertainer in the Brandon district. Born in the area, he began work at Browney Colliery at the age of eleven. Later he worked for fifty years at Brandon Colliery. Tom aged seventy-nine, died at his home, 12 Aged Miners' Homes, on the eve of the Big Meeting.

Heavy rain failed to dampen spirits on the occasion of the 67th Durham Miners' Gala. The re-elected Labour Government sent Aneurin Bevan M.P. as guest of the Durham miners; he, together with Emmanuel Shinwell M.P., Sir Hartley Shawcross K.C., M.P., and A. L. Horner, graced the platforms. Brandon's band and banner attended the Gala along with the other one hundred and fifty-six banners representing one hundred thousand Durham County miners.

Two bandsmen went to hear the championship contest in London. At the boarding house Geordie asked Tommy, 'What's that beuk for?'

'Why', says Tommy, 'It's for visitors to sign their nyems'.

'What's the letters for? There's M.P. after this nyem and C.C.'

'They stand for Member of Parliament and County Councillor', explained Tommy.

Then Geordie picked up a pen, wrote his name and added B.B.B.B.B.

'Why Geordie', said Tommy, 'Aa nivvor knew thoo had see many letters after thee nyem. What's them B's stand for?'

'Them', said Geordie, 'they stand for Best Bloomin' Blower i' Brandon Brass Band'.

A visitor from Belfast gave some of his impessions of the Gala,

'Accustomed as I am to huge demonstrations in Ulster', he writes, 'The size and splendour of the Durham Miners' Gala took my breath away. That the meeting is held in so beautiful and ancient a city is in itself sufficient to make the occasion one to be enjoyed by the visitor. The scene is forever printed on my memory. The banners are works of art.

'I was very impressed by the high standard of the colliery bands. It was moving to hear the hymn 'Gresford' played by three excellent bands in the cathedral.

'The things that are rooted in my memory: the high spirits and enthusiasm of the crowds who refused to be downhearted by heavy showers of rain, the variety of colour as one looked down on the scene at the racecourse, the patience and geniality of the Durham policemen, the balloons that shot into the air, became infinitesmal specks, then vanished to the west of the city, the "Niagara"—the expression used by the Minister of Health when referring to the amount of medicine being prescribed under the National Health Act—of tea and minerals consumed on the racecourse, the unfeigned emotion of Durham's Mayor on receiving a presentation from Mr. Sam Watson; Nye Bevan watching from a balcony as the Lodges passed his hotel.

'At home I will be able to tell of the industry and optimism of the Durham miner and of the Big Meeting that is big in every sense of the word'.

Two heavy showers of rain failed to dampen the spirits of the four thousand people who paid for admission to the fourth annual show held in Brandon Welfare Ground. The fancy dress parade was led by the 'Queen' (Miss Joyce Chance) and her six attendants. Herbert Winter was awarded the Jones Challenge Cup for the third successive year for gaining the highest number of points in the flower and vegetable sections.

Mr. J. P. Welsh has been manager of Brandon Colliery for nearly eight years; he is leaving to go to Silksworth Colliery as their new manager. His successor is Mr. Walter Everitt, manager of Brancepeth Colliery.

During Mr. Welsh's term at Brandon colliery a borehole was sunk from a Sub-station 251 feet down to the Busty Seam, the sinking took place near Littlewhite Farm, Brancepeth. Thick armoured electric cable took electricity direct to the pit, thus saving some two miles of underground equipment.

The architect (Mr. Fred Hedley) stated that approval had been received for the erection of forty-six houses at Brandon, and the installation of lighting, roads and sewers for ninety-two houses at a cost of over £74,141.

A man who had just moved into a new Council house met a friend, who inquired,

'How are you getting on?'

'Oh, fine', was the reply; 'we never have a quarrel now'.

'How's that?'

'Afraid to slam the doors'.

Sad Remembance Day. While the parade was passing through Meadow-field en route to St. John's Church for the armistice Day Service, one of the Brandon Colliery Prize Silver Band players collapsed and died shortly afterwards. He was thirty-nine year old Thomas William Ord, 30 Sunderland Street. A playing member of Brandon Silver Band since the age of thirteen, he will be greatly missed by his fellow bandsmen. He was colliery deputy and on the management board of Brandon Social Club.

Both underground and surface workers were granted a National Union of Mineworkers wage increase of five shillings making the underground minimum weekly wage £6 and the surface minimum £5.5s.

Brandon Welfare football team's highest score of the season came when they beat Coxhoe nine goals to one in a league game. Only a poor crowd witnessed the Christmas time glut of goals.

Laurie Moran was among the shotfirers transferred, on a temporary basis, to Brancepeth Colliery and Waterhouses Drift. When the River Browney burst into Littleburn Colliery water also penetrated into Brandon 'C' Pit. Soon the pit was unworkable, hence the transfer of men and shotfirers to the above named collieries.

1951

Laurie Moran spent most of December and part of the New Year working in Waterhouses Drift. Conditions were wet, the seam being near the surface, rain water settled in the workings. Laurie saw to the needs of a set of coal hewers; he was available if a coal hewer required shots firing. Working in a drift mine was a complete change for Laurie; smoking was allowed as naked lights were used throughout the drift, a warming drink was forthcoming, tin bottles containing tea being heated on the candle stove. Laurie's stay was pleasant as the men were very friendly towards the miners from across the Deerness Valley.

Alf was 'marra' to his father Abey, and the place in which they were hewing was very bad, so much so that they had to run out and in lest the stone came down upon them.

Abey: 'Howay, lad, is tha not gannen in ter face ter help me ter drill holes?'

Alf: (who is a nervous chapel lad) 'Wey, bless me soul, Aa'll tell that w'at ter dee. Thoo gan in and drill the hole an' Aa'll bide out here and pray for tha'.

Heavy falls of snow affected football fixtures throughout the North. Despite the adverse weather, Brandon's collieries produced 10,700 tons of coal, some 1,500 tons above their target. Output for the following week was even better when 10,718 tons were drawn to the surface.

During January underground miners were granted a further weekly increase of seven shillings and surface workers five shillings, making the underground minimum £6.7s. and the surface workers' minimum £5.10s.

Fish and chips make a popular meal. George Craythorne's wooden lock-up fish and chip shop sited at the end of Queen Street was busy; it was 1.30 p.m. The frying range took fire and the shop was gutted owing to there not being a water hydrant in the area. George suffered a serious loss.

Joseph Frost of Brandon, married Victoria Hughes from Alum Waters, at St. Joseph's Church, Ushaw Moor.

Councillor T. J. Dickinson (chairman of the governors) presented prizes at Brandon Modern School speech day. He said that it was gratifying that parents nowadays took more interest in their children's future sooner, and not just a short time before they were due to leave school.

Mr. Jim Robinson was of the opinion that children were of a better class, being better dressed and better mannered. Councillor Tom Metcalfe presided.

Horse lover Thomas Ridley died at 10 Albert Street. Born at Spennymoor, he had lived at Nevilles Cross, Langley Moor and Brandon. After seventeen years of farm work he became horse-keeper at the colliery, until the employment of pit ponies ceased. He was a well-known trainer and 'breaker' of horses. His son, Flight-Sergeant George Ridley, was killed on flying operations over Germany.

William Fenwick (Bill) (76), died after a brief illness at the residence of his daughter and son-in-law, Mr. and Mrs. J. Wilson, 10 Cobden Terrace.

He had resided for over half a century in Brandon Colliery. After working fifty years in the mine he was attacked by nystagmus. His wife, the late Catherine Fenwick, predeceased him by seven months. He leaves a family of five sons and two daughters.

Nystagmus (an afflication of the eye) like Miners' Asthma, attributed to bad working conditions; victims were at one time denied just compensation. When Laurie Moran worked as a datal hand Brandon 'C' Pit Busty Red Lion district, he helped the putter assigned to Bill Fenwick. On one occasion on leaving Bill's hewing place, Laurie asked the time. 'Twenty past one' came the quick response. Bill's outer pit garments were neatly bundled some twenty yards away from the hewing area. Curious, Laurie looked at the watch in Bill's waistcoat pocket. Time, one twenty-five. Later in the shift Laurie again asked the time. 'A quarter past four', answered Bill. On looking at the watch, Laurie found that the time almost coincided. On asking how he knew the time without looking at his watch, Bill remarked, 'I know the time by the number of tobacco chews I have used'. A puzzled Laurie Moran left Bill Fenwick's hewing place.

Two colliery officials were presented with a chiming clock and a wrist watch on their retirement. Mr. T. Green and Mr. R. Halkier were honoured at a reception held in Brandon's Ambulance Drill Hall.

Mr. Green has had fifty-seven years at the colliery, for thirty-six years he was manager of the Pipe and Brickworks, Brandon 'C' Pit.

Mr. Halkier was an engine-wright at Pit House Colliery for fifteen years, and succeeded Mr. John Brown as engineer at Brandon Colliery seven years ago.

After beating Page Bank Rovers by two goals to nil in the semi-final of the Brandon Aged Miners' Cup, Brandon Colliery Welfare took on Wolsingham Welfare in the final for the Cup at Willington. A crowd of a thousand saw Brandon Welfare gain a smart victory over Wolsingham by winning 1—0.

Another disastrous fire occurred in Brandon. Durham City Fire Brigade was called out to an outbreak of fire in a hut on the site of a former colliery pond near the Co-operative Stores Branch. The wooden structure, the property of Hopper Brothers, newsagents, was completely gutted, and two motor cycles were lost in the blaze.

During the week the 'C' Pit's target of 2250 tons was beaten by four tons, news reached the colliery of the frightful disaster at Easington Colliery when eighty-three men including two rescue workers, perished underground. A deputy in charge of Laurie Moran's district in the 'C' Pit, was one of the rescue men sent to the stricken pit. He returned to Brandon unhurt physically but his experiences underground at Easington left indelible memories.

A collection was taken for the Easington Pit Disaster Fund when Brandon Colliery Silver Band led by Joe Mains, gave a programme of music at Brandon Welfare Ground.

Another county pit disaster occurred, close on the heels of Easington Colliery; Eppleton's colliery explosion claimed nine lives.

Both colliery tragedies dampened spirits at the sixty-eighth Miners' Gala when Clem Attlee M.P., Herbert Morrison M.P., Michael Foot M.P., and A. L. Horner, Secretary of the National Union of Mineworkers, occupied the platforms. Sweltering heat greeted the largest crowd in the eighty years history of the 'Big Meeting'.

As usual the Gala attracted the fairground confraternity. Young miners and their girl friends congregated while their elders digested the words uttered by so many eminent politicians.

At Durham Miners' Gala a man went to a shooting gallery on the fairground. The 'sitting birds' were clay pipes. He paid for six shots and blazed away at the ornaments. Three were broken to fragments. 'That's three', he said to the man in charge of the stall, 'I'll have one of those clay pipes please'.

Three Brandon 'grooms wed three Brandon brides: R. Robinson married Miss E. Routledge. Both school teachers, they were married at Mount Calvary Church. Another Mount Calvary Church wedding took place between Beatrice Ann Bussey of Newcastle Street and Raymond Dixon of Red Courts. St. John's Church was chosen by Harold Reed and Elizabeth Gibbs for their wedding ceremony.

Brandon Colliery Welfare started the season in fine form by beating Wheatley Hill Social Club 5—2 at Brandon and playing a 1—1 draw with Bishop Auckland Reserves on their own ground.

Three hundred people witnessed retiring Beauty Queen Joyce Chance, welcome Brandon Colliery's fifth Annual Flower and Sports Show's Beauty Queen Ingrid Swinburne at the eve-of-the-show dance held in the British Legion Hall, Meadowfield. On the following day five thousand paid admission to the Flower Show.

Harry Dodds (51) died at his home, 9 Newcastle Street. He worked in the mine at Sacriston and came to Brandon thirty-four years ago and had been a colliery deputy-overman for the past fifteen years.

John William Kelley (Johnnie) met an early and tragic death. Forty-one year old Johnnie left his home, 22 Albert Street, to enjoy the final of a County Bowls Competition at Darlington some seventeen miles away. On his return home he was knocked down by a vehicle on the Great North Road at Aycliffe. He leaves a widow and six children.

George Glasgow of Briar Avenue, Sawmills Estate, travelled to London with workmate Thomas Burke of Langley Moor to receive the British Empire Medal awarded to them for gallantry when the River Browney, flood swollen, burst into the workings of Littleburn Colliery. It will be recalled that both men were prominent in saving men and ponies from the flooded pit galleries.

Well-known in Brandon Colliery, Joseph Clough and his wife Liza celebrated their golden wedding. They have five sons and four daughters, thirty-four grandchildren and five great-grandchildren.

Robert Foster of 94 Greta Street, Aberdare, New South Wales, Australia, submitted another report of Brandonians' activities in that far off continent.

The Brandonians met at Cessnock and there was a crowded hall with seventy-three adults and a number of juniors present.

Ike Hewitt opened the proceedings and said it was pleasing that they had a clean sheet as regards casualties during the war.

The entertaining artistes were better than ever; Bob Jones, Bob Lumley, Mrs. J. Robinson, Matt Armstrong, Mrs. Basil Basey, Bill Foster and Tom Brown all sang lustily. Everyone was sorry when midnight arrived.

With the singing of 'Auld Lang Syne' and 'Maori Farewell' the party ended. People from Western and Aberdare boarded their buses while taking part in community singing.

All said goodbye for another twelve months with the hope that they will be spared for many more Brandon reunions.

Robson Miller, Brandon Colliery, married Margaret Vest at St. John's Church, Meadowfield. Robson's grandfather, another Robson died at the age of eighty-two after a lifetime of toil. He had lived in Brandon Colliery for forty-eight years.

Catherine Humphries (78) had resided at Brandon for over sixty years and was the widow of Ralph Moody Humphries. She died at 28 Commercial Street and leaves six sons and four daughters.

Thomas Carr (42), 12 Red Ridges, died in hospital after a brief illness. A locomotive driver at the colliery, Thomas was born at Brandon one of twin sons of the late County Councillor Tom Carr.

Seventy-six year old Brandon Colliery veteran John George Wilkinson, died at the Aged Miners' Homes. Affectionately known as Geordie Wilkie, he was a pit deputy of the old breed; he knew how to deal with men and management. George had resided at Brandon for over sixty years. He began pit work at the age of twelve and retired after completing fifty years service to Messrs. Straker and Love. He held the position of deputy-overman for thirty years. He was a founder member of Brandon Social Club. Many years ago he kept goal for Brandon Albion Football Club.

A good game was seen at Langley Park when the home team drew 3—3 with Brandon Colliery Welfare in the Central League. Brandon are currently placed in the middle of the Durham Central League.

When Geordie came home from the football match he remarked to his wife that he had 'seen the game for nowt'.

The wife: 'Why, how did you manage that?'

Geordie replied, 'Ah climbed ower the wooden fencing'. His wife said it was a mean trick and made him sit down and send off the gate money.

This Geordie did, saying 'Ah saw the players on Saturday and am forwarding the money'.

The secretary promptly replied, 'I received your letter enclosing a shilling, but you didn't say which player you wanted!'

It is said that revenge is sweet, and it must have been to Dave Brandon, the Langley Park-based boxer, when he knocked out Charlie Curry, Coatbridge, in the first of a six round contest. This was a return bout, Dave having lost on points in September.

Dave has never been fitter than at present and he will add many more victories to his credit. He showed what a true sportsman he is by helping to assist Curry from the ring, the latter being injured when he fell to the canvas from a beautiful right hook.

Peter Kelly the hard-hitting Brandon miner, caused something of a sensation when he fought an Amateur Boxing Association representative at ten stones. Conceding weight, height and reach Kelly won on points after a gruelling four rounds bout. Peter who fights for New Brancepeth, took part in the eliminating bouts for the National Coal Board Championships.

Houghton Miners' Welfare Hall was full to capacity for the N.C.B. Boxing Contest. An interesting encounter was the welter-weight contest between Peter and W. Jefferson (Jarrow Community Centre) when after some spirited boxing, the latter was knocked out with only five seconds to go.

Dave Brandon had two wins in quick succession. He defeated Tommy Burns (Manchester) at Middlesbrough. The fight was stopped after three rounds when Burns had a badly cut lip. At that stage Brandon was well ahead on points. Dave's next fight took him to Darlington where he defeated Syd Plummer from Billingham by a technical knock-out in the fifth of an eight round contest.

The year saw two pay rises for miners. Underground workers were awarded seven shillings a week, making their minimum wage £6.7s. and the surface workers five shillings increase, making their minimum wage £5.10s. This rise was followed by a further increase of 13s.6d. and 11s. a week respectively.

Good Christmas news for miners! A further concession was granted—an entitlement to two weeks' annual holiday with pay. Miners are now head of the table of industrial workers' earnings.

1952

George Dobson, North Street, retired colliery official and Superintendent, Mid-Durham Corps, St. John's Ambulance Brigade, has retired from the Brigade after forty years' service. He is a serving Brother of the Order of St. John of Jerusalem. For twenty years he was a pit deputy-overman followed by twenty-three years as a pit overman.

Thomas Blenkinsop, 7 Aged Miners' Homes, has also retired from the St. John Ambulance Brigade after thirty-eight years' devoted service. Like George Dobson, he is a serving Brother of the Order of St. John of Jerusalem. He is seventy-seven years of age.

George Lee held the position as ambulance attendant at Brandon Colliery, where he had worked for fifty-three years. He had been an instructor in first aid and home nursing since 1912. Always on call day and night, he too, joined the foregoing in their retirement.

Another long service employee of Straker and Love has retired. Jim Spence has served their Brancepeth and Brandon Collieries as an electrician for forty-one years. He was appointed head electrician in 1918 and has been responsible for the electrification of the whole of Pit House Colliery, both on the surface and underground, as well as the remainder of Brandon Colliery. Mr. and Mrs. Spence live in Church Street.

National Coal Board Boxing Finals. Contests in every grade were arranged to be fought at St. James' Hall, Newcastle. Light welter-weight Peter Kelly, a Brandon 'C' Pit datal worker aged twenty-one, is a member of New Brancepeth Colliery Welfare Boxing Club and has been boxing for five years. In the divisional novices' finals last year he was narrowly outpointed by a more experienced boxer and is confident of going far this year in the national competition.

Peter fights an aggressive two-handed boxer in nineteen year old Dave Lumley of Langley Park who is a member of Hamsteels Boys' Club. The bout between Lumley, a member of one of the best amateur boxing families in the county, and Kelly should be one of the highlights of the divisional event.

Laurie Moran along with other boxing fans, was disappointed—yet proud—when a good knockout was gained by Peter (No. 5 Area) put down Dave (No. 5 Area) for the count in the first round of their national light welterweight fight. Peter will go forward to the next stage. His followers had expected to witness a long skilful fight.

'Sure', said Mike to Pat, 'you're a fine one. Why did yez run away whin Finnegan offered to fight ye? It's a coward ye are an' all!'

'Well Moike', returned Pat, 'Oi'd rayther be a coward foive minutes than a corpse for the rest ov me loife'.

A Communal Hall was opened on February 16th. Residents of the thirty-six bungalows erected by Brandon Urban Council at a cost of £36,000 are delighted with the hall which will serve as a communal recreation centre for aged residents.

A large congregation consisting of members of Brandon Urban Council, Women's Institutes, Old Aged Pensioners' Associations and other Associations attended a memorial service at St. John's Church in commemoration of the late King George VI who died on Wednesday February 6th.

Doctors fought for six months to save the life of twenty-one year old William Dodds, soldier son of Mr. and Mrs. George Dodds, 5 Victoria Avenue, before he died in King's College Hospital, London, suffering from a rare wasting disease that had defied the efforts of some of the finest medical brains in the country. William was one of only three people in the world known to be suffering from the disease, his father was told on his visit to see his son. One of the victims lives in America and some of the drugs used on this patient were flown to England. At the time he became ill, William was serving with the Buckinghamshire Light Infantry in Cyprus.

Two Brandon brothers serving with the Forces, Corporal Richard Clarke, Royal Army Ordnance Corps, and Lance-Corporal Edward Clarke, Royal Artillery, sons of Mr. and Mrs. Dicky Clarke, 23 Greyridge Estate, who had not seen each other for over three years, met in Hong Kong.

Good football was produced on a tricky pitch covered with snow and ice, witnessed by a meagre attendance when Brandon Colliery Welfare entertained Langley Park Colliery Welfare. Brandon emerged the winners 4—2.

Brandon were again worthy victors when they visited Chilton to play their Athletic for their Central League Cup game. The former reached their fourth semi-final. Brandon now entertain Wolsingham in this semi-final.

Alf Turner and Miss D. Irving, a Brandon couple, were married in St. John's Church. Vera Park, Brandon and John Nelson, New Brancepeth, were wed in the Wesley Church at Brandon. Austin Keenan and Sheila Byrne, Brandon were married at St. Patrick's Church, Langley Moor.

Geordie and Meg had been courting for many years, when she suddenly realised that they were getting old, and no sign of a match.

Next time they met she said, 'Geordie, dissent thoo think it was time we wor gettin' wed?'

'Wey, Meg, hinney', replied Geordie, 'Aa've often thowt of that, but, ye beggor, whe wad hev us?'

In the House of Commons J. D. Murray, M.P., asked the Minister of Housing and Local Government if he was aware that mining subsidence at Brandon Colliery is having a disturbing effect on one hundred and sixty miners and their families; if he will consult with the National Coal Board on this matter, and if he will also consider increasing the Council's allocation of houses to meet this situation.

Irene Dodds (26), daughter of Mr. H. Dodds, 9 Newcastle Street, and the late Harry Dodds, died in hospital at Chester-le-Street. She had been employed for seven years at Langley Moor. At her funeral a guard of honour was formed by forty of her colleagues from Hirst and Thackeray's factory.

Brandon Colliery Welfare entered their third and fourth final of the season when they defeated Kibblesworth Welfare by a goal to nil in the semi-final of the Birtley Aged Miners' Cup at Birtley; and when Lewellin United fell 2—1 in the semi-final of the Brancepeth Aged Miners' Cup. On both occasions a large crowd witnessed a good game.

Brandon's footballers, who have enjoyed much success this season, won their second trophy when more than a thousand spectators saw a keen encounter between the home club and Mackays Sports Club (one time Brandon's arch enemy) on the Brandon Welfare Ground in the Brandon Aged Miners' Cup. The home team won by the odd goal of three.

Brandon Colliery Welfare has formed a cricket club and thus became the first cricket team to operate in the area during the last seventeen years. Brandon showed promise by defeating Esh Winning II by three wickets in their first home match in Division B of the Mid-Durham League.

Sammy, the crack performer of the colliery cricket team, made a very short stay at the wicket and retired with a 'duck' to his discredit.

'Ah!' said the curate, who was captain of the eleven, 'you didn't do a well as last week, Sam'.

'Noa', agreed Sam significantly as he threw his bat into a corner of the pavilion. 'Last week Aa stopped in, Aa did, an' myeud hi-ty two, an' when Aa cam' oot Aa found thaat ye blighters had drunk arl the beor'.

Brandon gained their second victory in two attempts when they had forty-seven runs to spare over their Willington II visitors. Third time unlucky! Brandon found Tudhoe II too strong for them and went down by eight wickets after making sixty-eight against Tudhoe's seventy-three for two.

Bowlers versus cricketers at Brandon. The Colliery Welfare Bowls Club had a friendly match with Brandon Welfare cricketers, the latter winning an enjoyable match by thirteen runs.

Brandon Colliery Miners' Lodge made a gift of £1 each to all retired workmen and widows. The hand-out happily coincided with the annual outing to Seaburn of over three hundred pensioners of Brandon Old Aged Pensioners' Association. Ten motor coaches conveyed them to the coast.

The sixth annual Brandon Flower Show was an unqualified success. Six thousand sun soaked visitors shared the thrills pony scampering provided, along with an archery display, fancy dress parade, band contest, model aeroplane flying, photography exhibits, safety mining display, dog show, flower show and arts and crafts.

Teresa Wallace was Beauty Queen accompanied by attendants Elizabeth Richardson and Mary Dixon, was crowned by the retiring Beauty Queen Miss Ingrid Swinburne.

It is hoped that last year's deficit of £120.9s.1d. will be wiped out. The hard working committee of colliery folk deserve great credit.

Able Seaman William Jackson had time to reflect on home and parents left behind in Princess Street as he took up his duty as look-out aboard ship, he is a member of a Bofor gun's crew serving on the naval frigate 'Whitesand Bay' serving off the coast of Korea.

George Lee, retired Brandon Colliery ambulance attendant, made the long journey to London's St. Bartholomew's Hospital; his presence was required at an investiture. He was an Officer (Brother) of the Order of St. John of Jerusalem. The honour was bestowed on him in 1949, but the investiture has been deferred until now. George retired two years ago after completing fifty-four years at the colliery.

Another long serving Brandonian, Bill Bullows, eighty-one year old retired miner living at 17 Commercial Street, is the only survivor of the first Brandon Colliery Brass Band formed in 1889. He was employed at the colliery for fifty-five years, retiring two years ago.

Abel Hopkins, a retired Brandon Colliery miner, was presented with a badge and certificate by the National Brass Band Association to mark over fifty-five years' membership of Brandon Colliery Silver Band. He was made a member of the National Brass Band Club.

Abel is one of four brothers who have been connected with Brandon Band. One brother, who was killed in Italy during the first world war, was a bandsman with the Durham Light Infantry. Another brother, Councillor David Hopkins, is a former secretary. His youngest brother, the late Wilfred Hopkins, was a trombone player.

Both Abel Hopkins and William Bullows would attend the sixty-ninth Miners' Gala. They had proudly played the colliery banner onto Durham's racecourse on so many occasions.

The Gala was blessed with day long sunshine; Laurie Moran and his mate Steve Murthur joined the crowd, many of whom were in shirt sleeves, when Aneurin Bevan M.P., Sir Hartley Shawcross Q.C., M.P., Miss Margaret Herbison and A. L. Horner spoke.

Dave Brandon, the hard hitting Langley Park based welterweight, had an easy victory at West Hartlepool when he knocked out Fred Archer (Hucknall) in the first round of their scheduled six round contest. This augurs well for his meeting with Danny Molloy, the well-known Scottish welterweight, at St. James', Newcastle.

For the last fifteen years Elizabeth Ann Maddison has lived alone at 4 Aged Miners' Homes, Brandon. A life-long Methodist, she celebrated her ninetieth birthday at the home of Mr. and Mrs. Charles Brown of 9 Queen Street. Born at Willington, Elizabeth Ann has lived at Brandon Colliery for over forty years. In her younger days she had 'to work hard for very little'.

She was one of the first scholars of Mount Calvary Methodist Sunday School and of the church which was built seventy years ago. Guests at her party included nine life members of the Mount Calvary Church. Mrs. Cairns aged 88, Mrs. Maughan 88, Miss Pratt 85, Mrs. Taylor 79, Miss Beresford 76, Mrs. Sayer 74, Mrs. Smart 68, Mrs. Kirby 68. Miss Pratt, daughter of the late John Pratt, the first choirmaster, recalls how her father, along with other pioneers, hewed the stone out of the quarry at Brandon Village to build the church.

Mr. and Mrs. J. McMahan's children, Terence, Kathleen, Thersa and Anthony, all took home prizes at Durham St. Leonard's speech day. They live in Brandon's Red Courts.

Two Brandon girls had an August wedding when Miss F. Myers married William Atkinson at Brandon Independent Methodist Church, the bridegroom hails from West Rainton. Esther Stock wed Michael Brian Kelly of Sunderland Road, Durham at St. Patrick's Church, Langley Moor.

Norah Moran, the eldest of the Moran family, married Tom Maguire from nearby Meadowfield, in St. Patrick's Church, Langley Moor.

John Moran married in 1948 moved into a colliery house, 27 High Street, two years later. After two years John and his family have moved into their second home in the colliery's Albert Street.

While Brandon Colliery's population was spending the day at Redcar, Mrs. M. Richardson brought a title home to the village. She won the ladies' single bowls at the County National Coal Board finals at Blackpool.

Another local contingent visited South Shields, another popular resort. Alan Richardson, fourteen year old son of Mr. and Mrs. Dickie Richardson, 4 Queen Street, one of the party, is to be highly commended for his brave action in saving a girl from drowning. Alan, a keen swimmer, was assisted in his efforts by John Bell of Brandon, when Pat Pearson, on holiday with her grandmother at Meadowfield, got into difficulties while bathing.

Brandon 'C' Pit claimed yet another victim when William Dickinson (Maddison) not long returned to work after the pit's annual holiday, was fatally injured by a fall of stone. Forty-five year old Billy, of 21 Sunderland Street, was following his employment as a coal filler. He leaves a widow and three children.

Billy's one-time overman at the 'C' Pit, Joe Teasdale, died in hospital. He was sixty-nine and had been retired four years and lived in Fir Avenue, Sawmills Estate.

Another 'C' Pit worker succumbed to injuries received at the colliery. Steel officer Len Vickers aged fifty-nine, was descending the 'C' Pit shaft with shaft onsetter Herbie Hobson and Norman King. The cage had dropped about ten feet when its descent was suddenly arrested. Len Vickers sustained a fractured spine, Herbert a fractured pelvis and Norman a foot injury. Len died in hospital some six hours later.

Concern was expressed by members of Brandon Urban Council at their meeting concerning the question of damage and the worsening conditions of the National Coal Board houses at Brandon Colliery caused by the removal of a pillar of coal. Councillor David Hopkins said that another twenty to forty more houses were urgently needed for the people of Brandon Colliery who have been affected by the subsidence.

At the same meeting the clerk asked for authority to apply to the Ministry of Housing and Local Government for the loan of £15,878 to build twelve houses at Sawmills Lane.

William Dowdle seventy-five, worked in the mine for fifty-nine years and retired four years ago. He moved from the colliery's Sunderland Street, due for demolition, to Briar Avenue on the new Sawmills Estate where he died. For some years he was an auditor of Brandon Miners' Lodge. Since his retirement he had devoted much of his time in the interests of the old folk and served on the committee of Brandon Old Aged Pensioners' Association. William would have been interested in the proposed forming of an 'Over 60 Club' mooted at a meeting in the Communal Hall.

Christmas held new marvels for Laurie Moran and his wife Theresa. A new television set graced their sitting room. Laurie's back pay due from a rise in wages awarded to deputies and shot-firers, enabled him to become the fourth television owner to flaunt an aerial on the three rows of Browney Colliery.

Carol singers toured Brandon district on Christmas Eve. Brandon Colliery Silver Band played carols on Christmas Day.

1953

The Ambulance Drill Hall was crowded when three hundred aged pensioners attended the New Year party organised by Brandon Old Aged Pensioners' Association. Before the commencement of the party silence was observed in memory of two lately deceased members, William Dowdle and Mrs. R. G. Williams.

Spectators braved a strong wind and enjoyed the spectacular goal scoring New Year game of football when Brandon Colliery Welfare were at home to Chilton Athletic in a Central League fixture and ran out winners by six goals to four.

In February both underground and surface workers were granted a wage increase of six shillings. This latest rise makes the minimum weekly wage of the former £7.7s.6d. and that of the surface workers £6.7.6d.

Just as the racing fraternity was discussing the vaunted Grand National (a bus load of enthusiasts left Brandon bound for Liverpool), Mr. A. C. Longford was installed as new minister of Mount Calvary Methodist Church.

A curate had just been transferred to a country town. One day he was asked by one of his parishioners to offer prayers on the following Sunday for Phoebe Flynn.

The parson readily agreed and, on request, repeated the prayers on two more Sundays. After the third Sunday, the parishioners approached the curate and told him it was no longer necessary to pray for Phoebe Flynn.

'Why?' asked the curate. 'Has she died or recovered from her illness?'

'Oh, neither', replied the other. 'She's won the Grand National'.

Brandon 'C' Pit workmen and residents of New Brancepeth where Peter Kelly trains are interested in his progress in amateur boxing. He has followers from both colliery villages.

National Coal Board Boxing Finals scheduled to take place at Durham Ice Rink for the the first time include Peter of Red Ridges, Brandon Colliery, but due to a chain of unfortunate circumstances he will box in a special contest. Peter is a datal worker at Brandon 'C' Pit and has steadily improved as an amateur boxer. Since winning the novice title, he has always been a divisional finalist in the national competition. His two-handed boxing has made him a strong local favourite in the county and this season he won the lightweight A.B.A. finals in the division.

Dave Brandon, Langley Park boxer had a terrific battler with Bunty Adamson, the welterweight champion of Northern Ireland, in Belfast when they topped the bill in an eight round contest.

Brandon suffered a first round setback when his left eye was cut in a collision with Adamson. He carried on to give one of the best performances of his career. At the start of the last round there could not have been much in it, but misfortune again befell him when his right eye was cut and he had to retire. The crowd gave him a great ovation as he left the ring.

Peter Kelly was one of the guests at a dance organised by Brandon Colliery Amalgamated Sports Club in the Ex-servicemen's Hall. Peter, aged twenty-three, winner of the National Coal Board lightweight boxing championship held at Stoke, was presented with a wrist watch. Councillor David Hopkins made the presentation. Peter holds a string of trophies won at boxing. His proud parents, Mr. and Mrs. William Kelly, live at 18 Red Ridges.

Dave Brandon took time off from boxing when he was best man as his brother George's wedding. He and George journeyed to Doncaster where George married Miss L. Ford.

George Miller of 13 Princess Street married Norma Brown at St. John's, Meadowfield. William Lockey made up the trio of Brandon 'grooms when he married Maureen Whyalt in St. Giles' Church, Durham.

Three long-serving club officials with a total of seventy years to their credit, were presented with long service certificates. Arthur Stock presided at the presentation in Brandon Social Club. The recipients were Matty Wilkinson, chairman; Anty Howden, treasurer and Jack Higgins, secretary.

Edward Duffy of 32 Newcastle Street, died at the age of sixty-five in hospital after a long illness. He leaves a widow, four sons and five daughters.

Another miner invalid, Mick Robinson, 11 High Street, died in Dryburn Hospital after a long illness. Mick, aged sixty, was born at Brandon and began work in the mine at the age of thirteen. He retired from his work as waggon-way man in Brandon's 'C' Pit five years ago owing to ill health.

William McKay spent all his life in the area and had worked for half a century in the mine. A keen pigeon flyer, he was formerly a playing member of Brandon Swifts Football Club, and was a member of Brandon Social Club. William died at 9 Cobden Terrace in his sixty-eighth year.

On Coronation Day, May 2nd when Princess Elizabeth becomes Her Majesty Queen Elizabeth II, Brandon Urban Council will present a Coronation mug to every child, and a cup and saucer to each person sixty-five and over. The chairman Councillor Jack Milmore, will light a bonfire on the area's highest point, Pit House, at ten o'clock on Coronation night.

Dave Brandon once again figured in the boxing news. He was matched to fight Phil Mellish (Stalybridge) at the Durham Ice Rink; this being the first time the rink has been used for boxing.

Harry Warner (Dagenham) stood in for Dave on the night of the contest. About two thousand saw Warner and Phil Mellish provide the best bout of the evening.

Dave Brandon is now managed by Bruce Woodcock, Doncaster, where Dave now lives and trains.

A pitman from the age of twelve, a veteran of World War I awarded the Croix de Guerre for meritorious service on the battlefield, John Duncan Rutherford (Jack), 40 Albert Street, died in hospital. Jack, aged fifty-nine was forced to retire from the mine two years ago owing to ill-health.

During the second week of June Brandon 'C' Pit failed to reach its target of 2,525 tons by 495 tons.

Brandon Coronation Sports postponed from Coronation Day May 2nd, when the greatest amount of rain fell in one day, were held in the Welfare Ground.

A fance dress parade was led by the Centre Ward Queen, seventeen year old Mary Dixon of Queen Street and her attendants, headed by Brandon Silver Band. Brandon Modern School and St. Patrick's R.C. School provided a good display of sports. Each child received lemonade and a souvenir box of sweets. A bonfire was lit at 8 p.m. followed by fireworks which concluded a memorable event.

To mark the completion of their thousandth post war house, Brandon Urban Council held an official opening ceremony. They had built one thousand houses at an approximate cost of £1,500,000 or £1,600 per house.

A Durham miner who was difficult to suit with houses, was about to shift for the sixth time in a few months. He always got the same man to remove his belongings.

Up came the cart to the door, and Geordie noticed a hay fork on the flat, and said to the driver, 'What ivvor in the world hes thoo fetched the hay fork for?'

'What hev Aa fetched the hay fork for? Why', replied the driver, 'thoo knaas wat a job we had ter get the mattress on the cart the last time'.

Brandon Lodge banner attended the seventieth Miners' Big Meeting. The lodge was formed in 1882, and on July 18th 1884 a resolution was passed detailing a woman to stitch the lodge banner before proceeding to the gala at the end of that week. The membership of the lodge at that time was six hundred, today it is seventeen hundred.

Brandon Miners' Lodge appointed twelve banner carriers for this year's Gala, each man will receive two pounds. They are J. Burlison, E. Atkinson, J. Simpson, George Miller, Tommy Barnes, T. Robinson, W. Smith, Bill Prudhoe, E. Halliday, F. Johnson and Dicky Dennis.

It was decided at the annual meeting of the 'Welfare' to form a junior eleven and disband the seniors.

Brandon Colliery Welfare Juniors have selected for their first officials chairman, David White; secretary, J. J. Dixon; treasurer, G. Sykes; committee, F. Cooke, J. and G. Warriner, R. Holmes, R. Dixon, J. Collins, E. Staley, Jesse Marchant, S. Birchnall.

Brandon Welfare Committee has been very generous as regards equipment for the new junior club.

The Juniors opened their season with a visit from Ushaw Moor and gave a promising display in winning 11–2 after a good, fast game. Bullows netted six, Ditchburn two, Boal two and Jones one.

Charles McGarry died at the age of 63 at his home 11 Grey Gables, following a long illness. Born at Durham, he spent the greater part of his life at Brandon. He worked in the mine at Browney and Brandon. He was a former player with Durham City Rugby Club, and until his illness was a member of St. Patrick's R.C. Football Club.

Brandon Colliery veteran George Miller (88) died at his home, 22 Victoria Avenue. He began work in the mine at the age of eleven and completed sixty-five years' work there twelve years ago.

Something new in Brandon! A pony gymkhana attracted seven hundred people. A rider from Stanley was thrown and sustained a fractured collar bone. A line of bookies was present and was kept busy during the numerous races.

Mr. and Mrs. Nichol Westgarth celebrated their golden wedding. Nichol came to Brandon Colliery fifty years ago and rose to the position of fore-overman. He retired seven years ago after having filled an official position at the colliery for thirty-eight years.

During the first week of October Brandon 'C' Pit produced 2,910 tons of coal, thus beating their target of 2,525 tons by some 385 tons.

John Thomas Cauwood (47) of Grove Road, Sawmills Estate, died. Jackie was well known in the area in which he was born and spent all his life and worked in Brandon's 'C' Pit.

After a long illness fifty-eight year old Joseph Carroll died at his home, 31 Queen Street. He came to Brandon twenty-seven years ago. At the outbreak of the First World War he enlisted with the Durham Light Infantry and was invalided home in 1917.

The nation can look forward to a brighter Christmas now that sugar rationing is ended. Britain is slowly moving to normality after more than eight years of peace. Cheese, still rationed, is increased from one and a half ounces to two ounces per week over a period of eight weeks. Identity cards were abolished last year.

Dave Brandon

'Aa want an oonce o' cheese, hinney, an' Aa hope ye'll not be as impedent as the last one that wes in this shop. Ivvory time As axed for an ounce o' cheese he axed me if Aa was gan te git company'.

'Wey', answered the new boy with a amile, 'he must hev been daft, 'cos anybody wad knaa that ye wor just gettin' it to bait a mouse trap'.

When matchmaker Jack McBeth paired the hard-hitting Teesside fighter Malcolm Pidgeon of South Bank against the rugged Langley Park figher Dave Brandon, in an eight round welterweight contest, on November 10th 1953, at the Durham Ice Rink, he knew that he was on a winner.

The bout which was promoted by Mr. 'Icey' Smith, turned out to be the bloodiest and must punishing ever seen in the city.

Pidgeon, a teenage steelworker, was a walk-in exciting slugger, who would take two punches to land one of his devastating left hooks. As a successful amateur, Pidgeon had won 103 out of 105 bouts. Since turning professional under the management of Eric Munro, Malcolm has accounted for Johnny Delmore, Tom Cattman, Ray Dixon and Phil Mellish.

Brandon, a tough, hard-punching fighter from Langley Park, who is popular in the North East fight venues, has defeated Jack Thomas, Jimmy Brogden, Fred Archer, Dave Fisher, Rosco Long, Danny Malloy and Jerry Leary. Dave has also drawn with Peter Smith and lost on cuts to Ernie Vickers in a savage battle at Newcastle.

At the weigh-in Pidgeon scaled ten stones nine pounds, whilst the Langley Park fighter came in at ten stones seven and a half pounds.

From the start it was a rip-roaring contest. The fight was only a minute old, when Brandon landed two left jabs, then whipped over a hard right, which split the Teesside fighter's left eyebrow and the blood cascaded down his face. Pidgeon, his vision blurred, was off-target with the blows for the rest of the round, whilst Dave scored with his left.

Excellent corner work between the rounds, stemmed the flow of blood and round two saw Malcolm forcing the fight, stalking forward in his own inimitable style, scoring well with power-laden left and right hooks to the body and head. Brandon, bobbing and weaving fought on the retreat, drawing his rivals leads and countering with lightning left jabs and right crosses to the head. During the third, Pidgeon's left hooking to the head had the Langley Park fighter's nose bleeding profusely.

Round four saw the Teessider scoring with heavy hooks. Then the crowd applauded loudly as the Durham County fighter cracked over three hard rights in succession on his rival's injured eye. Rounds five and six were fought savagely as both fighters sought to dominate the contest, giving and taking heavy punishment and were covered in blood.

First, the Teessider would score with heavy lefts and rights, then the more versatile Brandon would reply with jolting left jabs and heavy rights to the head, which pulled Pidgeon up in his tracks. Rounds seven and eight were the most punishing, as both contestants who were both bleeding heavily, stood and exchanged heavy punches, both being rocked in turn, whilst the capacity crowd stood and applauded the two brave fighters.

As the final bell sounded, the referee walked over, separated the fighters and amidst tumultuous applause, declared the fight a draw. Both fighters later needed medical attention.

Dave is booked to fight Danny Cunningham (Glasgow), one of Scotland's best welterweights, at the Ice Rink.

To end a good year's boxing, Peter Kellly (National Coal Board Champion) beat Tommy Surplus (Joe Walton's Boys' Club).

1954

A New Year pay rise cheered Brandon Colliery miners when underground workers were granted 8s.6d. and surface workers 7s.6d. per week. Minimum weekly wage is now £7.15s. underground and £6.15s. for surface men.

Nurse Mary Jane Donegan Ramsey (66) died at Brandon. Daughter of the late Mr. and Mrs. Edward Ramsey, Brandon, Nurse Ramsey was at one time a pupil at the old Brandon Council School, and the Church of England School at Brandon Village. She was a Sunday School teacher at St. Agatha's Church, Brandon until she entered the nursing profession forty-two years ago.

Brandon Colliery lost a prominent figure with the death of Councillor Tom Dickinson. He was miners' checkweighman at Brandon for twenty-three years and had served sixty-one years in the mining industry. Native of Cumberland, he began work at the age of eleven as a surface worker and went into the mine at fourteen. He was chosen to succeed the late Thomas Carr as chairman of the miners' lodge.

Henry Blenkinsop (Harry) had lived in Brandon all his life until his sudden death at the age of fifty-nine. He began work at the colliery when he reached the age of fourteen. In the first world war he served in the D.L.I. and Royal Engineers and was gassed. He was actively associated with Brandon Flower Show and Sports Committee.

Charles Nixon Paulin (66) retired colliery winding-engineman of Grove Road, had a seizure while in a Durham theatre, he was removed to Dryburn Hospital where he died on admittance. He was well known in the district, highly esteemed, and took part in numerous activities.

The Ministry of Housing and Local Government approved an estimate for sixty-four houses to be built at Brandon's Carr Avenue.

Winding-engineman Joseph Howden was elected secretary of Brandon Colliery branch of the Durham County Enginemen's Association, a post held by the late Charles Paulin.

Peter Kelly successfully defended his lightweight title when he represented New Brancepeth Welfare Amateur Boxing Club, in the North-East Counties' Amateur Boxing Association Championships. Peter, a Brandon Colliery miner, had two fights, scoring a knock-out over Norman Holiday, Darlington, in the first round, and meeting in the final Tommy Surplis. Peter knocked out Surplis in the third round.

Brandon couple Michael Anderson and Margaret McGarry were married at St. Patrick's Church, Langley Moor. Another Brandon bridegroom, Martin Dowse, married Miss M. Robinson at St. Patrick's.

Easter-time saw four of Brandon's young men married when W. Brown wed Miss Jean Pickhard at Bearpark; R. Brown married Miss Marjorie Jones of Langley Moor; Ernest Buckley wed Enid Matthew and George Hesp took Marion Gough as his bride.

To the consternation of the guests the Vicar was very late for the ceremony.

Years afterwards he met the bridegroom, and taking him by the hand remarked, 'Well John, it's ten years since I gave you an awful fright'.

'Aye', said John sadly. 'Aa wish thoo hadn't turned up: Aa still hev hor'.

'So Geordie's gettin' married? Is the banns up?'
'Oh, aye — nee smokin', nee drinkin' and nee bettin'.''

James Henry Walton died at 29 Newcastle Street. Jim, a native of Stanhope, was sixty-seven, he had lived in Brandon for twenty-five years. After working fifty-one years in the mining industry he retired two years ago. He was an ex-amateur footballer and a pigeon fancier associated with Brandon Society. Four daughters and four sons survive.

Bachelor Robert Flather died at the premature age of thirty-three. His home was 27 Grey Ridge.

At weekends shaftsman Thomas Chicken would be standing astride the 'C' Pit cage as it left the silent heapstead to make his inspection of the pit shaft. A joiner by trade, he had lived in the Brandon area for thirty-six years. Tommy aged seventy-five, died in St. Margaret's Hospital, Durham.

John Robert Heron completed the quartet of deaths when he died twenty-five years after his retirement. Jack, aged ninety-three, died at his home, 6 Church Street. Born at Sunnybrow, he began work at the age of eleven as a messenger at the colliery owned by Straker and Love. He later became a colliery clerk and transferred to Brandon Colliery about seventy years ago. He was for many years manager of the hundreds of bee-hive coke ovens surrounding the two colliery shafts.

After representatives of the Centre Ward received complaints from residents of High Street and Newcastle Street the Council laid down rat poison in various parts of the two long streets. People spoke of a 'plague of rats' in the area.

A woman will preside for the first time at a Brandon Urban District Council meeting. Seven years ago Mrs. Phoebe Lidster became the first woman to be elected to B.U.D.C. Handing over the chain of office, Councillor Jack Millmore wished her good health for her term of office.

George Aither, rabbit fancier of local renown, added further honours to his lengthy list when his grey-brown Dutch rabbit won six firsts and a special for best in the show at Chester-le-Street and Birtley Fur and Feather Society's show.

A Brandon man was remanded a second time for the alleged stabbing of another colliery man after an argument in Brandon Social Club.

Brandon Co-operative Society was granted a lease of three hundred square yards of land near North Street, Brandon, for a three-year term at an annual rent of £5. Some of the buildings on the site are part of the first shops to be built in Brandon Colliery almost one hundred years ago.

Two Brandon girls opted for marriage in St. Patrick's R.C. Church, Langley Moor when Brenda Daglish wed Charles Kennick of Brandon, and when Elizabeth Taylor of Red Courts married James Mulhall of Meadowfield.

After a lingering illness Laurie Moran's mate, Steve Murthur, died at 56 Grove Road. Steve, aged thirty-eight, and Laurie were Brandon Colliery born and had been firm friends for a number of years. They had caddied at the golf links together; picked potatoes side by side; visited the sick and served in the wartime Home Guard together.

When Sam Watson opened the pit-head baths at Brandon Colliery Pit House, containing 2,128 lockers for the workers, he said that he had just returned from the Far East. 'There are two streets of houses to be abolished in Brandon. They are "palaces" to what the Chinese live in'. Brandon 'C' Pit did not qualify for pit head bathing facilities as it is deemed to have a short life.

Richard Wilson and Joseph Lonsdale, both from Brandon, married girls from neighbouring Browney Colliery and Langley Moor. Richard wed Jean Burns from Browney at St. Patrick's, Langley Moor, while Joseph took Joan Reed as his bride; they were married at St. John's, Meadowfield.

Jimmy Abson, Brandon Colliery Welfare crack bowls player, brought honour to the club when he won the county four-wood championship. The Bowls Club had another success when they entertained Addison Park, Meadowfield, in the second leg of the final of the district knock-out competition. In the first leg at Meadowfield, Brandon had won by 88 to 55 and gained the day 97 to 47 on this occasion. Isaac Pybus aged seventy-eight, one of the club's oldest playing members, was elected to play for an inter-league match on Gilesgate Welfare greens against a county side, while Harry Ball, another member, figured in the same game.

Twenty-three year old Dave 'Brandon' Ogilvie, professional boxer, second son of Mr. and Mrs. Ron Ogilvie, 29 Victoria Avenue, serving with the 2nd Battalion, the Durham Light Infantry in Germany, took part in the combined manoeuvres there. He had fought a match with a German boxer whom he disposed of in the second round. He is now a coach and physical training instructor to D. Company, and to the Battalion boxing team.

Richard Danby (Dickie) had lived all his life in the Brandon area. He began work in the mine at the age of thirteen, where he continued for fifty-two years, retiring eight years ago. He died suddenly at the home of his son-in-law and daughter, Mr. and Mrs. Dennis Harkin, Littleburn.

A large crowd saw Brandon Juniors masters in every department when they played local rivals Browney, in a Divisional Cup game. Brandon finished winners four goals to one. Browney lie third and Brandon occupy fifth place in the ten team league.

After appearing twice on remand, the Brandon Colliery miner accused of stabbing another miner was sentenced to two and a half years' imprisonment.

George Henry Jamieson was given the honour of unfurling the flag at Brandon Colliery 'C' Pit on Vesting Day. He was employed for over sixty years as an engine-plane man. He and Mrs. Jamieson celebrated their golden wedding last year. George died at the home of a daughter at Nevilles Cross, he was eighty-two.

Another old standard passed away when Councillor David Hopkins' mother died at his residence, 3 Hawthorn Park. Eighty-six years old Isabella Hopkins had lived in Brandon for seventy-eight years. Her husband, Joseph Henry Hopkins, predeceased her by eighteen years.

Once again George Aither of Albert Street secured six firsts and a special prize when he entered his young brown and grey Dutch rabbit at the Deerness Fur Society's open table show. The rabbit has won one hundred and six first prizes in fifteen months.

Brandon Miners' Lodge made a Christmas gift of one pound from the Aged People's Fund. All retired miners and widows over sixty qualified.

Brandon Social Club Committee remembered the old folks when they presented each aged member of the club with a Christmas gift of fifteen shillings.

1955

The New Year saw the customary 'first footing' and carol singing. All chapels and churches held services throughout the morning.

It was stated at the annual meeting of Brandon Colliery Silver Band that during 1953 the band secured four firsts, two seconds, two thirds and twelve specials for solo work. The band officials are: President, John D. Higgins; Chairman, Anty Howden; Secretary, W. Harvey; Assistant Secretary, James Foxcroft and Treasurer, Walter Harker.

National Savings volunteers decided to have first call on Brandon Colliery miners' pay packets. They sold savings stamps to miners as they left the colliery pay office on pay day.

Allan W. Madgin married Doris Myers in the Independent Methodist Church. John Burlison wed Margaret Maddison, both of Sawmills Estate. Both weddings were conducted by Mr. Laurie Simpson.

It was decided at the Council Meeting that Mr. W. Wilkinson, Sanitary Inspector, receive an additional sum of fifty pounds a year 'for extra responsibilities'.

Brandon Juniors were well worth their 1—0 win away over Lumley Juniors to qualify for the semi-final of the County Junior Cup. They went on to beat Seaton Holy Trinity in the semi-final. The Juniors had a successful programme over Easter when they won two and drew one of their three games. The Juniors' secretary and well-known local football referee, J. Dixon, living at 45 Red Courts, had to call Durham Fire Brigade to deal with a fire in the chimney stack which was quickly extinguished on the Brigade's arrival.

Peter Kelly, national light-weight division title holder, received a severe jolt in addition to a lot of good punches when he lost on points in a 'special bout' with seventeen year old Ernie Coates (Guisborough). When another contestant failed to appear at the National Coal Board divisional boxing championships at Birtley, Carter, who had gone to the contest as a spectator, found himself inside the ropes.

In years and appearance there looked to be a great difference, but it was a different tale when it came to exchanging punches. Kelly, who likes to mix it, must have been surprised when he found that appearances could not be taken for granted. Carter had the measure of Kelly in ringwork and was also able to take and give punishment.

Peter, one of eight Durham men, has been chosen to fight in the light-weight division at the mineworkers' national amateur boxing championships at the Royal Ordnance Factory, Barnbow, Leeds. This is the eighth season of miners' boxing and the standard has advanced so much that the championships are regarded as among the finest in Britain.

The National Union of Mineworkers recommends that Saturday working shall cease in May, June, July and August, with the provision that any lodge wishing to work during these months can do so. Full Saturday work will be restored in September. It was agreed that the extension of hours agreement should be continued for a further twelve months.

After a rousing cup-final Brandon Juniors carried off the Durham County Junior Cup, beating Leslies' Juniors from Hebburn 4–3. In addition to their victory, Brandon Juniors qualify for their league cup final when accounting for Dean and Chapter 2–0.

George Hewitt, Brandon's well-known football promoter, was awarded the British Empire Medal for service to the community.

Brandon Colliery Welfare honoured two members of the Welfare Bowls Club for outstanding success during last season. They are Mrs. N. Richardson, Brandon winner of Durham County Ladies' Singles Championship for the third year in succession, and James Abson, Brandon winner of the county open singles championship.

On behalf of the Welfare Committee, Mr. W. Everett, manager of Pit House Colliery, presented a wrist watch to the lady winner and a chromium breakfast set to Mr. Abson.

George Fairless could be seen pounding the streets of Brandon Colliery. He was the colliery caller, and his daily task was to knock on the miners' doors to ensure their presence at the pit. He retired four years ago. George, seventy-one, died at 24 North Street. He worked in the mine until the outbreak of the first world war, went to France with the Northumberland Fusiliers and lost an arm in the Battle of the Somme. After the war he became a surface worker at the colliery until his retirement.

Brandon lost three more veterans with the deaths of John Walker, seventy-nine, who had lived in Brandon since he was one year old. He had worked in the mine for more than half a century.

Thomas Underwood, the youngest of the trio at seventy-nine, began work underground at Brandon Colliery at the age of twelve and worked there for sixty-three years.

Ellen Kennedy, also seventy-nine, died at 12 College Terrace. She spent all her life in Brandon. Her husband John, four sons and three daughters survive.

The miners were in good heart on Gala Day, July 16th for the seventy-second Big Meeting. Glorious weather and a pay rise earlier in the year of 11s.6d. per week making the underground minimum weekly wage £8.6s.6d. and the surface wage £7.6s.6d. helped make their day.

Defiant speeches by Clem Attlee M.P., High Gaitskill M.P., Michael Foot and A. L. Horner, Secretary National Union of Mineworkers, made it a 'Big Meeting' to be long remembered.

Brandon's miners began their annual two weeks' holiday on 'Big Meeting' Saturday. A long hot spell was forecast for the annual break.

Chapel trips were in vogue during August which had a record one hundred and sixty hours of sunshine. There is a prolonged drought and water rationing is imminent.

The vicar of a certain mining village met one of his parishioners with her two children.

'I have not seen your two children at Sunday School for the past few Sundays', he said pleasantly.

'No, I don't suppose you have', tartly replied the mother. 'It's been so wet at the last two seaside trips that I've persuaded them to try the Wesleyans this year'.

Brandon Social Club through their able secretary Jack Higgins, arranged a trip to South Shields for four hundred old members. Twelve buses conveyed the happy crowd who each received ten shillings.

Patrick Moran now seventy-one and retired three years and Mary his wife aged sixty-nine with their son Frank, the only remaining member of the family living at home, moved from 5 Newcastle Street to number 2 Cobden Terrace. Mary, their second daughter working in Manchester, married miner Martin Healey from Browney Colliery.

Joe Defty, master leek grower, is on the warpath again with bigger and better leeks. He was top of the bench at the National Coal Board County Sports and Show held at Brandon.

Brandon showed its continued interest in flowers when it staged the Tenth Annual Exhibition of the Brandon Colliery and District Chrysanthemum Show which was an outstanding success, with blooms of a high standard. F. Whitwell, Brandon's new colliery manager, presented the prizes to the winners.

Winners of the National Coal Board Division Welfare Challenge Trophy, N.C.B. Northern Division Challenge Trophy, Dr. Crichton Challenge Cup, as well as two plaques, a third prize at Manchester, thirty medals and two miniature cups won by Kenneth Urwin for euphonium solos, is the impressive list of awards won by Brandon Colliery Silver Band.

Geordie was a trombone player in the local brass band, and had gone to see the bandmaster on important business. The following converation ensured:

Bandmaster: 'Noo Geordie, whaat's the trouble lad?'

Geordie: 'Ye'll hev te get a new trombone player, Jack'.

Bandmaster: 'Wey, whaat for? What's the matter wi thoo? Is thoo chuckin' it?'

Geordie: 'Aye, Aa'll hev te chuck it. Aa's shiftin' inter a council hoose an' there'll be ne room te practice'.

The Simpson family and North Street neighbours were plunged into mourning when a nineteen year old miner was fatally injured in a Christmas-time accident at Pit House Colliery. Thomas Simpson was caught in machinery and died in Durham County Hospital.

A well known Brandon Colliery man died at Acorn Place, Sawmills Estate. Seventy-one year old Adam Bailes was born at Sunnybrow but spent almost all of his life at Brandon, where he worked in the mine until his retirement, through ill health, twelve years ago. He was formerly a popular baritone vocalist.

Jackson Hewitson, Brandon, vice-president of Durham County Club Union and secretary of Langley Moor Social Club, has been re-elected for the twelfth year to represent Durham and Cleveland on the National Executive of the Club Union.

Brandon Social Club along with other clubs in the area, reduced the price of their drinks over the festive season. The normal price of beer is one shilling and sevenpence a pint.

Two miners were overheard discussing their experiences during the previous Saturday night:

'Aa was doon at the club', said one, 'and Aa didn't get hyem till eftor twelve o'clock'.

The other, who knew something of his friend's home life, gazed at him in astonishment. 'Ye divvent say so', he gasped. 'Why man, what aboot your wife? Did she miss ye?'

'Aye, she missed me alreet — but she put a hole in the fanleet ower the door!'

1956

Houses which had stood for almost one hundred years; one room up and one room down structures, which had seen generations of sometimes large families grow up in their restricted environs, were due for demolition. Sunderland Street and East Street came under the slum clearance order. Eager tenants left their one cold water tap for the luxury of the new estate; the luxury of an indoor bath with hot and cold running water and an indoor flush toilet held great appeal.

Miss F. Ecclestone, Brandon, married W. Richardson of New Brancepeth and Miss M. Hewitt, also of Brandon wed Alf Sherrington, Durham. Both parties were married at St. John's Church, Meadowfield.

Newcastle Street young woman Betty Brown, married Walter Cairns of the same street. They too had an Easter wedding at St. John's Parish Church.

Mr. and Mrs. William Henry Howden celebrated their diamond jubilee on Easter Monday. They were married at Brandon Parish Church by the late Rev. T. Lawson. Bill Howden, who is eighty-two, has lived all his life in Brandon. He started work at the age of twelve at Brandon Colliery, and worked until he reached the age of seventy-three, thus completing sixty-one years in the industry.

He recalls the Brancepeth Colliery 'A' Pit explosion of April 13th, 1896, when he and others from Brandon Colliery assisted in rescue work. He also remembers the 'C' Pit explosion at Brandon three years later. He had left the scene of the explosion about two hours before. Bill had played football for Brandon Albion and had been a keen bandsman for more that fifty years.

The small Independent Methodist Church built onto the end of Double North Street celebrated its Golden Jubilee. Will it survive when the North Streets are demolished?

After almost one hundred years the oldest chapel in Brandon is to close. Mr. Love, the co-partner of Brandon Colliery, built the chapel near the 'A' Pit heapstead for the Methodists of Brandon Colliery. The building was used as a school for colliery children, it obviated the steep climb to Brandon Village school.

It was unanimously agreed at a meeting of trustees and leaders of Trinity and Market Square Methodist Churches, that the two societies should amalgamate. The Sunday Schools have already joined forces for anniversary services.

June bride Sylvia Londsale, Brandon, married Ron Kelly at St. Patrick's Langley Moor.

One of the first secretaries with Brandon Colliery Silver Band and cornet player for thirty years with the band, William Bullows, died at 17 Commercial Street at the age of eighty-five. He retired eighteen years ago after more than half a century as a miner.

An overall increase of fourteen shillings to both underground and surface workers was granted the miners, making their minimum weekly wage £9.0s.6d. underground and £8.0s.6d. for surface workers.

The wage rise helped Brandon's miners when they started their annual holidays in early June. Many left for seaside resorts and some took advantage of an organised holiday to Northern Ireland arranged by the local Miners' Welfare Scheme. Others are spending stay-at-home holidays with daily bus excursions to nearby resorts.

Twelve buses conveyed about four hundred aged members, wives and widows of Brandon Social Club to Whitley Bay. Each club member and widow received ten shillings to spend as they pleased.

As shaft man Billy Deans worked astride the cage in Brandon 'C' Pit shaft, he was struck by a girder and knocked down the shaft to his death.

Joseph Kennedy (41) died at 6 High Street. Well known locally, Joe was a keen ambulance man formerly attached to Brandon Division St. John Ambulance Association. His mother, Ellen Kennedy died last year.

Brandon 'C' Pit failed to reach its weekly target of 2,025 tons at the end of the wettest summer for twenty-six years, 1,814 tons of coal being drawn. The colliery, after almost a hundred years of coal production, now relies on the low seams of coal, machine cut, filled away by fillers as they work horizontally at the coal face.

Brandon Social Club's concert room was crowded for a miners' lodge meeting on September 19th to discuss an unofficial stoppage which had laid three pits, Brandon 'C', Pit House and West Brandon, idle.

After a forty minute hearing the men agreed to return to work. Forty-seven men — cutters, fillers and stonemen, ceased work on Monday September 17th. The remainder of the 1,230 members of the Lodge came out on Tuesday night. Work resumed on Thursday, September 20th.

Three more weddings with Brandon participants took place when Joyce Firth of Cobden Terrace married John Henderson of Ushaw Moor, Jack Bell of Brandon wed Freda Myers of Brasside and Bernard Cairns married Gladys Graham of Willington.

The vicar was walking down the village steeet the other day. He was met by one of his parishioners, Geordie, who told him he had had a dream.

'What were you dreaming about?'

'Wey, Aa dreamt Aa was in Hivin'.

'And did you have a good time?' asked the vicar.

'Aye', Geordie replied, 'Aa met an aud sweetheart of mine and we travelled aboot for three weeks'.

'And did you not think of getting married?' asked the vicar.

'Aye, but there waas nee parasons there', replied Geordie.

Mary Elizabeth Carter, seventy-two years of age, died at Cobden Terrace; she came to Brandon more than forty years ago. Her husband, Edmund Carter, pre-deceased her by sixteen months.

George King died at the age of sixty. He had spent all his life in the Brandon area, and at the time of his death lived at 37 Albert Street. For twenty-six years he was an overman at the pit. Laurie Moran had worked under him as a shot-firer for a number of years. George was a well known Club man having been chairman of Meadowfield Club for fourteen years.

Dave Brandon discarded his boxing name for a day when he married Mary, younger daughter of Mr. and Mrs. James Robinson, 10 Commercial Square at Brandon Parish Church. The 'groom recently returned from Germany, where he has been a physical training instructor with the Durham Light Infantry.

Christmas time golden weddings were celebrated by two Sawmills Estate couples. Mr. and Mrs. Harry Harker were married on Christmas Day 1906. Harry who is seventy-five, came to Brandon forty years ago. Mr. and

Mrs. Fred Keepin, 19 Acorn Place, were married on Christmas Eve fifty years ago. Both parties celebrated with family gatherings.

1957

The tenth anniversary of the acquisition of Britain's coal mines by the State coincided with a further increase in the minimum wage. Nine shillings and sixpence being granted to both underground and surface workers. The minimum weekly wage now being £9.10s.0d. for the former and £8.10s.0d. for the surface men.

Mr. W. Wilkinson, after twenty-nine years of service as Public Health Officer of Brandon District Council, has retired. His home is the Lodge, Brandon Colliery, standing at the gates of Brandon Hospital.

The Inspector of Nuisances had called to investigate a report that Joe intended to keep a goat in his house and this annoyed the Inspector greatly. 'You must be mad to entertain such an idea', ejaculated the Inspector, and then he continued, 'Just think of the smell, man, just think of the smell!' Joe was not in the least perturbed. 'Oh, that's nowt, sor', he replied. The goat'll sharp get used te that!' (Collapse of Inspector).

John Thomas Pinkney (78) began work in the mine at the age of twelve at Brandon Colliery and rose to be a deputy-overman, a position he held for more than twenty-one years. He retired after completing fifty years in the industry. Jonti died at the home of his daughter and son-in-law, Mr. and Mrs. Leslie Cairns, 41 High Street.

For twelve years George Harvey, Pea Lea, Brandon has been a player as well as secretary of Brandon Colliery Band which at Gateshead Town Hall became runner-up in the Northern Area Third Division contest. This success means that Brandon Band has qualified for the first time to compete in the National Finals in October. George is forty-nine and is a deputy at the 'C' Pit.

Jack Bowes was a colliery slater, well known at Brandon Colliery, he could be seen daily at work repairing the colliery-owned houses. Sixty-seven year old Jack died in hospital. His home is 25 Greyridges, he had resided in Brandon for thirty-three years.

Brandon Juniors gave a fine display of teamwork at Bowburn when they played neighbouring rivals Browney Juniors in the National Association of Boys' Clubs Cup Final. Brandon scored three goals to Browney's two in an exciting game. The losers will no doubt look for revenge when they meet Brandon Juniors in the Old Aged Pensioners' Cup game.

David White, Brandon, married Miss Sowerby of Pity Me at Bethel Church, Durham.

Harry McKay, Brandon, married Doreen Miller, also of Brandon, at St. John's Church, Meadowfield.

Brandon couple Redvers Burnip and Margaret Anderson were also married at St. John's Church.

Geordie had just married at the register office and the blushing bride was on his arm. With them was Geordie's mother-in-law, stout and formidable, and a few friends each sporting a gay buttonhole. Geordie led the way to a nearby public house. 'What about a drink?' he asked. 'Aa'll pay'.

'Aye', quickly replied his mother-in-law, 'Aa think aa could tak a mouthful'.

Geordie looked at her, 'Now luk heor muther aa want nee fightin', ye'll be the syem as anybody else an tak a pint, see!'

Two old standards died in hospital. Mary Jane Blenkinsop, eighty-six, of 6 Aged Miners' Homes, came to Brandon sixty-six years ago. Her husband, Tom Blenkinsop, is a retired deputy-overman, and a past superintendent of Brandon Division of the St. John Ambulance Brigade.

Jack Goodall died a few days before his seventy-second birthday. Jack, who lived two doors away at 4 Aged Miners' Homes, had spent all his life in the area, starting work at the age of twelve. He had been deputy-overman for twenty years before retiring after completing half a century in the mine.

Brandon Social Club's able secretary Jack Higgins, after serving thirty-one years in that capacity, retired. His successor is Jack Stokoe the present compensation secretary of Brandon Miners' Lodge.

Eleven Brandon boys went on the rampage which landed them in Durham Juvenile Court. They admitted to a series of offences involving the smashing of windows, breaking and entering shops, stores and houses, stealing sums of money and some sweets. Two boys were sent to an approved school, another was put on three years' probation.

Fred Grayson (59) had been a deputy-overman for fifteen years. He left his home, 19 Dominion Road, Sawmills Estate, for work in the fifteen inch seam at Brandon 'C' Pit where he was currently employed as a shot-firer. During the course of his shift Fred was fatally injured. He was a well-known and popular man and great sympathy went out to his family on their sudden and grievous loss.

Brandon Social Club's seventh annual leek and flower show was a success. It attracted four thousand spectators during its two day duration. There were ninety-seven stands of pot leeks, and other classes attracted entries amounting to three hundred and fifty.

Patrick and Mary Moran celebrated their golden wedding. Paddy is seventy-three and his wife is seventy-one. Paddy retired five years ago from his job as coal conveyor attendant underground at Brandon's 'C' Pit, a job he took on after half a century of coal hewing. He was badly wounded during the First World War. A family of six sons and four daughters celebrated the occasion.

Brandon Colliery celebrated its centennial anniversary by producing 1,800 tons of coal — some 400 tons short of its present target.

```
Fifty years ago the 'A' Pit drew . . . . . . . . . . . . . . . . . . . . . 209440 tons
     Ballarat . . . . . . . . . . . . . . . . . . . . . . . . . . . . . . . . . . .459 tons
     'B' Pit Hutton. . . . . . . . . . . . . . . . . . . . . . . . . . . . 177422 tons
     'C' Pit Brockwell. . . . . . . . . . . . . . . . . . . . . . . . . . . 88650 tons
     Ballarat drew . . . . . . . . . . . . . . . . . . . . . . . . . . . . . 20036 tons
                                                                          ──────
     Total coals. . . . . . . . . . . . . . . . . . . . . . . . . . . . . 496016 tons
                                                                          ──────
'C' Pit Brockwell
     Seggar (fire-clay). . . . . . . . . . . . . . . . . . . . . . . . . . .8934 tons
                                                                          ──────
     Total for year. . . . . . . . . . . . . . . . . . . . . . . . . . . 504950 tons
                                                                          ──────
```

William Abson (76), 38 Princess Street was born at Penshaw and came to Brandon Colliery when he was five years of age. When he reached the age of twelve he started work at the colliery and was employed there for fifty-nine years.

Isabella Robson had spent all her long life of eighty-three years in Brandon. One of Brandon's oldest residents, she lived at 38 Russell Street. Brandon Colliery mourned the loss of two more true Brandonians.

A good number of the four hundred and four pupils on the roll of Brandon School took part in the fourth annual Carol Service and Nativity Play held in the Church of St. Brandon, Brancepeth. The singing and miming were much appreciated.

Last year one hundred and forty pupils in charge of Miss Raine, Mrs. Vann, Mrs. Forster and Headmaster joined other Durham County schools in the Carol Service held in Durham Cathedral.

Brandon Social Club once more showed its generous Christmastide attituade towards its aged members when over four hundred pounds was handed out to two hundred and ten of them who received thirty-five shillings each.

1958

Falls of snow greeted New Year 'first footers'. Snow continued to fall as Brandon Colliery Prize Band toured the colliery streets rendering much appreciated festive music.

Just two weeks into the New Year saw a fatal accident on the Brandon 'C' Pit to Pit House Colliery railway line. Forty-two year old Frank Robson a National Coal Board locomotive driver was crushed by trucks and died in hospital.

Three more old Brandonians died: Patrick Moran died at the age of seventy-four after having spent all his life at Brandon Colliery. He celebrated his golden wedding last year. Norah, Mary, Kathleen, Laurie, John, Eddie, Teresa, all married, with Frank and Joe, mourned the loss of their father.

Mary Moran now seventy-two and a widow, moved house once again; she and Frank are pleased with the new residence, 7 Oak Green Flats, one of a number being built by the Council alongside the Brandon Village road.

Catherine Higgins spent all her life in the Brandon area. Aged seventy-six, she died at Meadowfield. Catherine was the wife of John D. Higgins. Father Francis Jennings, the deceased's brother conducted Requiem Mass.

Jimmy Tones started work in the mine at the age of thirteen. He remained at the colliery and passed through the various grades to become a deputy overman, a position he held for thirty-one years. He retired six years ago after completing fifty-three years in the industry.

Jimmy and Mrs. Tones celebrated their golden wedding at 30 Princess Street. They were married at Brandon Parish Church by the late Rev. Harry Hayward.

Mr. and Mrs. George Prudhoe, 42 Princess Street, celebrated their golden wedding. George, seventy-one, was born at Witton Gilbert and came to Brandon where he has resided for seventy years. He started work at Browney Colliery at the age of twelve then transferred to Brandon Colliery where he worked for over half a century. He recalls an incident in the 'C' Pit when the seam he was working in fired. He and another pitman were compelled to run for safety.

Another ex 'C' Pit coal hewer, Charles Grice and Mrs. Grice, celebrated their golden wedding.

As slum clearance gets underway, families in the Brandon area are being re-housed. Thirty-two flats at Brandon costing £48,273 will consist of sixteen double storey houses with new roads and street lighting.

Isobel Bussey (52), wife of Sammy Bussey, died at 21 Newcastle Street. Her cremation took place at Sunderland.

David Hopkins, Hawthorn Park, Brandon, who has represented No. 1 Division of Brandon on the County Council for two years, is to be opposed by Mr. Dick Harle, of Brandon Hall, Brandon Village. He is contesting the election as a Conservative declaring that 'an increase in the anti-socialist members on the County Council can only do good, for a strong opposition makes for good local government'.

The coldest, bleakest Easter for over forty years saw Brandon 'C' Pit almost reach its target when 2,120 tons were drawn. Coal extracted from pillars of coal situated in the area of the shaft being the reason for the increased tonnage.

Flemming Farish (69), of 3 Red Courts, was buried at Brandon Village Cemetery. Flem, a native of South Shields, was a deputy overman for some years at Brandon 'C' Pit. He retired four years ago. During the First World War Flem was awarded the Military Medal for bravery on the battlefield.

Not many teams score five goals in a cup final and still lose, but Beamish and Tanfield Lea Juniors did in the final of the No. 5 Area National Coal Board Junior Cup. Opponents Brandon Colliery Welfare Juniors replied with eight goals to make it a thirteen goal final. The match was entertaining throughout, with plenty of goals to satisfy the seven hundred cash customers.

William Armstrong Ramsey (72), 39 Albert Street, was buried at Brandon Village Cemetery. He came to Brandon Colliery from Waldridge

Fell at the age of three. He worked at Brandon 'C' Pit for half a century. Billy was among the first young miners to leave Brandon Colliery to fight in the Great War 1914 – 1918.

Joseph Pouton (78) died at 31 Newcastle Street. Joe, born at Tow Law, had lived almost all his life at Brandon Colliery. He began work in the mine at the age of twelve and retired ten years ago after completing fifty-six years work in the mine.

George Fawbert has been a porter at Brandon Colliery railway station for forty years of his forty-six with the railway company. His devoted service was recognised when he was the recipient of gifts from the company and station staff. 'Old George' the porter was a familar figure seen patrolling the platforms.

A Brandon man was sent to prison for six months for breaking into Brandon Social Club and stealing £2.17s.6d. which he spent on beer and on playing the juke-box.

Arthur Shell and Irving Pigg had a good knock for Brandon Colliery when they entertained Stanhope in Division Three of the Mid-Durham Cricket League. Arthur reached the half century and Irving going in ninth was not out seventy-eight. The former was also in grand form with the ball for he took five wickets for seventeen in just seven overs.

The cricket match was very exciting, and Bill and Geordie began to talk about the marvels they were seeing.

'Excitin' match isn't it?' said Bill.

'Aye', was Geordie's reply. 'But Aa divvent like excitin' matches very much'.

Bill stared at him in amazement. 'What!' he exclaimed, 'thoo dissent like excitin' games? An wey on earth is that?'

'Wey', replied Geordie, 'it's like this. Aa chows a lot o' baccy, an' ivvery time the game gets varry excitin' Aa swallows aal Aa hev in me mouth. Excitin' matches is gettin' ower expensive for me'.

Brandon Colliery Welfare Juniors on the lookout for football talent, held a trial game on the Welfare ground. In honour of their winning of the No. 5 Area National Coal Board Cup, the players received plaques from the women's supporters' club, presented by Esther Bewley and William Harrison on behalf of Brandon Colliery Welfare.

The First Brandon Group of Boys Scouts and Cubs occupied their new headquarters. The building, formerly the premises of Brandon Social Club in Commercial Street, has been transformed into an attractive hall.

St. Patrick's Church, Langley Moor, was filled to capacity when an impressive service preceding the interment at Meadowfield Cemetery of a well-known Brandon Colliery couple took place. James Cummings (69) and his wife Amy (67) died within a few hours of each other. James died in Dryburn Hospital and when his coffin was carried into their home, 20 Grey Ridges, his wife collapsed and died a few hours later.

James had spent all his life in Brandon. In his earlier days he was a playing member of Langley Moor Shamrock Rovers Football Club, Langley Moor St. Patrick's F.C. and Littleburn Blackwatch F.C.

At No 23 Richard Clarke died at the age of sixty. Dickie moved to Brandon more than forty years ago. A keen sportsman, he was an enthusiastic follower of football, boxing and bowls. He was a keen gardener and leek grower.

Edith Rivers, Brandon, married Allan Morgan, Durham at St. John's, Meadowfield. Sidney Kay and Miss Beresford, both from Brandon, were wed at Brandon's Mount Calvary Church.

During the colliery holidays Brandon Social Club was once again host to its aged club members and their wives, and widows of past members, when four hundred and fifty travelled in thirteen buses to Whitley Bay. Each aged member and widow received a gift of ten shillings from the board of management.

The Rev. A. C. Langford officiated at the wedding at Mount Calvary Methodist Church of Irene, youngest daughter of Mr. and Mrs. Alf Firth, and Terence Eales, elder son of Mr. and Mrs. T. B. Eales, Meadowfield.

The Rev. Langford and his wife were recipients of gifts on their departure to Chester-le-Street Methodist Circuit after serving five years at Brandon. The Rev. Richard Davison took over duties as the twenty-third minister of Mount Calvary Methodist Church.

The new Murray Independent Methodist Church was opened at Brandon. The Brandon Colliery Silver Band led a parade to the new building and played a hymn for the large congregation present.

WANTED!! In Brandon area, mean, malicious person or persons; name and address a mystery; descriptions unknown; possibly armed with a knife; offence, stealing and viciously slashing prize pot leeks intended for show.

Two members of Brandon Workmen's Club leek show dug up their entries and found them slashed with a knife while a third member went to his garden and found his leeks had been stolen.

Brandon Colliery Prize Band posed for a picture in Kensington Town Hall, where they competed in the National Brass Band Championships.

Plans laid in 1948 for a new football field at Brandon Colliery Welfare are now beginning to take shape. Work has now started on the £4,000 project. It is expected that the football field will be ready in September for the 1959–1960 football season. The field will be more spacious than the present one.

Brandon Juniors had an easy passage in the second round of the County Cup when they beat Sherburn Road 13–2. The game became very one-sided after ten minutes.

Mary Alice Pinkney (83) died at the home of her daughter and son-in-law Mr. and Mrs. Leslie Cairns, 41 High Street. She has lived in Brandon for seventy years. Her husband John Thomas Pinkney (Jonti) died two years ago.

Seventy-nine year old Ada Howdon celebrated her diamond wedding two years ago. Ada died at 12 Station Avenue after living in Brandon for more than half a century. Her husband, W. H. Howdon, three sons and two daughters survive her.

Thomas Strong started work at eleven and retired at the age of seventy-four. He died at the age of eighty-one at his home, 1 North Street. Representatives of Brandon Colliery Deputies' Association and Brandon Colliery Silver Band were present at his funeral on Boxing Day at Brandon Village.

Brandon Colliery pigeon fancier Bob Garbutt of 17 Grey Ridges, is aiming for treble wins at the world's biggest show of racing pigeons in London. By entering a bird in Class 1 he has put himself in line for three top awards.

Couples married during the year include Harry Robinson and Rosemary Cowell, both of Brandon; Miss J. Myers, Brandon and F. Close of Sherburn; J. Wilson, Brandon and Miss L. Johnson, Ushaw Moor; Doreen Wilson, Brandon and Norman Green, Broompark; Robert Bird, Brandon and Elsie Crooks; Mary McGough, Brandon and Thomas McGough, Spennymoor; Owen Woods, Brandon and Jean Gibson, Durham; John Kennedy, Brandon and Winnie Davison, Durham and Albert Edward Bailes, Brandon and Anita Reay, Langley Moor.

Geordie was walking down the street looking very disconsolate and gloomy. Halfway down the street he met his friend Bill.

'Hulloa', said Bill. 'Thoo hes a varry glumpy leuk. What's up with tha?'

'Wey, man, Aa's fed up wi' one thing an' another'.

'Howay doon the raa an' liven thisel' up; thoo wants te droon thi trouble'.

'It's alreet thoo taalkin' aboot droonin' mi trouble, but she's fowerteen styen', replied Geordie.

1959

A recent wage increase of 9s.6d. to colliery workers makes the underground weekly minimum wage £9.17s.6d. and surface workers £8.17s.6d.

During the first two weeks of January long service certificates and a gift of ten shillings each have been presented to one hundred and fifty-one workmen at Brandon in recognition of more than fifty years each.

Brandon Urban District Council is to re-house many more families. About one hundred and sixty families will probably be re-housed from the 'black spots' in Brandon Colliery and Langley Moor. The Ministry of Housing has already granted a loan of £168,161 towards the cost of building another one hundred and eight houses on Brandon Estate during 1959.

The Bishop of Durham (Dr. M. H. Harland) paid his first visit to Brandon Parish Church and confirmed thirty-six candidates from the parishes of Brandon, St. Oswald's, Durham and Bow School, Durham.

Brandon made no mistake about reaching the semi-final of the Langley Park Aged Miners' Cup when they met Waterhouses. They won a very one-sided game. Waterhouses returned to the Deerness Valley the losers eleven goals to one.

Brandon Juniors reached the final of the Eden Cup when they beat Fishburn 2-1 while Brandon Boys' Club are strong challengers for league honours being top of the seven strong Durham Area Boys' Club League.

George Hewitt, secretary, Brandon Lodge, National Union of Mineworkers, sent a letter to the council complaining of the wording set out in the letter recently sent to each of its tenants.

He said, 'The members of Brandon Miners' Lodge protest against the letter sent out by the Brandon and Byshottles Urban District Council re the increase in rents from April 1959. The phrasing of the letter in our opinion was not graceful or diplomatic to the tenants of your housing scheme.

We therefore would like the Council to make a statement of reassurance to the tenants, that any future correspondence will not be a shock, but shall be worded in a different manner to the satisfaction of all concerned'.

William Wright Barlow (Billy) died at the age of seventy-seven. He came to Brandon Colliery as a young man of twenty and worked at the colliery for fifty years, retiring seven years ago.

Easter treat for Brandon aged members and wives. Brandon Social Club entertained them to tea and a concert, plus £1 to each club member. The chairman, Matt Wilkinson; secretary, Jack Stokoe; treasurer, Anty Howdon, supported by committee members made the arrangements.

Thomas Simpson (Bomber) forty-four years of age and a former miner at Brandon's 'C' Pit, was knocked down by a car at Stonebridge. He lay in the hospital in a critical condition for a week before his death there. Tommy who had to give up work owing to illness, lived with Mr and Mrs. Joseph Spirit.

James Campbell (62), 24 Grey Ridges, Brandon, died in Brandon Convalescent Hospital. He had spent all his life in the Brandon area and was a deputy-overman for some years, until he was compelled to give up work owing to illness eleven years ago. He served with the Seaforth Highlanders in Egypt during the 1939–45 war.

Maria Logan (77) died at 10 Station Avenue. She had lived all her life in the Brandon area. Her husband, James died ten years ago.

Another old Brandonian, Michael Tunney (78), died. He was a Boer War and Mons veteran. His son Norman Tunney was killed while serving in the Royal Navy during the 1939–45 World War.

Jimmy Twist (68) died at 25 North Street. He had spent all his life at Brandon Colliery and worked in Brandon 'C' Pit for half a century before retiring three years ago. He leaves a wife, four sons and two daughters. In his long coal hewing career Jimmy was regarded as being one of the best at 'hewing coals'.

Brandon horsekeeper Francis Graham Reid (56) died at his home, 33 Grey Ridges. Born at West Stanley he had spent most of his life in the Brandon area. He was for sixteen years employed as a horsekeeper with Brandon Co-operative Society, a position previously held by his father for some years.

Churches in the area were kept busy with the spate of Easter weddings. Jennie Bartle and Kenneth Carr were married at St. John's, Meadowfield. Matthew Wilson and Joyce Robinson at Brandon Independent Methodist Church. Miss M. Melia, Brandon married K. Lincoln at St. Patrick's R.C. Church, Langley Moor. Iris Strachan, Brandon and John Brown, Fence Houses, were wed at Mount Calvary Methodist Church, Brandon.

The final of the No. 5 Area N.C.B. Junior Cup between Brandon Colliery Welfare and Chester Moor Colliery Welfare was a tame affair. After ninety minutes there was no score and, as Brandon had more finals to play, extra time was agreed upon. There was still no score at the end of the first half of extra time, and shortly after, referee Tommy Lee of Consett had no option but to abandon the match due to failing light. The clubs decided to hold the cup for six months each. On the spin of a coin, Brandon will hold it for the first six months.

A mineral train became derailed near Brandon Colliery signal box. Five waggons ran down the line to a 'dumb end'. Railway traffic between Durham and Bishop Auckland was held up for some time until heavy lifting gear arrived on the scene.

Girl Guides of the 1st Brandon St. John's formed a guard of honour for Beryl Twist after her marriage to Barry Trowman, Sunnybrow at St. John's Church, Meadowfield. A reception was held in the Ex-Servicemen's Hall nearby.

Past and present officials of Brandon Colliery, representatives of Brandon Colliery Miners' Welfare Committee, and Bowling Clubs, together with offcials and members of Brandon Sawmills Estate Over-60 Club, joined relatives at the funeral of retired colliery engineer, seventy-five year old Robert Halkier.

He moved from Clara Vale Colliery forty-two years ago to be a fitter at Brandon 'C' Pit. He later became engine-wright at Pit House Colliery and then was appointed colliery engineer. After twenty-five years in that capacity he retired eight years ago.

The first annual miners' service in conjunction with Brandon Colliery Consultative Committee took place at Trinity Methodist Church, Station Avenue. The church was filled to capacity with officials and workmen of Brandon Colliery, members of the local authority, and other organisations.

In the church a large block of coal was placed on the communion table, together with a number of implements used in the production of coal, a number of lighted miners' safety and electric lamps, and miners' helmets.

After prayers, the congregation stood while Brandon Colliery Silver Band played the miners' hymn, 'Gresford' in memory of those who had lost their lives in the industry. Lessons were read by John Burlison and Frank Johnson.

Matt Wilkinson, chairman of Brandon Social Club, welcomed guests and club members on the re-opening of the club after alterations costing £4,000. Sid Lavers (chairman of the Northern Clubs' Federation Breweries) said that Brandon Club joined the Federation in 1941. Since then they had received £53,000 in dividends. Councillor Arthur Stock thanked the speakers.

Thomas Reavley, M.M., died. Brandon and district has lost one of its most popular residents. Tom, aged eighty-one, retired licensee, died at the home of his son and daughter-in-law, Mr. and Mrs. Robert Reavley, 2 Grey Ridges. During the 1914 – 18 World War Tom served with the 'Pals' (18th Battalion Durham Light Infantry). While in France on active service he became a corporal, and was awarded the Military Medal and bar for bravery on the battlefield. He had been a local rugby player and an amateur boxer, he took an interest in greyhound and whippet racing, as a trainer.

Early November brought good news for the Brandon area when the water supplied from Page Bank since the summer drought began, has been discontinued. The area's residents are looking forward to a better brew of tea.

This year the Durham miners, about half of them, were on their annual holiday at the time of the Miners' Gala. The Coal Board has agreed to arrange the 1961 holidays to enable more miners to attend the Gala, the times for 1960 have already been fixed.

Edna May Madgin died at the early age of forty-five. Three sons and husband Harry mourn her at 22 Princess Street.

Brandon Colliery's oldest resident, William Stock, ninety-one, died at the home of his daughter and son-in-law Mr. and Mrs. Thomas Lee. Four grandsons, James Arthur Mitchell, Walter, William and Raymond Stock, acted as underbearers when the funeral took place in the Trinity Methodist Church, Brandon.

James Atess left school at the age of eleven to start work at Brandon Colliery where he worked for sixty-one years until he retired at the age of seventy-two. Jimmy served with the 8th Durham Light Infantry during the 1914 — 18 World War, he was a keen pigeon flyer and fancier and was a pioneer member of Brandon Social Club.

He was eighty-three when he died in hospital. He leaves five sons and three daughters.

If the Miners' National Executive Committee's recommendation of compulsory retirement for miners at sixty-five years of age with a lump sum payment of £200 is accepted and put into operation, it will be the year's best news for a number of elderly miners still working.

1960

In early January fifty-eight year old Joseph Goodall died suddenly at his home, 2 Queen Street. He was a clerk at the colliery and had lived all his life in Brandon. He was a former member of the Market Square Methodist Church. A keen footballer, Joe had played in goal for Brandon United, Spennymoor and Wheatley Hill. He also played cricket for Brandon Colliery.

Brandon Juniors won their way into their third cup final when they beat Ushaw Moor in the Divisional Junior Cup.

The ceiling may shake and bits of lime flake into the glasses of beer in the four ale bar of the Red Lion (Blazer), Brandon, but the customers merely look up and say, 'It's just the lads; they're at it again'.

Making the old pub occasionally shake to its foundations are the lads, all Brandon lads, who have been encouraged by the breezy licensee, Arnold Taylor, to use an upper room as a gymnasium to keep fit.

John Taylor, the licensee's fifteen year old son, Jim Davis, and twins John and Roderick Strong, train three nights a week with punch bag, punch ball, bar-bells and skipping ropes.

Angela Minns, Red Courts, Brandon, married Danny Keenan of Meadowfield at St. Patrick's R.C. Church, Langley Moor.

A Brandon couple, Margaret Teggart and Thomas Gerrard, were married at Mount Calvary Methodist Church.

Four well known Brandon men died; George Turner (64), 36 High Street, a native of Willington. George started work in the mine at Page Bank and transferred to Brandon Colliery in 1920. He became involved in an accident at Pit House seven years ago. He had not been able to work since. George died at his home.

Nichol Huntley had lived all of his seventy-eight years in Brandon. After a spell of work at Browney Colliery he started work at Brandon Colliery and retired in 1948.

Thomas Blenkinsop (84), a retired deputy-overman had lived all his life in Brandon, he started work in the mine when he was twelve. He was an ardent ambulance worker and was a serving Brother of the Order of St. John.

Edward Mearman (74) died at his home in North Street. Little Teddy was well known as a local entertainer. He served as an officer in the Home Guard during the 1939 – 45 World War.

Mary Jane Sayer (81) had lived in Brandon for almost sixty years, during which time she was a member of Mount Calvary Methodist Church. She was the widow of Albert Sayer, also a keen local Methodist.

William Kennedy, Brandon, miner in the National Coal Board No. 4 Area, was one of the lucky fifty Durham miners who won the main awards in the prize draw organised by Durham Divisional Coal Board to stimulate even greater interest in their pit safety campaign.

Each of the main prizes, worth more than £30, comprised two return tickets to London with meals; hotel accommodation for two for two nights; theatre tickets and a sightseeing tour of London.

To qualify for the prize draw a miner had to be commensurable free (i.e. free from accident involving absence from work for a period exceeding three days) in the period January to April 2nd. In addition there were five hundred consolation prizes of £1 premium bonds.

Another life-long Brandonian, John William Lonsdale (67) died at his home, 7 Albert Street. John Willie started work in the mine at Brandon and after more than fifty years as a miner retired two years ago. He leaves his wife, seven daughters and six sons.

Streets patiently await demolition in the hottest and driest June for thirty-five years. As new houses are built on the Brandon Estate the colliery houses are vacated. Four Garbutt brothers, Bob, Tommy, John Henry and Billy, are members of the only family left in the district with earliest colliery connections.

William Garbutt, with his wife Sarah and daughters Mary and Margaret, together with three year old John Henry, came from Yorkshire in 1857 to occupy No. 14 Durham Street, the first long colliery row not yet complete.

Laurie Moran followed Brandon Cilliery banner onto Durham's racecourse for the 77th Miners' Gala held in July. Would it be the 'C' Pit's last Gala? After one hundred and four years it was becoming increasingly more difficult to provide the coal to keep the men fully employed.

Despite the uncertain future, Laurie joined the 250,000 strong crowd with its one hundred colourful banners. Eightpenny ham sandwiches, washed down with a fourpenny cup of tea, made an enjoyable meal under the cloudless July sky.

Laurie walked with Brandon Colliery Silver Prize Band led by band-master Mr. G. Brown, and Brandon Lodge banner as they joined Hetton and Eppleton bands for the Miners' Festival Service in Durham Cathedral.

I see them invade our fair city, their coloured banners high,
I hear the martial music, as each lodge goes marching by.
My heart is filled with northern pride, that all we miners know,
And I with teaming thousands more, reflect an inner glow.
Oh! come you Durham miners, come across the River Wear,
With many a laugh, and many a song, and many a hidden tear.
With banners fluttering in the breeze, and many a head held high,
Each Lodge comes gaily into view, and then goes marching by,
And as I pass the County, each band outplays the rest,
For there the miners' leaders stand, with many an honoured guest.
I wonder what our leaders feel, like generals, as they view,
The best shock troops of Europe were never quite as true.
They must be proud, Sam Watson, Jimmy Kelly and the rest,
To know that passing years have proved they really stood the test.
Above the River Wear so proud, erect, serene,
The beautiful Cathedral lends its grandeur to the scene,
As it has done through all the years, the miners rallied here,
A monument to all their hopes, and to their God so near.
So yearly let it still enfold, this pageantry so dear,
And let the miners' lodges march across the River Wear,
And we'll be there, we Durham men, to give a Durham greeting,
To welcome all the miners, as they come to their 'BIG MEETING'.

John McNally,
A miner of the Morrison Busty Colliery, Annfield Plain.

William Coope Birchnall, 79 of 1 Aged Miners' Homes, died in hospital. He had lived all his life in the area, at the age of twelve he started work at Brandon Colliery, and later became a deputy-overman, a position he held for forty years. He retired fourteen years ago. He was a keen first aid worker and held a medal as one of the winning team in a Brandon Ambulance competition as far back as 1904.

Miss Elizabeth Ramsey (53), 8 Station Road, died. She had spent all her life in Brandon. The eldest daughter of Mr. and Mrs. Edward Ramsey of Brandon, she was educated at Brandon School before going to Durham Girls' County School and Sunderland Training College. Miss Ramsey was a member of the teaching staff at Browney Council School Junior Department for twenty-five years.

Red Lion regulars and all his other friends were shocked on hearing of the sudden death of Arnold Taylor. Forty-eight year old Arnold came to Brandon Colliery twelve years ago. A keen sportsman, he took a keen interest in boxing, body building and weight lifting.

Isaac Pybus (83) moved to Brandon Colliery at the age of six and started work at the colliery when he was twelve. He retired seventeen years ago after completing fifty-four years in the industry. Ike has been a member of Brandon Lodge for seventy-one years. Hale and hearty, he has survived to see the demise of Brandon 'C' Pit where he had toiled for so many years. He and his wife celebrated their diamond wedding, they were married at Brandon Parish Church by the Rev. T. Lawson.

Brandon Colliery holidays were from 1st August to 13th August. Brandon took their holiday with Group 'A' in the National Coal Board's Group No. 3 list of holiday times.

Brandon 'C' Pit workmen had just worked one week after their annual holiday when they heard that the seams would officially cease to operate on August 19th.

John Moran after working twenty-two years at Brandon 'C' Pit was transferred to Pit House when the former pit closed.

A spacious Miners' Hall was built near the Aged Miners' Homes and opposite the colliery manager's residence, Hollygarth. The new building supersedes the corrugated sheet Miners' Hall erected in 1891 which cost £300 with seating for 300. The new hall will be much appreciated by Brandon's mining community.

Born at Brandon Colliery in 1916 during the First World War, Laurie Moran left school at fourteen. Work was scarce at the beginning of the 'hungry thirties'; after five months' search he landed a job as a screen hand at nearby Browney Colliery.

Laurie, after working on the screens for a few months, was given an ultimatum; go down the pit or leave the colliery. He had reached the age of fifteen.

It was 'Hobson's Choice' and despite the fact that Laurie's father, a coal hewer had often declared, 'I wouldn't let a dog go down the pit', Laurie entered the cage to work underground as a pony driver. He was hooked to mining.

Five years elapsed; on his twentieth birthday he descended the 'C' Pit shaft to work in the Busty Seam. After working the various grades – pony driver, putting, then coal hewing, Laurie took up shot-firing. Laurie was loath to leave coal hewing but his overman convinced him there was no future for coal hewers in the seam.

Laurie now at forty-four had been shot-firing for twelve years. He hadn't taken too kindly to the job, a shot-firer was the butt of men and management.

There was talk of an early closure of Brandon 'C' Pit as coal reserves were almost exhausted. Men and lads were to be transferred to Brandon's Pit House Colliery. Laurie decided, come what may, to refuse a transfer. Laurie was sick of the current manager's attitude towards his shot-firers. Laurie had been fined ten shillings on each of three infringements of the Coal Mines Act plus two weeks' on a datal wage – a total loss of some thirteen pounds. Another shot-firer charged at the same time with similar offences was fined a nominal ten shillings. Laurie was humiliated. He had been fined for offences on two occasions for petty things which were a daily occurrence among his workmates. His mind was made up. He would finish with the mines, draw the superannuation he had saved over the years and branch out on his own. He fancied joining the ranks of the self-employed.

All Brandon 'C' Pit's seams closed on August 19th. Men and lads were forthwith directed to Pit House Colliery. Laurie and another shotfirer declined the offer of transfer and were retained on salvage work.

Life changed completely for Laurie and his shot-firer friend. They joined Johnny Cummings and his gang of salvage men. An eight a.m. shift and an interesting job almost compensated for the sizeable drop in wages.

Laurie applied for his superannuated savings, he knew that salvage work would only last a few months. Then what?

Far off silent main headings and their tail gates were visited, their ringed girders had to be drawn and removed to the surface, steel was a valuable commodity. Coal cutting machines and other heavy gear were manhandled to the shaft bottom, these would be sent to other collieries. Finally lengths of waggonway rail would be pulled up and the void thereafter barred to man.

As he worked. Laurie reflected on man's ingenuity; massive caverns left when coal hewers' muscle and stonemen's skill had removed their contents were transformed into well-lit whitewashed and glistening pump house or hauler house where gigantic pump or mighty hauler operated.

Laurie visualised the daily activity in the one hundred or so individual stalls in the area of the shaft and as the districts advanced, the commodious stables built two miles underground, stables whose whitewashed walls and floors fresh straw strewn housed daily groomed perky pit ponies were a credit to the horsekeeper.

The 'A' Pit Busty Seam had South-West, Orton, First West, Fourth West, Second North, Crosscut and Tichborne Districts. The 'B' Pit or Hutton Seam named after James Hutton – Scottish geologist (1726-1797) is one of the most famous of the Durham seams and South-West ¾ mile from the shaft, Third South two miles 510 yards, Fourth South almost three miles inbye and Fifth North 2½ miles underground. The 'C' Pit boasted South-West, Second North, Third West, Ballarat, First North and Second North Districts.

All seams had contributed to the total of seventy-two men and boys killed at the colliery during its life of one hundred and four years. An unrecorded number of men had been crippled by falls of stone as they hewed at the coal-face; others permanently retired through Nystagmus which caused blindness, a disease happily obviated on the introduction of better coal-face lighting; men with lungs destroyed and a bleak future guaranteed through Miners' Asthma joined the anonymous group.

On December 13th, Laurie handed to his under-manager a precious slip of paper on which was written 'Fourteen days to terminate my employment'. He had acquired a building in which to set up business. He looked forward to the challenge.

Salvage men would shortly finish their task. The chasm of the shaft would be sealed and the plaintive lament of the harrassed putter, 'Fill the bloody pit in and give the farmer his bloody field back', would be answered.

BRANDON COLLIERY A, B, C & D PITS

MINERS & SURFACE WORKERS
FATAL ACCIDENTS

1861
Charles Bainbridge, aged 22, Screener – run over by truck

1865
Thomas Brady, aged 27, Hewer – crushed by descending cage

1866
John Connor, Surface Worker – crushed between trucks

1867
Luke Kirkup, aged 50, Plate Layer – knocked down by engine

1871
Frank Telford, aged 13, Screener – crushed by tub

1872
Thomas Evans, aged 13, Pony Driver – crushed by tubs

1873
Cuthbert Coulson, aged 12, Waler on Screens – crushed between trucks

1873
George Milner, aged 22, Coal Hewer – fall of stone

1877
Robert Holton, aged 11, Screener – killed at work

1877
Barnard McGlen, aged 31, Coal Hewer – fall of stone

1882
Alfred Cheesey, aged 38, Deputy Overman – fall of stone

1884
John Mills, aged 30, Coal Hewer – fall of stone

1885
Charles Holmes, aged 20, Putter – fall of top coal

1885
Thomas Wilson, aged 64, Surface Worker – crushed between truck and wall

1887
Michael Doyle, aged 14, Pony Driver – crushed by pony

1887
Ralph Harland, aged 40, Deputy Overman – fall of stone

1888
Thomas Ainsley, aged 30, Coal Hewer – fall of stone

1888
James Simpson, aged 14, Screener – caught in revolving drum

1889
Thomas Swaddle, aged 28, Coal Hewer — fall of stone

1889
Thomas Taylor, Surface Worker — crushed between trucks

1891
William Carroll, aged 22, Coal Hewer — fall of stone

1891
John Stoker, aged 28, Coal Hewer — fall of stone

1894
Robert Maughan, aged 31, Coal Hewer — fall of stone

1896
Matthew Peel, aged 55, Coal Hewer — fall of stone

1898
Adam Todd, Pony Driver — fall of stone

1899
John Stones, aged 22, Putter — crushed between tubs

1899
Francis Murphy, aged 20, Putter — explosion in 'C' Pit August 15th

1899
Enoch Griffiths, aged 30, Coal Hewer — explosion in 'C' Pit August 15th

1899
Ralph Broadbent, Coal Hewer — explosion in 'C' Pit August 15th

1899
George Robson, Putter — explosion in 'C' Pit August 15th

1899
William Carr, Deputy Overman — explosion in 'C' Pit August 15th

1899
Frank Robson, Putter — explosion in 'C' Pit August 15th

1901
James Wrightson, aged 40, Datal Hand — found in pit

1901
Alex Walsh, Engine Driver in the 'A' Pit

1902
James Liddle, aged 42, Deputy Overman — fall of stone

1903
Thomas Crozier, aged 27, Coal Hewer — killed by set of tubs

1903
Albert Peel, 13, killed by set of tubs

1903
Edward Rumley, aged 29, Coal Hewer — fall of stone

1904
Will Barnes, aged 37, Coal Hewer – fall of stone

1904
Thomas Coleman, aged 23, Coal Hewer – fall of stone

1904
William Crozier, aged 27, Coal Hewer – fall of stone

1905
Thomas Hunter, aged 46, Deputy Overman – fall of stone

1905
Philip McKenna, aged 17, Assistant Onsetter – crushed in shaft

1905
William Underwood, aged 28, Coal Hewer – fall of stone

1906
John Lee, aged 27, Coal Hewer – fall of stone

1906
Isaac Robertshaw, aged 23, Coal Hewer – fall of stone

1906
Joseph Hoyles, aged 25, Coal Hewer – hit by set of tubs

1908
George Burton, Coal Hewer – fall of stone

1909
John O'Neill, aged 18, Putter, fall of stone

1912
Joseph Graham, Truck Lowerer – crushed by trucks

1915
William Hamilton, aged 63, Shifter – killed by set of derailed tubs

1915
Thomas Parrish, aged 16, killed by set of derailed tubs

1919
Christopher Simpson, aged 42, Coal Hewer – knocked down by tub

1920
Sydney Lee, aged 17, Pony Driver – fall of stone in landing

1920
John Boyle, aged 46, Coal Hewer – fall of stone

1922
John Payne Cairns, aged 19, fall of stone in landing

1922
Charles Bell, aged 43, Coal Hewer – fall of stone

1922
Thomas Clennell, aged 15, Pony Driver – struck by loose band of curve
while riding men sett

1925
Paddy Cahill, Coal Hewer — fall of stone—lay seventeen years with broken back

1929
George Abson, Deputy Overman — fall of stone

1929
Sam Whitely, aged 56, Overman — crushed between tub and roof

1930
John Rutter, aged 36, Coal Hewer — gas explosion

1932
John Duffy, Coal Hewer — fall of stone

1937
Ernest Staley, aged 19, Shaft Datal Hand — fell down shaft

1938
Frederick Bowes, aged 49, Coal Hewer, crushed between tub and roof

1944
William Bromley, aged 59, Underground Mason — fall of stone

1950
Leonard Vickers, aged 45, Deputy Overman — cage accident

1952
William Maddison (Dickinson), aged 45, Face Cleaner — fall of stone

1956
William Deans, Bank Hand — knocked down shaft by swinging girder

1957
Frederick Grayson, aged 59, Shot-firer — killed in shot firing accident

1958
Francis Robson, aged 42, Surface Locomotive Driver — crushed between waggons

GLOSSARY

netty – cavity to hold household ashes, rubbish and excrement
quarls – bricks eight inches square and three inches thick
baulks – squared timber
heapstead – pithead structure built with baulks
peck – twenty pounds in weight
gig – a light two-wheeled carriage
hunkers – sitting on the heels
chow – a piece of tobacco to chew
score – 21 tubs – some collieries fix a score at 22 tubs
playing hell – tempters flare and strong language is used
off-takes – deductions from pay: house rent, house coal, fines, laid-outs etc.
short tubs – tubs, the contents of which, after reaching the surface, have settled below
    the rim of the tub, are deemed short tubs for which the hewer is fined or suffers
    confiscation of the tub's contents
gantrie – elevated wooden structure along which cone shaped iron tubs on four wheels,
    containing coal, are shoved to the coke ovens
patent safety cage – a recent invention which operates if the cage overshoots its mark.
    Safety levers are released which prevent the cage falling back
ganzie or jersey – a long sleeved woollen garment worn by most colliery lads
knurr and spell – game where a piece of wood is struck, similar to cricket
keeker – an under official – generally an elderly miner retired from the mine
waler – a young screen hand who climbs the full trucks to remove spoil
gallowa – slang for pit ponies bred in Galloway, a district in the South-west of Scotland
baff Saturday – the second Saturday of the two week period when no pay is drawn
band – bow legged
acting the game – the same as 'playing hell'
check-weighman – one who weighs the tubs of coal when they reach the surface
set-out – when the tub is set aside, it is liable to confiscation, supposedly not attaining
    the required weight
laid-out – a fine is imposed on the hewer if the tub is laid out, when it contains an ex-
    cess weight of stone
cracket – an essential part of the hewer's gear – a low wooden stool
bond – the worker signs an agreement which binds him to the colliery for one year
viewer – colliery manager
turnpike – gate across a road where a toll is paid
screen – moving belt on which the coal it tipped and the stone etc. is removed
stowed off – when the hewer has a surplus of coal hewed and waits for the putter
nowt gans reet – nothing goes right
arse – the bottom of the spine used to give leverage when a tub is derailed
set on – employed
form – a strong wooden plank set on legs, seats three or four people
cradle – a long coffin-like wooden object in which the baby sleeps; is has two curved
    piece of wood attached to its base for rocking purposes
truck or tommy shop – where workmen are paid in goods
outbye – going out towards the shaft
rodney – a tramp
headstock – wooden structure which houses the shaft pulley wheels
mat – floor covering, handmade from strips of old cloth woven on a frame
wall – where a pillar of coal had to be split a place called a wall was set away
fester – a painful, swollen condition e.g. hewers suffered the dreaded beat hand
settle – a long wooden seat fixed to the wall near the fireplace
cage hole – where the cage settles at the bottom of the shaft
chaldron – weight of coal, 85 lbs.
hawked phlegm – coughed up sticky mucus membrane
jenkin – a narrow place driven in or along a pillar of coal
skirtie – a place widened to make a flat or landing
winning – the main heading in any district; going forward

blacked – when a man suspected of union activity is sacked and his name is forwarded to other colliery owners

'set on' – when the strata breaks up and smashes wooden supports

limmers – portable shafts made of wood and iron, these are attached to the pony

come to bank – reached the surface

pit head – structure surrounding the shaft

keps – a movable ledge on which the cage rests while at the surface

choppy – chopped up food sent down the pit for the ponies

helper – a lad who helps the putter up a gradient

whole – advancing through solid coal

canny hands – good players

sump – well at the shaft bottom which stores water prior to pumping up the shaft

curving the jud – arduous work – when the top half of the seam of coal is hewed out to derive greater benefit from the shots

can – a tin containing explosives

breeched – out of baby clothes and into breeches or trousers at three or four

screener – one who removes stone, brass etc. from the coal tipped onto the screen

cracked out – challenged

harn – rough material like sacking

muffler – neck scarf

'tash – moustache

lying money – money paid to pitmen who cannot get on with their own work

stook – a strip of coal made easier to hew due to increased roof pressure

channel – open gutter running the length of the street

pitch and toss – a frowned on form of gambling – two pennies are spun into the air while bets are made as to which side the coin lands

brake – horse drawn four wheeled open vehicle with seats running lengthwise

idle the morn' – not working tomorrow

knicker bocker – loose fitting breeches gathered in at the knees

buntin – timber fastened into the shaft to give added strength

fustian – thick cotton cloth

goaf timber – timber which has to be drawn to enable the strata to fall thus removing excess roof pressure in the hewing area

hitch – fault in the seam – the coal or stone either rises or falls away from its course – at times entirely disappearing

drift – where the seam takes an upward or downward direction – similar to hitch

hop frog – the player leaps over the bent shoulders of the one in front and takes up a similar stance for the following player

stoved – term used when an infected house is cleaned

fathom – six feet

handball – two or more players use clenched fists to hit a ball against a wall

cholera – dreaded infectious disease

chromotrophe – pertaining to lantern show

privvies – posh name given to nettie

egg jarping – Easter ritual of cracking an opponent's boiled egg

duck – in cricket, when batsman is bowled without having scored

millenium – period of a thousand years; during which some claim Christ is to reign on earth

'Well kicked hinney' – 'Well done sonny'

quicklime – unadulterated lime

lockout – exclusion of workmen by employers as means of coercion

screenmen – men employed on the colliery screens to remove spoil from the coal

forbye – besides

scavenger – one who cleans out the netties or ashpits

quadrille – square dance

engine planeman – man who travels the underground road, keeps it in repair

erysipelas – disease causing deep red colouring of the skin

Yule-do – New Year gift of money which coal hewers bring for young pit lads

cafe chantant – tea and sing-song

conversazione – meeting for conversation

enteric fever — a form of typhoid fever
petticoat — long garment worn by boys until time for breeching
blazer — a sheet of thin metal placed before the fire to draw it
'I haven't a meg' — 'I'm broke, I haven't a penny'
'roll' in the roof — a fault in the strata — a rounded smooth stone which usually falls
    without warning. It is difficult to timber safely
trap — the same as 'gig' — a light two-wheeled horse drawn vehicle
heap-keeker — official who looks after the screen hands
game of fives — handball game where the players strike a ball with clenched fist
howked — pulled
agyen — again
heed — head
wint — with it

Thank you, dear reader for plodding through the fruit of a decade of research; you deserve a mention in the acknowledgements.

Mark Twain said, 'Find the truth then you can twist it to suit your needs'. Research revealed facts, which if twisted would have wrecked the truth. My exhaustive albeit exhilarating investigations unearthed treasures of interest which made the effort worthwhile. My two grandfathers were reared in colliery-owned houses denude of basic comforts. At the time of the 1871 National Census, Brandon Colliery boasted ten streets with a total of two hundred and eighty-one houses whose nineteen hundred and twenty-six inhabitants still carried water from springs fifteen years from the birth of the colliery. Vertical ladders leading to the upstairs rooms had been the vogue for a similar period.

To finish on a note of grief. News arrived from Yorkshire of the death on her June birthday of Teresa, aged sixty-two, forty years married, the fourth daughter and eighth in a family of ten. Her husband Ron with her three sisters and six brothers of the Moran family mourn her passing.

© Laurie Moran,
June 1987.